**Fifth Edition**

D1578942

# Research Methods in Psychology

**John J. Shaughnessy**
*Hope College*

**Eugene B. Zechmeister**
*Loyola University of Chicago*

**Jeanne S. Zechmeister**
*Loyola University of Chicago*

McGraw-Hill

Boston   Burr Ridge, IL   Dubuque, IA   Madison, WI   New York   San Francisco   St. Louis
Bangkok   Bogotá   Caracas   Kuala Lumpur   Lisbon   London   Madrid   Mexico City
Milan   Montreal   New Delhi   Santiago   Seoul   Singapore   Sydney   Taipei   Toronto

30130 117916063

# McGraw-Hill Higher Education ℵ

*A Division of The* **McGraw-Hill** *Companies*

RESEARCH METHODS IN PSYCHOLOGY, FIFTH EDITION
International Edition 2000

Exclusive rights by McGraw-Hill Book Co – Singapore, for manufacture and export. This book cannot be re-exported from the country to which it is sold by McGraw-Hill. The International Edition is not available in North America.

10  09  08  07  06  05  04  03  02
20  09  08  07  06  05  04  03  02  01
CTP    SLP

The credits section for this book begins on page 548 and is considered an extension of the copyright page.

**Library of Congress Cataloging-in-Publication Data**
Shaughnessy, John J., 1947--
    Research methods in psychology / John J. Shaughnessy, Eugene B. Zechmeister, Jeanne S. Zechmeister.—5th ed.
    p.    cm.
Includes bibliographical references and indexes.
ISBN 0-07-231260-2
    1.    Psychology—Research—Methodology. 2. Psychology, Experimental. I. Zechmeister, Eugene B., 1944—
II.        Zechmeister, Jeanne S. III. Title.
BF76.5S46   2000
150'.7'2—dc21                                          99-15858
                                                                        CIP

www.mhhe.com

When ordering this title, use ISBN 0-07-118466-X

Printed in Singapore

# About the Authors

**JOHN J. SHAUGHNESSY** is Professor of Psychology at Hope College, a relatively small, select, undergraduate liberal arts college in Holland, Michigan. After completing the B.S. degree at Loyola University of Chicago in 1969, he received the Ph.D. in 1972 from Northwestern University. He is a Fellow of the American Psychological Society whose recent research has focused on practical aspects of memory. He is coauthor, with Benton J. Underwood, of *Experimentation in Psychology* (Wiley, 1975). He was selected by students in 1992 as the Hope Outstanding Professor Educator; he serves as a mentor in the College's Faculty Development Program for younger faculty; and he has recently been chairperson of the Hope College Psychology Department.

**EUGENE B. ZECHMEISTER** is Professor of Psychology at Loyola University of Chicago, a large metropolitan university where he has taught both undergraduate and graduate courses since 1970. Professor Zechmeister completed his B.A. in 1966 at the University of New Mexico. He later received both the M.S. (1968) and Ph.D. (1970) from Northwestern University. A specialist in the field of human cognition, Professor Zechmeister authored, with S. E. Nyberg, *Human Memory: An Introduction to Research and Theory* (Brooks/Cole, 1982), and with J. E. Johnson, *Critical Thinking: A Functional Approach* (Brooks/Cole, 1992). He is a Fellow of both the American Psychological Association (Divisions 1, 2, and 3) and the American Psychological Society. In 1994, he was awarded the Loyola University Sujack Award for Teaching Excellence in the College of Arts and Sciences. Professor Zechmeister currently is the Undergraduate Program Director for the Loyola University of Chicago Psychology Department.

**JEANNE S. ZECHMEISTER** is Associate Professor of Psychology at Loyola University of Chicago where she has taught undergraduate and graduate courses in research methodology since 1990. Professor Zechmeister completed her B.A. at University of Wisconsin-Madison (1983) and her M.S. (1988) and Ph.D. (1990) in Clinical Psychology at Northwestern University. Her current research interests are in the area of psychology of religion, and she is conducting research on forgiveness. Her effectiveness as a teacher is evidenced by her many years of high teacher ratings and by her being identified consistently each year by graduating seniors as one of their best teachers at Loyola.

*To Paula
and to the Memory of
Martha,
two women to whom I am
greatly indebted
(J.J.S.)*

*To Ruth O'Keane
and to the Memory of
James O'Keane,
Kathleen O'Keane Zechmeister,
and My Mother
(E.B.Z.)*

*To Mom and Pop
(J.S.Z.)*

# Brief Contents

# Contents

# *Preface*

As research psychologists, we relish the opportunity to discover something new about behavior and mental processes. Our curiosity stirs, for example, when we consider what kinds of effects watching *Sesame Street* may have on the intellectual growth of children. We wonder, too, to what degree do genes determine personality? Or, on the social-psychological level, what are some outcomes of racial stereotyping? These are the types of inquiries into human behavior that engage us, keep us wondering, and prompt our exploration. For us, gathering, delving into, and analyzing research is a much anticipated venture. Like an eager child anxious to open up a brightly wrapped birthday present, we ask ourselves, "What will we discover?"

When we decided—two decades ago—to write a research methods textbook, we wanted to capture this excitement of psychological inquiry as well as the importance of understanding the methods by which research is conducted. Twenty years later, our greatest satisfaction from writing this textbook and teaching research methods is seeing students who enter the course feeling mild trepidations, leave not only feeling competent and confident but also excited about their understanding of the research process.

## ORGANIZATION AND APPROACH

As in previous editions, we begin with a general introduction to the scientific method and with suggestions for how to get started doing research in psychology. We then discuss descriptive, experimental, and applied methodologies. Although we have made some changes that we believe will benefit students in their study of research methods, the basic organization and content of the previous edition remains the same.

Our approach is based on our years of teaching experience. As instructors of research methods, we recognize that most students in our classes will be research consumers and not research producers. Yet we also understand that critical thinking skills are essential to both roles. As we have done in previous editions, we take a problem-solving approach to the study of research methods. Research begins with a question; an appropriate methodology must then be selected to answer that question. It is important to analyze the strengths and weaknesses of a methodology and to evaluate critically the nature of the evidence obtained.

We have drawn many examples from the rich psychology literature to help present research methods. Thus, students also learn much about psychology in general when studying research methodology. This approach is important because it helps students appreciate the critical link between research methods and psychological knowledge. We believe that it is this appreciation for research methods and their findings that makes the study of psychology even more fulfilling and meaningful.

## ABOUT THIS EDITION

Many years have past since the first edition was published, but we continue to keep this text current and exciting:

- This time around, we added more than 100 new references to this edition in order to show students the most recent psychological findings.
- New photos and drawings have been added to stimulate students' interest.
- We echo a message that was heard in previous editions: A multimethod approach to hypothesis testing is necessary to meet the goals of scientific psychology. All methodologies are limited and it is only by gathering evidence using many different approaches that we will succeed in our task.
- We include Challenge Questions at the end of each chapter that permit students to test their critical thinking skills. Many of these questions were developed from reports of research findings in the media. We urge instructors to provide students with additional examples of research findings from popular news outlets that not only will increase students' reasoning skills but also help them appreciate the relevance of understanding research to understanding their world.

## CHANGES IN THE FIFTH EDITION

The changes in this edition have made this text even more student-friendly and effective:

- **Bullet Points:** Users of previous editions will immediately recognize an important new pedagogical feature in this edition. Within each chapter we have added "bullet points" to the introduction of major sections. These bullet points represent summaries of the main ideas in each section and serve two major purposes. First, they provide an outline of the next section of text for the student. This alerts students to what will follow and guides their study. Over the years students have mentioned to us how much they like the many examples of "real" research methods and findings that we incorporate in the text, but they also have indicated that it is sometimes difficult to isolate what is the key idea of a text passage from what is meant to illustrate and amplify that idea. The bullet points should better enable students to identify the key ideas from their reading. A second purpose of the bullet points is to provide an easy method of review after the text has been studied. Students can make use of these outlines of key points to help summarize their knowledge of the chapter contents.

- **Tips and Strategies:** In Chapter 1 we expanded our coverage of "Getting Started Doing Research," making use of McGuire's (1997) interesting heuristics for generating testable hypotheses and Sternberg's (1997) guide to the selection of a research question. Most of us need help when learning to perform a complex task, and the tips given by these experts can help students begin to think about the complex task of doing psychological research. Instructors may wish to call attention to these strategies when discussing research studies used to illustrate various methodologies or to incorporate them when planning student research projects.
- **Approach to Statistical Analysis:** In the past few years there have been important challenges to the way psychologists traditionally analyze research results. A controversy has centered on the use of null-hypothesis significance testing. In fact, at one point, rumors of a "ban" by the APA on null-hypothesis testing were circulating in the field. At the same time, we have noticed an ever increasing sophistication in the statistical treatment of data. This is especially the case for correlational analyses. Path analysis and structural equation modeling techniques, for instance, are becoming more prevalent in the literature. As instructors we find it increasingly difficult to identify published articles that are approachable by undergraduates. And as authors of an introductory textbook on research methods, we find ourselves in a quandary. How do we introduce students to techniques of statistical analysis in a way that is sensitive to important issues in this area and also prepare them to digest current research reports? In part, this state of affairs represents the perennial problem of deciding how best to integrate research design and statistics, a problem every instructor of the research course (and every author of a methods textbook) has wrestled with. Recently, however, this challenge has become more salient and more difficult.

    Our response has been to make significant changes in the way in which we treat statistical analysis in this edition. The most obvious change will be seen in the appendix material, which has been completely rewritten. A new appendix is titled "Data Analysis and Interpretation" and replaces the previous appendix, which had mainly a how-to-do-it emphasis. The statistical appendix in this edition is a tutorial on analysis and interpretation of results based on our understanding of the issues as presented by experts in our field. We leaned heavily on Robert Abelson's ideas as elucidated in his published articles and book, *Statistics as Principled Argument* (1995/ Erlbaum), the trenchant arguments made by Geoff Loftus advocating the use of error bars and confidence intervals, the report by the APA Task Force on Statistical Inference co-chaired by Abelson, Jacob Cohen, and Robert Rosenthal (see, for example, Azar, 1997), as well as the views of many others who tutored us so we could tutor students.

    Students will find in the new appendix an introduction to what is recognized as a necessary three-stage approach to analysis: an exploratory stage (getting to know the data); a summary (descriptive) stage; and a confirmation stage (confirming what the data tell us). We describe techniques for analysis appropriate to all three stages (including stem-and-leaf displays, traditional descriptive statistics, and various methods of confirmation ranging from error bars to confidence intervals to traditional inferential techniques such as analysis of variance). We walk students through a research study using actual data from a published article, illustrating the stages of analysis and informing students what may and may not be said on the basis of analysis techniques. For instance, we discuss at length through a series of questions posed to students what they may conclude (or not conclude) on the basis of traditional null-hypothesis testing techniques. The appendix also presents the rationale and guidelines for obtaining measures of effect size as well as conducting a power analysis. Power tables are now included in this edition. We expect undergraduate students to find some of these statistical issues challenging, but we are optimistic that careful study of the material in this appendix will give them the necessary background both to read critically published research articles and to analyze data from their own research projects.

- **Improvement by Chapter:** In the chapter material we continue in this edition to identify for students how statistical analysis and methods are intertwined. In Chapter 4 we open the door to more complex correlational analysis with a (new) brief illustration of path analysis. In the experimental chapters (6–8) we again emphasize analysis of variance techniques in conjunction with effect size analyses, but also (in Chapter 6) illustrate graphical interpretation and the use of confidence intervals when confirming what data tell us. For this latter example, we had the gracious cooperation of Judy DeLoache and her colleagues who provided statistical summaries of actual data from her cross-cultural research on children's cognition. In this way we were able to illustrate difficult statistical concepts in the context of interesting contemporary psychological research, which is our never-ceasing goal when revising.

- **A New Sample APA Manuscript:** The topic of the new sample paper is false memory and is written to illustrate the most current recommendations of APA regarding report writing (e.g., including power analyses and effect size measures when reporting results). Like its predecessor, however, the manuscript details an actual research study.

- **Web Site:** Both students and instructors using this edition will also benefit from a new web site that was designed for this book. Much of the material that was published before in a workbook written to accompany the major text is now found on this web site. There are interactive exercises and quizzes for students to test their knowledge of text material, as well as links to other important psychology web sites. Instructors will find an image bank to prepare transparencies for class use, and both students and instructors may easily contact the authors via this site. Please come see us at www.mhhe.com/shaughnessy.

## WORDS OF THANKS

Many knowledgeable and discerning reviewers over the years contributed to this latest edition. Among the most recent to whom we are grateful are

Laura Bowman
   *Central Connecticut State University*
Angela Farris Watkins
   *Spelman College*
Joel Freud
   *University of Arkansas*
Brenda Kirby
   *LeMoyne University*

Laura Thompson
   *New Mexico State University*
Terri Bonebright
   *DePauw University*
David Basden
   *California State
   University–Fresno*

If a change that was recommended didn't appear, it wasn't because we didn't consider carefully what these reviewers were telling us. We did. Thanks for pushing us to be better.

The cumulative contributions of many others to this and earlier editions are by now beyond easy acknowledgment. Yet, some people stand out as helping to prepare this latest edition. They include our colleagues at Loyola University Chicago, Emil Posavac and Scott Tindale, who read and critiqued the new appendix dealing with data analysis and interpretation, and Joe Sherwin, Director of Research Services at Loyola, who read carefully the ethics chapter and made important suggestions for changes. The secretarial staff at Loyola made many things easier. In particular we want to acknowledge Lillian Hardison, Anita Sissac, and Marilyn Domingo. And many thanks go to Paula Shaughnessy, who stood in below-zero wind chill to snap a picture of three silly people running around in shorts one cold December day. Andy Apodaca, with just a little supervision from Liz Zechmeister, did a marvelous job of proofreading, checking references, and preparing the indexes.

We also would like to acknowledge the editorial and production staff at McGraw-Hill. Jane Vaicunas, as editorial director, has been with us for several editions now. Joe Terry was the senior sponsoring editor who brought things together, with a lot of help from his editorial assistant, Barbara Santoro. Susan Kunchandy and Jim Rozsa helped develop and market the book, respectively. Our project manager, Gloria Schiesl, and production supervisor, Sandy Hahn, got us through copy editing and page proofing, and then out the door. The supplement coordinator, Lai Moy, worked with John Shaughnessy to develop the instructor's manual. Cover designer, Rick Noel, made us look smart outside and Toni Michaels helped with photos inside. Our copy editor, Bea Sussman, was very helpful and did a superb job. Finally, these last two editions have benefited from the beautiful drawings by our good friend Fran Hughes. She makes research methods something to look at!

John J. Shaughnessy
Eugene B. Zechmeister
Jeanne S. Zechmeister

# General Issues

# Introduction

## CHAPTER OUTLINE

## PSYCHOLOGY AS A SCIENCE

- The scope of scientific psychology has increased dramatically in the 100-plus years since its inception.
- The American Psychological Association (APA) and the American Psychological Society (APS) promote the science of psychology.

There is no record of who first observed behavior carefully and systematically, who conducted the first public opinion survey, or even of who performed the first psychology experiment. We don't really know exactly when psychology first became an independent discipline. It emerged gradually, with its roots in the thinking of Aristotle (the "father" of all psychology; Keller, 1937), in the writings of later philosophers such as Descartes and Locke, and, even later, in the work of early 19th-century physiologists and physicists.

The date usually taken to mark psychology's official beginning is 1879. In that year Wilhelm Wundt established a formal psychology laboratory in Leipzig, Germany. Wundt, like many scientists of his time, had a doctoral degree in medicine. He even published for a while in the fields of anatomy and physiology. These experiences gave Wundt a basis for his ideas about a "physiological psychology" that led to his scientific approach to psychology. Dozens of researchers from around the world came to his psychology laboratory to learn about the "new" discipline. As a consequence, from Wundt's laboratory a scientific psychology spread quickly to the intellectual centers of the world. According to one noted historian, Wilhelm Wundt was the first person "who without reservation is properly called a psychologist" (Boring, 1950, p. 316).

Whatever exact date one accepts for the beginning of a scientific psychology, we can see that the enterprise is little more than 100 years old. Near the end of the 19th century, in 1892, the American Psychological Association (APA) was formed, with G. Stanley Hall as its first president. Hall had been a student at

Wilhelm Wundt
(1832–1920)

William James
(1842–1910)

Harvard of the well-known American philosopher and psychologist William James. In 1878, James bestowed upon Hall the first Ph.D. in psychology given in the United States. After receiving his degree, Hall left the United States to study with Wundt in Germany (Boring, 1950). Still later, in 1887, Hall founded the first psychology journal in the United States, the *American Journal of Psychology*. The APA had only a few dozen members in its first year; 100 years later, in 1992, when the APA celebrated its 100th birthday, there were approximately 70,000 members (see American Psychological Association, 1991).

Psychology has changed significantly since its beginnings. Wundt and his colleagues were primarily interested in questions of sensation and perception—for instance, visual illusions and imagery. Experiments on reaction time also were conducted with the goal of measuring the time necessary for various cognitive processes, such as those involved in making choices (Boring, 1950). Psychologists continue to be interested in sensation and perception, and Wundt's procedures form the basis of some of the experimental methods in use today. However, research on sensation and perception represents but a fraction of the research undertaken in contemporary psychology. Today psychologists are interested in a myriad of topics, including those in such general areas as clinical, social, industrial, counseling, physiological, cognitive, educational, and developmental psychology.

Psychology has also not developed strictly as a laboratory science. Although laboratory investigation remains at the heart of psychological inquiry, psychologists and other behavioral scientists do research in schools, clinics, businesses, hospitals, and other nonlaboratory settings, including the Internet (see, for example, Smith & Leigh, 1997). Many research psychologists, for instance, are engaged in program evaluation, a type of research in which the impact of large-scale interventions on groups or institutions is evaluated. Program evaluators confront questions such as whether a new management–labor relations program will lead to increased employee morale and company productivity, or whether the nationwide Head Start program has significantly raised the IQ of hundreds of thousands of preschoolers (see Chapter 10).

Promotion of psychological research is a concern of the APA as well as the American Psychological Society (APS). Formed in 1988 to emphasize mainly scientific issues in psychology, APS has grown at a phenomenal rate. When APS celebrated its 10th anniversary in 1998, there were more than 15,000 members (see Ruksznis, 1998). Although many psychologists choose to join either APA or APS, many join both. APA and APS both sponsor annual conventions, which psychologists attend to learn about the most recent developments in their fields; each organization also publishes scientific journals in order to communicate the latest research findings to its members and to society in general; and both organizations encourage student affiliation, which provides educational and research opportunities for both undergraduate and graduate psychology students. By affiliating with APA and APS, students can subscribe to major psychology journals at a relatively low cost as well as become involved at an early stage in a career in psychology. Information about joining APA and APS as a regular member or as a student affiliate can be obtained by writing to the respective head offices, or by consulting their World Wide Web pages on the Internet at:

(APA) http://www.apa.org
(APS) http://www.psychologicalscience.org

Both the APA and APS web sites provide news about important recent psychological research findings, information about psychology publications, and links to many psychology organizations. Take a look!

## THE SCIENTIFIC METHOD

- Psychologists use the scientific method to gain knowledge about human and animal behavior.
- The scientific method differs from nonscientific ("everyday") approaches to gaining knowledge.

There is one way in which psychology has not changed in the 100 years or so of its existence: The **scientific method** is still emphasized as the basis for investigation. The founding of Wundt's laboratory marked the beginning of the formal application of the scientific method to problems in psychology. This method is not identified with particular kinds of equipment, nor is it associated exclusively with specific research procedures. The scientific method is something abstract. It is an approach to knowledge that is best described by distinguishing it from what might be called *nonscientific* or "everyday" approaches to knowledge.

### Scientific and Nonscientific Approaches to Knowledge

- The scientific method is empirical and requires systematic, controlled observation.
- To achieve control in a research situation, researchers manipulate independent variables or select levels of individual differences variables to determine their effect on behavior.
- Dependent variables are measures of behavior used to assess the effects of independent variables.
- Scientific reporting is unbiased and objective; clear communication of concepts occurs when operational definitions are used.
- Scientific instruments are accurate and precise; physical and psychological measurement should be valid and reliable.
- A hypothesis is a tentative explanation for a phenomenon; testable hypotheses have clearly defined concepts (operational definitions), are not circular, and refer to concepts that can be observed.
- Scientists adopt a skeptical attitude and are cautious about accepting explanations until sufficient empirical evidence is obtained.

**TABLE 1.1**   CHARACTERISTICS OF SCIENTIFIC AND NONSCIENTIFIC (EVERYDAY) APPROACHES TO KNOWLEDGE*

|  | Nonscientific (everyday) | Scientific |
|---|---|---|
| General Approach: | Intuitive | Empirical |
| Observation: | Casual, uncontrolled | Systematic, controlled |
| Reporting: | Biased, subjective | Unbiased, objective |
| Concepts: | Ambiguous, with surplus meanings | Clear definitions, operational specificity |
| Instruments: | Inaccurate, imprecise | Accurate, precise |
| Measurements: | Not valid or reliable | Valid and reliable |
| Hypotheses: | Untestable | Testable |
| Attitude: | Uncritical, accepting | Critical, skeptical |

*Based in part on distinctions suggested by Marx (1963).

Several major differences between a scientific and a nonscientific approach to knowledge are outlined in Table 1.1. Collectively, the characteristics listed under "Scientific" define what is called the scientific method. The distinctions made in Table 1.1 between a scientific and a nonscientific approach are intended to highlight differences that frequently exist between an informal and casual approach that often characterizes our everyday thinking and thinking that is characteristic of the scientist's approach to knowledge. These distinctions are briefly summarized as follows.

General Approach   Many everyday judgments are made intuitively. This usually means that we act on the basis of what "feels right" or what "seems reasonable." Intuition is not based on a formal decision process, such as that of deductive logic, nor is it based on information that was taught to us or that we acquired through direct experience. The many everyday inferences and conclusions reached intuitively are the product of insight and of what we quickly perceive as true.

Intuition is a valuable cognitive process. We frequently have little to go on other than what intuition suggests is the right answer or the proper course to follow. Intuition can also help us make decisions in situations that we have not encountered before. Consider, for example, what intuition might suggest as the answer to a question based on the following situation:

Assume that on two different occasions you are the victim of a street crime. Let us say that you are walking down the street and someone tries to grab your wallet or purse. The thief begins to wrestle with you in order to get it. You find yourself in need of assistance. On one occasion there is a crowd of bystanders who witness the attempted robbery. On the other occasion there is only one person who sees the event. The question is: In which situation would you be more likely to receive help, when many people are present or when only one person is present?

Intuition would suggest that the more people present, the greater the chances that at least one person would help. Surprisingly, social psychologists have determined that just the opposite is true. A bystander is more likely to act in an emergency when alone than when a group of people is present (Latané & Darley, 1970; see also Chapter 3).

Our intuition about what is true does not always agree with what is actually true because we fail to recognize that our perceptions may be distorted by what are called cognitive biases or because we neglect to weigh available evidence appropriately (Kahneman & Tversky, 1973; Tversky & Kahneman, 1974). One such cognitive bias, for instance, is called *illusory correlation*. This is our tendency to perceive a relationship between events when none exists. To illustrate this bias, Ward and Jenkins (1965) showed people the results of a hypothetical 50-day cloud-seeding experiment. For each of the 50 days, the research participants were told whether cloud seeding had been done and whether it had rained on that day. Ward and Jenkins constructed the results such that there was actually no relationship between cloud seeding and the likelihood of rain—rain was equally likely on days when seeding had and had not been done. Nonetheless, people were convinced that the evidence supported their intuitive supposition that cloud seeding and rain varied together. One possible basis for the illusory-correlation bias is that we are more likely to notice events that are consistent with our beliefs than events that violate our beliefs. Thus, in Ward and Jenkins' study, people may have been more likely to notice and remember the days on which cloud seeding was followed by rain than the days on which clouds were seeded in vain because they believe cloud seeding produces rain.

The scientific approach to knowledge is empirical rather than intuitive. An **empirical approach** emphasizes direct observation and experimentation as a way of answering questions. This does not mean that intuition plays no role in science. Any scientist can probably recount tales of obtaining empirical results that intuition had suggested would emerge. On the other hand, the same scientist is also likely to have come up with just as many findings that were counterintuitive. Research at first may be guided by what the scientist's intuition suggests is the proper direction to take. Eventually, however, the scientist strives to be guided by what direct observation and experimentation reveal to be true.

Observation   We can learn a great deal about behavior by simply observing the actions of others. However, everyday observations are not always made carefully or systematically. Most people do not attempt to control or eliminate factors that might influence the events that they are observing. As a consequence, erroneous conclusions are often drawn. Consider, for instance, the classic case of Clever Hans. Hans was a horse who was said by his owner, a German mathematics teacher, to have amazing talents. Hans could count, do simple addition and subtraction (even involving fractions), read German, answer simple questions ("What is the lady holding in her hands?"), and give the date, and tell time (Watson, 1914/1967). Hans answered questions by tapping with his forefoot or by pointing with his nose at different alternatives shown to him. His owner considered Hans to be truly intelligent and denied using any tricks to guide his horse's behavior. And, in fact, Clever Hans was clever even when the questioner was someone other than his owner.

Newspapers carried accounts of Hans's performances, and hundreds of people came to view this amazing horse (Figure 1.1). In 1904 a scientific commission was established with the goal of discovering the basis for Hans's abilities.

**FIGURE 1.1**    Top: Clever Hans performing before onlookers. Bottom: Hans being tested under more controlled conditions when Hans could not see the questioner.

The scientists found that Hans was no longer clever if either of two circumstances existed. First, Hans did not know the answers to questions if the questioner also did not know the answers. Second, Hans was not very clever if he could not see his questioner. It was discovered that Hans was responding to very slight movements of the questioner. A slight bending forward by the questioner would start Hans tapping, and any movement upward or backward would cause Hans to stop tapping. The commission demonstrated that questioners were unintentionally cuing Hans in this way.

This famous account of Clever Hans illustrates the fact that scientific observation (unlike casual observation) is systematic and controlled. Indeed, it has been suggested that **control** is the essential ingredient of science, distinguishing it from nonscientific procedures (Boring, 1954; Marx, 1963). In the case of Clever Hans, investigators exercised control by manipulating, *one at a time*, conditions such as whether the questioner knew the answer to the questions asked and whether Hans could see the questioner (see Figure 1.1). By exercising control, taking care to investigate the effect of various factors one by one, the scientist seeks to gain a clearer picture of the factors that actually produce a phenomenon.

The factors that the researcher controls or manipulates in order to determine their effect on behavior are called the **independent variables.** In the simplest of studies, the independent variable has two levels. These two levels often represent the presence and the absence of some treatment, respectively. The condition in which the treatment is present is commonly called the *experimental condition*; the condition in which the treatment is absent is called the *control condition*. If we wanted to study the effect of drinking alcohol on the ability to process complex information quickly and accurately, for example, the independent variable would be the presence or absence of alcohol in a drink that participants were given. Participants in the experimental condition would receive alcohol, while participants in the control condition would receive the same drink without alcohol.

The levels of the independent variable do not always represent the presence and the absence of some treatment; moreover, an independent variable may have more than two levels. What is critical is that the levels differ with respect to the variable of interest. For example, Heath and Davidson (1988) recruited female college students to participate in a study designed to aid in the development of a rape-prevention pamphlet. When volunteers appeared in the laboratory, they were asked to review one of three packages of materials that they were told was being considered for possible inclusion in the pamphlet. The three packages of materials varied in the manner in which rape was described. Specifically, the materials to be reviewed presented rape as being very controllable, somewhat controllable, or not at all controllable. After reviewing the materials, the women were asked a series of questions regarding their own perceptions of the risk of rape. The independent variable in this study was the degree of control emphasized in the pamphlet materials; it had three levels (high, medium, low).

Sometimes the levels of the independent variable are selected by a researcher rather than manipulated. This is typically the case when an **individual differences variable** serves as the independent variable. An individual differences variable is a characteristic or trait that varies consistently across individuals. For example, a researcher may be interested in how depression affects perceptions of other people (e.g., Albright & Henderson, 1995). Do depressed individuals, for instance, perceive others more or less accurately than individuals who are not depressed? Level of depression would be the independent variable in this study. Level of depression is an individual differences variable and typically is not manipulated by a researcher; rather, the researcher controls this independent variable by systematically selecting individuals who exhibit varying levels of naturally occurring depression. Intelligence, age, aggressiveness, gender, and fraternity or sorority membership are other examples of individual differences variables. Because individuals are selected from preexisting groups, such as those who are depressed, female, aggressive, and so forth, these variables are also sometimes referred to as *natural groups variables*.

The term *independent variable* is used both for individual differences variables when levels of the variable are selected (e.g., level of depression) and for manipulated variables when the levels are implemented by the researcher (e.g., type of booklet describing rape). Nevertheless, as you will see later in Chapter 6, there are important differences between these two kinds of independent variables.

The measures of behavior that are used to assess the effect (if any) of the independent variables are called **dependent variables.** In our example of a study that investigates the effects of alcohol on processing complex information, the researcher might measure the number of errors made by control and experimental participants when playing a difficult video game. Errors, then, would be the dependent variable. Most studies in psychology are done in order to discover the nature of the relationship between particular independent and dependent variables. In the Heath and Davidson (1988) rape study, there were several dependent variables, represented by the women's responses to questions on the rape-perception questionnaire. The results showed that women who read materials emphasizing rape as an uncontrollable event reported higher anxiety when outside on the street or inside their homes, and a greater intention to take precautionary steps, than did women who reviewed the materials describing rape as more controllable. Interestingly, results of additional experiments carried out by Heath and Davidson (1988) indicated that although uncontrollable rape is definitely viewed as anxiety producing, the "intent" to be more cautious reported by their research participants may not always be followed by actual changes in behaviors. Unfortunately, when rape is perceived as an uncontrollable event some women may view attempts to reduce their vulnerability to attacks as futile.

If changes in the dependent variable are to be interpreted unambiguously as a result of the effect of the independent variable, proper control techniques must be used. The story of Clever Hans was used to show how scientists use control to eliminate alternative explanations for a phenomenon (e.g., that Clever Hans was, in fact, clever). Throughout this text, we will be describing specific control procedures used by psychologists when carrying out research (see especially Chapters 6 and 7).

Reporting    If we ask someone to *report* to us about events that occurred in our absence, we probably want the report to be unbiased and objective. Otherwise we will be unable to determine exactly what happened. As you might imagine, personal biases and subjective impressions often enter into everyday reports that we receive. Ask anyone to describe an event to you and you are likely to receive not merely details of the event but also personal impressions. You may also find that the details reported to you are not the ones that you would have reported. We often report events in terms of our own interests and attitudes. Obviously, these interests and attitudes do not always coincide with those of others. The next time you take a class examination, poll several classmates on their impressions of the test. Their reports are likely to vary dramatically, depending on such factors as how well prepared they were, what they concentrated on when they studied, and their expectations about what the instructor was going to emphasize on the test.

When scientists report their findings, they seek to separate what they have observed from what they conclude or infer on the basis of these observations. For example, consider the photograph in Figure 1.2. How would you describe to someone what you see there? One way to describe this scene is to say that two people are running along a path with another person running in front of them. You might also describe this scene as three people *racing* each other. If you use this second description, you are reporting an inference drawn from what

**FIGURE 1.2**    How would you describe this scene?

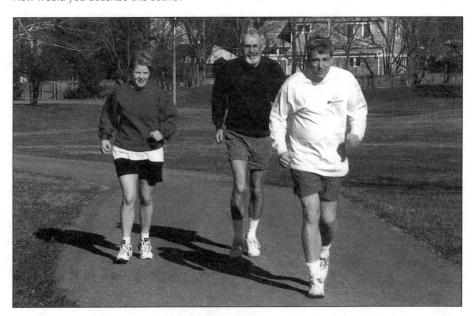

you have seen and not just reporting what you have observed. The description of three people running would be preferred in a scientific report.

This distinction between description and inference in reporting can be carried to extremes. For example, describing what is shown in Figure 1.2 as running could be considered an inference, the actual observation being that three people are moving their legs up and down and forward in rapid, long strides. Such a literal description also would not be appropriate. The point is that, in scientific reporting, observers must guard against a tendency to draw inferences too quickly. Further, events should be described in sufficient detail without including trivial and unnecessary minutiae. Proper methods for making observations and reporting them will be discussed in Chapter 3.

Scientific reporting seeks to be unbiased and objective. One accepted check on whether a report is unbiased is whether it can be verified by more than one independent observer. A measure of interobserver agreement, for example, is usually found in observational studies (see Chapter 3). Unfortunately, many biases are subtle and not always detected even in scientific reporting. Consider the fact that there is a species of fish in which the eggs are incubated in the mouth of the male parent until they hatch. The first scientist to observe the eggs disappear into their father's mouth could certainly be forgiven for assuming, momentarily, that he was eating them. That's simply what we expect organisms to do with their mouths! But the careful observer waits, watches for unexpected results, and takes nothing for granted.

Concepts   We use the term *concepts* to refer to things (both living and inanimate), to events (things in action), and to relationships among things or events, as well as to their characteristics (Marx, 1963). "Dog" is a concept, as is "barking," and so is "obedience." Concepts are the symbols by which we ordinarily communicate. Clear, unambiguous communication of ideas requires that we use concepts that are clearly defined. This means that the concepts we use should be free of unwarranted or surplus meaning. That is, a concept should not convey more meaning than was intended.

In everyday conversation we can often get by without having to worry too much about how we define a concept. Many words, for instance, are commonly used and apparently understood even though neither party to the communication knows *exactly* what the words mean. We are suggesting that people frequently communicate with one another without being fully aware of what they are talking about. This may sound ridiculous but, to illustrate our point, try the following.

Ask a few people whether they believe that intelligence is mostly inherited or mostly acquired. You might try arguing a point of view opposite to theirs just for the fun of it. After having engaged them in a discussion about the roots of intelligence, ask them what they mean by "intelligence." You will probably find that most people have a difficult time defining this concept. Yet people are frequently willing to debate an important point regarding intelligence, and even take a definite stand on the issue, without being able to say exactly what "intelligence" is. When someone does provide a definition, it is unlikely to be exactly the same as that given by another person. That is, "intelligence" means one thing to one person and something else to another. Clearly, in order to attempt to answer the question of whether intelligence is mainly inherited or mainly acquired, we must provide an exact definition that all parties involved can accept. On the other hand, we can talk about it, even argue about it, on an everyday basis without knowing exactly what it is we are talking about!

One way in which a scientist gives meaning to a concept is by defining it operationally. An **operational definition** explains a concept solely in terms of the operations used to produce and measure it. Intelligence, for instance, can be defined operationally by specifying a paper-and-pencil test emphasizing understanding of logical relationships, short-term memory, and familiarity with the meaning of words. Some may not like this operational definition of intelligence, but once a particular test has been identified, there can at least be no argument about what intelligence means *according to this definition*. Operational definitions facilitate communication, at least among those who know how and why they are used.

Although exact meaning is conveyed via operational definitions, this approach to communication has not escaped criticism. One problem has been alluded to already. That is, if we don't like one operational definition of intelligence, there is nothing to prevent us from giving intelligence another operational definition. Does this mean that there are as many kinds of intelligence as there are operational definitions? Each time a new set of questions is added to a paper-and-pencil test of intelligence do we have a new definition of intelligence? The answer, unfortunately, is that we don't really know. To determine whether a different procedure yields a new definition of intelligence, we would have to seek additional evidence. For example, do people who score high on one test also score high on the second test? If they do, the new test may be measuring the same thing as the old one.

Another criticism of using operational definitions is that the definitions are not always meaningful. For example, defining intelligence in terms of how long one can balance a ball on one's nose is an operational definition that most people would not find very meaningful. How do we decide whether a concept has been meaningfully defined? Once again, the solution is to appeal to other forms of evidence. How does performance on a balancing task compare to performance on other tasks that are commonly accepted as measures of intelligence? We must also be willing to apply common sense to the situation. Do people usually consider balancing a ball evidence of intelligence? Scientists are generally aware of the limitations of operational definitions; however, the clarity of communication that derives from this approach is assumed to outweigh the problems it raises.

**Instruments**    You depend on instruments to measure events more than you probably realize. The speedometer in the car, the clock in the bedroom, and the thermometer used to measure body temperature are all instruments that we would find it difficult to do without. And you can appreciate the problems that arise if one of these instruments is inaccurate. *Accuracy* refers to the difference between what an instrument says is true and what is known to be true. A clock that is consistently 5 minutes slow is not very accurate. Inaccurate clocks can make us late, inaccurate speedometers can earn us traffic tickets, and inaccurate thermometers can lead us to believe that we are ill when we are not. The accuracy of an instrument is determined by *calibrating* it, or checking it with another instrument known to be true. Thus, we periodically call the telephone company to check the accuracy of our clocks based on the recorded messages telling us the "time at the tone," which we assume represent the true time. The accuracy of speedometers can be checked using a combination of observations of roadside distance markers and the seconds ticking off on an accurate watch.

Measurements can be made at varying levels of *precision*. A measure of time in tenths of a second is not as precise as one that is in hundredths of a second. One instrument that yields imprecise measures is the gas gauge in most cars. Although reasonably accurate, gas gauges do not give very precise readings. Most of us have wished at one time or another that the gas gauge would permit us to determine whether we had that extra half gallon of gas that would get us to the next service station.

We also need instruments to measure behavior. Wundt used a reaction-time apparatus to measure the time required for cognitive processing. You can be assured that the precision, and even the accuracy, of instruments of this kind have improved significantly in the last 100 years. Today electronic counters provide precise measures of reaction time in milliseconds (thousandths of a second). Many other instruments are employed in contemporary psychology. To perform a psychophysiology experiment (e.g., when assessing a person's arousal level) requires instruments that give accurate measures of such internal states as heart rate and blood pressure. Tests of anxiety sometimes employ instruments to measure galvanic skin response (GSR). Other behavioral instruments are of the paper-and-pencil variety. Questionnaires and tests are popular instruments used by psychologists to measure behavior (see especially Chapter 4). So, too, are the rating scales used by human observers (see Chapter 3). For instance, rating aggression in children on a 7-point scale ranging from not at all aggressive (1) to very aggressive (7) can yield relatively accurate (although perhaps not too precise) measures of aggression. It is the responsibility of the behavioral scientist to use instruments that are as accurate and as precise as possible.

Measurement   Psychologists must deal with two types of measurement. The first type, *physical measurement*, involves dimensions for which there is an agreed-upon standard and an instrument for doing the measuring. Length is a dimension that can be scaled with physical measurement, and there are agreed-upon standards for units of length. For instance, 1 meter was at one time defined as 1/10,000,000 of the distance between the North Pole and the equator.

This proved impossible to measure precisely, so the definition of 1 meter was changed to the distance between two points on a platinum-iridium bar kept under controlled conditions near Paris, France. Although this provided accuracy to one part in a million, greater precision was sought. In 1960 the meter was defined as 1,650,763.73 wavelengths of the red-orange radiation of the inert gas krypton-86. But even this proved not precise enough for scientists. (When using the krypton measure to determine the distance from the earth to the moon, scientists found themselves in error by more than 1.5 meters.) The definition of the meter was changed to the length of the path traveled by light in a vacuum in 1/299,792,458 of a second.

In most research in psychology, however, the dimensions to be measured do not involve physical measurement. Rulers do not exist for measuring beauty, aggression, or intelligence. For these dimensions we must use a second type of measurement: *psychological measurement*. Agreement among a certain number of observers provides the basis for psychological measurement. If several independent observers agree that a certain action warrants a rating of 3 on a 7-point rating scale of aggression, we can say that we have a psychological measurement of the aggressiveness of the action. When Albright and Henderson (1995) asked individuals who were depressed and who were not depressed to evaluate other people, the researchers provided participants with an 8-point scale to judge the degree to which various statements about people were true. The rather counterintuitive finding was that depressed individuals provided more accurate ratings of other people than did those who were not depressed.

Of course, many dimensions that can be scaled physically can also be measured using psychological measurement. Observers can be asked to judge which of two lines is longer, and, if they consistently select the longer one, we know the observers can "measure" length. This type of measurement is called psychophysical measurement, and it represents one of the earliest areas of experimental investigation in psychology.

It is important that measurement be both valid and reliable. In general, **validity** refers to the "truthfulness" of a measure. A valid measure of a concept is one that measures what it claims to measure. We discussed this aspect of measurement when we mentioned possible operational definitions of intelligence. Intelligence, it was suggested, could be defined in terms of performance on a task requiring one to balance a ball on one's nose. According to the principle of "operationalism," this is a perfectly permissible operational definition. However, most of us would question whether such a balancing act is really a measure of intelligence. In other words, we would want to know if this is a valid measure of intelligence. Can intelligence actually be measured by how long we can keep a ball balanced on our nose? As we indicated earlier, evidence bearing on the validity of this definition would have to come from other sources. The validity of a measure is supported to the extent that people do as well on it as they do on independent measures that are presumed to measure the same concept. For example, if time spent balancing a ball is a valid measure of intelligence, then a person who does well on the balancing task should also do well

**FIGURE 1.3**    Balancing a ball on your nose may be an operational definition of intelligence, but is it a valid measure of intelligence?

on such measures as size of vocabulary, reasoning ability, and other accepted measures of intelligence.

The **reliability** of a measurement is indicated by its consistency. Several different kinds of reliability can be distinguished. When we speak of instrument reliability, we are discussing whether an instrument works consistently. The car that sometimes starts and sometimes doesn't when we engage the ignition is not very reliable. Observations made by two or more independent observers are said to be reliable if they show agreement—that is, if the observations are consistent from one observer to another. When several psychologists asked college students to rate the "happiness" of medal winners at the 1992 Summer Olympics in Barcelona Spain, they found that rater agreement was very high (Medvic, Madey, & Gilovich, 1995). They also found, somewhat counterintuitively, that bronze (third place) medal winners were perceived as happier than silver (second place) medal winners, a finding that was explained by a theory of counterfactual thinking. Apparently, people are happier just making it (to the medal stand) than they are just missing it (i.e., missing a gold medal).

In the context of psychological testing, researchers need to be concerned with test reliability. Are the results obtained on a test consistent from one administration of the test to another? When test scores are not reliable, we don't know what a particular score means. Suppose that in preparing to apply to graduate school in psychology you take the Graduate Record Examination (GRE), a test that is required of applicants to many graduate programs. Scores on this test are then sent to schools to which you are applying. Only if the GRE is a reliable test can a school trust that your score represents how you consistently perform on tests like this one. If a test is not reliable, then we have no way of knowing whether a particular score is high, low, or somewhere in the middle of scores you might possibly obtain on this test.

In subsequent chapters of this book, we will discuss various kinds of validity and reliability and introduce you to various methods for measuring them.

Hypotheses    A **hypothesis** is a tentative explanation for something. It frequently attempts to answer the questions "How?" and "Why?" At one level, a hypothesis may simply suggest how particular variables are related. For example, consider the phenomenon of "depressive realism," which we have alluded to previously. This refers to the idea that in many situations depressed individuals make more accurate (or realistic) judgments than do individuals who are not depressed. Albright and Henderson (1995) wondered whether depressive realism would extend to depressives' judgments about people. They hypothesized that depressed individuals would judge other people more accurately than would those who were not depressed. That is, they hypothesized that level of depression and accuracy of judgments were *related*. You may remember that when these researchers asked participants to rate the degree to which various statements about people were true, the results supported their hypothesis: Depressed individuals gave more accurate ratings of other people than did those who were not depressed.

At a more theoretical level, a hypothesis may offer a reason (the "why") for the way that particular variables are related. For example, Albright and Henderson (1995) suggested that many of us avoid symptoms of depression by perceiving other people less favorably than is actually true. (This way we always look good!) Such a strategy may help us to feel good about ourselves. These researchers further hypothesized that depressed individuals, in contrast, may lose this ability to view people unfavorably. That is, depressed individuals make more accurate (realistic) judgments *because* they have lost the ability to view others unfavorably. Moreover, consistent with their reasoning, individuals who were not depressed (unlike depressed individuals) rated others less favorably than was objectively true.

Nearly everyone has proposed hypotheses to explain some human behavior at one time or another. Why do people commit apparently senseless acts of violence? What causes people to start smoking cigarettes? Why are some students academically more successful than others? One characteristic often distinguishes the hypotheses proposed by the nonscientist from those offered by the scientist: testability. As attractive as it might be, if a hypothesis cannot be tested, it is of no immediate use to science (Marx, 1963).

Hypotheses are not testable *if the concepts to which they refer are not adequately defined*. To say that a would-be assassin shot a U.S. president or other prominent figure because he was mentally disturbed is not a testable hypothesis unless a definition of mentally disturbed can be agreed upon. Unfortunately, psychologists and psychiatrists cannot always agree on what terms such as "mentally disturbed" mean. Often this occurs because an accepted operational definition is not available for these concepts. You may have learned in a psychology class that many of Freud's hypotheses are not testable. One reason has to do with the lack of operational definition for such concepts as *id*. As one prominent researcher has commented, "a criterion of whether or not a so-called empirical concept is a scientific concept is whether or not it has been operationally defined" (Underwood, 1957, p. 52). Therefore, in addition to facilitating clarity in communication, operational definitions offer a means of evaluating whether our hypotheses contain scientifically acceptable concepts.

Hypotheses are also untestable if they are *circular*, in which case the event itself becomes an explanation for the event. One scientist has pointed out that using a definition of an event as an explanation for the event—that is, a *circular hypothesis*—is something you can "catch the late-night talk show hosts doing" all the time (Kimble, 1989). Consider these examples:

— Your eight-year-old son is distractable in school and having trouble reading because he has an attention deficiency disorder.
— The stock market crash of October 19, 1987, was caused by widespread economic panic. (Kimble, 1989, p. 495)

Do you see that by saying a boy is "distractable . . . *because* he has an attention deficiency disorder" doesn't explain anything? An attention deficiency disorder is defined by the inability to pay attention. Thus, such a statement simply says that he doesn't pay attention because he doesn't pay attention! Or that by saying a "stock market crash . . . was *caused* by widespread economic panic" simply suggests that economic panic (as defined by the stock market crash) is due to economic panic?

This scientist goes on to say that "If [he] could make just one change in what the general public (and some psychologists) understand about psychology, it would be to give them an immunity to such misuses of definitions" (Kimble, 1989, p. 495).

A hypothesis also may be untestable if it *appeals to ideas or forces that are not recognized by science*. As we have shown, science deals with the observable, the demonstrable, the empirical. To suggest that people who commit horrendous acts of violence are under orders from the Devil is not testable because it invokes a principle (the Devil) that is not in the province of science. Such hypotheses might be of value to philosophers or theologians but not to the scientist.

Hypotheses in scientific research are often derived from a theory. We'll discuss the nature of scientific theories, their function, and how they are constructed and tested later in this chapter. But now, let us complete this description of a scientific approach by discussing the attitude you must have as a scientist.

Attitude    More than anything else, scientists are skeptical. Not only do they want to "see it before believing it," but they are likely to want to see it again, and again, perhaps under conditions of their own choosing. Behavioral scientists come to this skepticism by recognizing two important facts. First, behavior is complex, and often many factors interact to give rise to a psychological phenomenon. Discovering these factors is often a difficult task. The explanations proposed are sometimes premature, not enough factors having been considered or the existence of one or more factors having gone unnoticed. Second, the behavioral scientist recognizes that science is a human endeavor. People make mistakes. Human inference, as we have suggested, is not always to be trusted. Therefore scientists are often skeptical about "new discoveries" and extraordinary claims.

The skepticism of scientists produces a cautiousness that is often lacking in those without scientific training. Too many people are apparently all too ready to accept explanations that are based on insufficient or inadequate evidence. This is illustrated by the widespread belief in the occult. Rather than approach cautiously the claims of those who promote belief in the paranormal, many people are uncritical in their acceptance. According to public opinion surveys, a large majority of Americans believe in ESP (extrasensory perception), and many people apparently are convinced that beings from outer space have visited earth. About 2 in 5 Americans give some credibility to astrology reports, and as many as 12 million adults report changing their behavior after reading astrology reports (Miller, 1986). Such beliefs are held despite minimal and often contradictory evidence of the validity of horoscopes. This human tendency to ignore certain kinds of evidence is not new. When scientists successfully demonstrated the means by which Clever Hans was so clever, many people continued to believe in his superior reasoning ability (Watson, 1914/1967).

What is responsible for this tendency to propose explanations based on the occult and to resist obvious evidence to the contrary? Singer and Benassi (1981) suggest that an uncritical attitude toward such events has several sources. First, there are many distortions in the media. The public is constantly exposed to television shows, newspaper accounts, and other reports of events presumably caused by supernatural forces. These reports are often presented with little critical evaluation, and scientific evidence for alternative explanations is frequently ignored. The sheer pervasiveness of such reports may lend credibility to them.

Another reason for the widespread acceptance of the occult may be deficiencies in human reasoning. As we emphasized earlier in this chapter, everyday inferences are susceptible to many biases, including the tendency to seek only confirmatory evidence, to jump to conclusions, and to perceive causality in events when none is actually present (see, for example, Zechmeister & Johnson, 1992). Finally, Singer and Benassi find fault with science education. Too often, they suggest, science is taught as a set of facts rather than as a way of approaching knowledge critically and systematically. Thus, people are often impatient with the scientific process and even confused when scientists appear to change their minds or when they attempt to clarify earlier findings. Singer and Benassi also find that the general public exhibits woefully little general scientific knowledge. Many people believe that islands float on the ocean surface, for instance, and that the moon is fixed in the sky but only visible at night. Belief in astrology reports and "lucky numbers," for example, is stronger among people with little formal education than it is among college-educated individuals (Miller, 1986).

Scientists do not, of course, automatically assume that unconventional interpretations of unexplained phenomena could not possibly be true. They simply insist on being allowed to test all claims and to reject those that are inherently untestable. Scientific skepticism is a gullible public's defense against charlatans and others who would sell them ineffective medicines and cures, impossible schemes to get rich, and supernatural explanations for natural phenomena.

## Goals of the Scientific Method

- The scientific method is intended to meet three goals: description, prediction, and understanding.
- Psychologists seek to describe events and relationships between variables; most often, researchers use the nomothetic approach and quantitative analysis.
- Correlational relationships allow psychologists to predict behavior or events, but do not allow psychologists to infer what causes these relationships.
- Psychologists understand the cause of a phenomenon when the three conditions for causal inference are met: covariation, time-order relationship, and elimination of plausible alternative causes.
- The experimental method, in which researchers manipulate independent variables to determine their effect on dependent variables, establishes time-order and allows a clearer determination of covariation.
- Plausible alternative causes for a relationship are eliminated if there are no confoundings in a study; a study free of confoundings has internal validity.
- External validity refers to the extent to which a study's findings may be used to describe different populations, settings, and conditions.

**Description**   Description refers to the procedures by which events and their relationships are defined, classified, cataloged, or categorized. Clinical research, for instance, has provided practitioners with many different sets of criteria for classifying mental disorders. Many of these are found in the American Psychiatric Association's *Diagnostic and Statistical Manual of Mental Disorders* (4th ed., 1994), also known as *DSM-IV*. Consider, as one example, the criteria used to define the disorder labeled *Dissociative Fugue* (formerly Psychogenic Fugue).

### Diagnostic Criteria for Dissociative Fugue

A The predominant disturbance is sudden, unexpected travel away from home or one's customary place of daily activities, with inability to recall one's past.

B Confusion about personal identity or assumption of a new identity (partial or complete).

C The disturbance does not occur exclusively during the course of Dissociative Identity Disorder and is not due to the direct physiological effects of a substance (e.g., a drug of abuse, medication) or a general medical condition (e.g., temporal lobe epilepsy).

D The symptoms cause clinically significant stress or impairment in social, occupational, or other important areas of functioning. (*DSM-IV*, 1994, p. 481)

The diagnostic criteria used to define dissociative fugue provide an operational definition for this disorder. Like many other unusual mental disorders, dissociative fugues are relatively rare; thus, we typically learn about these kinds of disorders based on individual descriptions of people exhibiting them. These descriptions are called "case studies." Clinical research frequently makes use of case studies, a procedure that will be discussed in detail in Chapter 9. Research also seeks to provide clinicians with descriptions of the prevalence of a mental disorder and their relationship to variables including, but not restricted to, gender and age. According to the *DSM-IV* (1994), for instance, dissociative fugue is seen primarily in adults, and although it is relatively rare, it is more frequent "during times of extremely stressful events such as wartime or natural disaster" (p. 482).

Another example of description in psychological research is the work of Levine (1990) who described the "pace of life" in various cultures and countries of the world. Measures of a country's tempo were made by noting the accuracy of outdoor bank clocks in a country's cities, by timing the walking speed of pedestrians over a distance of 100 feet, and by measuring the speed with which postal clerks processed a standard request for stamps. The investigator frequently enlisted the help of students to make observations while they traveled during summer vacations or semester breaks. The results of this study are shown in Figure 1.4. The citizens of Japan exhibited, overall, the fastest pace of life; the citizens of Indonesia were the slowest. U.S. citizens were second overall.

Psychology (like science in general) develops descriptions of phenomena using the *nomothetic approach*. The objective of the nomothetic approach is to establish broad generalizations and "universal laws" that apply to a wide population of organisms. As a consequence, psychological research frequently consists of studies involving large numbers of participants with the purpose of determining the "average," or typical, performance of a group. This average may or may not represent the performance of any one individual in the group. Not all citizens of Japan or the United States, for example, are on the fast track. In fact, Levine (1990) and his colleagues found wide differences in the pace of life among various cities within a country. Inhabitants of large cities walked faster than did those of medium-sized cities in the various countries that were visited. In the United States, differences in a city's tempo were found depending on the region of the country. Cities in the Northeast (e.g., Boston, New York) had a faster tempo than did cities on the West Coast (e.g., Sacramento, Los Angeles). Of course, there will be individual variations within cities as well. Not all citizens of Los Angeles are going to be slow-paced, nor are all New Yorkers going to be fast-paced. Nevertheless, the Japanese move *in general* at a faster

FIGURE 1.4    Measures of accuracy of a country's bank clocks, pedestrian walking speed, and the speed of postal clerks performing a routine task served to describe the pace of life in a country. In the graph a longer bar represents greater accuracy of clocks or greater speed of walking and performing a task (from Levine, 1990).

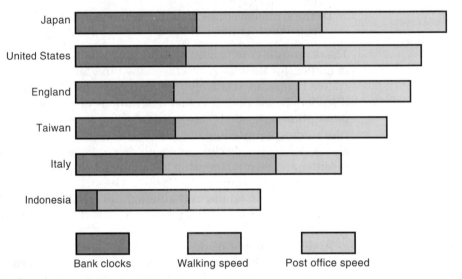

pace than do Indonesians, and Americans on the West Coast exhibit, *on the average*, a slower pace of life than do residents of the Northeast.

The nomothetic approach does not deny that there are important differences *among* individuals; it simply seeks to identify the similarities that exist among these differences. For example, a person's individuality is not threatened by our knowledge that that person's heart, like the hearts of other human beings, is located in the upper left chest cavity. Similarly, we do not deny a person's individuality when we state that that person's behavior is influenced by patterns of reinforcement. Researchers merely seek to describe what organisms are like in general on the basis of the average performance of a group of different organisms.

Although the nomothetic approach predominates in psychological research, there is an alternative. Some psychologists, notably Allport (1961), argue that the nomothetic approach is inadequate—that the individual cannot be represented by an average value. Allport argues that the individual both is unique and exhibits behavior that conforms to general laws, or principles. He maintains that study of the individual, called *idiographic research*, is important. A major form of idiographic research is the case study method, which we will describe in detail in Chapter 9.

Researchers decide whether to make generalizations about groups of individuals or to look for the lawfulness found in one individual's behavior. This decision is largely dictated by the nature of the question being asked. And although many researchers do mainly one or the other kind of research, others may do both. A clinical psychologist, for instance, may decide to pursue mainly idiographic investigations of a few clients in therapy but consider nomothetic issues when doing research with groups of college students. Another decision that the researcher must make is whether to do quantitative or qualitative research. *Quantitative research* refers to studies whose findings are mainly the product of statistical summary and analysis. *Qualitative research* produces research findings that are not arrived at by statistical summary or analysis and lack quantification altogether (see, for example, Strauss & Corbin, 1990).

The data of qualitative research are most commonly obtained from interviews and observations and can be used to describe individuals, groups, and social movements (Strauss & Corbin, 1990). Qualitative research is often about "naturally occurring, ordinary events in natural settings" (Miles & Huberman, 1994, p. 10). Powell-Cope (1995), for instance, used qualitative methods to "describe the experiences of gay couples when at least one was diagnosed with symptomatic HIV infection or AIDS" (p. 36). Van Meter, Yokoi, and Pressley (1994) used a qualitative research approach to develop a theory of student note-taking. The researchers met with university undergraduates in small discussion groups, conducted both directed and undirected interviews, then developed and administered formal questionnaires. According to the authors, this qualitative approach to research on student note-taking yielded "many insights into note-taking dynamics that have not been identified in previous research" (p. 323). Other examples of qualitative research are found in Chapter 3 when we discuss narrative records of observed behavior; case studies described in Chapter 9 also are a form of qualitative research. Just as psychological research is more frequently nomothetic than idiographic, it is also more typically quantitative than qualitative. And although both kinds of research can be usefully employed to describe behavior, our emphasis in this book is mainly on quantitative research.

**Prediction**   Description of events and their relationships often provides a basis for *prediction,* the second goal of the scientific method. There are important questions in psychology that call for predictions. For example: Does the early loss of a parent make a child especially vulnerable to depression? Are children who are overly aggressive likely to have emotional problems as adults? Do stressful life events lead to increased physical illness? Research findings suggest an affirmative answer to all of these questions. This information not only adds valuable knowledge to the discipline of psychology but is also helpful in both the treatment and the prevention of emotional disorders.

An important occupation of many psychologists is the prediction of later performance (e.g., on the job, in school, or in specific vocations) on the basis of earlier performance on various standardized tests. For instance, we mentioned earlier the Graduate Record Examination or GRE. Scores on this test, as well as undergraduate grade-point average (GPA), can be used to predict how well a student will do in graduate school. Yet Sternberg and Williams (1997) suggest that there are limitations on this prediction. They found that while GRE scores predicted fairly well the first-year grades of graduate students at their institution, the GRE was not predictive of other, important performance criteria such as advisors' ratings of a student's creativity, ability to teach, and ability to do research. Not surprisingly, these researchers have sparked a debate by questioning the validity of the GRE, which is so widely regarded as a predictor of students' later professional development (see, for example, "Comment" section of *American Psychologist*, 1998, 53, 566–577).

Interestingly, research has shown that faculty recommendations, which are usually required for graduate school admittance, are also a rather poor predictor of whether a student will successfully complete a doctorate degree (Willingham, 1974). On the other hand, there is research showing that the amount of undergraduate research activity and ratings by peers of a student's commitment to psychology are better predictors of later success in psychology (as measured, for example, by number of scientific publications) than are the more traditional measures, such as GRE scores and GPA (Hirschberg & Itkin, 1978).

When scores on one variable can be used to predict scores on a second variable, we say that the two variables are correlated. A **correlation** exists when two different measures of the same people, events, or things vary together—that is, when particular scores on one variable tend to be associated with particular scores on another variable. When this occurs, the scores are said to "covary." Consider a measure with which you likely have had some experience, namely teacher/course evaluations in classes that you have taken. College students are commonly asked to evaluate their instructors and the course material toward the end of a course. By the time a course is over, you probably have formed many impressions of a teacher (e.g., whether the instructor is supportive, enthusiastic, likeable). After all you have just spent as many as 12 or 14 weeks (perhaps more than 30 hours) in this instructor's classroom. Ambady and Rosenthal (1993) asked how well teacher evaluations by students *not* enrolled in the class would correlate with end-of-the-semester evaluations made by students in the class. They showed video clips (without sound) of teachers to a group of female undergraduates. But, and here is the interesting part, they showed the video clips for only 30 seconds, 10 seconds, or just 6 seconds (across several studies). The researchers found that teacher evaluations based on these "thin slices of nonverbal behavior" correlated well with end-of-the-semester teacher evaluations made by students who were enrolled in the class. These results indicate that people (in this case teachers) reveal much about themselves when their nonverbal behavior is seen only briefly, and also that we (as observers) can make relatively accurate judgments of affective behavior quite quickly. Ambady and Rosenthal's findings, of course, do not mean that all the information in teaching evaluations can be captured by this method as they focused only on judgments of affective behavior (e.g., likeableness).

We can cite one more example of correlational evidence from a study we introduced earlier. When studying the "pace of life," Levine (1990) found a positive correlation between a city's pace of life as measured by people's walking speed and its deaths from heart disease. This indicates that the faster the pace in a city, the more likely its inhabitants are to die from heart disease. Death rates from heart disease, in other words, can be predicted by simply measuring how fast a city's inhabitants typically walk 100 feet!

We are concerned with issues of correlation at various points in this text and discuss the more general topic of correlational research in Chapter 4. Correlational research, which seeks to describe predictive relationships among variables, is a major area of psychological research.

It is important to point out that successful prediction doesn't always depend on knowing why a relationship exists between two variables. Consider the report that the Chinese rely on observing animal behavior to help them predict earthquakes. Certain animals apparently behave in an unusual manner just before an earthquake. The dog that barks and runs in circles and the snake seen fleeing its hole, therefore, may be reliable predictors of earthquakes. If so, they could be used to warn people of forthcoming disasters. We might even imagine that in areas where earthquakes are likely, residents would be asked to keep certain animals under observation (as miners once kept canaries) to warn them of conditions of which they are as yet unaware. This would not require that we understand why certain animals behave strangely before an earthquake, or even why earthquakes occur.

You may remember that Levine (1990) showed that measures of the pace of a city can be used to predict death rates from heart disease. However, we can only speculate about why these measures are related. One possible explanation for this correlation suggested by the researchers is that people living in time-urgent environments engage in unhealthy behaviors, for example, cigarette smoking and poor eating habits, which increase their risk of heart disease (Levine, 1990). To account for the relationship between *non*student ratings and student teacher evaluations, Ambady and Rosenthal (1993) suggested that people are "attuned" to quickly picking up information about a person's affect because this information is important (adaptive) in real-life decision making. Without additional information, however, this idea must remain speculation.

Understanding    Although they are important goals in themselves, description and prediction are only the first steps in understanding a phenomenon. Understanding is the third and most important goal of the scientific method. It is achieved when the cause or causes of a phenomenon are identified. The scientist sets three important conditions for making a **causal inference** and, hence, of understanding: *covariation of events; a time-order relationship; and, the elimination of plausible alternative causes.*

If one event is the cause of another, the two events must vary together—that is, when one changes, the other must also change. This is the principle of covariation that we noted was the basis of the goal of prediction. Further, the presumed cause must occur before the presumed effect. This is the second condition, a time-order relationship. Finally, causal explanations are accepted only when other possible causes of the effect have been ruled out—when plausible alternative causes have been eliminated.

Unfortunately, people have a tendency to conclude that all three conditions for a causal inference have been met when really only the first condition is satisfied. For example, research has suggested that parents who are stern disciplinarians and who use physical punishment are more likely to have aggressive children than are parents who are less stern and use other forms of discipline. Parental discipline and children's aggressiveness obviously covary. Moreover, the fact that parents are typically assumed to influence how their children behave might lead us to think that the time-order condition has been met— parents use physical discipline and children's aggressiveness results. More recent research has shown, however, that infants vary in how active and aggressive they are and that the infant's behavior has a strong influence on the *parents'* responses in trying to exercise control. In other words, some children may be naturally aggressive and require stern discipline rather than stern discipline producing aggressive children. Therefore, the direction of the causal relationship may be opposite to what we thought at first.

It is important to recognize, however, that the causes of events cannot be identified unless covariation has been demonstrated. The first objective of the scientific method, description, can be met by describing events under a single set of circumstances. The goal of understanding, however, requires more than this. For example, suppose that a teacher wished to demonstrate that so-called "active learning strategies" help students learn. She could teach students using this approach and then describe the performance of the students who received instruction in this particular way. But at this point what would she know? How do we know that another group of students taught using an approach that did not use active learning strategies might not learn the same amount? Before the teacher could claim that the performance she observed was caused by the use of active learning strategies, she would have to compare this method with some other reasonable approach that did not employ active learning strategies. She would look for a difference in learning between the group using active learning strategies and a group not using this method. Such a finding would show that teaching strategy and performance covary. As you will see in Chapter 6, this is one reason why manipulation is such an important method of control for scientists. By manipulating independent variables, such as type of learning strategy, the investigator can determine more clearly whether any subsequent covariation occurs in the dependent variable. If it does, a bonus results from using manipulation: The time-order condition has also been met, because the researcher changes the independent variable (e.g., teaching method) and *subsequently* measures the changes, if any, in the dependent variable (e.g., a measure of student learning).

By far the most challenging condition to be met in making a causal inference is eliminating other plausible alternative causes. For example, consider a study in which the effect of two different teaching approaches (active and passive) is to be assessed. You can see that one way not to assign students to teaching conditions in this study would be to have all men in one group and all women in the other. If this were done, the independent variable of teaching method would be "confounded" with the independent variable of gender. **Confounding** occurs when two potentially effective variables are allowed to covary simultaneously. When research is confounded, it is impossible to determine what variable is responsible for any obtained difference in performance. If males were assigned to one condition of our hypothetical teaching experiment and females to another, then we would not know whether any difference we observed was due to gender of the participant or to the independent variable of type of teaching. When no confoundings are present, a research study is said to have **internal validity.** Much of the discussion in this book will focus on developing skills in performing internally valid research by learning to identify and eliminate confoundings.

The internal validity of a study, which relates to our ability to make causal inferences based on it, must be distinguished from the study's **external validity.** External validity involves the extent to which the research results can be generalized to different populations, settings, and conditions. A research finding may be internally valid and have little external validity. Although free of confoundings, the study may not be able to be generalized. Questions of external validity in science often arise, for instance, when results obtained with animal subjects are claimed to apply to human participants as well. Researchers frequently depend on experiments with animals to obtain information about human psychopathology and other illnesses. Animal models have been used to study drug addiction, minimal brain dysfunction, and various forms of mild to severe psychopathology (Maser & Seligman, 1977), as well as psychosomatic factors in various human illnesses (see Hofer & Myers, 1996). A frequent focus of animal research has been the effect of stress on the development of mental and physical illness. And while these studies have yielded valuable information about the effects of stress in animals, it is not clear whether these findings can be easily generalized to situations involving human responses to stress (e.g., Weiner, 1996). Nevertheless, as Hofer and Myers (1996) emphasize, the goal of animal research is the "enrichment of clinical and human research," and while "in themselves animal studies can never settle questions about human nature, . . . they can allow clinicians and those who study normal humans to ask more highly focused research questions that can be tested in the limited studies that are possible with our own species" (p. 522).

Because laboratory research, in general, is often conducted under more controlled conditions than are found in natural settings, an important task of the scientist is to determine whether laboratory findings generalize to the "real world." This is often the goal of what is called *field research*. By performing in the "field" (outside the laboratory) an experiment that is similar to an experiment that has been carried out in the laboratory, a researcher can provide evidence bearing on the external validity of laboratory results. Research conducted outside the laboratory often requires methods and procedures that are specifically designed for this less well controlled environment. Later in this book we will introduce some of the methods used by psychologists to conduct field research (see especially Chapters 3 and 10).

## Scientific Theory Construction and Testing

- Theories, proposed explanations for the causes of behavior, vary in their scope and their level of explanation.
- A scientific theory is a logically organized set of propositions that defines events, describes relationships among events, and explains the occurrence of events.
- Successful scientific theories organize empirical knowledge, guide research by offering testable hypotheses, and survive rigorous testing.
- Theories frequently posit intervening variables to explain observed behavior.
- Researchers evaluate theories by judging the theory's internal consistency, observing whether hypothesized outcomes occur when the theory is tested, and noting whether the theory makes precise predictions based on parsimonious explanations.

Theories are "ideas" about how nature works. Psychologists propose ideas about why behavior occurs the way it does (e.g., what causes schizophrenia), about the nature of cognition (e.g., how people solve problems), and so on. A psychological theory can be developed on different levels: For example, it can be developed on a physiological or on a symbolic level (see Anderson, 1990; Simon, 1992). A theory of schizophrenia may, in other words, propose biological causes (e.g., specific genetic carriers), psychological causes (e.g., patterns of emotional conflict, stress), or both. The propositions contained in theories may be expressed as verbal statements, as mathematical equations, or even as computer programs.

An important dimension on which theories differ is scope. The *scope* of a theory refers to the range of phenomena that it seeks to explain. A theory of "flashbulb memory," for instance, attempts to explain why the personal circumstances surrounding particularly surprising and emotional events, such as the explosion of the space shuttle *Challenger*, are remembered better than are details associated with everyday events (see, for example, Brown & Kulik, 1977; McCloskey, Wible, & Cohen, 1988). Many older adults, for instance, can apparently remember precisely what they were doing when they heard about the assassination of President Kennedy. The scope of a theory of flashbulb memory is relatively restricted, proposing as it does an explanation of the nature and cause of an interesting but very specific memory phenomenon. A theory of human love, such as that proposed by Sternberg (1986), is an example of a psychological theory of much greater scope. Sternberg shows how the amount and kind of love one experiences is a function of three critical behavioral components: intimacy, passion, and decision/commitment. Even broader in scope is Anderson's (1990; 1993; Anderson & Milson, 1989) theory of human cognition, which offers an account of how cognition works in general, including ideas about learning, memory, problem solving, and so on. Clearly, the scope of a theory can be quite large. In general, the greater the scope of a theory the more complex it is likely to be. Complexity may be a necessary characteristic of psychological theories

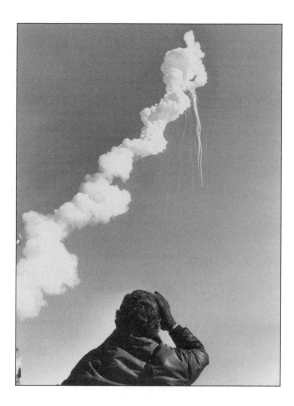

**FIGURE 1.5**    A theory of "flashbulb memory" seeks to explain why personal circumstances surrounding vivid, emotional events, such as the explosion of the space shuttle *Challenger*, are seemingly remembered so much better than are details of everyday events.

given the nature and range of phenomena psychologists try to understand. Complexity also can be a serious obstacle, however, to testing a theory. Most theories in contemporary psychology tend to be relatively modest in scope, attempting to account only for a limited range of phenomena.

The source of a scientific theory is a mixture of intuition, personal observation, and discovered knowledge (known facts and ideas). The famous philosopher of science, Karl Popper (1976, pp. 268–269), suggested that truly creative theories spring from a combination of "intense interest in a problem (and thus a readiness to try again and again)" and "critical imagination." *Critical imagination* is the ability to think critically, but there is more. It includes a readiness to challenge accepted ideas and an "imaginative freedom that allows us to see so far unsuspected sources of error" in previous thinking about a problem. Critical imagination, in other words, means traveling beyond what others have said are the boundaries (limits) of thinking about a problem. Assuming we have that important burning interest in a problem, one way we might approach constructing a scientific theory is by critically examining what is known, looking for flaws or unseen sources of error in that knowledge.

Whatever the nature and scope of a theory, whether it be expressed mathematically or verbally or developed at a physiological level or at some higher-order level, the theory includes certain assumptions and concepts that must be explained in order for it to be understood and tested. A theory of flashbulb memory, for instance, needs to state exactly what a flashbulb memory *is*, showing, for example, how flashbulb memory differs from other, more typical memory. A complete theory must also explain why in some cases a person's so-called flashbulb memory is clearly wrong, even though the individual expresses high confidence in the (inaccurate) memory (see Neisser & Harsch, 1992). To be complete, therefore, a theory must include definitions of various events or concepts (e.g., emotional events, test accuracy), information about relationships between these events (e.g., the relationship between degree of emotional involvement and amount remembered), and so forth. Thus, we can offer the following formal definition of a scientific **theory:** *a logically organized set of propositions (claims, statements, assertions) that serves to define events (concepts), describe relationships among these events, and explain the occurrence of these events.*

The major functions of a theory are to *guide* research and to *organize* empirical knowledge (Marx, 1963). In the early 1960s, Rotter (1966) developed a theory of internal versus external locus of control. In this theory, Rotter differentiates individuals who perceive a contingency between their behavior and what happens to them (internal locus of control) and those who perceive that their behavior has little consequence for what happens to them (external locus of control). Rotter developed a questionnaire to define this concept on the basis of the idea that individuals differ in locus of control because of the way they have been rewarded during their development. The theory suggests a relationship between perceived locus of control and anxiety, with greater anxiety associated with greater perceived external locus of control. The theory has guided researchers for many years and has served to organize a body of empirical literature regarding self-efficacy, or the feeling of being able to cope with the environment (see, for example, Myers, 1999). The success of a psychological theory such as the locus-of-control theory can be measured by the degree to which it achieves the two important goals of guiding research and organizing empirical findings.

A scientific theory guides research by suggesting testable hypotheses. You may remember that hypotheses, like theories, are explanations for behavior; however, a hypothesis typically is simpler and more tentative than is a scientific theory (Marx, 1963). We described earlier in this chapter several factors that affect the testability of hypotheses, including the important criterion of operational specificity of concepts. It is important that hypotheses derived from a theory attempt to meet these criteria.

Theories frequently require that we postulate intervening processes to account for observed behavior (Underwood, 1975). An intervening process is one that "mediates" between certain antecedent conditions and behavior. We have been discussing one such intervening process, memory. We can safely say that we have never "seen" memory. It is something that we infer based on observations of our own behavior and that of others when asked about a previous experience. We assume that there is some record of experiences somewhere inside us which we refer to when queried about a previous experience. The concept "memory" is proposed as an intervening process to explain the behavior we have observed. Mediating processes such as memory are called *intervening variables*. To be useful to the scientist, it is important that these concepts have a clear relationship to behavior (see Kimble, 1989). That is, although we might infer many kinds of unseen processes to help explain behavior, unless we tie down intervening processes to observed relationships between specific antecedents (independent variables) and behavior (dependent variables), our theories are scientifically weak. For example, a theory that proposes a "free-floating" process to explain behavior cannot be shown to be wrong. Because free-floating processes (e.g., "the little person inside me") are not tied to specific empirical relationships, they can be called into play in any and every situation to "explain" behavior.

How scientific theories should be evaluated and tested is one of the most complex and difficult issues in psychology and philosophy (e.g., Meehl, 1978, 1990a, 1990b; Popper, 1959). At least one scientist, however, suggests a rather straightforward procedure. Kimble (1989, p. 498) says quite simply, "The best theory is the one that survives the fires of logical and empirical testing." Although somewhat simplistic, this is a good starting point. A theory can be evaluated first on the basis of its organization, its logical consistency. Are its propositions arranged in a meaningful way? Is the theory free of contradictions? Can specific deductions about expected behavior be made from it easily? Theories are tested logically by exposing their internal structure to the critical eye of members of the scientific community. A particular theory's propositions, assumptions, and definitions are frequently the topic of debate in scientific journals. Ideas about the exact definition of flashbulb memories, for example, have been debated at length in the psychology literature (e.g., Cohen, McCloskey, & Wible, 1990; Pillemer, 1990; Winograd & Neisser, 1992).

Kimble (1989) suggests that a theory is strengthened or weakened according to the outcomes of empirical tests of hypotheses derived from it. Successful tests of a hypothesis serve to increase the acceptability of a theory; unsuccessful tests serve to decrease the theory's acceptability. The best theory, in this view, is the one that passes these tests successfully. But there are serious obstacles to testing hypotheses and, as a consequence, confirming or disconfirming scientific theories. For example, a theory, especially a complex one, may produce many specific testable hypotheses. Therefore, a theory is not likely to fall on the basis of a single test (e.g., Lakatos, 1978). Moreover, theories may include propositions and concepts that have not been adequately defined or suggest intervening processes that are related to behavior and to each other in complex and even mysterious ways. Such theories may have a long life, but their value to science is questionable (Meehl, 1978).

When constructing and evaluating a theory, scientists place a premium on parsimony (Marx, 1963). The *rule of parsimony* is followed when the simplest of alternative explanations is accepted. When choosing among theoretical propositions, scientists tend to favor the simplest of them. This rule is nicely illustrated by the comments made by Albert Einstein in response to a young psychology student's question about the cognitive "process that occurred when

[he] had [his] most productive thought" (Fromm, 1998, p. 1195). In 1932, Erika Fromm, who was then a student of Max Wertheimer, the founder of Gestalt psychology, wrote letters to 100 leading scientists and philosophers as part of a psychological study of productive thinking. Among the responses she received was one from Einstein. He described the nature of the thinking that led to his theory of relativity, a process which he then characterized in the following way:

> It was always the search for a logically simple meaning of empirically established relationships, propelled by the conviction that there existed a simple logical meaning. (Fromm, 1998)

*Precision of prediction* is another criterion by which a theory can be evaluated. Theories that make precise predictions about behavior are preferred to those that make only general predictions (Meehl, 1990a). For instance, a theory of flashbulb memory that predicts the precise nature and duration of a "forgetting function" for such a memory is clearly a better theory than one that simply states that these memories will be remembered "longer" than other memories. Stated another way, some tests are easier for theories to pass than are others. A good scientific theory is one that is able to pass the most rigorous tests. *Rigorous testing* includes more tests that seek to falsify a theory's propositions than ones that seek to confirm them (Cook & Campbell, 1979). While confirming a particular theory's propositions provides support for the specific theory that is being tested, confirmation logically does not rule out other, alternative theories of the same phenomenon.

Although theories can be difficult and challenging to work with, the process of constructing and evaluating scientific theories is at the core of the scientific enterprise and is absolutely essential for the continuation of the science of psychology.

## SCIENTIFIC INTEGRITY

- Psychologists are obligated to conduct research of the highest integrity.
- The American Psychological Association (APA) has adopted a code of ethics to guide the professional behavior of psychologists.

Science is a search for truth. Fraud, lies, and misrepresentations should play no part in a scientific investigation. But science is also a human endeavor, and frequently much more is at stake than truth. Both scientists and the institutions that hire them compete for rewards in a game with jobs, money, and reputations on the line. The number of scientific publications authored by a university faculty member, for instance, is usually a major factor influencing decisions regarding professional advancement through promotion and tenure. Under these circumstances, there are unfortunate, but seemingly inevitable, cases of scientific misconduct.

A variety of activities constitute violations of scientific integrity. They include data fabrication, plagiarism, selective reporting of research findings, failure to acknowledge individuals who made significant contributions to the research, misuse of research funds, and unethical treatment of humans or animals (see Adler, 1991). Some transgressions are easier to detect than others. Out-and-out fabrication of data, for instance, can be revealed when, in the normal course of science, results are not able to be reproduced by independent researchers, or when logical inconsistencies appear in published reports. However, more subtle transgressions, such as reporting only data that meet expectations or misleading reports of results, are difficult to detect. The dividing line between intentional misconduct and simply bad science is also not always clear.

To educate researchers about the proper conduct of science, and to help guide them around the many ethical pitfalls that are present, most scientific organizations have adopted formal codes of ethics. In Chapter 2 we will introduce you to the APA ethical principles governing research with humans and animals. As you will see, ethical dilemmas often arise. Consider the research by Heath and Davidson (1988) mentioned earlier in this chapter. You may remember that they asked groups of university women to help prepare a new rape-prevention pamphlet. Their participants reviewed materials that presented rape as very controllable, somewhat controllable, or not at all controllable. Women who read the uncontrollable version reported greater levels of anxiety about rape than did women who read the other versions. However, the researchers did not actually intend to produce a new rape-prevention pamphlet. Participants in this research were deceived regarding the true purpose of the study: to investigate how perceived controllability of rape influences women's perceptions of vulnerability to rape. Under what conditions should researchers be allowed to deceive research participants?

Deception is just one of many ethical issues that researchers must confront. As yet another illustration of ethical problems, we mentioned that animal subjects sometimes are used to help understand human psychopathology. This may mean exposing animal subjects to stressful and even painful conditions. Again, we must ask about the ethical issues involved with this type of research. Under what conditions should research with animal subjects be permitted? The list of ethical questions raised by psychological research is a lengthy one. Thus, *it is of the utmost importance that you become familiar with the APA ethical principles and their application at an early stage in your research career, and that you participate (as research participant, assistant, or principal investigator) only in research that meets the highest standards of scientific integrity.*

## GETTING STARTED DOING RESEARCH

— What to study?
— How do I find a hypothesis to test?
— Is my research question a good one?

There are many decisions that must be made before beginning to do research in psychology. The first one, of course, is, what to study. In what area of psychology do I wish to do research? Many students approach the field of psychology with interests in psychopathology and issues associated with mental illness. Others are intrigued with the puzzles surrounding human cognition, such as memory, problem solving, and decision making. Still others are interested in problems of developmental and social psychology. Psychology provides a smorgasbord of research possibilities to explore, as is illustrated by the literally hundreds of scientific journals that publish the results of psychological research. You can quickly find information about the many research areas within psychology by reviewing the contents of a standard introductory psychology textbook. More specific information can be found, of course, in the many classes offered by the psychology department of your college or university, such as abnormal psychology, cognitive psychology, and social psychology.

The next decision is a bit harder. How do I come up with a research hypothesis? McGuire (1997) believes that the ability to generate testable hypotheses can be described and taught to students. He identified 49 simple rules ("heuristics") for generating a hypothesis to be tested scientifically. We can not review all 49 suggestions here, but we can give you some insight into McGuire's thinking about scientific thinking by listing some of these heuristics. He suggests, for example, that we might generate a hypothesis for a research study by:

— thinking about deviations (oddities, exceptions) from a general trend or principle;
— imagining how *we* would behave in a task or faced with a specific problem;
— considering similar problems whose solution is known;
— making sustained, deliberate observations of a person or phenomenon (e.g., performing a case study);
— considering the opposite direction of plausible causality for a phenomenon;
— generating counterexamples for an obvious conclusion about behavior;
— exploring alternative labels for phenomena;
— "jolting one's conceptualizing out of its usual ruts" by shifting attention to the opposite pole of the problem or expressing a question in different modalities (e.g., pictures, words, symbols);
— coming up with multiple explanations for a given finding;
— thinking about how people need to function in a given environment;
— borrowing ideas or theories from other disciplines;
— looking for irregularities in previous results and attempting to reconcile conflicting outcomes;
— trying new modes of data collection such as performing qualitative analyses of a quantitative finding or carrying out new statistical analyses of old data.

No matter how or where you begin to develop a hypothesis for your research, at some point you will find yourself needing to peruse the published literature of psychological research. There are several reasons why you must search the psychology literature before beginning to do research. One obvious reason is that the answer to your research question may already be there. Someone else may have entertained the same question and provided an answer, or at least a partial one. It is highly unlikely that you will not find some research finding that is related to the research question you have chosen to answer. This should not discourage you; in fact, it should be a source of satisfaction. Finding that other people have done research on the same or similar idea will give you the "in" that is necessary to build the science of psychology. Doing research without a careful examination of what is already known may be interesting or fun (it certainly may be easy); perhaps you could call it a "hobby," but we can't call it science. Science is a cumulative affair: Current research builds on previous research. Once you have identified a body of literature related to your research idea, your reading may lead you to discover, as McGuire (1997) suggested, inconsistencies or contradictions in the published research. You may also find that the research findings are limited in terms of the nature of the participants studied or the circumstances under which the research was done, or that there is a psychological theory in need of testing. Having made such a discovery, you have found a solid research lead, a path to follow.

When reading the psychological literature and thinking about possible research questions, you might also consider how the results of psychological studies might be applied to societal problems. Later we discuss differences between basic and applied research (see especially Chapter 10). Suffice it to say that applied research typically focuses on improving the human condition. As you learn how to do research in psychology, you may want to consider ways this knowledge can be used to generate questions that when answered will make humankind just a little better off.

Searching the psychology literature is not the tedious task that it once was; computer-aided literature searches, including use of the Internet, have made identifying related research a relatively easy, even exciting task. In Appendix C of this book we outline how to search the psychology literature, including ways to use computer-based guides.

**FIGURE 1.6**  Computers have made reviewing psychological literature a relatively easy task.

Finally, as Sternberg (1997) points out, choosing a question to investigate should not be taken lightly. Some questions are simply not worth asking because their answers offer no hope of advancing the science of psychology. The questions are, in a word, meaningless, or at best, trivial. "How do I know if my research question is a good one?" Sternberg (1997) suggests that students new to the field of psychological research ask themselves several questions before deciding they have a good research question:

— Why might this question be scientifically important?
— What is the scope of this question?
— What are likely outcomes if I carry out this research project?
— To what extent will psychological science be advanced by knowing the answer to this question?
— Why would anyone be interested in the results obtained by asking this question?

As you begin the research process, finding answers to these questions may require guidance from research advisors and others who have successfully answered them in their own research. We also hope that your ability to answer these questions will be enhanced as you learn more about theory and research in psychology and as you read about the many examples of interesting and meaningful psychological research that we describe in this book.

Of course, identifying a research problem doesn't necessarily tell you *how* to do the research. What is it exactly that you want to know? Answering this question will mean that you must make other decisions as well. Should I do a qualitative or quantitative research study? What is the nature of the variables I wish to investigate? How do I find reliable and valid measures of behavior? What is the research method best suited to my research question? What kinds of statistical analyses will be needed? Do the methods I choose meet accepted moral and ethical standards?

A major goal of this book is to provide you with the information to help make these decisions and many others associated with the research process.

## THE ORGANIZATION OF THIS BOOK

This book provides an introduction to the way in which the scientific method is applied in psychology. As you are probably aware, the scope of psychology is quite large, encompassing many areas of study. Moreover, no single research methodology can be said to answer all the questions raised in a particular area. Thus, the best approach to answering a question about behavior or mental processes is frequently a *multimethod approach*—that is, searching for an answer using different research methodologies.

The organization of the book follows loosely the goals for the scientific method. Following a discussion of ethical issues in research (Chapter 2), we introduce you to what are called *descriptive methods*. Naturalistic observation, for instance, is an important tool of psychologists who want to describe behavior in a natural context (see Chapter 3). Questionnaires are among the most commonly used instruments in psychology and frequently are the basis for making *predictions* about behavior. The nature of questionnaires and their use in survey research are discussed in Chapter 4. Several less commonly used measures of behavior—those based on the examination of archival records and those derived from the study of physical traces—are treated in Chapter 5. In the third part of the book we deal with *experimental approaches* to the study of behavior. The emphasis is on experiments done with groups of participants (see Chapters 6–8). Experimental approaches are aimed chiefly at discovering cause-and-effect relationships. However, experimental methods used in the laboratory are not necessarily the same as those used outside the laboratory.

Finally, in the fourth section of the book we introduce you to the methods employed in *applied research*. In Chapter 9 there is a discussion of experiments conducted with small numbers of research participants, in fact, with single individuals ($N = 1$). In that chapter we also discuss the important case study method. The last chapter deals with quasi-experimental designs and with the important topic of program evaluation, which is concerned with assessing the effects of "treatments" applied in natural settings (see Chapter 10).

## SUMMARY

Psychology's official beginning is marked by the establishment, in 1879, of a formal psychology laboratory in Leipzig, Germany, under the direction of Wilhelm Wundt. With this beginning came the first applications of the scientific method to problems of psychology. As an approach to knowledge, the scientific method is characterized by a reliance on empirical procedures, rather than intuition, and by an attempt to control the investigation of those factors believed responsible for a phenomenon. Those factors that are systematically controlled in an attempt to determine their effect on behavior are called independent variables. The measures of behavior used to assess the effect (if any) of the independent variable are called dependent variables.

Scientists seek to report results in an unbiased and objective manner. This goal is enhanced by giving operational meaning to concepts. Scientists also seek to measure phenomena as accurately and precisely as possible. Measurement involves both physical and psychological measurement. Scientists seek both validity and reliability of these measures.

Hypotheses are tentative explanations of events. To be useful to the scientist, however, hypotheses must be testable. Hypotheses that lack adequate definition, that are circular, or that appeal to ideas or forces outside the province of science are not testable. Hypotheses are often derived from theories. More than anything else, scientists are skeptical. A skeptical attitude is not always found among nonscientists, who may rush to accept "new discoveries" and extraordinary claims.

The goals of the scientific method are description, prediction, and understanding. Both quantitative and qualitative research are used to describe behavior. Observation is the principal basis of scientific description. When two measures correlate, we can predict the value of one measure by knowing the value of the other. Understanding is achieved when the causes of a phenomenon are discovered. This requires that evidence be provided for covariation of events, that a time-order relationship exists, and that alternative causes be eliminated. When two potentially effective variables covary such that the independent effect of each variable on behavior cannot be determined, we say that our research is confounded. Confounding must be avoided if we wish to produce a study with internal validity. The external validity of a study involves the extent to which research results can be generalized to different populations, settings, and conditions.

Scientific theory construction and testing provide the bases for a scientific approach to psychology. Theories have the important function of guiding research and organizing empirical knowledge. Finally, many ethical questions are raised by psychological research; it is important that the science of psychology be carried out according to the highest standards of scientific integrity. Getting started doing psychological research requires us to make several important decisions, including those about what topic to investigate, what is the specific question I wish to answer, and is my question a good one? Finally, we must decide exactly how to *do* the research.

## KEY CONCEPTS

| | |
|---|---|
| scientific method | reliability |
| empirical approach | hypothesis |
| control | correlation |
| independent variable | causal inference |
| individual differences variable | confounding |
| dependent variable | internal validity |
| operational definition | external validity |
| validity | theory |

## REVIEW QUESTIONS

1 For each of the following characteristics, indicate how the scientific approach differs from nonscientific (everyday) approaches to knowledge: general approach, observation, reporting, concepts, instruments, measurement, hypotheses, and attitudes.

2 What is the major advantage of using operational definitions in psychology? What disadvantages are there in using operational definitions?

3 Distinguish between the accuracy of a measuring instrument and its precision.

4 What distinguishes physical measurement from psychological measurement?

5 What three shortcomings often keep hypotheses from being testable?

6 Why do behavioral scientists always seek to maintain a skeptical attitude?

7 What are the three goals of the scientific method?

8 What do we mean when we say that the nomothetic approach is used in science? How is the nomothetic approach different from the idiographic approach?

9   Provide an example both of quantitative research and of qualitative research.

10  What three conditions must be met if one event is to be considered the cause of another?

11  Distinguish between the internal validity and the external validity of a research study.

12  Describe how a scientific theory can be used to guide and organize empirical research.

13  Identify at least three characteristics used to evaluate a theory.

14  Explain the use of intervening variables in theory construction. What important quality should an intervening variable have?

## CHALLENGE QUESTIONS

1   In each of the following descriptions of research studies, you are to identify the independent variable(s). You should also be able to identify at least one dependent variable in each study.

A   A psychologist was interested in the effect of food deprivation on motor activity. She assigned each of 60 rats to one of four conditions differing in the length of time for which the animals were deprived of food: 0 hours, 8 hours, 16 hours, 24 hours. She then measured the amount of time the animals spent in the activity wheel in their cages.

B   A physical education instructor was interested in specifying the changes in motor coordination with increasing age in young children. He selected six groups of children and gave each child a test of motor coordination. The groups of children differed in age—that is, one group was made up of all 5-year-olds, the next group was all 6-year-olds, and so on up to the sixth group, which was all 10-year-olds.

C   A developmental psychologist was interested in the amount of verbal behavior very young children displayed depending on who else was present. The study he did involved selecting children who were either 2, 3, or 4 years old. These children were observed in a laboratory setting for a 30-minute period. Half of the children of each age were assigned to a condition in which an adult was present with the child during the session. The other half of the children were assigned to a condition in which another young child was present during the session with the child being observed. The psychologist measured the number, duration, and complexity of the verbal utterances of each observed child.

2   In the following description the independent variable of interest is confounded with a potentially relevant independent variable. Identify the confounding variable and explain clearly how the confounding occurred. Also state exactly what conclusion can be supported on the basis of the evidence presented. Finally, suggest ways in which the study could be done so that it would be internally valid.

A physiological psychologist developed a drug that she thought would revolutionize the world of horse racing. She named the drug Speedo, and it was her contention that this drug would lead horses to run much faster than they do now. (Forget, for the sake of this problem, that it is illegal to give drugs to racehorses.) She selected two groups of horses and gave one of the groups injections of Speedo once a week for 4 weeks. Because Speedo was known to have some negative effects on the horses' digestive systems, those horses given the Speedo had to be placed on a special high-protein diet. Those horses not given the Speedo were maintained on their regular diet. After the 4-week period, all the horses were timed in a 2-mile race and the mean times for the horses given Speedo were significantly faster than the mean times for those not given Speedo. The psychologist concluded that her drug was effective.

3  Two physicians did a study to try to determine why people who are allergic to cats still keep them as pets. They asked 67 patients (22 male and 45 female) with an average age of 40 years to complete a questionnaire concerning the nature of their attachment to their cat. Even though 11 people had a history of emergency room visits following exposure to cats, 38 said they would definitely replace their cat if it died, and an additional 16 reported they would have difficulty avoiding a new acquisition. Having someone to love and companionship were the most commonly selected reasons for having cats. The physicians concluded that cat ownership meets strong psychological needs in allergic patients. What comparison information is needed before reaching the conclusion that the psychological reasons for owning a cat are peculiar to allergic patients?

4  When presented with only correlational evidence, the investigator can only hypothesize about possible causal factors underlying a relationship between variables. A stage wherein the investigator thinks about possible causal factors and "tries them out" as explanations, perhaps during discussions with other researchers, is often a preliminary step to doing research that may provide evidence for the factors responsible for the reported relationship. For each of the following reports of covariation, identify a possible causal factor—that is, speculate on *why* these events are correlated.

A  A study of nearly 5,000 Swedish women (20 to 44 years old) revealed that couples who live together before marriage have an 80% higher probability of getting divorced than do married couples who do not live together before marriage.

B  Married women are found to suffer from depression more than men. However, the greater the marital compatibility, the less the risk of depression among women.

C  In the late 1980s the National Institutes of Health sponsored a conference to assess available data regarding the healing power of pets. The idea is that having pets is good for you. One investigator reported that among 92 coronary patients, pet owners were more likely to be alive 1 year after discharge from a coronary heart unit than were people who do not own a pet.

## Answer to Challenge Question 1

A  IV: hours of food deprivation with four levels; DV: time (in minutes) animals spent in activity wheel

B  IV: age of children with six levels (distinguish selection of levels from manipulation in part A); DV: scores on test of motor coordination

C  IV: age at three levels and additional person present with two levels (again, distinguish selection and manipulation); DV: number, duration, and complexity of child's verbal utterances

# Ethical Issues in the Conduct of Psychological Research

## CHAPTER OUTLINE

## INTRODUCTION

A scientist has an ethical responsibility to do the following:

— seek knowledge;
— carry out research in a competent manner;
— report results accurately;
— manage available resources honestly;
— fairly acknowledge, in scientific communications, the individuals who have contributed their ideas or their time and effort;
— consider the consequences to society of any research endeavor;
— speak out publicly on societal concerns related to a scientist's knowledge and expertise (Diener & Crandall, 1978).

In order to meet these obligations, the scientist must consider the numerous ethical issues and questions of proper scientific conduct. To help guide the ethical behavior of psychologists, the American Psychological Association (APA) has formulated an Ethics Code to aid ethical decision making in the context of doing research, as well as in other contexts, for example, when teaching, doing therapy, or serving as administrators (see American Psychological Association, 1992). The Ethics Code deals with such diverse issues as sexual harassment, fees for psychological services, test construction, classroom teaching, and expert witnesses.

As stated in the Preamble to the Ethics Code, psychologists are expected to make "a personal commitment to a lifelong effort to act ethically; to encourage ethical behavior by students, supervisees, employees, and colleagues, as appropriate; and to consult with others, as needed, concerning ethical problems" (p. 39). It is important for students of psychology also to make this commitment. They should familiarize themselves with the Ethics Code and make every effort to live up to its stated ideals and standards of behavior. (A copy of the complete APA Ethics Code can be obtained from the APA Order Department, American Psychological Association, 750 First Street, N.E., Washington, DC 20002-4242.)

Many of the ethical standards in the APA's Ethics Code deal directly with psychological research (see especially Sections 6.06–6.26 of the code), including the treatment of both humans and animals in psychological research. As with most ethical codes, the standards tend to be general in nature and require specific definition in particular contexts. Often more than one ethical standard applies to a research situation, and at times the standards may even appear to contradict one another. For instance, ethical research requires that human participants be protected from physical injury. Research, however, that involves drugs or other invasive treatments may place participants at risk of physical harm. The welfare of animal subjects should be protected; however, as we saw in Chapter 1, certain kinds of research may involve inflicting pain or other suffering on an animal. Solving these ethical dilemmas is not always easy and requires a deliberate, conscientious problem-solving approach to ethical decision making.

Ethical decisions are best made after consultation with others, including one's peers but especially those who are more experienced or knowledgeable in a particular area. In fact, review of a research plan by persons not involved in the research is legally required in some situations. In the remaining sections of this chapter, we identify those standards from the Ethics Code that deal specifically with psychological research. We also offer a brief commentary on some aspects of these standards and present several hypothetical research plans that raise ethical questions. By putting yourself in the position of having to make judgments about the ethical issues raised in these research proposals, you will begin to learn to grapple with applying particular ethical standards and with the difficulties of ethical decision making in general. We urge you to discuss these proposals with peers, teachers, and others who have had prior experience doing psychological research.

## Things You Need to Know Before You Begin to Do Research

- Prior to conducting any study, the research must be reviewed to determine if it meets ethical standards.

Because research psychologists must consider a host of ethical issues, problems can be avoided only by planning carefully and consulting with appropriate individuals and groups *prior to doing the research.* The failure to conduct research in an ethical manner undermines the entire scientific process, retards the advancement of knowledge, and erodes the public's respect for the scientific and academic communities. It can also lead to significant legal and financial penalties for individuals and institutions. The following ethical standards spell out some things researchers must keep in mind as they begin to do psychological research.

## APA Ethical Standards

### 6.06 Planning Research

1 **(a)** Psychologists design, conduct, and report research in accordance with recognized standards of scientific competence and ethical research.
   **(b)** Psychologists plan their research so as to minimize the possibility that results will be misleading.
   **(c)** In planning research, psychologists consider its ethical acceptability under the Ethics Code. If an ethical issue is unclear, psychologists seek to resolve the issue through consultation with institutional review boards, animal care and use committees, peer consultations, or other proper mechanisms.
   **(d)** Psychologists take reasonable steps to implement appropriate protections for the rights and welfare of human participants, other persons affected by the research, and animal subjects.

### 6.07 Responsibility

1 **(a)** Psychologists conduct research competently and with due concern for the dignity and welfare of the participants.

**(b)** Psychologists are responsible for the ethical conduct of research conducted by them or by others under their supervision or control.

**(c)** Researchers and assistants are permitted to perform only those tasks for which they are appropriately trained and prepared.

**(d)** As part of the process of development and implementation of research projects, psychologists consult those with expertise concerning any special population under investigation or most likely to be affected.

### 6.08 Compliance With Law and Standards

Psychologists plan and conduct research in a manner consistent with federal and state law and regulations, as well as professional standards governing the conduct of research, and particularly those standards governing research with human participants and animal subjects.

### 6.09 Institutional Approval

Psychologists obtain from host institutions or organizations appropriate approval prior to conducting research, and they provide accurate information about their research proposals. They conduct the research in accordance with the approved research protocol.

## Commentary

As you can see, the importance of consulting with others about ethical issues prior to doing research cannot be overemphasized. It is particularly critical that a researcher obtain prior approval from the proper institutional committee before doing research.

- Institutional Review Boards (IRBs) review psychological research to protect the rights and welfare of human participants.
- Institutional Animal Care and Use Committees (IACUCs) review research conducted with animals to ensure that animals are treated humanely.

The National Research Act, signed into law in 1974, resulted in the creation of the National Commission for the Protection of Human Subjects of Biomedical and Behavioral Research. This act requires that institutions, such as colleges and universities, seeking research funds from specific federal agencies, establish committees to review research sponsored by the institution. These committees, referred to as Institutional Review Boards (IRBs), review psychological research at these institutions in order to safeguard the rights and welfare of human participants. Federal regulations impose very specific requirements on the makeup and duties of these committees (see *Federal Register*, June 18, 1991). For example, an IRB must be composed of at least five members with varying backgrounds and fields of expertise. Both scientists and nonscientists must be represented, and there must be at least one IRB member who is not affiliated with the institution. Responsible members of the community, such as members of the clergy, lawyers, and nurses, are asked to serve on these committees.

**FIGURE 2.1**    Many ethical questions are raised when research is performed with humans and animals.

**FIGURE 2.1**     (*Continued*)

A psychology student seeking to do research with human participants is apt to be asked first to satisfy the regulations of a department committee charged with reviewing research conducted in the psychology department. Depending on the association of this departmental committee with an IRB, research falling into various well-defined categories is either reviewed at the departmental level or referred to the IRB, which has the authority to approve, disapprove, or require modifications prior to the approval of the research.

In 1985 the Department of Agriculture, as well as the Public Health Service, formulated new guidelines for the care of laboratory animals (Holden, 1987). As a result, institutions doing research with animal subjects are now required to have an Institutional Animal Care and Use Committee (IACUC), whose members minimally must include a scientist, a veterinarian, and at least one person not affiliated with the institution. Review of animal research by IACUCs extends to more than simply overseeing the research procedures. Federal regulations governing the conduct of animal research extend to specifications of animal living quarters and the proper training of personnel who work directly with the animals (Holden, 1987).

Nearly every college and university requires that all research conducted at the institution be reviewed at some stage by an independent committee. Violation of federal regulations regarding the review of research involving humans or animals can bring a halt to research at an institution, spell the loss of federal funds, and result in substantial fines (Holden, 1987; Smith, 1977). Given the complex nature of federal regulations and the policies of most institutions requiring review of research with humans and animals, *any individual who wants to do research should inquire of the proper authorities, prior to starting research, about the appropriate procedure for institutional review.*

## THE RISK/BENEFIT RATIO

- A subjective evaluation of the risks and benefits of a research project is used to determine whether the research should be conducted.

In addition to checking if appropriate ethical principles are being followed, a major function of an IRB is to arrive at a consensus regarding what is sometimes called the *risk/benefit ratio*. Despite use of the term *ratio*, the risk/benefit ratio is nothing like a mathematical ratio with easily calculable components. The decision to do research must rest on a subjective evaluation of the costs and benefits both to the individual and to society. Failure to do research may cost society the benefits of the knowledge gained from the research and, ultimately, an opportunity to improve the human condition. To do research may at times exact a cost from individual participants—for example, research participants risk injury when exposed to potentially harmful circumstances. The principal investigator must, of course, be the first one to consider these potential risks and benefits. Nevertheless, determining the ratio, and hence the decision to do research, is most appropriately made by knowledgeable individuals who do not have a personal interest in the research. As we have indicated, this is often the role played by a department ethics committee or an IRB.

In its simplest form, the **risk/benefit ratio** asks the question, Is it worth it? When the inconvenience and risks to participants are considered, is there sufficient potential benefit to the individual and to society to carry out this research? Many factors affect a decision regarding the proper balance of risks and benefits of a research activity. The most basic are the nature of the risk and the magnitude of the probable benefit to the participant as well as the potential scientific and social value of the research (Fisher & Fryberg, 1994). When the benefits to an individual are clear and immediate, or when there is obvious scientific and social value associated with the research, a greater risk can be tolerated than when the benefits are less clear or their application is less immediate. For instance, in the context of research investigating the antecedents of psychotic behavior, the possible benefits to both the participants and society may be substantial if a proposed treatment has a good possibility of having a beneficial effect. Society will also benefit as psychologists come to understand more completely such behaviors as aggression, altruism, eating disorders, deviance, and suicide. The benefits to be gained by investigating these behaviors, however, must be continually weighed against the risks to the participants.

In determining the risk/benefit ratio, a researcher must also take into account the probability that valid and interpretable results will be produced. An established scientist with a history of successful research in her field, for instance, would reasonably be judged to have a greater chance of obtaining important results than would an undergraduate psychology major. Rosenthal (1994b) makes a clear point in this regard: "Everything else being equal, research that is of a higher scientific quality is more ethically defensible" (p. 127). More specifically, "If because of the poor quality of the science no good can come of a research study, how are we to justify the use of participants' time, attention, and effort and the money, space, supplies, and other resources that have been expended on the research project?" (Rosenthal, 1994b, p. 128). Thus, *an investigator is obliged to seek to do research that meets the highest standards of scientific excellence.*

When research involves risk, there are considerations beyond making sure the research is planned competently. When risk is present, a researcher must confirm there are no alternative, low-risk procedures that might be substituted or that previous research has not already successfully addressed the research question being asked. Without careful prior review of the psychological literature, for instance, a researcher might carry out research that has already been done, thus exposing individuals to needless risk.

## Determination of Risk

- Potential risks in psychological research include risk of physical injury, social injury, and mental or emotional stress.
- Risks must be evaluated in terms of potential participants' everyday activities, their physical and mental health, and capabilities.

Determining whether research participants are "at risk" illustrates the difficulties involved in ethical decision making. Life itself is a risky affair. Commuting to work or school, crossing streets, and riding on elevators are all activities that have an element of risk. Simply showing up for an appointment to serve in a psychology experiment must be judged to entail some degree of risk. To say that human participants in psychological research can never risk injury would bring all research to a halt. Decisions about what constitutes risk must take into consideration those risks that are part of everyday life.

Any determination of risk must also consider the nature of the participants. Certain activities can reasonably be judged to pose a serious risk for some individuals but not for others. Running up a flight of stairs may substantially increase an elderly person's chance of suffering a heart attack; the same task would not be a serious risk for most young adults. Individuals who are exceptionally depressed or anxious might be expected to show more severe reactions to certain psychological tasks than would other people. Statements about what constitutes risk cannot be easily generalized to all individuals or populations.

Risk is often associated with the possibility of physical injury—that is, when bodily harm is threatened. More often, however, participants in social science research risk social or psychological injury. The potential for social risk exists when information gained about an individual through her or his participation in psychological research is revealed to others. Simply knowing that someone completed a questionnaire inquiring about deviant sexual practices could cause social injury if people react differently to that individual as a consequence of their knowledge. Information collected during the conduct of research may include important personal facts about intelligence, personality traits, and political, social, or religious beliefs. A research participant is not likely to want this information divulged to teachers, employers, or peers. Failure to protect the confidentiality of a participant's responses may significantly increase the possibility of social injury.

The potential for psychological injury exists whenever the procedures associated with a research activity are likely to induce serious mental or emotional stress in the participants. A participant in a social psychology experiment involving a simulated emergency, as when smoke enters a room where she is waiting, may experience a substantial amount of emotional stress until the true simulated character of the event is revealed. Merely participating in a psychology experiment is anxiety provoking for some individuals. After learning a list of nonsense syllables, a student participant once volunteered that he was sure the researcher now knew a great deal about him! The student assumed the psychologist was interested in his mental state as revealed by the associations he used when learning the list. In reality, this person was participating in a simple memory experiment designed to measure forgetting. *A researcher is under an obligation to protect participants from emotional or mental stress, including, when possible, that which might arise due to a participant's misconceptions about the nature of a psychological task.*

## Minimal Risk

- When a research study involves procedures or activities that are similar to those experienced by participants in their everyday life, the study is described as having "minimal risk."

A distinction is sometimes made between a participant "at risk" and one who is "at minimal risk." One definition of minimal risk is that followed by IRBs in their review of biomedical and behavioral research (*Federal Register*, January 26, 1981; amended *Federal Register*, June 18, 1991).

**Minimal risk** means that the probability and magnitude of harm or discomfort anticipated in the research are not greater in and of themselves than are those ordinarily encountered in daily life or during the performance of routine physical or psychological examinations or tests.

As an example of minimal risk, consider the fact that many psychology laboratory studies involve lengthy paper-and-pencil tests intended to assess various mental abilities. Participants are frequently under time pressure to complete the tests and may receive specific feedback regarding their performance. No doubt some degree of mental or even emotional stress is associated with participation in these kinds of activities. Within limits, however, the risk of psychological injury in this situation would generally be assumed to be no greater than that of being a student. Therefore, college students would be judged to incur only minimal risk in such experiments. When the possibility of injury is judged to be more than minimal, individuals are considered to be "at risk." When this occurs, more serious obligations fall on the researcher to protect the welfare of such participants.

## Dealing with Risk

- Whether "at risk" or "at minimal risk," research participants must be protected. More safeguards are needed as risks become greater.
- To protect participants from social risks, information they provide should be anonymous, or if that is not possible, the confidentiality of their information should be maintained.

Even when only a slight potential for injury exists, the researcher should try to minimize the risk and provide safeguards for the participants. For instance, stating at the beginning of a memory experiment that the tasks are not intended to measure intelligence or personality reduces the level of stress that some participants experience. When substances are to be taken internally, individuals should be screened prior to participation in order to identify and excuse any who might show unusual physical reactions. In situations where the possibility of harm is judged to be significantly greater than that occurring in daily life, the researcher's obligation to protect participants increases correspondingly. It is not unheard of for an IRB to require that a clinical psychologist be available to counsel individuals when, by participating in a psychology experiment, they are exposed to the possibility of serious emotional stress.

No research activity involving more than minimal risk to participants should be carried out unless alternative, low-risk methods of data collection have been explored. In some cases, descriptive approaches involving observation or questionnaires should be substituted for experimental treatments. It is also possible to take advantage of naturally occurring "treatments." For example, Anderson (1976) interviewed owner-managers of small businesses that had been damaged by hurricane floods. He found that the likelihood of problem-solving coping behaviors by the participants showed an inverted U-shaped function when related on a graph to perceived stress, indicating there is an optimal level of stress and that, when stress is higher or lower than this optimal level, performance decreases. A similar relationship has been demonstrated in a number of experimental laboratory tasks using experimenter-induced stress.

In order to protect research participants from social injury, the method of data collection should preserve the anonymity of participants or, when this is not possible, ensure the confidentiality of responses. Thus, if at all possible, a researcher should obtain information about participants in a manner that does not require individuals to be identified.

Simply not having participants sign their names to the test instruments is obviously one way to keep participation anonymous. When the researcher must test people on more than one occasion or otherwise track specific individuals, numbers can be randomly assigned to participants at the beginning of a study. Only these numbers need appear on participants' response sheets.

When anonymity cannot be preserved, confidentiality should be protected through some type of code system. If the information supplied by participants is particularly sensitive, such a scheme is necessary to minimize the risk of social injury. One procedure is to assign code numbers to participants. Names are then linked with the code numbers on a master list and access to this list restricted by keeping it under lock and key.

Assuring participants of their anonymity or the confidentiality of their responses can also benefit the researcher if such assurances lead the participant to be more honest and open when responding (Blanck, Bellack, Rosnow, Rotheram-Borus, & Schooler, 1992). It can be assumed that participants will be less likely to fabricate or withhold information if they do not have to worry about who will have access to their responses.

### What Do You Think?

For each of the following research situations, do you think only "minimal risk" is present (i.e., risk not greater than that of everyday life) or is more than minimal risk present? If more than minimal risk is present, then participants are judged to be "at risk." In this case, you might think of what safeguards could be employed to reduce that risk. As you do so, you will undoubtedly begin to anticipate some of the ethical issues yet to be discussed in this chapter.

1 College students are asked to complete an adjective checklist describing their current mood. The researcher is seeking to identify students who

are depressed so that they can be included in a study examining cognitive deficits associated with depression.

2 Elderly adults in a nursing home are given a battery of achievement tests in the dayroom at their home. A psychologist seeks to determine if there is a decline in mental functioning with advancing age.

3 Students in a psychology research methods class see another student enter their classroom in the middle of the class period, speak loudly and angrily with the instructor, and then leave. As part of a study of eyewitness behavior, the students are then asked to describe the intruder.

4 A researcher recruits students from introductory psychology classes to participate in a study of the effects of alcohol on cognitive functioning. The experiment requires that some students drink 2 ounces of alcohol (mixed with orange juice) before performing a computer game.

## Obtaining Informed Consent

- Researchers and participants enter into a social contract, often using an informed consent procedure.
- Researchers are ethically obligated to describe the research procedures clearly, identify any potential risks that might influence individuals' willingness to participate, and answer any questions participants have about the research.
- Research participants are ethically obligated to behave appropriately during the research by not lying, cheating, or engaging in other fraudulent behavior.

The success of most human psychological research depends on the willingness of students, patients, clients, and other members of the community to take part in a scientific investigation. At times, participants in psychological research are given money or other compensation for their time and effort. At other times, people simply respond to requests by researchers for volunteers to participate in a research endeavor and expect no compensation. Researchers obtain the **informed consent** of participants to ensure that the participants explicitly express a willingness to take part in the research after having been informed about the nature of the research, the consequences of not participating, and the factors that might be expected to influence their willingness to participate. Researcher and participant enter into a social contract. This contract is sometimes an informal one; however, in other circumstances, the contract includes statements signed by both researcher and participant, as well as by witnesses. As part of this contract, *a researcher has an ethical responsibility to make clear to the participant what the research entails, including any possible risk to the participant, and to respect the dignity and rights of the individual during the research experience.*

Although not often discussed, we wish to emphasize that the research participant also has an ethical responsibility to behave in an appropriate manner, for example, by paying attention to instructions and by performing tasks in the manner requested by the researcher. Taylor and Shepperd (1996) relate how in one study participants were briefly left alone by an experimenter who admonished them not to discuss the experiment among themselves. However, once alone, the participants talked about the experiment and obtained information from each other that in effect negated the value of the research. Moreover, when later asked by the experimenter about what they knew of the procedures and goals of the study, none admitted knowledge gained during their illicit conversation. We suggest that *lying, cheating, or other fraudulent behavior on the part of someone who has agreed to participate in a scientific investigation is as much of a violation of the scientific integrity of the research situation as is the failure of a researcher to fully explain to the participant the risks inherent in the research task.*

## APA Ethical Standards

### 6.10 Research Responsibilities

Prior to conducting research (except research involving only anonymous surveys, naturalistic observations, or similar research), psychologists enter into an agreement with participants that clarifies the nature of the research and the responsibilities of each party.

### 6.11 Informed Consent to Research

(a) Psychologists use language that is reasonably understandable to research participants in obtaining their appropriate informed consent (except as provided in Standard 6.12, Dispensing With Informed Consent). Such informed consent is appropriately documented.

(b) Psychologists inform participants of the nature of the research; they inform participants that they are free to participate or to decline to participate or to withdraw from the research; they explain the foreseeable consequences of declining or withdrawing; they inform participants of significant factors that may be expected to influence their willingness to participate (such as risks, discomfort, adverse effects, or limitations on confidentiality, except as provided in Standard 6.15, Deception in Research); and they explain other aspects about which the prospective participants inquire.

(c) When psychologists conduct research with individuals such as students or subordinates, psychologists take special care to protect the prospective participants from adverse consequences of declining or withdrawing from participation.

(d) When research participation is a course requirement or opportunity for extra credit, the prospective participant is given the choice of equitable alternative activities.

(e) For persons who are legally incapable of giving informed consent, psychologists nevertheless (1) provide an appropriate explanation, (2) obtain the participant's assent, and (3) obtain appropriate permission from a legally authorized person, if such substitute consent is permitted by law.

### 6.12 Dispensing With Informed Consent

Before determining that planned research (such as research involving only anonymous questionnaires, naturalistic observations, or certain kinds of archival

**FIGURE 2.2**    When college students are asked to participate in psychological research as part of a course they are taking, equitable alternative activities should be provided for those who do not wish to participate.

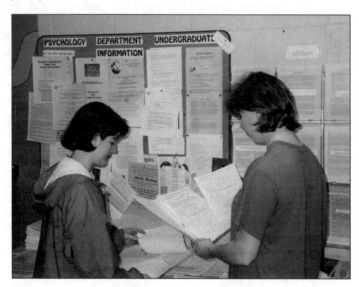

research) does not require the informed consent of research participants, psychologists consider applicable regulations and institutional review board requirements, and they consult with colleagues as appropriate.

### 6.13 Informed Consent in Research Filming or Recording

Psychologists obtain informed consent from research participants prior to filming or recording them in any form, unless the research involves simply naturalistic observations in public places and it is not anticipated that the recording will be used in a manner that could cause personal identification or harm.

### 6.14 Offering Inducements for Research Participants

**(a)** In offering professional services as an inducement to obtain research participants, psychologists make clear the nature of the services, as well as the risks, obligations, and limitations. (See also Standard 1.18, Barter [With Patients or Clients].)

**(b)** Psychologists do not offer excessive or inappropriate financial or other inducements to obtain research participants, particularly when it might tend to coerce participation.

## Commentary

- Potential research participants must be made aware of all aspects of the study that may influence their willingness to participate.
- Research participants must be allowed to withdraw their consent at any time without penalties.

- Individuals must not be pressured to participate in research.
- Informed consent must be obtained from legal guardians for individuals unable to provide consent (e.g., children, mentally impaired individuals); assent to participate should be obtained from individuals unable to provide informed consent.
- Researchers should consult with knowledgeable others, including an IRB, when deciding whether to dispense with informed consent, such as when research is conducted in public settings. These settings require special attention to protecting individuals' privacy.
- Privacy refers to the rights of individuals to decide how information about them is to be communicated to others.

Ethical research practice requires that research participants be informed of all features of the research that reasonably might be expected to influence their willingness to participate and that researchers respond to any inquiries the participants might make about the research. In this way individuals can make an informed decision about their participation. Participants should also be informed that they are free to withdraw their consent at any time without penalty or prejudice. Consent must be given freely, without undue inducement or pressure. *Informed consent should always be obtained and is absolutely essential when participants are exposed to the possibility of more than minimal risk.*

True informed consent cannot be obtained from certain individuals, such as the mentally impaired or emotionally disturbed, young children, and others who are recognized as having limited ability to understand the nature of research and the possible risks. In these cases, formal consent must be obtained from the participants' parents or legal guardians; however, when feasible "assent" always should be obtained from the participants themselves. Developmental psychologists who want to test schoolchildren are often faced with the task of contacting dozens (if not hundreds) of parents in order to secure permission for the children to participate in psychological research. We should mention that ethical restrictions such as those involving informed consent also raise methodological issues (see Adair, Dushenko, & Lindsay, 1985). For example, results of one study revealed that children of parents who did not provide parental consent for a research project were academically less successful and less popular with their peers than were children of parents who did provide consent (Frame & Strauss, 1987). Thus, data gathered from the children whose parents gave consent may not always be generalized to children who did not have parental consent.

Consider the dilemma faced by one graduate student who was seeking to interview adolescents receiving services from a family planning clinic (Landers, 1988). Parental permission was not required for the teens to attend the clinic; thus, if the investigator asked the parents for permission for their children to participate in the study, she would be revealing to the parents the teens' use of the clinic's services. Yet obtaining permission of parents before conducting research with minors is standard ethical practice and also is mandated by federal laws. To help make a decision regarding proper ethical procedures in this difficult case, the graduate student correctly sought advice from experts, specifically, from members of APA's Committee for the Protection of Human Participants in Research. (In 1990, this committee was renamed Committee on Standards in Research, and the scope of its ethical concerns was enlarged [Grisso et al., 1991].) The student used the information obtained from the experts to formulate the procedures that she proposed to use as part of her dissertation research. Although advice should be sought from knowledgeable others whenever ethical dilemmas arise, *final responsibility for conducting research ethically always rests with the investigator.*

It is not always easy to decide what constitutes undue inducement or pressure to participate. Paying college students $5 an hour to take part in a psychology experiment would not generally be considered improper coercion. Recruiting very poor or disadvantaged persons from the streets with a $5 offer may be more coercive and less acceptable (Kelman, 1972). Prisoners may believe that any refusal on their part to participate in a psychology experiment will be viewed by the authorities as evidence of uncooperativeness and will therefore make it more difficult for them to be paroled. Parents of schoolchildren may fear that their children will be less well treated by teachers if they refuse to give permission for their children to participate in research. When college students are asked to fulfill a class requirement by serving as participants in psychology experiments (an experience that presumably has some educational value), an alternative method of earning class credit should be made available to those who do not wish to participate in psychological research. Such options should be equivalent, in terms of time and effort, with the requirements of research participation. Frequently employed options include reading and summarizing journal articles describing research, making informal field observations of behavior, attending presentations of research findings by graduate students or faculty, and doing volunteer community service (see Kimmel, 1996).

Serious ethical problems can arise when a researcher withholds certain information about a psychological treatment from a research participant. The reason for withholding information may be a legitimate concern on the part of the researcher that informing participants of all the details of the experiment will negate the effect of a particular treatment. For example, research on conformity behavior often requires participants to believe that responses of other persons in the situation represent those individuals' own opinions. Telling individuals before the experiment that responses made by other people will be purposely misleading would appear to make this type of research impossible. (We discuss the use of deception in psychological research later in this chapter.)

IRBs require investigators to document that the proper informed consent procedure has been followed for any research involving human participants. A sample informed consent form for use with a normal adult population is shown in Box 2.1. This form may be submitted to an IRB for approval when deception is not present and when no more than minimal risk is anticipated. *If the research involves more than minimal risk or if deception is used, the investigator has the responsibility to seek advice from those with experience in the particular problem area under investigation.*

BOX 2.1

## SAMPLE INFORMED CONSENT FORM

[DATE]

I, [NAME OF PARTICIPANT], state that I am over 18 years of age and that I voluntarily agree to participate in a research project conducted by [NAME OF PRINCIPAL INVESTIGATOR, TITLE, INSTITUTIONAL AFFILIATION]. The research is being conducted in order to [BRIEF DESCRIPTION OF THE GOALS OF THE RESEARCH]. The specific task I will perform requires [DETAILS OF THE RESEARCH TASK, INCLUDING INFORMATION ABOUT THE DURATION OF PARTICIPANT'S INVOLVEMENT. ANY POSSIBLE DISCOMFORT TO PARTICIPANT MUST ALSO BE DESCRIBED.].

I acknowledge that [NAME OF PRINCIPAL INVESTIGATOR OR RESEARCH ASSISTANT] has explained the task to me fully; has informed me that I may withdraw from participation at any time without prejudice or penalty; has offered to answer any questions that I might have concerning the research procedure; has assured me that any information that I give will be used for research purposes only and will be kept confidential. [PROCEDURE FOR PROTECTING CONFIDENTIALITY OF RESPONSES SHOULD BE EXPLAINED.]

I also acknowledge that the benefits derived from, or rewards given for, my participation have been fully explained to me—as well as alternative methods, if available, for earning these rewards—and that I have been promised, upon completion of the research task, a brief description of the role my specific performance plays in this project. [THE EXACT NATURE OF ANY COMMITMENTS MADE BY THE RESEARCHER, SUCH AS THE AMOUNT OF MONEY TO BE PAID TO INDIVIDUALS FOR PARTICIPATION, SHOULD BE SPECIFIED HERE.]

_____

[Signature of Researcher]

_____

[Signature of Participant]

Members of an IRB also may be consulted to obtain advice on how to prepare a consent procedure that protects the rights of the participants. In some situations it may not be necessary to obtain informed consent. The most obvious example would be when researchers are observing individuals' behavior in public places without any intervention. An investigator, for instance, who wishes to gather evidence about race relations on a college campus by observing the frequency of mixed-race versus unmixed-race groups sitting at tables in the college cafeteria or walking across campus would not ordinarily need to obtain students' permission before making the observations. (We assume the identity of specific individuals will not be recorded.) Such student behavior can be considered public, and the method is naturalistic observation (see Chapter 3). However, deciding what is public or what is private behavior is not always easy.

Diener and Crandall (1978) identify three major dimensions to consider when deciding what information is private and what safeguards should be employed: sensitivity of the information, setting, and degree of dissemination of the information. Clearly, some kinds of information are more sensitive than others. Individuals interviewed about their sexual practices, religious beliefs, or criminal activities are likely to be more concerned about the dissemination of

**FIGURE 2.3**    Deciding what is public or what is private behavior is not always easy.

this information than those interviewed about who they believe will win the World Series. Similarly, organizations and businesses are likely to perceive some types of information about them as more sensitive than other types.

The setting in which behavior is observed is also a factor in defining what constitutes private activity. Individuals engaged in what reasonably might be considered public behaviors, such as attending a baseball game or other outdoor event, give up a certain degree of privacy. Yet, deciding what is public behavior is not always easy. Such behaviors as riding inside one's own car, using public bathrooms, or picnicking in a park are not easily classified. Decisions about ethical practice in these situations sometimes depend on the sensitivity of the data and the manner in which the information will be disseminated.

Dissemination of information in terms of group averages or proportions is unlikely to reflect on specific individuals. In other situations, code systems can be used to protect participants' confidentiality. *Dissemination of sensitive information about individuals or groups without their permission is a serious breach of ethics.* When information about individuals has been collected unobtrusively (e. g., by a concealed observer), one approach that has been suggested is to contact the individuals after the observations have been made and ask whether this information can be used by the researcher.

As Diener and Crandall indicate, the most difficult decisions regarding privacy involve situations in which there is an obvious ethical problem on one dimension but not on others and situations in which there is a slight problem on all three dimensions. For instance, the behavior of individuals in the darkened setting of a movie theater would appear to have the potential of yielding sensitive information about the individual, but the setting could be reasonably classified as public. **Privacy** refers to the rights of individuals to decide how information about them is to be communicated to others. Whenever possible, the manner in which information about participants will be kept confidential should be explained to participants in psychological research so they may judge for themselves whether the safeguards taken to ensure their confidentiality are reasonable. Implementing the principle of informed consent requires that the investigator seek to balance the need to investigate human behavior on the one hand with the rights of human participants on the other.

### WHAT DO YOU THINK?

Although the APA Code of Ethics suggests that informed consent is not necessarily required in studies involving naturalistic observation of public behavior or "similar research" (see Standard 6.10), as we have just seen, deciding what is "public" is not always easy. Consider the following research scenarios and decide whether you think informed consent of participants should be required before the researcher proceeds to do the research. It may be that you want more information from the researcher. If so, what additional information might you want before deciding? You will see that requiring informed consent can change a research situation dramatically, making it difficult, for example, for a researcher to record behavior under "natural" conditions. Such are the dilemmas of ethical decision making.

1  In a study of drinking behavior of college students, an undergraduate working for a faculty member attends a fraternity party and records the amount drunk by other students at the party.
2  As part of a study of the gay community, a gay researcher joins a gay baseball team with the goal of recording behaviors of participants in the context of team competition during the season. (All games are played outdoors and may be watched by the public.)
3  Public bathroom behavior (e.g., flushing, hand washing, littering, writing graffiti, etc.) of men and women is observed by male and female researchers concealed in the stalls of the respective washrooms.
4  A graduate student seeks to investigate cheating behaviors of college students by concealing himself in a projection booth in an auditorium used for administering exams to very large classes. From his vantage point he can see with the aid of binoculars the movements of most students. He records head movements, switching papers, passing notes, and other suspicious exam-taking behaviors.

During the 1980s, the APA Committee for the Protection of Human Participants in Research became involved in a number of controversies over the ethical issues related to psychosocial research on acquired immune deficiency syndrome (AIDS) (Melton, Levine, Koocher, Rosenthal, & Thompson, 1988). Particularly salient among the ethical dilemmas posed by this research is that related to privacy. Control over knowledge about oneself and one's body is basic to respect for persons and is even constitutionally protected; on the other hand, the courts have supported the government's police power to curb threats to public health (Melton & Gray, 1988). The transmission of AIDS is known to take place via the sharing of body fluids, such as sexual contact or sharing of needles for intravenous injections. Thus, to understand fully the spread of AIDS requires gathering data regarding individuals' sexual practices, drug use, medical history, travel, and acquaintances. Unfortunately, confidentiality cannot always be guaranteed to participants in AIDS research because of laws requiring the reporting of AIDS cases and the fact that records can sometimes be legally subpoenaed (Gray & Melton, 1985). As in other areas when ethical dilemmas arise, the investigator is obligated to seek advice from knowledgeable others regarding the appropriateness of a research procedure. For example, consultation with members of IRBs, experienced researchers, members of ethics committees, and representatives of the population at risk (Melton et al., 1988) will help ensure that the rights of participants are protected when the psychosocial aspects of communicable diseases are investigated.

## DECEPTION IN PSYCHOLOGICAL RESEARCH

- Deception in psychological research occurs when researchers withhold information or intentionally misinform participants about the research. By its nature, deception violates the ethical principle of informed consent, yet it is considered a necessary research strategy in certain areas of psychology.

No ethical issue related to research is more controversial than that of deception. There are those who would argue that participants should *never* be deceived in the context of psychological research. Deception runs counter to the principle of openness and honesty that ethical practice says should characterize the relationship between experimenter and participant. **Deception** can occur either through *omission*, the withholding of information, or *commission*, intentionally misinforming participants about an aspect of the research. Either kind of deception contradicts the principle of informed consent. To some, deception is morally repugnant; it is no different from lying. Nevertheless, despite the increased attention given to deceptive methodological practices over the last couple of decades, the use of deception in psychological research has not declined and remains a popular research strategy (Adair, Dushenka, & Lindsay, 1985; Sharpe, Adair, & Roese, 1992).

### APA Ethical Standards

#### 6.15 Deception in Research

(a) Psychologists do not conduct a study involving deception unless they have determined that the use of deceptive techniques is justified by the study's prospective scientific, educational, or applied value and that equally effective alternative procedures that do not use deception are not feasible.

(b) Psychologists never deceive research participants about significant aspects that would affect their willingness to participate, such as physical risks, discomfort, or unpleasant emotional experiences.

(c) Any other deception that is an integral feature of the design and conduct of an experiment must be explained to participants as early as is feasible, preferably at the conclusion of their participation, but no later than at the conclusion of the research. (See also Standard 6.18, Providing Participants With Information About the Study.)

## Commentary

- Deception is a necessary research strategy in some psychological research.
- Deceiving individuals in order to get them to participate in the research is always unethical.
- Researchers must carefully weigh the costs of deception against the potential benefits of the research when considering the use of deception.
- Researchers are ethically obligated to explain to participants their use of deception at the conclusion of the study and remove any harmful effects of the deception.

It is simply impossible to carry out certain kinds of research without withholding information from participants about some aspects of the research. In other situations, it may be necessary to misinform participants in order to have them adopt certain attitudes or behaviors. As we explain in Chapter 3, participant observers may find it necessary to give false information in order to gain access to a particular group or setting. Rosenhan (1973) and his colleagues, for instance, posed as patients in mental hospitals in order to investigate the manner in which psychiatric diagnoses are made. Or consider that Rosenthal's (1966) well-known research investigating experimenter bias was based on the assumption that the participants believed they were experimenters working for a principal investigator. The "experimenters" were actually the participants. The data collected by these participant-experimenters sometimes differed because of the expectations they had about the research outcome. The results helped researchers better understand the role of "experimenter bias" in the conduct of psychological research.

Although deception is sometimes justified on methodological grounds, deceiving participants for the purpose of getting them to participate in research in which they would not normally take part, or research that involves more than minimal risk, is always unethical.

A basic assumption underlying the use of deception is that it is necessary to conceal the true nature of an experiment so that participants will behave as they normally would or so that they will act in accordance with the stated instructions and cues provided by the experimenter. If people come to realize (and perhaps many already have) that psychologists often present misinformation and serving in a psychology experiment means they are likely to be deceived, then the very assumption on which the use of deception is based will be lost. Participants will no longer act in accordance with the instructions of the experimenter because they will no longer believe the experimenter is telling the truth. Frequent and casual use of deception undermines the usefulness of deception as a methodological tool (Kelman, 1967). In fact, Epley and Huff (1998) demonstrated that participants given knowledge in an experimental debriefing that they were deceived later exhibited more suspicion about future psychological research than did participants who were unaware of the deception.

The fact that psychologists are often identified with deceptive practices, and the fact that deception may be the basis for experimental manipulations in natural settings, also may affect the way people react to emergencies or other events they witness. On one college campus a student was attacked and shot by another student. Witnesses did not try to help, and the assailant was not pursued. When bystanders were asked why they did not intervene, some said they thought it was just a psychology experiment (Diener & Crandall, 1978).

Kelman (1972) suggests that, *before using deception, a researcher must give very serious consideration to (1) the importance of the study to our scientific knowledge, (2) the availability of alternative, deception-free methods, and (3) the "noxiousness" of the deception.* This last consideration refers to the degree of deception involved and to the possibility of injury to the participants. In Kelman's (p. 997) view: "Only if a study is very important and no alternative methods are available can anything more than the mildest form of deception be justified." *When deception is*

**FIGURE 2.4.** Deception is sometimes the basis for experimental manipulations in natural settings; for example, to investigate helping behavior, psychologists may create a situation involving what appears to be a person in distress.

*used, the researcher must inform participants after the experiment of the reasons for the deception, discuss any misconceptions they may have, and remove any harmful effects of the deception.* One goal of this debriefing is educating the participant about the need for deception. For example, after female participants were deceived about the true purpose of a study investigating women's perceptions of vulnerability to rape (see Chapter 1; Heath & Davidson, 1988), the researchers explained the reasons for the deception and corrected any misperceptions that had been created.

One final note regarding what is or is not deception should be made. Those who are just beginning to do research sometimes believe that unless they tell participants exactly what they expect to find—that is, the hypothesis being tested—they are deceiving participants. This is not necessarily the case. Information about the specific hypothesis being tested is usually withheld from participants in order not to bias them to behave in a certain way. For example, simply telling a group of control participants that comparisons will be made between their responses and those of a group receiving a particular treatment may introduce an unwanted spirit of competition. In most situations, not telling participants exactly what the researcher is testing is simply considered good experimental procedure. Of course, the researcher can never ethically withhold information that might seriously influence a participant's willingness to participate (APA Ethical Standard 6.15). Debriefing provides an opportunity to inform participants about the specific goals of a study and to educate them about the need to do psychological research.

### WHAT DO YOU THINK?

Deceptive practices in psychological research continue unabated (e.g., Sieber, Iannuzzo, & Rodriguez, 1995); however, debate in the scientific community concerning deception also has not abated (see, for example, Bröder, 1998; Fisher & Fryberg, 1994; Ortmann & Hertwig; 1997). It is a complex issue, with those taking part in the debate sometimes at odds over the definition of deception (see Ortmann & Hertwig, 1998). The debate was summarized by Fisher & Fryberg (1994) as follows: "Ethical arguments have focused on whether deceptive research practices are justified on the basis of their potential societal benefit or violate moral principles of beneficence and respect for individuals and the fiduciary obligations of psychologists to research participants" (p. 417). This is quite a mouthful; so let us see if we can break it down.

A moral principle of "beneficence" refers to the idea that research activities should be beneficent (bring benefits) for individuals and society. If deception is shown to harm individuals or society, then the beneficence of the research can be questioned. The moral principle of "respect for individuals" is just that: People should be treated as persons and not "objects" for study, for example. This principle would suggest that people have a right to make their own judgments about the procedures and purpose of the research in which they are participating (Fisher & Fryberg, 1994). "Fiduciary obligations of psychologists" refer to the responsibilities of individuals who are given trust over others, even if only temporarily. In the case of psychological research, the researcher is considered to have responsibility for the welfare of participants during the study and for the consequences of their participation.

These ideas and principles can perhaps be illustrated through the arguments of Baumrind (1985), who argues persuasively that "the use of intentional deception in the research setting is unethical, imprudent, and unwarranted scientifically" (p. 165). Specifically, she argues that the costs to the participants, to the profession, and to society of the use of deception are too great to warrant its continued use. Although these arguments are lengthy and complex, let us attempt a brief summary. First, according to Baumrind, deception exacts a cost to participants because it undermines the participants' trust in their own judgment and in a "fiduciary" (someone who is holding something in trust for another person). When research participants find they have been duped or tricked, Baumrind believes this may lead the participants to question what they have learned about themselves and to lead them to distrust individuals (e.g., social scientists) who they might have previously trusted to provide valid information and advice. A cost to the profession is exacted because participants (and society at large) soon come to realize that psychologists are "tricksters" and not to be believed when giving instructions about research participation. If participants tend to suspect psychologists of lying, then one may question whether deception will work as it is intended by the researcher, a point raised earlier by Kelman (1972). Baumrind also argues that the use of deception reveals psychologists are willing to lie, which seemingly contradicts their supposed dedication to seeking truth. Finally, there is harm done to society because deception undermines people's trust in experts and makes them suspicious in general about all contrived events. Of course, these are not the views of all psychologists (see Christensen, 1988; Kimmel, 1998). Milgram (1977), for instance, suggested that deceptive practices of psychologists are really a kind of "technical illusion" and should be permitted in the interests of scientific inquiry. After all, illusions are sometimes created in real-life situations in order to make people believe something. When listening to a radio program, people are not generally bothered by the fact that the thunder they hear or the sound of a horse galloping are merely technical illusions created by a sound effects specialist. Milgram argues that technical illusions should be permitted in the case of scientific inquiry. We deceive children into believing in Santa Claus. Why cannot scientists create illusions in order to help them understand human behavior?

Just as illusions are often created in real-life situations, in other situations, Milgram points out, there can be a suspension of a general moral principle. If we learn of a crime, we are ethically bound to report it to the authorities. On the other hand, a lawyer who is given information by a client must consider this information privileged even if it reveals that the client is guilty. Physicians perform very personal examinations of our bodies. Although it is morally permissible in a physician's office, the same type of behavior would not be condoned outside the office. Milgram argues that, in the interest of science, psychologists should occasionally be allowed to suspend the moral principle of truthfulness and honesty.

Those who defend deception point to studies showing that participants on the average do not appear to react negatively to being deceived (e.g., Christensen, 1988; Epley & Huff, 1998; Kimmel, 1996), and that although "suspiciousness" about psychological research may increase, the overall effects seem to be negligible (see Kimmel, 1998). Nevertheless, the bottom line according to those who argue for the continued use of deception is well summarized by Kimmel (1998): "An absolute rule prohibiting the use of deception in all psychological research would have the egregious consequence of preventing researchers from carrying out a wide range of important studies" (p. 805). No one in the scientific community suggests that deceptive practices be taken lightly; however, for many scientists the use of deception is less noxious (to use Kelman's term) than doing without the knowledge gained by such studies.

What do you think about the use of deception in psychological research?

## ADDITIONAL RESPONSIBILITIES TO RESEARCH PARTICIPANTS

- Researchers are ethically obligated to seek ways to benefit participants even after the research is completed, for example, by using debriefing procedures.

Over the years, many researchers have fallen into the trap of viewing human participants in research chiefly as means to an end, as "objects" used to obtain data in order to meet the goals of a research study. While perhaps conscientiously giving participants the opportunity to give their informed consent and carefully safeguarding them from serious injury, researchers sometimes have considered their responsibility to participants to end when the last response was made or the final piece of data collected. A handshake or "thank you" was frequently all that marked the end of the research session. This meant the research participants likely left with unanswered questions about specific aspects of the situation and with only the vaguest idea of the role they played in the scientific endeavor. It is important both in the planning and in the conduct of research to consider how the experience may affect the research participant and the participant's environment after the research is completed and to seek ways in which the participant will benefit from participation. As we have just seen, these concerns follow directly from the moral principles of beneficence and respect of individuals.

## APA Ethical Standards

### 6.16 Sharing and Utilizing Data

Psychologists inform research participants of their anticipated sharing or further use of personally identifiable research data and of the possibility of unanticipated future uses.

### 6.17 Minimizing Invasiveness

In conducting research, psychologists interfere with the participants or milieu from which data are collected only in a manner that is warranted by an appropriate research design and that is consistent with psychologists' roles as scientific investigators.

### 6.18 Providing Participants With Information About the Study

(a) Psychologists provide a prompt opportunity for participants to obtain appropriate information about the nature, results, and conclusions of the research, and psychologists attempt to correct any misconceptions that participants may have.

(b) If scientific or humane values justify delaying or withholding this information, psychologists take reasonable measures to reduce the risk of harm.

### 6.19 Honoring Commitments

Psychologists take reasonable measures to honor all commitments they have made to research participants.

## Commentary

- Debriefing benefits both participants and researchers.
- Debriefing informs participants about the nature of the research, their role in the study, and educates individuals about research. The goal of debriefing is to have individuals feel good about their participation.
- Debriefing allows researchers to learn how participants viewed the procedures, allows potential insights into the nature of the research findings, and provides ideas for future research.

Earlier we mentioned that protecting the confidentiality of a participant's responses brought benefits both to the participant (safeguarding from social injury) and to the researcher (increasing the probability of honest responding). **Debriefing** participants at the end of a research session also carries benefits both to participant and researcher (Blanck et al., 1992). As we saw when discussing the use of deception, *debriefing is necessary to remove any harmful effects or misconceptions about participation (although see Baumrind, 1985), as well as to explain to participants the need for deception; however, debriefing also has the important goals of educating participants about the research (rationale, method, results) and of leaving them with positive feelings about their participation.* Whenever possible, a researcher should take the time to explain the nature of the participant's specific performance and to show how it relates to group or normative data. If this is not feasible, participants should be given the opportunity at some future time to learn about the general outcome of the research. Some researchers take it upon themselves to mail a written report of a study's results to the participants; others, especially when testing captive populations such as college students, invite participants to come back later (for instance, at the end of a semester) to obtain a report summarizing the study's findings. In this way, participants can learn more about their particular contribution to the research study and, in doing so, feel more personally involved in the scientific process.

Debriefing is an opportunity for participants to learn more about research in general—by having the study's methodology explained to them, for instance, or by being introduced to various tests or instruments used in psychological research. Because the "educational value" of participation in psychological research is one reason given to justify the use of large numbers of volunteers from college introductory psychology classes, researchers testing students have an important obligation to attempt to educate participants about psychological research. In addition to being debriefed, student participants have sometimes been asked by classroom instructors to write brief reports about their research experience, including details about the study's purpose, the techniques used, and the significance of the research to understanding behavior. One evaluation of such a procedure revealed that students who wrote reports were more satisfied with the research experience and experienced a significantly greater overall educational benefit from it than did students who did not write reports (Richardson, Pegalis, & Britton, 1992).

Debriefing can help a researcher by providing an opportunity to find out how the participant viewed the procedures and treatments that were administered. For example, a researcher may wish to know whether a particular experimental procedure was perceived by the participant in the way the investigator intended (Blanck et al., 1992). Studies of what is called incidental learning involve exposing participants to certain kinds of critical material (e.g., the contents of a room, another person, a list of words, and so on) and then later asking them what they can remember of this material. It is important that participants, when exposed to the critical material, be unaware that a memory test will later be given (otherwise, intentional, not incidental, learning will take place). Debriefing enables the investigator to find out how participants perceived the tasks given to them and whether they were aware that their memory would be tested.

Debriefing that seeks to discover how participants perceive a specific task or situation must be done in a manner that avoids pressing them to reveal information they believe they are not supposed to possess. Research participants generally want to help with the scientific process, and many realize that in any valid psychological study information may be purposely withheld from them (Orne, 1962). To tell the researcher that they really *did* know about these details may seem to participants to threaten the study's validity and hence "ruin" it. Thus, if questioned directly, participants may withhold information about their perceptions in a misguided, albeit well-intentioned, attempt to protect the scientific integrity of the study. Debriefing should thus be carried out in an informal manner, with the participant carefully led by the investigator to respond honestly and openly. This is often best accomplished by using general questions in an open-ended format (e.g., What do you think this study was about?) and following up with more specific questions that, as much as possible, do not cue the participant about what responses are expected (Orne, 1962). Debriefing provides yet another benefit to researchers. It can provide them with "leads for future research and help identify problems in their current protocols" (Blanck et al., 1992, p. 962). Debriefing, in other words, can provide clues as to the reasons for a participant's performance, which may help when discussing the overall results or may set the stage for another study. Errors in experimental materials—for instance, missing information or ambiguous instructions—are sometimes detected through postexperimental interviews with participants. As we said, *debriefing is good for both the participant and the scientist.*

## RESEARCH WITH ANIMALS

Each year millions of animals are tested in laboratory investigations aimed at answering a wide range of important questions. New drugs are tested on animals before they are used with humans. Substances introduced into the environment must first be given to animals to test their effects. Animals are exposed to diseases in order that investigators may observe symptoms and test various cures. New surgical procedures—especially those involving the brain—are often first tried out on animals. Many animals are also used for behavioral research, for example, by ethologists and experimental psychologists. These investigations yield much information that contributes to human welfare (Miller, 1985). In the process, however, many animals are subjected to pain and discomfort, stress and sickness, and death. Although rodents, particularly rats and mice, are the largest group of laboratory animals, researchers use a wide variety of species in their investigations, including monkeys, fish, dogs, and cats. Specific animals are frequently chosen because they are good models of human responses. For example, psychologists interested in audition sometimes use chinchillas as subjects because their auditory processes are very similar to those of humans. In addition, animal models of the relationship between stress and diabetes have helped researchers to understand psychosomatic factors in this illness (Surwit & Williams, 1996).

Apparently, chimpanzees are the only nonhuman primates that can harbor the virus linked to AIDS (Landers, 1988). As a result, concern over the dwindling numbers of these animals has been expressed, not only by animal conservationists, who worry about the extinction of the species, but by biomedical researchers, who may have to depend on these animals for laboratory research aimed at finding a vaccine for AIDS (Booth, 1988; Goodall, 1987).

## APA Ethical Standards

### 6.20 Care and Use of Animals in Research

(a) Psychologists who conduct research involving animals treat them humanely.

(b) Psychologists acquire, care for, use, and dispose of animals in compliance with current federal, state, and local laws and regulations, and with professional standards.

**FIGURE 2.5**   Research with animals increases our understanding of mental and physical health.

(c) Psychologists trained in research methods and experienced in the care of laboratory animals supervise all procedures involving animals and are responsible for ensuring appropriate consideration of their comfort, health, and humane treatment.

(d) Psychologists ensure that all individuals using animals under their supervision have received instruction in research methods and in the care, maintenance, and handling of the species being used, to the extent appropriate to their role.

(e) Responsibilities and activities of individuals assisting in a research project are consistent with their respective competencies.

(f) Psychologists make reasonable efforts to minimize the discomfort, infection, illness, and pain of animal subjects.

(g) A procedure subjecting animals to pain, stress, or privation is used only when an alternative procedure is unavailable and the goal is justified by its prospective scientific, educational, or applied value.

(h) Surgical procedures are performed under appropriate anesthesia; techniques to avoid infection and minimize pain are followed during and after surgery.

(i) When it is appropriate that the animal's life be terminated, it is done rapidly, with an effort to minimize pain, and in accordance with accepted procedures.

## Commentary

- Animals are used in research to gain knowledge that will benefit humans, for example, by helping to cure diseases.
- Researchers are ethically obligated to protect the welfare of research animals and to treat them humanely.
- The use of animals in research is widely debated and involves complex issues.

The use of animals as laboratory subjects has often been taken for granted. In fact, the biblical reference to humankind's "dominion" over all lesser creatures is sometimes invoked to justify the use of animals as laboratory subjects (Johnson, 1990; Rollin, 1985). More often, however, research with animal subjects is justified by the need to gain knowledge *without putting humans in jeopardy* about aspects of nature that directly affect the human condition. Few cures, drugs, vaccines, or therapies have come about without experimentation on animals (Rosenfeld, 1981). It would be difficult to contemplate the consequences of doing research on such diseases as cancer or muscular dystrophy without the opportunity first to examine the course of the disease or try out a new cure on animal subjects. Feeney (1987), for example, has called attention to the contributions that basic research with animal subjects has made to the treatment of patients recovering from brain and spinal cord injury. He also points out that our understanding of the relationship between brain and behavior was advanced significantly by the now classic work in the 1960s of Roger Sperry, who won a Nobel Prize for his work on the "split brain" (the functioning of the brain after the corpus callosum has been cut). Early investigations by Sperry and others, using cats and monkeys as subjects, demonstrated that the two hemispheres of the brain can function independently in learning and memory. This knowledge permitted physicians to perform similar operations to treat humans suffering from intractable epilepsy. Maestripieri and Carroll (1998) suggest that investigation of naturally occurring infant maltreatment in monkeys can inform scientists about child abuse and neglect (see also Cicchetti, 1998).

Many questions, however, have been raised about the role of animal subjects in psychological studies (Novak, 1991; Shapiro, 1998; Ulrich, 1991). These questions include the most basic one, whether animals should be used at all in scientific investigations, as well as important questions about the care and protection of animal subjects. Clearly, according to the APA principles, *the researcher who uses animal subjects in an investigation has an ethical obligation to look out for their welfare and to treat them humanely.* Only individuals qualified to do research and to manage and care for the particular species being used should be allowed to participate. When the research exposes the animals to pain or discomfort, it must be justified by the potential scientific, educational, or applied goals. As we noted earlier when institutional review was discussed, animal review boards (IACUCs) are now in place at research facilities receiving funds from the Public Health Service. These committees are charged with determining the adequacy of the procedures for controlling pain, carrying out euthanasia, housing animals, and training personnel, as well as determining whether the experimental design is sufficient to gain important new information and whether the animal model is appropriate or whether nonanimal models could be used (Holden, 1987).

Partly in response to calls from members of animal rights groups during the 1980s, investigators must now meet a host of federal and state requirements, including inspection of animal facilities by veterinarians from the U.S. Department of Agriculture (Landers, 1987a, 1987b; see also National Research Council, 1996). These regulations are often welcomed by members of the scientific community, and many animal researchers belong to groups such as the APA Committee on Animal Research and Experimentation (CARE) that seek to protect laboratory animals. CARE has developed a list of specific guidelines to be followed when animal subjects are used in psychological research. (A copy of these guidelines may be obtained by writing CARE, c/o Science Directorate, American Psychological Association, 750 First Street, N.E., Washington, DC 20002-4242.) As with any ethically sensitive issue, however, it is clear that compromises must be made. For example, until alternatives to animal research can be found, the need to conduct research using animal subjects in order to battle human disease and suffering must be balanced against the need for adequate control over the way animals are treated in laboratory research (Goodall, 1987). As APA's chief executive officer, Raymond Fowler, pointed out, it is also important that the use of animal subjects not be restricted because the application of the research is not readily apparent (Fowler, 1992). "The charges that animal research is of no value because it cannot always be linked to potential applications is a charge that can be made against all basic research." Such an indictment "threatens the intellectual and scientific foundation" of all psychology, including both "scientists and practitioners" (p. 2).

Although few scientists would disagree that restrictions are necessary to prevent needless suffering in animals, most want to avoid a quagmire of bureaucratic restrictions and high costs that will undermine research. Feeney (1987) suggests that severe restrictions and high costs, as well as the negative publicity (and occasional terrorist acts) directed toward individuals and institutions by extremists within the animal activist groups, may deter young scientists from entering the field of animal research (see also Azar, 1994a). If such is the case, the result possibly could be to deprive the (presently) incurably ill or permanently paralyzed of the hope that comes through scientific research.

Clearly, the issues surrounding the debate over the relevance of animal research to the human situation are many and complex. As Ulrich (1992) has commented, discussion of these issues must be approached with "wisdom and balance" (p. 386).

## WHAT DO YOU THINK?

Ethical decision making often pits opposing philosophical positions against one another. This is clearly seen in the debate over the use of animals in research. At the center of this debate is the question of the "moral status" of humans and nonhuman animals. As the Australian philosopher Peter Singer (1990, p. 9) points out, two generally accepted moral principles are:

1 All humans are equal in moral status.
2 All humans are of superior moral status to nonhuman animals.

Thus, Singer continues, "On the basis of these principles, it is commonly held that we should put human welfare ahead of the suffering of nonhuman animals; this assumption is reflected in our treatment of animals in many areas, including farming, hunting, experimentation, and entertainment" (p. 9).

Singer, however, does not agree with these commonly held views. He argues that "there is no rational ethical justification for always putting human suffering ahead of that of nonhuman animals" (p. 9). Unless we appeal to religious viewpoints (which Singer rejects as the basis of decisions in a pluralistic society), there is, according to Singer, no special moral status to "being human." This position has roots in the philosophical tradition known as utilitarianism, which began with the writings of David Hume (1711–1776) and Jeremy Bentham (1748–1832), as well as John Stuart Mill (1806–1873) (Rachels, 1986). Basically, this viewpoint holds that whenever we have choices between alternative actions we should choose the one that has the best overall consequences (produces the most "happiness") for everyone involved. What matters in this view is whether the individual in question is capable of experiencing happiness-unhappiness, pleasure-pain; whether the individual is human or nonhuman is not relevant (Rachels, 1986).

What do you think about the moral status of humans and animals and its relation to psychological research?

## REPORTING OF PSYCHOLOGICAL RESEARCH

- Investigators attempt to communicate their research findings in peer-reviewed scientific journals, and the APA Code of Ethics provides guidelines for this process.

Generally, once a psychological investigation is completed, the principal investigator prepares a manuscript for submission to one of the dozens of psychology-related scientific periodicals. Publication in a psychology journal not only achieves the goal of communicating the results of a study to members of the scientific community and to society in general but, as we have seen, may also enhance the researcher's reputation and even the reputation of the institution that sponsored the research. But getting the results of a scientific investigation published is not always an easy process, especially if the researcher wishes to publish in one of the more prestigious scientific journals. Journals sponsored by APA, such as the *Journal of Abnormal Psychology, Journal of Educational Psychology, Journal of Experimental Psychology: Learning, Memory, and Cognition*, and *Psychological Review*, can have rejection rates approaching 90% (American Psychological Association, 1998). Manuscripts submitted for publication must be prepared according to strict stylistic guidelines (see Appendix C), meet rigorous methodological and substantive criteria, and be appropriate for the particular journal to which the manuscript is submitted.

Problems in any of these three areas may be sufficient to deny publication; however, manuscripts are more commonly rejected because of problems in the methodology of the study, problems in the statistical treatment of the results, or because the results do not make a significant enough contribution to scientific progress in the field. Decisions about the acceptability of a scientific manuscript are made by the journal's editors, usually on the basis of comments made by the experts in the field who have been asked by the editors for their opinions about the manuscript's scientific worth. This process is known as peer review, and many scientists have had their hopes of being published dashed along this difficult path. Despite the many pressures to publish in order to earn promotion or tenure at a university, it is imperative that all scientists adhere strictly to the code of ethics governing the reporting of results.

## APA Ethical Standards

### 6.21 Reporting of Results

(a) Psychologists do not fabricate data or falsify results in their publications.

(b) If psychologists discover significant errors in their published data, they take reasonable steps to correct such errors in a correction, retraction, erratum, or other appropriate publication means.

### 6.22 Plagiarism

Psychologists do not present substantial portions or elements of another's work or data as their own, even if the other work or data source is cited occasionally.

### 6.23 Publication Credit

(a) Psychologists take responsibility and credit, including authorship credit, only for work they have actually performed or to which they have contributed.

(b) Principal authorship and other publication credits accurately reflect the relative scientific or professional contributions of the individuals involved, regardless of their relative status. Mere possession of an institutional position, such as Department Chair, does not justify authorship credit. Minor contributions to the research or to the writing for publications are appropriately acknowledged, such as in footnotes or in an introductory statement.

(c) A student is usually listed as principal author on any multiple-authored article that is substantially based on the student's dissertation or thesis.

### 6.24 Duplicate Publication of Data

Psychologists do not publish, as original data, data that have been previously published. This does not preclude republishing data when accompanied by proper acknowledgment.

### 6.25 Sharing Data

After research results are published, psychologists do not withhold the data on which their conclusions are based from other competent professionals who seek to verify the substantive claims through reanalysis and who intend to use such data only for that purpose, provided that the confidentiality of the participants can be protected and unless legal rights concerning proprietary data preclude their release.

### 6.26 Professional Reviewers

Psychologists who review material submitted for publication, grant, or other research proposal review respect the confidentiality of and the proprietary rights in such information of those who submitted it.

## Commentary

- Decisions about who should receive publication credit are based on the scholarly importance of the contribution.
- Ethical reporting of research requires recognizing the work of others using proper citations and references; failure to do so may result in plagiarism.
- Proper citation includes using quotation marks when material is taken directly from a source and citing secondary sources when an original source is not consulted.

The ethical standards governing the reporting of the results of a scientific investigation seem more straightforward than in other areas of ethical concern. Even here, however, the lines cannot always be drawn clearly. Consider, for example, ethical issues related to assigning *publication credit* to those who make contributions to a research project. Research is often a collaborative effort, involving, for instance, colleagues who offer suggestions about a study's design, graduate or undergraduate students who assist a principal investigator by testing participants and organizing data, technicians who construct specialized equipment, and expert consultants who give advice about computer programs needed for statistical analyses. Because authorship of a published scientific study frequently is used to measure an individual's motivation and competence in a scientific field, *it is important to acknowledge fairly those who have contributed to a project.* However, deciding whether an individual should be credited by being an "author" of a scientific paper or whether that individual's contribution should be acknowledged in a less visible way, such as in a footnote, is not always easy (see, for example, Murray, 1998). If authorship is granted, then the order of authors' names must also be decided. "First author" of a multiple-authored article generally signifies a greater contribution than does "second author" (which is greater than third, etc.). There is a general consensus that contributions leading to authorship should be based mainly in terms of their scholarly importance (e.g., aiding the conceptual aspects of a study) and not by the time and energy invested in the study (Bridgewater, Bornstein, & Walkenbach, 1981; Fine & Kurdek, 1993).

A rather troublesome area of concern, not only for some professionals but frequently for students, is that of **plagiarism.** Again, the ethical standard seems clear enough: Don't present substantial portions or elements of another's work as your own. But what constitutes "substantial portions or elements," and how does one avoid giving the impression that another's work is one's own? This can be like walking a tightrope. On one side is the goal of achieving recognition for contributing to the solution of a problem; on the other side is the goal of recognizing others who have previously contributed to its solution. The fact that both professionals and students are too often caught in the act of plagiarizing suggests that many veer from the tightrope by seeking their own recognition at the expense of giving due credit to the work of others. Sometimes acts of plagiarism result from sloppiness (failing to double-check a source to verify that an idea that is presented did not originate with someone else, for example). Errors of this kind are still plagiarism; *ignorance is not a legitimate excuse.* On other occasions, especially among students, plagiarism can result from failure to identify literal passages through the use of quotation marks or to acknowledge the use of secondary sources. A *secondary source* is one that discusses other (original) work. Most textbooks can be considered secondary sources. Again, ignorance concerning the proper form of citation is not an acceptable excuse, and on unfortunate occasions researchers—professors as well as students—have seen their careers ruined by accusations of plagiarism.

Mistakes can be made all too easily. For example, what constitutes a "substantial" element of another's thinking is not always determined by quantity, as is sometimes assumed. That is, researchers occasionally ask "how much" of a passage can be used without putting it in quotation marks or otherwise identifying its source. A substantial element can be a single word or short phrase if that element serves to identify a key idea or concept that is the result of another's thinking. Students and other novices in an academic discipline, who may not yet be cognizant of important concepts and ideas in an area of knowledge, must be particularly careful when referring to the work of others. *Whenever material is taken directly from a source, it should be placed in quotation marks and the source properly identified.*

Because students and others new to a scientific field frequently rely on secondary sources, it is very important that they understand how to use and cite such sources, which include not only textbooks, but published reviews of research such as those that appear in scientific journals like the *Psychological Bulletin*, and other sources whose authors refer to another's findings and ideas. It is always unethical to present an idea or result from an article or publication found in a secondary source *in a manner that suggests you consulted the original work* when your only source of information about the critical material comes from the secondary source. For example, suppose you wish to discuss the interesting work done by Levine (1990) on pace of life that we discussed in Chapter 1 of this text. Unless you are able to locate and peruse the original article, it is unethical for you simply to acknowledge Levine when citing his work; you must also cite the authors of the textbook who discussed his work. It is also bad scholarship because if your readers rely on your report, they will be relying on your interpretation of the textbook authors' interpretation of the original (Levine's) work. It isn't difficult to see how building a base of scientific knowledge on interpretations of interpretations (and so on, when others interpret *your* work) would quickly produce inconsistencies and contradictions.

Citing work mentioned in a secondary source should be avoided whenever possible (e.g., by taking the time to locate and consult the original), but when it is necessary to do so, proper citation means informing your reader that you did *not* consult the original work (e.g., by using the phrase "as cited in . . ." when referring to the original work). This gives your reader fair warning that the identification and interpretation of the critical material did not originate with you. (Students of psychology are expected to be familiar with the stylistic rules and guidelines for manuscript preparation found in the *Publication Manual of the American Psychological Association*, 4th ed., 1994. See also Appendix C in this textbook.) As with other areas of ethical decision making, when in doubt get advice from others with experience in the area in which you have questions.

### What Do You Think?

Ethical concerns associated with the assigning of authorship can take many forms. For example, not only is it unethical for a faculty member to take credit for a student's work, it is also unethical for students to be given undeserved author credit. This latter situation may arise, for instance, in a misguided attempt by a faculty mentor to give a student an edge when competing for a position in a competitive graduate program. According to Fine and Kurdek (1993), awarding students undeserved author credit may falsely represent the student's expertise, give the student an unfair advantage over peers, and, perhaps, lead others to create impossible expectations for the student. These authors recommend that faculty and students collaborate in the process of determining authorship credit and discuss early on in the project what level of participation warrants author credit.

As with many ethical issues, the process of making a good decision is not always easy. Consider the following scenario presented by Fine and Kurdek (1993) as part of their discussion of this important issue:

> An undergraduate student asked a psychology member to supervise an honors thesis. The student proposed a topic, the faculty member primarily developed the research methodology, the student collected and entered the data, the faculty member conducted the statistical analyses, and the student used part of the analyses for the thesis. The student wrote the thesis under very close supervision by the faculty member. After the honors thesis was completed, the faculty member decided that data from the entire project were sufficiently interesting to warrant publication as a unit. Because the student did not have the skills necessary to write the entire study for a scientific journal, the faculty member did so. The student's thesis contained approximately one third of the material presented in the article. (pp. 1141–1142)

> What do you think? Should the student be an author on any publication resulting from this work? Or, perhaps, should the student's work only be acknowledged in a footnote to the article? If you think the student should be given author credit, do you think the student should be first author or second author?

## STEPS FOR ETHICAL DECISION MAKING

Should research participants be placed at risk of serious injury to gain information about bystander apathy? Should psychologists use deception to learn about the causes of date rape? Is it acceptable to make animals suffer in order to learn about human drug addiction? These questions require answers; however, you no doubt realize by now that the answers do not come easily. Moreover, it is often unclear what the "right" answer is or even if there *is* a right answer. More often than not, at least in the context of doing psychological research, the answer is based on the reflective judgment of a group of individuals with varying backgrounds and experiences who are asked to review the study. The people who comprise a university IRB or IACUC, for instance, are one such group. Recommendations can be made regarding the steps to be taken in this review process (Keith-Spiegel & Koocher, 1985). We have prepared one set of recommendations based on our readings and on discussions with philosophers involved in ethical decision making.*

1  Find out all the facts of the situation. In other words, determine exactly what is involved in terms of procedure, nature of participants, and so on.

2  Identify the relevant ethical issues. An important part of this inquiry will be consulting ethical guidelines that are available, such as the APA Ethics Code we have excerpted in this chapter, as well as policy statements from various professional organizations. Also, make sure you are aware of local, state, and federal regulations or laws in this area.

3  Decide what is at stake for all parties involved (participants, researchers, institutions). This will mean taking different viewpoints, for example, by asking what is at stake from a scientific point of view, from society's viewpoint, from the view of participants, and from an overall moral viewpoint.

4  Identify alternative methods or procedures, discussing the consequences of each alternative, including their ethical implications. As part of this discussion, consider the consequences of *not* doing the proposed research. Examine the practical constraints of each alternative.

5  Decide on the action to be taken. Judge the "correctness" of your decision not in terms of whether it makes you feel happy (you may not), but, rather, in terms of the process that was followed. Is it the best that can be done given the circumstances?

## SUMMARY

Psychological research raises many ethical questions. Thus, before beginning a research project, you must consider the specific ethical issues, as well as the various federal and state laws, relevant to your project. In most cases formal institutional approval—for example, from an IRB or IACUC—must be obtained

*We wish to acknowledge the contributions in this section of various members of the Loyola University of Chicago Center for Ethics, especially David Ozar, Mark Waymack, and Patricia Werhane.

before beginning to do research. One function of an IRB is to reach a consensus regarding the risk/benefit ratio of the proposed research. Risk can involve physical, psychological, or social injury. Informed consent must be obtained from human participants in most psychological research. Researchers must take special safeguards to protect human participants when more than minimal risk is present and to provide appropriate debriefing following their participation. Debriefing can also help human participants feel more fully involved in the research situation as well as help the researcher learn how the participants perceived the treatment or task. Serious ethical questions arise when researchers withhold information from participants. When deception is used, debriefing should include providing information concerning the reasons for having used deception.

Psychologists testing animal subjects must obey a variety of federal and state guidelines and, in general, must treat the animals humanely. Animals may be subjected to pain or discomfort only when alternative procedures are not available and when the goals of the research are judged to justify such procedures. Reporting of psychological findings should be done in a manner that gives appropriate credit to the individuals who helped with the project. Appropriate acknowledgment must also be made of those individuals whose ideas or findings have previously been reported in the published literature and who therefore contributed to the investigator's planning or thinking about the study.

## Key Concepts

risk/benefit ratio                      deception
minimal risk                            debriefing
informed consent                        plagiarism
privacy

## Review Questions

1 Briefly summarize the role of Institutional Review Boards (IRBs) and Institutional Animal Care and Use Committees (IACUCs) in overseeing psychological research.
2 How is the risk/benefit ratio used in ethical decision making?
3 Differentiate among the following possible types of injury in psychological research: physical, psychological, social.
4 How is the possibility of social risk typically safeguarded against?
5 Under what conditions do the APA ethical standards indicate that informed consent may not be necessary?
6 What do Diener and Crandall (1978) say are three important dimensions to consider when making decisions about what information is private?
7 When is it unethical to deceive human participants?
8 What are the major benefits of debriefing, both to the participant and to the researcher?
9 What kinds of special knowledge are required by the APA standards for those working with animal subjects?

10  According to the APA standards, what circumstances must be present before animals may be subjected to stress or pain?

11  What allows an individual to claim "authorship" of a published scientific report?

12  What specific ethical procedure should be followed when it is necessary to cite information from a secondary source?

## CHALLENGE QUESTIONS

NOTE: Each of the challenge questions for Chapter 2 includes a hypothetical research proposal involving a rationale and method similar to that of actual published research. To answer these questions, you will need to be familiar with the APA ethical principles and other material on ethical decision making presented in this chapter, including the recommended steps for ethical decision making that were outlined at the end of this chapter. As you will see, your task is to decide whether specific ethical standards have been violated and to make recommendations regarding the proposed research, including the most basic recommendation of whether the investigator should be allowed to proceed. Unlike other chapters, no answers to the questions are provided. To resolve the ethical dilemmas, you must be able not only to apply the appropriate ethical standards but also to reach an agreement regarding the proposed research after discussion with others whose backgrounds and knowledge differ from your own. You will therefore have to consider points of view different from your own. We urge you to approach these problems as part of a group discussion of these important issues.

### Proposal 1

I. Assume you are a member of an Institutional Review Board (IRB). Besides yourself, the committee includes a clinical psychologist, a social psychologist, a social worker, a philosopher, a Protestant minister, a history professor, and a respected business executive in the community. The following is a summary of a research proposal that has been submitted to the IRB for review. You are asked to consider what questions you might want to ask the investigator and whether you would approve carrying out the study at your institution in its present form, whether modification should be made before approval, or whether the proposal should not be approved. (An actual research proposal submitted to an IRB would include more details than we present here.)

Rationale   Psychological conformity occurs when people accept the opinions or judgments of others in the absence of significant reasons to do so or in the face of evidence to the contrary. Previous research has investigated the conditions under which conformity is likely to occur and has shown, for example, that conformity increases when people anticipate unpleasant events (e.g., shock) and when the pressure to conform comes from individuals with whom the individuals identify. The proposed research examines psychological conformity in the context of discussions about alcohol consumption among teenage students. The goal of the research is to identify factors that contribute to students' willingness to attend social events where alcohol is served to minors and to allow obviously intoxicated persons to drive an automobile. This research seeks to investigate conformity in a natural setting and in circumstances where unpleasant events (e.g., legal penalties, school suspension, injury, or even death) can be avoided by not conforming to peer pressure.

## Method

The research will involve 36 high school students between the ages of 16 and 18 who have volunteered to participate in a research project investigating "beliefs and attitudes of today's high school students." Participants will be assigned to four-person discussion groups. Each person in the group will be given the same 20 questions to answer; however, they will be asked to discuss each question with members of the group before writing down their answers. Four of the 20 questions deal with alcohol consumption by teenagers and with possible actions that might be taken to reduce teenage drinking and driving. One member of the group will be appointed discussion leader by the principal investigator. Unknown to the participants, they will be assigned randomly to three different groups. In each group, there will be either 0, 1, or 2 students who are actually working for the principal investigator. Each of these "confederates" has received prior instructions from the investigator regarding what to say during the group discussion of the critical questions about teenage drinking. (The use of confederates in psychological research is discussed in Chapter 3.) Specifically, confederates have been asked to follow a script which presents the argument that the majority of people who reach the legal driving age (16), and all individuals who are old enough (18) to vote in national elections and serve in the armed forces, are old enough to make their own decisions about drinking alcohol; moreover, because it is up to each individual to make this decision, other individuals do not have the right to intervene if someone under the legal age chooses to drink alcohol. Each of the confederates "admits" to drinking alcohol on at least two previous occasions. Thus, the experimental manipulation involves either 0, 1, or 2 persons in the four-person groups suggesting they do not believe students have a responsibility to avoid situations where alcohol is served to minors or to intervene when someone chooses to drink and drive. The effect of this argument on the written answers given by the actual participants in this experiment will be evaluated. Moreover, audiotapes of the sessions will be made without participants' knowledge, and the contents of these audiotapes will be analyzed. Following the experiment, the nature of the deception and the reasons for making audiotapes of the discussions will be explained to the participants.

## Proposal 2

II. Assume you are a member of an Institutional Animal Care and Use Committee (IACUC). Besides yourself, the committee includes a veterinarian, a biologist, a philosopher, and a respected business executive in the community. The following is a summary of a research proposal that has been submitted to the IACUC for review. You are asked to consider what questions you might want to ask the investigator and whether you would approve carrying out this study at your institution in its present form, whether modification should be made before approval, or whether the proposal should not be approved. (An actual research proposal submitted to an IACUC would include more details than we present here.)

Rationale   The investigators seek to investigate the role of subcortical structures in the limbic system in moderating emotion and aggression. This proposal is based on previous research from this laboratory which has shown a significant relationship between damage in various subcortical brain areas of monkey subjects and changes in eating, aggression, and other social behaviors (e.g., courtship). The areas under investigation are those that sometimes have been excised in psychosurgery with humans when attempting to control hyperaggressive and assaultive behaviors. Moreover, the particular subcortical area that is the focus of the present proposal has been hypothesized to be involved in controlling certain sexual activities that are sometimes the subject of psychological treatment (e.g., hypersexuality). Previous studies have been unable to pinpoint the exact areas thought to be involved in controlling certain behaviors; the proposed research seeks to improve on this knowledge.

## Method

Two groups of rhesus monkeys will be the subjects. One group ($N = 4$) will be a control group. These animals will undergo a sham operation, which involves anesthetizing the animals and drilling a hole in the skull. These animals then will be tested and evaluated in the same manner as the experimental animals. The experimental group will undergo an operation to lesion a small part of a subcortical structure known as the amygdala. Two of the animals will have lesions in one site; the remaining two will receive lesions in another site of this structure. After recovery, all animals will be tested on a variety of tasks measuring their food preferences, social behaviors with same and opposite-sex monkeys (normals), and emotional responsiveness (e.g., reactions to a novel fear stimulus: an experimenter in a clown face). The animals will be housed in a modern animal laboratory; the operations will be performed and recovery monitored by a licensed veterinarian. After testing, the experimental animals will be sacrificed and the brains prepared for histological examination. (Histology is necessary to confirm the locus and extent of lesions.) The control animals will not be killed; they will be returned to the colony for use in future experiments.

PART

# II

# *Descriptive Methods*

# *Observation*

## CHAPTER OUTLINE

## OVERVIEW

As was mentioned in Chapter 1, scientists and nonscientists alike rely on observation to learn about behavior. What distinguishes scientific observation from nonscientific observation is the manner in which observations are made. Nonscientists are likely to observe casually and are often unaware of personal and situational biases that may influence their observations. Nonscientists rarely keep formal records of what they observe and consequently depend on memory for information about an event. Unfortunately, what one remembers about an event is not likely to be a literal record of what one experienced, and memory can be affected by information added after an event is observed (Bartlett, 1932; Loftus, 1997a, 1997b; Pezdek, Finger, & Hodge, 1997). Scientific observation, on the other hand, is made under precisely defined conditions, in a systematic and objective manner, and with careful record keeping. When observations are made in this manner, valuable information about behavior and its antecedents can be obtained. And, although observation is basic to all of psychology, we can distinguish among several types of observational studies.

An important task of the psychologist is to describe behavior in its natural context and to identify relationships among variables that are present. Changes in behavior are frequently observed to result from the context in which behavior occurs. For example, Schaller (1963) observed that mountain gorillas regularly eat meat when in captivity, but he found no evidence of meat eating by gorillas in the wild. Preschool children give longer and more evaluative narratives when reminiscing with their father than with their mother (Haden, Haine, & Fivush, 1997). By describing behavior in natural settings, the psychologist seeks to establish a basis for predicting future behavior.

Often, observation is also the first step in discovering the reasons why organisms behave the way they do. Observation, in other words, is an important step in hypothesis generation. For example, both animals and humans are known to display distinctive reactions to novel or unfamiliar situations. Observing a group of 2- and 3-year-old children in the presence of an unfamiliar person or object, Kagan, Reznick, and Snidman (1988) identified those children who were consistently shy, quiet, and timid and those who were consistently sociable, talkative, and affectively spontaneous. When the same children were observed at 7 years of age, a majority of the children in each group exhibited similar behaviors. The researchers hypothesized that shyness in childhood as well as extreme social anxiety in adulthood are the result of temperamental differences present at birth. In a similar vein, Caspi and associates (1997) used observational measures made at age 3 to successfully predict health-risk behaviors (e.g., abusing alcohol) of young adults. These results also support the idea that temperamental differences observed early in childhood are linked to distinct adult behavior patterns.

Systematic observation is an important tool not only of psychologists but of anthropologists, sociologists, and ethologists. In this chapter we examine observational methods used to investigate behavior—especially, but not exclusively, in natural settings. As you will see, the scientist-observer is not always passive, present merely to record behavior. Researchers sometimes intervene in the situation in which they are observing behavior. We'll take a look at scientists' reasons for intervening in natural settings. Methods for recording data and techniques for analyzing data are also illustrated, and some limitations and problems associated with the observation of behavior are explained.

## CLASSIFICATION OF OBSERVATIONAL METHODS

- Observational methods can be classified as "observation with intervention" or "observation without intervention."
- Methods for recording behavior can be classified in terms of how much of behavior is recorded.

Observational methods can be classified according to the degree to which an observer intervenes in an observational setting as well as according to the way in which that behavior is recorded (see Willems, 1969). Hence we make an important distinction between observation with intervention and observation without intervention. Methods of recording behavior also generally differ in terms of whether all (or nearly all) of the behavior exhibited in a given setting is recorded or only particular units of behavior are recorded. In some situations an observer may seek a comprehensive description of behavior. This may be accomplished by the use of film, tapes, or lengthy verbal descriptions. More often, a researcher records specific units of behavior that are related to the goals of a particular study. An investigator, for instance, who is interested in prosocial behavior likely will concentrate on specific behaviors that define this type of behavior. For example, Chambers and Ascione (1987) observed children while they played either an aggressive video game or a video game with prosocial content. Children who played the aggressive game were later observed to put less money in a donation box and to volunteer to help sharpen pencils significantly less than did those who played the prosocial game.

We will discuss observational methods first in terms of the extent of observer intervention and then in terms of methods of recording behavior.

## OBSERVATION WITHOUT INTERVENTION

- The goals of naturalistic observation are to describe behavior as it normally occurs and to examine relationships among variables.
- Naturalistic observation helps to establish the external validity of research findings.
- When ethical and moral considerations prevent experimental control, naturalistic observation is an important research strategy.
- Ethologists use naturalistic observation to describe innate patterns of behavior in animals and humans.

Observation of behavior in a more or less natural setting, without any attempt by the observer to intervene, is frequently called **naturalistic observation.** An observer using this method of observation acts as a passive recorder of what occurs. The events witnessed are those occurring naturally and have not been manipulated or in any way controlled by the observer. What exactly constitutes a natural setting is not easily identified (see Bickman, 1976; Willems & Raush, 1969). In general, we can consider a natural setting one in which behavior ordinarily occurs and that has not been arranged specifically for the purpose of recording behavior. Observing people in a psychology laboratory would not, for instance, be considered naturalistic observation. The laboratory situation has been created specifically to study behavior and, in a manner of speaking, is an artificial rather than a natural setting. In fact, an important reason for doing naturalistic observation is to verify relationships between variables that have been identified in the psychology laboratory. Observation in natural settings serves, among other functions, as a way of establishing the external validity of laboratory findings.

The major goals of observation in natural settings are to describe behavior as it ordinarily occurs and to investigate the relationship among variables that are present. Hartup (1974), for instance, chose naturalistic observation to investigate the frequency and types of aggression exhibited by preschoolers in a St. Paul, Minnesota, children's center. He distinguished hostile aggression (person-oriented) from instrumental aggression (aimed at the retrieval of an object, territory, or privilege). Although he observed boys to be more aggressive overall than girls, his observations provided no evidence that the types of aggression differed

**FIGURE 3.1** Naturalistic observation is frequently the basis of psychologists' investigations of childhood behavior.

between the sexes. Thus Hartup was able to conclude that, with respect to hostile aggression, there was no evidence that boys and girls were "wired" differently.

Hartup's study of children's aggression illustrates why a researcher may choose to use naturalistic observation rather than to manipulate conditions related to behavior. There are certain aspects of human behavior that moral or ethical considerations prevent us from controlling. Researchers may be interested in the relationship between early childhood isolation and later emotional and psychological development. However, we would object strenuously if they tried to take children from their parents in order to raise them in isolation. Alternative methods of data collection must be considered if this problem is to be investigated. For example, the effect of early isolation on later development has been studied through experimentation on animal subjects (Harlow & Harlow, 1966), descriptions of so-called feral children raised outside of human culture, presumably by animals (Candland, 1993), case studies of children subjected to unusual conditions of isolation by their parents (Curtiss, 1977), and systematic observation of institutionalized children (Spitz, 1965). The nature of children's aggression is another aspect of behavior the investigation of which is subject to moral and ethical limitations. We would not want to see children intentionally harassed and picked on simply to record their reactions. However, as anyone knows who has observed children, there is plenty of naturally occurring aggression. Hartup's study shows how observation without intervention can be a useful alternative to methods of data collection that attempt to manipulate the behavior of interest.

Psychologists are not the only researchers who observe behavior in natural settings. Observation is a fundamental method of ethologists. Although related to psychology, **ethology** is generally considered a branch of biology (Eibl-Eibesfeldt, 1975). Ethologists study the behavior of organisms in relation to their natural environment. A major question they seek to answer is how natural selection has worked to produce particular behavior patterns in an animal species. The focus of an ethological investigation is often the development of an **ethogram.** This is nothing less than a complete catalog of all the behavior patterns of an organism, including information on frequency, duration, and context of occurrence for each behavior.

Ethologists adopt a comparative approach to understanding behavior and often seek to explain behavior in one animal species on the basis of innate patterns of behavior observed in species lower on the evolutionary scale. Speculations about the role of innate mechanisms in determining human behavior are not uncommon among ethologists. For instance, Barash (1977) observed whether male and female human pedestrians visually scanned both directions before crossing a dangerous intersection in Seattle, Washington. When a male adult and a female adult were together, adult males scanned more than females. This was true regardless of whether children were also present. The ethologist-observer suggested an evolutionary explanation: Adult male monkeys and baboons in the wild generally function as lookouts to warn the rest of the group of approaching danger. An ethological perspective has proved important for the understanding of both normal and abnormal human behavior. An interesting example is the ethological analysis of psychiatric problems based on comprehensive descriptions of facial behavior of schizophrenic patients (see Pitman et al., 1987).

## OBSERVATION WITH INTERVENTION

- Most psychological research uses observation with intervention.
- The three methods of observation with intervention are participant observation, structured observation, and the field experiment.

It is characteristic of the scientist to "tamper" with nature, to intervene, in order to make a point or to test a theory. Intervention rather than nonintervention characterizes most psychological research. Kinds of intervention vary widely in psychological studies, depending on such things as the purpose for investigating behavior, the nature of the behavior under observation, and the ingenuity of the researcher.

Although the types of intervention employed by psychologists are too numerous and diverse to classify, their reasons for intervening are generally one or more of the following:

**1** To precipitate or cause an event that occurs infrequently in nature or that normally occurs under conditions that make it difficult to observe.

**2** To investigate the limits of an organism's response by varying systematically the qualities of a stimulus event.

**3** To gain access to a situation or event that is generally not open to scientific observation.

**4** To arrange conditions so that important antecedent events are controlled and consequent behaviors can be readily observed.

**5** To establish a comparison by manipulating one or more independent variables to determine their effect on behavior.

These reasons for intervening are illustrated in three methods of observation: participant observation, structured observation, and the field experiment. As we review these major observational techniques, the investigator's reasons for intervening will become clear.

## Participant Observation

- Undisguised participant observation is often used to understand the culture and behavior of groups of individuals.
- Disguised participant observation is often used when researchers believe individuals would change their behavior if they knew it was being recorded.
- Participant observation allows researchers to observe behaviors and situations that are not usually open to scientific observation.
- Participant observers may sometimes lose their objectivity or may unduly influence the individuals whose behavior they are recording.

Observation of behavior by someone who also plays an active and significant role in the situation or context in which behavior is recorded is called **participant observation.** In *undisguised* participant observation, individuals who are being observed know that the observer is present for the purpose of collecting information about their behavior. This method is used frequently by anthropologists who seek to understand the culture and behavior of groups by living and working with members of the group.

When the observer's role is not known to those who are being observed, we speak of *disguised* participant observation. As you might imagine, people do not always behave in the way they ordinarily would when they know their behavior is being recorded. Politicians, for instance, often make different statements when speaking to the press, depending on whether their comments are "for" or "off" the record. Our own behavior is likely to be affected by knowing that we are being watched. This problem associated with observational methods will be discussed more fully later in the chapter. For now, let us simply say that researchers may decide to disguise their role as observers if they believe that people being observed will not act as they ordinarily would if they know their activities are being recorded. Disguised participant observation typically raises ethical issues, for example, of privacy and of informed consent, which must be addressed prior to implementing the study. We will discuss these issues later in this chapter (see also discussion in Chapter 2).

Disguised participant observation was used by Rosenhan (1973) to investigate the basis of psychiatric diagnosis in the context of a mental institution. Eight individuals (including psychologists, a pediatrician, and a housewife) misrepresented their names and occupations and sought admission to twelve different mental hospitals. Each complained of the same general symptom: that he or she was hearing voices. Rosenhan (p. 251) described these symptoms and the rationale for their selection by the observers as follows:

> Asked what the voices said, he replied that they were often unclear, but as far as he could tell they said "empty," "hollow," and "thud." The voices were unfamiliar and were of the same sex as the pseudopatient. The choice of these symptoms was occasioned by their apparent similarity to existential symptoms. Such symptoms are alleged to arise from painful concerns about the perceived meaninglessness of one's life. It is as if the hallucinating person were saying, "My life is empty and hollow." The choice of these symptoms was also determined by the *absence* of a single report of existential psychoses in the literature. Beyond alleging the symptoms and falsifying name, vocation, and employment, no further alterations of person, history, or circumstances were made.

Immediately after being put in the mental ward, the researchers stopped complaining of any symptoms and refrained from acting abnormally. In addition to observing patient-staff interactions, the observers were interested in how long it took for a "sane" person to be released from the hospital. Length of hospitalization ranged from 7 to 52 days. The researchers were never detected as sane and, when they were discharged, their schizophrenia was said only to be "in remission." Apparently, once the pseudopatients were labeled schizophrenic, they were stuck with that label no matter what the nature of their subsequent behavior.

Participant observation allows an observer to gain access to a situation that is not usually open to scientific observation. In addition, the participant observer is often in a position to have the same experiences as the people under study. This may provide important insights and understanding of individuals or groups. The pseudopatients in the Rosenhan study, for instance, felt what it was like to be labeled schizophrenic and not to know how long it would be before they could return to society. In the fall of 1959, John Howard Griffin set out to research "what it was like to be a Negro in a land where we keep the Negro down." Griffin, a White man, darkened his skin using medication and stain in order to pass himself off as Black. For more than a month he traveled (walking, hitchhiking, riding buses) through Mississippi, Alabama, and Georgia. He described his experiences as a participant observer in his book *Black Like Me* (1960), which was an important precursor of the civil rights movement of the 1960s.

A participant observer's role in a situation can produce certain methodological problems. By identifying with the individuals under study, it is possible for an observer to lose the scientific objectivity that accurate and valid observation requires. Changes in a participant observer are sometimes dramatic and are not easily anticipated. Witness the experiences of a criminologist who used undisguised participant observation to study police officers at work. Kirkham (1975) went through police academy training like any recruit and became a uniformed patrol officer assigned to a high-crime area in a city of about half a million. His immersion in the daily activities of an officer on the beat led to marked changes in his attitudes and personality. As Kirkham (p. 19) himself noted:

> As the weeks and months of my new career as a slum policeman went by, I slowly but inexorably began to become indistinguishable in attitudes and behavior from the policemen with whom I worked. . . . According to the accounts of my family, colleagues and friends, I began to increasingly display attitudinal and behavioral elements that were entirely foreign to my previous personality—punitiveness, pervasive cynicism and mistrust of others, chronic irritability and free-floating hostility, racism, a diffuse personal anxiety over the menace of crime and criminals that seemed at times to border on the obsessive. A former opponent of capital punishment, I became its vociferous advocate in cases involving felony murder, kidnapping and the homicide of police officers—even though as a criminologist I continued to recognize its ineffectiveness as a deterrent to crime.

Participant observers must be aware of the threat to objective reporting that arises due to their involvement in the situation wherein they are recording behavior. This threat necessarily increases as degree of involvement increases.

Another problem with observer involvement is the effect the observer has on the behavior of those being studied. It is more than likely that the participant observer will have to interact with other people, make decisions, initiate activities, assume responsibilities, and otherwise act like everyone else in that situation. Whenever observers intervene in a natural setting, they must ask to what degree participants and events are affected by the intervention. Is what is being observed the same as it would have been if the observer had never appeared? It is difficult to generalize results to other situations if intervention produces behavior that is specific to the conditions and events created by the observer.

In the case of participant observation, the extent of an observer's influence on the behavior under observation is not easily assessed. Several factors must be considered, such as whether participation is disguised or undisguised, the size of the group entered, and the role of the observer in the group. Griffin, for example, was not known to be a White man even by most of the Blacks he associated with, and his entry into a subculture of literally thousands of disadvantaged Blacks could not reasonably be expected to influence the nature of Black-White interactions that he observed. Similarly, it does not appear that Rosenhan and his associates significantly affected the natural environment of the mental ward by assuming the role of mental patients. (However, some of the patients—though none of the staff—apparently detected the sanity of the pseudopatients, suggesting to the observers that they were there to check up on the hospital.)

When the group under observation is small or the activities of the participant observer are prominent, the observer is more likely to have a significant effect on participants' behavior. This problem confronted several social psychologists who infiltrated a group of people who claimed to be in contact with beings from outer space (Festinger, Riecken, & Schachter, 1956). A leader of the group said he had received a message from the aliens predicting a cataclysmic flood on a specific date. The flood was to stretch from the Arctic Circle to the Gulf of Mexico. The prophecy was reported in the newspapers, and certain psychologists who read the account saw an opportunity to test a theory of group cohesion and reaction in the face of unfulfilled prophecy. (The psychologists assumed that the flood was not going to occur.) Because of the attitudes of members of the group toward "nonbelievers," the researchers were forced to make up bizarre stories in order to gain access to the group. This tactic worked too well. Not only were the disguised participant observers welcomed into the group, which never consisted of more than a dozen hard-core believers, but their stories were taken as signs from the extraterrestrial beings. One of the observers was even thought to be a spaceman bringing a message. The researchers had inadvertently reinforced the group's beliefs and influenced in an undetermined way the course of events that followed. By the way, the flood never occurred, but at least some of the group members came to use this disconfirmation as a means of strengthening their initial belief. They began to seek new members by arguing that their faith had prevented the prophesied flood.

Thus, although participant observation may permit an observer to gain access to situations not usually open to scientific investigation, the observer using this technique must seek ways to deal with the possible loss of objectivity and the potential effects that a participant observer may have on the behavior under study.

## Structured Observation

- Structured observations are set up to record behaviors that may be difficult to observe using naturalistic observation.

- Structured observations are often used by clinical and developmental psychologists.
- Problems in interpreting structured observations can occur when the same observation procedures are not followed across observations or observers, or when important variables are not controlled.

There are a variety of observational methods using intervention that are not easily categorized. Because researchers exert some control over the events, these procedures differ from naturalistic observation without intervention. However, the degree of control in these instances is often less than that seen in field experiments, which we will consider later. We have labeled these procedures **structured observation.** Often the observer intervenes in order to cause an event to occur or to "set up" a situation so that events can be more easily recorded than they would be without intervention. In other cases the observer may create quite elaborate procedures to investigate a particular behavior more fully.

Structured observations may occur in a natural setting or in a laboratory setting. Structured laboratory observations are often used by clinical psychologists when making behavioral assessments of parent-child interactions (see, for example, Hughes & Haynes, 1978). A parent and child who are seeking some sort of help come to a diagnostic clinic or laboratory and are asked to engage in specific tasks while being observed (often from behind a one-way window). Observations are made of various specific behaviors (for instance, tantrums or other emotional outbursts by the child) and of the general nature of the parent-child interactions. Partly on the basis of the results of this structured observation, the therapist plans a strategy to address the behavioral problems that exist. Leavens and Hopkins (1998) used structured observations of chimpanzees to investigate "gaze alternation," the behavior of alternating looking at a distant (and desired) object and the face of an experimenter who is in a position to retrieve the object. A banana was placed outside the cage of the chimpanzee by one experimenter, who then left the scene. A second experimenter approached, gave verbal greetings and established eye contact with the chimpanzee while ignoring the banana. Communication via gaze alternation was defined as alternating looking by the chimpanzee at the banana and the face of the experimenter. Vocal and pointing gestures were also recorded. The chimpanzees revealed high levels of what appears to be a form of intentional communication in goal-directed activities—a behavior, however, that clearly was present more often among older than younger animals.

Structured observations are also frequently used by developmental psychologists. Perhaps most notable are the methods of Jean Piaget (1896–1980). In many of Piaget's studies a child is first given a problem to solve and then given several variations on the problem to test the limits of the child's understanding. The observer acquaints the child with the nature of the problem and then usually asks questions to probe the child's reasoning processes. These structured observations have provided a wealth of information regarding children's cognition and are the basis for Piaget's "stage theory" of intellectual development. Piaget-type tasks are also frequently used by animal researchers to investigate

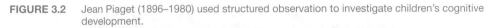

**FIGURE 3.2**    Jean Piaget (1896–1980) used structured observation to investigate children's cognitive development.

aspects of animal cognition. In one such study, orangutans outperformed squirrel monkeys on a classic test of the ability to represent the existence of an unperceived object or what has been called object permanence (de Blois, Novak, & Bond, 1998).

Structured observation is a compromise between the passive nonintervention of naturalistic observation and the systematic manipulation of independent variables and precise control that characterize laboratory methods. Such a compromise permits observations to be made under conditions that are more natural than those imposed in a laboratory. Nevertheless, there may be a price to pay. The failure to follow similar procedures each time an observation is made may make it difficult for other observers to obtain the same results when investigating a problem. Uncontrolled, and perhaps unknown, variables may play an important part in producing the behavior under observation. For example, the fact that structured observations like those used by Piaget do not always follow the same procedure from one observation to another can be viewed as a problem with these techniques (see Brainerd, 1978).

To reinforce this point regarding the possible influence of uncontrolled variables in structured observation, let us relate a historical anecdote about two well-known psychologists in the first half of the 20th century (see Cohen, 1979). In 1913, the same year he launched psychology on a new course with his remarks entitled, "Psychology as the Behaviorist Views It," John B. Watson set sail for the Tortugas islands off the coast of Florida. On a previous visit to the islands, he had begun observations of noddy and sooty terns in their natural habitat. Accompanying him was Karl Lashley, a student of Watson's who later did important physiological studies of brain function. Lashley went with Watson to help him make his observations and to help test the homing abilities of terns. At one point during the summer, Lashley removed 30 birds from their nests and took them with him on a boat trip to Mobile, Alabama, where he released 15 of them. Traveling more than 100 miles farther to Galveston, Texas, Lashley set free the remaining 15 birds. Watson waited on the island to record the arrival of the birds if, indeed, they were able to make it back as popular stories of the time suggested. Four days after Lashley released them, the birds began returning to the island. Watson and Lashley had demonstrated that terns could safely navigate across an open sea with no obvious landmarks from a distance of 1,000 miles. They were at a loss to explain how the birds managed their remarkable feat, and, as events transpired, Watson did not have the opportunity to carry out any more tests of the birds' homing abilities.

Suppose, however, that the procedure of taking the terns on board a ship caused some of the birds to become ill (something that had actually happened on a previous occasion, when the birds died in transit) and that their illness affected their homing behavior. When no birds returned to their nests after being released, the observers might have wrongly concluded that the animals had no homing instinct. This possibility does not seem that farfetched when you consider that more recent observations of bird navigation have revealed that homing pigeons make use of airborne odors to recognize the location of their lofts (see Wallraff & Sinsch, 1988). Birds who were allowed to smell only filtered air before being released did not show any tendency to return home.

Although structured observations are often important for gathering information about behavior, and even for testing specific hypotheses, researchers must be aware of the limitations they impose when they allow some variables to remain uncontrolled and when procedures differ with the circumstances or the behavior of the subject under observation.

Ethologists frequently use structured observation to study the limits of an organism's response by varying systematically the characteristics of a stimulus event. For example, observations by Nobel Prize-winning ethologist Konrad Lorenz led to the discovery of imprinting (see Eibl-Eibesfeldt, 1975). Imprinting is a process by which certain animal species form an attachment to an object encountered during a critical or sensitive period in their lives. Immediately after hatching, for example, the young graylag gosling will imprint on almost any moving object in its environment and follow that object for some time afterward. Under ordinary conditions, the object of the bird's imprinting is its parent, and the innately triggered response is important for the young bird's survival. To understand the imprinting response better, ethologists sometimes create models of both male and female parents and test the young animal's response when the models move, when they make a noise, or when the imprinting response is punished (see Eibl-Eibesfeldt, 1975). Lorenz himself served as a model; many students of psychology have been introduced to ethology by scenes of the famous ethologist being energetically pursued over land and water by the young birds who attached themselves (imprinted) to him.

## Field Experiments

- In a field experiment, researchers manipulate one or more independent variables in a natural setting to determine the effect on behavior.
- A confederate is a research assistant who behaves in specified ways to create an experimental condition.

When an observer manipulates one or more independent variables in a natural setting in order to determine their effect on behavior, the procedure is called a **field experiment.** Although experimental methods will be discussed extensively in later chapters of this book, we mention the field experiment here because it represents one end of the nonintervention-intervention dimension that characterizes observational methods. In conducting a field experiment, the observer (now usually called the experimenter) seeks to control the antecedents of an event in order to measure systematically the effect of a variable on behavior. Control or comparison groups are used, and the experimenter usually dictates the assignment of participants to conditions. The field experiment is probably the most frequently used field-observation technique in social psychology (Bickman, 1976). In most cases individuals are unaware that they are participating in an experiment. In a field experiment researchers also typically make use of **confederates.** A confederate is someone in the research situation who is instructed to behave in a certain way in order to produce an experimental situation. Confederates, for example, have been employed by social psychologists to pose as robbers when bystander reaction to a crime has been investigated (Latané & Darley, 1970) and to mimic the behavior of individuals cutting into a waiting line in order to study the reactions of those in line (Milgram, Liberty, Toledo, & Wackenhut, 1986).

Field experiments sometimes yield valuable practical knowledge. For example, research by Latané and Darley and others helps us to understand the variables that affect a bystander's willingness to come to the aid of a victim. Interestingly, many studies show that a bystander is more likely to aid a victim when the bystander is alone than when other bystanders are present. Crusco and Wetzel (1984) also conducted a field experiment with the potential for practical application. They investigated the effect of touching on restaurant customers. Waitresses working as confederates touched restaurant customers on either the hand or the shoulder while returning change. The researchers speculated that a touch on the hand would produce positive affect toward the waitress whereas a touch on the shoulder, which may be seen as a sign of dominance, would not be viewed positively, especially by male diners. The participants were 114 diners from two restaurants who were randomly assigned to three levels of the independent variable: Fleeting Touch, when the waitress twice touched the diner's palm for 1/2 second when returning change; Shoulder Touch, when she placed her hand for 1 to 1 1/2 seconds on the diner's shoulder as she gave back change; and No Touch, when no physical contact was made with the customers. The major dependent variable was the size of the tip. Results showed that males tipped overall more than females but that both male and female diners gave a significantly larger tip after being touched than when not touched. The results did not show, as the researchers had expected, that the nature of the touch made a difference; male and female diners were affected equally by both kinds of touches.

## RECORDING BEHAVIOR

- Researchers choose whether to obtain a comprehensive behavioral record or to record selected behaviors depending on the goals of the observational research.
- How the results of a study are ultimately summarized, analyzed, and reported depends on how behavioral observations are initially recorded.

We have mentioned two important characteristics of observational methods. One is the degree of observer intervention, the other the method of recording behavior. As we have tried to show, intervention is a dimension anchored at one end by the absence of any intervention, as is associated with passive observation in a naturalistic setting, and at the other end by the active and systematic manipulation of antecedent events that characterizes field experiments. Observational methods also differ in the manner in which behavior is recorded, particularly the degree to which behavior is abstracted from the situation in which it is observed (see Willems, 1969, for a thorough discussion of this aspect of observational methods).

In general, methods of recording behavior can be classified as those that seek a comprehensive description of behavior and the situation in which it occurs and those that focus on only certain kinds of behavior or events. Whether all behavior in a given setting or only selected aspects are to be observed depends on the purposes or goals of an observational study. Decisions regarding the manner in which behavior is recorded also depend on whether the investigator is doing qualitative or quantitative research. As we saw in Chapter 1, the results of a qualitative study are presented chiefly in the form of verbal description and logical argument, whereas quantitative research emphasizes statistical description and analysis of data to support a study's conclusions. The important point for you to remember is that how the results of a study are eventually summarized, analyzed, and reported hinges on the way in which the behavior is initially recorded.

## Obtaining Qualitative Records of Behavior

- Narrative records in the form of written descriptions of behavior, audiotapes, and videotapes are comprehensive records of observed behavior.
- Researchers classify and organize data from narrative records to test their hypotheses about behavior.
- Narrative records sometimes include observers' inferences about individuals' motives or feelings, as in ethnography or ecological psychology.
- Field notes are records made by trained observers that describe particular events and behaviors of interest rather than comprehensive accounts of behavior.
- Narrative records should be made during or soon after behavior is observed, and observers must be carefully trained to record behavior according to established criteria.

**Narrative records** are intended to provide a more or less faithful reproduction of behavior as it originally occurred. Written descriptions of behavior made by an observer are one major type of narrative record. So are the spoken records produced by using a tape recorder and the visual records obtained with videotape or movie cameras. Ethologists are often interested in every detail of a behavioral event, so motion picture film turns out to be one of their most important means of recording behavior (Eibl-Eibesfeldt, 1975). For example, to study the function of the "eyebrow flash" in social interactions, ethologists made use of 67 hours of film showing individuals in naturally occurring social situations (Grammar, Schiefenhovel, Schleidt, Lorenz, & Eibl-Eibesfeldt, 1988). Across three different cultures, the eyebrow flash, usually accompanied by a smile, was found to be a universal social signal, for example, as a sign of factual "yes."

Once narrative records are obtained, the observer can study, classify, and organize the records at leisure. Particular hypotheses or expectations about the behaviors under observation can be tested by examining the data. This constitutes an important difference between narrative records and other forms of behavior measurement wherein the classification or coding of behaviors is done at the time of observation. Thus, researchers must choose methods for obtaining narrative records that will capture the particular information necessary for evaluating a study's hypotheses.

We have already mentioned how Piaget used structured observation to study the cognitive development of children. Having selected a problem to present to the child, Piaget then made a rather literal record of the child's attempts to solve the problem. The following narrative record was obtained by Piaget when investigating a 4-year-old child's understanding of volume.

In this structured observation, the child is given two containers, A and L, of equal height. A is wide and L is narrow. A is filled to a certain height (one-quarter or one-fifth) and the child is asked to pour the same quantity of liquid into L. The dimensions are such that the level will be four times as high in L as in A for the same amount of liquid. In spite of this striking difference in the proportions, the child at this stage proves incapable of grasping that the smaller diameter of L will require a higher level of liquid. Those children who are clearly still at this stage are satisfied that there is "the same amount to drink" in L when they have filled it to the same level as A. Here is a narrative record of one child's (Blas) response to this situation:

> Blas (4.0): "Look, your mummy has poured out a glass of lemonade for herself (A) and she gives you this glass (L). We want you to pour into your glass as much lemonade as your mummy has in hers.—(She poured rather quickly and exceeded the level equal to that in A that she was trying to achieve.)—Will you both have the same like that?—*No.*—Who will have more?—*Me.*—Show me where you must pour to so that you both have the same.—(She poured up to the same level.)—Will you and mummy have the same amount to drink like that?—*Yes.*—Are you sure?—*Yes.*" (Piaget, J. [1965]. *The child's conception of number,* pp. 11–12. New York: Norton. First published in French in 1941 under the title *Le Genèse du nombre chez l'enfant.*)

The narrative begins with the observer's comments to the child, Blas. The observer says, "Look, your mummy has poured out a glass of lemonade. . . ." After that follows an exact reproduction of what the observer said, what the child said, and what happened in this situation. The narrative contains little observer inference and the exact sequence of behaviors is recorded. His many observations of children's behavior led Piaget to a number of important conclusions about human cognitive development. As you can see, Piaget used the narrative record to illustrate that the 4-year-old has not yet mastered the principle of "conservation of volume." The two containers, which were of equal height but different width, were perceived by the child to hold the same amount of liquid when the level of the liquid was the same.

Hartup (1974) obtained narrative records as part of his naturalistic study of children's aggression. He investigated a number of different aspects of children's aggression, including the relationship between particular kinds of antecedent events and the nature of the aggressive episodes that followed. Consider this sample narrative record from Hartup's study (p. 339):

> Marian [a 7-year-old]. . . is complaining to all that David [who is also present] had squirted her on the pants she has to wear tonight. She says, "I'm gonna do it to him to see how he likes it." She fills a can with water and David runs to the teacher and tells of her threat. The teacher takes the can from Marian. Marian attacks David and pulls his hair very hard. He cries and swings at Marian as the teacher tries to restrain him; then she takes him upstairs. . . . Later, Marian and Elaine go upstairs and into the room where David is seated with a teacher. He throws a book at Marian. The teacher asks Marian to leave. Marian kicks David, then leaves. David cries and screams, "Get out of here, they're just gonna tease me."

Hartup (1974) instructed his observers to avoid making inferences about the intentions, motives, or feelings of the participants and to use precise language in describing behavior. Note that we are not told why David might want to throw a book at Marian or how Marian feels about being attacked. Hartup believed that certain antecedent behaviors were related to specific types of aggression. Because any inferences or impressions of the observers were strictly excluded, the content of the narrative records could be classified and coded in an objective manner. Thus, individuals coding the narrative would not be influenced by what the observer inferred was going on.

Not all narrative records are as focused as those obtained by Piaget or Hartup, nor do narrative records always avoid inferences and impressions of the observer. An important goal of **ecological psychology** involves the comprehensive description of individuals in everyday contexts. This approach has much in common with **ethnography,** which has long been a major descriptive tool of anthropologists and sociologists. Ethnographers frequently combine data obtained through various observational methods, such as naturalistic observation and participant observation, as well as that obtained through the examination of documents and interviews, in order to describe the context and meanings of everyday social situations (see Taylor & Bogdan, 1998). One example of ecological research is a study of "a day in the life" of a midwestern school girl (Barker, Wright, Schoggen, & Barker, 1978, pp. 56–58). Eight different observers took turns observing an 8-year-old girl from the time she awoke in the morning until she went to sleep at night. Because the researchers wanted to include information about the girl's motives, feelings, and perceptions, they required that the observers make a number of inferences. Generally, only the inferences that two or more observers agreed on were included. For example, people can often agree as to when someone is sad or happy or excited or calm. The narrative record of this little girl's day was about 100,000 words in length and was later determined to contain 969 different behavior episodes.

Narrative records are not always meant to be comprehensive descriptions of behavior as we have seen illustrated in the context of structured observations used by Piaget, or in the study of the day in the life of a young schoolgirl. Often the narrative records of an observer are merely running descriptions of the participants, events, settings, and behaviors. These records are generally called **field notes.** Field notes are nothing more than the verbal records of a trained observer. Used by journalists, social workers, anthropologists, ethnographers, ethologists, and others, they do not always contain an exact record of everything that occurred. Events and behaviors that especially interest the observer are recorded and are likely to be interpreted in terms of the observer's specialized knowledge or expertise. For example, in making notes about a particular patient, a psychiatrist might compare the client's symptoms with those of other patients or with a textbook definition. An ethologist might record how the behavior of one species appears to parallel that of another.

Field notes tend to be highly personalized (Brandt, 1972), but they are probably used more frequently than any other kind of narrative record. Field notes have generated numerous revelations about behavior; they are the basis of Darwin's theory of evolution as well as Rosenhan's description of being sane in insane places. Their usefulness as scientific records depends on the accuracy and precision of their content. These characteristics will be related to the training of the observer and the extent to which the observations that are recorded can be verified by independent observers and through other means of investigation.

Practical, as well as methodological, considerations dictate the manner in which narrative records are made. As a general rule, records should be made during or as soon as possible after behavior is observed. The passage of time blurs details and makes it harder to reproduce the original sequence of actions. Adjang (1986) used a portable cassette recorder to make narrative records of his spoken observations of the teasing behavior of young chimpanzees; however, he then transcribed these spoken reports onto paper "as soon as possible" (p. 139). This rule is sometimes not easy to follow when observations are made in natural settings. An ethologist who is trying to record the behavior of animals in the wild is sometimes hampered by bad weather, animal migration, dwindling daylight, and so forth. Notes may have to be made quickly—even while the observer is quite literally on the run. At other times observers may have to wait until they return to camp to make written records of behavior. When Festinger et al. (1956) infiltrated the group of people waiting for spacemen to rescue them from a cataclysmic flood, the participant observers sometimes found it difficult to take notes without being seen by members of the group. Excuses had to be made to leave the group (to go to the bathroom, for example) in order to make written records of the group's activities.

Decisions regarding the content of a narrative record must be made prior to observing behavior. We have seen, for example, that verbal narratives may differ according to the degree of observer inference or the completeness of the behavioral record. Thus, these aspects of a narrative record, as well as others, must be decided on prior to beginning a study (see, for example, Brandt, 1972). Once the content of narrative records is decided, observers must be trained to record behavior according to the criteria that have been set up. Practice observations may have to be conducted and records critiqued by more than one investigator before "real" data are collected.

## Obtaining Quantitative Measures of Behavior

- When researchers seek to describe *specific* behaviors or events, they often obtain quantitative measures of behavior such as frequency of occurrence or duration of a behavior.
- Quantitative measures of behavior use one of the four levels of measurement scales: nominal, ordinal, interval, and ratio.
- Rating scales, often used to measure psychological dimensions, are frequently treated as if they are interval scales even though they usually represent ordinal measurement.
- Electronic recording devices may be used in natural settings to record behavior and pagers sometimes are used to signal participants to report their behavior (e.g., on a questionnaire).

When only certain behaviors or specific aspects of individuals and settings are of interest, the behaviors need to be defined prior to beginning an observational study. Decisions also should be made as to exactly how characteristics of their occurrence should be measured—that is, how the behavior can be *quantified*. For example, assume you wish to observe reactions to individuals with obvious physical disabilities by those who do not have such disabilities. In order to conduct your study, it would be necessary to define what constitutes a "reaction" to a physically disabled individual. Are you interested, for example, in helping behaviors, approach/avoidance behaviors, eye contact, length of conversation, or in some other behavioral reaction? As you consider what behaviors you will use to define people's "reactions," you will also have to decide how you will measure these behaviors. Assume, for instance, you are planning a study using naturalistic observation and that you have chosen to measure people's reactions by observing eye contact between individuals who do not have obvious physical disabilities and those who do. Exactly how should you measure eye contact? Should you simply measure whether a passerby does or does not make eye contact, or do you want to measure the *duration* of any eye contact? Of course, you may wish to make multiple measures, a research strategy that is recommended whenever it is feasible. The decisions you make will depend on the particular hypotheses or goals of your study, but they will also be influenced by information gained by examining previous studies that have used the same or similar behavioral measures. (Unfortunately, previous research indicates that reactions to physically disabled individuals frequently can be classified as unfavorable. See, for example, Thompson, 1982.)

Measurement Scales    Defining a behavioral measure involves deciding what scale of measurement to use. Thus, it is important for you to be familiar with the types of measurement scales used in behavioral research. There are four levels of measurement, or **measurement scales,** that apply to both physical and psychological measurement. The lowest level, or scale, is called a *nominal scale;* it involves categorizing an event into one of a number of discrete categories. For instance, we could measure the color of people's eyes by classifying them as "brown eyed" or "blue eyed." When studying people's reactions to individuals with obvious physical disabilities, a researcher might use a nominal scale by measuring whether persons make eye contact or do not make eye contact with someone who has an obvious physical disability. This type of category system is called a **checklist.** A checklist is used to record the presence or absence of specific behaviors, such as whether individuals make eye contact with a physically disabled person, whether children in a classroom are talking or are quiet, whether people use seat belts or do not use seat belts.

Characteristics of participants—such as age, race, and sex—are also frequently recorded using a checklist, as are features of the setting—such as time of day, location, and whether other people are present. It is often informative to observe behavior as a function of participant and context variables. Do males use seat belts more than females? Are people who drive inexpensive automobiles more likely to share a ride than people who drive expensive automobiles? These questions can be answered by observing the presence or absence of certain behaviors (seat-belt use or car pooling) for different categories of participants and settings (male and female, expensive and inexpensive automobiles).

Jenni (1976; also Jenni & Jenni, 1976) used a checklist to study the book-carrying behavior of male and female college students. Three types of book-carrying behaviors were defined: two major types and an "other" category. Figure 3.3 illustrates the two major types of carrying behavior. Students using Type I wrap one or both arms around the books, with the short edges of the books resting on the hip or in front of the body. Students using Type II support the books by one arm and hand at the side of the body, with the long edges of the books approximately horizontal to the ground. The "other" category included a variety of book-carrying methods that did not fit either Type I or Type II. For example, students occasionally hold books by the edges with both hands in front of the body (for instance, when reading while walking).

Observations of 2,626 individuals were made on six college campuses (three in the United States, one in Canada, and two in Central America). Individuals were observed as they passed a certain point on campus. Type of carrying behavior and sex of the student were noted. In terms of the arithmetic operations that we can perform on data recorded on a nominal scale, we can use only the relationships "equal" and "not equal." A common way of summarizing nominal data is to report frequency in the form of proportion or percent of instances in each of the several categories. Across the six college campuses, 82% of the females were observed to use the Type I method, whereas only 3% of the males used this method. On the other hand, the observers found that 96% of the males used the Type II carrying method compared with 16% of the females. The "other" methods were used 2% of the time or less by both male and female students. It appears that book-carrying behavior among college students is almost totally sex specific. Do you think there are sex-specific ways in which students carry backpacks?

**FIGURE 3.3**  Two methods that students were observed to use to carry books. In the Type I method, the short edges of the book rest on the hip or in front of the body. In the Type II method, the books are either pinched from above or supported from below by the hand or by both the hand and the arm (from Jenni & Jenni, 1976).

Type I                    Type II

The second level, or scale, called an *ordinal scale,* involves ordering or ranking events to be measured. Ordinal scales add the arithmetic relationships "greater than" and "less than" to the measurement process. One common example of an ordinal scale is class rank. We can order students in a class from highest to lowest, but if we know only their ranks we have no information about how far apart the students are in academic performance. When we know that an Olympic distance runner won a silver medal, we do not know whether she finished second in a photo finish or trailed 200 meters behind the gold-medal winner. Tassinary and Hansen (1998) showed line drawings of female figures to male and female undergraduates. The figures varied on physical dimensions such as height, weight, and hip size. The undergraduates rank ordered sets of figures in terms of attractiveness and fecundity (i.e., capability of bearing children). According to evolutionary psychology theory, female attractiveness is defined on the basis of cues simultaneously signaling both physical attractiveness and reproductive potential. Interestingly, results of this study using ordinal measures did not particularly support this aspect of evolutionary psychology theory.

The third level, or scale, called an *interval scale,* involves specifying how far apart two events are on a given dimension. On an ordinal scale, the difference between an event ranked first and one ranked third does not necessarily equal the distance between those events ranked third and fifth. For example, the difference in grade-point averages (GPAs) between the first and third students in a class may not be the same as the difference in GPAs between the third- and fifth-ranked students. On an interval scale, however, differences of the same numerical size in scale values are equal. For example, the difference between 50 and 70 correct answers on an aptitude test is equal to the difference between 70 and 90 correct answers, and the ratio of these scale intervals is also meaningful. What is missing from an interval scale is a meaningful zero point. For instance, if your score were zero on a verbal aptitude test, you would not necessarily have absolutely zero verbal ability. On the other hand, the standard arithmetic operations of addition, multiplication, subtraction, and division can be performed on data that are measured on an interval scale. Whenever possible, therefore, psychologists try to measure psychological dimensions using interval scales.

In the context of an observational study, observers sometimes are called on to make ratings of behaviors and events. This usually involves making subjective judgments about the degree or quantity of some trait or condition (see Brandt, 1972). Generally a rating system requires an observer to evaluate some characteristic of an individual or situation on a psychological dimension. For example, Dickie (1987) asked observers to rate parent-infant interactions in the context of a study designed to assess the effects of a parent training program. The observers visited the home and rated both the mother and the father while the parents interacted with their infant child. During most of the observation period, the observers sat in the room with the infant and asked the parents to "act as normal as possible—just as if we [the observers] weren't here." Structured observations involving assigned play with each parent were also used.

Parent-infant interactions were rated on 13 different dimensions, including degree of verbal, physical, and emotional interaction. For each dimension a continuum was defined that represented different degrees of this variable. A 7-point scale was used, whereon 1 represented the absence or very little of the characteristic and larger numbers represented increasingly more of the trait. Table 3.1 outlines one of the dimensions used by the observers in this study: warmth and affection directed toward the child. Note that precise verbal descriptions are given with the four odd-numbered scale values to help observers define different degrees of this trait. The even-numbered values (2, 4, 6) are used by observers to rate events that they judge fall between the more clearly defined values. The investigators found that parents who had taken part in a program aimed at developing competency in dealing with an infant were rated higher than were untrained parents on many of the variables.

At first glance, a rating scale such as that used by Dickie would appear to represent an interval scale of measurement. There is no true zero, and the intervals seem to be equal. And, in fact, many researchers treat such rating systems *as if* they represented interval scales of measurement. Closer examination, however, reveals that most of the rating scales used by observers to evaluate people or events on a psychological dimension really yield only ordinal information. For a rating system to be truly an interval level of measurement, a rating of 2, for instance, would have to be the same distance from a rating of 3 as a rating of 4 is from 5 or a rating of 6 is from 7. It is highly unlikely that human observers can make subjective judgments of traits such as warmth, pleasure, aggressiveness, anxiety, and so forth in a manner that yields precise interval distances

**TABLE 3.1**  EXAMPLE OF RATING SCALE USED TO MEASURE A PARENT'S WARMTH AND AFFECTION TOWARD AN INFANT CHILD*

| Scale Value | Description |
| --- | --- |
| 1 | There is an absence of warmth, affection, and pleasure. Excessive hostility, coldness, distance, and isolation from the child are predominant. Relationship is on an attacking level. |
| 2 | |
| 3 | There is occasional warmth and pleasure in interaction. Parent shows little evidence of pride in the child, or pride is shown in relation to deviant or bizarre behavior by the child. Parent's manner of relating is contrived, intellectual, not genuine. |
| 4 | |
| 5 | There is moderate pleasure and warmth in the interaction. Parent shows pleasure in some areas but not in others. |
| 6 | |
| 7 | Warmth and pleasure are characteristic of the interaction with the child. There is evidence of pleasure and pride in the child. Pleasure response is appropriate to the child's behavior. |

*From materials provided by Jane Dickie.

between ratings. Classification of measures according to level of measurement is not always easy, and advice should be sought from knowledgeable experts when in doubt. In this way you will be prepared to make the correct choices regarding the statistical description and analysis of your data.

The fourth level of measurement is a *ratio scale*. A ratio scale has all the properties of an interval scale with the important additional quality of an absolute zero point. In terms of arithmetic operations, a zero point makes the ratio of scale values meaningful. For example, temperature as expressed on the Celsius scale represents an interval scale of measurement. A reading of 0 degrees Celsius does not really mean absolutely no temperature. Therefore it is not meaningful to say that 100 degrees Celsius is twice as hot as 50 degrees, or that 60 degrees is three times as warm as 20 degrees. On the other hand, the Kelvin scale of temperature does have an absolute zero, and the ratio of scale values can be meaningfully calculated. Physical scales measuring time, weight, and distance can usually be treated as ratio scales.

As an example of ratio measurement, consider an interesting study by LaFrance and Mayo (1976). They investigated racial differences in amount of eye contact between individuals of the same race engaged in conversation. Pairs of Black individuals and pairs of White individuals were observed in natural settings. The amount of time each member of the pair spent looking into the face of the other member was recorded. Duration of eye contact represents a ratio level of measurement. The researchers found that Blacks gazed less at another person while listening to conversation than did Whites. LaFrance and Mayo suggest that subtle differences in eye contact may be a source of social misunderstandings. White speakers may feel that lack of eye contact by a Black listener indicates untrustworthiness or lack of interest when it may merely be a manifestation of a cultural difference between the races.

Another important measure of behavior is *frequency* of occurrence. This measure sometimes produces confusion when attempting to identify the level of measurement. For example, in observing book-carrying behavior, Jenni (1976) made only one observation of each individual. As was noted, this represents a nominal level of measurement: Behaviors were recorded as falling in one of several mutually exclusive categories. Frequency of book-carrying behavior, therefore, was described in terms of the number (or percentage) of *different* individuals who used one method or another.

Checklists also can be used to obtain information about the frequency of particular behaviors in the same individual or group of individuals. In this case, repeated observations of the same individual or group are made over a period of time. The presence or absence of specific behaviors is noted at the time of each observation. In these situations, frequency of responding can be assumed to represent a ratio level of measurement. That is, if "units" of some behavior (e.g., occasions when a child leaves a classroom seat) are being counted, then zero represents an absence of that specific behavior. Ratios of scale values would be meaningful as long as, for instance, an individual with 20 units had twice as many units as someone with 10.

Consider, for instance, the Schedule for Classroom Activity Norms (SCAN), which is a checklist that divides classroom behavior into 27 discrete categories (McKinney, Mason, Perkerson, & Clifford, 1975). At repeated intervals of time, an observer records what each child in the classroom is doing. Many observations of the same child show which categories of behavior are most frequent for that child. In one study using the SCAN checklist, researchers looked for relationships between the frequency of certain classroom behaviors and performance on standard tests of academic achievement. Combining information obtained from observing the children's behavior with information obtained from IQ tests yielded a more accurate prediction of school achievement than could be obtained by using either observation or IQ information alone.

Table 3.2 summarizes the characteristics of levels of measurement that we discussed. You will need to keep these four types of scales in mind as you select statistical procedures for analyzing the results of the research you will be doing (see Appendix A).

**Electronic Recording and Tracking**   Behavior is sometimes measured by the use of various electronic recording and tracking devices. For example, in an observational study of family interactions of depressed women, the observers used portable microcomputers to record relevant behavior (see Hops et al., 1987). Family members were given codes, as were various behaviors and characteristics of the family interaction, and these were recorded using the hand-held electronic recording devices. As part of a study investigating the relationship between cognitive coping strategies and blood pressure among college students, participants were outfitted with an ambulatory blood pressure monitor (Dolan, Sherwood, & Light, 1992). College students wore the electronic recording device during two "typical" school days, one of which, however, included an exam. Participants also completed a questionnaire assessing coping strategies and kept detailed logs of their daily activities. The researchers compared blood pressure readings for different times of the day and as a function of coping style. Students classified as exhibiting "high self-focused coping" (that is, who showed tendencies "to

**TABLE 3.2**   CHARACTERISTICS OF MEASUREMENT SCALES

| Type of Scale | Operations | Objective |
|---|---|---|
| Nominal | Equal/not equal | Sort stimuli into discrete categories |
| Ordinal | Greater than/less than | Rank-order stimuli on a single dimension |
| Interval | Addition/multiplication/ subtraction/division | Specify the distance between stimuli on a given dimension |
| Ratio | Addition/multiplication/ subtraction/division/ formation of ratios of values | Specify the distance between stimuli on a given dimension and express ratios of scale values |

keep to themselves and/or blame themselves in stressful situations," p. 233), had higher blood pressure responses during and after an exam than did those who were classified as low in self-focused coping strategies.

Using an innovative procedure known as the Experience Sampling Method (ESM), researchers outfit participants with electronic beepers, usually for a week at a time, with the request they provide reports of their activities when signaled by the pagers (e.g., Csikszentimihalyi & Larson, 1987; Larson, 1989). In one study of adolescent interactions with their families, 220 middle-class youth provided reports at two periods in their lives, grades 5 to 8 and grades 9 to 12 (Larson, Richards, Moneta, Holmbeck, & Duckett, 1996). When "beeped," the adolescents used a checklist to indicate whom they were with, responded on 7-point scales regarding their emotional state and perceptions of the people they were with, and answered open-ended questions about their activities. As might be expected, the data revealed a sharp decline in the time adolescents spend with family members across grades 5 to 12. A surprising finding was that amount of adolescent-family conflict was not related to changes in family time, something *not* seen in other primates where conflict frequently leads to disengagement from the family group. The researchers argued that for human adolescents "the negative experience with family is as likely to be a stimulus for continued interaction—like one might see in an embattled, enmeshed family—as it is to be a stimulus for physical withdrawal" (p. 752). The ESM procedure also has been used to study the emotional states of chronic mental patients (e.g., Delespaul, 1995).

Because the ESM procedure relies on participants' self-reports of mood and activities, and not on direct observation of their behavior, it is important that techniques be devised to detect biases in data collection (e.g., possible omission or misrepresentation of personal activities by participants) (see Larson, 1989, for a discussion of possible biases using this method). Experience sampling has some of the problems associated with behavioral self-reports using survey methodology, which will be discussed in the next chapter. These problems can be weighed against the time and labor costs sometimes required to obtain a comprehensive description of behavior through direct observation (e.g., Barker et al., 1978).

## SAMPLING TECHNIQUES

- When a complete record of behavior cannot be obtained, researchers seek to obtain a representative sample of behavior.
- The extent to which observations may be generalized, or external validity, depends on how behavior is sampled.

Before conducting an observational study, a researcher must make a number of important decisions about "when" and "where" observations will be made. In some cases, it might be possible to observe all the behavior of interest—for instance, the behavior patterns of certain short-lived organisms. In most cases, however, something considerably less than "all" of behavior will be observed. Imagine the task, if you will, that Barker et al. (1978) would have faced had they tried to record the behavior exhibited by an 8-year-old every day for a year. If she exhibited 969 behavioral episodes in a single day, we would expect more than 350, 000 episodes in 365 days!

Needless to say, in the vast majority of observational studies, the investigator must be satisfied with something considerably less than a complete record of behavior. Only certain behaviors occurring at particular times and in specific settings can generally be observed. In other words, behavior and settings must be sampled. The nature of these samples determines the extent to which generalizations are possible. Observations made of classroom behavior at the beginning of a school year, for instance, may not yield results that are typical of behavior seen at the end of the school year. Nor, for that matter, do observations made in the morning necessarily reveal the same pattern of classroom behavior as observations made in the afternoon. The frequency and type of aggression observed in children who are required to wear school uniforms may not be representative of the aggression found in children who do not wear school uniforms. As we saw in Chapter 1, our ability to generalize research findings depends upon the study's external validity. Results reasonably can be generalized only to participants, conditions, and situations similar to those in the study in which the results were actually observed. Time sampling, event sampling, and situation sampling are used to lend external validity to observational findings.

## Time and Event Sampling

- Time sampling, systematic or random, refers to researchers' choice of time intervals for making observations.
- When researchers are interested in events that happen infrequently, they rely on event sampling to sample behavior.

Hartup (1974) used a combination of time and event sampling when studying children's aggression. In **time sampling,** the intervals at which observations are made are chosen either systematically or randomly with the goal of obtaining a representative sample of behavior. As examples, we might consider the application of these techniques in the context of observing a child's classroom behavior.

Suppose that observations are to be made for a total of 2 hours each day. As we indicated, restricting observations to certain times of the day (say, mornings only) would not necessarily permit us to generalize our findings to the rest of the school day. One approach to obtaining a representative sample is to schedule observation periods *systematically* throughout the school day. Observations might be made during four 30-minute periods beginning every 2 hours. The first observation period could begin at 9 A.M., the second at 11 A.M., and so forth. Another possibility would be to schedule 10-minute observation periods every half hour during the school day. A *random* time-sampling technique could be used in the same situation by distributing four 30-minute periods (or a dozen 10-minute periods) randomly over the course of the day. A different random schedule would be determined each day on which observations are made. Times would vary from day to day but, over the long run, behavior would be sampled equally from all times of the school day. A major advantage of the Experiential Sampling Method, discussed above, is that electronic beepers can be programmed to signal participants on a random time schedule (normal sleeping times are excluded). In their study of middle-class youth, Larson et al. (1996) obtained reports on the adolescents' experiences at "16,477 random moments" in their lives.

Systematic and random time-sampling procedures are often combined, as when observation intervals are scheduled systematically but observations within an interval are made at random times. For example, having scheduled four 30-minute observation periods at the same time each day (e.g., 9:00 A.M., 11:00 A.M., etc.), an observer might then decide to observe only during 20-second intervals that are randomly distributed within each 30-minute period. Or observation periods might be scheduled randomly during certain weeks of the school year but with weeks selected systematically from the early, middle, and late parts of the year. Whatever method is used, the observer must carefully scrutinize the schedule, noting both its limitations and its advantages in terms of yielding *a representative record of behavior*. Sampling plays a central role in conducting surveys. Many issues related to the topic of sampling are discussed in Chapter 4 when survey methods are introduced.

**Event sampling** may be a more efficient method of sampling behavior than time sampling when the event of interest occurs infrequently. In this case researchers want to maximize their opportunities to observe an event in order to get enough information about its occurrence to make investigating it worthwhile. Not only may time sampling cause precious instances of an event to be missed, but if the event is of significant duration, time sampling may not permit an observer to be present at the beginning of an event or to witness an event in its entirety. In event sampling the observer records each event that meets a predetermined definition. Researchers interested in children's reactions to special events in school, such as a Christmas play, would want to use event sampling. The special event defines when the observations are to be made. Researchers would certainly not want to use time sampling in this situation in the hope that a special event might occur during one of their randomly selected observation periods.

In many situations in which event sampling is used, a formally scheduled event like a school play is not the event of interest. Instead, researchers are often interested in events that occur unpredictably, such as natural or technical disasters. Researchers, for example, who are interested in victims' reactions to violent crimes are dependent on event sampling in selecting the occasions for making their observations. Whenever possible, observers try to be present in those situations and at those times when an event of interest has occurred or is likely to occur. Thus, in an ethological study of children's "rough-and-tumble" play, an observer positioned herself in the corner of a playground to observe members of a nursery school class (Smith & Lewis, 1985). Event sampling was the method of choice due to the relatively low frequency of this behavior, and the researcher made observations whenever rough play began. However, this manner of observing behavior can easily introduce biases into the behavioral record—as when, for instance, an observer samples at the times that are most "convenient" or only when an event is certain to occur. Characterization of events at these times may not be the same as at other times. In most situations, only through some form of time sampling is an observer likely to guarantee a representative sample of behavior.

## Situation Sampling

- Situation sampling involves studying behavior in different circumstances, locations, and conditions and often with different participants.
- Situation sampling enhances the external validity of findings.

The external validity of observational findings can be significantly increased through **situation sampling.** Whenever possible—and when it is in keeping with the goals of a study—behavior should be observed under many different circumstances, locations, and conditions. By sampling different situations researchers reduce the chance that their results will be peculiar to a certain set of circumstances or conditions. It is clear that behavior often changes as a function of the context in which it is observed. Animals do not behave the same way in zoos as they do in the wild. Children do not always behave the same way with one parent as they do with the other parent. By sampling different situations, a researcher can also increase the diversity of the subject sample and hence achieve greater generality than could be claimed if only particular types of individuals were observed. As part of a naturalistic observation of beer drinking among college students, investigators purposely sampled behavior in various settings where beer was served, including five town bars, a student center, and a fraternity party (see Geller, Russ, & Altomari, 1986). When LaFrance and Mayo (1976) investigated racial differences in eye contact, they sampled many different situations. Pairs of individuals were observed in college cafeterias, business-district fast-food outlets, hospital and airport waiting rooms, and restaurants. By using situation sampling the investigators were able to include in their sample people who differed in age, socioeconomic class, sex, and race. Their observations of an apparent cultural difference in eye-contact behavior have considerably greater external validity than if only certain types of participants, or behavior in only a specific situation, had been studied.

## ANALYSIS OF OBSERVATIONAL DATA

### Data Reduction

- Observational data are summarized through the process of data reduction.
- Researchers quantify the data in narrative records by coding behaviors according to specified criteria, for example, by categorizing behaviors.
- Data are summarized using descriptive measures such as frequency counts, means, and standard deviations.

Analysis of Narrative Records   Once they have been collected, narrative records can provide a wealth of information about behavior in natural settings. However, for meaningful information to emerge, data relevant to the goals of an observational study must be abstracted from the lengthy behavioral descriptions included in most narrative records. Results must be organized, and statements summarizing important findings must be prepared. This process of abstracting and summarizing behavioral data is called **data reduction.**

The first step in quantitative analysis of the content of narrative records often consists of identifying units of behavior, or particular events. This stage of data reduction involves **coding** behavioral records according to specific criteria. For instance, we previously noted that a narrative record describing a day in the life of a schoolgirl was found to contain 969 different behavior episodes (Barker et al., 1978, pp. 56–58). Hartup's (1974) 10-week observation of children's aggression yielded information about 758 units of aggression. As part of an ethological study of preschool children, McGrew (1972) identified 115 different behavior patterns. He classified patterns of behavior according to the body part involved, ranging from facial expressions such as bared teeth, grin face, and pucker face, to locomotion behaviors such as gallop, crawl, run, skip, and step. Coders classified these behavioral patterns while watching videotape records showing interactions of children attending nursery school.

Relevant units of behavior or events often are classified in terms of their apparent function or their particular antecedents. For instance, Hartup used nine categories to classify the nature of aggressive episodes. Antecedents of aggression were described using 18 different categories. Relationships between antecedent events and types of aggression were then summarized, and comparisons were made between different age groups. When derogation ("put-down") elicited aggression, more younger children than older children retaliated via some form of physical aggression (such as hitting). McGrew (1972) found that children exhibit a "pout face" after losing a fight over a toy. This ethologist-observer noted that young chimpanzees show a similar expression when seeking reunion with their mother. A "pucker face" was observed in children particularly after being frustrated (and often just prior to weeping). Interestingly, there seems to be no record of a pucker face in nonhuman primates.

**Descriptive Measures**   When events are classified into mutually exclusive categories (nominal scale), the most common descriptive measure is one of relative frequency. The proportion or percentage of times that various behaviors occur is expressed in terms of the total frequency of events observed. We have already seen several examples of this type of descriptive measure. Jenni (1976), for instance, reported the percentage of times that male and female students were observed to use three different book-carrying methods. Barash (1977) summarized his observations of pedestrian behavior in terms of the percentage of people in various social groupings who looked both ways.

When behavior is recorded on at least an interval scale of measurement, as frequently is the case when ratings are made, and when ratio measures of time (duration, latency) are used, one or more measures of central tendency are generally reported. The most common measure is the *arithmetic mean*, or *average*. The mean describes the "typical" score in a group of scores and is an important summary measure of group performance. Measures of variability or dispersion of scores around the mean are necessary to describe group performance completely. The *standard deviation* approximates the average distance of a score from the mean. (Measures of central tendency and variability, as well as confidence intervals for the mean, are discussed in Appendix A, as are additional guidelines for data summary and description.)

The mean and standard deviation as descriptive measures are illustrated in the results of the study by LaFrance and Mayo (1976). You may remember that these investigators observed other-directed looking behavior in pairs of Black and White conversants. The number of seconds that each listener in a pair spent looking into the speaker's face was recorded. Table 3.3 gives the means and standard deviations summarizing the results of this study. As we noted previously, White listeners spent more time looking into the faces of White speakers than Black listeners spent looking into the faces of Black speakers. This was found for same-sex pairs as well as mixed-sex pairs.

## Observer Reliability

- Interobserver reliability refers to the extent to which independent observers agree in their observations.
- Interobserver reliability is increased by training observers and providing feedback about discrepancies, and by providing clear definitions about behaviors and events to be recorded.
- High interobserver reliability increases researchers' confidence that observations about behavior are accurate (valid).
- Interobserver reliability is assessed by calculating percentage agreement or correlations, depending on how the behaviors were measured and recorded.

In assessing the results of an observational study, we need to inquire about reliability of an observer. Would another observer viewing the same events obtain the same results?

**TABLE 3.3**   MEANS AND STANDARD DEVIATIONS DESCRIBING THE TIME (IN SECONDS) THAT LISTENERS SPENT LOOKING INTO THE FACE OF A SPEAKER PER 1-MINUTE OBSERVATION UNIT*

| Group | Mean | Standard Deviation |
| --- | --- | --- |
| Black conversants | | |
|    Male pairs | 19.3 | 6.9 |
|    Female pairs | 28.4 | 10.2 |
|    Male-female pairs | 24.9 | 11.6 |
| White conversants | | |
|    Male pairs | 35.8 | 8.6 |
|    Female pairs | 39.9 | 10.7 |
|    Male-female pairs | 29.9 | 11.2 |

*From LaFrance and Mayo (1976).

Interobserver Reliability   The degree to which two independent observers are in agreement is referred to as **interobserver reliability.** Lack of agreement from one observer to another leaves us uncertain about what is being measured and prevents us from generalizing research results. Low interobserver reliability can be due to characteristics of the observers or to the procedures and methods of observing. When behavior is recorded, differences between observers in terms of experience, attitude, fatigue, boredom, and outcome expectancies are possible reasons for low interobserver reliability. Observer reliability is generally increased by training observers and giving them specific feedback regarding any discrepancies between their observations and those of other observers (Judd, Smith, & Kidder, 1991).

Low interobserver reliability may also result when the event to be recorded is not clearly defined. Imagine Hartup (1974) asking his observers to record aggressive episodes among children without giving them an exact definition of aggression. What exactly is aggression? Some observers might decide to define aggression as one child's physical attack on another; other observers might include verbal assaults in their definition of aggression. What is a playful push and what is an angry shove? Without a clear definition of behavior or of the events to be recorded, observers do not always agree—and hence show low interobserver reliability. In addition to providing precise verbal definitions, giving concrete examples of a phenomenon generally helps increase reliability among observers. Showing observers the pictures of book-carrying methods in Figure 3.3, for example, could be assumed to improve their ability to classify behavior according to this characteristic.

High observer reliability is not necessarily sufficient evidence that observations are accurate. We can imagine two observers of behavior who are both "in error" to the same degree. For instance, both might be influenced in a similar way by what they expect the outcome of the observational study to be. It is conceivable that the two observers would agree about what they saw but neither observer would provide an accurate record of behavior. Instances are occasionally reported in the media of several observers claiming to see the same thing (for instance, an unidentified flying object, or UFO), only to have the event or object turn out to be something other than what observers claimed it to be (for instance, a weather balloon). Nevertheless, when two independent observers agree, we are generally more inclined to believe that their observations are valid than when data are based on the observations of a single observer. In order for observers to be independent, each must be unaware of what the other has recorded. The chance of both observers being influenced to the same degree by outcome expectancies, fatigue, or boredom is generally so small that we can feel confident that what was reported actually occurred. Of course, the more independent observers who agree, the more confident we become.

Measures of Reliability   How observer reliability is measured depends on the way in which behavior is measured. When events are classified according to mutually exclusive categories, such as when individuals are classified in terms of whether they show a certain behavior, observer reliability is generally assessed via a percentage agreement measure.

A formula for calculating percentage agreement between observers is:

$$\frac{\text{Number of times two observers agree}}{\text{Number of opportunities to agree}} \times 100$$

Barash (1977) reported that observers were 100% reliable when classifying pedestrians as to the type of social group that was present (adult male and female, female with children, and so on) and in agreement 97% of the time when deciding whether pedestrians scanned both directions before crossing the street. Hartup (1974) reported measures of reliability that ranged from 83% to 94% for judges who coded narrative records according to type of aggression and nature of antecedent events. Although there is no hard-and-fast percentage of agreement that defines low interobserver reliability, a perusal of the literature reveals that researchers generally report estimates of reliability that exceed 85%, suggesting that agreement much lower than that is unacceptable.

Because in many observational studies most of the data are collected by one observer, or by several observers who collect data at different times, measures of reliability are often based only on a sample of observations for any one observer. For example, two observers might be asked to record behavior according to some time-sampling procedure and there might be only a subset of times during which both observers are present. Amount of agreement for the times when both observers were present can be used to indicate the degree of reliability for the study as a whole. For example, when studying beer drinking among college students, investigators reported the percent agreement for two independent observers who were present at slightly fewer than half of the 243 total observation periods; during the remaining periods only one observer was present (Geller et al., 1986). Observer reliability for home observations of family interactions involving depressed women was based on 86 (17%) of the 520 sessions (Hops et al., 1987).

When observational data are of at least an interval nature, as is often assumed when subjective ratings are made or when some variable such as time is measured, observer reliability can be measured using a Pearson Product-Moment Correlation Coefficient $r$. (Correlational measures, including the Pearson $r$, are discussed more fully in Chapter 4.) LaFrance and Mayo (1976) obtained measures of reliability when observers recorded how much of the time a listener gazed into the speaker's face during a conversation. The average correlation for observer reliability between pairs of observers was .92 in their study.

## PROBLEMS IN THE CONDUCT OF OBSERVATIONAL RESEARCH

### Influence of the Observer

- When individuals change their behavior when they know they are being observed ("reactivity"), their behavior may no longer be representative of their normal behavior.

- Research participants may use demand characteristics in the research situation to guide their behavior.
- Methods to control reactivity include unobtrusive (nonreactive) measurement, adaptation (habituation, desensitization), and indirect observations of behavior.
- Researchers must consider ethical issues when attempting to control reactivity.

Reactivity    The influence that an observer has on the behavior under observation is referred to as **reactivity.** Generally, we can think of reactive research situations as situations in which individuals "react" to the presence of an observer. Behavior in these situations may not be representative of behavior when an observer is not present. Underwood and Shaughnessy (1975) relate how a student, as part of a class assignment, set out to observe whether drivers came to a complete stop at an intersection with a stop sign. The student had hypothesized that drivers of high-priced cars would be less likely than drivers of low-priced cars to stop at the sign. The observer located himself on the street corner with clipboard in hand. However, he soon observed that all cars were stopping at the stop sign. He then realized that his presence was influencing the driver's

**FIGURE 3.4**    Reactivity refers to the influence that an observer has on the behavior under observation; for example, motorists are more likely to stop at a stop sign if an observer is visibly present.

behavior. When he concealed himself near the intersection, he found that drivers' behavior changed and he was able to gather data regarding his hypothesis.

Although human research participants may not exhibit innate reactions to an observer, as is the case with certain animals (e.g., see Moore & Stuttard, 1979), they can respond in very subtle ways when they are aware that their behavior is being observed. For instance, participants are sometimes apprehensive and more than a little anxious about participating in psychological research. Measures of arousal, such as heart rate and galvanic skin response (GSR), may show changes simply as a function of an observer's being present. Wearing an electronic beeper that signals when to record behavioral activities and mood also can be expected to affect participants' behavior (e.g., Larson, 1989).

Social psychologists have long been aware that behavior is affected by the presence of another person. Research has shown that performance on simple tasks can be facilitated by the presence of another person, a so-called facilitation effect, whereas performance on more complex tasks is often inhibited, a so-called social-impairment effect (see, for example, Bond & Titus, 1983). As you might suspect, whether social-facilitation and impairment effects are found depends not only on the complexity of the task but on who is present. For example, if the other person present is someone whose job it is to evaluate performance, as would be the case if an experimenter or observer were present, then effects due to another's presence are rather robust (see Guerin, 1986). In this case, social facilitation is usually attributed to increased arousal brought about by anticipation of being evaluated or to an increased desire on the part of the participant to gain approval and do what is socially acceptable. Social impairment would be produced if increased arousal interfered with performance, as sometimes happens when an individual facing tough competition "chokes," or if the presence of an observer distracts an individual and brings about poorer performance than that found when the person is alone. Although of interest as social psychological phenomena, these effects, of course, also help to define reactivity in a research situation and must be guarded against by the researcher.

Research participants may also attempt to behave in the way they think the researcher wants them to behave. Knowing that they are part of a scientific investigation, individuals usually want to cooperate and to be "good" participants. Being a good participant may be seen as doing what is expected by the observer. Orne (1962) has referred to the cues and other information used by research participants to guide their behavior in a psychological study as the **demand characteristics** of the research situation. Orne suggests that individuals generally ask themselves the question, "What am I supposed to be doing here?" By paying attention to cues present in the setting, including those that are part of the research procedure itself, or even by attending to implicit cues given by the researcher, the research participants can perhaps figure out what is "expected" of them and attempt to modify their behavior accordingly. An individual's reactions to the demand characteristics of a research situation pose threats to both the external and the internal validity of psychological research. When research participants behave in a manner that is not representative of their behavior outside the psychological research setting, our ability to generalize the results is restricted. Also, by behaving in a manner that they think is expected of them, participants may unintentionally make a research variable look more effective than it actually is or even nullify the effects of an otherwise significant variable. The problem of demand characteristics is often cited as a reason for limiting individuals' knowledge about their role in a study or about the study's hypothesis. By keeping participants unaware of important details regarding the study, the investigator hopes to obtain more representative behavior. However, limiting an individual's information about a study raises ethical concerns, which we discussed in Chapter 2, and about which we will have more to say later in this chapter.

Controlling Reactivity    Problems of reactivity can be approached in several ways. Reactivity can be eliminated if observations are made in such a way that the presence of the observer is not detected by research participants. Measures of behavior in such circumstances are referred to as **unobtrusive (nonreactive) measures.** Obtaining unobtrusive measures may involve concealing the observer or hiding mechanical recording devices such as tape recorders and videotape cameras. LaFrance and Mayo (1976) observed people in conversation without their knowledge. Observations were made in a variety of natural settings, such as restaurants and waiting rooms, so we can imagine that observers had to keep their stopwatches and data sheets hidden behind menus and potted plants in order to obtain unobtrusive measures of behavior. Yet another approach is for researchers to use disguised participant observation and adopt a role in the situation other than that of observer. You may remember this procedure was used by social psychologists studying the behavior of individuals who claimed to be in contact with aliens from outer space (Festinger et al., 1956). Participants do not know that an observer is present, so we assume that they act as they ordinarily would. To investigate honesty, Hays (1980) worked as a clerk in a college student union. When patrons asked for change for a dollar bill, he gave them a nickel extra. Only 45% of those patrons who were judged by the observer to be aware of the extra nickel returned the extra money.

Another way of dealing with reactivity is to adapt participants to the presence of an observer. It can be assumed that, as participants get used to an observer being present, they will come to behave normally in that person's presence. Adaptation can be accomplished through either habituation or desensitization. In a *habituation* procedure observers simply introduce themselves into a situation on many different occasions until the participants cease to react to their presence. In order to film a documentary entitled *An American Family*, which was shown on public television in the early 1970s, observers (with their cameras) literally moved into a California home and recorded the activities of a family over a 7-month period. Although it is impossible to tell how much of their behavior was influenced by the observers' presence, the events that unfolded and remarks made by family members gave evidence of a habituation process having taken place. During filming the family broke up, the mother asking the father to move out of the house. When interviewed later about having the divorce announced to millions of television viewers, the father admitted that they could have asked the camera crew to get out but that, by this time, "we had gotten used to it" (*Newsweek,* 1973, p. 49).

Habituation may result when undisguised participant observers spend a great deal of time with the participants they are observing. Although they are still aware that an observer is present, participants may begin to behave as though the observer were not present. As part of a study of aggressive behavior in preschool children, Addison (1986) reported that before actual data were collected, a 5-day adaptation period was used to adapt the children to the presence of both the observer and the videotape equipment. Because the children often experienced classroom observers in the form of student teachers and other adults, there appeared to be no effect due to the presence of the researcher. Moreover, Addison (1986) stated that the children's interest in the videotape equipment diminished after a few days. Hart and Risley (1995) recorded children's vocabulary growth in their homes for more than 2 years. They began, however, "when the children were 7–9 months old so we would have time for the families to adapt to observation before the children actually began talking" (p. 28). Later, they were able to report that "Although no parent was unaware that the observer was there, over time the observer tended to fade into the furniture" (p. 35).

*Desensitization* as a means of dealing with reactivity is similar to the desensitization used in the behavioral treatment of phobias. In a therapy situation, an individual with a specific fear (say, an irrational fear of spiders) is first exposed to the feared stimulus at a very low intensity. The patient may be asked to think of things that are related to spiders, such as dusty rooms and cobwebs. At the same time the therapist helps the patient practice relaxation. Gradually the intensity of the stimulus is increased until the patient can tolerate the actual stimulus itself.

Desensitization is often used by ethologists to adapt animal subjects to the presence of an observer. Prior to a violent death in the land of her beloved subjects, Fossey (1981, 1983) conducted fascinating observational studies of the mountain gorilla in Africa. Over a period of time she moved closer and closer to the gorillas so that they would get used to her presence. She found that by imitating their movements—for instance, by munching the foliage they ate and by scratching herself—she could put the gorillas at ease. Eventually she was able to sit among the gorillas and observe them as they touched her and explored the research equipment she was using.

Finally, nonreactive measures of behavior can be obtained by observing behavior indirectly (see Webb, Campbell, Schwartz, Sechrest, & Grove, 1981). This may involve examining physical traces left behind or examining archival information, which are records kept by society about individuals and events. One researcher investigated the drinking behavior of people living in a town that was officially "dry" by counting empty liquor bottles in their trash cans. Another researcher used the records kept by a library to assess the effect on a community of the introduction of television. Withdrawals of fiction titles dropped, but the demand for nonfiction was not affected (see Webb et al., 1981). Physical traces and archival data are important unobtrusive measures that can be valuable sources of information about behavior. In Chapter 5 we discuss more fully these indirect methods of observation.

Ethical Issues    Whenever individuals are observed without their knowledge, as we saw may occur when an investigator seeks to control for reactivity, important ethical issues arise. For instance, in many circumstances, observing people without their consent can represent a serious invasion of privacy. As you saw in Chapter 2, deciding what constitutes an invasion of privacy is not always easy, and must include a consideration of the sensitivity of the information, the setting where observation takes place, and the degree of dissemination of the information obtained (e.g., Deiner & Crandall, 1978).

When individuals are involved in situations that are deliberately arranged by an investigator, as might happen in a field experiment, ethical problems associated with placing participants at risk may arise. Consider, for instance, a field experiment designed to investigate how college students' attitudes toward racial harassment are affected by hearing other students either condone or condemn racism (Blanchard, Crandall, Brigham, & Vaughn, 1994). More than 200 White undergraduate women attending various universities were "naive participants." The women were approached by a White interviewer as they walked across campus and were invited to answer a short series of questions about "how their college should respond to acts of racism" (p. 994). A female confederate, posing as a student, approached the interviewer so that she arrived at the same time as the naive participant. The interviewers asked both "students" the same five questions; however, the interviewer always questioned the confederate student first. At this point, the confederate responded by either condemning or condoning racists' acts. Of interest was the effect of these statements on the naive participants' responses to the same questions. The results were clear: Hearing another student condemn racism produced more condemning responses relative to a no-influence control group, and hearing another student condone racism produced more condoning reactions to racism than hearing no one else express an opinion. Thus, as the authors suggest, the findings "imply that a few outspoken people can influence the normative climate of interracial social settings in either direction" (p. 997).

Were the naive participants "at risk?" If you think the participants were at risk, what degree of risk was present? Did the goals of the study, and the knowledge potentially obtained, outweigh any risk? Although participants were "debriefed immediately" in this study, is that sufficient to address any concerns that the naive students might have about how they behaved when confronted with racist opinions, or even to restore confidence in a science that seeks knowledge through deception? Attempting to provide answers to these kinds of questions highlights the difficulty of ethical decision making. (Recommended steps in the process of ethical decision making are outlined in Chapter 2.)

## Observer Bias

- Observer bias occurs when observers' expectations about behavior lead to systematic errors in identifying and recording behavior, and when researchers' biases determine which behaviors they choose to observe.
- Expectancy effects can occur when observers are aware of hypotheses for the outcome of the study or the outcome of previous studies.
- The first step in controlling observer bias is to recognize that it may be present.
- Observer bias may be reduced by keeping observers unaware ("blind") of the goals and hypotheses of the study.

You may remember that when Rosenhan (1973) and his colleagues observed the interaction between staff members and patients in mental hospitals, they found a serious bias on the part of the staff. Once patients were labeled schizophrenic, their behavior was interpreted solely in light of this label. Behaviors that might have been considered normal when performed by sane individuals were interpreted by the staff as evidence of the patients' insanity. For instance, note taking by the participant observers, which was done openly, was later discovered to have been cited by members of the staff as an example of the pseudopatients' pathological state. As a result of the staff's tendency to interpret patients' behavior in terms of the label that had been given them, the sanity of the pseudopatients was not detected. This example clearly illustrates the danger of **observer bias,** the systematic errors in observation that result from an observer's expectations.

Expectancy Effects    Although we might hope that scientific observations are free from the kind of observer bias documented by Rosenhan, we know that this is not always the case. In many scientific studies the observer has some expectancy about what behavior should be like in a particular situation or should result from a specific psychological treatment. This expectancy may be created by knowledge of the results of past investigations or perhaps by the observer's own hypothesis about behavior in this situation. Expectancies can be a source of observer bias—*expectancy effects*—if they lead to systematic errors in observation (Rosenthal, 1966, 1976).

An example of a study designed to document observer bias will illustrate this problem (see Cordaro & Ison, 1963). The study required college student observers to record the number of head turns and body contractions made by two groups of flatworms. The observers were led to expect different rates of turning and contracting in the two groups. The worms in the groups were, however, essentially identical. What differed was the observers' expectations about what they would see. Results showed that the observers reported twice as many head turns and three times as many body contractions when a high rate of movement was expected than when a low rate was expected. Apparently, the students interpreted the actions of the worms differently depending on what they expected to observe.

Other Biases   An observer's expectancies regarding the outcome of a study may not be the only source of observer bias. You might think that using automated equipment such as movie cameras would eliminate observer bias. Although automation reduces the opportunity for observer bias, it does not necessarily eliminate it. Consider the fact that, in order to record behavior on film, the observer must determine the angle, location, and time of filming. To the extent that these aspects of the study are influenced by personal biases of the observer, such decisions can introduce systematic errors into the results. Altmann (1974) describes an observational study of animal behavior in which the observers biased the results by taking a midday break whenever the animals were inactive. Observations of the animals during this period of inactivity were conspicuously absent from the observational records. Furthermore, using automated equipment generally only postpones the process of classification and interpretation, and it is perfectly possible for the effects of observer bias to be introduced when narrative records are coded and analyzed.

Controlling Observer Bias   Observer bias cannot be eliminated, but it can be reduced in several ways. As we mentioned, the use of automatic recording equipment can help, although the potential for bias is still present. *Probably the most important factor in dealing with observer bias is the awareness that it might be present.* That is, an observer who knows about this bias will hopefully take steps to reduce its effect.

Observer bias also can be reduced by limiting the information provided to observers. When Hartup (1974) analyzed the results of his observational study of children's aggression, the individuals who performed the analysis were not permitted to see all the narrative records. When the nature of the aggressive act was classified, the antecedent events were blacked out; and when antecedent events were coded, the nature of the aggressive act was blacked out. Therefore, in making their classifications, the coders could not be influenced by information related to the event that they were coding. In a manner of speaking, the coders were "blind" to certain aspects of the study. Observers are *blind* when they do not know why the observations are being made or the goals of a study. When Burns, Haywood, and Delclos (1987) observed the problem-solving strategies of children from two different socioeconomic groups, they first videotaped the children while they worked on five tasks selected from standardized intelligence tests. When task strategies were observed and coded from the videotape records, however, the observer-coder was blind to which group the child was from. When LaFrance and Mayo (1976) investigated eye contact between individuals conversing in natural settings, their observers did not know that possible differences along racial lines were being probed. Using "blind" observers greatly reduces the possibility of introducing systematic errors due to observer expectancies.

## SUMMARY

Observational methods can be characterized in terms of both the degree of observer intervention and the manner in which behavior is recorded. Observation in a natural setting without observer intervention is called naturalistic observation. On the other hand, both structured observation (frequently used by developmental psychologists) and field experiments (often used by social psychologists) depend on some degree of observer intervention. The manner of record keeping in an observational study varies according to whether a comprehensive description of behavior is sought or the observer seeks only to describe certain predefined units of behavior. Whereas narrative records, including field notes, are used to provide comprehensive descriptions of behavior, checklists are typically used when it is simply of interest whether a specific behavior has occurred (and under what conditions). Frequency and duration of behaviors also may be recorded, and observers are sometimes called on to make subjective judgments, in the form of ratings, about the quality or degree of a characteristic of the subject or situation.

How quantitative data are described and analyzed depends on the scale of measurement used. The four levels of measurement used by psychologists are nominal, ordinal, interval, and ratio.

Observations can rarely be made of all behavior that occurs. Consequently, some form of behavior sampling (time or situation sampling) must be used. An important goal of sampling is to achieve a representative sample of behavior. When narrative records are made, some type of coding system is generally used as one step in the process of data reduction. Measures of frequency and duration, as well as ratings, are typically summarized, using descriptive statistics such as the mean and standard deviation.

It is essential to provide measures of observer reliability when reporting the results of an observational study. Depending on the level of measurement that has been used, either a percentage agreement measure or a correlation coefficient can be used to assess reliability. Possible influences of reactivity and observer bias must be controlled in any observational study. Finally, ethical issues must be addressed prior to beginning a research study, and they are especially salient when conducting observational studies using disguised participant observation, unidentified confederates, or other forms of participant deception.

## KEY CONCEPTS

| | |
|---|---|
| naturalistic observation | checklist |
| ethology | time sampling |
| ethogram | event sampling |
| participant observation | situation sampling |
| structured observation | data reduction |
| field experiment | coding |
| confederate | interobserver reliability |
| narrative records | reactivity |
| ecological psychology | demand characteristics |
| ethnography | unobtrusive (nonreactive) |
| field notes | measures |
| measurement scale | observer bias |

## REVIEW QUESTIONS

1 What three characteristics distinguish scientific observation from nonscientific observation?
2 What critical characteristics distinguish among naturalistic observation, participant observation, structured observation, and a field experiment?
3 What two dimensions can be used to classify observational methods?
4 There are five general reasons for intervening in conducting an observational study. Identify a study illustrating each reason—either from the studies cited in this chapter or from research you have read about in other psychology courses.
5 What factors in participant observation can be expected to influence the extent of the observer's influence on the behavior being observed?
6 What is the principal advantage of the structured observation method?
7 Name the four scales of measurement, and give an example of each.
8 What aspect of an observational study is the proper use of time sampling and situation sampling intended to ensure?
9 What are the most common descriptive measures (a) when events are classified into mutually exclusive categories and (b) when behavior is recorded on at least an interval scale?
10 What factors contribute to low interobserver reliability, and how can interobserver reliability be increased?
11 Does high interobserver reliability ensure the validity of observations? Why or why not?
12 Why are participants' reactions to demand characteristics a threat to both the internal and the external validity of psychological research?
13 What ethical issues must one address when using unobtrusive measures such as concealing the presence of an observer?
14 Give an example of each of the two ways in which investigators attempt to mitigate reactivity by adapting individuals to the presence of the observer.
15 What is the best procedure to reduce observer bias?

## CHALLENGE QUESTIONS

1 Students in a developmental psychology lab course conducted an observational study of parent-infant interactions in the home. When they first entered the home on each of the 4 days they observed a given family, they greeted both the parents and the infant (and any other children at home). They instructed the family to follow its daily routine and they asked a series of questions about the activities of that day to determine whether it was a "normal" day or something unusual had happened. The students tried to make the family feel comfortable, but they also tried to minimize their interactions with the family and with each other. For any given 2-hour observation period there were always two student observers present in the home, and the two observers recorded their notes independently of each other. There were six pairs of students who were randomly assigned to carry out the 8 hours of observation on each of the 12 families who volunteered to serve in the study. The same pair of observers always observed a given family, and two families were assigned to each pair of observers. The observers used checklists to record behaviors on a number of different dimensions, such as mutual warmth and affection of the parent-infant interaction.

   **A**  Cite two specific procedures used by the students to ensure the reliability of their findings.

   **B**  Cite one possible threat to the external validity of the findings of this study; once again, cite a specific example from the description provided.

   **C**  Cite one specific aspect of their procedure that indicated that the students were sensitive to the possibility that their measurements might be reactive. What other methods might they have used to deal with this problem of reactivity?

**2** A naturalistic observation study was done to assess the effects of environmental influences on drinking by college students in a university-sponsored pub. Eighty-two students between the ages of 18 and 22 were observed. Observations were differentiated on the basis of whether the person being observed was with one other person or was in a group of two or more other people. The observations were made over a 3-month period; sessions were always from 3 P.M. to 1 A.M., and observations were made Monday through Saturday. Each participant was observed for up to 1 hour from the time he or she ordered the first beer. Two observers were always present during any observation session. The results showed that in terms of number of beers drunk per hour men drank more and faster than did women. Men drank faster when with other men, and women also drank faster with men present. Both men and women drank more in groups than when with one other person. These results do indicate that the environment within which drinking occurs plays an important role in the nature and extent of that drinking.

   **A**  Identify the independent and dependent variables in this study.

   **B**  What is the operational definition of a group in this study?

   **C**  Identify one specific aspect of this study that increases the external validity of the findings.

**3** A friend of yours is absolutely convinced that he has a positive influence on the friendliness of conversations in which he is a participant. He has reached this conclusion on the basis of his everyday observations. You convince him that a systematic study is needed to confirm his hypothesis. Your friend (still smiling) carefully develops an operational definition of the friendliness of a conversation and records a rating for each of the next 50 conversations in which he is a participant. His results show that 75% of these conversations are rated "very friendly," 20% are rated "friendly" and 5% are rated neutral. Your friend returns to you—now convinced beyond a shadow of a doubt that he has a positive effect on the friendliness of a conversation. Although your friend won't be pleased with you, explain to him why the results of his study are essentially useless as a means of confirming his hypothesis. While you have this chance to teach your friend about research methods, explain to him why it would be better for you or someone else to rate the friendliness of the conversations in a proper study testing your friend's hypothesis.

**4** The following description is based upon a study that was done as an assignment in a research methods class. You are to use this description to answer the questions that follow it.

    The study was conducted to investigate one aspect of the pace of life at a small college. The measure of pace of life was the time it took a person to walk a distance of 70 feet. Researchers compared the walking speeds of people who did (called passers) or did not pass (called the nonpassers) someone while going through an area designated as the passing zone—the main path from the administration building continuing through the path that leads past the admissions office. Participants walked west in the passing zone up to a marker that indicated the start of the timing zone, which was 70 feet long. Observers worked in pairs with one observer timing the passer and the second observer timing the nonpasser. There were 24 pairs of observers who made a total of 83 paired observations (passer/nonpasser pairs). Observers positioned themselves so that they could see the passing zone and the timing zone but so they would not be noticed by the people walking along the path. The observers recorded the gender of the observed person, the context in which the observation took place (e.g., how crowded it was, weather conditions), and the date and time of the observation. Observations were distributed across the days of the week during which the study was done with more observations on Monday, Wednesday, and Friday than on Tuesday and Thursday. The results indicated that the passers' times through the 70-foot timing zone were faster than the times for the nonpassers.

A   Identify the type of observational method that was used in this study.

B   What is the operational definition of the dependent variable in this study?

C   Identify one aspect of the procedures in this study that would likely increase the reliability of the observations.

D   Identify one aspect of the procedures in this study that would likely limit the external validity of the findings of this study.

E   Identify one aspect of the procedures in this study that would likely decrease the reactivity of the observations.

F   What possible interpretations do you think are appropriate for the finding that passers walked faster than nonpassers? Try to come up with at least one interpretation based on a characteristic of the people in the categories of passer and nonpasser and at least one based on characteristics of the situation.

## Answer to Challenge Question 1

A   The students' procedures that enhanced reliability were as follows: observing each family for 8 hours, using two independent observers, and using checklists to provide operational definitions.

B   One possible threat to the external validity of the findings was that the 12 families volunteered for the study and such families may differ from typical families.

C   The students' efforts to minimize interactions with the family and with each other suggested that they were sensitive to the problem of reactivity. Two other methods they might have used are habituation and desensitization.

# Correlational Research:
# Surveys

## CHAPTER OUTLINE

## Overview

Campaigns for political offices frequently are accompanied by media reports revealing the results of the "latest poll." A poll supposedly tells us which candidate is "ahead" at any particular time. Media analysts spend a lot of time interpreting poll results, giving us their opinions about what the latest "figures" mean for the candidates. You may even have seen debates about whether polls influence the political process; for example, analysts have argued that some people "switch sides" to support a front runner in the poll in order to be on the winning side. Although polls are intended to describe people's voting preferences at the time the poll is taken, they are also used to predict how people will vote at the time of the actual election. Candidates use poll results to help orchestrate their campaigns, for example, by identifying places they should visit and key public issues. Political polls involve the use of survey-research methods. As you will see in this chapter, however, surveys have a much broader application than their use in political polling; they are an important research tool of psychologists.

Survey research represents a more general approach to psychological research called correlational research. Correlational research, unlike experimental research (see Chapter 6), does not involve the manipulation of independent variables. Instead, **correlational research** assesses relationships among naturally occurring variables with the goal of identifying predictive relationships. The predictive relationships found in correlational research have implications for decisions such as diagnosing psychological disorders and selecting among job applicants. A decision to admit you to a university was likely made with the help of correlational research showing the relationship between various predictors (e.g., high school rank, academic test scores) and a measure of success in college (e.g., first-year college GPA).

Larose and Roy (1995) identified a predictive relationship in their study of students who were beginning college. Students completed a questionnaire that measured their personal approach to learning. For example, the questionnaire included items asking about students' attitudes toward teachers and the students' priorities regarding their use of time. Using students' responses to this questionnaire, Larose and Roy (1995) found they could predict students' academic success in the first year of college better than when only high school grade point average was used to predict college success. Their questionnaire was also useful in predicting which students were likely to be at risk academically in their first year of college. Correlational findings such as these can play an important role in decision making.

In this chapter we also introduce the basic logic and techniques of *sampling*—the process of selecting a subset of a population to represent the population as a whole—which is so often critical to successful prediction. You will then learn about the advantages and disadvantages of various survey-research methods and survey-research designs. We conclude the chapter with a brief discussion of the correspondence between people's reported behavior when completing surveys and their actual behavior. Do people really do what they say they do?

## CORRELATIONAL RESEARCH

### The Nature of Correlations

- A correlation assesses the extent to which two variables covary; the correlation coefficient is a quantitative index of the direction and magnitude of this relationship.
- The direction of a correlation coefficient can be negative or positive.
- The magnitude of a correlation coefficient ranges from $-1.0$ (a perfect negative relationship) to $+1.0$ (a perfect positive relationship); a correlation coefficient of 0.00 indicates no relationship.
- Scatterplots are graphical displays of the relationship between two variables.

Prediction, as you saw in Chapter 1, is an important goal of the scientific method. Correlational research frequently provides the basis for this prediction. A **correlation** exists when two different measures of the same people, events, or things vary together—that is, when scores on one variable covary with scores on another variable. For example, a widely known relationship exists between smoking and lung disease. The more individuals smoke (e.g., measured by duration of smoking), the greater their likelihood of contracting lung disease. Thus, smoking and lung disease covary, or go together. This correlation also can be expressed in these terms: The less people smoke, the lower their chances for contracting lung disease. Based on this correlation we can make predictions about lung disease. For example, if we know how long an individual has smoked, we can predict (to some degree) his or her likelihood of developing lung disease. The nature of our predictions and the confidence we have in making them depends on the direction and the strength of the correlation.

The direction and strength of a correlation are determined by computing a **correlation coefficient.** The correlation coefficient is a quantitative index of how well we are able to predict one set of scores (e.g., likelihood of lung disease) using another set of scores (e.g., duration of smoking). A correlation coefficient expresses the relationship between two variables in terms of both the *direction* and the *magnitude* of that relationship.

The direction of a correlation coefficient can be either positive or negative. A positive correlation indicates that, as the values for one measure increase, the values for the other measure also increase. As we've seen, measures of smoking and lung disease are positively correlated (more smoking, more lung disease). Another predictive relationship concerns Scholastic Aptitude Test (SAT) scores: SAT scores and college students' first-semester GPAs are positively correlated. Thus, we can predict that students with higher SAT scores should have higher first-semester GPAs, and students with lower SAT scores should have lower first-semester GPAs. With correlations, the "reverse" prediction can be made too. If we know only the first-semester GPAs of students, we can "predict" what their SAT scores were prior to entering college. Students with higher GPAs would be more likely to have higher SAT scores, and students with lower GPAs would be likely to have lower SAT scores.

In a negative correlation, as the value of one measure increases, the value of the other measure *decreases*. A national survey of high school seniors showed a negative correlation between the amount of time spent watching TV and the number of correct answers on an academic achievement test (Keith, Reimers, Fehrmann, Pottebaum, & Aubrey, 1986). Students who spent *more* time watching TV answered *fewer* questions correctly on an achievement test. What about the reverse prediction? Based on this finding, if you knew that a student scored very high on the achievement test, would you predict that the student had spent a "a lot" of time or "a little" time watching TV?

The magnitude (degree) of a correlation coefficient can range in absolute values from 0.0 to 1.00. A value of 0 indicates there is no correlation and there is no basis for making predictions. The relationship between intelligence and mental illness, for example, exhibits a zero correlation; we cannot predict the likelihood that a person will become mentally ill by knowing the person's IQ (nor can we predict a person's IQ based on his or her mental health). A value of +1.00 indicates a perfect positive correlation, and a value of −1.00 indicates a perfect negative correlation. When a correlation coefficient is either +1.00 or −1.00, we can make predictions with absolute confidence. Values between 0 and 1.00 indicate predictive relationships of intermediate strength and, therefore, we have less ability to predict confidently. Remember, the sign of the correlation signifies only its direction; a correlation coefficient of −.46 indicates a stronger (more predictive) relationship than one of +.20. (Note: In practice, only the sign of negative correlation coefficients is indicated; a coefficient without a plus or minus sign is treated as positive, that is, +.20 = .20.)

The nature of a correlation can be represented graphically using a scatterplot. Scores for the two variables are represented on the x-axis and y-axis. Each individual has a value (or score) for each variable (e.g., SAT score and first-semester GPA). A scatterplot shows the intersecting points for each pair of scores. Hypothetical examples of scatterplots showing strong positive, practically zero, and moderate negative correlations are shown in Figure 4.1. The magnitude or degree of correlation is seen in a scatterplot by determining how well the points correspond to a straight line; stronger correlations seem to form a straight line of points. Thus, the correlation is stronger in the first example (a) than in the other two examples; however, the correlation represented in the third example (c) is stronger than the second example (b). The direction of a correlation can be seen in the scatterplot by noting how the points are arranged. When the pattern of points seems to move from the lower left corner to the upper right (a), then the correlation is positive (low scores on the x-axis go with low scores on the y-axis and high scores on the x-axis go with high scores on the y-axis). When the pattern of points is from the upper left to the lower right (c), the correlation is negative (low scores on the x-axis go with high scores on the y-axis and high scores on the x-axis go with low scores on the y-axis). Whether represented in a scatterplot or in a correlation coefficient, the purpose of a correlation is to

**FIGURE 4.1**    Three scatterplots illustrating a strong positive (a),.a zero (b), and a moderate negative (c),
correlation between scores on two variables: X and Y.

(a) Positive relationship     (b) Zero relationship     (c) Negative relationship

determine how well we can predict one measure based on its covariation with
another measure. A formula for calculating the most commonly used correlation coefficient, the Pearson $r$, may be found at the end of this chapter.

## Correlation and Causality

- When two variables are related (correlated), we can make predictions for
  the variables; however, we cannot make inferences about the cause of the
  relationship.
- When a relationship between two variables can be explained by a third
  variable, the relationship is said to be "spurious."

A study by Lubin and his colleagues (1988) illustrates how useful correlational studies can be in psychological research. They investigated correlations
among measures of physical and psychological health in their survey of 1,543
adults living in the United States. Respondents rated their physical health and
provided information about health-related factors such as how often they visit
a physician and the nature and frequency of any medications they were taking.
The interviewers also collected data regarding respondents' occupation and religious affiliation, frequency of volunteer and social activities, and so forth.
Each of the respondents also completed a paper-and-pencil test measuring both
positive affect (e.g., happiness) and negative affect (e.g., depression). Measures
of psychological health and physical health were found to be correlated. For instance, positive affect was positively correlated with self-ratings of physical
health; happier people were more healthy. Additionally, frequency of volunteer
activities correlated negatively with a measure of depression; people who were
more active with volunteer activities experienced less depression. Correlations
like these can be useful for predicting physical and psychological health-related
problems.

Correlational studies are the method of choice when the goal of the research is prediction. There are serious limitations, however, on using results of correlational studies to infer causal relationships: "*Correlation does not imply causation.*" For instance, there is a reliable correlation between being outgoing (socially active) and being satisfied with one's life (Myers & Diener, 1995). Based on this correlation alone, however, we could *not* argue convincingly that being more outgoing and socially active *causes* people to be more satisfied with their lives. Although it is possible that being outgoing causes people to be more satisfied with their lives, the "reverse" causal relationship also may be true: Being satisfied with life may cause people to be more outgoing and socially active. The causal relationship could go either way—being more outgoing causes greater life satisfaction *or* being more satisfied with life causes people to be more outgoing. It is impossible to determine the correct causal direction simply by knowing the correlation between the two variables.

Another causal interpretation may exist for this relationship. It's possible that a third variable, having more friends, leads people to be more outgoing *and* more satisfied with their lives. A correlation that can be explained by a third variable is called a *spurious relationship* (Kenny, 1979). In this particular example, "number of friends" is a possible third variable that could account for the relationship between being outgoing and being satisfied with one's life. Individuals with more friends may be more likely to be outgoing and satisfied with life than people with fewer friends. This isn't to say that the original positive correlation between being outgoing and life satisfaction doesn't exist (it certainly does), it just means that other variables (e.g., number of friends) may explain *why* the relationship exists. These problems with understanding causal relationships based on correlations should make it clear that *more than mere correlational evidence is necessary to make causal statements.*

## Path Analysis

- Path analysis is a statistical technique used to help researchers understand potential causes of correlational relationships.
- Mediators are variables that help to explain the relationship between two variables.
- A moderator variable affects the strength and direction of the relationship between two variables.
- Although path analysis helps researchers to interpret correlational studies, they cannot make definite causal statements about the relationships between variables.

There are sophisticated statistical techniques that can be used to help with causal interpretations of correlational studies (Baron & Kenny, 1986; Holmbeck, 1997). One technique involves the identification of mediator variables and moderator variables. A *mediator variable* is a variable that is used to explain the correlation between two variables. A *moderator variable* is a variable that affects the direction or strength of the correlation between two variables. A study by

Valentiner, Holahan, and Moos (1994) nicely illustrates these concepts. The researchers carried out a correlational study to examine the relationship between parental support and students' adjustment to college. Parental support was measured by asking first-year students questions about their mother and father, such as "Does she (he) really understand how you feel about things?" and "Is she (he) critical or disapproving of you?" They measured changes in well-being and distress over a 2-year period, and observed a correlation between parental support and changes in psychological adjustment: Students' perceptions of positive support from their parents were associated with greater well-being and less distress over the 2-year period. In analysis terms, this relationship is called "direct" because one variable (parental support) is directly correlated with another variable (changes in adjustment); this is illustrated as Path a in Figure 4.2.

Valentiner and his colleagues sought to explain why this relationship exists, and predicted that how students cope with stress might mediate, or help to explain, the relationship between parental support and adjustment. Specifically, they measured the extent to which these students coped using "approach coping" more than "avoidance coping" for "the 'most important problem' they experienced in the past 12 months" (p. 1096). Approach coping strategies involve active efforts to solve problems or change one's thinking about a problem, whereas avoidance coping strategies involve trying to forget the problem exists or behaving in ways that don't address the root of the problem (e.g., yelling "to let off steam"). Generally, approach coping is viewed as more adaptive than avoidance coping. Consistent with their predictions, Valentiner et al. found that parental support was positively correlated with the percent of approach coping students used; this is illustrated as Path b in Figure 4.2. Thus, students' perception that their parents are supportive was associated with more adaptive, approach coping.

This is only part of the story, however. Valentiner et al.'s next step was to show that approach coping is associated with positive changes in psychological adjustment (Path c in Figure 4.2). This is exactly what their correlations demonstrated: Students who used more approach coping than avoidance coping had

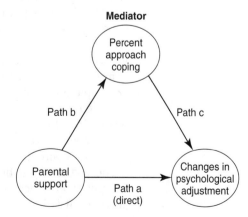

**FIGURE 4.2** Illustration of direct (Path a) and indirect (Paths b and c) relationships between parental support and changes in psychological adjustment to college. Adapted from Figure 1 of Valentiner et al. (1994).

improved well-being and less distress over the 2-year period. With this pattern of relationships, Valentiner and his colleagues were able to say that parental support was directly associated with students' adjustment (Path a), and also that approach coping partially mediated, or explained, the relationship between parental support and psychological adjustment (Paths b and c). Thus, one possible reason why parental support was associated with positive adjustment is because parental support also was associated with the use of adaptive, approach coping strategies. In analysis terms, parental support is said to be associated with psychological adjustment *indirectly*, through the mediating variable of coping strategies.

Valentiner et al. (1994) also identified a moderator variable that affected the observed relationships between parental support, coping, and changes in students' adjustment. The moderator variable in their study was how controllable the participants thought their "most important problem" was, and the sample was divided into two groups: students who thought the occurrence of their problem was controllable and students who thought the event's occurrence was uncontrollable. The correlational analyses were then repeated separately for each group of students to determine if the same pattern of correlations would be obtained. Basically, researchers try to identify a moderator variable to discover the conditions under which a relationship exists and the conditions under which the relationship is weaker or does not exist.

What happened with students who reported their life event was *controllable?* The pattern of correlations changed: Perceptions of parental support were no longer directly related to changes in psychological adjustment (Path a). However, the indirect relationship between parental support and adjustment, through approach coping, was still observed (Paths b and c). Thus, for controllable problems, perceptions of parental support may help students to use more effective coping strategies, which are associated with positive changes in psychological adjustment.

Precisely the opposite picture emerged for students who reported their event was *uncontrollable*. In these analyses, parental support directly predicted changes in students' psychological adjustment over the 2-year period (Path a). Now, however, the indirect path involving correlations with approach coping was not associated with students' adjustment (Paths b and c). How can it be that adaptive, approach coping was not associated with students' adjustment in the face of uncontrollable events? Valentiner et al. explain this rather unintuitive finding by arguing that when events are uncontrollable, coping strategies that emphasize active problem solving may be counterproductive—much like hitting your head against a brick wall. When events are uncontrollable, the best strategy may be to *not* try to solve the problem because it can't be solved. In this situation, perceptions of supportive parents seem to be more important for students' positive adjustment.

The use of sophisticated statistical techniques like those we just described can greatly enhance our ability to interpret the results of correlational studies. However, it is important to remember that we still can't make definite causal statements based on an analysis of mediator and moderator variables.

## MEASURES IN CORRELATIONAL RESEARCH

### Questionnaires as Instruments

- Most survey research relies on questionnaires to measure variables.
- Demographic variables describe the characteristics of people who are surveyed.
- Self-report scales are used to assess people's judgments or to identify individual differences among respondents.
- Two methods to develop individual differences scales are the Likert method and factor analysis.
- The accuracy and precision of questionnaires requires expertise and care in their construction.

The value of correlational research (and any research) ultimately depends on the quality of the measurements that researchers make. The quality of these measurements, in turn, depends on the quality of the instruments used to make the measurements. The primary research instrument in survey research is the questionnaire. On the surface, a questionnaire may not look like the high-tech instruments used in much modern scientific research; but, when constructed and used properly, a questionnaire is a powerful scientific instrument for measuring different variables.

*Demographic Variables* Demographic variables are an important type of variable frequently measured in survey research. Demographic variables are used to describe the characteristics of the people who are surveyed. Religious affiliation and occupation, which Lubin and his colleagues (1988) measured in their study of psychological and physical health, are demographic variables. Measures such as race, ethnicity, age, and socioeconomic status are also examples of demographic variables. Whether we decide to measure these variables depends on the goals of our study, as well as on other considerations. Entwisle and Astone (1994), for example, provide a practical reason for including race and ethnicity as demographic variables in survey research. This practical reason is the ever-increasing diversity of the U.S. population. Entwisle and Astone (1994) point out that "The ethnic and racial diversity of the U.S. population is now projected to increase through the middle of the next century, so that by then the majority of the U.S. population will be persons whose ethnicity would now be classified as 'nonwhite'" (p. 1522). By asking respondents to identify their race we are able to document the racial mix of our sample and, if part of the research goals, compare racial groups.

Measuring a demographic variable such as race may at first seem very easy. One straightforward method is simply to ask respondents to identify their race in an open-ended question: What is your race? _____ Such an approach may be straightforward, but the resulting measurement of race may not be satisfactory. For example, some respondents may mistakenly confuse "race" and "ethnicity." Important distinctions in identifying ethnic groups may go unrecognized by respondents and researchers. For instance, Hispanic does not identify a race; Hispanic designates all those whose country of origin is Spanish speaking.

So, a person born in Spain would be classified as Hispanic. *Latino* is a term that is sometimes used interchangeably with Hispanic, but Latino designates people whose origin is from the countries of North and South America, excluding Canada and the United States. Distinctions like these can be confused. For example, a person known to the authors is of European Spanish heritage and correctly considers himself a Caucasian, and not Latino. His ethnicity is Hispanic.

In general, "quick and dirty" approaches to measurement in survey research tend to yield messy data that are hard to analyze and interpret. Entwisle and Astone (1994) recommend a more deliberate—and effective—approach when measuring race. They outline a series of nine questions to measure a person's race. One of these questions is, What race do you consider yourself to be? Other questions seek information such as what countries the person's ancestors came from, and whether Latino respondents are Mexican, Puerto Rican, Cuban, or something else. This more detailed series of questions allows researchers to measure race less ambiguously, more accurately, and more precisely. We use this example of measuring race to illustrate a more general principle: *The accuracy and precision of questionnaires as survey-research instruments depends upon the expertise and care that go into their construction.*

**Preferences and Attitudes**    Individuals' preferences and attitudes are frequently assessed in surveys. For example, a marketing researcher may be interested in consumers' preferences for different brands of coffee, or a political group may be interested in potential voters' attitudes regarding controversial public issues. Psychologists have long been interested in measuring people's thoughts and feelings on a vast array of topics, and often develop *self-report scales* for people to provide verbal or written responses to items on the scale.

Self-report scales are commonly used to measure people's judgments about items presented on the scale (e.g., coffee, divorce, political candidates, life events) and to determine differences among people on some dimension presented on the scale (e.g., personality traits, amount of stress). For example, respondents may be asked to rate different life events according to how stressful they perceive the events to be. The researcher then may develop a list of life events that vary on the dimension of stressfulness. This type of scale focuses on differences among the items on the scale. To measure individual differences, respondents may be asked to report how often during the past year they experienced different stressful life events listed on a scale. A total stress score can be obtained for each individual by summing responses to the items on the scale. Individuals can then be compared according to the amount of stress experienced during the past year.[1] Rozin, Markwith, and Stoess (1997) investigated individual differences among people who were "meat avoiders, vegetarians, and people reluctant to eat meat" (p. 68). They found that vegetarians who avoid meat for moral reasons find meat

---

[1]The area of psychological measurement concerned with scaling items or stimuli is known as psychophysics, and the area of measurement concerned with individual differences is referred to as psychometrics.

more disgusting and avoid a wider range of animal foods than do those who avoid meat for health reasons. Interestingly, though, both groups showed similar levels of dislike for the taste and smell of meat.

Individual differences scales are used to identify differences among respondents on the dimension measured in the scale (e.g., degree of meat avoidance) and are perhaps the most common scales in psychology. Two frequently used methods to develop individual differences scales are the Likert method and factor analysis. In the Likert method, a number of items are written to reflect the construct or domain of interest. For example, a researcher may be interested in individuals' willingness to forgive others. A 5-point rating scale is typically provided for individuals to respond by circling a number on the scale. One item that could be used to measure forgiveness is:

When people hurt me or make me angry, I can usually forgive them.

1————————2————————3————————4————————5
Strongly                                                                Strongly
disagree                                                                agree

Many such items are administered to a large group of people (at a minimum, 100), and each individual's responses are summed to derive a total score. Items are then selected from the whole set of items to best represent the domain. Items are discarded if they don't discriminate individuals who are high on the dimension from individuals who are low (based on their total score). Each selected item should correlate well with the total scale score. Once the best items are chosen, an individual's scale score is obtained by summing her responses to these items. An important goal of scale development is reliability, and in the Likert method, each time the scale is used the researcher must demonstrate that the items in the scale consistently measure the domain of interest (reliability is discussed in greater detail later in this chapter). It is important to note that measures with 5-point rating scales are often called "Likert scales" (instead of, most correctly, "Likert-type scales," or more simply, "5-point rating scales"). A scale is only a Likert scale if it follows the method for scale development that we just outlined.

Factor analysis is similar in that it is designed to select the best items to represent the construct or domain of interest. An advantage of factor analysis is that a measure can be developed that assesses more than one construct. For example, the forgiveness researcher may be interested in "other-forgiveness" and "self-forgiveness," so her questionnaire may have items intended to represent each "factor." In factor analysis, responses for each item are correlated with responses for every other item (this represents many "intercorrelations," which is why factor analysis is best accomplished using a computer). The pattern of intercorrelations among items is used to determine which items are related to the factor(s) represented in the scale. Items that correlate poorly are dropped. As with Likert scales, the reliability of scales developed using factor analysis should be analyzed each time they are used.

Self-report measures, often in the form of a questionnaire, are among the most frequently used tools in psychology. Given their importance, it is critical that these measures be developed carefully. Important information on questionnaire construction, such as wording of questions, response options, questionnaire format, and order of questions, is found in Appendix B.

## Margin of Error

- Although survey researchers select a sample to represent a population, they recognize that it is unlikely the sample will exactly describe the population due to sampling error.
- The margin of error represents a quantitative estimate regarding the difference between sample results on a measure and the likely population values.
- The margin of error is influenced by the sample size and the confidence level researchers choose for estimating the population value.
- Although the margin of error indicates how well survey results may describe a population, whether these results can be interpreted depends on the quality of the survey-research methods.

Survey results are often reported in terms of the percentage of respondents who prefer a certain candidate, agree or disagree with a certain position, or possess some particular demographic characteristic. We must be careful, however, when we translate this numerical information into a verbal description of the results. For example, a major metropolitan newspaper reported on the National Collegiate Athletic Association's (NCAA) 1995 Division I Graduation-Rates Report. The overall graduation rate within 6 years for all students entering in 1988 (both athletes and nonathletes) was 57%. For football players the graduation rate was 56%, and the newspaper reported the good news that this represented an increase from the 1987 graduation rate. In 1987, the graduation rate for football players was 55%. It turns out that the percentage increase in the graduation rate for football players, 1%, was not particularly impressive. The graduation rates for 1987 and 1988 were included in the newspaper article so there wasn't an effort to mislead the reader about the size of the increase. However, survey researchers need some way to translate these differences in percentages into appropriate verbal statements. Is a change from 55% to 56% a "meaningful" or "significant" increase? When it comes to describing survey results, an increase is not always an increase.

As we will describe more fully later in this chapter, survey research relies heavily on sampling. Survey research is conducted when we would like to know the characteristics of a population (e.g., preferences, attitudes, demographics), but often it is impractical to survey the entire population (we'd spend all of our time completing surveys!). Responses from a sample are used to describe the larger population. Well-selected samples will provide good descriptions of the population, but it is unlikely that the results for a sample will describe the population *exactly*. For example, if the average age in a classroom of 33 college students is 26.4, it's unlikely that the mean age for a sample of 10 students from the class will be exactly 26.4. Similarly, if it were true that 65% of a city's population favor the present mayor and 35% favor a new mayor, we wouldn't necessarily expect an exact 65:35 split in a sample of 100 voters randomly selected from the city population. We expect some "slippage" due to sampling, some "error" between the actual population values and the estimates from our sample. At issue, then, is how accurately the responses from the sample represent the larger population.

It is possible to estimate the **margin of error** between the sample results and the true population values. Rather than providing a precise estimate of a population value (e.g., "65% of the population prefer the present mayor"), the margin of error presents a *range* of values with the idea that the true population value is likely to be within the range (e.g., "between 60% and 70% of the population prefer the present mayor"). What specifically is this range?

The margin of error provides an estimate of the difference between the sample results and the population values due simply to chance or random factors. Let's consider a specific example using the hypothetical mayoral election referred to above. Assume that in a random sample of 100 voters, 63 people said they favor the present mayor and 37 said they want her replaced. (Let us assume we "know" that 65% of the people in the population favor the incumbent and 35% want a new mayor.) The question we must ask is, Is the difference between 63 and 65 (the sample estimate and population value, respectively) a *real* difference? That is, is the sample value of 63% an accurate description of the population, given that we expect some error? Another way of stating this is: Is the sample value of 63 *within the margin of error* that is expected when random samples of this size are taken? If it is, then the difference between 63 and 65 may not be a real difference but one due to sampling error.

The margin of error gives us the range of values we can expect due to sampling error—remember that we expect some error; we don't expect to describe the population exactly. To stay with the mayoral election example, let us assume that a poll of many voters is taken and a media spokesperson gives the following report: "Results indicate that 63% of those sampled favor the incumbent, and we can say with 95% confidence that the poll has a margin of error of 5%." The reported margin of error with the specified level of confidence (usually 95%) indicates that the percentage of the actual population who favor the incumbent is estimated to fall between 58% and 68% (5% is subtracted from and added to the sample value of 63%). Because the population value (65%) falls within the range of values indicated by the margin of error, it is reasonable to assume that the sample value of 63% accurately describes the population. It's important to remember, however, that we usually don't know the true population value. The information we get from the sample and the margin of error is the following: 63% of the sample favor the incumbent, and we are 95% confident that if the entire population were sampled, between 58% and 68% of the population would favor the incumbent. This can be represented on a graph by plotting the value obtained for the sample (63%), with error bars

**FIGURE 4.3**  Error bars are used to represent the margin of error for the estimate of the population value.

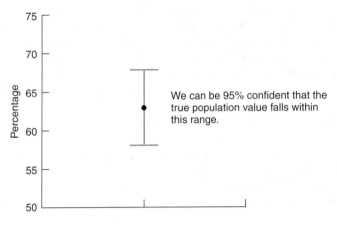

representing the margin of error. Figure 4.3 displays error bars around the sample estimate.

The margin of error is primarily determined by the size of the sample—the larger the sample size, the smaller the margin of error. This is because a larger sample is more likely to represent the diverse characteristics of the population. Thus, in order to reduce the margin of error (and more precisely describe the population), an obvious decision is to increase the size of the sample. This may make sense in some situations, but increasing sample sizes can make the cost of doing a survey too high. For example, if our margin of error is 5% with a sample size of 100, we would have to quadruple the sample size to 400 to decrease the margin of error by half!

The margin of error is influenced also by how confident we want to be when estimating the population value. Given a sample of specific size, we can be more confident about our estimate when we have a larger margin of error. As an illustration, think of what your weight is right now. Can you confidently estimate your weight within 5 pounds (a margin of error)? Would you be more confident of your estimate if you were allowed to be within 10 pounds? We could express the differences in the sizes of the intervals in terms of confidence. A person might say, "I am 99% confident that my weight is between 160 and 180, but I'm only 90% confident that my weight is within 165 and 175." When describing survey results, a 99% confidence level results in a larger margin of error (i.e., a larger range of values) than does a 90% confidence level (assuming the same sample size for the two different confidence levels).

The margin of error for a given sample can be computed using the sample size and a specified confidence level. In practice, however, a desired margin of error (e.g., 3%) and confidence level (e.g., 95%) are selected and the sample size necessary to achieve these two objectives is then calculated.

Margins of error are routinely included in media reports of national surveys. At this point, you should be able to estimate the population values from sample information presented in media reports. Remember that you can not know for sure the true population value based on sample information. The goal of surveys is to tell you "with a margin of error" what the true population value is.

Knowing the margin of error for a survey is not sufficient to assure that the survey results can be interpreted. Interpretable results also depend on factors such as how the survey sample was selected, how many selected for the sample actually responded to the survey, how the questions on the questionnaire are worded, and the training of the interviewers who administer the questionnaire (Converse & Traugott, 1986). Unfortunately, these important aspects of survey research usually are not reported in the media. Thus, we should be cautious in accepting interpretations of survey results unless we are well informed about critical characteristics of the survey. As you will soon see, problems can arise even in a carefully conducted survey.

## Reliability and Validity

- Reliability refers to the consistency of measurement, and is frequently assessed using the test-retest reliability method.
- Reliability is increased by including many similar items on a measure, by testing a diverse  sample of individuals, and by using uniform testing procedures.
- Validity refers to the truthfulness of a measure: Does it measure what it intends to measure?
- Construct validity represents the extent to which a measure assesses the theoretical construct it is designed to assess; construct validity is determined by assessing convergent validity and discriminant validity.

As we learned in Chapter 1, reliability and validity are vital characteristics of all psychological measurement. Thus, it makes sense that measurements in survey research must be reliable and valid. In this section we will describe some procedures researchers use to determine whether measures are reliable and valid.

We first discuss examples of assessing the reliability and validity of *tests*. Tests, like surveys, are commonly used instruments in correlational research. We chose to use tests for our examples because you already know a great deal about tests—they're probably a routine part of your life. You may even prefer a particular type of test because you believe you perform better on that type of test. Most of us experience emotional reactions when taking tests, ranging from exhilaration to terror! There are good reasons for these emotional reactions. Important decisions frequently are based in part on test results—admission to college, passing or failing courses, admission to graduate or professional schools. Although you have considerable experience with tests, what else do you know about the tests you take? For example, have you ever wondered whether the tests you take are reliable and valid? Consider that question for a moment. How would you be able to tell whether a test was reliable and valid? Asked a different way, what are the fundamental characteristics of a reliable and valid test?

Reliable tests, like reliable observers or any other reliable measurements, are characterized by consistency. A reliable test is one that yields similar (consistent) results each time it is taken. Tests must be reliable if they are to be used to make predictions about who will be selected for a scholarship, who will be hired for a competitive job, or who should be fired from a job. For example, Powell and Whitla (1994) developed a test they call MicroCog to measure normal changes in cognitive processes as people age. As part of the natural aging process, older adults experience some changes in memory and other cognitive functions. For instance, they may have trouble remembering people's names, which leads some older adults to wonder if they are "losing it." This question is important in the workplace. In 1994, it became illegal in the United States for an employer to compel a worker to retire because of age. Tests like MicroCog can be useful to older adults to allay their fears about memory loss and to employers when they make difficult decisions about the performance of older employees. When test results are used as part of the process of making such important personal decisions, it is essential that the tests be as reliable as possible—reliability is no longer just a measurement issue.

There are several ways to measure a test's reliability. One common method is to compute a *test-retest reliability*. Usually, test-retest reliability involves administering the same test to a large sample of people at two different times (hence, test and retest). For a test to be reliable, people need not obtain identical scores on the two administrations of the test, but a person's relative position in the distribution of scores should be similar at the two test times. The consistency of this relative positioning is determined by computing a correlation coefficient using the two test scores for each person in the sample. A desirable value for test-retest reliability coefficients is .80 or above, but the size of the coefficient depends on factors such as the number and types of items.

As we just mentioned, the reliability of a test is affected by the number of items on the test; in this case, more items is better. We are likely to have unreliable measures if we try to measure a student's understanding of material based on a single test item, or a baseball player's hitting ability based on a single time at bat, or a person's attitude toward the death penalty based on a single question on a survey. The reliability of our measures will increase greatly if we average the behavior in question across a large number of observations—many test items, many at-bats, and many survey questions (Epstein, 1979).

In general, measurements will also be more reliable when there is greater variability on the factor being measured among those individuals being tested. Often the goal of measurement is to determine the extent to which individuals differ. A sample of individuals who vary a great deal from one another are easier to differentiate reliably than are individuals who differ by only a small amount. Consider this example. Suppose we wish to assess soccer players' ability to pass the ball effectively to other players. We will be able to differentiate more reliably good players from poor players if we include in our sample a wider range of players—for example, professionals, high school players, and peewee players. It would be much harder to differentiate players reliably if we only tested professional players—they'd all be good! The range of skill level would not be that great. Thus, a test is often more reliable when administered to a diverse sample than when given to a restricted sample of individuals.

A third and final factor affecting reliability is related to actual test administration. Tests will be more reliable when the testing situation is free of distractions and when clear instructions are provided for completing the test. (You may wish to think about times when your own test performance was hindered by noise or when you weren't sure what a question was asking.) These three factors affecting the reliability of tests (number and type of items, variability in the sample, and testing procedures) apply equally to measurements made using questionnaires in survey research.

The reliability of a test is easier to determine and to achieve than the validity of a test. The definition of validity is deceptively straightforward—a valid test measures what it is intended to measure. For example, a valid test of research methods knowledge might ask you about the terms *reliability* and *validity*; we suspect you would question the validity of a research methods test that asked about the classical counterpoint in the fugue of Mozart's Symphony No. 4 in C Major (finale). Have you ever heard students complain that questions on a test didn't seem to address the material covered in class? This is an issue of validity.

At this point, we will focus on construct validity, which is just one of the many ways in which the validity of a test is assessed. The *construct validity* of a test represents the extent to which the test measures the theoretical construct it is designed to measure. Quantitative reasoning, intelligence, self-esteem, anxiety, and depression represent examples of theoretical constructs psychologists measure using tests. One approach to determining the construct validity of a test relies on two other kinds of validity: convergent validity and discriminant validity. These concepts can best be understood by considering an example.

Table 4.1 presents data showing how we might assess the construct validity of a measure of "life satisfaction." Lucas, Diener, and Suh (1996) note that psychologists are increasingly examining factors such as happiness, life satisfaction, self-esteem, optimism, and other indicators of well-being. However, it's not clear whether these different indicators all measure the same construct (e.g., well-being) or whether each is a distinguishable construct. Lucas and his colleagues conducted several studies in which they asked individuals to complete questionnaire measures of these different indicators of well-being. For our purposes we will focus on a portion of their data from their third study, in which they asked participants to complete three scales: two life satisfaction measures, the Satisfaction with Life Scale (SWLS) and a 5-item Life Satisfaction measure (SL-5), and a measure of Positive Affect (PA). At issue in this example is whether the construct of life satisfaction—the quality of being happy with one's life— can be distinguished from being happy more generally (positive affect).

The data in Table 4.1 are presented in the form of a correlation matrix. A correlation matrix is an easy way to present a number of correlations. Look first at

**TABLE 4.1**   EXAMPLE OF CONSTRUCT VALIDITY*

|        | SWLS  | LS-5  | PA    |
|--------|-------|-------|-------|
| SWLS   | (.88) |       |       |
| LS-5   | .77   | (.90) |       |
| PA     | .42   | .47   | (.81) |

*Data from Lucas et al. (1996), Table 3.
*Note:* SWLS = Satisfaction with Life Scale; LS-5 = 5-item Life
Satisfaction scale; PA = Positive Affect scale.

the values in parentheses that appear on the diagonal. These parenthesized correlation coefficients represent the test reliabilities of the three measures appearing in the table (Satisfaction with Life Scale, 5-item Life Satisfaction, and Positive Affect, respectively). As you can see, the three measures show good reliability (each is above .80). Our focus, however, is on measuring the construct validity of "life satisfaction," so let's look at what else is in Table 4.1.

It is reasonable to expect that scores on the Satisfaction with Life Scale (SWLS) should correlate with scores on the 5-item Life Satisfaction measure; after all, both measures were designed to assess the life satisfaction construct. In fact, Lucas et al. observed a correlation between these two measures of .77, which indicates that they correlate as expected. This finding provides evidence for *convergent validity* of the tests; the two tests converge (or "go together") as measures of life satisfaction.

The case for the construct validity of life satisfaction can be made even more strongly when the measures are shown to have discriminant validity. As can be seen in Table 4.1, the correlations between the Satisfaction with Life Scale (SWLS) and Positive Affect (.42) and between the 5-item Life Satisfaction measure (LS-5) and Positive Affect (.47) are lower. These findings show that life satisfaction tests do not correlate as well with a test designed to measure another theoretical construct—namely, positive affect. The lower correlations between the life satisfaction tests and the positive affect test indicate that *different* constructs are being measured. Thus, there is evidence for *discriminant* validity of the life satisfaction measures because they seem to "discriminate" life satisfaction from positive affect—being satisfied with one's life is not the same as general happiness. The construct validity of life satisfaction gains support in our example because there is evidence for both convergent validity and discriminant validity.

## Predictions and Decisions

- Actuarial prediction relies on correlational data to make predictions about people's average behavior.
- Predictions are improved when multiple sources of information are used.
- Statistical predictions, based on correlations, have been shown to be superior to predictions based on clinical judgment.

The results of correlational research have implications for decision making. Predictive relationships can be used in making diverse decisions such as who should pursue a career as a salesperson or who should be admitted to a psychiatric hospital. Making predictions based on correlational data is called **actuarial prediction.** As we described in the previous section, predictive relationships must be reliable in order to make good decisions. Based on highly reliable predictive relationships (i.e., strong correlations), we can accurately predict what people's average behavior will be. For example, students who score in the highest 20% on an academic aptitude test are *on average* more likely to succeed in college than are students who score in the lowest 20%. However, actuarial predictions do not necessarily tell us what an *individual* person will do in a particular situation. Thus, knowing a particular student's score on an academic aptitude test does not allow us to predict with certainty whether *that* student will graduate from college. We can only predict what students "like this student" will typically (on the average) do. Nonetheless, actuarial prediction can still be extremely useful.

Important decisions are rarely based on a single source of information. Instead, when more than one measure has been shown to have predictive value, we combine the information across measures to improve predictions. This is similar to the multimethod approach to research described in Chapter 1. When several different research methods are used to investigate a problem, we're more likely to achieve a valid conclusion. The same is true when making decisions: The use of several different predictors in the decision-making process increases the likelihood of making good decisions.

For example, applications to graduate and professional schools comprise several pieces of predictive information: GRE (MCAT, LSAT) test scores, undergraduate GPA, letters of recommendation, and personal essays. Similarly, employers selecting applicants in more applied settings rely on the use of multiple predictors. Broach (1992) reported that predictions of air traffic controllers' performance in radar-based training after 1 or 2 years in that occupation were better when biographical data (such as age and prior experience) were included than when the predictions were based solely on a civil service test.

Statistical prediction based on correlational research is sometimes contrasted with clinical prediction. Specifically, Meehl (1954) studied the task that clinical psychologists routinely face when they diagnose their clients' disorders. Statistical prediction and clinical prediction represent two different ways to combine information when making a decision. Clinical prediction occurs when a clinician reviews the available evidence pertinent to a case, including impressions gained from interviewing the client, and then makes a diagnosis (prediction) of the client's disorder. Clinical prediction relies heavily on the personal and professional *judgment* of the clinician.

Statistical prediction is essentially the same as actuarial prediction: Correlational research is used to identify predictive relationships. For example, a large amount of research has shown that the occurrence of "depression" is correlated with low energy, difficulty sleeping, and crying; the occurrence of "schizophrenia" is correlated with withdrawal and disordered thinking. Information about a given client is entered into this predictive (correlational) system, and a statistical prediction is made about which disorder is most likely experienced by the client. The distinguishing characteristic of statistical prediction is that it is based on empirical evidence (e.g., results of paper-and-pencil tests) rather than on the individual judgment of a clinician. Which of these two approaches yields more accurate predictions of psychological disorders?

Meehl (1954) compared the accuracy of statistical prediction versus clinical prediction when clinicians make these challenging diagnostic decisions. He found that, in an absolute sense, *neither* clinical prediction nor statistical prediction was very accurate—a not surprising finding given the complexity involved in diagnosing psychological disorders. Meehl did find, however, that statistical prediction was more accurate than clinical prediction. In fact, research has shown that statistical prediction is superior to clinical prediction (personal judgments) across a wide variety of areas, including predictions about who to admit to graduate school, who is a good risk for a bank loan, who is at risk for a heart attack, and who should be paroled from prison (Dawes, Faust, & Meehl, 1993). We should generally trust, therefore, what the data "say" more than what one person says when making important decisions.

Although this evidence suggests that we should rely on statistical prediction whenever possible, it is not always practical to do so. As Meehl (1993) emphasizes, "You could not choose a graduate school, buy a car, get married (or divorced), let alone invest money or vote for president, if you required all your choices to be derived rigorously from scientific proof" (p. 727). Empirical evidence simply is not available for many important decisions. When we have no basis for making a statistical prediction, then we must make the best decision we can based on our own judgment. However, when we do have the data for a statistical prediction, we face a different situation. Meehl (1993) argues that, *ethically*, we are making a questionable choice if we ignore the data and rely on personal judgment. Our hope is that the knowledge you have gained about correlational research and predictions will allow you to make a more informed decision about how you make decisions in your life.

## USES OF SURVEYS

- Survey research is used to assess people's thoughts, opinions, and feelings.
- Surveys can be specific and limited in scope or more global in their goals.
- The best way to determine whether a survey is biased is to examine the survey procedures and analyses.

We discussed in Chapter 3 how psychologists use observational methods to infer what people must have been thinking or feeling to have behaved in a certain way. Survey research is designed to deal more directly with the nature of people's thoughts, opinions, and feelings. On the surface, survey research is deceptively simple. If you want to know what people are thinking, ask them! Similarly, if you want to know what people are doing, observe them! As we have seen, however, when we hope to infer general principles of behavior, our observations must be more sophisticated than our everyday, casual observations. So, too, survey research requires more than simply asking people questions.

The deceptive ease of conducting a survey is illustrated in a report by a young girl named Bridgette that was published in a suburban grammar school's newsletter. The report read, "I surveyed 50 people on which candy bar they liked best. Here are my results in order of preference: Hershey bar—35, Snickers—10, Whachamacallit—5." These results may please the makers of Hershey bars, but the supplier for the school's vending machine should be wary of stocking it based on Bridgette's findings. Who were the "50 people" surveyed? How were they selected? How was the survey conducted? Was each child interviewed separately? If other children were present during the interview, were they eating candy bars? If so, what brands? Do the children who claim to like Hershey bars best really eat them most often? These and many other questions must be answered before we can confidently interpret the results of this survey.

You may be thinking at this point that we are taking Bridgette's survey too seriously, and you are probably right. Nonetheless, these questions are typical of those that should be asked when we read or hear reports of surveys. A goal of this chapter is to help you to ask the right questions about surveys and to aid you in evaluating the answers provided to these questions.

Social scientists, such as political scientists, psychologists, and sociologists, use surveys for a variety of reasons. For example, Cherlin et al. (1991) conducted national surveys in Great Britain and the United States to investigate the effects of divorce on children. Myers and Diener (1995) reported the results of many studies that used surveys to study factors affecting people's personal sense of well-being.

Surveys are also used to meet the more pragmatic needs of political candidates, public health officials, professional organizations, and advertising and marketing directors. The scope and purpose of surveys can be limited and specific, or they can be global. For example, the Practice Directorate of APA conducted a survey with a limited and specific purpose (Peterson, 1995). The Practice Directorate is a branch of APA that focuses primarily on the concerns of clinical psychologists. Their national survey of 1,087 adults was designed to understand better what the public thinks psychologists do, what kind of education psychologists have, and in what settings psychologists practice. The survey produced many observations, including that 46% of respondents reported having seen a mental health professional or that someone in their family had, and 80% said that psychologists usually work in private practice. In fact, although more than half of psychologists do work in the mental health field, fewer than half of those work in private practice. Clearly, the public's estimate of 80% is high. Results from this survey will be useful to the Directorate in focusing their public education strategies.

Myers and Diener (1995), on the other hand, conducted a survey with a more global scope. They reported the results of a survey sampling people from 24 countries representing every continent but Antarctica. One of the research questions was whether people in wealthy countries have a greater sense of well-being than those in not-so-wealthy countries. Is being "well-off" associated with greater "well-being"? The survey results showed that national wealth, as measured by gross national product per capita, is positively correlated with well-being (.67). But this relationship is not simple because national wealth is also correlated with other variables that are themselves highly correlated with well-being, such as number of continuous years of democracy (.85). Thus, surveys can be used to address issues of global concern such as democracy, wealth, and well-being.

One of the ways that surveys can be used deserves mention because of ethical issues. An ethical dilemma arises when sponsors of survey research have vested interests in how the results turn out. Crossen (1994) highlighted this by stating, ". . . more and more of the information we use to buy, elect, advise, acquit, and heal has been created not to expand our knowledge but to sell a product or advance a cause" (p. 14). Crossen (1994) cites examples such as a national survey sponsored by the zinc industry showing that 62% of respondents wanted to keep the penny (which is zinc based), and a survey sponsored by a manufacturer of cellular phones showing that 70% of respondents (all of whom used cellular phones) agreed that people who use cellular telephones are more successful in business.

Is it reasonable to conclude that survey results are biased anytime the outcome of the survey is favorable for the sponsoring agency? Answers to ethical questions are rarely simple and the answer to this one certainly is not. High-quality and ethical research can be done when the sponsor has an interest in the outcome. Knowing the sponsor of the research is important when evaluating survey results, but is not sufficient for judging whether the study is biased. It is much more important to know whether a biased sample has been used, or whether the wording of questions has been slanted, or whether the data have been selectively analyzed or reported. Any of these aspects of survey research can bias the results, and unethical researchers can use these techniques to make the results "turn out right." The best protection against unethical researchers and poor-quality research is to examine carefully the procedures and analyses used in the survey research.

## CHARACTERISTICS OF SURVEYS

- Survey research involves selecting a sample (or samples) and using a predetermined set of questions.

Though they differ in how they can be used, all surveys have some characteristics in common. These shared characteristics make properly conducted surveys an excellent method for describing people's attitudes and opinions. First, surveys generally involve sampling, a concept we introduced in our discussion of observational methods (Chapter 3) and will discuss more in the next section of this chapter. Surveys also are characterized by their use of a set of predetermined questions for all respondents. Oral or written responses to these questions constitute the principal data obtained in a survey. By using the same phrasing and ordering of questions, it is possible to summarize the views of all respondents succinctly.

When a representative sample of people is asked the same set of questions, we can describe the attitudes of the population from which the sample was drawn. Furthermore, when the same questions are used, we can compare the attitudes of different populations or look for changes in attitudes over time. An example of the latter comes from two surveys of animal rights activists, one taken at a national march in Washington, DC, in 1990, and another of activists attending a similar event in 1996 (Plous, 1998). Results revealed that a change had taken place in the priorities of people in the animal rights movement during this time. Specifically, in 1990 a majority of activists viewed animal research as the most important issue facing the movement; in 1996, animal agriculture was viewed as the most important issue. The researcher suggested that there now may be more room for dialogue between activists and researchers than there was previously. Thus, survey research can be used to study changes in people's attitudes by presenting the same questions to samples selected at different times.

## SAMPLING TECHNIQUES

- Careful selection of a survey sample allows researchers to generalize findings from the sample to the population.

Assume you've decided your research question is best answered using a survey, and you've determined the population of interest for your survey. The next step is to decide who to interview. This involves selecting a sample of respondents to represent the population. The power and efficiency of sampling are aptly summarized by survey researcher Angus Campbell (1981, p. 17):

> The method of choice for portraying all the variety of a large heterogeneous population is clearly that of the sample survey. Ever since statisticians and social scientists learned how to draw a sample from a large universe in such a way that every member of the universe has an equal chance of being chosen, it has been possible to describe the national population accurately by obtaining information from a few thousand carefully selected individuals.

Whether we are describing a national population or a much smaller one (e.g., the students of one university), the procedures are the same. We explain in this section how to make that careful selection of individuals which Campbell describes.

### Basic Terms of Sampling

- The identification and selection of elements that will make up the sample is at the heart of all sampling techniques; the sample is chosen from the sampling frame, or list of all members of the population of interest.

- Researchers are not interested simply in the responses of those surveyed; instead, they seek to describe the larger population from which the sample was drawn.
- The ability to generalize from a sample to the population depends critically on the representativeness of the sample.
- A biased sample is one in which the characteristics of the sample are systematically different from the characteristics of the population.
- Selection bias occurs when the procedures used to select a sample result in the overrepresentation or underrepresentation of some segment(s) of the population.

As we begin to talk about sampling techniques, we need to be clear about the definitions of four terms: *population, sampling frame, sample,* and *element.* The relationships among the four critical sampling terms are summarized in Figure 4.4. A **population** is the set of all cases of interest. If you were interested in the attitudes of students on your campus toward services provided by the library, your population would be all students on your campus. In a survey, we select a subset of the population to represent the population as a whole.

**FIGURE 4.4**   Illustration of relationships among four basic terms in sampling.

Next, we need to develop a specific list of the members of the population. This specific list is called a **sampling frame** and is, in a sense, an operational definition of the population of interest. In a survey of students' attitudes toward library services, the sampling frame might be a list obtained from the registrar's office of all currently enrolled students. The extent to which the sampling frame truly reflects the population of interest determines the adequacy of the sample we ultimately select. The list provided by the registrar should provide a good sampling frame, but some students might be excluded, such as students who registered late.

The subset of the population actually drawn from the sampling frame is called the **sample.** We might select 100 students from the registrar's list to serve as the sample for our library survey. How closely the attitudes of this sample of students will represent all students' attitudes depends critically on how the sample is selected. Each member of the population is called an **element.** The identification and selection of elements that will make up the sample is at the heart of all sampling techniques.

It is important to emphasize at this point that samples are of little or no interest in themselves. A new library is not going to be built for the sole use of the 100 students surveyed. Similarly, the social psychologist is not interested solely in the racial attitudes of the 50 people he surveyed, nor is the marketing director interested only in the preferences of the 200 consumers she surveyed. Populations, not samples, are of primary interest. The "power" of samples to describe the larger population is based on the assumption that survey responses in a sample are applicable to the population from which the sample was drawn.

The ability to generalize from a sample to the population depends critically on the **representativeness** of the sample. Clearly, individuals in a population differ in many ways, and populations differ from each other. For example, one population might be 40% male and 60% female, whereas in another population the distribution might be 75% female and 25% male. *A sample is representative of the population to the extent that it exhibits the same distribution of characteristics as the population.* If a representative sample of 200 individuals has 80 males and 120 females, which of the above-mentioned populations does it represent?

The major threat to representativeness is bias. A **biased sample** is one in which the distribution of characteristics in the sample is *systematically* different from the target population. A sample of 100 individuals that included 80 females and 20 males would be biased if the population was 60% female and 40% male. In this case, females would be overrepresented and males would be underrepresented in the sample. There are two sources of bias: selection bias and response bias. (We will discuss selection bias now and deal with response bias in the Survey Method section.) **Selection bias** occurs when the procedures used to select the sample result in the overrepresentation of some segment of the population or, conversely, in the exclusion or underrepresentation of a significant segment.

Charles Madigan, a senior writer for the *Chicago Tribune,* documented a selection bias in samples surveyed for the 1994 national election. He identified the selection bias by comparing the demographic characteristics of the voters interviewed in exit polls to characteristics of the population drawn from U.S. census data. Note that the U.S. census data, representing the entire population, includes voters and nonvoters, whereas the exit-poll sample comprises voters only. Madigan determined that the exit-poll sample differed in systematic ways from the U.S. population in terms of age, race, education, income, and the proportion of working women. These differences indicate that the sample was not representative of the population due to a selection bias. Although the voter poll accurately reflects the interests and attitudes of those people who voted, their votes and survey responses may not be used to characterize the attitudes of the population (which includes people who did not vote). Clearly, politicians cannot assume a "mandate" based on a biased sample of individuals who voted.

A general lesson from the above example is that what constitutes a representative sample depends on the population of interest. For example, if exit polls are concerned (as they usually are) only with people who vote, then an unbiased sample is one that is representative of *probable voters,* not all eligible voters. Similarly, when a university wishes to know college students' opinions about on-campus parking, then the target population is college students who bring cars to campus (not college students in general). An unbiased sample would, in this case, be one that is representative of the subset of students who have cars on campus.

Selection bias also threatens the results of surveys posted on the World Wide Web. As Schmidt (1997) notes, the web "presents survey researchers with an unprecedented opportunity to examine groups of people with questionnaires tailored to the investigation of both broad and narrow domains" (p. 274). Nevertheless, there are some problems and risks. For example, although the number of people using the web is increasing at a fast fate, the majority of users in the late 1990s could be characterized as young males (late teens to early thirties) with above-average socioeconomic status (Schmidt, 1997). Those who wish to use the web for survey research must therefore be aware of the characteristics inherent to the population of web users. But this is not something new. Survey researchers must be constantly alert to the threat of selection bias in sampling. Fortunately, as we will see, they have developed techniques that can minimize the risk.

## Approaches to Sampling

- Two approaches to selecting a survey sample are nonprobability sampling and probability sampling.
- With nonprobability sampling techniques, accidental sampling and purposive sampling, there is no guarantee that every element in the population has an equal chance of being included in the sample.
- Accidental sampling relies on individuals' availability and willingness to respond to a survey; in purposive sampling, researchers select elements for the sample based on their special characteristics.

- With the probability sampling techniques, simple random sampling and stratified random sampling, researchers can estimate the likelihood their findings for the sample differ from the population.
- In simple random sampling each element of the population has an equal chance of being included in the sample; in stratified random sampling, the population is divided into subpopulations (strata), and random samples are drawn from the strata.
- Probability sampling is the method of choice for obtaining a representative sample.

There are two basic approaches to sampling—nonprobability sampling and probability sampling. In **nonprobability sampling** we have no guarantee that each element has some chance of being included and no way to estimate the probability of each element's being included in the sample. In our library survey, if a researcher interviewed the first 10 students who entered the library, she would be using nonprobability sampling. Clearly, not all students would be equally likely to be at the library at that particular time, and some students would have essentially no chance of being included in the sample.

By contrast, if the researcher were to select 10 students randomly from the registrar's list of enrolled students, she would be using probability sampling. In **probability sampling** all students (elements) have an equal chance of being included in the sample. We can describe this researcher's approach as probability sampling because her sampling procedure (i.e., random selection from a predetermined list) allows all students to have an equal chance of being selected for the survey. Probability sampling is preferred because it allows researchers to estimate the likelihood that their sample findings differ from the findings they would have obtained by studying the whole population. Probability sampling is far superior to nonprobability sampling in ensuring that selected samples represent the population. Thus, the researcher who selects 10 students randomly from the registrar's list of students is more likely to have a representative sample than the researcher who bases her survey results on the first 10 students who show up at the library.

Nonprobability Sampling    Two types of nonprobability sampling are accidental sampling and purposive sampling. **Accidental sampling** involves selecting respondents primarily on the basis of their availability and willingness to respond. Newspapers often interview "the person on the street" and publish their comments. Their comments may make interesting reading, but their opinions are not likely to represent those of the wider community because accidental sampling was used. Accidental sampling also is involved when people respond to surveys in *Cosmopolitan* or other magazines because the magazine has to be available (and purchased), and people must be willing to send in their responses.

Crossen (1994) describes the drawbacks of another variation of accidental sampling, call-in surveys. Call-in surveys are used by TV and radio shows to poll the views of their audience. Those who happen to be "tuned in" and who are willing to call (and sometimes to pay the charge for calling a 900 number) make up the sample for these call-in surveys. Thus, it should be kept in mind that people who make calls in response to a call-in request differ from the general population not only because they are part of the particular show's audience, but they are motivated enough to make a call.

Crossen (1994) discusses a prime-time TV-news show that conducted a call-in survey with a question concerning the preferred location for the United Nations. It turns out that another survey research study involving about 500 randomly selected respondents also asked the same question. The question was whether the United Nations (UN) headquarters should remain in the United States. Of the 186,000 callers who responded, a solid majority (67%) wanted the UN *out of the United States*. Of the respondents to the survey research study (a random sample of individuals), a clear majority (72%) wanted the UN *to stay in the United States*. How could these two surveys yield such different—even opposite—results? Should we put more confidence in the results of the call-in survey because of the massive sample size? Absolutely not! A large accidental sample is just as likely to be an unrepresentative sample as is any other accidental sample. As a general rule, you should consider that accidental sampling will result in a biased sample unless you have strong evidence confirming the representativeness of the sample.

A second type of nonprobability sampling is **purposive sampling,** in which the investigator selects the elements to be included in the sample on the basis of their special characteristics. The individuals selected are commonly those who have an expertise or experiences related to the purpose of the study. You can think of these people being selected, on purpose, so as to understand their special experiences.

Connors and his colleagues selected a purposive sample in their study of "restraint" in alcohol and substance use (Connors, Collins, Dermen, & Koutsky, 1998). Restraint was first studied with overeaters, and in that context, refers to individuals' preoccupation with food and methods used to control and regulate food intake. Importantly, when regulation methods fail, highly restrained individuals may be more likely to binge. Connors et al. thought the restraint construct could describe alcoholics and substance abusers. Their survey sample consisted of 193 individuals seeking inpatient treatment for alcohol and other drug abuse. The patients completed questionnaires and interviews as part of admission procedures. Correlations among their measures allowed the researchers to conclude that the restraint concept may also be applied to individuals who abuse alcohol or other substances, as their survey responses indicated they are preoccupied with their substance and likely to abuse when their regulation methods fail. As you can see, Connors et al. were not interested in restraint in the general population, but in a very specific population. So, purposive sampling was ideally suited to the purpose of their study.

Probability Sampling    The distinguishing characteristic of probability sampling is that the researcher can specify, for each element of the population, the probability that it will be included in the sample. Two common types of probability sampling are simple random sampling and stratified random sampling. **Simple random sampling** is the basic technique of probability sampling. The most common definition of random sampling is that every element has an equal chance of being included in the sample. The procedures for simple random sampling are outlined in Box 4.1.

One critical decision that must be made in selecting a random sample is how large it should be. Earlier in this chapter we described the relationship between margin of error and sample size; the smaller the desired margin of error, the larger the sample size needs to be. For now, we will simply note that the size of a random sample needed to represent a population depends on the homogeneity (variability) of the population. College students in Ivy League schools represent a more homogeneous population than college students in all U.S. colleges in terms of their academic abilities. At one extreme, the most homogeneous population would be one in which all members of the population are identical. A sample of one would be representative of this population regardless of the size of the population. At the other extreme, the most heterogeneous population would be one in which each member was completely different from all other members on all characteristics. No sample, regardless of its size, could be representative of this population. Every individual would have to be included to describe such a heterogeneous population. Fortunately, the populations with which survey researchers work typically fall somewhere between these two extremes. Thus the representativeness of samples, like the joy of eating a piece of chocolate cake, increases with increasing size—up to a point.

The representativeness of a sample can often be increased by using stratified random sampling. In **stratified random sampling,** the population is divided into subpopulations called *strata* (singular, *stratum*) and random samples are drawn from each of these strata. There are two general ways to determine how many elements should be drawn from each stratum. One way (illustrated in the last example of Box 4.1) is to draw equal-sized samples from each stratum. The second way is to draw elements for the sample on a proportional basis. Consider a population of undergraduate students made up of 30% freshmen, 30% sophomores, 20% juniors, and 20% seniors (class years are the strata). A stratified random sample of 200 students drawn from this population would include 60 freshmen, 60 sophomores, 40 juniors, and 40 seniors. In contrast, drawing equal-sized samples from each stratum would result in 50 students for each class year. Which sample of 200 better represents the population?

In addition to its potential for increasing the representativeness of samples, stratified random sampling is useful when you want to describe specific portions of the population. For example, a simple random sample of 100 students would be sufficient to survey students' attitudes on a campus of 2,000 students. Suppose, however, your sample included only 2 of the 40 chemistry majors on campus, and you wish to describe the views of students according to different majors. Although this accurately reflects the proportion of chemistry majors in the campus population, it would be risky to use the views of only 2

**BOX 4.1**

## SAMPLES OF RANDOM SAMPLES

The following names represent a scaled-down version of a sampling frame obtained from the registrar's office of a small college campus. Procedures for drawing both a simple random sample and a stratified random sample from this list are described below.

| | | |
|---|---|---|
| Adamski | F | Jr |
| Alderink | F | Sr |
| Baxter | M | Sr |
| Bowen | F | Sr |
| Broder | M | So |
| Brown | M | Jr |
| Bufford | M | So |
| Campbell | F | Fr |
| Carnahan | F | So |
| Cowan | F | Fr |
| Cushman | M | Sr |
| Dawes | M | Jr |
| Dennis | M | Sr |
| Douglas | F | Fr |
| Dunne | M | So |
| Fahey | M | Fr |
| Fedder | M | Fr |
| Foley | F | So |
| Grossman | F | Jr |
| Harris | F | Jr |
| Hedlund | F | So |
| Johnson | F | Fr |
| Klaaren | F | Jr |
| Ludwig | M | Fr |
| Nadeau | F | Sr |
| Nowaczyk | M | Jr |
| O'Keane | F | Sr |
| Osgood | M | So |
| Owens | F | So |
| Penzien | M | Jr |
| Powers | M | Sr |
| Ryan | M | Fr |
| Sawyer | M | Jr |
| Shaw | M | Sr |
| Sonders | F | Sr |
| Suffolk | F | So |
| Taylor | F | Fr |
| Thompson | M | Fr |
| Watterson | F | Jr |
| Zimmerman | M | So |

### Drawing a simple random sample

**Step 1.** Number each element in the sampling frame: Adamski would be number 1, Harris number 20, and Zimmerman number 40.

**Step 2.** Decide on the sample size you want to use. This is just an illustration, so we will use a sample size of 5.

**Step 3.** Choose a starting point in the Table of Random Numbers in Appendix A (a finger stab with your eyes closed works just fine—our stab came down at column 8, row 22 at the entry 26384). Because our sampling frame ranges only from 1 to 40, we had decided *prior* to entering the table to use the left two numbers in each set of five and to go across the table from left to right. We could just as easily have decided to go up, down, or from right to left. We could also have used the middle two or the last two digits of each set of five, but one should make these decisions before entering the table.

**Step 4.** Identify the numbers to be included in your sampling by moving across the table. We got the numbers 26, 06, 21, 15, and 32. Notice that numbers over 40 are ignored. The same would be true if we had come across a repetition of a number we had already selected.

chemistry students to represent all 40 chemistry majors (2 is too few). In this case (and more generally when a stratum is small in number), you could sample more chemistry majors to describe their views better. We can't say precisely how many to sample because, as we learned earlier, the sample size needed to represent a population depends on the heterogeneity of the population.

**Step 5.** List the names corresponding to the selected numbers. In our case the sample will include Nowaczyk, Brown, Hedlund, Dunne, and Ryan.

An even easier system, called *systematic sampling,* can be used to obtain a random sample. In this procedure you divide the sample size you want into the size of the sampling frame to obtain the value $k$. Then you select every $k$th element after choosing the first one randomly. In our example we want a sample size of 5 from a sampling frame of 40, so $k$ would be 8. Thus we would choose one of the first eight people randomly and then take every eighth person thereafter. If Alderink were chosen from among the first 8, the remaining members of the sample would be Cowan, Foley, Nowaczyk, and Shaw. Note: This system should *not* be used if the sampling frame has a periodic organization—if, for example, you had a list of dormitory residents arranged by room and every tenth pair listed occupied a corner room. You can readily see that, in such a list, if your sampling interval was 10 you could end up with all people from corner rooms or no people from corner rooms.

**Drawing a stratified random sample**

**Step 1.** Arrange the sampling frame in strata. For our example we will stratify by class standing, so our sampling frame now looks like this:

| Freshmen | Sophomores |
|---|---|
| 1 Campbell | 1 Broder |
| 2 Cowan | 2 Bufford |
| 3 Douglas | 3 Carnahan |
| 4 Fahey | 4 Dunne |
| 5 Fedder | 5 Foley |
| 6 Johnson | 6 Hedlund |
| 7 Ludwig | 7 Osgood |

| Freshmen | Sophomores |
|---|---|
| 8 Ryan | 8 Owens |
| 9 Taylor | 9 Suffolk |
| 10 Thompson | 10 Zimmerman |

| Juniors | Seniors |
|---|---|
| 1 Adamski | 1 Alderink |
| 2 Brown | 2 Baxter |
| 3 Dawes | 3 Bowen |
| 4 Grossman | 4 Cushman |
| 5 Harris | 5 Dennis |
| 6 Klaaren | 6 Nadeau |
| 7 Nowaczyk | 7 O'Keane |
| 8 Penzien | 8 Powers |
| 9 Sawyer | 9 Shaw |
| 10 Watterson | 10 Sonders |

In our example the strata are equal in size, but this need not be the case.

**Step 2.** Number each element within each stratum, as has been done in the foregoing list.

**Step 3.** Decide on the overall sample size you want to use. For our example we will draw a sample of 8.

**Step 4.** Draw an equal-sized sample from each stratum such that you obtain the desired overall sample size. For our example this would mean drawing 2 from each stratum.

**Step 5.** Follow the steps for drawing a random sample and repeat for each stratum. We used the previously determined starting point (column 8, line 22) in the Table of Random Numbers, but this time we used the last digit in each set of five. The numbers identified for each stratum were: Freshmen (4 and 1), Sophomores (6 and 4), Juniors (7 and 9), and Seniors (2 and 9).

**Step 6.** List the names corresponding to the selected numbers. Our stratified random sample would include Fahey, Campbell, Hedlund, Dunne, Nowaczyk, Sawyer, Baxter, and Shaw.

## SURVEY METHODS

- Three methods for obtaining survey data are mail surveys, personal interviews, and telephone interviews.

Selecting the sample is only one of several important decisions to make when conducting survey research. You also need to decide how you will obtain information from the respondents. There are three general methods: mail surveys, personal interviews, and telephone interviews. As was true of sampling techniques, there is no one best method for all circumstances; each survey method has its own advantages and disadvantages. The challenge you face is to select the method that best fits the problem you are studying.

## Mail Surveys

- Although mail surveys are quick and convenient, they may have the problem of response bias when individuals fail to complete and return the survey.
- Due to response bias, the final sample for the survey may not represent the population.

Mail surveys are used to distribute self-administered questionnaires that respondents fill out on their own. One advantage of mail surveys is that they usually can be completed relatively quickly. Because they are self-administered, mail surveys also avoid the problems due to interviewer bias (to be defined in the next section). Among the three survey methods, mail surveys are the best for dealing with highly personal or embarrassing topics, especially when anonymity of respondents is preserved.

Unfortunately, there are many disadvantages to mail surveys. Some of these disadvantages are less serious than others. For instance, because respondents will not be able to ask questions, the questionnaire must be completely self-explanatory. A second less serious disadvantage is that the researcher has little control over the order in which the respondent answers the questions. The order of questions may affect how respondents answer certain questions. A serious problem with mail surveys, however, is one of bias—namely, response bias.

**Response bias** is a threat to the representativeness of a sample because not all respondents complete the survey. There are many reasons why this occurs. For example, respondents with literacy problems, low educational background, or vision problems may not complete the questionnaire; therefore, people with these characteristics may not be represented well in the final sample of respondents. Often, people included in a sample are too busy or not interested enough in the study to return a completed questionnaire. Low response rate (i.e., failure to complete and return the survey) is the major factor leading to response bias in mail surveys.

Low response rates necessarily produce smaller samples than the researcher intended. Generally, however, the size of the sample is not the most serious concern. The problem is that low response rates typically suggest response bias. Because of response bias, a carefully selected probability sample may become a nonprobability sample—an accidental sample in which individuals' availability and willingness determine whether they complete the survey. For example, for a survey concerning introductory psychology courses, Zechmeister and

Zechmeister (2000) used *Peterson's Guide to Four-Year Colleges 1998* to randomly select 250 universities and colleges in the United States and then sent surveys to their psychology departments. The response rate was 56%—surveys were returned from 140 psychology departments.

Unless the return rate is 100%, the potential for response bias exists regardless of how carefully the initial sample was selected. The researcher must demonstrate the absence of response bias. That is, the researcher needs to show that the sample of respondents who returned the survey is representative of the population, and that no segment of the population is overrepresented or underrepresented. For example, in Zechmeister and Zechmeister's survey, information from *Peterson's Guide to Four-Year Colleges 1998* allowed them to demonstrate that colleges for which a survey was returned were not different from colleges for which a survey was not returned.

The typical return rate for mail surveys is only around 30%. There are things you can do, however, to increase the return rate. Return rates will be highest when the questionnaire has a "personal touch," when it requires a minimum of effort for the respondent, when the topic of the survey is of intrinsic interest to the respondent, and when the respondent identifies in some way with the organization or researcher sponsoring the survey. Warwick and Lininger (1975) describe a survey that met these requirements. About 100,000 members of women's religious congregations in the United States were surveyed. The study was sponsored and supported by the religious congregations, it was conducted by a visible and respected member of one of the religious orders, and the subject matter was of great interest to the respondents. The result was an almost saintly response rate.

**FIGURE 4.5**    The three general methods for conducting surveys (telephone interviews, personal interviews, and mail surveys) have both advantages and disadvantages.

## Personal Interviews

- Although costly, personal interviews allow researchers to gain more control over how the survey is administered.
- Interviewer bias occurs when survey responses are recorded inaccurately or when interviewers guide individuals' responses.

When personal interviews are used to collect survey data, respondents are usually contacted in their homes or in a shopping mall, and trained interviewers administer the questionnaire. The personal interview allows greater flexibility in asking questions than does the mail survey. In a personal interview the respondent can obtain clarification when questions are unclear and the trained interviewer can follow-up incomplete or ambiguous answers to open-ended questions. The interviewer controls the order of questions and can ensure that all respondents complete the questions in the same order. Traditionally, the response rate to personal interviews has been higher than for mail surveys.

The advantages of using personal interviews are impressive, but there are also a few disadvantages. Increasing fear of urban crime and an increasing number of households with no one home during the day have reduced the attractiveness of using personal interviews in the home. A significant disadvantage of conducting personal interviews is the cost. The use of trained interviewers is expensive in terms of both money and time. Perhaps the most critical disadvantage of personal interviews involves the potential for interviewer bias. The interviewer should be a neutral medium through which questions and answers are transmitted. **Interviewer bias** occurs when the interviewer records only selected portions of the respondents' answers or tries to adjust the wording of a question to "fit" the respondent. For example, suppose a respondent in a survey about television states, "The biggest problem with TV shows is too much violence." Interview bias would occur if the interviewer writes down "problem with TV is violence" instead of the respondent's full response. In a follow-up question, interview bias also would occur if the interviewer asked, "By violence do you mean murders, muggings, and rapes?" A more neutral probe would allow the respondent to describe what he or she means by asking, "Could you elaborate on what you mean by violence?"

The best protection against interviewer bias is to employ highly motivated, well-paid interviewers who are trained to follow question wording exactly, to record responses accurately, and to use follow-up questions judiciously. Interviewers should also be given a detailed list of instructions about how difficult or confusing situations are to be handled. Finally, interviewers should be closely supervised by the director of the survey project. The decision to use personal interviews is not one survey researchers take lightly.

A frequently used variation of the personal interview is the *focused interview* (also called *focus group*). Rather than interviewing a single person, the focused interview is done in a group setting, and the researcher tries to learn from the respondents the reasons for the attitudes or opinions they hold. Focused interviews are used extensively in market research to determine consumers' reactions to current or new products and services. Focused interviews are increasingly being used as part of the strategic planning process by civic organizations, colleges and universities, and churches. There is less emphasis in this approach on obtaining a quantitative summary of the views across all respondents. Instead, the goal is to obtain a qualitative description of the ideas that emerge from a guided group discussion.

## Telephone Interviews

- Despite some disadvantages, telephone interviews have become the method of choice for completing brief surveys.

The prohibitive cost of personal interviews and difficulties supervising interviewers have led survey researchers to turn to telephone interviews. Phone interviewing met with considerable criticism when it was first used because of serious limitations on the sampling frame of potential respondents. Many people had unlisted numbers, and the poor and those in rural areas were unlikely to have a phone. By 1979, however, more than 95% of all households had telephones, and households with unlisted numbers could be reached using random-digit dialing. Telephone interviewing also provides better access to dangerous neighborhoods, locked buildings, and respondents available only during evening hours (have you ever been asked to complete a telephone survey during dinner?). Interviews can be completed more quickly when contacts are made by phone, and interviewers can be better supervised when all interviews are conducted from one location.

The telephone survey, like the other two survey methods, is not without its drawbacks. A possible selection bias exists when respondents are limited to those who have telephones and the problem of interviewer bias remains. There is a limit to how long respondents are willing to stay on the phone, and individuals may respond differently when talking to a "faceless voice." Hippler and Schwarz (1987) suggest that people take less time to form judgments during phone interviews and they may have difficulty remembering the response options offered by the interviewer. Moreover, extensive use of phone solicitation for selling products and requesting contributions has led many people to be less willing to be interviewed. And many people who are working two jobs are rarely at home to answer the phone. In spite of these limitations and perhaps others you can think of, the telephone interview is the method of choice for nearly all brief surveys.

## SURVEY-RESEARCH DESIGNS

- The three types of survey design are the cross-sectional design, successive independent samples design, and the longitudinal design.

You are no doubt developing a sense that doing survey research, like doing all types of research, requires making a series of choices and decisions. For example, survey researchers decide who to survey when they choose a sampling plan, and they decide how to administer the survey when they choose a survey method. In this section we describe one of the most important decisions survey researchers must make—the choice of a research design. A survey-research design is the overall plan or structure used to conduct the entire study. There are three general types of survey-research designs: the cross-sectional design, the successive independent samples design, and the longitudinal design. As you probably already suspected, there is no all-purpose research design that meets every survey need; the choice of design must be tailored to the objectives of the study.

## Cross-Sectional Design

- In the cross-sectional design one or more samples are drawn from the population(s) at one point in time.
- Cross-sectional designs allow researchers to describe the characteristics of a population or the differences between two or more populations, and researchers can make predictions based on the correlational survey data.

One of the most commonly used survey-research designs is the cross-sectional design. In a **cross-sectional design,** one or more samples are drawn from the population *at one time.* Information collected from the sample(s) is used to describe the population at that point in time. A researcher who gave questionnaires to samples of 20-year-olds, 30-year-olds, and 40-year-olds, asking about solutions to the homeless problem in the United States, would be using a cross-sectional design. So, too, would a researcher who sampled male and female college students and asked their opinions about various career possibilities following graduation.

Goodman and her colleagues (1997) used a cross-sectional design in their nationwide study of mental disorders in 9- to 17-year-olds. The purpose of their study was to determine if youths who receive outpatient mental health services for their disorder differ in systematic ways from the larger population of children and adolescents with mental disorders. They questioned whether previous research findings observed for samples of youths who receive treatment ("clinical samples") may be generalized to describe youth who do not obtain treatment, particularly because only a small proportion of children and adolescents with mental disorders receive treatment.

To answer this question they examined data collected in a study sponsored by the National Institute of Mental Health (NIMH) on mental disorders in children and adolescents. A community-based sample of parent-youth pairs from Connecticut, Georgia, New York, and Puerto Rico completed surveys and were interviewed in their homes. A total of 1,285 parent-youth pairs participated. (Thus, you can see that even cross-sectional designs are not necessarily simple or quick.) The focus in a cross-sectional survey is description—describing the characteristics of a population or the differences among two or more populations. Goodman et al. made many observations to describe differences between youths with mental disorders who received outpatient mental health services and youths with mental disorders who did not receive treatment.

Of their sample, 747 (58%) of the youths had no mental disorder (within the past 6 months); however 25 (3%) of these had received mental health services. A total of 535 (42%) were diagnosed with some type of mental disorder based on the structured interview; of these, only 69 (13%) received outpatient mental health services. How did the 69 children and adolescents with mental disorders who received treatment differ from the 466 who did not? Goodman et al. looked at a number of variables, and found that the youths who received mental health services were more likely to be identified as non-Hispanic White relative to other ethnic groups, and were less likely to be prepubertal girls. They were also judged to be more impaired, less competent, and more likely to have two or more disorders. Their parents differed too. Parents of youths who received treatment were more educated but were less satisfied with their family life, did not monitor their children, and were more likely to use mental health services themselves. Based on these data, Goodman et al. concluded that research samples of youths who receive treatment are not representative of all youths who have a mental disorder. Thus, research based on clinical samples may have limited generalizability to the larger population of children and adolescents with mental disorders.

Cross-sectional designs are ideally suited for the descriptive and predictive goals of correlational research. Surveys are also used to assess changes in attitudes or behaviors over time and to determine the effect of some naturally occurring event, such as the passage of a law to raise the drinking age. For these purposes the cross-sectional design is not the method of choice. Rather, research designs are needed that systematically sample respondents over time. Two such designs are discussed in the next two sections.

## Successive Independent Samples Design

- In the successive independent samples design, different samples of respondents from the population complete the survey over a time period.
- The successive independent samples design allows researchers to study changes in a population over time.
- The successive independent samples design does not allow researchers to infer how individual respondents have changed over time.
- A problem with the successive independent samples design occurs when the samples drawn from the population are not equally representative of the population—that is, the samples are not comparable.

In the **successive independent samples design,** a series of cross-sectional surveys are conducted over time (successively). The samples are independent because a different sample of respondents completes the survey at each point in time. There are two key ingredients: (1) the same set of questions should be asked of each sample of respondents, and (2) the different samples should be drawn from the same population. In this way, responses can be compared over time. This design is most appropriate when the major goal of the study is to describe changes in the attitudes or behaviors of members of a population over time. We already mentioned one such successive independent samples design, that by Plous (1998), who surveyed different groups of animal rights activists who attended a national march in 1990 and 1996.

As another example, consider how a researcher might examine the changes in values and goals of male and female college freshmen over time. One way to do this would be to survey students at one point in time (e.g., 1990), then 10 years later (i.e., in 2000) ask *different samples* of college freshmen the same questions. In fact, such a study has been conducted since 1966, and every year some 350,000 full-time freshmen from a nationally representative sample of over 700 colleges and universities are surveyed (Astin, Parrott, Korn, & Sax, 1997). This research represents the largest and longest empirical study of higher education in the United States, with over 1,500 universities and over 9 million students participating during the 30-plus years of the study. Students are asked approximately 40 questions covering a number of topics, and although some changes have occurred in the survey over the 30 years, many questions have been asked each year, making this an excellent example of a successive independent samples design.

What can be said about changes in students' values and goals during this time period? Astin et al. (1997) reported the results for the portion of the survey in which students are asked to rate the importance of different values. Two values were of particular interest: "the importance of developing a meaningful philosophy of life" and "the importance of being very well off financially" (p. 12). Figure 4.6 displays the results for the percentage of students who endorsed these values as "essential" or "very important." In the late 1960s over 80% of students indicated that developing a meaningful philosophy of life was essential—in fact, this was the top value endorsed by students. In contrast, being well-off financially was essential to less than 45% of the students, and ranked fifth or sixth among students' values during the late 1960s. In 1996, the position of these values was reversed. Being well-off financially was the top value, with 74.1% of students endorsing this as essential. At sixth place in 1996 was developing a meaningful philosophy of life, with 42.1% of students endorsing this as an essential value. As can be seen in Figure 4.6, these contrasting trends in values began to shift in the early 1970s, crossed in 1977, and traded places in the late 1980s. Since then they have remained relatively unchanged. Using mediational analyses (described earlier), Astin et al. attributed some of these changes to increases in television viewing during the same time period, and suggested that the materialistic values celebrated in televisions shows such as *Dallas* and *Lifestyles of the Rich and Famous* promote materialistic values among viewers. Astin et al. concluded that "for many young people today, the making of money has become a kind of 'philosophy of life' in itself" (p. 14).

The successive independent samples design does have limitations. As way of illustration, the data presented in Table 4.2 represent the results of a successive independent samples design measuring people's trust in government in 1972 and 1978 (You may recall that Watergate occurred during this time period). Clearly, more Americans were cynical in 1978 than in 1972. How can we interpret

**FIGURE 4.6** Contrasting trends in values for college freshmen from 1966–1996.
*Source:* Figure 7 (p. 13), Astin et al. (1997).

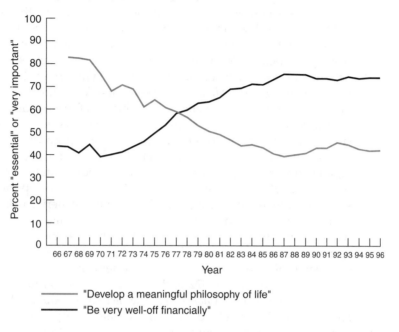

"Develop a meaningful philosophy of life"

"Be very well-off financially"

this finding? Consider the change from 36% to 52% in the "cynical" category from 1972 to 1978. We might be tempted to conclude 36% of the population still maintained their cynical views, and to that group we can add 16% of the population who changed their view to become more cynical by 1978. Who are these additional people? Well, we could also see that 38% of the population was trusting in 1972, but this dropped by 19% in 1978 (down to 19% "trusting" in 1978). Wouldn't it be easy to conclude that among the 19% of individuals who were no longer trusting, 16% changed their views to be cynical, 2% changed their views to "mixed" feelings, and 1% failed to answer? After all, that's how the numbers seem to add up!

**TABLE 4.2** TRUST IN GOVERNMENT, 1972–1978*

|  | 1972 | 1978 |
|---|---|---|
| Cynical | 36% | 52% |
| Mixed | 24% | 26% |
| Trusting | 38% | 19% |
| Not answered | 2% | 3% |
| Number of cases | (2,285) | (2,304) |

*Data taken from Campbell (1981), Appendix Table 8.

What we must remember, however, is that the people surveyed in 1978 were not the same people surveyed in 1972! The extent to which individuals change their views over time can be determined only by testing the *same* individuals on both occasions. We cannot determine in the successive independent samples design who has changed their views or by how much. The purpose of the successive independent samples design is to describe changes over time in the distribution of *population* characteristics (e.g., cynicism in the population), not to describe changes in *individual* respondents. Accordingly, the successive independent samples design is not very helpful in ferreting out the reasons for observed changes like those shown in Table 4.2. (As you will soon see, another survey design, the longitudinal design, is more appropriate in these situations.)

A second potential problem with the successive independent samples design arises when the successive samples are not representative of the same population. Imagine that the researchers who did the surveys reported in Table 4.2 had sampled affluent Americans in 1972 and poor Americans in 1978. Their comparisons of Americans' attitudes toward government over this time period would be meaningless. That is, they wouldn't be able to state that the population had become more cynical over time because it's possible that the degree of cynicism differs for affluent and poor Americans, which could also account for the difference between 1972 and 1978 results. The affluent and poor samples illustrate the problem of *noncomparable successive samples*. Changes in the population across time can be described accurately only when the successive independent samples represent the same population. Thus, it is important to assure that the successive independent samples are comparable. Although sophisticated statistical procedures exist to help unravel the problems associated with noncomparable successive samples, the best solution is to avoid the problem by carefully selecting successive samples that represent one population.

## Longitudinal Design

- In the longitudinal design, the same respondents are surveyed over time in order to examine changes in individual respondents.
- Because of the correlational nature of survey data, it is difficult to identify the causes of individuals' changes over time.
- As people drop out of the study over time (respondent mortality), the final sample may no longer be comparable to the original sample or represent the population.
- Individuals' survey responses may be influenced by the fact that they have completed the survey on more than one occasion.

The distinguishing characteristic of the **longitudinal design** is that the *same* sample of respondents is surveyed more than once. For example, a researcher interested in changes in college students' attitudes about their college experience might give a questionnaire to a sample of students when they begin their college studies, and then give *the same questionnaire to the same individuals* after they complete each year of college.

The longitudinal design has two important advantages. First, the investigator can determine the direction and extent of change for individual respondents. Also, because changes in individuals' responses are assessed, it's easier to investigate reasons for attitude or behavior changes. Second, the longitudinal design is the best survey design when a researcher wishes to assess the effect of some naturally occurring event. For example, by measuring people's attitudes before and after a national election, the researcher can assess the effect of this event. (For further discussion of assessing the effects of naturally occurring events, see Chapter 10.)

Heatherton, Mahamedi, Striepe, Field, and Keel (1997) used the longitudinal design to investigate changes in attitudes and behaviors related to eating during the transition from college to early adulthood. Although much is known about eating disorders in adolescents and college students, Heatherton and his colleagues were interested in learning how disordered eating may progress over time as individuals settle down, marry, establish careers, begin families, and importantly, gain a stronger sense of identity. These researchers hypothesized that as individuals change their roles and life goals during their 20s, an emphasis on physical appearance may decrease, which would decrease the prevalence of eating problems. To test their hypothesis they randomly selected a sample of 800 women and 400 men from a private northeastern college in 1982 to complete a survey about eating and dieting. Their response rate was 78% ($N = 625$) for women and 69% ($N = 276$) for men. In 1992, they contacted these same individuals (with the help of the alumni office) and surveyed them again about their eating attitudes and behaviors. The distinguishing characteristic of the longitudinal design is the fact that the same individuals were surveyed in each phase of the study.

As you may imagine, longitudinal designs involve a massive effort. The potential power of such an effort, however, is that researchers can examine changes within individuals over time. In Heatherton et al.'s (1997) study, results indicated different changes in eating and weight gain for women and men. Survey responses suggested that during the decade since college, women's eating disorder symptoms, chronic dieting, and body dissatisfaction decreased. However, despite these decreases, women's dissatisfaction with their body and their desire to lose weight remained high. Men, in contrast, rarely had problems with eating and weight during college. Ten years later, however, they had experienced weight gain (an average of almost 12 pounds, compared to women's average gain of 4 pounds). Men also reported increased dieting and symptoms of disordered eating on the 1992 survey, although this was still low relative to women.

Heatherton et al. (1997) made some interesting observations that are relevant to our understanding of longitudinal surveys. Heatherton et al. proposed that decreases in women's eating problems reflect their maturation during their 20s, changes in their roles, and being away from the college campus (and the pressures to be thin that occur on college campuses). It's possible, however, that other processes may account for changes within the individuals in the sample. Using a successive independent samples design in which *separate* samples of college students were surveyed in 1982 and 1992, Heatherton, Nichols, Mahamedi, and Keel (1995) noted that eating-disordered symptoms and body dissatisfaction also were lower for the college students in the 1992 sample relative to the 1982 sample. These findings suggest that decreases in eating-disordered attitudes and behaviors may reflect changes that are occurring at a societal level. Heatherton et al. (1997) suggested that increasing information about eating disorders presented in the media (e.g., accounts of the late Princess Diana's struggle with bulimia) may explain these decreases. As you can see, one potential problem with longitudinal survey designs is that it is difficult to pinpoint the exact *causes* for individuals' changes over time, as it is not clear whether the longitudinal changes reflect maturational processes within the individuals, or societal changes about eating attitudes and behaviors.[2]

Another potential problem with longitudinal designs is that it can be difficult to obtain a sample of respondents who will agree to participate in a longitudinal study, which more often than not means a long-term study. In many studies the respondents may be asked to complete several lengthy surveys at regular intervals over a number of years. People are often hesitant to make the commitment of time necessary to complete such an extensive project.

Even when the respondents do agree to participate, there can be further problems. You might think this design solves the problem of noncomparable samples (i.e., when samples are drawn from different populations) that can occur when successive independent samples are used. After all, in the longitudinal design the same people participate over and over, so of course the sample represents the same population each time. Unfortunately, successive samples in a longitudinal design are identical *only if* all members of the original sample participate throughout the study. This is not likely to be the case. For example, in the Heatherton et al. (1997) study there were 901 participants in the original 1982 sample. In 1992, only 724 (80%) of the original participants returned a useable survey. Unless all the respondents in the original sample complete all phases of a longitudinal design, there is a possible problem due to *respondent mortality* (sometimes literal, but most often figurative). Respondent mortality is probably the most serious disadvantage of the longitudinal design because as samples decrease over time, they are less likely to represent the original population from which the sample was drawn. It is usually possible, however, to determine whether the final sample is comparable to the original sample in a longitudinal design. The characteristics of nonrespondents in the follow-up phase(s) are known because they participated in the original sample. Therefore, we can look at their original responses to see how these individuals may differ from those who continued their participation.

---

[2]Heatherton et al. (1997) noted that because the decreases in problem eating were larger among individuals in the longitudinal survey than in the successive independent sample survey, maturational processes likely were operating to decrease individuals' problem eating over time, in addition to societal changes.

Paradoxically, problems can also arise in longitudinal designs because the same respondents are interviewed more than once. One possible problem is that respondents may strive heroically to be consistent across interviews. This can be particularly troublesome if the study is designed to assess changes in respondents' attitudes! Although their attitudes have actually changed, people may report their original attitudes in an effort to appear consistent (perhaps they know researchers value reliability). Another potential problem is that the initial interview may sensitize respondents to the issue under investigation. For example, consider a longitudinal design used to assess students' concern about crime on campus. Once the study starts, participants may pay more attention to crime reports than they normally would. You might recognize this as an illustration of reactive measurement—people behaving differently because they know they are participating in a study (see Chapter 3).

Rather than trying to be heroically consistent in their eating attitudes and behaviors over time, Heatherton et al. (1997) noted that their participants may have been reluctant to report that they were having the same problems with eating as when they were in college. Thus, the decreases the researchers observed in problem eating during the 10-year period may be due to the fact that "women who are approaching their thirties may be embarrassed to admit they are experiencing problems typically associated with adolescence" (p. 124). When survey respondents are asked to report their attitudes and behaviors, researchers must be alert to reasons why their respondents' reports may not correspond to their actual behavior.

## Correspondence between Reported and Actual Behavior

- Survey research involves reactive measurement because individuals are aware their responses are being recorded.
- Social desirability refers to pressure respondents sometimes feel to respond as they "should" believe rather than how they actually believe.
- Researchers can assess the accuracy of survey responses by comparing these results with archival data or behavioral observations.

Regardless of how carefully survey data are collected and analyzed, the value of these data depends on the truthfulness of the respondents' answers to the survey questions. Should we believe survey responses reflect people's true thoughts, opinions, feelings, and behavior? The question of the truthfulness of verbal reports has been debated extensively, and no clear-cut conclusion has emerged. Judd et al. (1991) note, however, that in everyday life we regularly accept the verbal reports of others as valid. If a friend tells you she enjoyed reading a certain novel, you may ask why, but you do not usually question whether the statement accurately reflects your friend's feelings. However, in everyday life there are some situations in which we *do* have reason to suspect the truthfulness of someone's statements. When shopping for a used car, for instance, we might not always want to trust the "sales pitch" we receive. Generally, however, we accept people's remarks at their face value unless we have reason to suspect otherwise. We apply the same standards to the information we obtain from survey responses.

By its very nature, survey research involves reactive measurement. Respondents not only know their responses are being recorded, but they may also suspect their responses may prompt some social, political, or commercial action. Hence, pressures are strong for people to respond as they "should" believe and not as they actually believe. The term often used to describe these pressures is **social desirability** (the term "politically correct" refers to similar pressures). For example, if respondents are asked whether they favor giving help to the needy, they may respond affirmatively because they believe this is the most socially acceptable attitude to have. As suggested in Chapter 3, the best protection against reactive measurement is to be aware of its existence.

Sometimes researchers can examine the accuracy of verbal reports directly by using archival data or unobtrusive measures (topics described more fully in Chapter 5). Judd et al. (1991) describe research by Parry and Crossley (1950) wherein responses obtained by experienced interviewers were subsequently compared with archival records for the same respondents kept by various agencies. Their comparisons revealed that 40% of respondents gave inaccurate reports to a question concerning contributions to United Fund (a charitable organization), 25% reported they had registered and voted in a recent election (but they did not), and 17% misrepresented their age. A pessimist might find these figures disturbingly high, but an optimist would note that a majority of respondents' reports were accurate even when social desirability pressures were high, as in the question pertaining to charitable contributions.

Researchers also assess the accuracy of verbal reports by directly observing respondents' behavior. The field experiment done by Latané and Darley (1970) illustrates the problem. They found that bystanders are more likely to help a victim when the bystander is alone than when other witnesses are present. Subsequently, a second group of participants was asked whether the presence of others would influence the likelihood they would help a victim. They uniformly said that it would not. Thus, individuals' verbal reports may not correspond well to behavior. A similar example comes from Milgram's (1974) series of experiments on people's obedience to authority. In one of his experiments, Milgram found that 63% of the men he tested (ages 20 to 50) complied fully with instructions to administer increasing levels of shock to a learner each time the learner made a mistake. The 63% who complied fully applied the highest level of shocks used in the experiment. Prior to doing this experiment Milgram asked a different group of people what they would do in this situation. Most said they would certainly stop before reaching the highest level of shock. Research findings such as these should make us extremely cautious of reaching conclusions about people's behavior solely on the basis of verbal reports. Of course, we should be equally cautious of reaching conclusions about what people think solely on the basis of direct observation of their behavior.

We want to make one final point about the usefulness of survey results. The process of doing a survey has much in common with the process of writing an essay. You often begin with a grand topic that must be focused so that it can be covered manageably. As you narrow your focus, you may sometimes have the feeling that your original topic has been lost or at least made trivial. No essay can capture all aspects of a given topic, nor can a 20-item or even 200-item questionnaire. Survey research, like the rest of the scientific enterprise, is built on faith that compiling reliable findings in a series of limited studies will eventually lead to increased understanding of the important broader issues we face.

## SUMMARY

Correlational research represents a general approach to research that focuses on assessing the covariation among naturally occurring variables. The goal of correlational research is to identify predictive relationships by using correlations or more sophisticated statistical techniques. The results of correlational research also have implications for decision making, as reflected in the appropriate use of actuarial prediction. The greatest limitation of correlational research is the problem of interpreting causal relationships.

Survey research illustrates the principles of correlational research and it provides an accurate and efficient means for describing people's thoughts, opinions, and feelings. Surveys differ in purpose and scope, but they generally involve sampling. Results obtained for a carefully selected sample are used to describe the entire population of interest. Surveys also involve the use of a predetermined set of questions, generally in the form of a questionnaire.

Sampling is a procedure whereby a specified number of elements are drawn from a sampling frame that represents an actual list of the possible elements in the population. Our ability to generalize from the sample to the population depends critically on the representativeness of the sample, the extent to which the sample has the same characteristics as the population. Representativeness is best achieved by using probability sampling rather than nonprobability sampling. In simple random sampling, the most common type of probability sampling, every element is equally likely to be included in the sample. Stratified random sampling is used when analysis of subsamples is of interest.

There are three general survey methods: mail surveys, personal interviews, and telephone interviews. Mail surveys avoid problems of interviewer bias and are especially well suited for examining personal or embarrassing topics. The problem of response bias is a serious limitation of mail surveys. Personal interviews and phone surveys usually have higher response rates and provide greater flexibility. The phone survey is the method of choice for most brief surveys.

Survey research is carried out according to an overall plan called a research design. There are three survey research designs: the cross-sectional design, the successive independent samples design, and the longitudinal design. Cross-sectional designs focus on describing the characteristics of a population or the differences between two or more populations at one point in time. Describing changes in attitudes or opinions over time requires the use of successive independent samples or longitudinal designs. The longitudinal design is generally preferred because it allows the researcher to assess changes for specific individuals and avoids the problem of noncomparable successive samples.

Survey results, like those of other verbal reports, can be accepted at face value unless there is reason to do otherwise, such as pressures on respondents to give socially desirable responses. People's behavior does not always conform to what they say they would do, so survey research will never replace direct observation. However, survey research does provide an excellent way to examine people's attitudes and opinions.

## KEY CONCEPTS

correlational research
correlation
correlation coefficient
margin of error
actuarial prediction
population
sampling frame
sample
element
representativeness
biased sample
selection bias
nonprobability sampling

probability sampling
accidental sampling
purposive sampling
simple random sampling
stratified random sampling
response bias
interviewer bias
cross-sectional design
successive independent
   samples design
longitudinal design
social desirability

## REVIEW QUESTIONS

1 Describe the major goal of correlational research, and briefly explain how correlational research is different from experimental research.

2 What two types of information do you gain by knowing the sign and the numerical value of a correlation coefficient?

3 Describe the difference between a mediating variable and a moderating variable.

4 Describe the Likert method for developing a scale.

5 Identify at least two factors beyond the margin of error of the sample that you would need to know to be sure that a survey's results are interpretable.

6 Describe briefly one way you could measure a test's reliability and one way you could measure a test's validity.

7 Explain how clinical and actuarial prediction could be used in deciding which students to admit to your college or university. What is the relative predictive accuracy of these two approaches?

8 What information is needed to address the ethical issue that arises when the sponsoring agency of a survey has a vested interest in how the results turn out?

9 What two characteristics do surveys have in common regardless of the purpose for which the survey has been done?

10 What is the greatest threat to the interpretability of the results of a survey when an accidental sample is used?

11 Explain the relationship between the homogeneity of the population from which a sample is to be drawn and the size of a sample needed to ensure representativeness.

12 What factors would you consider in deciding whether to use a mail survey, personal interviews, or telephone interviews for your survey research project?

13 What aspect of a survey research project is threatened by response bias and what factor contributes most to the potential for response bias?

14 What would you need to be assured of before interpreting group changes in attitudes over time that were found in using a successive independent samples design?

15 Which survey research design would you choose if you want to assess the direction and extent of change over time in the opinions of individual respondents?

16 How would you respond if someone told you that survey results were useless because people did not respond truthfully to questions on surveys?

## CHALLENGE QUESTIONS

1 Survey research is difficult to do well, and this can be especially the case when the topic is people's sexual attitudes and practices. For a book focusing in part on women's sexuality, an author mailed 100,000 questionnaires to women who belonged to a variety of women's groups in 43 states. These groups ranged from feminist organizations to church groups to garden clubs. The author's questionnaire included 127 essay questions. The author received responses from 4,500 women. Findings in this survey included that 70% of respondents married five years or more reported having extramarital affairs and that 95% of respondents felt emotionally harassed by the men they love.

  A The final sample in this study is large (4,500). Is this sufficient to assure the representativeness of the sample? If not, what survey research problem lessens the sample's representativeness?

  B Is it possible on the basis of your response to Part A of this question to argue that any conclusions drawn by the author from her data are incorrect? What could you do to determine whether the results were correct?

2 Dual-income couples now outnumber those with single incomes, and this has led researchers to examine how dual career demands affect relationships. A survey research study on this topic was described in *Psychology Today* (1988). The researchers found that among dual-career couples there was a positive correlation such that couples who spent greater amounts of time together found their relationship more satisfactory.

  A Presume that this finding is a reliable one. What two alternative explanations would you propose for why this correlation exists.

  B What moderator variables could you use to explore possible causal relationships underlying this correlation? Be sure to specify how you think the size or direction of the original correlation will change as you change the values of the moderator variable.

3 Two student researchers have been asked to do a survey to determine the attitudes of other students toward fraternities and sororities on campus. There are 2,000 students in the school. About 25% of the students belong to the Greek organizations and 75% do not. The two student researchers agree that they should use a cross-sectional

design for their study. But they disagree about what sampling plan is best for the study. One researcher thinks they should draw a stratified random sample of 200 students: 100 from among those students who belong to Greek organizations and 100 from among the independent students. The second researcher thinks they should draw one simple random sample of 100 students from the campus as a whole. Comment critically on these two sampling plans. Finally, develop your own sampling plan if you decide that neither of the ones proposed so far is optimal.

4   A task force has been established at a small liberal arts college under the direction of the Dean of Students to examine the quality of students' experiences on their campus. The task force decides to do a survey to determine students' knowledge of and their perceptions of the fairness of the judicial system used to enforce the rules in the living units on campus. The questionnaire for the survey included personal questions asking students to describe their own experiences when they had violated college policies or when they had known other students who had violated college policies. A stratified random sample was drawn from the Registrar's list of full-time students living on and off campus. The sample size was 400 on a campus with 2,000 full-time students. Questionnaires were returned by 160 students for a response rate of 40%. One important finding from the survey was that over a third of the respondents rated the judicial system as unfair. The task force met to decide whether to include the survey findings such as this one in its final report to the Dean of Students.

A   Was the initial sample of 400 students likely to be representative of the population of 2,000 full-time students? Why or why not?

B   Identify a potential survey research problem that could be present in this study that would lead the task force to be concerned that the final sample was not representative of the population of 2,000 students.

C   Using only the evidence that the response rate for the survey was 40% the task force concluded that the final sample was not representative of the population of students. They further decided that the ratings of the judicial system as unfair by more than a third of the students was an incorrect overestimate. Do you agree that the finding represents an incorrect estimate? Why or why not?

D   While the task force was meeting to discuss their final report, one member of the task force expressed the opinion that students' responses were unlikely to have been truthful and so the results of the survey were useless and should not be reported at all. The director of the task force calls on you to respond to this statement. What would you say?

## Answer to Challenge Question 1

A   In general, larger sample sizes do make it more likely that the sample will be representative. The problem in this study is that the final sample (though large) represents a low response rate from the original sample of 100,000 (4.5%). The low response rate and the topic of the survey make it likely that a response bias is present in this survey such that the sample of 4,500 women cannot be considered representative.

B   The likely problem of response bias does not make it possible to argue that the conclusions drawn by the author are incorrect. Neither can the author argue on the basis of this sample that the conclusions are correct. We simply cannot know based on this evidence whether the conclusions are correct or incorrect. There is at least one good way to determine if the results of this survey were correct. You would need to obtain from the literature the results of one or more surveys on women's sexual attitudes and practices. It would be essential that these other surveys had used representative samples of women. Then, you would compare the results of this survey with those of the other surveys. Only if the results of the present survey corresponded to those of the surveys with the representative samples would we consider the results of the present survey correct. Of course, you could also carry out your own survey, one that avoids the problems that are present in this survey, and determine whether your results are similar to those of this author-researcher!

## PEARSON PRODUCT-MOMENT CORRELATION COEFFICIENT *r*

The degree of relationship between two variables for the same sample of subjects is determined by calculating a correlation coefficient. If the two measures both represent at least an interval scale of measurement (see Chapter 3), then the Pearson Product-Moment Correlation Coefficient *r* is used. The computational formula for the Pearson *r* is as follows:

$$ r = \frac{\Sigma XY - \dfrac{(\Sigma X)(\Sigma Y)}{n}}{\sqrt{\left(\Sigma X^2 - \dfrac{(\Sigma X)^2}{n}\right)\left(\Sigma Y^2 - \dfrac{(\Sigma Y)^2}{n}\right)}} $$

where
X = raw scores for the first variable,
Y = raw scores for the second variable,
$\Sigma$ = sum of scores, and
n = number of pairs of scores.

# Unobtrusive Measures of Behavior

## OVERVIEW

Thus far, we have emphasized how the behavioral scientist learns about behavior through some form of direct observation (Chapter 3) or from data obtained through survey research (Chapter 4). In this chapter we consider some alternatives to these major approaches to studying behavior. The alternatives, called **unobtrusive measures,** tell us about behavior indirectly. The researcher obtains data unobtrusively, frequently with the individuals being studied not present during the investigation. Although these alternative methods are often important in themselves, they also frequently provide a means of confirming the validity of conclusions reached on the basis of direct observation or surveys. Thus, unobtrusive measures can make important contributions to the multimethod approach to research.

One type of unobtrusive measure is the examination of **physical traces** produced by individuals' behavior. Consider, for example, the possibility that Latin Americans differ from North Americans in their concern for punctuality. Possible cultural differences in the importance of punctuality could be investigated by surveying people in both North American and Latin American countries as to how they feel about concerts or sporting events that begin later than the scheduled starting time. However, an alternative, unobtrusive, method would be to examine clocks in cities of North America and South America. It seems reasonable to assume that people's concern for time will be reflected in how accurately they set their clocks. In fact, researchers found that public clocks (those located in banks) in a Brazilian city were less accurate than those in a similar-sized city in the United States (Levine, West, & Reis, 1980). Although there may be alternative explanations for this finding, differences in this physical-trace measure support the notion that cultural differences in concern for being on time do exist. You may remember from the discussion in Chapter 1 that Levine (1990) also used accuracy of public clocks to help define the "pace of life" of cities and countries around the world. Direct observation revealed that the walking speed of a country's citizens correlated positively with the accuracy of the country's public clocks.

Archives constitute another important unobtrusive source of information about behavior. **Archival data** are obtained by inspecting the records and documents produced by society, as well as by analyzing reports in the media. For example, researchers have claimed that analyses of mortality data reveal a lower than expected frequency of deaths before important events, such as birthdays and religious holidays, and a higher than expected frequency of deaths after these important events. The general procedure for investigating the relationship between death and important occasions is to examine archival data revealing the death dates of individuals in relation to certain important events (see, for example, Schulz & Bazerman, 1980). Three major positive events have been examined by researchers: birthdays, national elections, and religious holidays. For instance, one of the early studies to offer data supporting a "death-dip hypothesis" used birth dates and death dates of persons listed in the book *Four*

*Hundred Notable Americans* (Schulz & Bazerman, 1980). Based on chance alone, one would expect that an individual's death is equally likely in any of the 12 months. However, the number of deaths during the month prior to the month of an individual's birth was found to be lower than the death rate for other months, thus, supporting the death-dip hypothesis. According to Schulz and Bazerman, a general explanation for this type of finding is that people somehow prolong their lives or delay death until a special event, such as a birthday, has been experienced. Exactly how one might do this is not particularly clear. One suggestion is that looking forward to a positive event creates a state of positive anticipation that precipitates beneficial neurochemical changes. Another possible explanation is that elderly persons are more likely to follow their health and medical regimens closely as an important date nears, so as to reduce the chances of dying before the event arrives.

In this chapter we present the rationale for using physical traces and archival data. Particular kinds of physical traces are identified and examples of their use in psychological studies are offered. Types of archives and the kinds of data that can be drawn from archival sources are also reviewed. Several important advantages of the use of physical traces or archival data are highlighted. There are some limitations and problems with these unobtrusive measures, and they, too, are discussed.

## PHYSICAL TRACES

### Rationale

- Unobtrusive measures of behavior such as physical traces do not have the problem of reactivity, in which people change their behavior because they know they are being observed.
- The investigation of physical traces represents a valuable component of the multimethod approach to hypothesis testing.

As everyone who has read a few detective stories knows, examining physical evidence of past behavior can provide important clues to the characteristics (or even identity) of individuals, as well as information about the conditions under which an event occurred. The size of footprints in the ground says something about the size and age of the person who stepped there. The distance between footprints can indicate whether the person was walking or running, and so on. As we have seen, physical evidence (in the form of clock settings) can be of value to behavioral scientists. Physical traces (as well as archival data discussed later in this chapter) are especially valuable because they provide nonreactive measures of behavior (Webb et al., 1981).

You will recall from Chapter 3 that a behavioral measure is reactive when participants' awareness of an observer affects the measurement process. This is often the case when direct observations are made, and it is nearly always the case when surveys are conducted. Aware that their responses are being recorded, participants may behave in a way that does not correspond to their normal behavior.

Survey data are particularly susceptible to reactive effects, because respondents may give answers that they feel the researcher wants to hear or may answer in a way that makes them (the respondents) look good. For instance, social scientists are well aware that responses to surveys asking about degree of political activity, such as past voting behavior, typically overestimate this activity (e.g., Endersby & Towle, 1996).

Physical-trace measures are unobtrusive because they are obtained indirectly, in the absence of the subject; thus, they are valuable alternatives to the reactive measures obtained via direct observation or surveys. Although a physical-trace measure might be the only measure of behavior in some studies, physical traces are more commonly used in combination with other measures. As we have emphasized previously, a research study can be strengthened considerably by including several different measures of behavior. A **multimethod approach** to hypothesis testing is recommended because it reduces the likelihood that research findings are due to some artifact of a single measurement process (Webb et al., 1981). There are few (if any) perfect measures in the social sciences. Therefore, the results of a study must be carefully scrutinized to determine whether some characteristic of the measurement instrument (such as its reactivity) has contributed to the results. Even then, it is possible that some artifact has been overlooked. *The most persuasive argument supporting the validity of a particular research hypothesis is one based on evidence obtained by applying a combination of measures.*

Researchers investigating cultural differences in time perception used such a multimethod approach. They surveyed individuals living in Latin America and in the United States to find out how frequently their subjects were late for appointments and to discover their attitudes toward being late (Levine et al., 1980). Citizens of Brazil reported themselves more often late for appointments and expressed less regret at being late than did citizens of the United States. However, a bias in these responses could be present if people described themselves in a way that fit their cultural "image," rather than as they actually behaved. As already noted, however, the researchers also found that public clocks were less accurate in Brazil than in the United States. Further, the researchers observed that watches worn by people in the United States deviated less from the correct time than watches worn by people in Brazil. The data obtained by examining public clocks and the watches worn by citizens of each country tended to confirm the validity of the survey responses and, in combination with the survey results, provided impressive evidence for the research hypothesis.

## Types of Physical Traces

- Two categories of physical traces are "use traces" and "products."
- Use traces reflect the physical evidence of use (or nonuse) of items, and can be measured in terms of accretion or erosion and in terms of natural or controlled use.
- By examining the products people own or the products produced by a culture, researchers test hypotheses about attitudes and preferences.

Physical traces are the remnants, fragments, and products of past behavior. Two broad categories of physical traces are "use traces" and "products." *Use traces* are what the label implies—the physical evidence that results from use (or nonuse) of an item. Clock settings are an example of a physical-use trace. So are the remains of cigarettes in ashtrays and the marks made in textbooks. *Products* are the creations, constructions, or other artifacts of earlier behavior. Anthropologists are often interested in the surviving products of ancient cultures. By examining the types of vessels, paintings, and other artifacts that remain, the anthropologist can often describe precisely the pattern of behavior exhibited in a setting that is thousands of years old. Psychologists may also examine physical products in order to describe behavior or to test hypotheses. Psychologists who study animal behavior, for instance, may learn about the behavior of different species by examining the types of nests that are constructed. Newhagen and Ancell (1995) examined bumper stickers used by Black and White residents of a Washington, DC, suburb to investigate racial differences in degree of emotional expressiveness.

Use Traces    An examination of physical evidence provides measures of both accretion and erosion (Webb et al., 1981). *Accretion measures* are based on the accumulation of material. Measuring the amount of litter found on a college campus, for example, would be taking an accretion measure. *Erosion measures* are obtained when the physical evidence is the result of selective wear and tear. The degree to which a young child's dolls show signs of wear is an erosion measure that might indicate which dolls the child likes best. The distinction between accretion measures and erosion measures is not always so obvious. Settings of clocks, for instance, resist easy classification. Nevertheless, classifying physical-use traces in terms of accretion or erosion is often a meaningful description of physical traces, and the distinction calls our attention to two important dimensions of use traces.

Physical-use traces are also classified as either natural or controlled (planned). *Natural* use traces are produced without any intervention by the investigator. Their appearance is the result of naturally occurring events. *Controlled,* or planned, measures result to some degree from the intervention or manipulation of an investigator. A study by Friedman and Wilson (1975) illustrates the distinction between these two types of measures.

The investigators employed both controlled and natural accretion measures to investigate college students' use of textbooks. They affixed tiny glue seals between adjacent pages of textbooks before the students purchased the books for a course. At the end of the semester the investigators obtained the books from the students and recorded how many seals in the textbooks had been broken and where the broken seals were located. Because the researchers controlled the presence of glue seals in the books, this constituted a controlled (accretion) measure. It may be judged to be an accretion measure in that the researchers recorded the accumulation of broken seals (although one might reasonably argue that "erosion" was being measured). The investigators also analyzed the frequency and nature of underlining by students in the textbooks, something, of course, that is typically associated with textbook use. This constituted a natural accretion measure. Analysis of these physical-use measures indicated that students more often read (and presumably studied) the chapters that appeared early in the book than those appearing later in the book.

Table 5.1 contains examples of physical-use traces and the variables being measured. These measures either were used as part of an actual scientific study or represent suggestions by researchers of possible novel and nonreactive measures of behavior (see Webb et al., 1981). The examples given in Table 5.1 are organized according to whether they are accretion or erosion measures and whether their

**TABLE 5.1**   EXAMPLES OF PHYSICAL-USE TRACES AND VARIABLES BEING MEASURED*

| Trace | Variable |
| --- | --- |
| Natural accretion | |
| Inscriptions (graffiti) on walls of public rest rooms | Sexual preoccupation |
| Radio dial settings | Popularity of radio stations |
| Fingerprints or smudges on pages of books | Book usage |
| Liquor bottles in trash cans | Alcohol consumption of households |
| Odometer readings in cars | Conservation of gasoline |
| Litter | Effectiveness of antilitter posters |
| Dust on books | Frequency or recency of use |
| Garbage | Food use and lifestyle |
| Locked/unlocked cars | Concern for property |
| Lengths of cigarette butts | Cultural differences in death rate due to cancer |
| Controlled accretion | |
| Glue seals broken (seals inserted prior to distribution) | Index of specific pages read |
| Nose prints on windows of museum exhibit (windows wiped clean each night) | Popularity (frequency) and age (height of points) of viewers |
| Natural erosion | |
| Wear on floor or steps | Amount of foot traffic |
| Wear on library books | Frequency of use |
| Food consumed | Eating behavior |
| Spots (produced by rubbing) on statues or religious objects | Level of religious belief |
| Controlled erosion | |
| Wear on children's shoes (measured at two points in time) | Activity level of children |
| Removal of "tear-away" tags on ads or notices | Interest in notice |
| Wear on mats or other floor coverings placed in specific areas | Amount of foot traffic |
| Change in statues or objects coated with substances sensitive to touching | Superstitious behavior |

*From Webb et al. (1981).

use is natural or controlled. As you examine the contents of Table 5.1, can you think of other possible physical traces that could serve as measures of the variables listed?

Products    Physical products have been examined less frequently in psychological studies than have physical-use traces. Nevertheless, this category of physical traces has been used in interesting and meaningful ways to test hypotheses about behavior. A particularly good example of the use of physical products is found in a study by Coren and Porac (1977). They investigated the extent of human right-handedness in various cultures since ancient times. To determine manual preference, they examined more than 12,000 works of art, including paintings, sculpture, and other products that spanned more than 50 centuries of human endeavor. The researchers recorded instances of unambiguous tool or weapon use depicted in the artworks. They looked for any differential trend in the depiction of right- or left-handers in different cultures and at different times in human history. No differences were evident. Rather, across many cultures and in every epoch, 93% of the artworks examined showed persons using their right hand. The results provide evidence for a physiological rather than a sociocultural theory of handedness.

Brandt (1972) points out that the products that people own provide important clues to their lifestyle and behavior patterns. What personality differences, for instance, are reflected in the purchase of different models of cars or in the extras and options that are ordered with a car? Besides serving as a measure of social status or personality, the products a person owns can be used to assess the validity of certain kinds of verbal reports. Are individuals' statements about their attitude toward energy conservation, for instance, related to the kinds of products they own and use?

Consider the American driving public's interest in bumper stickers. You probably have seen stickers that state "Guns Don't Kill, People Do," or "Stop Abortion." As Newhagen and Ancell (1995) point out, bumper stickers are unique in that they "allow for the expression of highly personal opinions about strongly held views to a large audience without any real commitment to interact with them" (p. 313). And, unlike graffiti, which is often illegal and socially undesirable, bumper stickers permit an acceptable outlet for the expression of public emotion. When Newhagen and Ancell analyzed bumper sticker messages of suburban Blacks and Whites in the Washington, DC, area, they found overall frequency of bumper sticker usage was highest in low-income areas regardless of race. High-income White neighborhoods showed most evidence of positive and intense stickers, whereas bumper stickers were least frequently observed and, when they were, the messages were the most subdued, in high-income Black neighborhoods. The researchers suggested that the results illustrate examples of discretely different forms of public expression of emotion as a function of race and income. This conclusion seems to fit with Endersby and Towle's (1996) characterization of bumper stickers as reflecting "a form of identification and solidarity with a group sharing common beliefs" (p. 307).

## Problems and Limitations

- Before concluding that a measure of physical traces is a valid indicator of behavior or attitudes, a researcher should make sure no sources of bias exist.
- Validity of physical-trace measures can be ascertained by examining converging evidence.

Physical measures offer a researcher valuable and sometimes novel means to study behavior, and the measures available are limited only by the ingenuity of the investigator. However, the validity of physical traces must be carefully examined and verified through independent sources of evidence. Bias can be introduced in the way physical-use traces are laid down and in the manner in which traces survive over time. Does a well-worn path to the right indicate people's interest in objects in that direction or simply a natural human tendency to turn right? Is the setting of clocks a good measure of people's regard for punctuality, or do inaccurate clock settings indicate poor artisanship, inadequate maintenance, or irregular electrical service? To what extent is frequency of bumper sticker usage affected by the recent success of local sports teams?

Problems associated with the analysis of physical traces are illustrated in a classic study of honesty carried out using the "lost-letter technique" (see Merritt & Fowler, 1948). We can consider the method as controlled accretion. The investigators "accidentally" dropped postcards and envelopes at various locations in cities of the East and Midwest. Two types of envelopes were "lost." One contained a written message, and the other contained a lead slug the size of a 50-cent

**FIGURE 5.1**   The classic "lost-letter technique" illustrates some of the problems with the analysis of physical traces (see text).

piece. All the letters were addressed and bore proper postage, but no return address was shown. Although 85% of the empty envelopes were returned, only 54% of the envelopes with a slug found their way to a mailbox. Further, more than 10% of the envelopes with a slug were returned after having been opened.

Before the researchers could conclude that the return rates represented a valid measure of the public's honesty (or dishonesty), several possible biases associated with this physical trace had to be considered. Postcards, for instance, were less likely than sealed envelopes to be returned, but the fact that postcards may be more easily disturbed by natural conditions than are larger envelopes may have contributed to this difference. On the other hand, envelopes with a slug are heavier and less likely to be blown away—and these were still less likely to be returned. Letters that were dropped in certain locations (e.g., where many children are present) or at certain times of the day (e.g., just before nightfall) are also likely not to be returned for reasons other than the public's dishonesty or apathy.

Some of these possible biases associated with the lost-letter technique were avoided by the methods of dispersal used by the researchers, whereas others were checked via direct observation of a letter's fate. Observation of a sample of dropped letters revealed that a letter was picked up 90% of the time by the first person who saw it, suggesting that dropped letters were soon in the hands of unknowing participants.

In an interesting twist on the lost-letter technique, Stern and Faber (1997) used the Internet to produce a "lost e-mail" technique. In one study the researchers investigated people's attitudes toward the 1996 presidential candidate, Ross Perot, by sending messages to randomly selected e-mail addresses across the country. They sent two different versions of what was supposed to look like a misdirected e-mail message. Both messages went to "Steve" and asked for help with fund raising; however, one version mentioned that the fund raising was for Ross Perot. Although return rates did not differ between the two versions, the researchers analyzed the contents of messages included with the returned e-mail. A number of people returning the Ross Perot message went out of their way to say they were voting for someone else, while none said they planned to vote for him. That informed consent is not part of this procedure, and that returned e-mail typically includes the sender's e-mail address, making an anonymous response impossible, introduces ethical concerns. What do you think? How would you address these ethical concerns?

Whenever possible, supplementary evidence for the validity of physical traces should be obtained (see Webb et al., 1981). Alternative hypotheses for changes in physical traces must be considered, and data must be collected that allow different interpretations to be dismissed. Care must also be taken when comparing results across studies to make sure that measures are defined similarly. When Newhagen and Ancell (1995) tallied bumper stickers, they included only those literally found on car bumpers; Endersby and Towle (1996) operationally defined bumper stickers as any message visible from the rear of the vehicle, which included rear window decals. Different operational definitions of a concept can easily lead to different results.

# ARCHIVAL DATA

## Rationale

- Archival data comprise the records or documents of the activities of individuals, groups, institutions, and governments.
- Archival data are used to test hypotheses as part of the multimethod approach, to establish the external validity of laboratory findings, and to assess the effects of natural treatments.
- Archival data represent a rich, plentiful source of observations for psychological studies.

When we were born, a record was made of our birth. Information on the birth record probably included the city and state in which we were born, the date and time of our birth, our parents' names, and our name. When we die, another record will be made. It will include such details as probable cause of death, date and time of death, and our age. In between these two events, innumerable records are made of our behavior. Physicians record visits. Hospitals keep a record of when we enter and when we leave. Schools record our grades and extracurricular activities. Businesses may record the number of times we are late or how often we fail to show up for work. Newspapers describe notable successes and failures. Local governments record when we get married and to whom, as well as when we buy a house and how much it costs. The federal government records, among other things, what we pay in income taxes.

Records are kept not only of individuals but also of countries, institutions, cities, and businesses. The gross national product of a country, its major exports and imports, the size of its defense budget, the distribution of its population, and the number of television sets owned by its populace are but a few of the facts that are frequently recorded. How much profit a company makes is part of its report to stockholders. Voting behaviors of state and federal legislators are recorded, as is the amount of money a city spends on social services. Analysis and interpretation of local and world events flood the media. The contents of the media and of documents and books (published and unpublished) are a source of information about current fads and prejudices, changing patterns of belief, and the ideas of important (and not so important) members of society.

*Archives* are records or documents recounting the activities of individuals or of institutions, governments, and other groups. As measures of behavior, archival data share some of the same advantages as physical traces. Archival measures are nonreactive and therefore provide an alternative to data collection via surveys. Like physical-trace measures, archival data can be used to check the validity of other measures as part of a multimethod approach to hypothesis testing. A nice illustration of the use of archival data in the context of a multimethod approach to hypothesis testing is Frank and Gilovich's (1988) investigation of the strong cultural association that exists between the color black and "badness," or evil.

As Frank and Gilovich point out, in vintage American Western movies you could always tell the good guys from the bad guys. The good guys, of course, wore white hats and the bad guys wore black hats. There is a strong cultural association between black and badness. We speak of people being "blackballed," "blacklisted," "blackmailed," and a person's reputation's being "blackened." When terrible things happen it is a "black day." Black is seen in many cultures as the color of death. The good and bad sides of human nature are also contrasted using black-and-white images, as was illustrated by the characters of the famous *Star Wars* movies. Viewers of these classic films likely will remember the confrontation between the villain, Darth Vader (dressed completely in black), and the young hero, Luke Skywalker (dressed in white or light colors). Vader, unfortunately, had "gone over" to the dark side.

Frank and Gilovich wanted to find out if this strong cultural association between black and evil would affect the way people behave. Specifically, they asked whether professional sports teams that wear black uniforms are more aggressive than those that wear nonblack uniforms. Using archival data obtained from the central offices of the National Football League (NFL) and the National Hockey League (NHL), Frank and Gilovich analyzed penalty records of each major professional team in these sports between 1970 and 1986. Yards penalized were analyzed in the NFL, and minutes that a player was assigned to the penalty box were calculated in the NHL. These particular measures were deemed more appropriate given the study's hypothesis than was number of infractions. Penalties for overaggressiveness are generally more severe (in yards or minutes) than are those for simple rule violations. The operational definition of a "black uniform" was that the colored version of the team's uniform (the one used typically for away games in the NHL and for home games in the NFL) was more than 50% black. (An exception was made for the Chicago Bears of the NFL, who wear dark-blue uniforms but whose uniforms many people mistakenly remember as black; thus, they were included among the black-uniform teams.) According to the authors' hypothesis, teams wearing black should be penalized more than would be expected simply by chance. And they were. Thus, teams with black uniforms, such as Oakland, Chicago, and Cincinnati in the NFL, and Philadelphia, Pittsburgh, and Vancouver in the NHL, were reliably more aggressive than were many other teams.

What psychological processes might account for these effects? Frank and Gilovich suggest that both social-perception and self-perception processes are at work. They argue that others (specifically, referees) "see" players in black as more aggressive than players not wearing black (and therefore award more penalties to players in black), and that players themselves behave more aggressively when they put on black uniforms. As part of their multimethod approach to this issue, they provided support for these explanations by collecting data from laboratory experiments. In one experiment, both college students and referees watched staged football games between teams wearing black or white uniforms and rated their aggressiveness. In a second study, students donned either black or white uniforms in anticipation of an athletic competition before choosing a game from a list of aggressive and nonaggressive games. In the first experiment, both referees and college students were more likely to rate a team wearing black as aggressive. The second experiment showed that students who donned black uniforms chose more aggressive games. By combining data obtained from archival analyses and laboratory experiments, the investigators provide an unusually strong case for their explanations of this interesting cultural phenomenon.

An examination of archival information may also provide a way to test the external validity of laboratory findings. Lau and Russell (1980) analyzed the contents of the sports pages in eight daily newspapers in order to test whether results obtained from laboratory-based experiments investigating *causal attributions* (the reasons people give for a certain outcome, or the cause they attribute the outcome to) were relevant to "real-world" settings. A major finding from laboratory studies of attributions is that people tend to make internal attributions (assuming that the outcome is due to some characteristic within themselves) for success and to make external attributions (assuming that the outcome is due to something beyond their control) for failure. Lau and Russell's analysis of explanations given by sportswriters or team members for the outcome of baseball and football games supported this conclusion. Specifically, they identified 594 explanations for success and failure involving 33 major sporting events. From the perspective of the winning team, 75% of the attributions were internal, whereas only 55% of the attributions of the losing team were internal. Support for this laboratory-based attribution theory also was obtained by analyzing letters and replies published in two widely syndicated newspaper advice columns: "Ann Landers" and "Dear Abby" (see Fischer, Schoeneman, & Rubanowitz, 1987; Schoeneman & Rubanowitz, 1985).

Other reasons for using archival data are to test hypotheses about past behavior and to assess the effect of a natural treatment. For example, given that sports teams typically play "at home" and "away" over the course of a season, researchers repeatedly ask how this difference affects a team's performance. Archival records play a central role in studies of the "home advantage" in sports competitions (see, for example, Courneya & Carron, 1992). The *home advantage* refers to the fact that in many sports competitions a team wins consistently more games played at home than it does games played away. An interesting and somewhat counterintuitive finding (because it goes against the well-documented home advantage), is that teams playing at home do not necessarily perform well in key games, such as those that decide a championship (Baumeister, 1995; Baumeister & Steinhilber, 1984). The "home choke" phenomenon, nevertheless, has not always found support through archival analyses (Schlenker, Phillips, Boniecki, & Schlenker, 1995a, 1995b).

*Natural treatments* are naturally occurring events that have significant impact on society at large or on particular members. Because it is not always possible to anticipate these events, the investigator who wishes to assess their impact must be prepared to use a variety of behavioral measures, including archival data. Assassinations of world leaders, drastic changes in the stock market, and the passage of new laws are examples of the kinds of events that may have important effects on behavior and that might be investigated using archival data.

**FIGURE 5.2**   Archival records permit psychologists to study the "home advantage" in sports competitions.

So, too, are the naturally occurring events of a natural life history, such as death or divorce of parents, a chronic illness, or marital difficulties.

In 1921, Lewis Terman began a longitudinal study of intelligence by recruiting more than 1,500 above average children in the San Francisco and Los Angeles schools (see Friedman et al., 1995; also Terman & Oden, 1947). The children, 856 boys and 672 girls, were preadolescents at the time and have been followed at 5- to 10-year intervals since that time. The archival records associated with Terman's study of gifted children, and interviews with surviving members of this group, enabled investigators to study "psychosocial and behavioral predictors of longevity" (Friedman et al., 1995). One particular focus is the effect of parental divorce on individual behavior and longevity. Many studies in the psychology literature indicate that children experiencing parental divorce or conflict have more conduct and behavioral problems, greater academic difficulties, and poorer health than children whose parents did not divorce (see Tucker et al., 1997). Researchers used the archival records from Terman's study to examine the effect of parental divorce on mortality rates. The data are clear, at least in this homogeneous group of very bright (IQs greater than 135), nearly all White, mostly middle-class individuals: Parental divorce leads to premature death. Men from divorced homes were predicted to die at age 76, whereas those from intact homes were predicted to die at age 80; for women the corresponding predicted ages of death were 82 and 86 (Friedman et al., 1995). Reasons for this effect are complex and not completely understood. For example, children from divorced homes were also more likely to be divorced themselves, men were more likely to die from physical injuries, and women from divorced homes smoke more (Tucker et al., 1997). Results of these archival analyses indicate, nevertheless, that "parental divorce sets off a negative chain of events, which contribute to a higher mortality risk among individuals from divorced homes" (Tucker et al., 1997, p. 389).

Another reason for considering archival data as a behavioral measure is simply because archival data are so plentiful. We noted earlier the extensive records that society keeps on individuals, groups, and institutions. Through careful analysis of archival information, the industrious researcher can seek evidence to support numerous hypotheses. There are practical advantages as well. Archival data represent data that have already been collected; at times, initial summary descriptions may also be provided in archival records. Thus, an extensive data-collection stage may be circumvented. Because archival information is frequently part of the public record and is usually reported in a manner that does not identify individuals, ethical concerns are less worrisome. One goal of this chapter is to alert you to the possible rich rewards of analyzing archival data in the context of psychological studies of behavior. As more and more archival sources become available through the Internet, researchers will find it even easier to examine behavior in this way.

## Types of Archival Data

- Types of archival data include running records, news media, and other types of records; archival data can consist of public or private documents.

The sheer diversity and extent of archival sources make their classification rather arbitrary. Records that are continuously kept and updated are frequently referred to as *running records*. Tax records and records of various government agencies are good examples, as are the myriad records of sports teams. Because of their continuous nature, running records are particularly useful in longitudinal studies or in the documentation of trends. Other records, such as personal documents, are more likely to be discontinuous or episodic (see Webb et al., 1981). Archival records can also be distinguished by the degree to which they are available for public inspection. Many records kept by government agencies are easily obtainable. Most records of private institutions and businesses, however, are not open to public scrutiny or can be obtained only after many requests and considerable patience on the part of the researcher.

The news media are yet another important source of archival information. Various records, ranging from stock market reports to crime statistics, are published in newspapers and reported on television. The content of media reports is also a form of archival record and is subject to analysis. Earlier we described how the contents of sports pages were used to test a theory of causal attribution.

The placement of "Found" advertisements in the Lost and Found section of a newspaper can be used to measure public altruism (see Goldstein, Minkin, Minkin, & Baer, 1978).

Phillips (1977) used running records of motor vehicle fatalities kept by the California Highway Patrol and a measure of suicide publicity derived from California newspapers to determine whether there is a significant suicidal component to motor vehicle fatalities. He hypothesized that a substantial number of deaths arising from motor vehicle accidents are actually the result of individuals using their cars to commit suicide. To test this hypothesis, Phillips investigated whether motor vehicle fatalities would, like suicides in general, increase after a well-publicized suicide story. Components of the publicity measure included the daily circulation of each newspaper and the number of days the newspaper carried the suicide story. This measure correlated significantly with changes in motor vehicle fatalities after each story. The number of motor vehicle fatalities increased significantly during the few days after a well-publicized suicide story, reaching a peak on Day 3. This result is shown in Figure 5.3. Changes in frequency were determined by comparing experimental periods (the week right after the story) with control periods that were free from suicide stories and were matched with the experimental periods in terms of day of the week, presence or absence of holidays, and time of the year. Phillips concluded that "suicide stories stimulate a wave of imitative suicides, some of which are disguised as motor vehicle accidents" (p. 1464).

Table 5.2 contains a list of selected sources of archival information and the nature of the data that might be obtained from them. The types of archival data shown in Table 5.2 are rather arbitrarily classified as running records, those pertaining to the media, and "other records," including records of businesses, schools, and other private institutions. An examination of the sources described in Table 5.2 will introduce you to the variety of possible measures that can be obtained from archival sources. Then, following a discussion of content analysis of archival sources, we will review several specific illustrations of the use of archival data in the context of hypothesis testing.

**FIGURE 5.3**    Daily fluctuations in motor vehicle accident fatalities for a 2-week period before, during (Day 0), and after publication of suicide stories. (From Phillips, 1977.)

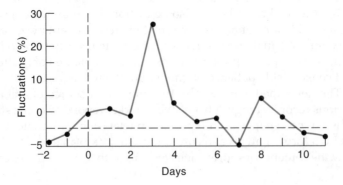

**TABLE 5.2** SELECTED SOURCES OF ARCHIVAL INFORMATION AND ILLUSTRATIVE DATA FOR THREE TYPES OF ARCHIVES*

| Source | Illustrative data |
|---|---|
| **Running records** | |
| *Congressional Record* | Statements of position on particular issues |
| Telephone directories | Community ethnic group membership |
| Salaries of teachers or government employees | Community support |
| Government agency records (labor, commerce, agriculture departments) | Living trends |
| Judicial record | Uniformity in sentencing for antisocial behavior |
| *Moody's Handbook* | Corporate financial structure |
| *Who's Who in America* | Nature of cited accomplishments of successful people |
| Tax records | Regional differences in patterns of living |
| City budgets | Perceived value or extent of support of various activities |
| **Media** | |
| Society section of metropolitan newspaper | Upper-middle-class and lower-upper-class activities |
| Children's books on sale | Qualities of models (heroes and heroines) |
| Movie announcements in newspapers | Changing taboos and enticements |
| Want ads | Employer inducements |
| Obituary columns | Charity preferences |
| Published speeches | Political, social, economic attitudes |
| Newspaper headlines | Press bias |
| **Other records[†]** | |
| Absentee and tardiness records | Work habits or motivation |
| Military reenlistment and longevity figures | Morale indicator |
| Pay increase and promotion lists | Perceived value of individuals to an organization |
| Number of people one supervises | Measure of management responsibility |
| Production and other output figures | Performance of individuals, departments, and so on |
| Sales contest records | Selling effectiveness, effectiveness of incentive plans |
| Sales slips at Delegates' Lounge bar in UN | Tension indicator |
| Peanut sales at ball games | Excitement indicator (greater after than before seventh inning) |
| Sales level of consumer goods | Effectiveness of display location, advertisement, or style of packaging |
| Air trip insurance figures | Public concern before and after air crashes |
| Sales of layettes by color (blue or pink) | Sex preference in different social classes |
| Sale price of autographs | Popularity indicator |
| Club membership list | Indicator of segment of society involved |
| Committee reports | Institutional modification attempts |
| Actuarial records: birth, baptismal, death records; marriage licenses | Comparative demographic data (occupation, religion, time of day, cause of death, and so on) |
| Cemetery documents, burial-lot records | Family membership |

*Adapted from Brandt (1972).
[†]Institutions, business, hospitals, schools, and so on; may or may not be opened to public inspection.

## Content Analysis

- Content analysis refers to the process of making inferences based on objective coding of archival records.
- Steps for content analysis include identifying a relevant source of archival data, sampling data from the records, and then coding the contents of the records.
- Content coding includes classifying events and behaviors from archival records into clearly defined categories and recording the amount of time or words devoted to events and behaviors.
- Trained coders use rating scales to make qualitative judgments about the contents of archival records.

Although many sources of archival data can be identified, the usefulness of these sources depends ultimately on how their content is analyzed. In the simplest case, the analysis required may be minimal. Recording the votes of state legislators may be as simple as transcribing vote tallies found in legislative documents. Similarly, determining the win-loss record of sports teams playing at home or away is simply a matter of working with data found in one of the many sports digests that are on the market. In many cases, however, extracting relevant data from an archival source requires careful procedures and relatively complex analysis of the source's content. Furthermore, problems of sampling, reliability, and validity of measures must be addressed, just as these problems are addressed in situations where behavior is observed directly.

**Content analysis** is generally defined as any technique for making inferences by objectively identifying specific characteristics of messages (Holsti, 1969). Although it is associated primarily with written communications, content analysis may be used with any form of message, including television and radio programs, speeches, films, and interviews. Weigel, Loomis, and Soja (1980) used content analysis to study race relations as they are depicted on prime-time television. They analyzed the frequency of appearances of Blacks and Whites on evening television shows carried by all three major networks. In addition, they rated the quality of Black-White and White-White interactions. Carroll and Russell (1997) analyzed four major Hollywood films to test a biological theory of facial expression. An analysis of actors' portrayal of emotions such as disgust and fear did not provide evidence for "patterns" of facial components predicted by some theories. Finally, in a content analysis of a popular form of written communication, personal ads, researchers analyzed the descriptions of partner preferences among homosexual and heterosexual individuals (Bailey, Kim, Hills, & Linsenmeier, 1997). They related their findings to theories of sexual orientation and psychological adjustment of homosexual individuals who are not typically masculine or feminine.

There are several discernible steps in conducting research using content analysis. First is the identification of a relevant archival source. What is relevant, of course, depends on the goals of the study and the questions the researcher is asking. In some cases merely a statement of the purpose of the study is sufficient to pinpoint an appropriate archival source. A researcher who sets out to study humor in tombstone messages, the manifest content of suicide notes, or race relations on television has already identified the general source for content analysis. In other situations the identification of relevant sources depends on the ingenuity of the researcher. Lau and Russell's (1980) choice of the sports page represented an appropriate and clever use of archival sources as a test of the external validity of laboratory findings related to attribution. In the absence of films depicting emotional expression in everyday life, Carroll and Russell (1997) selected Hollywood films, such as *Ordinary People* (1980) and *Dead Poets Society* (1989), "noted for their realistic portrayal of modern life and for their highly emotional content" (p. 167).

Having identified an archival source, the researcher must sample selections from this source appropriately. Sampling procedures similar to those described in previous chapters can be used. As is the case when behavior or events are sampled, the goal of sampling is to obtain a sample that is representative of all the data of interest. To investigate race relations on television, Weigel et al. (1980) videotaped a full week's broadcasts by the three major networks in the spring of 1978. Only programs with a story line, but all product commercials, were included in the sample. The decision not to use documentaries, news broadcasts, and sports shows reduced the sample of viewing time by about 20%. As always, the extent to which the results of an archival study can be generalized depends on the nature of the sample that is used. Terman's study of genius was, as we saw, based on data collected from high IQ, mainly White, middle-class individuals. Thus, the external validity of subsequent, archival studies of longevity is necessarily less than it would be had a more heterogeneous sample been represented in the archives. Moreover, we might question whether the impact of parental divorce on children's lives at the beginning of the 20th century, when divorce was less frequent and less socially acceptable, is the same as it is today.

The next step in performing a content analysis is *coding*. This step is similar to the scoring of narrative records (see Chapter 3) and requires that relevant descriptive categories and appropriate units of measure be defined (see Holsti, 1969). As with the choice of the archival source itself, what determines a relevant descriptive category is related to the goals of the study. This aspect of a content-analysis task can be illustrated by examining the categories used by Weigel et al. (1980) in their study of race relations. Four major categories were defined: (1) human appearance time, (2) Black appearance time, (3) cross-racial appearance time, and (4) cross-racial interaction time. Each category was operationally defined. For instance, cross-racial interaction was defined as "the time during which black and white characters were engaged in active, on-screen interactions (talking, touching, or clear nonverbal communication)" (p. 886). The use of precise operational definitions permitted coders viewing the sample broadcasts to make reliable judgments of events.

In many content-analysis studies, the communication is written. The units of classification for quantitative analysis generally include single words, characters, sentences or paragraphs, themes, or particular items (Holsti, 1969). Lau and Russell (1980), for instance, determined the frequency of attribution statements that were categorized as either internal or external and were made by members of the winning or losing team. In a study of bereavement, researchers performed a content analysis of interview transcripts of men who had lost a partner to AIDS (Pennebaker, Mayne, & Francis, 1997). Use of insight and causal words predicted emotional well-being a year later.

Another unit of measure often used when newspaper content is analyzed is that of space—for instance, number of column inches devoted to a particular topic. This measure was used by Phillips (1977) when studying the relationship between publicized suicides and frequency of motor-vehicle fatalities. When television or radio broadcasts are studied, the unit of measure may be time. Such was the case for the study by Weigel et al. (1980). Both Black appearances and Black-White appearances were expressed in terms of the percentage of total human appearance time.

Qualitative measures are also used as part of content analysis. These qualitative assessments are frequently in the form of ratings. For example, in addition to measuring time of cross-racial interactions on prime time television, Weigel et al. sought to determine the "degree to which cross-racial interactions on television were characterized by the conditions that promote friendliness and mutual respect in face-to-face encounters" (pp. 886–887). To do this, they developed a series of rating scales that emphasized the interpersonal dimensions found to be important in previous race-related research. Broadcasts videotaped a year earlier were used to define levels of the scales, and coders were trained in the use of the scales before real data were collected. Newhagen and Ancell (1995) asked raters to judge on a 10-point scale the emotional valence (positive or negative) and intensity of bumper sticker messages.

Satterfield and Seligman (1994) used the CAVE technique to investigate the explanatory styles of George Bush and Saddam Hussein during several historical periods of conflict, including the Persian Gulf Crisis. The acronym, CAVE, stands for "content analysis of verbatim explanations" (see Schulman, Castellon, & Seligman, 1989). The CAVE guidelines help researchers identify causal statements in written or spoken verbatim messages. The statements can then be rated on dimensions of explanatory style, similar to those used by Lau and Russell in their study of causal attributions in sports. The content analysis of verbatim explanations by Bush and Hussein for periods preceding military actions or political conflicts produced an interesting result:

> When the leaders were pessimistic (relative to themselves), their subsequent actions were more cautious and passive. When the leaders were relatively optimistic, their subsequent actions were more aggressive and risky. (Satterfield & Seligman, 1994, p. 79)

The authors noted the many limitations of their study (e.g., a relatively small sample of verbatim messages and world events was analyzed). They also appropriately acknowledge that the correlational nature of their study means they must "leave open the large class of third-variable accounts before concluding that explanatory style itself causes cautious versus risky actions" (p. 79). For example, before a definitive conclusion regarding the relationship between explanatory style and political action can be reached, such issues as political demands on the leaders or cultural differences in rhetorical style need to be investigated further. Nevertheless, the data suggest that "shifts in explanatory style seem at least to signal corresponding shifts in aggressivity and risk taking" (p. 80). Archival research of this kind may help us better understand the psychological nature of political decision making and perhaps even help predict the course of world events.

Whenever possible, judges (coders or raters) should be blind to important aspects of the study, such as the main hypotheses, the source of the messages, and the immediate surrounding context. Judges in the Satterfield and Seligman (1994) study of explanatory style, for example, rated the world leaders' statements only after "all potentially biasing date information was removed" (p. 78) and after source material had been assigned random number codes. Measures of interjudge (interobserver) reliability also should be presented as part of a content analysis. (Measures of interobserver reliability are discussed in Chapter 3.)

## Illustrative Uses of Archival Data

- Archival data are used to analyze communications and trends over time, and to assess the effects of natural treatments.

**Analysis of Communications**   Satterfield and Seligman's (1994) analysis of the explanations by George Bush and Saddam Hussein for world events is a good example of the use of archival data to analyze communications. So, too, is an interesting study by Osgood and Walker (1959), who compared the content of real suicide notes, simulated suicide notes (notes deliberately faked), and ordinary letters. Working under the assumption that language behavior changes as a function of heightened motivation, they suggested that suicide notes should differ from ordinary letters and faked notes in several ways. The investigators chose 16 different measures to test their hypotheses regarding the content of these messages (e.g., number of syllables per word and number of distress-expressing phrases). Many of these measures revealed significant differences between suicide notes and ordinary letters. Interestingly, suicide notes did not show greater disorganization. When quantitative measures that were successful in distinguishing between suicide notes and ordinary letters were used to differentiate between faked and real suicide notes, the analysis correctly predicted the real suicide note in 10 of 13 matched pairs.

**Analysis of Trends**   Over the years, women have frequently been underrepresented in businesses and professions. In the last few decades, however, significant attempts have been made to reduce any gender bias affecting hiring and promotion as well as entry into various professions. Scientific organizations, such as those in psychology, have taken steps to reduce discriminatory practices. The *APA Publication Manual* (American Psychological Association, 1994), for instance, includes specific guidelines for using inclusive language in APA journals (see also Appendix C). The APA Ethics Code, which was discussed in Chapter 2, clearly promotes respect for people's rights and for the dignity of all individuals without regard to gender (as well as to other cultural, social, or physical factors). According to General Principle D of the Ethics Code, "Psychologists try to eliminate the effect on their work of biases based on these factors, and they do not knowingly participate in nor condone unfair discriminatory practices" (American Psychological Association, 1992, p. 1600).

To what extent have psychologists been successful in reducing gender bias in their research activities? To attempt to answer this question, researchers reviewed nearly 5,000 scientific articles from eight psychology journals published between 1970 and 1990 (Gannon, Luchetta, Rhodes, Pardie, & Segrist, 1992). The journals were selected so as to represent various topic areas (developmental, abnormal, and so on) within psychology. With the exception of one journal that did not begin publication until 1978, the contents of all articles published in these journals in 1970, 1975, 1980, 1985, and 1990 were examined. Eight different variables were identified, and the contents of the articles were coded according to these variables. Among them were the gender of the first author, gender of the participants, the type of language (i.e., sexist or nonsexist) used, and the existence of generalizations based on gender (e.g., generalizations of results obtained from participants of one gender to both genders).

The results of this trend analysis of gender bias in published psychology articles revealed that while "sexism has clearly diminished in the past two decades," there is "continued evidence of discriminatory practices" (p. 389). For example, on the positive side, significant increases between 1970 and 1990 in the percentages of articles with female first authors were found in nearly every journal, while the percentages of studies that had male-only participants declined significantly in most journals. In addition, sexist language in these psychology journals was all but totally eliminated by 1990. On the negative side, a substantial percentage of articles showing gender bias were still being published in 1990. An article was considered gender-biased "if participants included only one gender for no obvious reason or with no reason explicitly stated, if sexist language was used, or if the discussion section contained inappropriate generalizations" (p. 393). Under this definition, gender-biased studies averaged about 85% in 1970 and about 30% in 1990. As the authors indicated, the archival analysis revealed an obvious reduction in gender bias in psychological studies during the period of this study, but it is evident from the data that, as of 1990, there was still room for improvement.

An analysis of APA journals by Graham (1992) revealed that there also is room for improvement in the manner in which psychologists approach the study of African Americans. Archival data obtained from six major APA journals indicated that the presence of empirical articles on African Americans decreased during the period between 1970 and 1989. The bottom line was highlighted in the title of her article: "Most of the Subjects Were White and Middle Class." This trend seems unfortunate when, as the author notes, "social concerns demand increased understanding of the psychological functioning of Black Americans, and pedagogical needs call for cultural diversity in our academic curricula"

(p. 629). In terms of publishing sex-biased studies and empirical studies of minority groups, one might well ask, where is psychology now?

Assessing the Effect of a Natural Treatment   A study investigating the effect of a natural treatment (one that we have mentioned previously) is that of Phillips (1977). In this study, the "treatment" was the publicity given by major newspapers to suicides, and the effect of this publicity on motor vehicle fatalities was assessed. In a subsequent study, Phillips (1978) used records of the U.S. National Transportation Safety Board (*Briefs of Accidents: U.S. Civil Aviation*) to show a relationship between well-publicized murder-suicides and changes in fatal aircraft accidents. This archival study revealed a sharp increase in multifatality crashes (implying both a murder and a suicide component) in the period following the widespread publicizing of a murder-suicide story. Interestingly, the peak increase in aircraft fatalities occurred on Day 3 following the story, just as was found when suicide stories were related to motor vehicle fatalities (see Figure 5.3). In yet another study, Phillips (1983) showed homicides increased significantly following heavyweight championship prize fights during the period between 1973 and 1978. Particularly intriguing is the fact that deaths due to homicides peaked 3 days following the prize fight, as had been found in previous analyses of motor vehicle and airplane fatalities following well-publicized suicide stories. As evidence that this effect is due to some type of modeling of aggression, Phillips carried out additional analyses showing that homicides increased as the level of publicity surrounding the event increased. He operationally defined level of publicity in terms of whether the fight was discussed on television network news. He found that the increase in homicides was significantly greater when the fight was given more publicity on the network news.

This series of studies by Phillips and his colleagues is an impressive demonstration of the use of archival data to provide external validity to the results of laboratory findings. Phillips noted that laboratory studies have shown that exposure to violent films and television produces brief increases in aggression by laboratory subjects. Often, however, neither the setting nor the nature of the violence studied (e.g., hitting inflatable toys) is similar to that found in the real world. In contrast, studies using archival data, although lacking the rigorous control possible in the laboratory, provide evidence of what happens to people who are exposed to real media instances of aggression.

## Problems and Limitations

- Archival data may be biased due to selective deposit and selective survival.
- Selective deposit occurs when biases influence what information is recorded (deposited) in an archival record, or whether a record is made at all; selective survival occurs when archival records are missing or incomplete.
- Archival records are subject to errors and changes in record-keeping procedures.

- Although archival data are considered nonreactive, reactivity can influence the production of archival records; this is particularly true for public records.
- When interpreting the results of correlational analyses of archival data, researchers must be alert to the possibility of spurious relationships.

When discussing the validity of physical traces, we mentioned that biases may result from the way physical traces are established and from the manner in which they survive over time. These biases are referred to as selective deposit and selective survival, respectively, and they are no less a problem for archival records (see Webb et al., 1981). Either of these biases can impose severe limitations on the generality of research findings.

Problems of **selective deposit** arise when biases exist in the production of archival sources. An interesting example of selective deposit is that associated with suicide notes. We mentioned earlier the research of Osgood and Walker (1959), who performed a content analysis of suicide notes and compared real suicide notes to ordinary letters and to faked suicide notes. We might ask whether the thoughts and feelings expressed in suicide notes are representative of all suicides. It happens that fewer than a fourth of all individuals who commit suicide leave notes, so it is possible that those who do leave notes are not representative of no-note individuals (Webb et al., 1981).

Problems of selective deposit may also arise when individuals associated with archival sources have the opportunity to edit and alter records before they are permanently recorded. This is illustrated by legislators' use of the *Congressional Record*. Though the *Congressional Record* is ostensibly a spontaneous record of speeches and remarks made before the Congress, legislators actually have the opportunity to edit their remarks before they are published (Webb et al., 1981) and even to enter into the record documents and accounts that were never really read aloud. No doubt remarks that are, in hindsight, viewed as less than politically expedient are changed prior to publication in the *Congressional Record*. Researchers who use archival data must be aware of the biases that may occur when an archive is produced. Consider, for example, what types of biases might cause selective recording of crime statistics, income expense accounts, or sales figures.

Problems associated with **selective survival** arise when records are missing or incomplete (something an investigator may or may not even be aware of). It is important to consider whether there are reasons to suspect systematic biases in the survival of certain records. Are documents missing that are particularly damaging to certain individuals or groups? Following a change of presidential administrations, are some types of archives destroyed or misplaced? Are "letters to the editor" representative of all letters that were received? Schoeneman and Rubanowitz (1985) cautioned that when analyzing the contents of advice columns, they could not avoid the possibility of a preselection bias because advice columnists print only a fraction of the letters they receive. As one prominent group of researchers has commented, when one examines archival data, "the gnawing reality remains that archives have been produced for someone else and by someone else" (Webb et al., 1981, p. 140).

In addition to problems arising from selective deposit and survival, the researcher using archival sources must be aware of possible errors in the record keeping and changes over time in the manner in which the records were kept. It is important to demonstrate that the record keeping was relatively constant and stable over the period of the study. When running records are kept, there is always the possibility that the definitions of categories have been changed midstream. For example, had the U.S. National Transportation Safety Board made important changes in the definition of "noncommercial" aircraft during the period of Phillips' (1978) study, it would have seriously affected the statistics he used to implicate murder-suicides in aircraft fatalities. An interesting example of unintended bias appears in the debate over the "home choke" hypothesis. Critics argue that the archival data do not support the hypothesis that sports teams choke in key games when playing at home (Schlenker, et al., 1995a, 1995b). When defending the archival analyses supporting the hypothesis, Baumeister (1995) pointed out that during the archival period there had been a rule change for the World Series regarding the use of a designated hitter. The rule change favored the home team, and could have worked against the "home choke" hypothesis.

Although archives represent nonreactive measures of behavior, their classification as such applies only to archival analysis; it does not imply that reactivity was not a problem when the archive was produced. Statements made by public figures and printed in newspapers or reported by other media must be evaluated for their reactive components. Politicians and others who are constantly exposed to media publicity no doubt learn how to "use" the media, and their public stance may not match their private views. Lau and Russell (1980) had to consider whether the public statements made by players and coaches about a team's performance were really the same as those they made in private. They concluded that differences between public and private statements of attribution no doubt existed but that these differences do not invalidate their generalization of laboratory findings to real-world settings. The only way to control for reactive effects in archival data is to be aware that they may exist and, when possible, to seek other forms of corroborative evidence.

Yet another problem in the analysis of archival data is identifying spurious relationships. A **spurious relationship** exists when evidence falsely indicates that two or more variables are associated. Such evidence may be the result of inadequate or improper statistical treatment. This problem may exist in studies showing a relationship between frequency of deaths and important occasions. Although many people appear to endorse the view that individuals can somehow prolong their life in order to experience certain important events, such as birthdays, Schulz and Bazerman (1980) reanalyzed data from several studies to show that supportive evidence may be the result of statistical artifacts—for example, the way in which the period of time before and after a death was measured. This reanalysis of the data eliminated any evidence for the death-dip hypothesis. These researchers also reanalyzed data from other studies supporting the death-dip and death-rise hypotheses and showed how statistical artifacts could account for the results. Nevertheless, Schulz and Bazerman suggested that data supporting the death-dip hypothesis "may well be within reach if we use the proper methodologies and carefully select important events" (p. 261).

Spurious relationships can also exist when variables are accidentally or coincidentally related. This is sometimes the case when changes in two variables are the result of another, usually unknown, third variable. For instance, it has been noted that ice cream sales and the crime rate are positively correlated. However, before concluding that eating ice cream prompts people to commit crimes, it is important to consider the fact that both variables are affected by increases in temperature; neither eating ice cream nor committing crime directly affects the other.

Several studies (e.g., Baron & Reiss, 1985) have been done to determine whether Phillips' (1983) finding of a relationship between heavyweight prize fights and homicides in the United States is a spurious one. Critics suggested that statistical artifacts are present, while others questioned whether important variables were controlled. Baron and Reiss, for instance, suggested that the third-day peak, which Phillips (1983) admitted he could not readily interpret, was quite possibly due to the occurrence of holidays or weekends near prize-fight dates or even to fluctuations in the unemployment rate. Nevertheless, extensive reanalysis of Phillips' original data tended to reaffirm a link between violence portrayed in the media and violence acted out in society (see Miller, Heath, Molcan, & Dugoni, 1991; Phillips & Bollen, 1985).

There is no easy way to deal with spurious relationships except to gather, from independent sources, additional data that will help confirm a relationship and to subject the available archival data to more than one kind of analysis. This often is no easy task and explains why, as we have noted on more than one occasion, that researchers are appropriately cautious when giving their final conclusions about the outcome of an archival study (see, for example, Baumeister, 1995).

As one last example of the difficulties associated with interpretations based on archival data, consider the problems involving the outcome of archival studies examining the relationship between temperature and aggression (see, for example, Anderson, 1989). Psychologists frequently have used archival records of temperatures and of frequencies of aggressive or violent acts—such as assaults, rapes, and homicides—in order to test the hypothesis that aggression increases with increases in temperature. Data supporting the temperature-aggression hypothesis have been around for years. Nevertheless, researchers have also been aware of possible artifacts of tests of this hypothesis. For example, are aggressive incidents more likely when more people are outdoors, interacting in groups (shopping, playing sports, taking vacations)? If this is the case, and if we assume people are more likely to be outside in the warmer months, then a relation between temperature and aggression may be a spurious one. Temperature and violence would not be directly related but accounted for by some third variable such as opportunity for outdoor activities (see Anderson, 1989). You may recognize this argument as a variation on the ice cream sales–crime rate relationship mentioned earlier. Researchers responded to this criticism by looking at a wide variety of measures, collected during different historical periods, and across cultures. The relationship between temperature and aggression was similar in these studies, making an alternative explanation less plausible (Anderson, 1989).

The manner in which spurious relationships appear can be illustrated with another set of data collected to test the temperature-aggression hypothesis. One way to test this hypothesis is to examine frequency of violent acts as a function of month of the year, the expectation being that violent acts will be most frequent during the hottest months of the year, such as July and August. Anderson (1989) summarized the results of several studies that looked at this relationship. In the bottom panel of Figure 5.4, you can see data revealing the frequency of assaults across the 12 months of the year. The data in this figure appear to support the temperature-aggression hypothesis, frequency of assaults is least during the cold months and peaks during July and August. Now look at the data at the top of Figure 5.4. In this graph the monthly frequencies of homicides are graphed.

**FIGURE 5.4**   Summaries of data relevant to tests of the temperature-aggression hypothesis. Data on the bottom show monthly distribution of assaults; data on the top describe monthly distribution of homicides. (From Anderson, 1989.)

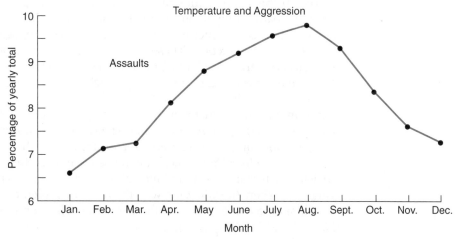

The frequencies of homicides and assaults are similar for the first few months of the year and, in fact, July and August reveal peak periods for both kinds of violent acts. However, the frequency of homicides is also very high in the cold month of December. Is the temperature-aggression hypothesis invalidated? Or, is there an artifact in these data? One possibility is that homicides increase in December due to an increase in family disputes during the holidays (see Anderson, 1989). Researchers must be constantly alert to possible artifacts in a data set and seek corroborative evidence for an hypothesis. For instance, showing that temperature is related to assaults and not to property crime argues for a specific relationship between temperature and aggression (Anderson, Bushman, & Groom, 1997). Finally, as we have emphasized previously, it is important to take a multimethod approach to hypothesis testing.

## ETHICAL ISSUES AND UNOBTRUSIVE MEASURES

- Unobtrusive measures such as physical traces and archival data represent an important research method for psychologists to fulfill their ethical obligation to improve individual and societal conditions.

The APA Ethics Code makes clear that psychologists have an obligation to "promote integrity in the science," be "concerned about the ethical compliance of their colleagues' scientific and professional conduct," seek to "broaden knowledge of behavior and, where appropriate, to apply it pragmatically to improve the condition of both the individual and society." Moreover, "when undertaking research, they [should] strive to advance human welfare and the science of psychology" (see Preamble, Principles B, C, and F, of the *APA Ethics Code;* American Psychological Association, 1992, pp. 1599–1600). These goals apply, of course, to scientists in general and not simply when they use of one particular methodology, such as that associated with unobtrusive measures. Nevertheless, because several studies reviewed in this chapter highlight nicely the *proactive* nature of scientific research, these ethical principles are worth emphasizing. Research reviewed in this chapter illustrates, for instance, how psychologists have contributed meaningfully to our understanding of suicide, race relations, effects of parental divorce, conflict resolution, societal violence, sexual discrimination, and fair scientific practices. These contributions arise from one small part of psychological research, that having to do with physical traces or archival data. This impressive list testifies to the way in which psychologists strive to meet their ethical responsibilities.

It is important to remember that there may be a cost to society of *not* doing research (see Chapter 2). A better understanding of such social problems as violence, suicide, and race relations, for example, has the potential to improve many people's lives. Yet, ethical dilemmas arise when there are serious risks to participants that make certain kinds of research difficult to justify when considering a risk/benefit ratio. One way in which this dilemma may be resolved is to seek alternative, low-risk methods of data collection (see Chapter 2). In the present chapter, you saw how research can be carried out on important psychological problems under conditions where ethical issues are often minimal relative to more intrusive methods. Thus, in some situations, unobtrusive measures may represent an important low-risk methodology for research on important social issues.

## SUMMARY

Unobtrusive measures such as physical traces and archival data are important alternatives to direct observation and surveys. Physical traces are the remnants, fragments, and products of past behavior. Physical-use traces are based on the accumulation of evidence (accretion measures) or are the result of selective wear (erosion measures). Furthermore, use traces can either result naturally, without any intervention by the investigator, or be planned by the investigator. Physical traces may provide important nonreactive (unobtrusive) measures of behavior and can be used as the sole dependent variable or in combination with other measures of behavior. Multimethod approaches to the study of behavior are particularly recommended because they reduce the chance that results are due to some artifact of the measurement process. In obtaining physical traces, an investigator must be aware of possible biases in the way in which traces accumulate or survive over time.

Archival data are found in records and documents that recount the activities of individuals, institutions, governments, and other groups. These sources of information are valuable because they provide a way of investigating the external validity of laboratory findings, assessing the effect of a "natural treatment" (such as a political assassination), analyzing the content of communications, and describing trends. Archival records are nonreactive measures of behavior and, like physical traces, can be used in multimethod approaches to hypothesis testing. The analysis of archival data typically requires some form of content analysis, a process that can involve problems of sampling and coding that are not unlike those that arise in the analysis of narrative records (see Chapter 3). Problems of selective deposit and selective survival must be investigated when archival data are used, and evidence should be presented showing that observed relationships are not spurious.

Unobtrusive measures can be an important alternative to more intrusive methodologies, permitting psychologists to do research on important issues with minimal risk to the participants.

## KEY CONCEPTS

unobtrusive measures
physical traces
archival data
multimethod approach

content analysis
selective deposit
selective survival
spurious relationship

## REVIEW QUESTIONS

1 What characteristic of physical traces and archival data makes them especially attractive alternatives to the direct-observation and survey method of measuring?

2 Why are multimethod approaches to hypothesis testing recommended?

3 What are the different kinds of physical-trace measures used by psychologists, and in what ways do they differ?

4 What possible sources of bias exist when physical-use traces are the dependent variable in a research study, and how can the validity of these measures be verified?

5 Identify and give an example of one of the four reasons for using archival data.

6 What dimensions distinguish the various types of archival sources used by psychologists?

7 What three basic steps must be taken in any research in which content analysis is done?

8 Explain the role of precise operational definitions in content analysis, and give one example of a quantitative unit and one example of a qualitative unit of measurement in content analysis.

9 Identify and give an example of the problems that researchers must be aware of when they make use of archival sources.

10 Explain the two ways in which evidence indicating spurious relationships most often arises.

## CHALLENGE QUESTIONS

1 Suggest two sources of archival data for each of the following variables. Be sure to specify an operational definition of each variable.
   A   Public's interest in cultural events
   B   Students' political attitudes
   C   Community concern about crime
   D   Amount of mobility in a corporation
   E   Citizens' attitudes toward their schools
   F   Ethnic grouping of neighborhoods
   G   Current fads in dress

2 For each of the following archival sources, specify two kinds of data that might be useful in a psychological study. Once again, be sure to specify the operational definition that could be used for the variable you have identified.
   A   Weekly news magazine
   B   Television soap operas
   C   Classified section of newspaper
   D   Annual city budgets
   E   Student yearbooks
   F   List of donors to a university
   G   Television commercials

3 A bright female graduate student in psychology has been offered a job with both *Newsweek* and *Time*. The salary offers of the two companies are basically the same, and it appears that both the working conditions and the job responsibilities are similar. To help her decide which job to accept, she resolves to determine whether one magazine has a better attitude toward women than the other. She appeals to you to

help her with a content analysis of these two news magazines. What specific advice would you give her regarding each of the following steps of her content analysis?

**A** Sampling

**B** Coding

**C** Reliability

**D** Quantitative and qualitative measures

4 An educational specialist was convinced that schoolyard fights among young boys were more violent than those among young girls. To gather evidence relevant to her hypothesis, she checked the records at the nurse's office of her school. She found that, of the 100 injuries resulting from fights which were reported to the school nurse, 75% involved boys and only 25% involved girls. The investigator was convinced on the basis of these findings that her hypothesis was correct. Criticize this conclusion by showing how these very same findings could result if exactly the opposite of the investigator's hypothesis were true—namely, that fights among young girls are more violent. (Be sure to confine your answer to the adequacy of the data that the investigator has presented to support her conclusion.)

5 A researcher wishes to test the hypothesis that children attending private grade schools are not as "dirty-minded" as students attending public grade schools. He chooses two schools (one a parochial school and one public) that are located in the same neighborhood, approximately one mile apart. Both schools include grades 1 through 8. To test the hypothesis, the investigator decides to use measures both of natural accretion and of controlled accretion. Specifically, he operationally defines "dirty-mindedness" as the number of obscene words (from a predetermined list) that are found in the restrooms of each school. The natural accretion measure is simply the number of new target words appearing on the walls of the restrooms at the end of each week. As a measure of controlled accretion, the investigator obtains permission from the school authorities to place pads of paper and pencils in the toilet stalls of the restrooms at each school. On each pad of paper is written "Leave me a note." At the end of each week the investigator replaces the pad with a fresh one and examines the pages that have been written on for the appearance of obscene words.

**A** Comment on possible problems of selective deposit and survival for the physical-trace measures proposed in this study.

**B** Frame questions that might be asked concerning the external validity of this study.

**C** Suggest ways in which the investigator might use a multimethod approach to this problem.

## Answer to Challenge Question 1

The sources of archival data listed below for each of the variables represent only illustrations and not definitive answers. Operational definitions are only sketched here; they should be developed more fully through discussion in class.

**A** Public's interest in cultural events—attendance figures for theater and concerts in the past calendar year; membership lists of organizations that support cultural events

**B** Students' political attitudes—records of participation by students at local, state, and national conventions; membership lists of organizations that advocate political positions

**C** Community concern about crime—police records of all calls reporting "suspicious" activities in the community; sales records for locks, burglar alarms, and firearms

**D** Amount of mobility in a corporation—company records of average time spent by employees in various positions; company records with annual lists of promotions within the company

**E** Citizens' attitudes toward their schools—records of the election results for millage requests for schools, including number of millage votes that passed and number of times each had to come up for a vote; membership lists for parent-teacher organizations with the implication that active participation suggests positive attitudes

**F** Ethnic grouping of neighborhoods—analysis of the ethnic origins of the names in neighborhood phone directories; city licensing records for restaurants and food stores in the neighborhoods

**G** Current fads in dress—sales records for selected articles of clothing that typify a particular fad; magazine, newspaper, and television advertisements for clothing

PART

III

# Experimental
# Methods

# Independent Groups Designs

## CHAPTER OUTLINE

## OVERVIEW

In previous chapters we discussed research methods that primarily fulfill the descriptive and predictive functions of the science of psychology. Psychologists use observational methods to develop detailed descriptions of behavior, often in natural settings. Survey-research methods allow psychologists to describe people's attitudes and opinions. Successful prediction is achieved when we discover measures of behavior that covary reliably; for instance, people who have many significant changes in their lives are also more stressed. Converging evidence for the validity of behavior descriptions based on observation and survey research can be obtained by analyzing archival data and physical traces, nonreactive means for describing behavior. However, as essential as they are to the scientific study of behavior, description and prediction are not sufficient. Psychologists also seek understanding—the "why" of behavior. Scientific understanding is achieved when the causes of a phenomenon have been identified. The next three chapters focus on the best available research method for identifying causal relationships—the experimental method. We will explore how the experimental method is used to test psychological theories as well as to answer questions of practical importance (e.g., whether an intervention worked to increase children's reading proficiency).

The distinction between experimental methods and descriptive methods should not be drawn too sharply. Observation, survey research, and archival data can certainly contribute to our understanding of the causes of behavior, and experiments certainly require observation. In fact, experiments are a kind of structured observation. Field experiments and longitudinal designs in survey research also embody the principles of the experimental methods, although we have discussed them in the context of descriptive research methods. Similarly, experimental methods can be used effectively to develop accurate descriptions of behavior, especially when the methods are applied to practical research problems such as the effectiveness of a behavior modification program (see Chapter 9).

As we have emphasized, the best overall approach to research is the multimethod approach. If we obtain comparable answers to a research question after using different methods, our confidence in our conclusions increases. Our conclusions are then said to have *convergent validity*. Each method has different shortcomings, but the methods have complementary strengths that overcome these shortcomings. The special strength of the experimental method is that it is especially effective for establishing cause-and-effect relationships.

In the present chapter we discuss the most commonly used experimental design—the random groups design. You will be introduced to the underlying logic of this design, the procedures for forming random groups, the ways in which the external validity of experiments can be established, and the challenges to internal validity that apply specifically to the random groups design. Two alternative experimental designs involving independent groups also will be considered: the matched groups design and the natural groups design. We conclude this chapter by describing how the results of experiments are analyzed.

Statistical analysis gives us the evidence we need to decide if our experiment worked to reveal the process we are investigating.

## CHARACTERISTICS OF EXPERIMENTS

- Researchers manipulate an independent variable in an experiment to observe the effect on behavior, as assessed by the dependent variable.
- Good experiments can be identified by their internal validity, reliability, sensitivity, and external validity.

Imagine you are observing adults while they are reading. Would you be able to tell whether individuals are saying the words to themselves as they read silently? Most adult readers don't move their lips when reading, so it's unlikely you could tell whether they are saying words silently to themselves. Think now as you read these words. Can you mentally "hear" the words as you read them? This process of "hearing" words while reading is literally unobservable. However, Haber and Haber (1982) constructed a clever situation to study this unobservable process. The term they used for talking to oneself while reading was *subvocal articulation*. To examine this process, they gave college students two types of sentences to read, tongue-twisters (Francis Forbes' father fries five flounders) and control sentences that were not tongue-twisters (Mary Wright's uncle cooks red lobsters). Haber and Haber reasoned that, if the students did say the words to themselves as they read silently, the tongue-twister sentences would be harder to read and thus take longer to read than the control sentences. This is exactly what they found, so they concluded that we do "talk to ourselves" as we read.

Haber and Haber never did observe subvocal articulation directly. They constructed a situation in which a difference in behavior (reading time) was observed indirectly as a result of a process they presumed was occurring. The situation the researchers created allowed this process to "show itself." Much of the experimental research in psychology is like that of the Haber and Haber study. Theoretical processes are proposed [*we talk to ourselves when we read*], experiments are done in which outcomes are predicted on the basis of these explanatory processes [*tongue-twister sentences should take longer to read than control sentences*], and the outcomes of the experiments are used to make decisions about the existence of these unobservable theoretical processes [*because the tongue-twister sentences did take longer to read, we conclude that we do talk to ourselves when we read*].

A true experiment involves the *manipulation* of one or more factors and *measurement* (observation) of the effects of this manipulation on behavior. The factors the researcher controls or manipulates are called the **independent variables.** The measures used to observe the effect (if any) of the independent variables are called **dependent variables.** When Haber and Haber (1982) investigated subvocal articulation, they manipulated the independent variable of the type of sentence students read (tongue-twister or control). The dependent variable they observed was the amount of time it took students to read each sentence. (Although the term *experiment* is also used to describe studies with independent variables whose levels are selected [e.g., gender of participant or grade level in school] rather than manipulated, for reasons that will become clear, we treat these kind of "experiments" separately later in this chapter.)

There are many ways to distinguish experiments that are done properly from those done improperly, but we will emphasize four characteristics of experiments to consider: internal validity, reliability, sensitivity, and external validity. An experiment has *internal validity* when the cause and effect relationship is interpretable—that is, we can conclude that manipulating the independent variable caused a change in the dependent variable, and we can rule out other plausible causes for the outcome. In all cases, we want our experiments to have good internal validity because only then can we make claims about the causes of behavior. Second, the purpose of an experiment is to produce a difference in behavior; a *reliable experiment* is one in which this difference is likely to be observed again if the experiment is repeated. When our experiments are reliable, we can state with confidence that our conclusions are not arbitrary or due to chance factors. Third, independent variables differ in terms of how large an effect they have on behavior; a *sensitive experiment* is likely to detect the effect of an independent variable even when the effect is small. For example, Haber and Haber found that students take more time to read tongue-twisters compared to control sentences. However, a smaller mean difference in reading time might be observed when comparing students' reading times for sentences with familiar words and sentences with unfamiliar words. Our goal is to design sensitive experiments that allow us to observe the effects of our manipulation, even when those effects might be small. Finally, when an experiment has *external validity* the findings can be generalized to individuals, settings, and conditions beyond the scope of the specific experiment. That is, questions of external validity ask whether the findings observed in an experiment would be observed when other individuals participate, when other settings and conditions are used.

You will want to learn ways to enhance each of these characteristics in the experiments you do. However, this may not be easy because these four important characteristics of a good experiment cannot always be maximized simultaneously. For instance, procedures that increase the sensitivity of an experiment can reduce its external validity. Thus, planning an experiment is something of a juggling act. In what follows you'll find directions for managing this complex task.

## WHY PSYCHOLOGISTS CONDUCT EXPERIMENTS

- Researchers conduct experiments to test hypotheses about the causes of behavior.
- Experiments allow researchers to decide whether a treatment or program effectively changes behavior.

A major purpose of conducting experiments is to test empirically the hypotheses derived from psychological theories. A hypothesis is a tentative explanation (e.g., an explanation for why some behavior occurs). If the results of the experiment are consistent with what is predicted by the hypothesis, then the explanation receives support. Such was the outcome of the experiment by Haber and Haber (1982). On the other hand, if the results differ from what was expected, then the proposed explanation may need to be modified and a new hypothesis developed and tested in the next experiment. Although testing and revising hypotheses can sometimes be a long and painstaking process, much like combining the pieces to a puzzle to form a picture, the self-correcting interplay between experiments and proposed explanations can become a challenging and satisfying approach to understanding the causes of the way we think, feel, and behave.

Besides providing empirical tests of proposed explanations derived from theories, experiments can be used to test the effectiveness of a treatment or program. For instance, experiments are often used to test the effects of medical treatments on particular illnesses. This role of experiments in this area has a long history (Thomas, 1992). Consider the fact that near the beginning of the 19th century, typhoid fever and delirium tremens were often fatal. The standard medical practice at that time was to treat these two conditions by bleeding, purging, and the administration of other, similar "therapies." An experiment was performed to test the effectiveness of these supposedly beneficial treatments. One group was randomly assigned to receive the standard treatment (bleeding, purging, etc.), and a second group was randomly assigned to receive nothing but bed rest, good nutrition, and close observation. Thomas (1992) describes the results of this experiment as "unequivocal and appalling" (p. 9): The group given the standard medical treatment of the time did *worse* than the group left untreated. Treating such conditions using early 19th-century practices was worse than not treating them at all! Experiments such as these contributed to the insight that many medical conditions are self-limited; the illness runs its course, and patients recover on their own. Many psychological disorders also will disappear when left untreated, a process known as spontaneous remission. Well-conducted experiments can provide vital information about the effectiveness of treatments and programs in a wide variety of areas. Seligman and his associates, for example, initiated an impressive series of experiments looking at the effect of teaching cognitive and social problem solving techniques on the prevention of childhood depression (e.g., Gillham, Reivich, Jaycox, & Seligman, 1995), a process they call "psychological immunization." Thus, experiments serve a useful purpose not only when we are testing theories but also when we are seeking solutions to society's problems.

## EXPERIMENTAL CONTROL

- Control is the essential ingredient of experiments; experimental control is gained through manipulation, holding conditions constant, and balancing.
- Experimental control allows researchers to make the causal inference that the independent variable *caused* the observed changes in the dependent variable.

- An experiment has internal validity when it fulfills the three conditions required for causal inference: covariation, time-order relationship, and elimination of plausible alternative causes.
- Manipulation of an independent variable is used to establish a time-order relationship and allows for a clearer determination of covariation.
- When confounding occurs, a plausible alternative explanation for the observed covariation exists, and therefore, the experiment lacks internal validity.
- Plausible alternative explanations are ruled out by holding conditions constant and balancing.
- In an independent groups design, each group of participants in the experiment represents a different condition of the independent variable.

Experiments are effective for testing hypotheses because they allow us to exercise a relatively high degree of control in a situation. Control is used in experiments to meet the three conditions necessary for a causal inference—that is, to be able to state with confidence that the independent variable *caused* the observed changes in the dependent variable. The three conditions needed to make a causal inference are covariation, time-order relationship, and elimination of plausible alternative causes. When these three conditions are met, the experiment has internal validity.

The covariation condition is met when we observe a relationship between the independent and dependent variables. For example, when Haber and Haber (1982) manipulated the tongue-twister and control sentences, the time it took students to read the sentences differed. We can say that the time needed to read a sentence was related to (covaried with) the type of sentence (tongue-twister or control). The second condition, time-order relationship, is met when we manipulate an independent variable in an experiment and *then* observe changes in the dependent variable. We make a causal inference when the cause precedes the effect. Imagine bumping your head and experiencing a headache (a covariation). The time-order relationship is usually one in which you bump your head and then experience the headache, so you infer that bumping your head caused the subsequent headache. Similarly, in controlled experiments, the condition of time-order relationship will be met when manipulation is used and a subsequent change in behavior is observed.

The key to meeting the conditions of covariation and time-order relationship is the control technique of *manipulation*. When some factor (e.g., type of sentence) is presumed to cause an effect on behavior (e.g., time to read a sentence), the factor is manipulated as an independent variable with at least two levels. In Haber and Haber's experiment the investigators introduced two types of sentences: tongue-twister and control. Many experiments involve more than two levels of an independent variable; however, at least two conditions of the independent variable are necessary in order to compare the differences in observed behavior (the dependent variable).

The most challenging condition for making causal statements is the elimination of plausible alternatives. To infer that some factor caused an effect on behavior we must be sure that other explanations are not possible. To do this, we use two additional methods of control: *holding conditions constant* and *balancing*. These control techniques can be illustrated in an experiment investigating eyewitness behavior conducted by Loftus and Burns (1982).

Their experiment concerned the effect of viewing a violent scene on a person's memory for information in the film that was presented seconds before the individual witnessed the mentally shocking event. The experiment was done at the University of Washington, and 226 students volunteered to participate in order to fulfill a course requirement. The students participated in small groups, and each small group was randomly assigned to view one of two films. Approximately half of the students (115) were assigned to view a violent version of a film. Near the end of the film, these students saw a robber, while running to a getaway car, turn and fire a shot toward two men who were pursuing him. The shot hit a boy in the face, and the boy fell bleeding to the ground. The other half of the students viewed a nonviolent version of the film that was identical to the violent version until just before the shooting. At this point in the film, the camera switched back to inside the bank, where the students saw the bank manager telling the customers and employees what happened and asking them to remain calm. The two versions of the film (violent and nonviolent) represent the levels of the independent variable in the experiment.

After viewing the film, students in both groups answered 25 questions about events in the film. One question was critical: It asked for the number on the

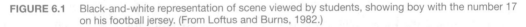

**FIGURE 6.1**    Black-and-white representation of scene viewed by students, showing boy with the number 17 on his football jersey. (From Loftus and Burns, 1982.)

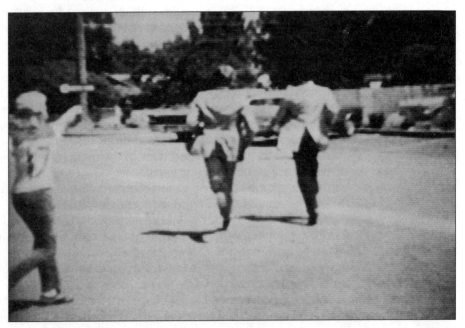

football jersey worn by a boy playing in the parking lot outside the bank. The boy wearing the jersey (see Figure 6.1) was visible for 2 seconds during the film—the 2 seconds before the shooting (violent version) or the 2 seconds before the scenes back in the bank (nonviolent version). The dependent variable was the percentage of students who correctly recalled the jersey number. The results were clear-cut: Just over 4% of the students correctly recalled the number in the violent condition, whereas nearly 28% did so in the nonviolent condition. Thus, Loftus and Burns concluded that a mentally shocking event can impair memory for details immediately preceding the event.

How did Loftus and Burns (1982) use the control techniques of holding conditions constant and balancing? *Holding conditions constant* is used to make sure that the independent variable is the only factor that differs systematically across the groups. In their experiment, the students viewed exactly the same film except for the critical incident; they were given the same experimental instructions at the beginning of the experiment and received the exact same questionnaire at the conclusion.

If the two groups had differed on a factor other than the film manipulation, then the results of the experiment would have been uninterpretable (i.e., lacking internal validity). For example, if the participants in the violent version had viewed a film depicting a boy in the background wearing a different jersey than that seen in the nonviolent version, then we wouldn't know whether the difference in recall was due to viewing the violent version of the film or to the fact that the jersey was different (e.g., a smaller number or less distinct). When the independent variable of interest and a different, potential independent variable are allowed to covary, a **confounding** is present. Holding conditions constant is used to avoid confoundings. By holding constant the boy playing in the background and the jersey (among other things) in the two versions of the film, Loftus and Burns avoided a confounding. A factor that is held constant so it does not change cannot possibly covary with the intended independent variable. More importantly, a factor that is held constant cannot possibly covary with the dependent variable either, making it possible to rule out the variable as a potential explanation for the observed results.

It is important to recognize, however, that we choose to control only those factors we think might influence the behavior we are studying—what we consider *plausible* alternative causes. For instance, Loftus and Burns held the setting constant by testing all their participants in the same room, but it is unlikely they specifically controlled the room temperature to be constant between groups because room temperature probably would not affect memory (at least when varying only a few degrees). They also tested students in "small groups," but there was no apparent attempt to hold constant the size of the group. Again, it doesn't seem plausible that small variations in the size of groups watching the film would have an effect on recall. The point is that we control only those factors we believe are potentially relevant—that is, those additional factors that might affect the behavior of interest. Nevertheless, we should constantly remain alert to the possibility that there may be confounding factors in our experiments whose influence we had not anticipated or considered.

Another example of holding conditions constant is apparent in the sentences used by Haber and Haber (1982) to examine subvocal articulation. The tongue-twisters (Francis Forbes's father fries five flounders) and control sentences (Mary Wright's uncle cooks red lobsters) have several features in common. Two important features held constant are the number of words in the sentences (six) and the number of syllables (nine). Imagine what would happen to our conclusions if the tongue-twister sentences always had more words and syllables than the control sentences; in this case, type of sentence (tongue-twister or control) would be confounded with number of words/syllables in the sentence. When the results indicate that tongue-twisters take longer to read than control sentences, would you be able to conclude subvocal articulation caused the difference? Could it be simply that longer sentences take longer to read? By holding constant the number of words and syllables in the sentence, we can rule out the plausible explanation that more time is needed to read tongue-twisters because they are longer. Can you see any other features of the sentences that were held constant?

The control technique of *balancing* is required because not all factors we want to control can be held constant. The most important factors in psychological research that cannot be held constant are the characteristics of the participants who are tested. Individual differences among participants cannot be eliminated—we simply can't make everyone exactly the same. As a result, differences across conditions on the dependent variable measure may be due to the fact that different people participated in the various conditions. An experimenter must find a way to make sure these individual differences do not confound the independent variable being investigated.

In an **independent groups design,** each group represents a different condition as defined by the independent variable. The experiment on eyewitness behavior is an example of an independent groups designs: The independent variable (i.e., the version of the film) varied across different groups of participants. To have internal validity it is important to balance individual differences among the different groups of the experiment. That is, we must make sure that one group is not smarter, more motivated, more conscientious, contains more females, has fewer psychology majors, and so forth, than another group. In the Loftus and Burns study of eyewitness behavior, if participants viewing the nonviolent film were also shown to be more attentive or have better recall ability than participants viewing the violent version, a plausible alternative explanation for the findings exists. It's possible that attentiveness (or memory ability) and not the version of the film could explain why participants in the nonviolent condition recalled more. By balancing subject characteristics across the groups, we rule out the alternative explanation that group differences on the dependent variable are due to characteristics of the participants. Exactly how this is done will be the major topic of the next section, where we will examine the most commonly used design involving independent groups of subjects, the random groups design.

Before turning to the next topic, however, consider one other characteristic of the methodology used in the Loftus and Burns experiment. The experimental manipulation involved a form of deception because the experimenters did not tell participants that they would see a boy being shot in the face. Moreover, we can imagine that this scene might be emotionally disturbing for some students. No doubt the researchers would argue that deception was necessary in order for memory following a traumatic event to be investigated in this manner. If participants knew they would see an emotionally disturbing event, then they might act differently than they would without that knowledge. For example, they might try to prepare themselves mentally for such an event. This may not only cause them to act differently from the way they would otherwise, but the event itself would perhaps no longer be as shocking as it would be without fore-warning. As you learned in Chapter 2, debriefing participants about the experiment is always necessary when deception is used in order to help the participants understand the reasons why they were deceived and to clear up any misunderstandings that might arise from their role in the experiment. Does the experimenters' use of deception in this study of eyewitness behavior seem justified? Do you believe that participants viewing the film were placed "at risk"? If so, do you think the risk was justified?

## RANDOM GROUPS DESIGN

### Random Assignment

- One type of independent groups design, the random groups design, has comparable groups of individuals participate in different levels of the independent variable.
- The logic of the random groups design allows researchers to make causal inferences about the effect of the independent variable on the dependent variable.
- Random assignment to conditions is used to form comparable groups by balancing or averaging subject characteristics across the conditions of the independent variable manipulation.
- Block randomization balances subject characteristics and potential confoundings that occur during the time in which the experiment is conducted, and creates groups of equal size.

The simplest experiments involve one independent variable with two levels and one measure of the dependent variable. The effect of the independent variable is assessed by observing the difference in the dependent variable between these two levels. In the independent groups design, a different group of subjects participates in each level (i.e., the groups are independent of each other). In the experiment done by Loftus and Burns (1982), for example, one group of participants was assigned to view a violent version of a film while a second group of participants viewed a nonviolent version of the same film. Both groups' memory for details of the films was compared. The logic of the design is straightforward. *If* the two groups are similar on all important characteristics at the start of the experiment *and if*, in the experiment itself, the two groups are treated the same *except* for the level of the independent variable (e.g., violent or nonviolent film), *then* any difference in the performance (e.g., memory for details) between the two groups must be caused by the independent variable.

Clearly, one key to this logic behind the experimental method is forming comparable (similar) groups at the start of the experiment. In the **random groups design,** comparable groups are formed prior to implementing the independent variable. One way to do this is by sampling subjects in a way that ensures each subject in the population has an equal likelihood of being included in each group of the experiment. One possible procedure for accomplishing this goal is random selection, as, for example, when we sample randomly from a registrar's list of students to obtain a representative sample of students for a survey (see Chapter 4). Actually, random selection is rarely used to establish comparable groups in a psychology experiment. Random selection requires well-defined populations (e.g., a registrar's list of students), but psychology experiments usually involve accidental samples from ill-defined populations. For example, human adult participants are often students from introductory psychology courses who volunteer for experiments as part of the course. Individuals enrolled in a general psychology course just happen to be those students who are taking this course in a given school term. Similarly, animal subjects typically are those that happen to be shipped to the researcher by a supplier. The animal researcher may not be aware of the precise nature of the population from which the animals were obtained or how they were selected.

The most common solution to the problem of forming comparable groups when ill-defined populations are involved is to use **random assignment** to place subjects in the conditions of the experiment. A closer look at the details of the Loftus and Burns experiment illustrates both the procedures of random assignment and the power of the random groups design. The major benefit of randomly assigning subjects to groups is to balance or average out the characteristics of the students in the two groups. For example, as we noted previously, if the groups of participants viewing the two versions of the film differed in their memory ability, then we could reasonably argue that the observed difference in memory for details of the film was due simply to this characteristic of the participants and not due to the type of film viewed. In this example, participants' memory ability, and type of film would be confounded. However, because the two samples of over 100 students in the Loftus and Burns experiment were randomly assigned to conditions, they are unlikely to differ (on the average) in memory ability, in attentiveness, or in any other way that might influence individuals' performance on the memory test. That is, random assignment to conditions is used to ensure that the average memory ability, the average attentiveness, and so forth, were comparable for the two groups. Because other potential causal factors were controlled by holding them constant and because individual differences among the students in the two groups were controlled by balancing them using random assignment, we can conclude that the different versions of the film caused the difference in students' memory performance.

A common procedure for carrying out random assignment is block randomization. First, let us describe exactly how block randomization is carried out, and then we will look at what it accomplishes. Suppose we have an experiment with five conditions. A "block" is made up of a random order of all five conditions.

*One block of conditions*  ➔  *Random order of conditions*

A  B  C  D  E  C  A  E  B  D

In block randomization, one subject is assigned to *each* condition in the block before a second subject is assigned to *any* one condition. That is, we assign subjects to conditions one block at a time. For example, if we want to have 10 subjects in each of five conditions, then there would be 10 blocks in the block-randomized schedule. Each block would consist of a random arrangement of the five conditions. You might think of this procedure as one where you take the first five people who show up for the experiment and assign each one randomly to one of the five conditions, then take the next five people and assign each to one of the five conditions, and so on, until you have done this 10 times. This procedure is illustrated below for the first 11 participants.

| 10 Blocks | Participants | Condition | |
|---|---|---|---|
| 1) C A E B D | 1) Cara | → C | |
| 2) E C D A B | 2) Andy | → A | |
| 3) D B E A C | 3) Jacob | → E | First block |
| 4) B A C E D | 4) Molly | → B | |
| 5) A C E D B | 5) Emily | → D | |
| 6) A D E B C | 6) Eric | → E | |
| 7) B C A D E | 7) Anna | → C | |
| 8) D C A E B | 8) Laura | → D | Second block |
| 9) E D B C A | 9) Sarah | → A | |
| 10) C E B D A | 10) Lisa | → B | |
| | 11) Tom | → D | |

and so on for 50 participants

**Block randomization** is an important technique for randomly assigning subjects to groups because it produces groups that are of equal size while controlling for time-related variables. The number of observations in each group influences the reliability of the descriptive statistics for each group. Because you will be comparing descriptive statistics across groups in your experiment, you want these measures to be of comparable reliability. So, each group should ideally be of similar size. Block randomization accomplishes this. Also, because subjects are assigned to conditions one block at a time, events that occur during the time when the experiment is being done are likely to be experienced by equal numbers of subjects in all conditions of the experiment. This is important because experiments often take a substantial amount of time to complete and the behavior of participants can be affected by events that occur during the time the experiment is conducted.

For example, suppose that you are doing a Loftus-and-Burns-type experiment that requires 100 participants assigned randomly to four conditions (e.g., four types of film segments). Assume further that you are drawing participants from introductory psychology classes. Given the availability of participants and your own personal schedule, such an experiment may take several weeks to complete. What if, after beginning the experiment, an instructor in one of the introductory psychology classes happens to describe the Loftus and Burns experiment? An experiment just like yours! Some students participating in your experiment may now recognize the film of the bank robbery and be prepared for a memory test, which could affect their performance. If all participants with knowledge of the experiment are assigned to one particular experimental condition, this would produce a serious confounding. The beauty of block randomization is that it will balance (or average) any effect of participants' prior knowledge of the experiment across the four conditions. That is, participants from that particular introductory psychology class will be randomly assigned to the different conditions of your experiment in approximately equal numbers. Thus, although there may be more variability in the groups' performances (which, you will see, can be troublesome), you will avoid a confounding. Block randomization works to balance other time-related variables, such as changes in experimenters or even changes in the populations from which subjects are drawn. An experiment conducted across two semesters of a school year (e.g., both fall and spring semesters) is perfectly acceptable if a block randomization schedule is used.

The procedure of block randomization, like many procedures, is best learned by doing it. You can get an idea of what using block randomization is like by doing Challenge Question 1A at the end of the chapter.

## Establishing External Validity

- When findings from an experiment can be applied to other individuals, settings, and conditions, the experiment has external validity.
- Although random assignment to conditions improves the internal validity of an experiment, it does not lead to representative samples that would increase the experiment's external validity.
- In some investigations (e.g., theory-testing), researchers may choose to emphasize internal validity over external validity; other researchers may choose to increase external validity using sampling or replication.
- Replication (usually partial replication) is an important method for establishing the reliability and external validity of research findings.
- Researchers often seek to generalize results about conceptual relationships among variables rather than specific conditions, manipulations, settings, and samples.

External validity refers to the extent to which findings from an experiment can be generalized to individuals, settings, and conditions beyond the scope of the specific experiment. Think for a moment about the Loftus and Burns experiment that we have been discussing. Can these findings be used to help us understand eyewitness behavior that might occur in a natural setting (and not on film)? When eyewitnesses are alone? When a different type of traumatic incident is involved? These are questions that ask about the external validity of the eyewitness study.

Although random assignment is the most commonly used procedure for carrying out a random groups design, it does not provide representative samples that allow researchers to generalize the results of an experiment beyond the particular subjects who happened to participate in the experiment. For example, we previously pointed out that participants in many psychology experiments form an accidental sample from an ill-defined population (introductory psychology students). Random assignment of subjects to conditions of an experiment will establish comparable groups *within* this accidental sample and, thus, help assure the internal validity of the experiment. But, how do we establish the external validity of experiments that involve random assignment? How do we generalize the findings for the different groups across individuals, settings, and conditions?

One answer to this question is a bit unsettling, at least initially. Quite simply, for some experiments we do not establish external validity. Mook (1983) argued that, when the purpose of an experiment is to test a specific hypothesis derived from a psychological theory, the question of external validity of the findings is irrelevant. An experiment is often done to determine whether subjects *can* be induced to behave in a certain way. The question whether subjects *do* behave that way in their natural environment is secondary to the question raised in the experiment. The issue of the external validity of experiments is not a new one, as reflected in the following statement by Riley (1962, p. 413): "In general, laboratory experiments are not set up to imitate the most typical case found in nature. Instead, they are intended to answer some specific question of interest to the experimenter."

There are circumstances, however, in which it is critical to obtain results that can be generalized beyond the boundaries of the experiment itself. There are several ways to proceed. First, and most obviously, you can attempt to include in your experiment characteristics of the situation to which you wish to generalize. For example, Ceci (1993) described a research program that he and his colleagues conducted on children's eyewitness testimony. He described how their research program was motivated in part because previous studies on this topic did not capture all the dimensions of an *actual* eyewitness situation. Ceci described how their research program included factors such as multiple suggestive interviews, very long retention intervals, and recollections of stressful experiences. Including these factors made the experiments more representative of situations that are actually involved when children testify.

Ceci (1993) also pointed out, however, that important differences remained between the experiments and real-life situations:

> High levels of stress, assaults to a victim's body, and the loss of control are characteristics of events that motivate forensic investigations. Although these factors are at play in some of our other studies, we will never mimic experimentally the

assaultive nature of acts perpetrated on child victims, because even those studies that come closest, such as the medical studies, are socially and parentally sanctioned, unlike sexual assaults against children. (pp. 41–42)

As Ceci's comments reveal, in some situations, such as those involving eyewitness testimony about despicable acts, there may be important ethical constraints on establishing the external validity of experiments.

A second way to increase external validity is by sampling people or events. When the external validity of an experiment can be established ethically and when external validity is a high priority for the research, a simple general rule should be followed: Include a representative sample on any dimension (individuals, settings, or conditions) in your experiment to which you want to generalize your results. For example, when you wish to generalize beyond the particular subjects who participated in the experiment, then random selection (when that is possible) is preferable to random assignment. However, even when a truly representative sample on a relevant dimension is not feasible, you can increase the external validity of your study beyond a particular version of a violent event in an eyewitness study, beyond a specific word list in a memory experiment, or beyond a single photograph in a facial recognition study, by including multiple instances of these events. Participants can be randomly assigned to the different versions of each condition and the results then averaged across the different versions. Our belief that the results will generalize to other situations is strengthened when we observe similar results across a variety of stimulus types.

A third way to demonstrate external validity is through replication. **Replication** means repeating all of the procedures used in a particular experiment in order to determine whether the same results will be obtained a second time with different participants. Most replications are done when an initial finding is unexpected or is judged to be especially important. Typically, replication is said to occur if the effect of the independent variable is present in both the original study and in the replication study. *Replication serves the important goal of providing evidence for the reliability of an experimental finding.* Establishing the reliability of experimental findings from experiments posted on the World Wide Web, for instance, has become a matter of serious concern since more research is now being done online by Web users who happen upon experiments at psychology-related sites (e.g., the site maintained by the American Psychological Society). A major question is: Are the results obtained from traditional laboratory experiments with college student participants the same or similar to those results obtained from experiments posted on the Web (see, for example, Krantz, Ballard, & Scher, 1997).

As you might imagine, an exact replication is almost impossible to carry out. The subjects tested in the replication will be different from those tested in the original study; the testing rooms, experimenters, and even apparatus also may be different. Thus, when attempting to replicate an experimental result, in nearly every instance the replication will be a partial replication. Nevertheless, there are distinct advantages to carrying out a partial replication. *Partial replications*, in fact, are commonly done as a routine part of the process of investigating the conditions under which a phenomenon reliably occurs. Let us examine why.

A partial replication can help to establish both experimental reliability (by demonstrating that a similar experimental result occurs when the *same* basic experimental procedures are repeated) and external validity (by showing that a similar experimental result occurs when slightly *different* experimental procedures are used). Consider the same basic experiment done in both a large metropolitan public university and in a small rural private college; the participants and the settings in the experiments are very different. If the same results are obtained even with these different participants and settings, we can say the findings can be generalized across these two populations and settings. Notice that neither experiment alone has external validity; it is the findings that occur in *both* experiments that have external validity.

In partial replications, some but not all of the conditions of the original experiment are repeated. This may also occur when an experimenter chooses to repeat some levels of an independent variable, and also add some new levels not previously tested. When the same results are observed for the levels of the independent variable that are repeated (replicated), evidence for the reliability of the findings is obtained (remember that reliability indicates *consistency*). For conditions that are different from the original experiment, observing similar findings demonstrates the external validity of those findings. For instance, suppose you decided to follow up the interesting results on subvocal speech obtained by Haber and Haber (1982). If you designed a new experiment that included their two types of sentences (control and tongue-twisters) but also included a new type of sentence that varied in some theoretically important way from the original ones, then you would be able to obtain information about the reliability of their results (did you find the same thing when using their sentences?) as well as the external validity of their results along the dimension you chose to vary.

A frequently asked question concerning external validity of psychological research findings is related to the nature of the "subjects." As you are aware, many studies in psychology involve college students who participate in experiments as part of their introductory psychology course. Dawes (1991), among others, argues that college students are a select group who may not always provide a good basis for building general conclusions about human behavior and mental processes. He suggests that the college environment tends to protect students from external problems, thereby enhancing their feeling of control over their lives. People living outside the college environment may not have the same sense of control that college students do. Thus, research on "locus of control" done with college students may not generalize to people living outside the college environment. On the other hand, research involving fundamental processes such as sensation or perception might reasonably be judged to generalize well to noncollege students despite the differences in environment. In general, the arguments raised by Dawes and others should lead us to exercise care in generalizing conclusions from all studies in which college students are participants.

**FIGURE 6.2**    Questions of external validity include those related to the nature of the participants in psychological research; for example, we might ask whether results of studies done with college students will generalize to people not in a college.

It would be virtually impossible to establish the external validity of each finding in psychology by performing partial replications across each of the dimensions over which we want to generalize (e.g., subjects, settings, tasks, and so on). But if we take arguments like those of Dawes seriously, as indeed we should, it would appear that we have an impossible task in front of us. How, for instance, do we show that an experimental finding obtained with a group of college students will generalize to groups of older adults, working professionals, less educated individuals, and so forth? Underwood and Shaughnessy (1975) provide an answer, or at least an approach worth considering. Their notion is that we should assume that behavior is relatively continuous across time, subjects, and settings unless we have reason to assume otherwise. For instance, most experiments are carried out in individual laboratory rooms, but we are not likely to argue that the results of the experiment apply only to those particular rooms. Similarly, the particular subjects tested in an experiment are considered, according to this reasoning, to be generally representative of other, similar individuals who might have been tested.

Underwood and Shaughnessy's (1975) assumption is not a call to blind faith in any experimental finding. The boundaries for generalizing experimental findings are set by consensus of the research community. The research community may agree, for example, that introductory psychology students who volunteer for experiments are representative of college students in general but not representative of young children or the elderly. Or, agreement may be reached for some phenomena and not others. For instance, generalizing results of a vision experiment based on a college student sample may be safer than generalizing results of a locus of control experiment. Underwood and Shaughnessy (1975) argued that the burden of proof regarding questions of external validity rests with the person claiming we should *not* generalize. Consider criticisms questioning the generalizability of results based on college students. One response to such criticisms is to place the burden of proof on the critics by requiring them to provide an empirical demonstration that results based on college students are, in fact, limited. Such direct tests using partial replications represent perhaps the best way to establish the external validity of experimental findings.

Yet another way to establish the external validity of experimental research conducted in laboratory settings is demonstrated by Anderson and Bushman's (1997) analysis of aggression research. They used meta-analysis, a procedure described at the end of this chapter, to compare findings from aggression experiments conducted in laboratory settings to correlational findings from "real-world" settings. Critics of laboratory experiments argue that "artificial" laboratory situations in which, for example, college students may be "aggressive" by rating a rude experimenter negatively, do not tell us much about real-life aggression in which people threaten, assault, and murder others. Critics of real-world studies argue that correlations, for example, between violence presented in media and crime statistics, do not tell us about the causes of aggression. Anderson and Bushman's approach to this controversy was to argue that both types of studies potentially tell us about aggression if we look at the psychological processes these studies are attempting to examine. That is, what we wish to generalize from any one study are *conceptual relationships* among variables, not the specific conditions, manipulations, settings, samples, etc. (see also Banaji & Crowder, 1989; Mook, 1983).

An example provided by Anderson and Bushman (1997) illustrates the idea of generalizing at the level of psychological processes. We could conduct a study with 5-year-old children to determine if a specific name-calling manipulation induces anger and aggression, and then conduct another study to determine if this name-calling manipulation generalizes to 35-year-old adults. As Anderson and Bushman state, this type of research is likely to have low external validity regardless of whether the studies are conducted in the laboratory or the real world because the specific name-calling manipulation, " 'Pooh-pooh head' just doesn't pack the same 'punch' for 5- and 35-year-old people" (p. 21). However, if we wish to generalize the general psychological process, "*insults increase aggressive behavior*," we could use different words that would be meaningful insults for each population to determine if the psychological process regarding insults generalizes across populations.

To examine psychological processes related to aggression, Anderson and Bushman (1997) identified a list of individual differences variables and situational variables they believed are related to aggression. They then searched the psychological literature for laboratory studies and real-world studies to compare the effects of these variables in the two settings. Importantly, they focused on conceptual relationships in the studies rather than comparing studies that used the same specific operationalizations of variables. For each individual differences variable they examined, they found the setting of the research did not change the nature of the effect. In both laboratory settings and real-world settings, males were more physically aggressive than females, but males and females did not differ in verbal aggressiveness; trait aggressiveness was positively correlated with aggression; and people with Type A personalities were more aggressive than people with Type B personalities. Also, for each situational variable they examined, with the exception of temperature, they found the nature of the effects was the same in laboratory and real-world studies. In both settings, provocation, alcohol, violent media, and anonymity of the aggressor were found to increase aggression. Anderson and Bushman concluded that "artificial" laboratory experiments do provide meaningful information about aggression because they demonstrate the same conceptual relationships that are observed in real-world aggression. Furthermore, laboratory experiments allow researchers to isolate the potential causes of aggression and to investigate boundary conditions for when aggression will or will not occur.

What about when results in the lab and the real world disagree? In real-world studies (as was observed in the archival data presented in Chapter 5), hot temperatures are associated consistently with aggression, but temperature effects are inconsistent in laboratory studies. Anderson and Bushman (1997) argue that these discrepancies, rather than evidence for the weakness of either method, should be used to help us refine our theories about aggression. That is, the discrepancies should make us recognize that different psychological processes may be at work in each setting. When we increase our understanding of these discrepancies, we will increase our understanding of aggression.

## Challenges to Internal Validity

- Randomly assigning intact groups to different conditions of the independent variable creates a potential confounding due to individual differences among participants in the intact groups.
- Block randomization increases internal validity by balancing extraneous variables across conditions of the independent variable.
- Whether extraneous variables are controlled by balancing or by holding conditions constant influences the external validity and sensitivity of an experiment.
- Selective subject loss, but not mechanical subject loss, threatens the internal validity of an experiment.
- Placebo control groups are used to control for the problem of demand characteristics, and double-blind experiments control both demand characteristics and experimenter effects.

Testing Intact Groups    Random assignment is used to assure comparable groups in the random groups design. There are times, however, when noncomparable groups are formed even when random assignment appears to have been used. This problem occurs when intact groups (and not individual subjects) are randomly assigned to the conditions of an experiment. *Intact groups* are those that were formed prior to the start of the experiment. For example, the different sections of an introductory psychology class are intact groups. Students are not randomly assigned to different sections of introductory psychology classes (although sometimes scheduling classes seems random!). Students often choose to be in a particular section because of the time the class meets, the instructor, friends who will be in the class, and any number of other factors. Problems arise, however, when individuals differ across the intact groups. For example, students who choose to take an 8:00 A.M. section may differ from students who prefer an 11:00 A.M. section. Random assignment of these intact groups to experimental conditions is simply not sufficient to balance the systematic differences among the intact groups. These individual differences, then, are almost guaranteed to confound the independent variable under investigation. The solution to this problem is simple—do not use intact groups in a random groups design. (As you will see in Chapter 10, there are situations when researchers use intact groups because random assignment of participants to conditions is not possible; however, this means that the problem of confounding must be dealt with, and is always a less desirable alternative to a random groups design.)

**Balancing Extraneous Variables**   A number of factors in an experiment may vary as a result of practical considerations when carrying out the study. For example, to complete an experiment more quickly, a researcher might decide to have several different experimenters test small groups of participants. The sizes of the groups and the experimenters themselves become potentially relevant variables that could confound the experiment, making the results uninterpretable. For example, if all the individuals in the experimental group are tested by one experimenter and all those in the control group are tested by another experimenter, the levels of intended independent variable become confounded with the experimenters. One would not be able to determine whether an observed difference between the control group and experimental group on the dependent variable was due to the independent variable manipulation or to the fact that different experimenters implemented the study.

   Potential variables that are not directly of interest to the researcher, such as different experimenters and sizes of groups, are such vexing sources of confounding that they have a special name: **extraneous variables.** But don't let the term fool you! An experiment confounded by an extraneous variable is no less confounded than if the confounding variable were of considerable inherent interest. For example, Evans and Donnerstein (1974) studied one such extraneous variable—the differences between participants who volunteer early in the term and those who volunteer late in the term. Their results indicated that those who volunteer early are more academically oriented and are more likely to have an internal locus of control (i.e., they emphasize their own responsibility for their actions rather than external factors). Their findings suggest it would not be wise to test participants in the experimental condition at the beginning of the term and participants in the control condition at the end of the term, as this would potentially confound the independent variable with participants' locus of control. As we have seen, block randomization should be used to balance characteristics of participants across the conditions of an experiment.

Block randomization provides an easy and effective way to control numerous extraneous variables by balancing them across groups. All that is required is that entire blocks be tested at each level of the extraneous variable. For example, if there were four different experimenters, entire blocks of the block-randomized schedule would be assigned to each experimenter. Because each block contains all the conditions of the experiment, this strategy guarantees that each condition will be tested by each experimenter. Usually, we would assign the same number of blocks to each experimenter, but this is not essential. What is essential is that entire blocks be tested at each level of the extraneous variable, which, in this case, is experimenter. The balancing act can become a bit tricky when there are several extraneous variables, but careful advance planning can avoid confounding by such factors.

Even when their potential effects have been controlled through balancing, extraneous variables affect the sensitivity and external validity of an experiment. For example, if five different experimenters test an equal number of participants in each of two conditions, the experiment will be free of confounding due to any differences across experimenters. However, the performance of the participants within each condition is likely to vary more than if one experimenter had tested all the participants. Participants are likely, after all, to respond differently to the different experimenters, even when the experimenters try to treat all participants within a condition the same way. Similarly, using two different word lists in a memory experiment or five different perceptual displays in a perception experiment will increase variability relative to a situation in which only one instance was used. This increased variability within each group makes it harder to detect differences between the groups, thus reducing the sensitivity of the experiment. If a difference is obtained between the two conditions, however, this finding has greater external validity than, for example, if only one experimenter had done the testing (because the findings can be generalized across different experimenters).

This is the general principle that emerges: *Controlling extraneous variables by holding them constant leads to more sensitive experiments with less external validity, whereas controlling extraneous variables by balancing them leads to lower sensitivity but increased external validity.* Both balancing and holding constant extraneous variables are equally effective control techniques, however, in ensuring that an experiment is internally valid.

**Subject Loss**   Internally valid experiments involving the random groups design need to have comparable groups of subjects not only at the beginning of an experiment but, except for the addition of the independent variable, also at the end. When subjects begin an experiment but fail to complete it successfully, the internal validity of the experiment can be threatened. There are two types of subject loss: mechanical and selective. It is important to distinguish between these two ways by which subjects are lost because selective subject loss poses a threat to internal validity (Underwood & Shaughnessy, 1975).

**Mechanical subject loss** occurs when a subject fails to complete the experiment because of an equipment failure (in this case, the experimenter is considered part of the equipment). If a light bulb burns out, or if someone inadvertently interrupts an experimental session, or if the experimenter reads the wrong set of instructions, the subject who was being tested represents a mechanical subject loss. Mechanical loss is unrelated to any characteristic of the subject, so it should not lead to systematic differences between the characteristics of the subjects who successfully complete the experiment in the various conditions of the experiment. In a real sense, mechanical subject loss represents the effect of chance events (e.g., a projector bulb happens to burn out) and, thus, should be expected to occur equally across conditions of an experiment. Hence, internal validity is not typically threatened when data from such subjects are excluded from the experiment. When mechanical subject loss occurs, the name of the dropped subject and the reason for the loss need to be recorded. The lost subject is then replaced by the next subject tested.

Selective subject loss is a far more serious matter. **Selective subject loss** occurs (1) when subjects are lost differentially across the conditions of the experiment; (2) when some characteristic of the subject is responsible for the loss; and (3) when this subject characteristic is related to the dependent variable used to assess the outcome of the study. Selective subject loss destroys the comparable groups that are essential to the logic of the random groups design, and can thus render the experiment uninterpretable. This problem can arise in a variety of experimental situations, for example, physiological studies involving surgical or drug treatments, memory experiments testing retention over days or weeks, and longitudinal designs in survey research (see Chapter 4).

The problems associated with selective subject loss can be illustrated by considering a fictitious but realistic example. Assume that the directors of a local fitness center decide to do an experiment to test the effectiveness of a one-month fitness program they have developed. They identify 80 people who are willing to volunteer for the experiment, and they randomly assign 40 to each of two groups. Random assignment to conditions is used to create comparable groups by balancing characteristics such as weight, fitness level, motivation, and so on across the two groups. Members of the control group are simply asked to come to the center at the end of the month. When they arrive, they are given a fitness test. Those in the experimental group participate in a vigorous fitness program for one month prior to the test at the end of the month. Assume all 40 control participants show up for the fitness test, but only 25 of the experimental participants stay with the rigorous fitness program for the full month, and only these 25 people are given the test. The average fitness score is significantly higher for the experimental group, leading the directors of the fitness center to make the claim that: "A scientifically based research study has shown that our program leads to better fitness."

**FIGURE 6.3**   Selective subject loss occurs when participants fail to complete an experiment for reasons related to the dependent variable.

Do you think the fitness center's claim is justified? It's not. At least not on the basis of the study we have described. This hypothetical study represents a classic example of selective subject loss. The loss occurred differentially across conditions; participants were lost only from the experimental group. The problem is not that the groups ended up different in size. The results would have been interpretable if 25 people had been randomly assigned to the experimental group and 40 to the control group and all the individuals had completed the experiment. The problem is that the 25 experimental participants who completed the fitness program are not likely to be comparable to the 40 control participants. It is likely that only the more naturally fit experimental participants could complete the rigorous program; the less fit individuals likely dropped out. Thus, the loss is traceable to a characteristic of the participants—their original level of fitness—and this characteristic is relevant to the outcome of the study. The final fitness scores of the experimental participants might have been higher even if they had not participated in the fitness program because they were more fit when they began!

If selective subject loss is not identified until after the experiment is completed, little can be done except to chalk up the experience of having conducted an uninterpretable experiment. You can take some preventive steps, however, if you realize in advance that selective loss may be a problem. One alternative is to administer a pretest and screen out subjects who are likely to be lost. In our example, an initial test of fitness could have been given, and only those participants who scored above some minimal level allowed into the experimental and control groups. The cost associated with this alternative is decreased external validity because the results could be generalized only to people above the minimal fitness level. This cost may be well worth paying because an interpretable study of limited external validity is still preferable to an uninterpretable study.

The second way to minimize the risk of selective subject loss also involves a pretest. Here all subjects are given the pretest but are then simply randomly assigned to one of the conditions. Then, if a subject is lost from the experimental group, a subject with a comparable pretest score is dropped from the control group. In a sense, this approach tries to restore the comparability of the groups. This approach also entails a cost of decreased external validity because those subjects who finally end up in the study may differ from those in the original sample. The advantage of this approach is that external validity is lost *only if* selective subject loss *does* occur. When a pretest is used to check for selective subject loss, it is essential that the pretest measures the dimension responsible for the loss. In our example, a fitness pretest would be preferable to a pretest of visual acuity (which is likely to be unrelated to subject loss in this study). Thus, the researcher must be ready to anticipate possible reasons for selective subject loss and measure these factors prior to beginning the study.

Placebo Control and Double-Blind Experiments    The final challenge to internal validity we will describe arises because of expectations held by both participants and experimenters. In our discussion of the problem of reactivity in observational research (Chapter 3), we introduced the concept of demand characteristics (Orne, 1962). **Demand characteristics** refer to the cues and other information used by individuals to guide their behavior in a psychological study. For example, if research participants know they have been given alcohol, they may expect certain effects, such as relaxation or giddiness, and behave accordingly. In addition to potential problems due to demand characteristics, there are also potential biases traceable to the expectations of the experimenters. The general term used to describe these biases is **experimenter effects** (Rosenthal, 1963). Experimenter effects may lead the experimenters to treat subjects differently in the different groups of the experiment in ways other than those required to implement the independent variable. In the context of our example experiment involving alcohol, experimenter effects could occur if the experimenters treated people in the different groups differently by, for example, reading the instructions more slowly to individuals who had been given alcohol. Experimenter effects also include biased observations by experimenters when they know which treatment the subject has received. Biased observations due to experimenter effects would arise in the alcohol study, for example, if the experimenters were more likely to notice unusual motor movements or slurred speech among the "drinkers" (because they "expect" drinkers to behave this way).

The problems of demand characteristics and experimenter effects can never be eliminated, but there are special research designs that control these problems. Demand characteristics may be controlled using a research design that involves **placebo control** groups. A *placebo* (from the Latin word meaning "I shall please") is a substance that looks like a drug or other active substance but is actually an *inert*, or inactive, substance. Pishkin and Shurley (1983) used a placebo control group to demonstrate the effectiveness of two drugs (doxepin and hydroxyzine). The drugs were tested to determine if they reduce arousal levels of psychiatric patients in response to stress. The placebo participants were given capsules identical to the two drugs, but the placebo capsules contained only lactose, a sugar found in milk. None of the participants in the placebo control group realized their pill contained no medicine so all groups had the same "awareness" of taking a drug, and therefore, the same expectations. That is, the demand characteristics were the same for the groups—all participants expected to experience effects of the drug. Any differences between the experimental groups and the placebo control group could legitimately be attributed to the *actual* effect of the drug taken by the experimental participants, and not the participants' expectations about receiving a drug. One group of researchers claims that a placebo effect is significantly related to the therapeutic effect of antidepressant drugs such as Prozac (Kirsch & Sapirstein, 1998).

Placebo control groups can be used in combination with a technique that controls for both demand characteristics *and* experimenter effects. The technique is called a **double-blind** procedure because both the participant *and* the observer are blind to (unaware of) what treatment is being administered. In an experiment such as the Pishkin and Shurley (1983) study, two researchers would be needed to accomplish the double-blind procedure. The first researcher would prepare the drug capsules and code each capsule in some way; the second researcher would distribute the drugs to the participants, recording the code for each drug as it was given to an individual. This procedure ensures there is a record of which drug each person received, but neither the participant nor the experimenter who actually administers the drugs (and observes their effects) knows which treatment the participant received. Thus, experimenter expectancies about the effects of the treatment are controlled because the researcher who makes observations is unaware of who received the treatment and who received the placebo. Similarly, demand characteristics are controlled because participants remain unaware of whether they received the drug or placebo. Note that using placebo control groups raises special ethical concerns, as research participants who expect to receive a drug may instead receive a placebo. Typically, the ethics of this procedure are addressed in the informed consent procedure prior to the start of the experiment. Participants are told they may receive a drug or a placebo. Only individuals who consent to receiving the placebo or the drug participate in the research.

## ALTERNATIVE INDEPENDENT GROUPS DESIGNS

### Matched Groups Design

- A matched group design may be used to create comparable groups when there are too few subjects available for random assignment to work effectively.
- Matching subjects on the dependent variable task is the best approach for creating matched groups, followed by matching subjects on a task that is from the same category as the dependent variable.
- After subjects are matched on the matching task they should then be randomly assigned to the conditions of the independent variable.

The random groups design is by far the most common type of independent groups design. To work effectively, however, the random groups design requires samples of sufficient size to guarantee that individual differences among subjects will be balanced through random assignment. Specifically, the assumption behind the random groups design is that individual differences "average out" across groups. But how many subjects are required to ensure that this averaging process works as it should? The answer is, "It depends." More subjects will be needed to average out individual differences when sampling from a heterogeneous population than from a more homogeneous one.

We can be relatively confident that random assignment will *not* be effective in balancing the differences among subjects when small numbers of subjects are tested from heterogeneous populations. However, this is exactly the situation researchers face in several areas of psychology. For example, some developmental psychologists study newborn infants; others study elderly people. These psychologists often have available only limited numbers of participants, and both newborns and the elderly certainly represent diverse populations.

**FIGURE 6.4** Random assignment is not likely to be effective in balancing differences among subjects when small numbers of subjects from heterogeneous populations are tested (e.g., newborns). In this situation, researchers may want to consider the matched groups design.

One alternative that researchers have in this situation is to administer all the conditions of the experiment to all the subjects, using a repeated measures design (to be discussed in Chapter 7). Nevertheless, some independent variables require separate groups of subjects for each level. For instance, assume you are trying to assess the effects of participation in a special program for senior citizens. You will need to have a separate control group that does not participate in the program. Or suppose you wish to administer two types of postnatal care to different groups of premature infants. In these situations a repeated measures design is of no use.

The matched groups design is a good alternative when neither the random groups design nor repeated measures design can be used effectively. The logic of the **matched groups design** is simple and compelling. Instead of trusting random assignment to form comparable groups, the researcher makes the groups equivalent by matching subjects. In most uses of the matched groups design a pretest task is used to match subjects. The challenge is to select a pretest task (also called a matching task) that equates the groups on a dimension that is relevant to the outcome of the experiment. *The matched groups design is useful only when a good matching task is available.*

Researchers have several options when selecting a matching task. The most preferred option is to match subjects using the same task that will be used in the experiment itself. For example, if the dependent variable in the experiment is blood pressure, participants should be matched on blood pressure prior to the start of the experiment. The matching is accomplished by measuring the blood pressure of all participants and then forming pairs or triples or quadruples of subjects (depending on the number of conditions in the experiment) who have identical or similar blood pressures. After these matched sets are formed, the investigator must assign subjects within a set randomly to the different conditions of the experiment such that each subject in a matched set is assigned to a different condition. Random assignment (after matching the subjects) is used to balance individual differences other than those for which subjects were matched. The logic of the design is again straightforward. Participants in the different matched groups begin the study with average blood pressure equivalent across the groups. Assume, then, some treatment is applied to one group but not to others. Blood pressure is assessed again at the end of the treatment to determine the outcome of the study. Because average blood pressure across the groups was equivalent at the start of the study, any group differences in blood pressure at the end of the study may be attributed to the treatment (presuming other potential variables have been held constant or balanced).

In some experiments, the primary dependent variable cannot be used to match subjects. For example, consider an experiment that examines different approaches to solving a puzzle. If a pretest were given to see how long it took individuals to solve this puzzle, the participants would likely learn the solution to the puzzle during the pretest. If so, then it would be impossible to observe differences in the speed with which different groups of participants solved the puzzle in the experiment itself. After having experience with the puzzle in the pretest, all participants would likely solve the puzzle very quickly. In this situation the next best alternative to using the experimental task as the matching task is to use a task from the same class or category as the experimental task. In our problem-solving experiment, participants could be matched on their performance when solving a different puzzle from the experimental puzzle. However, it is important that performance on the experimental puzzle correlates positively with performance on the matching puzzle. The least preferred alternative for matching is to use a task from a class different from the experimental task. For our problem-solving experiment, participants could be matched on some test of general ability, such as an intelligence test. As is true for all effective matching tasks, this general matching task must correlate positively with performance on the experimental task. One must keep in mind that as the correlation between the matching task and the dependent variable decreases, the advantage of the matched group design, relative to the random groups design, also decreases.

There is an additional important issue that arises with the matched groups design even when a good matching task is available. Consider an experiment comparing two different methods of caring for premature infants. The matched groups design would work well for this type of experiment. Six pairs of premature infants could be matched on their body weight and on measures such as their scores on an infant motor coordination test. This experiment illustrates the conditions when a matched groups design is most helpful—the need to test separate groups with only small numbers of participants and good matching tasks available. We began our discussion of the matched groups design by saying it is useful when we have too few participants to allow randomization to form comparable groups. A matching task like the body weights of the premature infants ensures comparable groups *only* on the dimension measured by the matching task. Although the matched groups design serves a very important purpose by allowing us to form comparable groups on the significant dimensions reflected in good matching tasks (e.g., body weights of premature infants), there remain potentially relevant characteristics of the participants that are not matched. For example, the two groups of premature infants may not be comparable in their general health or in their degree of parental attachment. It is important, therefore, to use random assignment in the matched groups design to balance other potential factors beyond the matching task. For instance, after matching the infants on body weight and motor coordination, the pairs of infants would be randomly assigned to one of the two groups. In conclusion, *the matched groups design is a better alternative than the random groups design when a good matching task is available and when only a small number of (heterogeneous) subjects is available for an experiment that requires separate groups for each condition.*

## Natural Groups Design

- Individual differences variables (or subject variables) are selected rather than manipulated to form natural groups designs.
- The natural groups design represents a type of correlational research in which researchers look for covariations between natural groups variables and dependent variables.

- Causal inferences cannot be made regarding the effects of natural groups variables because plausible alternative explanations for group differences exist.

Researchers in many areas of psychology are interested in independent variables that are called *individual differences variables* or *subject variables*. Individual differences variables such as gender, introversion-extraversion, or aggressiveness, are important independent variables in personality psychology, abnormal psychology, developmental psychology, and social psychology. These variables cannot be manipulated. We cannot randomly assign someone to be 20 years old or to be an introverted or aggressive person, or to be male or female. Instead, we *select* the levels of these independent variables.

It is important to differentiate experiments involving independent variables whose levels are selected from those involving independent variables whose levels are manipulated. Experiments involving independent variables whose levels are selected—like individual differences variables—are called **natural groups designs.** The natural groups design is frequently used in situations in which ethical and practical constraints prevent us from directly manipulating independent variables. No matter how interested we might be in the effects of traumatic events such as major surgery on subsequent depression, we could not ethically perform major surgery on a randomly assigned group of introductory psychology students and then compare their depression symptoms with those of another group who did not receive surgery! Similarly, if we were interested in the relationship between divorce and emotional disorders, we could not randomly assign some people to get divorced. By using the natural groups design, however, we can compare people who have had surgery with those who have not. Similarly, people who have chosen to divorce can be compared with those who have chosen to stay married.

The intent of studies using the natural groups design is to determine whether these natural "treatments" result in systematic differences in behavior. For example, studies have shown that people who are separated or divorced are much more likely to receive psychiatric care than are those who are married, widowed, or have remained single. In general, the natural groups design involves looking for *correlations* between subjects' characteristics and their performance. Because of this, the natural groups design represents a type of correlational research (see also Chapter 4).

Natural groups designs are highly effective in meeting the first two objectives of the scientific method—description and prediction. Serious problems can arise, though, when the results of natural groups designs are used to make causal statements. For instance, the finding that divorced persons are more likely than married persons to receive psychiatric care shows that these two factors covary. This result could be taken to mean that divorce causes emotional disorders that lead to the need for psychiatric care. Before reaching this conclusion, however, we must assure ourselves that the time-order condition for a causal inference has been met—namely, that divorce preceded

**FIGURE 6.5**   Do individuals who join fraternities differ in important ways from individuals who do not? This question can be answered using the natural groups design.

the emotional disorder. Demonstrating covariation does nothing to specify the direction of the causal relationship. Perhaps those who suffer from emotional disorders are more likely to get divorced because the disorder placed strain on the relationship or because the emotional disorder contributed to marrying unwisely in the first place.

The most critical problem in drawing causal inferences based on the natural groups design is meeting the third condition for demonstrating causality: eliminating plausible alternative causes. Do you see how this problem is especially troublesome with the natural groups design? Eliminating plausible alternative causes requires a high degree of control and the experimenter has far less control in the natural groups design. The individual differences studied in the natural groups design are usually confounded. This is because groups of individuals are likely to differ in many ways in addition to the variable used to classify them. For example, individuals who divorce and individuals who stay married may differ with respect to a number of characteristics other than their marital status. For example, they may differ in their religious practices or financial circumstances. Any differences observed between divorced and married individuals may be due to these other characteristics, and not divorce. The manipulation done by "nature" is rarely the controlled type we have come to expect in establishing the internal validity of an experiment.

In Chapter 8 we will discuss an effective approach for drawing causal inferences in the natural groups design. The approach requires that *individual differences be studied in combination with independent variables that can be manipulated.* This combination of more than one independent variable in one experiment requires the use of a complex design, which we cover in Chapter 8. For now, recognize that drawing causal inferences based on the natural groups design can be a treacherous enterprise. While we frequently refer to such designs as "experiments," there are important differences between an experiment involving an individual differences variable and an experiment involving a manipulated variable.

## ANALYSIS OF EXPERIMENTS

### Overview

- Descriptive statistics are not sufficient to summarize the results of a study because they provide no indication of whether the findings are reliable.
- Inferential statistics are used to determine whether an independent variable has a reliable effect on a dependent variable.
- Two methods to make inferences about sample data are null hypothesis testing and confidence intervals.

The purpose of an experiment is to determine whether an independent variable has had an effect on behavior as indicated by changes in the dependent variable. The foundation of the analysis of an experiment is the description of the results. Descriptive statistics begin to answer the question, "What happened in your experiment?" (See Appendix A for an overview of the major steps in data analysis.) Nevertheless, descriptive statistics are rarely sufficient to answer this question. The problem is that the data we typically are describing are based on samples we have selected and assigned to the conditions of our experiment. The situation would be entirely different if we were describing populations and not samples. A population represents all the data of interest; a sample is just part of those data. Rarely, however, do psychologists work with populations. Most of the time they sample behavior and seek to make a conclusion about the effect of an independent variable based on these samples. Sample characteristics can vary from one sample to another simply due to chance variation. Knowing this requires us to be very cautious about drawing conclusions based simply on calculating descriptive statistics for our samples. How do we know that the differences we "see" among our sample means are reliable?

The best way to determine whether the differences in means obtained in an experiment are reliable would be to replicate the experiment and see if the same outcome is obtained. We noted earlier that replications provide evidence both for the external validity of a finding and the reliability of the finding. Although replications, especially partial replications, do occur in the natural course of research on a topic, they would be a cumbersome and inefficient way to establish the reliability of experimental findings if they were to be required for every experiment done in psychology. Participants for experiments are a scarce resource, and each replication costs us a study that could be done to ask new and different questions about behavior. We need some alternative to replication for determining whether the differences obtained in a single experiment are larger than would be expected on the basis of error (chance) variation alone.

The typical approach to drawing conclusions based on sample data has been through the use of inferential statistics, and more specifically, the approach called null hypothesis testing. **Inferential statistics** provide a way to test whether the differences in a dependent variable associated with various conditions of an experiment can be attributed to an effect of the independent variable. Null hypothesis testing is the most common form of inferential statistics used to make these decisions. There are many critics of this approach, however, and psychologists have been urged to seek other ways to draw inferences about sample data (e.g., Cohen, 1995; Loftus, 1996; Schmidt, 1996). Thus, in what follows, we first introduce you to an important alternative to null hypothesis testing, one that makes use of confidence intervals around the means. Then, we will discuss the more common approach, one based on null hypothesis testing. At that time, we will identify some of the important limitations to null hypothesis testing that critics have highlighted. Our introduction will be brief; you will find more about these two approaches to the analysis of experiments in Appendix A.

## Confidence Intervals

- Samples are used to estimate population values.
- Confidence intervals for a sample identify the range of values in which we can expect a population value to fall with a specified level of confidence.
- Researchers determine whether populations differ by noting whether the confidence intervals for different samples in a study overlap.

To illustrate the use of confidence intervals to analyze and interpret results, we consider a study on how infants "grasp the nature of pictures" (DeLoache, Pierroutsakos, Uttal, Rosengren, & Gottlieb, 1998). Have you ever wondered whether infants understand that a picture of an object is not the same thing as the object itself? DeLoache and her colleagues were intrigued by research demonstrating that infants as young as 5 months seem to recognize the similarity between objects and their pictures, but also seem to recognize they're not the same. However, these research findings do not correspond well to anecdotes of infants' behavior toward pictures in which infants and young children try to grasp or pick up the objects represented in pictures, and even try to step into a picture of a shoe! These anecdotal reports suggest that infants and children treat pictured objects as if they are real objects, despite the two-dimensional representation in the picture. In four studies, DeLoache et al. examined "to what extent infants would treat depicted objects as if they were real objects" (p. 205).

**FIGURE 6.6**    Infants' understanding of the nature of pictures was examined by observing how they investigate and point to pictured objects. (From DeLoache et al., 1998; used with permission.)

Although we will focus on the results presented for DeLoache et al.'s (1998) fourth study, it is helpful to highlight the findings from their first three studies. In Study 1, a structured observation, 10 9-month-old infants were observed as they explored a picture book with "eight highly realistic color photographs of individual objects (common plastic toys)" (p. 206). The results indicated that each infant manually explored at least one picture and 8 of the 10 infants tried to grasp a pictured object at least once (the average was 3.7 attempts). In their second study, the investigators sought to make sure that infants could distinguish between pictured objects and their real-life counterparts. In this study, eight 9-month-olds were presented with the pictured object and the real object simultaneously. Overwhelmingly, the infants reached first for the object instead of the picture (86% of the trials), indicating that infants' grasping at pictures in Study 1 was not because the infants could not discriminate between two- and three-dimensional objects. The purpose of Study 3 was to determine the external validity of these findings by observing the grasping of pictures by "Beng infants from severely impoverished and largely nonliterate families living in a rural village in the West African nation of Côte d'Ivoire (Ivory Coast)" (p. 207). (See Figure 6.6.) The results indicated that Beng infants manually explored and grasped at the pictures (including pictures of objects common in the Beng community) in the same way as American infants.

The purpose of the fourth study was to determine how children's behavior toward pictures changes with age. Three age groups were tested: 9-month-olds, 15-month-olds, and 19-month-olds. Each group had 16 children, 8 girls and 8 boys. In addition to observing children's behaviors of investigating the pictures with their hands (grasping and other investigative behaviors), the

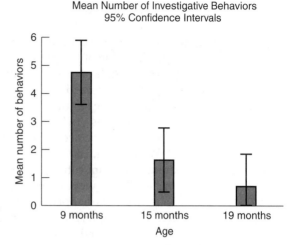

**FIGURE 6.7**  Mean number of investigative behaviors with 95% confidence intervals for 9-month-olds, 15-month-olds, and 19-month-olds. (From DeLoache et al., 1998; used with permission.)

researchers also coded instances of pointing at pictured objects. Their results for infants' investigative behaviors are shown in Figure 6.7.

The independent variable, age of the children, is a natural groups design with three levels: 9 months, 15 months, and 19 months. This variable appears on the horizontal axis (*x*-axis). The dependent variable was number of investigative behaviors and the mean number of these behaviors appears on the vertical axis (*y*-axis). As you can see in Figure 6.7, the mean number of investigative behaviors is highest for 9-month-olds, and much lower for 15-month-olds and 19-month-olds. The other important piece of information in the figure is the "bars" that surround each mean. We can use these bars to make decisions about whether the effect of the independent variable, age, is reliable.

The bars around each mean in Figure 6.7 represent confidence intervals. A **confidence interval** tells us the range of values in which we can expect a population value to fall with a specified level of confidence (see also "margin of error" in Chapter 4). We cannot estimate the population value precisely because of sampling error; the best we can do is estimate a range of probable values. The smaller the range of values expressed in our confidence interval, the better is our estimate of the population value. The bars in Figure 6.7 represent a 95% confidence interval. For 9-month-olds, the mean number of investigative behaviors for the sample was 4.75, and we can be 95% confident that the interval 3.61 and 5.89 (4.75 ± 1.14) contains the population mean for 9-month-olds. Thus, the sample of 16 9-month-old infants in this study is used to estimate the average number of investigative behaviors that would be demonstrated if the larger population of 9-month-olds were tested in this situation. For 15-month-olds, the mean number of investigative behaviors was 1.63, and we can be 95% confident that the interval between .49 and 2.77 (1.63 ± 1.14) contains the population mean. The sample mean for 19-month-olds was .69, and the 95% confidence interval has a lower bound of 0.0 (restricted by the range of permissible values) and an upper bound of 1.83 (.69 ± 1.14). Information about how to calculate and interpret confidence intervals is presented in Appendix A.

In many psychology studies, we are not really interested in estimating the specific value of the population mean. For example, we aren't really interested in knowing the average number of times 9-month-olds can be expected to grasp at pictures. Instead, we are interested in the *pattern* of population means and comparing the relationships among population means (Loftus & Masson, 1994). That is, we wish to be able to compare the behavior of the different age groups. This, too, can be accomplished using confidence intervals.

We can ask, do infants in the different age groups demonstrate different amounts of investigative behaviors, given our estimates of the population means? To answer this question, we examine the overlap of the bars in Figure 6.7. When the bars do not overlap, we can be confident that the population means differ. For example, the confidence interval for 9-month-olds does not overlap with the interval for 15-month-olds. From this, we can conclude that 9-month-olds differ from 15-month-olds in the number of investigative behaviors when looking at pictures (the means tell us that 9-month-olds investigate pictures more than 15-month-olds). The same conclusion can be made when comparing 9-month-olds and 19-month-olds. However, a different conclusion must be made when comparing 15-month-olds and 19-month-olds. Figure 6.7 demonstrates that the bars for these two groups overlap, indicating that the population means may not differ. For example, given our 95% confidence interval, it is possible that the true population mean for 15-month-olds is 1.63 (1.63 falls within the range of probable values, .49–2.77). It is also possible, given our 95% confidence interval, that the true population mean for 19-month-olds is also 1.63. Thus, even though the *sample* means differ (1.63 and .69, respectively), we cannot conclude that the *population* means differ (and in psychological research, we are more interested in describing the population than the sample). Based on the means and confidence intervals presented in Figure 6.7, we can conclude that 9-month-old infants investigate pictures with their hands more than 15-month-olds and 19-month-olds, and that these two older groups may not differ in the amount of investigative behavior they demonstrate.

DeLoache et al.'s (1998) data for infants' pointing at pictures are presented in Figure 6.8. What conclusions can you draw about the effect of age on infants' pointing based on the means and confidence intervals presented in this figure? Do 15-month-old infants differ from 9-month-old infants in their pointing behavior? Why or why not? Do 19-month-old infants differ from 15-month-old infants? Why or why not?

A final word of caution is necessary. Bars presented in graphs of data in journal articles sometimes represent *confidence intervals*, but may also represent the *standard error of the mean* or *standard deviations* (see Appendix A). Importantly, inferences about differences between means can only be made using confidence intervals. (A quick technique for *approximating* confidence intervals is to multiply the standard error of the mean by 2.) To complicate matters further, authors sometimes fail to inform readers what is presented. When bars are presented, it

**FIGURE 6.8**  Mean number of pointing behaviors with 95% confidence intervals for 9-month-olds, 15-month-olds, and 19-month-olds. (From DeLoache et al., 1998; used with permission.)

is important to inform readers what they represent and how they were calculated (Estes, 1997). (In Appendix A we discuss more fully the advantages of using confidence intervals when analyzing experiments.)

## Null-Hypothesis Testing

- Null hypothesis testing is used to determine whether mean differences among groups in an experiment are greater than the differences that are expected simply because of error variation.
- The first step in null hypothesis testing is to assume that the groups do not differ—that is, that the independent variable did not have an effect (the null hypothesis).
- Probability theory is used to estimate the likelihood of the experiment's observed outcome, assuming the null hypothesis is true.
- A statistically significant outcome is one that has a small likelihood of occurring if the null hypothesis is true.
- Because decisions about the outcome of an experiment are based on probabilities, Type I or Type II errors may occur.

We introduce the idea of null hypothesis testing with the results from a classic series of studies by Asch (1951, 1955) on conformity to group pressure. The task in Asch's experiments was simple. Male participants were shown two cards. The first card contained one line, called the standard. The second card contained three lines of different lengths, only one of which matched the standard. The participants' task was to select the line that was the same length as the standard. Eighteen tests of this kind were given to each participant. During a test session, varying numbers of other men were present, all seated around a table. These men were introduced to the participant as fellow participants in the experiment, but they were actually working as confederates of the experimenter (see Chapter 3 for a discussion of the ethics of using confederates). For each card, the men were asked in turn which line they believed matched the standard. The confederates responded with incorrect responses on 12 of the 18 trials. When more than one confederate was present, each confederate gave the same incorrect response. Thus, the independent variable was the number of confederates present, and there were seven levels of this variable (0, 1, 2, 3, 4, 8, and 16). Participants were randomly assigned to a group representing one of these seven levels. The dependent variable was the degree to which the participant conformed to group pressure; this was measured by counting the number of trials in which the participant chose the incorrect response instead of the obviously correct choice. The maximum number of trials on which participants could conform by choosing the incorrect line was 12.

Two questions were addressed in Asch's experiment. First, would participants conform? That is, would they choose the incorrect line more in the conditions when others were present than when they were alone? Second, would conformity increase with increasing size of the dissenting (incorrect) majority? Asch conducted a properly controlled experiment, so it is possible to use the results of the study to answer these two questions.

As we have already seen in our discussion of confidence intervals, the first and most important step in analyzing an experiment is to summarize the results using appropriate descriptive statistics. The mean numbers of errors for the participants who had been randomly assigned to each of the seven groups in Asch's experiment are presented in Figure 6.9. The results seem clear. Fewer errors, on the average, were made when the participants were alone than when they were confronted with the incorrect responses of other "participants." And mean errors increased with increasing size of the dissenting majority, at least up to groups of four.

Descriptive statistics alone are not sufficient, however, to answer the two questions Asch's experiment addressed. In a random groups design, the problem rests with the nature of the control provided by balancing through random

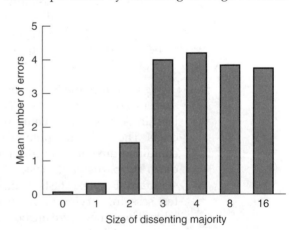

**FIGURE 6.9**    Mean number of errors as a function of the size of the dissenting majority. (Adapted from Asch, 1951.)

assignment. Random assignment does not eliminate the differences among subjects. Random assignment simply distributes the differences among subjects (comparably, we hope) across the groups in the experiment. That is, the differences among subjects are not allowed to vary systematically across groups.

The nonsystematic variation due to differences among subjects within each group is called *error variation*. The individual differences within each group are reflected in the range of errors present in each condition. For example, Asch reported that when 16 confederates chose the incorrect line, at least one participant made no errors, while another participant made 10 errors. Thus, even though all the participants in this group received the same instructions and heard 16 confederates choose an incorrect line on 12 of the 18 trials, not all of the participants responded in the same way. This error variation is due in part to the different characteristics of the participants in the group (e.g., some may be more sensitive to social pressure). The presence of error variation in experiments poses a problem because the means of the different groups in the experiment may differ simply because of error variation, and not because the independent variable has an effect. Recall that we assess the effect of our independent variable by looking for differences among the means for the different conditions. However, if the means can differ because of error variation, and not necessarily because of the independent variable, we cannot be sure if the independent variable has had an effect. You will note that this is the same dilemma faced by researchers using a natural groups design (see our example above); however, in a natural groups design the chance variation between samples is due to the way samples were selected (not assigned). Thus, by themselves, the mean results of the best-controlled experiment do not permit a definite conclusion about the effectiveness of the independent variable. We have already examined one way out of this dilemma, the use of confidence intervals. Now let's look at another.

The primary approach in psychology to making a decision about the effect of an independent variable is called null hypothesis testing. This form of statistical inference is both inductive and indirect. It is inductive because we draw general conclusions about populations on the basis of the specific samples we test in our experiments, as we do when constructing confidence intervals. However, unlike the approach using confidence intervals, this form of statistical inference is also indirect because it begins by assuming the null hypothesis. The **null hypothesis** is the assumption that the independent variable has had *no* effect. Once we make this assumption, we can use probability theory to determine the likelihood of obtaining the difference observed in our experiment if the null hypothesis were true. If this likelihood is small, we reject the null hypothesis and conclude that the independent variable did have an effect on the dependent variable measure. Outcomes that lead us to reject the null hypothesis are said to be **statistically significant.** A statistically significant outcome means only that the difference we obtained in our experiment is larger than would be expected if error variation alone (i.e., chance) were responsible for the outcome.

Perhaps you can appreciate the process of statistical inference by considering the following dilemma. A friend, with a sly smile, offers to toss a coin with you to see who pays for the meal you just enjoyed at a restaurant. Your friend just happens to have a coin ready to toss. Now it would be convenient if you could directly test whether your friend's coin is biased (by asking to look at it). Not willing to appear untrusting, however, the best you can do is test your friend's coin indirectly by assuming it is not biased and seeing if you consistently get outcomes that differ from the expected 50-50 split of heads and tails. If the coin does not exhibit the ordinary 50-50 split (after several trials of flipping the coin), you might surmise that your friend is trying, by slightly underhanded means, to get you to pay for the meal. Similarly, we would like to make a direct test of statistical significance for an obtained difference in our experiments. The best we can do, however, is to compare our obtained outcome with the expected outcome of no difference. *The key to understanding null-hypothesis testing is to recognize that we can use the laws of probability to estimate the likelihood of an outcome only when we assume that chance factors are the sole cause of that outcome.* This is not different from flipping your friend's coin several times to make your conclusion. You know that, based on chance alone, 50% of the time the coin should come up heads, and 50% of the time it should be tails. Anything different from this probable outcome would lead you to conclude that something other than chance is working—that is, your friend's coin is biased.

*A statistically significant outcome is one that has only a small likelihood of occurring if the null hypothesis is true.* But just how small is small enough? Although there is no definitive answer to this important question, the consensus among members of the scientific community is that outcomes associated with probabilities of less than 5 times out of 100 (or .05) if the null hypothesis were true are judged to be statistically significant. The probability we elect to use to indicate an outcome is statistically significant is called the *level of significance*. The level of significance is indicated by the Greek letter alpha ($\alpha$). Thus, we speak of the .05 level of significance, the .10 level, or the .01 level, which we report as $\alpha = .05$, $\alpha = .10$, $\alpha = .01$.

You must choose the level of significance *before* you begin your experiment, not after you have done the statistical analysis. Choosing the level of significance before doing the analysis allows you to avoid the temptation of using the probability of your obtained outcome as the level of significance you *would have chosen*. Strictly speaking, there are only two conclusions possible when you do an inferential statistics test: You either reject the null hypothesis or you fail to reject the null hypothesis.

When we take a strict approach to null-hypothesis ($H_0$) testing, we are essentially acknowledging the fact that it is impossible to prove something does not exist. For example, if we propose there is a monster in Lake Michigan, you would be unable to prove to us this is not so. Putting ecological considerations aside for the moment, you might drain Lake Michigan to show no monster is there, but we could simply assert that the monster dug into the bed of the lake. You might then begin to dredge the lake, and if you still came up with no monster, we could argue that our monster is digging faster than you are dredging. Becoming more desperate, you might fill the lake with explosives and if, after detonating them, you found no remains of the monster, we could calmly propose that our monster is impervious to explosives. So long as we are free to add characteristics to our monster, there is simply no test you could perform that would convincingly show us the monster does not exist. Practically speaking, however, if we continued to believe in our monster after reasonable efforts failed to yield evidence of its existence, we would be judged unreasonable and would lose credibility with other members of the community.

A similar practical problem faces the community of researchers in psychology. When we conduct an experiment and observe the effect of the independent variable is not statistically significant, we do not reject the null hypothesis. However, we do not accept the null hypothesis of no difference either. It's the same problem as occurs with the monster. There may have been some factor in our experiment that prevented us from observing an effect of the independent variable (e.g., few subjects, poor operationalization of the independent variable). Although we recognize the logical impossibility of *proving* that $H_0$ is true, we also must have some method of deciding which independent variables are not worth pursuing (to avoid losing credibility with our colleagues). Most often, experiments are done to show that an independent variable causes a change in behavior. We should not get too discouraged, however, if the particular independent variable we are studying does not produce a statistically significant difference in internally valid experiments with sufficient power. The discipline of psychology also progresses by identifying factors that do not influence behavior in particular situations.

Somewhat ironically, the standards for experiments that show an independent variable is irrelevant for behavior are even higher than the standards for those that show the independent variable is relevant. A *relevant variable* is one that influences behavior. Experiments that show effects are likely to be replicated, which allows researchers to determine the reliability of the effect. When an independent variable does not produce an effect, investigators may not pursue research with that variable any further. All too often, however, after failing to reject $H_0$, researchers do a small (and insensitive) "replication" to confirm their original conclusion of no effect. If anything, the second experiment should be *more* sensitive than the first if it is to strengthen the conclusion that the independent variable has had no effect (Tversky & Kahneman, 1971).

There are some instances in which researchers may choose to *accept* the null hypothesis (rather than simply fail to reject $H_0$). Yeaton and Sechrest (1986, pp. 836–837) argue persuasively that findings of no difference are especially critical in applied research. A few of the questions they cite to illustrate their point:

> "Are children who are placed in day-care centers as intellectually, socially, and emotionally advanced as children who remain in the home? Is a new, cheaper drug with fewer side effects as effective as the existing standard in preventing heart attacks?"

These important questions clearly illustrate situations in which accepting the null hypothesis (no effect) involves more than a theoretical issue—life and death consequences rest on making the correct decision. Frick (1995) argues that never accepting the null hypothesis is neither desirable nor practical for psychology. There are times when we want to be able to state with confidence that there is no difference. As a community, we need some way to assure ourselves that some monsters are just not worth searching for.

There is a troublesome aspect to the process of statistical inference and our reliance on probabilities for making decisions. No matter what decision you reach, and no matter how carefully you reach it, there is always some chance you are making an error. The two possible "states of the world" and the two possible decisions an experimenter can reach are listed in Table 6.1. The two "states of the world" are that the independent variable either does or does not have an effect on behavior. The two possible correct decisions the researcher can make are represented by the upper-left and lower-right cells of the table. If the independent variable does have an effect, the researcher should reject the null hypothesis; if it does not, the researcher should fail to reject the null hypothesis.

The two potential errors are represented by the other two cells of Table 6.1, and these two types of errors have the highly descriptive names of Type I error and Type II error. These errors arise because of the probabilistic nature of statistical inference. When we decide an outcome is statistically significant because the outcome's probability of occurring under the null hypothesis is less than .05, we acknowledge that in 5 out of every 100 tests, the outcome *could* occur even if the null hypothesis were true. The level of significance, therefore, represents the probability of making a *Type I error:* rejecting the null hypothesis when it is true. The probability of making a Type I error can be reduced simply by making the level of significance more stringent, perhaps .001. The problem with this approach is that it increases the likelihood of making a *Type II error:* failing to reject the null hypothesis when it is false.

The problem of Type I errors and Type II errors should not immobilize us. But it should help us understand why researchers rarely use the word *prove* when they describe the results of an experiment that involved inferential statistics. Instead, they describe the results as "consistent with the hypothesis," or "confirming the hypothesis," or "supporting the hypothesis." These more tentative statements are a way of indirectly acknowledging that the possibility of making a Type I error or a Type II error always exists. The .05 level of significance

**TABLE 6.1**    POSSIBLE OUTCOMES OF DECISION MAKING WITH INFERENTIAL STATISTICS

|  | States of the world | |
| --- | --- | --- |
|  | Null hypothesis is false | Null hypothesis is true |
| Reject null hypothesis | Correct decision | Type I error |
| Fail to reject null hypothesis | Type II error | Correct decision |

represents a compromise position that allows us to strike a balance and avoid making too many of either type of error. The problem of Type I errors and Type II errors also reminds us that statistical inference can never replace replication as the ultimate test of the reliability of an experimental outcome.

## Limitations of Null-Hypothesis Testing

- Null-hypothesis testing is frequently misinterpreted in terms of the meaningfulness of the results, the internal validity of the experiment, the truth of the null hypothesis, and the reliability of experiment outcomes.

Unfortunately, there are many misuses and misunderstandings of null-hypothesis testing. There are some common problems of null-hypothesis testing that you should avoid. For instance, you should be aware that:

— A statistically significant result is not the same as a practically meaningful result.
— A statistically significant result does not mean that the result is interpretable.
— A statistically significant result does not tell us whether the null hypothesis is true.
— A statistically significant result also does not tell us whether the experiment will replicate.

We will consider each of these problems in turn.

One common misuse of null hypothesis testing occurs when we confuse the statistical significance of a finding with the practical significance, or meaningfulness, of the conclusion based on that finding. The likelihood of obtaining a statistically significant finding is directly related to the sample size tested in the experiment. If we do an experiment with a very large number of subjects, almost any finding will be statistically significant. For example, suppose you ask participants to rate their life satisfaction on a 1 to 7 scale, with "1" indicating "not satisfied" and "7" indicating "very satisfied." Suppose further that a statistically significant difference was observed between mean ratings for a sample of 1,000 males and 1,000 females, with hypothetical mean ratings of 5.5 and 5.6. Although this difference in mean ratings may be "statistically significant," one may question the meaningfulness of such a difference in ratings. Later in this chapter we discuss ways to report the magnitude of an effect (measures of "effect size") which complement results from null-hypothesis testing. A measure of effect size tells us how big an effect our independent variable had on the dependent variable. We can use our knowledge of effect size to judge just how meaningful an effect is.

The statistical significance of a finding also says nothing about the internal validity of the experiment. Although we might be tempted to accept a conclusion if it is based on a "statistically significant" finding, we must remember that our ability to draw appropriate conclusions depends, most of all, on the internal validity of the study. In other words, confounded experiments can easily produce statistically significant outcomes! These "significant outcomes" should, of course, never be interpreted as valid when an experiment lacks internal validity.

J. Cohen (1995) points out two other common misunderstandings of what null-hypothesis testing tells us. The first misunderstanding is that a statistically significant finding tells us the probability that the null hypothesis is true. This misunderstanding is illustrated by the (incorrect) conclusion that "The probability of obtaining these results by chance alone is less than .05." With null-hypothesis testing, we never know the probability of the null hypothesis. What a statistically significant finding *does* tell us is the probability of our obtained difference *given that the null hypothesis is true*. Remember, our first step is to assume the null hypothesis is true; we do not determine the probability that the null hypothesis is true nor do we determine the probability that our obtained results are due to chance. An appropriate conclusion could be phrased, "The results occur with a probability less than .05 assuming the null hypothesis to be true."

A second misunderstanding involves the replicability of a finding that is associated with a certain probability under the null hypothesis. Suppose you conduct an experiment and the statistical analyses indicate the probability of your finding is $p = .01$. This probability *does not* indicate that the outcome would be replicated 99% of the time if the experiment were repeated. Or, stated slightly differently, we *can not say* with 99% confidence that the outcome is reliable—that is, it would be replicated. What we can say is that the finding we obtained in our experiment is an unlikely one if the independent variable had no effect. The only way to find out for sure if a finding will replicate is to replicate it!

You may be wondering at this point how null-hypothesis testing continues to be used when it has so many limitations. As Cohen (1995) says, "don't look for a magic alternative to NHST [null hypothesis significance testing], [or] some other objective mechanical ritual to replace it. It doesn't exist" (p. 1001). He advocates that researchers seeking to generalize from their data should use a variety of analysis techniques such as graphic data analysis and confidence intervals, as well as estimates of effect sizes (described at the end of this chapter). He also argues that improved statistical analysis in psychology requires improvements in psychological measurement and theory construction so that the hypotheses psychologists test will be more specific. Cohen (1995) concludes his critique of null-hypothesis testing with some sage advice: ". . . we have a body of statistical techniques, that, used intelligently, can facilitate our efforts. But given the problems of statistical induction, we must finally rely, as have the older sciences, on replication" (p. 1002).

## Analysis of Variance (ANOVA)

- Analysis of variance (ANOVA) is an inferential statistics test used to determine whether an independent variable has had a statistically significant effect on a dependent variable.

- The logic of analysis of variance is based on identifying sources of error variation and systematic variation in the data.
- The *F*-test is a statistic that represents the ratio of between-group variation to within-group variation in the data.
- The results of the initial overall analysis of an omnibus *F*-test are presented in an analysis of variance summary table; analytical comparisons can then be used to identify specific sources of systematic variation in an experiment.
- Although analysis of variance can be used to decide whether an independent variable has had a statistically significant effect, researchers examine the descriptive statistics to interpret the meaning of the experiment outcome.

Statistical inference requires a test to determine whether or not the outcome of an experiment was statistically significant. The most commonly used inferential statistics test in the analysis of experiments is the *analysis of variance* (or ANOVA). As its name implies, the analysis of variance is based on analyzing different sources of variation in an experiment. In this section we will briefly introduce how the analysis of variance is used to analyze experiments that involve the random groups design.

There are two sources of variation in any random groups experiment. First, variation *within* each group can be expected because of individual differences among subjects who have been randomly assigned to a group. The variation due to individual differences can not be eliminated, but this variation is presumed to be balanced across groups when random assignment is used. In a properly conducted experiment, the differences among subjects within each group should be the only source of error variation. Subjects in each group should be given instructions in the same way, and the level of the independent variable to which they've been assigned should be implemented in the same way for each member of the group.

The second source of variation in the random groups design is variation *between* the groups. If the null hypothesis is true (no differences among groups), any observed differences among the means of the groups can be attributed to error variation (e.g., the different characteristics of the participants in the groups). As we've seen previously, however, we don't expect group means to be exactly identical. Fluctuations produced by sampling error make it likely that the means will vary somewhat—error variation. Thus, the variation among the different group means, when the null hypothesis is assumed to be true, provides a second estimate of error variation in an experiment. If the null hypothesis is true, this estimate of error variation between groups should be similar to the estimate of error variation within groups. Thus, the random groups design provides two independent estimates of error variation, one within the groups and one between the groups.

Now suppose that the null hypothesis is false. That is, suppose the independent variable has had an effect in your experiment. If the independent variable has had an effect, should the means for the different groups be the same or different? You should recognize that they should be different. An independent variable that has an effect on behavior should produce *systematic differences* in the means across the different groups of the experiment. That is, the independent variable should introduce a source of variation among the groups of the experiment—it should cause the groups to vary. This systematic variation will be added to the differences in the group means that are already present due to error variation.

The *F*-Test    We are now in a position to develop a statistic that will allow us to tell whether the variation due to our independent variable is larger than would be expected on the basis of error variation alone. This statistic is called *F*; it is named after Ronald Fisher, the statistician who developed the test. The conceptual definition of the **F-test** is the following ratio:

$$F = \frac{\text{Variation between groups}}{\text{Variation within groups}} = \frac{\text{Error variation} + \text{Systematic variation}}{\text{Error variation}}$$

If the null hypothesis is true, there is no systematic variation between groups (no effect of the independent variable) and the resulting *F* ratio has an expected value of 1.00 (since error variation divided by error variation would equal 1.00). As the amount of systematic variation increases, however, the expected value from the *F*-test becomes greater than 1.00.

The analysis of experiments would be easier if we could isolate the systematic variation produced by the independent variable. Unfortunately, the systematic variation between groups comes in a "package" along with error variation. Consequently, the value of the *F* ratio may sometimes be larger than 1.00 simply because our estimate of error variation between groups happens to be larger than our estimate of error variation within groups (the two estimates should be similar but can differ due to chance factors). How much greater than 1.00 does the *F* statistic have to be before we can be relatively sure that it reflects true systematic variation due to the independent variable? Our earlier discussion of statistical significance provides an answer to this question. To be statistically significant, the *F* value needs to be large enough so that its probability of occurring if the null hypothesis were true is less than our chosen level of significance, usually .05.

We are now ready to apply the principles of null-hypothesis testing and the procedures of the analysis of variance to analyze a specific experiment. We will use the Asch experiment we described earlier. The first step in doing an inferential statistics test like the *F*-test is to state the research question the analysis is intended to answer. Typically, this takes the form of "Did the independent variable have any overall effect on performance?" In the Asch experiment this question would be, "Did varying the size of the dissenting majority have any effect on the number of errors participants made?" Once the research question is clear, the next step is to develop a null hypothesis for the analysis.

The initial overall analysis of the experiment is called an *omnibus F-test*. The null hypothesis for such omnibus tests is that all the group means are equal (remember that the null hypothesis assumes no effect of the independent variable). The formal statement of a null hypothesis ($H_0$) is always made in terms of population characteristics. These population characteristics are indicated by Greek letters, and the population mean is symbolized as $\mu$ (mu). We can use a subscript for each mean in the Asch experiment to reflect the size of the dissenting majority (the levels of the independent variable). Our null hypothesis then becomes

$$H_0: \mu_0 = \mu_1 = \mu_2 = \mu_3 = \mu_4 = \mu_8 = \mu_{16}$$

The alternative to the null hypothesis is that one or more of the means of the groups are not equal. In other words, the alternative hypothesis states that $H_0$ is wrong, there is a difference somewhere. If the size of the dissenting majority does have an effect on conformity (i.e., if the independent variable produces systematic variation), we will reject the null hypothesis.

Analysis of Variance Summary Table    The next step in an analysis of variance is to do the computations to obtain the estimates of variation that make up the numerator and denominator of the $F$-test. Computing $F$-tests is best done using a computer. Our focus now is on interpreting the results of the computations. The results of an analysis of variance are presented in an Analysis of Variance Summary Table. The summary table for the Asch experiment is presented in Table 6.2.

The means for each group that were presented earlier in Figure 6.9 are repeated at the bottom of the table. We examine the components of the summary table before looking at the outcome of the $F$-test for the experiment.

The left column of a summary table lists the two sources of variation described earlier. In this case the independent variable of the dissenting majority is a source of variation *between* the groups and the *within-groups* differences provide an estimate of error variation. The total variation in the experiment is the sum of the variation between and within the groups. The next column is the degrees of freedom ($df$). In general, the statistical concept of degrees of freedom is defined as the number of entries of interest minus one. Since there are 7 levels

**TABLE 6.2**    ANALYSIS OF VARIANCE SUMMARY TABLE

| Source of Variation | $df$ | SS | MS | $F$ | $p$ |
|---|---|---|---|---|---|
| Between Groups (Majority Size) | 6 | 198.98 | 33.16 | 27.2 | .0001 |
| Within Groups (Error) | 63 | 77.13 | 1.22 | | |
| Total | 69 | 276.11 | | | |

| | Size of dissenting majority | | | | | | |
|---|---|---|---|---|---|---|---|
| | 0 | 1 | 2 | 3 | 4 | 8 | 16 |
| Mean Number of Errors | .08 | .33 | 1.53 | 4.00 | 4.20 | 3.84 | 3.75 |

of the dissenting majority independent variable, there are 6 *df* between groups (7 − 1 = 6). There are 10 participants within each group, and so there are 9 *df* within each of the 7 groups. Because all 7 groups are the same size, we can determine the within-groups *df* by multiplying the *df* within each group by the number of groups (9 × 7) for 63 *df*. The total *df* is the number of subjects minus one (and also the sum of *df* between groups plus *df* within groups).

The sums of squares (SS) and the mean square (MS) are computational steps in obtaining the *F* statistic. The MS between groups (row 1) is an estimate of systematic variation plus error variation, and is calculated by dividing the SS between groups by the *df* between groups (198.98 ÷ 6 = 33.16). The MS within groups (row 2) is an estimate of error variation only, and is computed by dividing the SS within groups by the *df* within groups (77.13 ÷ 63 = 1.22). The *F* ratio is obtained by dividing the MS between groups by the MS within groups (33.16 ÷ 1.22 = 27.2). We are now ready to use the information in the summary table to test for the statistical significance of the outcome in the Asch experiment. You may anticipate the conclusion already, knowing that when the null hypothesis is assumed to be true (i.e., no effect of the independent variable), the estimate of systematic variation plus error variation (numerator of the *F*-test) should be approximately equal to the estimate of error variation only (denominator of the *F*-test). As we see here, the estimate of systematic variation plus error variation (33.16) is quite a bit larger than the estimate of error variation alone (1.22).

The obtained *F* value in this analysis appears in the second to last column of the summary table, and is reported as, $F(6,63) = 27.2$. An *F* statistic is identified by its degrees of freedom. In this case there are 6 *df* between groups and 63 *df* within groups. The probability of obtaining an *F* as large as 27.2 if the null hypothesis were true is shown in the last column of the summary table (.0001). The obtained probability of .0001 is less than the level of significance ($\alpha = .05$), so we reject the null hypothesis and conclude that the overall effect of the size of the dissenting majority is statistically significant.

Just what have we learned when we find a statistically significant outcome in an analysis of variance testing an omnibus null hypothesis? In one sense, we have learned something very important. We are now in a position to state that manipulating the independent variable produced a change in performance (i.e., participants' errors about the lines). In another sense, merely knowing our outcome is statistically significant tells us nothing about the *nature* of the effect of the independent variable. The descriptive statistics (in our example, the mean number of errors in Figure 6.9) allow us to describe the nature of the effect: As the size of the dissenting majority increased, up to 4 dissenters, the mean number of errors made by participants increased; with 8 and 16 dissenters, the number of errors decreased. Imagine if participants had made the most errors when they were alone. The results of the *F*-test could also have been statistically significant. The means, however, would lead us to draw a very different conclusion from the one we would reach based on the means in Figure 6.9. The point is, *never try to interpret a statistically significant outcome without referring to the corresponding descriptive statistics.*

Knowing that the omnibus test is statistically significant also does not tell us the *location* of the effect. We only know there is systematic variation *somewhere* in our experiment. On the basis of the omnibus test, we can only respond to a person who asked, "What happened in your experiment?" by saying,"Something." This response is not very satisfying and would almost surely prompt the exasperated reply, "Yes, but what?" Based on the omnibus *F*-test alone, however, we are unable to state which of the group means differed. Fortunately, there are analysis techniques that allow us to locate more specifically the sources of systematic variation in our experiments. These techniques are called analytical comparisons, and they are linked directly to the hypotheses that led Asch to do the experiment in the first place.

Analytical Comparisons   Asch did not do his experiment simply to find out whether something would happen when he manipulated the size of the dissenting majority. Instead, he had at least two specific questions to address in the experiment: Would participants choose the incorrect line more in the conditions when others were present than when they were alone? And would conformity increase with increasing size of the dissenting majority? **Analytical comparisons** are a way to translate these research questions into a form that allows us to locate a specific source of systematic variation in our experiment. We will illustrate this process with the first of Asch's two research questions.

The first step in doing an analytical comparison, like the first step in doing an omnibus analysis, is to state the null hypothesis for the analysis. The verbal statement of the null hypothesis for Asch's first research question is: The mean number of errors for the group when participants are alone is equal to the mean of all the groups in which other participants were present. This analytical comparison contrasts the performance of participants who are alone with the performance of participants when they are in a group. Note that we are not concerned with the particular number (1–16) of other people present, so we consider the mean for all individuals who participated with confederates present. More formally, the null hypothesis is:

$$H_0: \mu_0 = (\mu_1 + \mu_2 + \mu_3 + \mu_4 + \mu_8 + \mu_{16})/6$$

We can compute a mean square for this particular comparison. The mean square for the comparison reflects a combination of error variation and systematic variation due to this specific comparison. An *F* ratio can then be formed with the comparison mean square in the numerator and the mean square within groups in the denominator (estimate of error variation alone). Because this analytical comparison essentially involves the contrast between two means (participants alone and participants in groups), it has only 1 degree of freedom. We then determine the probability of the resulting *F* ratio by using the same procedures we described earlier for omnibus *F*-tests.

The computations for the first analytical comparison in the Asch experiment result in $F(1,63) = 57.53$ with a $p = .0001$. The obtained $p$ is less than the conventional .05 level of significance, and so the analytical comparison is statistically significant. This outcome allows us to state that one source of systematic variation in the Asch experiment was that participants in groups performed differently from participants who were alone. Because the mean number of errors for participants in groups (2.94) was higher than that for participants alone (.08), we can conclude that Asch's first hypothesis was confirmed: Participants chose the incorrect line more in the conditions when others were present than when they were alone, suggesting these participants conformed to group pressure. Think again about your friend's question about "what happened" in your experiment. Can you see why you would be glad you know about analytical comparisons when you try to answer your friend's question?

## Effect Size

- A problem with inferential statistics is that they are influenced by the sample size in an experiment.
- Measures of effect size indicate the strength of the relationship between the independent and dependent variables, but are not affected by sample size.
- One commonly used measure of effect size, *d,* examines the difference between two group means relative to the within-group variability.
- In addition to providing information about the amount of impact an independent variable has had, measures of effect size allow quantitative comparisons of results across experiments and estimates of the average effect of an independent variable.

When we do an inferential statistics test we are interested in determining whether the independent variable had an effect. One limitation of inferential statistics tests, however, is that the outcome of such tests is influenced by the sample size used in the experiment. That is, given an independent variable with an effect of a certain size, the value from the $F$-test used to test the effect of that independent variable will increase as the sample size increases. In other words, the $F$ ratio can increase even when the effect size does not! Thus, the $F$-test (and other inferential statistics) does not directly tell us the effect size of the independent variable. This means that we need something other than an inferential statistics test to measure the size of the effect of an independent variable. What is needed to measure **effect size** is an indicator that reflects the strength of the relationship between the independent and the dependent variables and is independent of sample size. Several measures of effect size meet these criteria (e.g., Keppel, 1991). We describe how these different measures of effect size are computed in Appendix A. What we will do here is use one of these measures to describe the nature of an effect size and the way an effect size generally is interpreted.

One commonly used measure of effect size in experimental research is called *d.* It is a ratio that measures the difference between the means for the levels of the independent variable divided by the within-group standard deviation. The standard deviation tells us approximately how far, on the average, scores vary from a group mean. It is a measure of the "dispersal" of scores around a mean and, in the case of the within-group standard deviation, tells us about the degree of "error" due to individual differences (i.e., how individuals vary in their responses). The standard deviation serves as a useful metric to assess a difference between means. That is, the "size" of the effect of the independent variable (the difference between group means for the independent variable) is always in terms of the average dispersal of scores occurring in an experiment. If there is a lot of within-group variability (i.e., the within-group standard deviation is large), the denominator for $d$ is large. To be able to observe the effect of the independent variable, given this large within-group variability, the difference between two group means must be large. When the within-group variability is small (the denominator for $d$ is small), the same difference between means will reflect a larger effect size. Because effect sizes are presented in standard deviation units, they can be used to make meaningful comparisons of effect sizes across experiments using different dependent variables.

There are some guidelines to help us interpret $d$ ratios. J. Cohen (1992) provided a useful classification of effect sizes with three values—small, medium, and large. Cohen (1992) describes the rationale for his classification of effect size (ES) as follows:

> My intent was that medium ES represent an effect likely to be visible to the naked eye of a careful observer. (It has since been noted in effect-size surveys that it approximates the average size of observed effects in various fields.) I set small ES to be noticeably smaller than medium but not so small as to be trivial, and I set large ES to be the same distance above medium as small was below it. Although the definitions were made subjectively, with some minor adjustments, these conventions . . . have come into general use. (p. 156)

Each of the classes of effect size can be expressed in quantitative terms; for example, a medium effect for a two-group experiment is a $d$ of .50; a small and large effect are $d$s of .20 and .80, respectively. These expressions of effect magnitude are especially useful when comparing results from similar studies.

There are several advantages of using measures of effect size (see, for example, Chow, 1988):

**1** Measures of effect size provide information about the *amount* of impact an independent variable has had. Thus, they complement tests of statistical significance which give only an indication of the presence or absence of an effect of an independent variable. In this way, we can use measures of effect size to rank several independent variables within the same experiment in terms of their relative importance.

**2** Measures of effect size can be used to summarize a series of experiments that have included the same independent variable or dependent variable. This allows for a quantitative comparison of the outcomes across the series of experiments. For example, effect size can be used to find out whether a particular independent variable consistently had about the same amount of impact across the experiments.

**3** Effect sizes can be averaged to provide an estimate of the overall effect size of an independent variable across a series of similar experiments. This comparison is especially important in applied research examining the effectiveness of treatments like an educational innovation or a new approach to psychotherapy.

None of the important questions addressed using effect size can be answered using the $F$ ratios or $p$ values obtained when inferential statistics tests are done. Nonetheless, measures of effect size and inferential statistics tests are complementary (Chow, 1988). For example, measures of effect size are more informative than are "$p$ values" in helping researchers determine the substantive importance of experimental outcomes. At times, we want to know just how much of an "effect" our treatment had. Knowing the answer may help us decide whether to actually implement this treatment in an applied setting. When an experiment is being done to test predictions derived from a theory, however, the size of the effect of an independent variable is less critical. In this case, we are usually content with knowing that the independent variable "worked" in the way a theory said it should. In fact, as tests of a theory become more sophisticated, it is likely that small effects will be more critical. Inferential statistics tests are useful when experiments are done to test theories by confirming that an effect is present.

There is another reason not to discount small effect sizes. Consider the fact that studies have indicated there is a small positive effect of taking aspirin to try to prevent second heart attacks. Considering the large number of people who are at risk for recurrent heart attacks, the small positive effect of taking aspirin could still have an impact on thousands of people. In terms of the potential numbers of people who could benefit, the small beneficial effect of taking aspirin would not be a small effect at all.

Abelson (1985) identified another subtle aspect of interpreting small effect sizes. Abelson argues there are processes with tiny individual influences that can cumulate to produce meaningful outcomes. He uses a sports analogy to make his point. Abelson calculated how much of the variation in whether a batter got a hit in a single time at bat could be predicted on the basis of skill differences in major league batters. The skill differences were measured using the major league players' batting averages over 5 years. Basically, Abelson wanted to know if players' 5-year batting averages could be used to predict whether they got a hit on a particular occasion when facing a pitcher. Abelson found that less than 1% of the variation in a single at bat could be predicted by the batters' skill. If we interpreted the small value of this effect size at face value we would come to the very improbable conclusion that batting skill has almost nothing to do with batting success! However, when averages over 5 years are used to predict a subsequent *season's* batting average, rather than a single time at bat, batting skill is a much stronger predictor of batting success.

The problem here is a familiar one; Abelson is illustrating what happens if we try to predict the outcome of single observations—in this case, single at bats. Although researchers may be able to predict behavior *on average*, it is often quite difficult to predict behavior for a specific occasion. Abelson draws an apt analogy to the situation researchers face when interpreting an effect size based on a single experiment. A small effect size need not indicate that an independent variable is unimportant. Effect sizes can be used more effectively when they are based on a series of experiments. We conclude this chapter by describing a procedure for just this purpose: meta-analysis.

## Meta-Analysis

- Meta-analysis uses measures of effect size to summarize the results of many experiments investigating the same independent variable or dependent variable.
- A critical aspect of meta-analysis is deciding which experiments to include in the analysis: The value of a meta-analysis depends on the methodological quality of the experiments that are included.

Each strand contributes to the strength of a rope. But the rope is stronger than any strand. Similarly, each properly done experiment strengthens our confidence in a particular psychological principle. But the principles of psychology are stronger than the results of any individual experiment. This is because principles of psychology (laws, if you will) emerge only after looking at the relationships among the results of many individual experiments. When a particular finding is found again and again under many different experimental situations, we are in a position to state with confidence a general law of behavior. This is the procedure used by Anderson and Bushman (1997) to identify the variables that consistently have been shown to impact aggression.

Meta-analysis is a valuable tool that makes it easier to summarize the results of experiments investigating the same independent variable or dependent variable. **Meta-analysis** is the analysis of the results of several independent experiments. In any experiment, the unit of analysis is the responses of individual subjects. In a meta-analysis, the unit of analysis is the results of individual experiments. These results are summarized using measures of effect size like those described in the previous section. Meta-analyses are used to answer questions like: Are there gender differences in conformity? What are the effects of class size on academic achievement? Is cognitive therapy effective in the treatment of depression? The results of individual experiments, no matter how well done, are not likely to be sufficient to provide answers to questions about such important general issues. We need to consider a body of literature (i.e., many experiments) pertaining to each issue. (See Hunt, 1997, for a good and readable introduction to meta-analysis.)

Prior to the use of meta-analysis, the results of previous research on a particular topic were summarized using some form of narrative review. These reviews were typically published in the *Psychological Bulletin*. The reviewers were often experts in the area of research under investigation. After reading and thinking about the relevant studies, the reviewers would draw conclusions that they thought were supported by the evidence. Meta-analysis is not intended to replace these narrative reviews; instead, it is meant to strengthen the evidence used to reach conclusions. For example, reviewers previously would tally the number of experiments that did or did not show a statistically significant effect of an independent variable. This "voting method" was a crude measure of the effect of the independent variable, particularly because of "publication bias." Publication bias occurs because research reports are more likely to be published (rather than filed in a cabinet) when statistically significant findings are reported; therefore, the "voting method" may overestimate the effect size of variables. Meta-analysis allows us to measure directly the average effect size for a given independent variable across experiments.

Rosenthal (1994a) used meta-analysis to summarize the results of 345 experiments on experimenter effects. Experimenter effects occur when the participants in an experiment respond in ways that correspond to the expectancies of the experimenter (see earlier section in this chapter on placebo control and double-blind experiments, as well as Chapter 3). Experimenter effects represent a specific instance of the more general category of interpersonal expectancy effects, which represent the effects of people's expectations on others' behavior. Table 6.3 presents the mean effect sizes for each of eight domains in which interpersonal expectancy effects have been studied. The table also includes a brief description of an example of a type of study done in each domain. The mean effect size across all 345 studies is .70, a medium effect using J. Cohen's (1992) scale. For four of the eight domains the mean effect size is greater than .80, indicating a large effect. Table 6.3 also shows that the interpersonal expectancy finding has considerable external validity because there is at least a medium size effect in six of the eight domains. Thus, we are in a position to state with confidence a general principle: Interpersonal expectancies can influence people's behavior.

Meta-analyses like the one summarized in Table 6.3 provide an efficient and effective way to summarize the results of large numbers of experiments. Nevertheless, the sophisticated statistical techniques that are used in meta-analyses are powerful only when the data from the studies being analyzed have been gathered in appropriate ways. The results of meta-analyses can be misleading

**TABLE 6.3**   ILLUSTRATION OF USE OF MEAN EFFECT SIZE IN META-ANALYSIS

| Domain | $d$ | Example of type of study |
|---|---|---|
| Laboratory interviews | .14 | Effects of sensory restriction on reports of hallucinatory experiences |
| Reaction time | .17 | Latency of word associations to certain stimulus words |
| Learning and ability | .54 | IQ test scores, verbal conditioning (learning) |
| Person perception | .55 | Perception of other people's success |
| Inkblot tests | .84 | Ratio of animal to human Rorschach responses |
| Everyday situations | .88 | Symbol learning, athletic performance |
| Psychophysical judgments | 1.05 | Ability to discriminate tones |
| Animal learning | 1.73 | Learning in mazes and Skinner boxes |
| Overall mean | .70 | |

Adapted from Rosenthal, R. (1994a). Interpersonal expectancy effects: A 30-year perspective. *Current Directions in Psychological-Science*, 3, 176–179.

when experiments with poor internal validity are included. Thus, important questions regarding meta-analyses ask: Which experiments should be included in the meta-analysis? Will only experiments reported in journals with high editorial standards be included, or will the meta-analysis include research reports that have not undergone editorial review? In general, the methodological quality of the experiments included in the meta-analysis will determine its ultimate value (see Judd et al., 1991).

Our hope is that this brief introduction to the analysis of experiments gives you an appreciation of the variety of ways statistical analysis can be done. Appendix A provides more details about statistical analysis, as well as a plan to follow when analyzing data. One theme emerges from our discussion of statistical analysis. There is no one best approach to analyzing an experiment, just as there is no one best research method. Analysis techniques, like any tools, are best used when we know their strengths and weaknesses. We need to recognize that statistical analysis does not determine the conclusions we draw from our experiment—we do that! Statistical analysis does help us constrain the conclusions we reach. Most of all, statistical analysis is not a necessary evil in experimental research; it is a critical step on the path from asking a research question to answering it.

## SUMMARY

Experimental research allows us to observe the unobservable. Predictions based on proposed explanatory processes can be either confirmed or refuted by experimental outcomes. Properly done experiments are internally valid, reliable, sensitive, and externally valid. A major purpose of experiments is to test hypotheses derived from theories, but experiments can also be used to test the effectiveness of treatments or programs in applied settings. The experimental method is ideally suited to identifying cause-and-effect relationships when the control techniques of manipulation, holding conditions constant, and balancing are properly implemented.

In this chapter we have focused on applying these control techniques in experiments in which different groups of subjects are given different treatments representing the levels of the independent variable. In the most common design of this type, the random groups design, the groups are formed using randomization procedures such that the groups are comparable at the start of the experiment. If the groups perform differently, it is presumed that the independent variable is responsible. Random assignment is the most common method of forming comparable groups. By distributing subjects' characteristics equally across the conditions of the experiment, random assignment is an attempt to ensure that the differences among subjects are balanced across groups in the experiment. The most common technique for carrying out random assignment is block randomization.

Random assignment contributes to the internal validity of an experiment, but external validity must be established in some other way. One approach to enhancing external validity is to select representative samples of all dimensions on which you wish to generalize. Replication serves primarily as a check on the reliability of experimental findings, but replication also plays a key role in establishing external validity. When we obtain the same outcomes in two partial replications of the same experiment done in two widely different settings with different subjects, our confidence in the external validity of that finding increases. A partial replication, including the dimension on which you want to generalize as an independent variable, is perhaps the best way to establish external validity.

Testing intact groups even when the groups are randomly assigned to conditions should be avoided because the use of intact groups is highly likely to result in a confounding. Extraneous variables, such as different rooms or different experimenters, must not be allowed to confound the independent variable of interest. Even when such extraneous variables are controlled, however, they can contribute to the sensitivity and external validity of an experiment. Holding extraneous variables constant increases sensitivity and decreases external validity, whereas balancing extraneous variables decreases sensitivity and increases external validity.

A more serious threat to the internal validity of the random groups design is involved when subjects fail to complete the experiment successfully. Selective subject loss occurs when subjects are lost differentially across the conditions and some characteristic of the subject that is related to the outcome of the experiment is responsible for the loss. We can help prevent selective loss by restricting subjects to those likely to complete the experiment successfully, or we can compensate for it by selectively dropping comparable subjects from the group that did not experience the loss. Demand characteristics and experimenter effects can be minimized through the use of proper experimental procedures, but they can best be controlled by using placebo control and double-blind procedures.

The matched groups design is an alternative to the random groups design when only a small number of subjects is available along with a good matching task and when the experiment requires separate groups for each treatment. The biggest problem with the matched groups design is that the groups are equated only on the characteristic measured by the matching task. In the natural groups design, researchers select the levels of independent variables (usually individual differences or subject variables) and look for systematic relationships between these independent variables and other aspects of behavior. Essentially, the natural groups design involves looking for correlations between subjects' characteristics and their performance. Such correlational research designs pose problems in drawing causal inferences.

The purpose of analyzing an experiment is to determine whether an independent variable has had an effect on behavior as reflected by differences in the dependent variable across the levels of the independent variable. The identification of such differences begins with descriptive statistics. Because differences in the dependent variable can arise because of error variation alone, we need a way to help decide whether the obtained differences represent simply chance or also represent the effect of the independent variable. Confidence intervals may be constructed to help determine what happened in the experiment. Moreover, the inductive and indirect process of null-hypothesis testing provides a set of guidelines for deciding on the statistical significance of a finding. There are important limitations of null-hypothesis testing that prevent it from ever replacing replication; replication remains the ultimate test of the reliability of a research finding. The most commonly used inferential statistics test in the analysis of experiments is the analysis of variance.

Measures of effect size provide important information that cannot be obtained from inferential statistics tests. One strength of effect size is that it is a measure that is independent of the sample size in an experiment. Measures of effect size do have limitations, but effect size can be especially useful in meta-analysis. Meta-analysis provides a quantitative summary of the results of a large number of experiments on an important research problem.

## KEY CONCEPTS

| | |
|---|---|
| independent variables | placebo control |
| dependent variables | double-blind |
| confounding | matched groups design |
| independent groups designs | natural groups designs |
| random groups design | inferential statistics |
| random assignment | confidence intervals |
| block randomization | null hypothesis |
| replication | statistically significant |
| extraneous variables | *F*-test |
| mechanical subject loss | analytical comparison |
| selective subject loss | effect size |
| demand characteristics | meta-analysis |
| experimenter effects | |

## REVIEW QUESTIONS

1 Briefly outline the logic of the random groups design.
2 What issues would you consider if you wanted to establish the external validity of an experiment you were planning to do that involved random assignment?
3 Describe the role of partial replications and that of conceptual relationships among variables in establishing the external validity of a research finding.
4 What impact do extraneous variables have on the sensitivity and external validity of an experiment?
5 What preventive steps could you take if you anticipate that selective subject loss may pose a problem in your experiment?
6 Explain the logic of the two techniques that are used to control demand characteristics and experimenter effects.

7 Describe the conditions under which you would recommend that the matched groups design be used.

8 How do individual differences variables differ from manipulated independent variables, and why does this difference make it difficult to draw causal inferences on the basis of the natural groups design?

9 How would you use confidence intervals to reach conclusions about differences in performance across the conditions of an experiment?

10 How would you explain to a friend that statistical inference is inductive and indirect?

11 Explain what you have learned about the effect of an independent variable when you find out it has produced a statistically significant outcome. Is a statistically significant finding necessarily an important finding?

12 Distinguish between the information you gain from an omnibus $F$-test and from an analytical comparison.

13 Describe one advantage and one limitation of using measures of effect size.

14 What is the major difference between meta-analysis and narrative review in summarizing the results of previous research on a particular topic?

## CHALLENGE QUESTIONS

1 An experimenter is planning to do a random groups design experiment to study the effect of the rate of presenting stimuli on people's ability to recognize the stimuli. The independent variable is the presentation rate, and it will be manipulated at four levels: Very Fast, Fast, Slow, and Very Slow. The experimenter is seeking your help and advice with the following aspects of the experiment:

A The experimenter asks you to prepare a block randomized schedule such that there will be four participants in each of the four conditions. To do this you can use the following random numbers that were taken from the random number table in Appendix A.

1-5-6-6-4-1-0-4-9-3-2-0-4-9-2-3-8-3-9-1-9-1-1-3-2-2-1-9-9-9

5-9-5-1-6-8-1-6-5-2-2-7-1-9-5-4-8-2-2-3-4-6-7-5-1-2-2-9-2-3

B The experimenter is considering restricting participants to those who pass a stringent reaction time test so as to be sure that they will be able to perform the task successfully with the Very Fast presentation rate. Explain what factors the experimenter should consider in making this decision, being sure to describe clearly what risks, if any, are taken if only this restricted set of participants is tested.

C The experimenter discovers that it will be necessary to test participants in two different rooms. How should the experimenter arrange the testing of the conditions in these two rooms so as to avoid possible confounding by this extraneous variable?

2 A researcher was conducting a series of experiments on the effects of external factors on people's persistence in exercise programs. In one of these experiments, the researcher manipulated three types of distraction while subjects walked on a treadmill. The three types of distraction were concentrating on one's own thoughts, listening to a tape of music, and watching a video of people engaging in outdoor recreation. The dependent variable was how strenuous the treadmill exercise was at the time the subject decided to end the session (the incline of the treadmill was regularly increased as the person went through the session, thereby making the exercise increasingly strenuous).

In an introductory psychology course, 120 students volunteered to participate in the experiment, and the researcher randomly assigned 40 students to each of the three levels of the distraction variable.

After only 2 minutes on the treadmill, each subject was given the option to stop the experiment (this option came before any of the subjects could reasonably be expected to be experiencing fatigue). Data for the subjects who decided to stop after only 2 minutes were not included in the analysis of the final data. Twenty-five subjects who were concentrating on their own thoughts completed the experiment; 30 subjects in the music condition completed the experiment; and 40 subjects in the video group completed the experiment. The mean strenuousness score was highest for the concentration group ($n = 25$), next highest for the music group ($n = 30$), and lowest for the video group ($n = 40$). These results did not support the researcher's prediction that the mean strenuousness score would be highest in the video group.

**A** What methodological problem may threaten the internal validity of this experiment? What factors indicate that this problem occurred?

**B** Assume that a pretest measure was available for each of the 120 subjects and that the pretest measured the degree to which each subject was likely to persist at exercise. Describe how you could use these pretest scores to confirm that the problem you identified in part A had occurred.

3 The newspaper headline summarizing research that had been reported in a medical journal read: "Study: Exercise Helps at Any Age." The research described in the article involved a 10-year study of nearly 10,000 men—and only men. The men were given a treadmill test between 1970 and 1989. Then they were given a second treadmill test 5 years after the first test and their health was monitored for another 5 years. Men who were judged unfit on both treadmill tests had a death rate over the next 5 years of 122 per 10,000. Men judged fit on both treadmill tests had a 5-year death rate of only 40 per 10,000. Most interestingly, men judged unfit on the first treadmill test but fit on the second had a death rate of 68 per 10,000. The benefits of exercise were even greater when only deaths from heart attacks were examined. The benefits from exercise were present across a wide range of ages—thus, the headline.

**A** Why is the newspaper headline for this article potentially misleading?

**B** Why do you think the researchers tested only men?

**C** Identify two different ways of obtaining evidence that you could use to decide whether the results of this study could be applied to women. One of the ways would make use of already published research and the other way would require doing a new study.

4 An experiment was done to test the effectiveness of a drug that is being considered for possible use in the treatment of people who experience chronic anxiety. Fifty people who are chronically anxious are identified through a local health clinic and all 50 people give their informed consent to participate in the experiment. Twenty-five people are randomly assigned to the experimental group, and they receive the drug. The other 25 people are randomly assigned to the control group, and they receive a placebo. The participants in both groups are monitored by a physician and a clinical psychologist during the 6-week treatment period. After the treatment period, the participants provide a self-rating on a reliable and valid 20-point scale indicating the level of anxiety they are experiencing (higher scores indicate greater anxiety). The mean self-rating in the experimental group was 10.2 and the mean rating in the control group was 13.5. The $F$-test for the mean difference between the two groups was $F(1,48) = 7.50$, $p = .01$.

**A**   Explain why a double-blind procedure would be useful in this experiment and describe how the double-blind procedure could be carried out in this experiment.
**B**   What information would you use to begin to describe "what happened" in this experiment?
**C**   Is the $F$-test for this experiment statistically significant? Be sure to provide the evidence on which you base your decision.
**D**   The effect size for this experiment is $d = .37$. What does this effect size tell you about the effectiveness of the drug beyond what you know from the test of statistical significance?

## Answer to Challenge Question 1

**A**   The first step is to assign a number from 1 to 4 to the respective conditions: 1 = Very Fast; 2 = Fast; 3 = Slow; and 4 = Very Slow. Then, using the random numbers, select four sequences of the numbers from 1 to 4. In doing this you skip any numbers greater than 4 and any number that is a repetition of a number already selected in the sequence. For example, if the first number you select is a 1, you skip all repetitions of 1 until you have selected all the numbers for the sequence of 1 to 4. Following this procedure and working across the rows of random numbers from left to right, we obtained the following four sequences for the four blocks of the randomized block schedule. The order of the conditions for each block is also presented. The block randomized schedule specifies the order of testing the conditions for the first 16 participants in the experiment.

Block 1: 1-4-3-2   Very Fast, Very Slow, Slow, Fast

Block 2: 4-2-3-1   Very Slow, Fast, Slow, Very Fast

Block 3: 1-3-2-4   Very Fast, Slow, Fast, Very Slow

Block 4: 2-3-4-1   Fast, Slow, Very Slow, Very Fast

**B**   The investigator is taking a reasonable step to avoid selective subject loss, but restricting participants to those who pass a stringent reaction time test entails the risk of decreased external validity of the obtained findings.
**C**   The rooms can be balanced by assigning entire blocks from the block randomized schedule to be tested in each room. Usually, the number of blocks assigned to each room is equal, but this is not essential. For effective balancing, however, several blocks should be tested in each room.

# Repeated Measures Designs

267

## OVERVIEW

As we have emphasized, the experimental method involves at least two conditions (often a "treatment" condition and a "control" condition) in order to determine the differential influence of these conditions, if any, on behavior. Thus far we have considered experimental designs in which each condition is represented by a separate group of subjects. These independent groups designs (random groups, matched groups, and natural groups) are powerful tools for studying the effects of a wide range of independent variables. There are times, however, when it is inefficient to have conditions represented by different groups of participants. In such circumstances, it is still possible to do an interpretable experiment by having each participant experience all the conditions of an experiment. These designs are called **repeated measures designs** (or *within-subjects designs*). In an independent groups design, there is a separate group that serves as a control for the group given the experimental treatment. In a repeated measures design, subjects *serve as their own controls* because they participate in both the experimental and control conditions.

We begin this chapter by exploring the reasons why a researcher might choose a repeated measures design. We next examine practice effects in the repeated measures designs. Practice effects arise because participants undergo changes as they are repeatedly tested. Participants may improve with practice, for example, because they learn more about the task or because they become more relaxed in the experimental situation. They also may get worse with practice—for example, because of fatigue or reduced motivation.

We described in Chapter 6 that individual differences among participants cannot be eliminated in the random groups design, but they can be balanced by using random assignment. Similarly, temporary changes participants experience due to repeated testing in the repeated measures designs (i.e., practice effects) cannot be eliminated. Like individual differences in the random groups design, however, practice effects can be balanced across the conditions of a repeated measures design experiment. When practice effects are balanced the effect of an independent variable in a repeated measures design experiment is interpretable. Balancing *does not eliminate* practice effects from repeated measures designs. Balancing works by *averaging out* the practice effects across conditions. By doing this, we avoid confounding practice effects with the conditions of the experiment. This chapter discusses various techniques for accomplishing this balancing. We also describe potential limitations of repeated measures designs. We conclude the chapter with an introduction to procedures for analyzing the results of repeated measures designs.

## REASONS FOR USING REPEATED MEASURES DESIGNS

- Researchers may decide to use a repeated measures design when few participants are available, to be more efficient when conducting the experiment, to increase the sensitivity of the research, or to study differences within subjects over time or across stimuli.

- Repeated testing of individuals to establish reliability of measurement differs from the repeated measures design because researchers manipulate an independent variable across the conditions of a repeated measures design.

There are at least four reasons why a researcher might choose a repeated measures design. First, repeated measures designs require fewer participants, so they are ideal for situations in which only a small number of participants is available.

The second reason for choosing a repeated measures design applies even when sufficient numbers of participants are available for an independent groups design. A researcher might choose to use a repeated measures design for the sake of convenience or efficiency. For example, Ludwig, Jeeves, Norman, and DeWitt (1993) conducted a series of experiments studying communication between the two hemispheres of the brain. The investigators measured how long it took participants to decide whether two briefly presented letters had the same name. The letters came from the set AaBb. Participants were to press the "match" key when the letters had the same name (AA, aa, Bb) and the "no match" key when the letters had different names (AB, ab, Ab). There were several different ways in which the pairs of letters were presented across four experiments, but there were two major conditions in these experiments. Either both letters were presented to one hemisphere (unilateral) or one letter of the pair was presented to each hemisphere (bilateral). Across the four experiments bilateral presentation led to faster response times than did unilateral presentation. In these experiments, two hemispheres were better than one!

Each trial in the Ludwig et al. (1993) experiment required only a few seconds to complete. They could have tested separate groups of participants for the unilateral and bilateral conditions, but this approach would have been horribly inefficient. It would have taken more time to instruct participants regarding the nature of the task than it would have to do the task itself! A repeated measures design in which each participant was tested on both unilateral and bilateral trials provided the experimenters with a far more efficient way to answer their question about how the brain processes information.

The third reason for choosing a repeated measures design for an experiment is that the experiment will generally be more sensitive than one that uses an independent groups design. As was noted in Chapter 6, sensitivity refers to the extent an experiment is able to detect differences in the dependent variable as a function of the independent variable. In repeated measures designs, the investigator tries to detect differences in the performance of the same participants under different conditions. In independent groups designs, researchers try to detect differences in the performance of different participants under different conditions. Repeated measures designs are generally more sensitive than are independent groups designs because the two types of designs differ in the amount of error variation that is present. Simply speaking, there is usually more variation *between* people than there is *within* people. That is, participants will vary within themselves over time (in a repeated measures design) less than participants will vary from other participants (in an independent groups design), and, thus, error variation is less in a repeated measures design. The less error variation, the easier it is to see the effect of an independent variable. The increased sensitivity of repeated measures designs is especially attractive to researchers who are studying independent variables that have small (hard-to-see) effects on behavior.

The fourth reason for choosing a repeated measures design is that some areas of psychological research require its use. When the research question involves studying changes in participants' behavior over time, such as in a learning experiment or in a longitudinal design (see Chapter 4), a repeated measures design is needed. Further, whenever the experimental procedure requires that participants compare two or more stimuli relative to one another, a repeated measures design must be used. For example, a repeated measures design would have to be used if a researcher wanted to measure the minimum amount of light that must be added before participants could detect that a spot of light had become brighter. It would also be called for if a researcher wanted participants to rate the relative attractiveness of a series of photographs. In general, the research areas of psychophysics (illustrated by the light-detection experiment) and scaling (illustrated by the ratings of attractiveness) rely heavily on repeated measures designs. Journals such as *Perception & Psychophysics* and *Journal of Experimental Psychology: Human Perception and Performance* frequently publish results of experiments using repeated measures designs.

Before continuing our discussion of repeated measures designs, we want to make a distinction between this type of design and other situations in which subjects are tested repeatedly. Psychologists frequently measure subjects on more than one occasion. There are important reasons for doing this, and these reasons usually have to do with reliability. First, as you saw in earlier chapters, a researcher may obtain two (or more) measures of the same individual in order to establish the reliability (consistency) of a measure. For example, a group of participants may be given the same aptitude test on two different occasions in order to assess the test-retest reliability of such an instrument. A correlation coefficient would likely be used to measure reliability in this situation. Another reason for testing subjects repeatedly is to obtain a more stable and, hence, reliable measure of behavior. For example, consider a study of individuals' current level of depression based on a self-report inventory. An investigator who measures depression would probably not want to use a questionnaire that has only one item asking about depression. Rather, such a measure will be more reliable if it is based on people's responses to many different items asking about their current mood. These situations, in which we test subjects repeatedly in order either to measure reliability, or to increase the reliability of our measurement, should be differentiated from repeated measures designs in which we contrast subjects' behavior in two or more conditions of an experiment.

## PRACTICE EFFECTS

- In repeated measures designs, confoundings due to individual differences variables are eliminated because the same individuals participate in each condition (level) of the independent variable.

- In repeated measures designs, participants' performance may change across conditions simply because of repeated testing, not because of the independent variable manipulation; these changes are called practice effects.
- Practice effects may threaten the internal validity of a repeated measures experiment when the different conditions of the independent variable are presented in the same order to all participants.

At first glance, repeated measures designs might appear far superior to independent groups designs. The repeated measures designs require fewer participants than do the independent groups designs, and experiments can usually be completed more quickly when repeated measures designs are used. In addition to their greater efficiency, the repeated measures designs offer another advantage—the problem of confounding the conditions of the experiment with the characteristics of the participants within each condition is avoided. That is, in an independent groups design, one must take care to ensure that participants in different conditions of the experiment are essentially equivalent in terms of important characteristics (e.g., motivation, aptitude, etc.). An experiment is confounded if participants in various groups differ in ways other than the levels of the independent variable. In a repeated measures design, the same participants are tested in all conditions, so it is impossible to end up with brighter, more aggressive, or more anxious participants in one condition than in another condition. Stated formally, there can be no confounding by individual differences variables in the repeated measures designs.

The apparent superiority of repeated measures designs diminishes, however, when we realize that these designs require that the same participant must be tested more than once. Participants may change across repeated testings even if all tests are done under the same conditions. That is, participants may get better and better at doing a task if a skill is being developed, or they may get worse and worse at the task because of such factors as fatigue and boredom. The repeated testing of each participant in the repeated measures designs gives the participants practice with the experimental task. The changes participants undergo with repeated testing are called **practice effects.**

Kahneman, Frederickson, Schreiber, and Redelmeier (1993) used a repeated measures design in a series of experiments investigating people's perception of pain. They argued that the duration of an aversive experience plays a much smaller role in our perception of pain than do two other factors. They demonstrated that our evaluations of pain are influenced most by the worst moments and the final moments of the experience. In other words, we judge how painful an experience was by judging how painful it was at the point of most intense pain and by how painful it was at the end of the experience. These two factors were shown to be more important in the perception of pain than the amount of time the pain lasted. We will illustrate the balancing of practice effects using one of the experiments that Kahneman et al. (1993) did to determine the influence of the intensity of the pain in the final moments of the experience. Other experiments in the series addressed the second factor, the point of the most intense moments of pain in an experience.

There were two conditions in the experiment. In the first condition (short trial) students immersed one hand in cold water (14 degrees Celsius) for 60 seconds. In the second condition (long trial) the students also immersed their hand in 14-degree water for 60 seconds, but they then kept their hand immersed 30 seconds longer while the temperature of the water was gradually raised 1 degree (warmed) to 15 degrees. Each participant experienced both the short trial and the long trial only once. There was a 7-minute interval filled with another activity after each trial. One dependent variable was people's ratings of their degree of pain after each trial. The most important measure in the experiment, however, was the choice students made when they were asked to choose which trial they preferred to repeat.

The researchers found that the students' ratings of pain indicated that the 15-degree water was painful, but noticeably less painful than the 14-degree water. Overall, the long trial was rated by students as more painful than the short trial. Nonetheless, when students were asked which trial they preferred to repeat, 69% chose the more painful long trial. Kahneman et al. (1993) argued that the students chose the long trial because it was less painful in the final moments of the experience. The overall duration of the long trial was less critical in determining students' choice than was the fact that it was less painful at the end of their experience. To reach this intriguing insight the researchers had to make sure that practice effects were balanced in the experiment.

Suppose that Kahneman et al. (1993) had tested all the students by giving them the short trial first and then the long trial. In this case, practice effects would not have been balanced. The problem with using only one testing order is that differences between the two types of trials would be confounded with

**FIGURE 7.1**    In order to examine people's perceptions of pain, students in Kahneman et al.'s (1993) experiment immersed their hand in cold water.

the order in which they occurred: The short trial would always be the first trial and the long trial would always be the second trial. Students might become more familiar with the sensations resulting from having their hand immersed in cold water as they move from one trial to the other. Or maybe they would be less apprehensive about possible pain after they had experience with one trial. There are many important ways in which the students could change over the two trials. We call the summation of these changes *practice effects*. If only one order had been used, practice effects and the conditions of the experiment would be confounded. Thus, if people rated the two conditions differently, we wouldn't know if the difference in ratings was due to the type of trial (short or long) or the temporal order (first or second) in which the conditions appeared.

Kahneman et al. (1993) balanced practice effects by administering the conditions in two different orders. Half of the students received the short trial followed by the long trial and half received the long trial followed by the short trial. Since both orders were used equally often, the students' preference to repeat the long trial rather than the short trial cannot be attributed to the long trial always having been presented last. The changes due to practice effects that occurred for the students from the first trial to the second trial are likely to fall equally on each of the two conditions because half the students experienced practice effects during a long trial, and half on a short trial. Practice effects should average out across conditions. Any difference in performance, therefore, between the two conditions is the result of the nature of the short and long trials and not the result of practice effects.

## BALANCING PRACTICE EFFECTS

- In the complete repeated measures design, individuals participate in each condition of the independent variable manipulation several times (in different orders) to balance practice effects *within* each individual.
- In the incomplete repeated measures design, individuals participate in each condition only once, and different individuals receive different orders of the conditions in order to balance practice effects *across* individuals.
- Because counterbalancing techniques differ for complete and incomplete designs, researchers must first choose which design they will use.

There are two types of repeated measures designs. In the *complete design*, practice effects are balanced for each participant. Balancing practice effects for each participant is accomplished by administering the conditions to each participant several times, using different orders each time. Each participant can thus be considered a "complete" experiment. In the *incomplete design*, each condition is administered to each participant *only once*. The order of administering the conditions is varied across participants rather than for each participant as is the case in the complete design. Practice effects in the incomplete design average out when the results are combined for all participants. This may seem a bit confusing at this point, but hopefully it will become clearer as we discuss these types of designs. The specific techniques for balancing practice effects, called **counterbalancing,** differ in the two repeated measures designs, so we will discuss the two designs separately. Just keep in mind that a major goal when using a repeated measures design is to control for practice effects; exactly how we do that depends on the specific repeated measures design that is used. Thus, the first step in controlling practice effects is to determine whether your experiment is based on a complete repeated measures design or an incomplete design.

## Complete Design

- Practice effects are balanced in complete designs within each participant using block randomization or ABBA counterbalancing.
- In block randomization, the conditions of the experiment (a block) are randomly ordered each time they are presented.
- ABBA counterbalancing is preferred when it is not possible to administer conditions often enough for practice effects to be balanced using block randomization.
- In ABBA counterbalancing, a random sequence of all conditions is presented, followed by the opposite of the sequence.
- Block randomization is preferred over ABBA counterbalancing when practice effects are not linear, or when participants' performance can be affected by anticipation effects.

Does one side of your face express emotion more intensely than the other side? Sackheim, Gur, and Saucy (1978) used a repeated measures design to attempt to answer this question. Earlier research had shown that participants given photographs depicting posed facial expressions of six basic human emotions (happiness, surprise, fear, sadness, anger, and disgust) could readily and accurately identify the expressed emotion. Sackheim and coworkers took advantage of a technique developed in earlier work on facial recognition whereby a full photograph of a face can be constructed using only one side of a person's face. The technique involves developing both a photograph of a full face and a photograph of its mirror image. These two photographs are then split down the middle and two composite photographs are made—one from the two versions of the left side of the face and one from the two versions of the right side. Illustrative photographs are presented in Figure 7.2. In the center is a photograph of a person expressing disgust. The two composite photographs made from the center photograph are presented on either side of the original. Does one of the two composites in Figure 7.2 look more disgusted than the other?

Participants were shown slides of photographs like those in Figure 7.2 and were asked to rate each slide on a 7-point scale indicating the intensity of the expressed emotion. The slides were presented individually for 10 seconds, and participants were then given 35 seconds to make their rating. To increase the external validity of their experiment, the investigators had photographs of 14 different people depicting the 6 identifiable emotions and 1 neutral expression. The critical independent variable in the experiment, however, was the *version* of

**FIGURE 7.2** (a) Left-side composite, (b) original, and (c) right-side composite of the same face. The face is expressing disgust. (From Sackheim et al., 1978.)

the photograph (left composite, original, or right composite). Each participant rated 54 slides: 18 left composites, 18 originals, and 18 right composites.

Participants' ratings of emotional intensity were consistently higher for the left composite than for the right composite. Sackheim et al. interpreted these findings in terms of hemispheric specialization of the brain. In general, the left hemisphere controls the right side of the body and the right hemisphere controls the left side of the body. Thus, the left composite reflects control by the right hemisphere, and the right composite reflects control by the left hemisphere. The higher ratings of emotional intensity for the left composite photographs suggest that the right hemisphere may be more heavily involved than the left hemisphere in the production of emotional expression.

The interpretation of the differences in the ratings depends critically on the order in which the slides were presented to participants. If all the original versions were presented first, followed by all the right composites, then by all the left composites, higher ratings for the slides shown at the end of this long sequence may reflect the intensity of the participants' boredom and fatigue rather than the intensity of the emotions actually depicted in the photographs. If you imagine yourself in this experiment making a rating for each of the slides in this long sequence (over 40 minutes), you will get a sense of what we mean by practice effects. Surely your attention, motivation, and experience in rating the emotionality of photographs will change as you work through the sequence of slides. Sackheim et al. used balancing techniques specifically developed for use with the complete design in repeated measures experiments to ensure that each of the three versions of the photographs was equally likely to appear at any point in the long series of slides.

In the complete design, participants are given each treatment enough times to balance practice effects for each participant. Of course, this is possible only when each treatment can be administered more than once. When the task is simple enough and not too time-consuming (such as judging the emotional intensity of photographs), it is possible to give one participant several experiences with each treatment. In fact, in some complete designs, only one or two participants are tested and each participant experiences literally hundreds of trials. More commonly, however, researchers use procedures like those used by Sackheim et al. That is, several participants are tested, and each participant is given each treatment only a relatively small number of times. In Sackheim et al.'s experiment, participants completed 18 trials with left composites, 18 trials with original composites, and 18 trials with right composites. Researchers have two choices in deciding how to arrange the order in which the treatments in a complete design are administered: block randomization and ABBA counterbalancing.

**Block Randomization**   We introduced block randomization in Chapter 6 as an effective technique for assigning participants to conditions in the random groups design. *Block randomization* can also be used to order the conditions for each participant in a complete design. For instance, Sackheim et al. administered each of the three versions of their photographs (left composite, original, and right composite) 18 times to each participant. The sequence of trials shown in Table 7.1 illustrates how block randomization could be used to arrange the order of the three conditions in their experiment. The sequence of 54 trials is broken up into 18 blocks of 3 trials. Each block of trials contains the three conditions of the experiment in random order. In general, *the number of blocks in a block-randomized schedule is equal to the number of times each condition is administered, and the size of each block is equal to the number of conditions in the experiment.*

If a participant rated the photographs following the sequence in the block-randomized schedule shown in Table 7.1, it is unlikely that changes in the participant's attention, motivation, or experience with rating photographs would affect any one of the conditions more than any other. The practice effects can reasonably be expected to average out over the three experimental conditions. Determining the average position of each of the three conditions in the block-randomized sequence gives a rough indication of the balancing of practice effects. This can be done by summing the trial numbers on which each condition appears and dividing by 18. For instance, the original version of the photographs appeared on trials 1, 5, 8, 11, 13, 18, 21, 24, 27, 28, 33, 34, 39, 40, 44, 48, 49, and 53. The average position of the original photographs, therefore, was 27.6. The corresponding values for the left and right composite photographs are 27.7 and 27.2, respectively. That these average values are so similar tells us that any one version of the photographs was not more likely to appear at the beginning, middle, or end of the sequence of 54 trials.

Block randomization is effective in balancing practice effects, but each condition must be repeated several times before  we can expect practice effects to average out. We should not expect practice effects to be balanced after two or three blocks—any more than we would expect sample sizes of two or three in the random groups design to result in comparable groups. Fortunately, a technique is available to balance practice effects when it is not possible to administer each

**TABLE 7.1** BLOCK-RANDOMIZED SEQUENCE OF TRIALS IN AN
EXPERIMENT WITH THREE CONDITIONS ADMINISTERED
18 TIMES EACH

| Trial | Conditions | Trial | Conditions |
|-------|-----------|-------|-----------|
| 1 | O | 28 | O |
| 2 | L | 29 | L |
| 3 | R | 30 | R |
| 4 | R | 31 | R |
| 5 | O | 32 | L |
| 6 | L | 33 | O |
| 7 | R | 34 | O |
| 8 | O | 35 | R |
| 9 | L | 36 | L |
| 10 | L | 37 | L |
| 11 | O | 38 | R |
| 12 | R | 39 | O |
| 13 | O | 40 | O |
| 14 | L | 41 | R |
| 15 | R | 42 | L |
| 16 | R | 43 | R |
| 17 | L | 44 | O |
| 18 | O | 45 | L |
| 19 | R | 46 | R |
| 20 | L | 47 | L |
| 21 | O | 48 | O |
| 22 | L | 49 | O |
| 23 | R | 50 | R |
| 24 | O | 51 | L |
| 25 | R | 52 | R |
| 26 | L | 53 | O |
| 27 | O | 54 | L |

*Note:* The conditions are the three versions of the photographs
used by Sackheim et al. (1978): L = left composite, O = original,
R = right composite.

condition often enough for the averaging process of block randomization to
work effectively.

ABBA Counterbalancing   In its simplest form, ABBA counterbalancing can be
used to balance practice effects in the complete design with as few as two administrations of each condition. **ABBA counterbalancing** involves presenting
the conditions in one sequence (i.e., A then B) followed by the opposite of that
same sequence (i.e., B then A). Its name describes the sequences when there are

only two conditions (A and B) in the experiment, but ABBA counterbalancing is not limited to experiments with just two conditions. Sackheim et al. could have presented the versions of their photographs according to the ABBA sequence outlined in the top row of Table 7.2 labeled "Condition." Note that in this case it literally would be ABCCBA since there are three conditions. The order of the three conditions on the first three trials is simply reversed for trials 4 to 6.

The row of Table 7.2 labeled "Practice effect (linear)" illustrates how ABBA counterbalancing can balance practice effects. ABBA counterbalancing is appropriately used when practice effects are linear. If practice effects are linear the same amount of practice effects is added to or subtracted from performance on each successive trial. In our example, suppose that one "unit" of hypothetical practice effects is added to performance on each trial. Because there would be no practice effect associated with the first trial, the amount of practice added to Trial 1 in the table is zero. Trial 2 has one unit of hypothetical effects added because of participants' experience with the first trial; in Trial 3 there are two units added because of participants' experience with two trials, and so on. If you add up these hypothetical practice effects for each condition, you will see that all the totals are the same, namely, 5. The left composite condition gets the least (+0) and the greatest (+5) influence from practice effects; the right composite condition gets two intermediate amounts (+2 and +3). The ABBA cycle can be applied with any number of conditions, but there must be an even number of repetitions of each condition. (An unequal number of repetitions would end in the middle of an ABBA sequence—that is, AB would be the last two conditions of an ABBA series.) It balances practice effects even more effectively with larger numbers of repetitions of the cycle. Usually, however, ABBA counterbalancing is used when the number of conditions and the number of repetitions of each condition are relatively small.

Although ABBA counterbalancing provides a simple and elegant means to balance practice effects, it is not without limitations. For example, when practice effects for a task are not linear but involve abrupt initial changes followed by relatively little change thereafter, ABBA counterbalancing is ineffective. This is illustrated in the last row of Table 7.2, labeled "Practice effect (nonlinear)." In this example, the left composite receives a total of only 6 hypothetical units of practice effects, and the other two conditions receive a total of 12 units each. When practice effects of this type are anticipated, researchers often ignore performance on the early trials and wait until the practice effects reach a "steady

**TABLE 7.2**    ABBA COUNTERBALANCED SEQUENCE OF TRIALS IN AN EXPERIMENT WITH THREE CONDITIONS (LEFT COMPOSITE, ORIGINAL, AND RIGHT COMPOSITE)

|  | Condition: | Trial 1<br>Left | Trial 2<br>Original | Trial 3<br>Right | Trial 4<br>Right | Trial 5<br>Original | Trial 6<br>Left |
|---|---|---|---|---|---|---|---|
| Practice effect (linear) |  | +0 | +1 | +2 | +3 | +4 | +5 |
| Practice effect (nonlinear) |  | 0 | +6 | +6 | +6 | +6 | +6 |

state." Reaching a steady state is likely to take several repetitions of each condition, so researchers tend to use block randomization to balance practice effects in these situations. This problem should alert you to the fact that there are situations when you should not choose a repeated measures design, for example, if nonlinear changes cannot easily be eliminated from your analysis.

A second limitation of ABBA counterbalancing is the problem of anticipation effects. *Anticipation effects* occur when a participant develops expectations about which condition should occur next in the sequence. The participant's response to that condition may then be influenced more by this expectation than by the actual experience of the condition itself. For example, consider a time-perception experiment in which the participant's task is to estimate the length of time that has passed between when the experimenter said "Start" and when the experimenter said "Stop." (Of course, participants have to be prevented somehow from marking off time during the interval by counting or rhythmically tapping.) If the time intervals in such an experiment are 12, 24, and 36 seconds, then one possible ABBA sequence of conditions could be 12-24-36-36-24-12. If this cycle were repeated several times, participants probably would recognize the pattern and expect a series of increasing and then decreasing intervals. Their time estimates might soon begin to reflect this pattern rather than their perception of each independent interval. In general, block randomization should be used if anticipation effects are likely.

## Incomplete Design

- Practice effects are balanced *across* subjects in the incomplete design rather than *within* subjects, as in the complete design.
- The rule for balancing practice effects in the incomplete design is that each condition of the experiment must be presented in each ordinal position (first, second, etc.) equally often.
- The best method for balancing practice effects in the incomplete design with four or fewer conditions is to use all possible orders of the conditions.
- Two methods for selecting specific orders to use in an incomplete design are the Latin Square and random starting order with rotation.
- Whether using all possible orders or selected orders, participants should be randomly assigned to the different sequences.

In the incomplete design, each participant is given each treatment *only once*. The results for any one participant, therefore, are uninterpretable because the levels of the independent variable for each participant are perfectly confounded with the order in which those levels were presented. For instance, the first participant in an incomplete design experiment might be tested first in the experimental condition (E) and second in the control condition (C). Any differences in the participant's performance between the experimental and control conditions could be due to the effect of the independent variable *or* to the practice effects resulting from the EC order. To break this confounding of the order of conditions and the independent variable, we can administer different orders of the conditions to different participants. For example, we could administer the conditions of our incomplete design experiment to a second participant in the CE order, testing the control condition first and the experimental condition second. In this way, we could balance the effects of order across the two conditions using two participants instead of one.

To illustrate the techniques for balancing practice effects in the incomplete design, we will use an experiment by Erber (1991) on the effects of people's moods on their perceptions of other people. There were two stages in this experiment. In the first stage, the independent variable of mood was manipulated using independent groups—that is, each participant was in only one mood group. In this first stage, participants read one of three stories about events in the life of a young female artist. These stories were previously shown to be effective in inducing positive, neutral, or negative moods in people. The story for the positive-mood condition included several events culminating in the artist's receiving a scholarship to college. The neutral-mood story described how the artist decided which college to attend. The negative-mood story described how the artist was overcome by a rare disabling illness at the end of her first year in college. Thus, after the first stage, participants are assumed to be in one of three moods: positive, neutral, negative.

At this point, the second stage of the experiment began. The participants believed that the second stage was a separate experiment, one in which they were asked to rate the likelihood of a person engaging in a particular behavior (welcoming a friend with a hug, getting depressed over the weather, and so on). Four individuals were described to the participants, and then the participants were asked to rate the likelihood that these individuals would demonstrate various behaviors. Four brief descriptions were provided to each participant, one for each "target" individual whom they would rate. For reasons that will become apparent, the descriptions were based on somewhat contradictory traits. Each of the four "target people" was described as (1) either moody and warm; (2) pessimistic and understanding; (3) unselfish and unsociable; or (4) trustworthy and possessive. A repeated measures design was used to implement the independent variable of the target person, which, of course, had four levels. Specifically, an incomplete design was used in which each participant rated all four target people *once*.

Before describing the techniques that can be used to balance practice effects for an independent variable in the incomplete design, we will take a brief look at the results of the Erber study. The dependent variable in this study was the participants' ratings of the likelihood that the target people would engage in certain behaviors. The researcher hypothesized that these ratings would be influenced by *participants'* mood (positive, neutral, or negative) as manipulated in the first stage of the experiment. Because the target people were described using both a positive (e.g., warm) and a negative (e.g., moody) trait, the researchers wanted to see if the participants' mood would determine which of the two traits most influenced their ratings. For example, the participants' task was to rate how likely it was for someone described as "warm and moody" to engage in positive behavior, such as "welcoming a friend with a hug," or in negative behavior, such as "getting depressed over the weather." Welcoming someone with a hug is something a "warm" person might do, while getting depressed is something a "moody" person is more likely to do. Perhaps you can anticipate what happened in this experiment.

The results revealed that if a participant was in a positive mood, then a "warm and moody" person was rated as more likely to engage in positive behavior (e.g., welcoming with a hug) than in negative behavior (e.g., getting depressed over the weather). If the participant was in a negative mood, the same "warm and moody" individual was rated more likely to engage in negative behavior than in positive behavior. The effect of mood on ratings of negative behaviors was larger than was the effect of mood on ratings of positive behaviors. These findings (along with other findings reported in the study) indicate that mood can influence the way we perceive other people in important ways. One such influence, Erber (1991) argues, is that negative mood may facilitate the accessibility of negative information about others. In other words, if you're in a bad mood, you're more likely to accentuate someone's negative traits!

The repeated measures independent variable in the Erber (1991) experiment was the four types of target people. In order to rule out practice effects as an alternative explanation for the findings it is essential that the order in which the targets are rated is balanced. We turn now to the balancing techniques that are used in the incomplete design. The general rule for balancing practice effects in the incomplete design is a simple one: *Each condition of the experiment must appear in each ordinal position equally often*. Several techniques are available for satisfying this general rule. These techniques differ in what additional balancing they accomplish, but so long as the techniques are properly used, the basic rule will be met and the experiment will be interpretable. That is, if appropriate balancing is carried out, then we will be in a position to determine whether the independent variable, and not practice effects, influenced the participants' behavior.

**All Possible Orders**   The preferred technique for balancing practice effects in the incomplete design is to use all possible orders of the conditions. Each participant is randomly assigned to one of the orders. With only two conditions there are only two possible orders (AB and BA); with three conditions there are six possible orders (ABC, ACB, BAC, BCA, CAB, CBA). In general, there are $N!$ (which is read "$N$ factorial") possible orders with $N$ conditions, where $N!$ equals $N(N - 1)(N - 2) \ldots (N - [N - 1])$. As we just saw, there are six possible orders with three conditions, which is 3! ($3 \times 2 \times 1 = 6$). The number of required orders increases dramatically with increasing numbers of conditions. For instance, for only five conditions there are 120 possible orders of the conditions, and for six conditions there are 720 possible orders. Because of this, the use of all possible orders is usually limited to experiments involving four or fewer conditions. With four conditions, how many possible orders are there?

Because there were four target people in the Erber (1991) experiment, 24 sequences would be required to obtain all possible orders of the conditions. These sequences are presented in the left half of Table 7.3. Using all possible orders

**TABLE 7.3**   ALTERNATIVE TECHNIQUES TO BALANCE PRACTICE EFFECTS IN AN INCOMPLETE REPEATED MEASURES DESIGN EXPERIMENT WITH FOUR CONDITIONS

| | | | | | | | | Selected orders | | | | | | | |
| --- | --- | --- | --- | --- | --- | --- | --- | --- | --- | --- | --- | --- | --- | --- | --- |
| All possible orders | | | | | | | | Latin Square | | | | Random starting order with rotation | | | |
| Ordinal position | | | | Ordinal position | | | | Ordinal position | | | | Ordinal position | | | |
| 1st | 2nd | 3rd | 4th | 1st | 2nd | 3rd | 4th | 1st | 2nd | 3rd | 4th | 1st | 2nd | 3rd | 4th |
| M | P | U | T | U | M | P | T | M | P | U | T | P | U | T | M |
| M | P | T | U | U | M | T | P | P | T | M | U | U | T | M | P |
| M | U | P | T | U | P | M | T | T | U | P | M | T | M | P | U |
| M | U | T | P | U | P | T | M | U | M | T | P | M | P | U | T |
| M | T | P | U | U | T | M | P | | | | | | | | |
| M | T | U | P | U | T | P | M | | | | | | | | |
| P | M | U | T | T | M | P | U | | | | | | | | |
| P | M | T | U | T | M | U | P | | | | | | | | |
| P | U | M | T | T | P | M | U | | | | | | | | |
| P | U | T | M | T | P | U | M | | | | | | | | |
| P | T | M | U | T | U | M | P | | | | | | | | |
| P | T | U | M | T | U | P | M | | | | | | | | |

*Note:* The four conditions are identified by the first letter of the first adjective describing each of the four target people in the Erber (1991) experiment: Moody-Warm (M), Pessimistic-Understanding (P), Unselfish-Unsociable (U), and Trustworthy-Possessive (T).

certainly meets the general rule of ensuring that all conditions appear in each ordinal position equally often. The first ordinal position shows this balancing most clearly: The first six sequences begin with the Moody-Warm (M) target, and each succeeding set of six sequences begins with one of the other three targets. The same pattern applies at each of the four ordinal positions. For example, the "M" target also appears six times in the second ordinal position, six times in the third ordinal position, and six times in the fourth ordinal position.

There is one other issue that must be addressed in deciding to use all possible orders. For this technique to be effective, it is essential that at least one participant be tested with each of the possible orders of the conditions. That is, at least one participant should receive the MPUT order, at least one should receive the MPTU order, and so on. Therefore, the use of all possible orders requires at least as many participants as there are possible orders. That is, if there are four conditions in the experiment, you must test 24 participants (or 48 or 72 or some other multiple of 24). This restriction makes it very important that you have a good idea of the number of potential participants available to you before testing the first participant.

**Selected Orders**   We have just described the preferred method for balancing practice effects in the incomplete design, all possible orders. There are times, however, when the use of all possible orders is not practical. For example, if we wanted to use the incomplete design to study an independent variable with seven levels, we would need to test 5,040 participants if we used all possible orders—one participant for each of the possible orders of the seven conditions (7! orders). We obviously need some alternative to using all possible orders if we are to use the incomplete design for experiments with five or more conditions.

Practice effects can be balanced by using just some of all the possible orders. The number of selected orders will always be equal to some multiple of the number of conditions in the experiment. For example, to do an experiment with one independent variable with seven levels, we need to select 7, 14, 21, 28, or some other multiple of seven orders to balance practice effects. The two basic variations of using selected orders are illustrated in Table 7.3. To allow you to compare the types of balancing more directly, we have illustrated the techniques for selected orders with the four-level independent variable from Erber's (1991) experiment that we described in the previous section.

---

**BOX 7.1**

## HOW TO CONSTRUCT A LATIN SQUARE

More than one valid Latin Square can be constructed for an experiment. A simple procedure for constructing a square *with an even number (N) of conditions* is as follows:

**1** Randomly order the conditions of the experiment.
**2** Number the conditions in your random order 1 through *N*.

> Thus, if you had *N* = 4 conditions (A,B,C,D) and the random order (from Step 1) was B, A, D, C, then B = 1, A = 2, D = 3, C = 4.

**3** To generate the first row (first order of conditions), use the rule:

> 1, 2, *N*, 3, *N* − 1, 4, *N* − 2, 5, *N* − 3, 6, etc.
> In our example, this would yield 1, 2, 4, 3.

**4** To generate the second row (second order of conditions) add 1 to each number in the first row but with the understanding that 1 added to *N* = 1.

> We would then have 2, 3, 1, 4.

**5** The third row (third order of conditions) is generated by adding 1 to each number in the second row and again *N* + 1 = 1.

> The third row would be 3, 4, 2, 1.

**6** A similar procedure is carried out for each successive row.

Can you construct the fourth row in this 4 × 4 square?

**7** Assign the conditions to their corresponding numbers as determined in Step 2.

The Latin Square for this example would be:

> B A C D
> A D B C
> D C A B
> C B D A

If there is an odd number of conditions, then two squares must be constructed. The first can be made according to the rule given above for even-numbered squares. The second square is generated by reversing the rows in the first square. For example, assume *N* = 5 and the first row of the first square is B A E C D. The first row of the second square would then be D C E A B. The two squares are joined to make a *N* × 2*N* square. In either case, even or odd, subjects should be assigned randomly to the rows of the square. Thus, you must have available at least as many subjects as there are multiples of rows. (Procedures for selecting or constructing Latin Squares are also described in Winer, Brown, and Michels [1991, pp. 674–679].)

The first type of balancing using selected orders is called the Latin Square. In a *Latin Square,* the general rule for balancing practice effects is met. That is, each condition appears at each ordinal position once. For example, just to the right of the center of Table 7.3, we can see that in the Latin Square, condition "M" appears exactly once in the first, second, third, and fourth ordinal positions. This is true for each condition. Additionally, in a Latin Square each condition precedes and follows each other condition exactly once. Examination of the Latin Square in Table 7.3 shows that the order "MP" appears once, as does the order "PM." The order "PV" appears once, as does the order "VP," and so on, for every combination of conditions. (See also Box 7.1 on p. 283.)

The second balancing technique using selected orders requires you to begin with a random order of the conditions and to rotate this sequence systematically with each condition moving one position to the left each time (see the example on the right in Table 7.3). Using a random starting order with rotation effectively balances practice effects because, like the Latin Square, each condition appears in each ordinal position. However, the systematic rotation of the sequences means that each condition always follows and always precedes the *same* other conditions, which is not like the Latin Square technique. The simplicity of the random starting order with rotation technique and its applicability to experiments with more than four conditions are its primary advantages.

The use of all possible orders, Latin Squares, and random starting orders with rotation are equally effective in balancing practice effects because all three techniques ensure that each condition appears in each ordinal position equally often. Regardless of which technique one uses to balance practice effects, the sequences of conditions should be fully prepared prior to testing the first participant, and participants should be randomly assigned to these sequences.

## LIMITATIONS OF REPEATED MEASURES DESIGNS

- There are some variables that cannot be studied using a repeated measures design.

The first obvious limitation of repeated measures designs is that they cannot be used to study individual differences variables such as age and gender. A 40-year-old person cannot be 20 years old, then 60 years old, and then 40 years old again (though we've all known people who act that way!). Second, repeated measures designs also are not appropriate when the levels of the independent variable represent an unfolding sequence of successive events. For example, a study of brain lesions would require controls such as Anesthesia Only and a Sham-Operated condition, and the sequential nature of these treatments seems to demand separate groups. That is, an animal could not be tested in the Anesthesia Only group once the animal was lesioned. Third, experiments in which each condition takes a great deal of time to implement are not likely to be suitable for repeated measures designs. For example, if the treatment involved participation in a year-long program, one ABBA sequence in a repeated measures design would take 4 years to implement! Finally, as you saw, a repeated measures design should not be used when practice effects are not apt to be linear. It is unlikely that the random groups design will be completely replaced by the repeated measures designs.

## Irreversible Tasks

- Because individuals participate more than once in repeated measures designs, irreversible tasks cannot be used; instead, different versions of the task should be used.
- To balance practice effects when different versions of a task are used, the conditions of the independent variable of interest *and* the different versions of the task must be balanced.

We will consider a hypothetical but realistic experiment looking at the effects of marijuana use to illustrate a problem sometimes encountered in a repeated measures design, that of irreversible tasks. Participants in this hypothetical experiment are asked to come to the laboratory on four different days. Each day the participants smoke two cigarettes that contain one of four dose levels of marijuana—a placebo control (0) and doses of 50, 100, and 200 units. The experiment is an incomplete repeated measures design so each participant is given each dose once.

The experiment examines the effects of marijuana on people's ability to learn and remember new information. One way to carry out an experiment like this would be to give each participant a different list of words to learn under each dose of marijuana. A different list of words would be needed each time because a memory task of this type is an *irreversible task*—one that cannot be administered more than once without risking that the participant will master the task. Once participants master the task, their performance under subsequent conditions is not likely to vary. In a sense, irreversible tasks result in a "ceiling effect" for all conditions after the first one under which the task has been performed. When performance hits a "ceiling" there is no way to measure any further improvement in performance in the other conditions (see Chapter 8).

Suppose in this example that the researchers had given the *same* list of words to participants on each of the four days. Consider the performance of a participant who received the following sequence of doses: 0, 50, 200, and 100. Performance may not be all that good on the first day (0 dose) because the participant is learning the list of words for the first time. However, on the second, and following days, his or her performance is likely to be better because the list had been learned on Day 1. Note that this "improvement" would be seen just when the participant is receiving doses (50, 200, 100) of marijuana. This may make marijuana look like a drug that enhances memory! Of course, it would not be a valid finding because of the problem with irreversible tasks. Because the list was mastered early in the experiment, it would be impossible to know if marijuana had any effects on memory.

Thus, to control for problems associated with this irreversible task, memorizing a list of words, a *different* list of words should be used each time individuals participate in the experiment. This, however, creates a new problem if the same list is used for each condition of the independent variable manipulation. That is, if List A is always used for the 0-dose condition, and List B is always used for the 50-dose condition, and so on, the particular version of the list becomes confounded with dosage level. If the lists differ in important ways, for example, if one list is easier than the others, the effect of dosage level (the primary independent variable) cannot be interpreted.

The solution to the problem of irreversible tasks is outlined in Table 7.4. The solution requires two steps. The first step is to balance practice effects for the primary independent variable (in our case, the marijuana variable). A random starting order with rotation has been used to accomplish the balancing of the four dose levels (0, 50, 100, and 200 units); that is, each dosage condition appears in each ordinal position of the experiment. The sequences for the first four participants appear in the upper-left quadrant of the table. The first subject receives the conditions in the order 50, 200, 0, and 100 units with Lists A, B, C, and D, respectively. This order is then rotated for the second subject (200, 0, 100, 50), but note that this subject receives List A with the 200 dose, List B with the 0 dose, and so on. When the sequence of dosage levels is rotated for the third and fourth subjects, they too receive different lists for the dosage conditions. Because each dose appears with each of the four lists exactly once, the marijuana variable is also balanced for the possible effects of the list variable. Thus, if one

**TABLE 7.4**    BALANCING EXPERIMENTS WITH IRREVERSIBLE TASKS IN REPEATED MEASURES DESIGNS

| | Ordinal position | | | | | Ordinal position | | | |
|---|---|---|---|---|---|---|---|---|---|
| | 1st | 2nd | 3rd | 4th | | 1st | 2nd | 3rd | 4th |
| | | List | | | | | List | | |
| Subject | A | B | C | D | Subject | B | C | D | A |
| 1 | 050 | 200 | 000 | 100 | 5 | 050 | 200 | 000 | 100 |
| 2 | 200 | 000 | 100 | 050 | 6 | 200 | 000 | 100 | 050 |
| 3 | 000 | 100 | 050 | 200 | 7 | 000 | 100 | 050 | 200 |
| 4 | 100 | 050 | 200 | 000 | 8 | 100 | 050 | 200 | 000 |
| | Ordinal position | | | | | Ordinal position | | | |
| | 1st | 2nd | 3rd | 4th | | 1st | 2nd | 3rd | 4th |
| | | List | | | | | List | | |
| Subject | C | D | A | B | Subject | D | A | B | C |
| 9 | 050 | 200 | 000 | 100 | 13 | 050 | 200 | 000 | 100 |
| 10 | 200 | 000 | 100 | 050 | 14 | 200 | 000 | 100 | 050 |
| 11 | 000 | 100 | 050 | 200 | 15 | 000 | 100 | 050 | 200 |
| 12 | 100 | 050 | 200 | 000 | 16 | 100 | 050 | 200 | 000 |

*Note:* The numbers 000, 050, 100, and 200 refer to dose levels.

list happens to be easier for participants to learn, any one dosage level would not have an advantage due to being associated consistently with the easier list.

A problem would arise, however, if the researcher were to try to assess differences among the four lists. The lists for the first four participants are perfectly confounded by the ordinal position. That is, List A is always learned first, List B is learned on Day 2, List C on the third day, and List D is always last. The confounding of lists and ordinal position can be overcome by taking the second step in dealing with the problem of irreversible tasks. In general, this second step requires testing additional participants so that the list variable and ordinal position are also balanced. In our example, 12 additional participants need to be tested, with the order of the lists systematically rotated for each successive set of four participants. This also is illustrated in Table 7.4. Each quadrant of the table includes the same four orders of marijuana doses. However, by comparing the upper left quadrant with the three remaining quadrants, you can see that the order of the lists for each quadrant is different. The order of the lists has been determined using a random starting order with rotation, such that four different orders of the lists are used: ABCD, BCDA, CDAB, DABC. Thus, across the 16 subjects, each condition appears in each ordinal position with each version of the list. The two-step process of balancing in experiments involving irreversible tasks ensures that each of three variables (the independent variable of interest, stage of practice, and task) are balanced for the other two. Thus, the effects of all three variables are interpretable.

## Differential Transfer

- Differential transfer occurs when the effects of one condition persist and influence performance in subsequent conditions.
- Because differential transfer threatens the internal validity of repeated measures designs, variables that may lead to differential transfer should be tested using a random groups design.
- Differential transfer can be identified by comparing the results for the same independent variable when tested in a repeated measures design and in a random groups design.
- An efficient method for determining whether differential transfer has occurred in an incomplete design is to compare the results for the independent variable at the first stage of practice to the results for the overall repeated measures design.

The most consistent and vocal critic of repeated measures designs has been E. C. Poulton (1973, 1975, 1982; Poulton & Freeman, 1966). While conceding that balancing techniques control practice effects, Poulton has argued that they do not eliminate a more serious problem. This problem arises when performance in one condition differs depending on the condition that precedes it. We call this **differential transfer.**

Consider a problem-solving experiment in which two types of instructions are being compared in a repeated measures design. One set of instructions (A) is expected to enhance problem solving, whereas the other set of instructions (B) serves as the neutral control condition. It is reasonable to expect that participants tested in the order AB will be unable or unwilling to abandon the approach outlined in the A instructions when they are supposed to be following the B instructions. Giving up the "good thing" participants had under instruction A would be the counterpart of successfully following the admonition "Don't think of pink elephants!" When participants fail to give up the instruction from the first condition (A) when they are supposed to be following instruction B, any difference between the two conditions is reduced. For those participants, after all, condition B was not really tried, and it becomes similar to a situation in which they participated in an "AA" condition, not an "AB" condition.

In general, the presence of differential transfer threatens internal validity because it becomes impossible to determine if there are true differences between the conditions. It also tends to underestimate differences between the conditions and thereby reduces the external validity of the findings. *Thus repeated measures designs should not be used when differential transfer may arise.* Differential transfer is sufficiently common with instructional variables to advise against the use of repeated measures designs for these variables (Underwood & Shaughnessy, 1975). Unfortunately, differential transfer can arise in any repeated measures design. For instance, the effect of 50 units of marijuana may be different if administered after the participant has received 200 units than if administered after the participant has received the placebo (e.g., if the participant has an increased tolerance for marijuana after receiving the 200 dose). There are ways, however, to determine whether differential transfer is likely to have occurred.

Poulton (1982) maintains that the best way to determine whether differential transfer is a problem is to do two separate experiments. The same independent variable would be studied in both experiments, but a repeated measures design would be used in one experiment and a random groups design in the other. The random groups design cannot possibly involve differential transfer because each participant is tested in only one condition. Poulton argues that differential transfer is not a problem if the repeated measures design shows the same effect of the independent variable as that shown in the random groups design. If the two designs show different effects for the same independent variable, however, differential transfer is likely to be responsible for producing the different outcome in the repeated measures design. When differential transfer does occur, the results of the random groups design should be used to provide the best description of the effect of the independent variable.

Perhaps the most efficient way to follow Poulton's advice is to do experiments involving a relatively large repeated measures experiment using the incomplete design. For example, if 48 participants were tested in a four-condition experiment with all possible orders of the conditions (i.e., 24 different orders), there would be 12 participants tested in each of the four conditions at the first stage of practice (i.e., the first ordinal position). That is, with 24 possible orders, each of four conditions (A, B, C, D) would appear six times in the first ordinal position, and since there are 2 participants tested in each sequence, there would be 12 receiving A first, 12 B first, and so on. So long as participants have been randomly assigned to sequences, the repeated measures design contains a random groups design for the first condition given to each participant. In other words, at this point in your repeated measures design (the first stage of practice), you have 12 participants assigned randomly to each of four conditions, making a random groups design within the first ordinal position. By comparing the results for the independent variable in the first ordinal position with the overall results for the independent variable in the repeated measures design, we can achieve the comparison Poulton recommends in one experiment.

## ANALYSIS OF REPEATED MEASURES DESIGNS

### Sensitivity and Power

- Sensitivity refers to the likelihood that an *experiment* will detect the effect of an independent variable when, in fact, the independent variable truly has an effect.
- Power refers to the likelihood that a *statistical test* will allow researchers to reject correctly the null hypothesis of no group differences.
- The power of statistical tests is influenced by the level of statistical significance, the size of the treatment effect, and the sample size.
- Repeated measures designs are likely to be more sensitive and to have more statistical power than independent groups designs because estimates of error variation are likely to be smaller in repeated measures designs.
- The primary means for researchers to increase statistical power are increasing sample size or using a repeated measures design, or both.

Before we describe the use of the *F*-test in the analysis of repeated measures designs, we will describe the concept of power in statistical analyses. The **sensitivity** of an experiment is the likelihood that it will detect an effect of the independent variable if the independent variable does, indeed, have an effect. As we have mentioned, repeated measures designs are generally more sensitive than independent groups designs. An experiment is said to have sensitivity; a statistical test is said to have power. The **power** of a statistical test is the probability that the null hypothesis will be rejected when it is false. The null hypothesis is the hypothesis of "no difference," and, thus, is false and should be rejected when the independent variable has made a difference. You may remember that in our discussion of Type I and Type II errors (see Chapter 6), we defined a Type II error as the probability of failing to reject the null hypothesis when it is false. Power can also be defined as 1 minus the probability of a Type II error. It is important to be aware of the factors in an experiment that affect the power of the statistical test that will be used to analyze the data *before* beginning to collect the data.

Keppel (1991) provides an excellent description of the factors affecting the power of a statistical test such as the analysis of variance. The power of a statistical test is determined by the interplay of three factors: the level of statistical significance, the size of the treatment effect, and the sample size. Keppel goes on to argue, however, that for all practical purposes sample size is the primary factor that researchers can use to control power. He describes how to use power charts to select an appropriate sample size for a given level of power with a certain level of significance and with an expected treatment effect that is either small, medium, or large. (We described the nature of small, medium, and large effects when we describe the measurement of effect sizes in Chapter 6.) The differences in sample size that are needed to detect effects of different sizes can be dramatic. For example, Cohen (1988) reports the sample sizes that are needed for an independent groups design experiment with one independent variable manipulated at three levels. It takes a sample size of 30 to detect a large treatment effect; it takes a sample size of 76 to detect a medium treatment effect; and it takes a sample size of 464 to detect a small treatment effect. It thus takes over 15 times more participants to detect a small effect than it does to detect a large effect!

Sample size is the major factor researchers can control to affect the power of the statistical analyses they use to analyze their experiments. Using repeated measures experiments can also affect the power of the statistical analyses researchers use. Repeated measures experiments are generally more sensitive than are independent groups experiments. This is because, as was mentioned earlier, the estimates of error variation are generally smaller in repeated measures experiments (see also next section). The smaller error variation leads to an increased ability to detect small treatment effects in an experiment. And that is just what the power of a statistical analysis is—the ability to detect small treatment effects when they are present.

To conduct a power analysis you must first estimate the effect size anticipated in your experiment. An examination of the effect sizes obtained in previous studies for the independent variable of interest should guide your estimate. Once an effect size is estimated, you must then turn to "power tables" to obtain information about the sample size you should use in order to "see" the effect. These steps for conducting a power analysis are described more fully in Appendix A. Power tables are also included at the end of Appendix A for you to consult. (Should you wish to investigate this issue further, Cohen [1992] provides a brief introduction to power, and, Cohen [1988] provides a more thorough introduction.)

## Repeated Measures Analysis of Variance

- The general procedures and logic for null hypothesis testing using repeated measures analysis of variance are similar to those used for independent groups analysis of variance.
- Before beginning the analysis of variance for a complete design, a summary score (e.g., mean, median) for each participant must be computed for each condition.
- Descriptive data are calculated to summarize performance for each condition of the independent variable across all participants.

- The primary way that analysis of variance differs for repeated measures is in the estimation of error variation, or residual variation; residual variation is the variation that remains when systematic variation due to the independent variable and participants is removed from the estimate of total variation.

The analysis of experiments using repeated measures designs involves the same general procedures used in the analysis of independent groups design experiments. The principles of null-hypothesis testing are applied to determine whether the differences obtained in the experiment are larger than would be expected on the basis of error variation alone. The analysis begins with an omnibus analysis of variance to determine whether the independent variable has produced any systematic variation among the levels of the independent variable. Should this omnibus analysis prove statistically significant, analytical comparisons can be made to find the specific source of the systematic variation—that is, to determine which specific levels differed from each other. Because we have already described the logic and procedures for this general analysis plan in Chapter 6, we will focus in this section on the analysis procedures specific to repeated measures designs.

The first step in analyzing an experiment is preparing a matrix summarizing participants' performance in each condition of the experiment. In random groups designs, this means simply listing the scores of the participants tested in each of the conditions of the experiment and then summarizing these scores with some descriptive statistic such as the mean. Similarly, in complete repeated measures designs, we prepare a matrix in which the scores for each participant in each condition of the experiment are listed. An example of such a matrix appears in the upper portion of Table 7.5. The data represent performance of the five participants tested in a time-perception experiment done as a classroom demonstration of a complete repeated measures design. The purpose of the experiment was not to test the accuracy of participants' time estimates compared with the actual interval lengths. Instead, the purpose of the experiment was to determine whether participants' estimates of time increased systematically with increasing lengths. In other words, could participants discriminate between intervals of different lengths? Each participant was tested using all four interval lengths (12, 24, 36, and 48 seconds).

Each of the four interval lengths was tested six times in the experiment, and block randomization was used to determine the order in which the intervals were presented. Thus, each participant provided 24 time estimates, 6 estimates for each of the four interval lengths. Any one of the 6 estimates for a given time interval is contaminated by practice effects, so some measure that combines information across the 6 estimates is needed. Typically, the mean across the 6 estimates for each interval would be calculated for each participant to provide a single estimate of performance in each condition. As you may remember, however, the mean is influenced by extreme scores; it is quite possible that participants gave extreme estimates of the time intervals for at least one of the six tests of each interval. Thus, for this particular set of data, the median of the 6 estimates probably provides the best measure to reflect the participants' estimates

**TABLE 7.5**   DATA MATRIX AND ANALYSIS OF VARIANCE SUMMARY TABLE FOR A REPEATED MEASURES DESIGN EXPERIMENT

| | Data matrix | | | |
|---|---|---|---|---|
| | Interval length | | | |
| Participant | 12 | 24 | 36 | 48 |
| 1 | 13 | 21 | 30 | 38 |
| 2 | 10 | 15 | 38 | 35 |
| 3 | 12 | 23 | 31 | 32 |
| 4 | 12 | 15 | 22 | 32 |
| 5 | 16 | 36 | 69 | 60 |
| Mean | 12.6 | 22.0 | 38.0 | 39.4 |

*Note:* Each value in the table represents the median of the participants' six responses at each level of the interval length variable.

| Source of Variation | df | SS | MS | F | p |
|---|---|---|---|---|---|
| Subjects | 4 | 1553.5 | — | — | — |
| Interval Length | 3 | 2515.6 | 838.5 | 15.6 | .0004 |
| Residual (error variation) | 12 | 646.9 | 53.9 | | |
| Total | 19 | 4716.0 | | | |

of the time intervals. These median estimates (rounded to the nearest whole number) are listed in Table 7.5. The point of this illustration is that you must compute a score for each participant in each condition before you begin to do an analysis of variance.

Once an individual score for each participant in each condition has been obtained, the next step is to summarize the results across participants, using an appropriate descriptive statistic. The mean estimates across participants for each of the four intervals are listed in the row labeled "Mean" in Table 7.5. Even though the data for only five participants are included in the table, these mean estimates are reasonably accurate reflections of the actual interval lengths, at least for intervals up to 36 seconds. (Note that the mean is an average of medians. You may be used to seeing the mean and median as descriptive statistics summarizing a group's performance; however, as this example illustrates, these summary statistics also can be used to represent one person's performance when that performance is an "average" across trials or test occasions.)

The focus of the analysis was on whether the participants could discriminate intervals of different lengths. As you have probably already realized, we cannot confirm the participants' ability to discriminate intervals of varying lengths until we know that the mean differences in Table 7.5 are greater than would be expected on the basis of error variation alone. That is, even though it may *appear* that participants were able to discriminate between the different intervals, we do not know if their performance was different from that which would occur by chance. The null hypothesis for an omnibus analysis of variance for the data in

Table 7.5 is that the mean estimates for each interval are the same. To perform an *F*-test of this null hypothesis, we need an estimate of error variation plus systematic variation (the numerator of an *F*-ratio). The variation among the mean estimates across participants for the four intervals provides the information we need for the numerator. Even if these five participants had been tested on only one interval length several times, we would not expect their mean estimates to be identical. Thus, we know the mean estimates we have for each level of the interval variable reflect error variation as well. We also know, however, that if the different interval lengths did systematically affect the participants' judgments, then the mean estimates for the intervals would reflect this systematic variation. To complete the *F*-ratio, we also need an estimate of error variation alone (the denominator of the *F*-ratio).

One distinctive characteristic of the analysis of repeated measures designs is the way in which error variation is estimated. We described in Chapter 6 that for the random groups design individual differences among participants that are balanced across groups provide the estimate of error variation that becomes the denominator of the *F*-ratio. Because individuals participate in only one condition in these designs, differences among participants cannot be eliminated—they can only be balanced. In repeated measures designs, on the other hand, there is systematic variation among participants. Some participants consistently perform better across conditions, and some participants consistently perform worse. Because each individual participates in each condition of repeated measures designs, however, differences among participants contribute equally to the mean performance in each condition. Accordingly, any differences among the means for each condition in repeated measures designs cannot be the result of systematic differences among participants. In repeated measures designs, however, differences among participants are not just balanced—they are actually eliminated from the analysis. The ability to eliminate systematic variation due to participants in repeated measures designs makes these designs generally more sensitive than random groups designs.

If differences among participants cannot be the basis of estimating error variation in repeated measures designs, how do we get an estimate that involves only error variation in these designs? The source of error variation in the repeated measures designs is the differences in the ways the conditions affect different participants. Perhaps the best way to describe the way we get these estimates is to say that we do it "by default." We first determine how much total variation there is in our experiment. Then we subtract the two potential sources of systematic variation: the independent variable and participants. The remainder is called *residual variation,* and it represents our estimate of error variation alone. (For a more complete discussion of residual variation and why it is an estimate of error variation alone, see Keppel [1991].) As was the case in the random groups design when we used variation within groups as our estimate of error variation alone, residual variation serves as the denominator for the *F*-ratio in repeated measures designs (i.e., as an estimate of error variation alone).

The analysis of variance summary table for this analysis is presented in the lower portion of Table 7.5. As described in Appendix A, the computations of a repeated measures analysis of variance would be done using a statistical software package on a computer. Our focus now is on interpreting the values in the summary table and not on how these values are computed. Table 7.5 lists the four sources of variation in the analysis of a repeated measures design with one manipulated independent variable. Reading from the bottom of the summary table up, these sources are (1) total variation, (2) residual variation, (3) variation due to interval length (the independent variable), and (4) variation due to subjects.

As in any summary table, the most critical pieces of information are the $F$-test for the effect of the independent variable of interest and the probability associated with that $F$-test under the null hypothesis. The important $F$-test in Table 7.5 is the one for interval length. The numerator for this $F$-test is the mean square (MS) for interval length; the denominator is the residual MS. There are four interval lengths, so there are 3 degrees of freedom ($df$) for the numerator. There are 12 $df$ for the residual variation. We can obtain the $df$ for the residual variation by subtracting the $df$ for subjects and for interval length from the total $df$ ($19 - 4 - 3 = 12$). The obtained $F$ of 15.6 has a probability under the null hypothesis of .0004, which is less than the .05 level of significance we have chosen as our criterion for statistical significance. So we reject the null hypothesis and conclude that the interval length was a source of systematic variation. This means that we can conclude that the participants' estimates did differ systematically as a function of interval length.

As we mentioned previously (in Chapter 6), it is good statistical practice to include measures of effect size for your analyses. A typical measure of effect size for a repeated measures design is the strength of association measure called eta squared ($\eta^2$) (see Appendix A). This measure is calculated by dividing the sum of squares for the independent variable by the sum of squares for the independent variable plus the sum of squares error. For our sample study, eta squared is $2515.6/(2515.6 + 646.9) = .80$. This indicates the proportion of variance accounted for by the independent variable. Appendix A provides more information about the calculation of effect sizes and their interpretation.

This omnibus analysis of variance would almost certainly be followed by analytical comparisons (such as comparing the mean for each interval to the mean for the succeeding interval) to determine more exactly that mean estimates increased with increasing interval lengths. Once again, the logic of these analytical comparisons corresponds to the logic we discussed in Chapter 6 when we considered analytical comparisons in the random groups design. In most instances, the residual MS can be used as an estimate of error variation alone in computing the $F$-tests for the analytical comparisons. (See Keppel [1991], however, for a discussion of the complications that can arise in doing analytical comparisons in repeated measures designs.)

## Summary

Repeated measures designs provide an effective and efficient way to conduct an experiment by administering all the conditions in the experiment to each participant. Repeated measures designs are useful when only very few participants are available or when an independent variable can be studied most efficiently by testing fewer participants several times. Particular areas of psychological research (e.g., psychophysics) may also require the use of repeated measures designs. Finally, repeated measures designs may be used when a more sensitive experiment is required.

For any repeated measures design experiment to be interpretable, however, practice effects must be balanced. Practice effects are changes that participants undergo because of repeated testing. In a complete repeated measures design, practice effects are balanced for each participant. In an incomplete repeated measures design, each participant receives each treatment only once, and the balancing of practice effects is accomplished across participants.

Block randomization and ABBA counterbalancing can be used to balance practice effects in a complete repeated measures design. ABBA counterbalancing should not be used, however, if practice effects are expected to be nonlinear (and cannot be eliminated from the analysis) or if anticipation effects are likely. Techniques for balancing practice effects in an incomplete repeated measures design involve either the use of all possible orders or selected orders (the Latin Square and rotation of a random starting order). When irreversible tasks are used, three independent variables must be balanced (the independent variable of interest, stage of practice, and the task variable). The most serious problem in any repeated measures design is differential transfer—when performance in one condition differs depending on which condition it follows. Procedures for detecting the presence of differential transfer are available, but there is little that can be done to salvage a study in which it occurs.

The analysis of the results of repeated measures designs follows the same principles of null-hypothesis testing used to analyze independent groups designs. Estimates of error variation are determined differently, however, in the analyses of variance for repeated measures designs. The generally smaller estimates of error variation in repeated measures designs increases the sensitivity of these designs. The greater sensitivity of the experiments generally increases the power of the resulting statistical analyses in repeated measures experiments.

## KEY CONCEPTS

| | |
|---|---|
| repeated measures designs | differential transfer |
| practice effects | sensitivity |
| counterbalancing | power |
| ABBA counterbalancing | |

## REVIEW QUESTIONS

1. Researchers choose to use a repeated measures design for several different reasons. What are four of those reasons?
2. Distinguish between a complete design and an incomplete design for repeated measures designs.
3. What options do researchers have in balancing practice effects in a repeated measures experiment using a complete design?

4 Under what two circumstances would you recommend against the use of ABBA counterbalancing to balance practice effects in a repeated measures experiment using a complete design?

5 State the general rule for balancing practice effects in repeated measures experiments using an incomplete design.

6 What techniques can be used to balance practice effects in the repeated measures experiments using an incomplete design? Which technique is preferred?

7 Explain what is meant by an irreversible task in a repeated measures design?

8 For which types of independent variables are repeated measures designs unlikely to prove useful?

9 Describe how researchers can determine if differential transfer has occurred in a repeated measures experiment using an incomplete design.

10 Explain the different roles played by systematic differences across participants in the analysis of random groups designs and repeated measures designs.

11 What three factors determine the power of a statistical test? Which factor is the primary one that researchers can use to control power?

12 What is a common measure of effect size for a repeated measures analysis and what does this measure indicate about the independent variable?

## CHALLENGE QUESTIONS

1 The following problems represent different situations in the repeated measures designs in which practice effects need to be balanced.

A Consider a repeated measures experiment using a complete design involving one independent variable. The independent variable has three levels (Low, Medium, and High). You are to prepare an order for administering the conditions of this experiment so that the independent variable is balanced for practice effects. You are first to use block randomization to balance the variable and then to use ABBA counterbalancing to balance the variable. Each condition should appear twice in the order you prepare. Use the first row of the random number table in Appendix A to determine your two random orders for block randomization.

B Consider a repeated measures experiment using an incomplete design. One independent variable is to be manipulated at six levels (A, B, C, D, E, and F). Present a table showing how you would determine the order of administering the conditions to the first six participants of the experiment. Be sure that practice effects are balanced for these participants.

2 Consider a repeated measures experiment using an incomplete design to manipulate an environmental variable, room temperature. There are three levels of the variable (60 degrees, 65 degrees, and 70 degrees). The dependent variable of interest is the amount of time taken to solve a list of word problems. Thus, three different word problem lists are required (designated as Lists A, B, and C). Present a table showing how you could administer the conditions of the experiment in order to determine the effect of the three independent variables: room temperature, stage of practice, and list. You have only nine people available for participants, but previous research indicates that you need not be concerned with problems of differential transfer.

3 The pursuit rotor is a test of perceptual-motor coordination. It involves a turntable with a disk about the size of a dime embedded in it. The participant is given a pointer and is asked to keep the pointer on the disk while the turntable is rotating. The dependent variable is the percentage of time on each trial that the participant keeps the pointer on the disk. Learning on this task in linearly related to trials over many

periods of practice, and the task generally takes a long time to master. A researcher wants to study the influence of time of day on the performance on this task with four different times (10 a.m., 2 p.m., 6 p.m., and 10 p.m.). The participants will receive a constant number of trials under each of the four conditions, and participants will be tested in one condition per day over four consecutive days. The researcher has 96 participants available.

   **A**   What design is being used for the time-of-day variable in this experiment?

   **B**   What research design is included in the first stage of practice of this experiment? How could the researcher use the results of the design in the first stage of practice as an indication of whether differential transfer had occurred?

**4** The following table represents the order of administering the conditions to participants in a repeated measures experiment using an incomplete design in which the independent variable was the difficulty of the task given to the participant (High, Medium, or Low Difficulty). The values in parentheses represent the number correct for each participant in each condition. Use this table, when necessary, to answer questions that follow.

| Participant | Order of conditions | | |
|---|---|---|---|
| 1 | High (2) | Medium (9) | Low (9) |
| 2 | Medium (3) | Low (5) | High (7) |
| 3 | Low (4) | High (3) | Medium (5) |
| 4 | High (6) | Low (10) | Medium (8) |
| 5 | Medium (7) | High (8) | Low (6) |
| 6 | Low (8) | Medium (4) | High (4) |

   **A**   What method was used to balance the stage-of-practice effects?

   **B**   Present the values you would use to describe the overall effect of the task difficulty variable. Include a verbal description of the effect along with the descriptive statistics that you use as a basis of your description.

   **C**   What would you conclude if the $F$-test for the effect of task difficulty was $F(2,10) = 4.25, p = .04$?

## Answer to Challenge Question 1

**A** Assigning the values 1, 2, and 3 to the Low, Medium, and High conditions, respectively, and using the first row of the random number table in Appendix A beginning with the first number in the row, the block-randomized sequence is Low-High-Medium-Low-Medium-High. One possible ABBA counterbalanced sequence is Low-Medium-High-High-Medium-Low.

**B** Because there are six conditions, all possible orders is not feasible. Therefore, either a Latin Square or a random starting order with rotation is needed to balance practice effects. A possible set of sequences using rotation is:

| Participant | Position | | | | | |
|---|---|---|---|---|---|---|
| | 1st | 2nd | 3rd | 4th | 5th | 6th |
| 1 | B | D | E | C | A | F |
| 2 | D | E | C | A | F | B |
| 3 | E | C | A | F | B | D |
| 4 | C | A | F | B | D | E |
| 5 | A | F | B | D | E | C |
| 6 | F | B | D | E | C | A |

# Complex Designs

## CHAPTER OUTLINE

OVERVIEW

In the last two chapters we described the basic experimental designs that psychologists use to study the effect of an independent variable. We discussed how an independent variable could be implemented with a separate group of participants in each condition (Chapter 6) or with each participant experiencing all the conditions (Chapter 7). We limited our discussion in these two chapters to experiments involving only one independent variable because we wanted you to concentrate on the characteristics of each research design. Experiments involving only one independent variable are not, however, the most common type of experiment in current psychological research. Instead, researchers most often use **complex designs** in which two or more independent variables are studied simultaneously in one experiment.

Consider, for example, a study by May, Hasher, and Stoltzfus (1993). These researchers used a complex design to study the effects of time of day on memory performance of younger and older people. In a preliminary study they determined that most younger adults (ages 18–22) were classified as "evening types" and most older adults (ages 66–78) were classified as "morning types." They reasoned on the basis of these results that the optimal time of day for doing a memory task would be in the afternoon for younger adults and in the morning for older adults. In their experiment they tested 11 older adults in the morning and 11 in the afternoon. Similarly, they tested 10 younger adults in the morning and 10 in the afternoon. All the participants first read 10 short stories. Immediately after reading the last story they were tested for their recognition of sentences that either were included in the story (old sentences) or were not included in the story (new sentences).

As indicated in the following diagram, this experiment involved four conditions: (1) older adults tested in the morning; (2) older adults tested in the afternoon; (3) younger adults tested in the morning; and (4) younger adults tested in the afternoon.

|                | Time of Testing | |
| Age Group      | Morning | Afternoon |
| -------------- | ------- | --------- |
| Older Adults   | 1       | 2         |
| Younger Adults | 3       | 4         |

In this complex design, one independent variable is an individual differences variable (age), with two levels: older adults and younger adults. The second independent variable is a manipulated independent groups variable, the time of testing, which also has two levels: morning or afternoon. In a complex design such as this one, the levels of each of the two independent variables are combined *factorially*. Factorial combination involves pairing each level of one independent variable with each level of a second independent variable. For example, older and younger adults are tested both in the morning and in the afternoon. The number of conditions in a complex design is always equal to the product of the number of levels for each independent variable included in the experiment. In the May et al. (1993) experiment there are two levels of age and two levels of time of testing so there are four conditions ($2 \times 2 = 4$). If these two age groups had been tested at three times of day, there would have been six conditions ($2 \times 3 = 6$).

Factorial combination in complex designs makes it possible to assess the effect of each independent variable alone (*main effect*) and the effect of the independent variables in combination (*interaction*). For example, May et al. found, as expected, that younger adults performed better overall on the recognition memory test than did older adults. This represents a main effect of the age variable. That is, "collapsed" across time of testing, younger adults performed better on the dependent variable than did older adults. More importantly, they found that recognition performance did not differ for younger and older adults in the morning (older adults' optimal time); but younger adults did much better than older adults in the afternoon (younger adults' optimal time). In other words, being tested at their nonoptimal time hurt older adults more than it did younger adults. This type of effect, called an *interaction effect*, can be discovered only when two or more independent variables are included in the same experiment. In general, an **interaction** occurs when the effect of one independent variable differs depending on the level of a second independent variable.

Complex designs may seem a bit complicated at this point, but the concepts will become clearer as you progress through this chapter. In what follows we describe the procedures for producing, analyzing, and interpreting main effects and interactions. We begin with a review of guidelines for identifying or selecting an experimental design. We then describe the basic concepts of main effects and interactions in complex designs. The analysis plans for complex designs are introduced along with the application of analysis of variance to complex designs. We give special attention to the interpretation of interactions in complex designs.

## GUIDELINES FOR IDENTIFYING AN EXPERIMENTAL DESIGN

- Researchers use complex designs to study the effects of two or more independent variables in one experiment.
- In complex designs, each independent variable can be studied with an independent groups design or with a repeated measures design.

An experiment with a complex design has, by definition, more than one independent variable. Each independent variable in a complex design must be implemented using either an independent groups design or a repeated measures design according to the procedures described in Chapters 6 and 7. When a complex design has both an independent groups variable and a repeated measures variable it is called a *mixed design*. Before examining complex designs themselves, we need to review briefly the characteristics of the various experimental designs that can be used to study a single independent variable. You will be better able to understand descriptions of complex designs if you can quickly and accurately identify the independent variables, their levels, and the design used to implement each independent variable. Similarly, your ability to carry out your own experiments using complex designs will be enhanced if you can confidently select the most appropriate design for each independent variable in which you are interested.

The flowchart in Figure 8.1 summarizes the distinctions among experimental designs by taking you through a series of questions. The diagram will probably

**FIGURE 8.1**    Flowchart for identifying experimental designs.

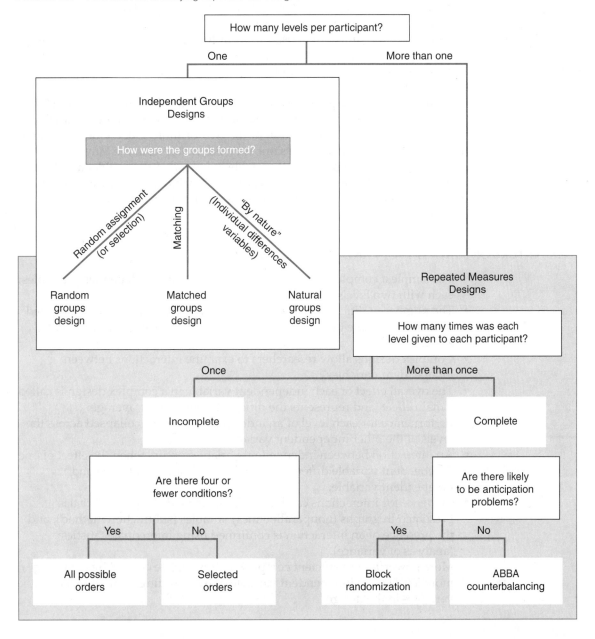

prove most useful to you when you are reading about a particular experiment in either your text or a journal article. As you identify each independent variable in an experiment, you can track the variable through Figure 8.1 to determine what design has been used to implement the independent variable. The first question at the top of the flowchart is the most critical one. The answer to the question, How many levels of the independent variable were administered to each participant?, determines whether an independent groups or repeated measures design has been used. Answering the subsequent questions for the independent groups designs will allow you to identify the particular type of design by examining the procedures used to form the groups. For the repeated measures designs, we have included questions to help you distinguish complete and incomplete repeated measures designs and to identify the appropriate balancing techniques for each type.

Complex designs require that you go through the flowchart in Figure 8.1 as many times as necessary to identify the design for each independent variable in the experiment. In a complex design, the two or more independent variables need not be implemented in the same way. For example, in the May et al. (1993) study, the age group independent variable (younger adults or older adults) represented a natural groups design. The time of day independent variable (morning or afternoon) was manipulated using the random groups design.

## THE NATURE OF MAIN EFFECTS AND INTERACTIONS

- The simplest complex design is a 2 × 2 design—two independent variables, each with two levels.
- The number of different conditions in a complex design can be determined by multiplying the number of levels for each independent variable (e.g., 2 × 2 = 4).
- Complex designs allow researchers to examine interactions between independent variables.
- The overall effect of each independent variable in a complex design is called a main effect, and represents the differences among the average performance for each level of an independent variable collapsed across the levels of the other independent variable.
- An interaction between independent variables occurs when the effect of one independent variable differs depending on the levels of the second independent variable.
- Evidence for interactions can be identified using descriptive statistics presented in graphs (nonparallel lines) or tables (subtraction method), and the presence of an interaction is confirmed using inferential statistics (analysis of variance).
- More powerful and efficient complex designs can be created by including more levels of an independent variable or by including more independent variables in the design.

The simplest possible experiment involves one independent variable manipulated at two levels. Similarly, the simplest possible complex design involves two independent variables, each of which is manipulated at two levels. Complex designs are identified by specifying the number of levels of each of the independent variables in the experiment. A 2 × 2 (which is read "2 by 2") design, then, identifies the most basic complex design. Conceptually, there is an unlimited number of complex designs because any number of independent variables can be studied and each independent variable can have any number of levels. In practice, however, it is unusual to find experiments involving more than four or five independent variables. Regardless of the number of independent variables, the number of conditions in a complex design can be determined by multiplying the number of levels of the independent variables. For instance, as we saw in the May et al. study of age and time of day, there are two independent variables with each having two levels in a 2 × 2 design; thus, there are four conditions in a 2 × 2 design. In a 3 × 3 design there are two independent variables with 3 levels each so there are nine conditions. In a 3 × 4 × 2 design there are three independent variables with 3, 4, and 2 levels, respectively, and a total of 24 conditions. The primary advantage of all complex designs is the opportunity they provide for identifying interactions between independent variables.

The nature of main effects and interactions is essentially the same in all complex designs, but they can be seen most easily in a 2 × 2 design. Consider an experiment by Hass, Katz, Rizzo, Bailey, and Eisenstadt (1991). They used a 2 × 2 design to investigate cross-racial evaluations. Cross-racial evaluations of performance is a research topic of both theoretical and practical importance. When given comparable information about a White and a Black applicant for a job, for instance, do evaluators rate the candidate of their own race (in-group) more favorably than the candidate of the other race (out-group)?

The students in the Hass et al. (1991) experiment (all of whom were White) were told by a White female experimenter that the researchers were developing a new quiz game for college students called Trivia Challenge. The participants were tested in small groups but one member of the group was always a confederate of the experimenter. The race of the group captain was the first independent variable. The two levels were Black and White captains. The experimenter made sure that an election among the group members always resulted in the confederate being selected as the captain of the group. The captain selected the questions that the group had to answer in the quiz game. The nature of these questions defined the second independent variable in the experiment, outcome, which also had two levels. In the success outcome conditions, the captain selected easy questions and the group easily reached the criterion for correct answers in the allotted time. In the failure outcome condition, the captain selected questions of such difficulty that the group failed to meet the criterion. Groups of participants were randomly assigned to the four groups formed by the factorial combination of the race of the captain (Black, White) and the outcome (success, failure). Can you identify the conditions of the experiment?

**TABLE 8.1**    EXAMPLE OF A 2 × 2 DESIGN WITH AN INTERACTION
(Mean Evaluation Scores for Captains in Each Group)

|  | Race of Captain | |
| --- | --- | --- |
| Outcome | Black | White |
| Success | 309.6 | 280.9 |
| Failure | 155.3 | 196.1 |

Adapted from Hass et al. (1991).

After the quiz game, participants completed a questionnaire that included several items requiring them to evaluate the captain of their group. The responses to these questions were combined into an overall evaluation score, with higher scores indicating more favorable evaluations of the captain. The mean evaluation scores for the four conditions of the experiment are presented in Table 8.1. We will use the data in this table to illustrate two critical concepts in complex designs: *main effects* and *interactions.*

In any complex factorial design it is possible to test predictions regarding the overall effect of each independent variable in the experiment while ignoring the effect of the other independent variable(s). The overall effect of an independent variable in a complex design is called a **main effect.** For example, the overall mean for success outcomes (295.2) can be obtained by averaging the two values for the Black and White captains in the two success conditions: [(309.6 + 280.9)/2] = 295.2. Similarly, the mean of the failure outcomes can be computed to be 175.7.[1] *The means for a main effect represent the overall performance at each level of a particular independent variable collapsed across (averaged over) the levels of the other independent variable.* In this case we collapsed over the race of the captain variable to obtain the means for the main effect of the outcome variable. The main effect of the outcome variable is the difference between the means for the two levels of the outcome variable—(295.2 − 175.7). In the Hass et al. (1991) experiment, the main effect of the outcome variable indicates that, overall, the evaluation scores for all captains were higher for success outcomes (295.2) than for failure outcomes (175.7).

Similarly, we can also determine whether there is a main effect of the second independent variable, race of captain. The procedure is exactly like that outlined for determining the effect of the outcome variable, but, of course, this time we must average across the success and failure conditions. The main effect for captain is the difference between the mean evaluation ratings for the two types of captains. You should be able to determine for yourself that these means were 232.4 and 238.5 for Black and White captains, respectively. Thus, it appears that

[1]The simple averaging of the values within each row and column to obtain the means for the main effects is possible *only* when there are equal numbers of participants contributing to each mean in the table. For procedures to use when the cells of the table involve different sample sizes, see Keppel (1991).

in the Hass et al. experiment, White captains were rated overall more favorably than Black captains. However, the difference was not great, and one would have to test whether the difference is statistically significant.

Analysis procedures for determining the statistical significance of main effects will be described in the next section. For now, we need only note that the interpretation of main effects is critically dependent on whether an interaction is or is not present. In general, main effects should be interpreted with caution whenever an interaction is present in the experiment. When no interaction occurs, the main effects of each independent variable can be interpreted as though they had been manipulated in two separate experiments, each of which involved only one independent variable.

The most important aspect of Table 8.1 is that it reflects an interaction between the two independent variables, race of the captain and outcome. If only successful outcomes had been tested in the experiment (first row of Table 8.1), we would have concluded that Black captains are evaluated more favorably than White captains. On the other hand, if only outcomes involving failure had been tested (second row of Table 8.1), we would have concluded that White captains are evaluated more favorably than Black captains. These results indicate that whether Black or White captains are evaluated more favorably *depends* on the type of outcome, success or failure. We discuss the statistical analysis of interactions in complex designs in the next section. For now, it is sufficient if you recognize that *an interaction is likely to have occurred when the effect of one independent variable changes depending on the levels of the second independent variable.*

When one independent variable interacts with a second independent variable, the second independent variable must interact with the first one (that is, the order of the independent variables doesn't matter). For example, we described the interaction in Table 8.1 by stating that the effect of the race of the captain varies with the type of outcome. The reverse is also true; the effect of the type of outcome varies with the race of the captain. Black captains were evaluated more favorably than White captains in the success condition, but White captains were evaluated more favorably than Black captains in the failure condition. Hass et al. (1991) chose to describe the interaction by emphasizing that the evaluation of the Black captains was more extreme than was the evaluation of the White captains (the Black captains' evaluation was more positive with success and more negative with failure). How you choose to describe the results of an interaction depends on which aspect of the interaction you want to emphasize. For example, Hass et al. emphasized the more extreme ratings given to the Black captains because they were testing the hypothesis that cross-race evaluation leads to more polarized (more extreme) responses for out-group members (White participants rating Black captains) than for in-group members (White participants rating White captains).

Mastering the concepts of main effects and interactions requires practice in identifying the various types of outcomes that can arise in a complex design. Box 8.1 provides an exercise that gives you an opportunity to begin to practice identifying main effects and interactions in 2 × 2 designs using only descriptive statistics. Inferential statistics would be required to confirm the statistical significance of any obtained effects, but the effects themselves can best be seen in a table or graph of the means for the conditions of the experiment.

There are three common ways to report a summary of the descriptive statistics in a complex design: tables, bar graphs, and line graphs. The procedures for preparing such tables and figures and the criteria for deciding which type of presentation to use are described in Appendix C. In general, tables can be used for any complex design and are most useful when the exact values for each condition in the experiment need to be known. Bar graphs and line graphs, on the other hand, are especially useful for showing patterns of results without dwelling on the exact values. Line graphs are particularly useful for depicting the results of complex designs because an interaction can be seen so readily in a line graph. *Nonparallel lines in the graph suggest an interaction; parallel lines suggest no interaction.*

---

BOX 8.1

## HERE AN INTERACTION, THERE AN INTERACTION, EVERYWHERE AN INTERACTION

In the spirit of practice makes perfect, let us now turn our attention to the exercise we have prepared to help you learn to identify interactions. Your task is to identify main effects and interactions in each of six complex design experiments (A through F). In each table or graph in this box, you are to determine whether the effect of each independent variable differs depending on the level of the other independent variable. In other words, is there an interaction? After checking for the interaction, you can also check to see whether each independent variable produced an effect when collapsed across the other independent variable. That is, is there a main effect of one or both independent variables? The exercise will be most useful if you also practice translating the data presented in a table (Figure 8.2) into a graph and those presented in graphs (Figures 8.3 and 8.4) into tables. The idea of the exercise is to become as comfortable as you can with the various ways of depicting the results of a complex design.[2]

FIGURE 8.2    Mean number of correct responses as a function of task difficulty and anxiety level.

A.

| Anxiety level | Task difficulty | |
|---|---|---|
| | Easy | Hard |
| Low | 3.34 | 3.34 |
| High | 5.55 | 1.19 |

B.

| Anxiety level | Task difficulty | |
|---|---|---|
| | Easy | Hard |
| Low | 6.25 | 3.10 |
| High | 4.25 | 1.10 |

[2]Answer key for exercises in this box: An interaction occurs in A, D, and E.

When the results of a 2 × 2 design are summarized in a table, it is easiest to assess the presence or absence of an interaction by using the subtraction method. One determines the differences between the means in each row (or column) of the table and then compares these differences. If the differences are different, an interaction is likely. In applying the subtraction method, it is essential that the differences be calculated in the same direction. For example, to use the subtraction method for the data reported in Table 8.1, you could subtract the evaluation score for the White captain from that of the Black captain for the success outcome (+28.7) and then for the failure outcome (−40.8). The sign of the obtained difference should also be carefully noted. The subtraction method shows you that these differences are very different and, thus, an interaction between the two variables is likely. You can practice applying the subtraction method by determining the mean differences for the columns of Table 8.1. For more practice, see Box 8.1.

**FIGURE 8.3**   Mean number of errors as a function of type of task and brain hemisphere tested.

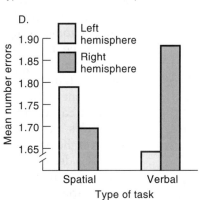

**FIGURE 8.4**   Mean reaction time as a function of set size and response type.

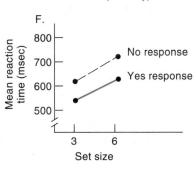

The opportunity to identify an interaction makes the 2 × 2 design more useful analytically than designs involving only one independent variable. Nonetheless, the 2 × 2 design barely scratches the surface when it comes to tapping the potential of complex designs. The 2 × 2 design can be extended in one of two ways. Additional levels of one or both of the independent variables can be included in the design, yielding designs such as the 3 × 2, the 3 × 3, the 4 × 2, the 4 × 3, and so on. Or additional independent variables can be studied in the same experiment with the number of levels of each variable ranging from 2 to some unspecified upper limit. The addition of a third or fourth independent variable yields designs such as the 2 × 2 × 2, the 3 × 3 × 3, the 2 × 2 × 4, the 2 × 3 × 3 × 2, and so on. We will describe one example of each of the two ways that a complex design can be extended beyond the 2 × 2.

Social psychologists are interested in the stereotypic beliefs people have about others. Eagly and Steffen (1984) describe one such stereotype pertaining to beliefs about men and women: "women are more communal (selfless and concerned with others) and less agentic (self-assertive and motivated to master) than men" (p. 735). In a series of experiments testing college students, Eagly and Steffen examined whether the social roles that women and men hold may contribute to the gender stereotypes. That is, if women are more likely to be working at home caring for children and men more likely to be employed outside the home, then men may be seen as more agentic and women are seen as more communal. Eagly and Steffen obtained results consistent with their social role interpretation.

In 1997, one of your textbook author's research methods classes tried to replicate one of Eagly and Steffen's (1984) experiments. They reasoned that Eagly and Steffen's results might not replicate because of the changes that had occurred over the past decade in men's and women's social roles. The experiment was a 2 × 3 design. College students were given a brief description of a target person and were asked to rate the target on 18 different traits. The first independent variable was the gender of the target: male or female. The second independent variable was the role assigned to the target person; there were three levels: unspecified, employed, or home care. The description for the employed male target, for example, was "An average man who is employed full-time." The measure participants used to rate the targets included 18 bipolar trait adjectives like "Not at all Aggressive" at one end of the scale and "Very Aggressive" at the other end of the scale. The participants marked one of five points along the scale to indicate which point best described the target person for that scale. The lowest possible score on the trait measure was 18 (a value of 1 for all 18 adjectives) and the highest possible score on the measure was 90 (a value of 5 for all 18 adjectives). Targets rated higher on the measure were judged to have more agentic characteristics; targets rated lower were judged to have more communal characteristics. Fifteen participants were randomly assigned to each of the six conditions of the experiment.

The results of the replication experiment are presented in Figure 8.5. An interaction is present in this experiment; the difference between the ratings for

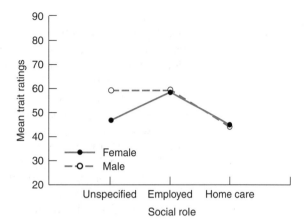

**FIGURE 8.5** Illustration of an interaction in a complex design (2 × 3).

female and male targets varies with the different social roles. For the unspecified role, female targets are rated less agentic than are the male targets; this finding replicates a gender stereotype similar to that found by Eagly and Steffen (1984)—males are perceived as more agentic than females. For the employed role, however, female and male targets received comparable ratings, and both male and female employed targets were rated as agentic as the male target in the unspecified role. Similarly, for the home care role female and male targets were rated about the same and at about the same level as the female targets in the unspecified role. One way to summarize these findings is to say that if you are employed you are perceived to be more agentic (and more like a male) and if you are caring for children at home you are perceived as less agentic (and more like a female).

The experiment we just described illustrates how complex design experiments can be used to study intriguing issues like gender stereotypes. For our purposes now, however, the experiment illustrates that the concept of an interaction can be extended to complex designs beyond the 2 × 2, in this case to a 2 × 3 design. You should now be beginning to see how complex designs allow psychologists to test how two independent variables can work together to produce an interaction.

An even more powerful extension of complex designs arises when there are three independent variables in the experiment. Pingitore, Dugoni, Tindale, and Spring (1994) examined three independent variables in their study of possible discrimination against moderately obese people in a mock job interview. Participants in the experiment viewed videotapes of job interviews. The role of the applicant for the job in the videotapes was played by professional actors who were of normal weight. In the moderately obese conditions, the actors wore makeup and prostheses so that they appeared 20% heavier. Three of the independent variables in the experiment were: the weight of the applicant (normal or overweight); the gender of the applicant (male or female); and the participants' concern about their own body (high or low). The degree of concern with one's own body was called the body-schema variable. It was based on the participants' satisfaction-dissatisfaction with their own bodies and the importance of body awareness to their self-concept. For this part of the study, then, Pingitore et al. (1994) used a 2 × 2 × 2 design. The dependent variable was the participants' rating on a 7-point scale of whether they would hire the applicant (1 = definitely not hire and 7 = definitely hire).

As a first step in describing the results of the Pingitore et al. (1994) study we will examine an interaction of two independent variables that manipulated characteristics of the applicant: the applicant's weight and the applicant's gender. For normal weight applicants, male and female applicants were given very similar hiring ratings (means of 6.0 and 5.5 for males and females, respectively). For overweight applicants, however, mean hiring ratings were lower, especially the ratings of female applicants (means of 4.8 and 3.6 for males and females, respectively). The pattern of this interaction effect indicates that female applicants who are overweight may experience more job discrimination than male applicants who are overweight.

Pingitore et al. (1994) were able to refine their understanding of possible discrimination based on the applicant's weight even further when they included the independent variable of participants' body schema in their analysis. The interaction of the applicant's weight and gender described above occurred only with participants who were high in concern about their own bodies. That is, those high on the body-schema variable gave overweight female applicants especially low ratings. Participants who were low on the body-schema variable, on the other hand, gave lower ratings to overweight applicants, but their ratings for male and female applicants were about the same.

The results of the Pingitore et al. experiment for these three variables are shown in Figure 8.6. As you can see, displaying the means for a three-variable experiment requires a graph with more than one "panel." One panel of the figure shows the results for two variables at one level of the third variable and the other panel shows results for the same two variables at the second level of the third independent variable. Because there are only two levels of the third variable, we can show the means for all eight conditions in these two panels. If the third variable had three levels (i.e., 2 × 2 × 3 or 12 conditions), then we could use three panels in our graph for this comparison, one for each combination of the first two variables at each level of the third independent variable.

One way to summarize the Pingitore et al. (1994) findings we have just described is to say that the interaction of the independent variables of the applicants' weight and the applicants' gender *depended upon* the participants' body schema. We call this type of finding a three-way (or triple) interaction. As you can see, when we have a three-way interaction, all three independent variables must be taken into account when describing the results.

Let us summarize by saying that, in general, *when there are two independent variables, an interaction occurs when the effect of one of the independent variables*

**FIGURE 8.6** Illustration of an interaction for a 2 × 2 × 2 complex design.

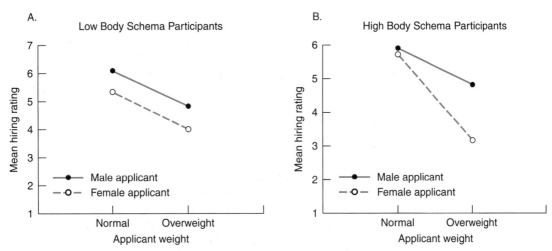

*differs depending on the level of the second independent variable. When there are three independent variables in a complex design, a three-way interaction occurs when the interaction of two of the independent variables differs depending on the level of the third independent variable.* Look again at Figure 8.6. You should easily see that the pattern of results for the first two independent variables (applicants' body weight and gender) differs depending on the level of the third variable (participants' body schema).

The power and complexity of complex designs increase substantially when the number of independent variables in the experiment increases from two to three. In the two-factor design there can be only one interaction, but in the three-factor design each independent variable can interact with each of the other two independent variables and all three independent variables can interact together. Thus, the change from a two-factor to a three-factor design introduces the possibility of obtaining four different interactions. If the three independent variables are symbolized as *A*, *B*, and *C*, the three-factor design allows a test of the main effects of *A*, *B*, and *C*; the two-way interactions of *A* × *B*, *A* × *C*, *B* × *C*; and the three-way interaction of *A* × *B* × *C*. The efficiency of an experiment involving three independent variables is remarkable. Pingitore et al. (1994) would have had to perform three experiments involving two variables at a time (applicant's gender and applicant's weight; applicant's gender and participant's body schema; and applicant's weight and participant's body schema) in order to assess the three main effects and the three two-way interactions that they could examine in a single three-factor design. Furthermore, they could assess the simultaneous interaction of all three independent variables only by including all three variables in the same experiment. Complex designs are a very powerful tool in psychological research.

## ANALYSIS OF COMPLEX DESIGNS

### Logic of Analysis Plan

- In a complex design with two independent variables, the sources of systematic variation are the main effects for each independent variable and the interaction between the two independent variables.
- Descriptive statistics are needed to interpret the results of inferential statistics.
- How researchers interpret the results of a complex design differs depending on whether a statistically significant interaction is present or absent in the data.

The analysis of complex designs builds on the logic used in the analysis of experiments with only one independent variable (see Chapter 6). You may remember that the first step in analyzing such single-factor experiments is to perform an omnibus *F*-test to determine whether the independent variable has produced any systematic variation in the dependent variable. If the omnibus test is statistically significant, analytical comparisons can be used to pinpoint more precisely the source of the systematic variation.

The tracking of sources of systematic variation applies equally to the analysis of complex designs that involve more than one independent variable. The same basic tool—the analysis of variance—can be used for complex designs. In complex designs with two independent variables, however, there are three potential sources of systematic variation. Each independent variable can produce a main effect, and the two independent variables can combine to produce an interaction effect.

The experiment we will use to illustrate the analysis plan for a complex design involved a 3 × 3 design with nine groups of participants. Children of three

**FIGURE 8.7**    The experiment used to illustrate the analysis of a complex design involved a 3 × 3 design. One variable was an individual differences variable, age, and it had three levels: Children were 4, 5, and 6 years of age. The other variable was a manipulated variable, and it also had three levels: Children were tested with another child, alone, or with a parent. The dependent variable was time spent playing with unfamiliar toys.

different ages (4, 5, and 6) were tested under one of three situations (alone, with a parent, and with another child). Thus, the first independent variable, age, is an individual differences variable with three levels, and the second independent variable, situations, is manipulated using three levels. The dependent variable in the experiment was the amount of time the child spent playing with novel (unfamiliar) toys. There were 10 children of each age tested under each of the three conditions, so there were 90 participants in the experiment, 10 participants in each of the nine conditions.

Table 8.2 shows the mean times children in each group spent playing with novel toys. An analysis of variance summary table for this complex design is presented in Table 8.3. It was generated on a computer using a statistical software package that performs complex analyses of variance.

Let's look first at the analysis of variance summary table. There are three potential sources of systematic variation in this experiment: the main effect of age, the main effect of situation, and the interaction between the age and situation variables. The summary table indicates the degrees of freedom (*df*) for each of these effects. For the main effects, the degrees of freedom are equal to the number of levels of the independent variable minus one. Since there are three levels for both age and situation, the degrees of freedom for both main effects are 2. The degrees of freedom for the interaction are obtained by multiplying the degrees of freedom for each independent variable entering into the interaction. Thus, there are 4 degrees of freedom for the Age × Situation interaction (2 × 2 = 4). The degrees of freedom for the Mean Square Within Groups (the estimate of error variation for all three effects in the complex design) are obtained by multiplying the degrees of freedom within each group times the number of groups. In our example, there are 10 participants in each group and

**TABLE 8.2**  TABLE OF MEAN TIMES (IN MINUTES) SPENT PLAYING WITH NOVEL TOYS IN A 3 × 3 DESIGN

| | Age | | | Means for main |
| Situation | 4 | 5 | 6 | effect of condition |
|---|---|---|---|---|
| Alone | 5 | 5 | 10 | 6.7 |
| With a parent | 15 | 25 | 35 | 25.0 |
| With another child | 10 | 15 | 15 | 13.3 |
| Means for main effect of age | 10.0 | 15.0 | 20.0 | |

**TABLE 8.3**  ANALYSIS OF VARIANCE SUMMARY TABLE FOR A 3 × 3 DESIGN

| Source of Variation | *df* | MS | F | p | $\eta^2$ |
|---|---|---|---|---|---|
| Age (A) | 2 | 35 | 3.5 | .03 | .07 |
| Situation (B) | 2 | 92 | 9.2 | .0005 | .19 |
| Age × situation (A × B) | 4 | 48 | 4.8 | .002 | .19 |
| Error variation within groups | 81 | 10 | | | |
| Total | 89 | — | | | |

therefore 9 degrees of freedom within each group. Because there are nine groups in the experiment, there are 81 *df* within groups.

The three *F*-tests entered in the summary table were computed by dividing the mean square (MS) within groups into the mean square for age, for situation, and for the interaction. The specific probabilities for each of the *F*-tests were part of the computer output for this analysis. If they had not been provided, we would have to use the value of *F* and the appropriate degrees of freedom for each effect (2 and 81 for each of the two main effects and 4 and 81 for the interaction) and consult a table of *F* values (see end of Appendix A) in order to determine their probabilities. Using the criterion of $\alpha = .05$ to determine statistical significance, we can see that the *F*-tests for each main effect and the interaction are statistically significant because the *p* value associated with each *F*-test is less than .05. A measure of effect size, eta squared ($\eta^2$) or proportion of variance accounted for, is also reported for each effect.

The information in the analysis of variance summary table is useful only in conjunction with the means reported in Table 8.2. The statistically significant *F*-test for the interaction indicates that the pattern of results across age differs for the three situations. As you can see in Table 8.2, the means reveal a larger increase across age in the time spent playing with a novel toy when the child is with a parent than when the child is either alone or with another child. The interaction can be seen clearly in the pattern of nonparallel lines shown in Figure 8.8. The means for the main effects of age and of situation on the outside of Table 8.2 also appear to differ, and these apparent differences are supported by the statistically significant *F*-test for each main effect.

The three *F*-tests in the summary table represent the counterpart of the omnibus *F*-tests we described when discussing the analysis of experiments with only one independent variable. In a complex design, just as in a single-factor design, follow-up analyses are needed to interpret the initial omnibus tests. The analysis plan for complex designs differs depending upon whether a statistically significant interaction is present.

Table 8.4 provides guidelines for interpreting a complex design experiment when an interaction does occur and when one does not. We will go through Table 8.4 twice, once describing an experiment in which there is an interaction and once describing a study in which there is no interaction.

## Analysis with an Interaction

- If the omnibus analysis of variance reveals a statistically significant interaction, the source of the interaction is identified using simple main effects analyses and tests of simple comparisons.
- A simple main effect is the effect of one independent variable at one level of a second independent variable.
- If an independent variable has three or more levels, simple comparisons can be used to examine the source of a simple main effect by comparing means two at a time.

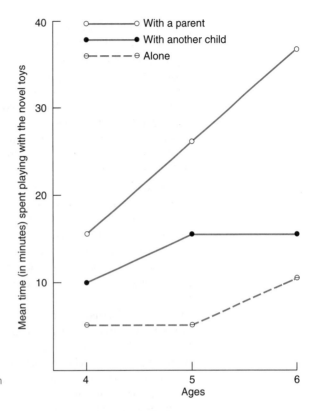

**FIGURE 8.8**   This graph shows results of complex design involving two independent variables, each with three levels.

**TABLE 8.4**   GUIDELINES FOR THE ANALYSIS OF A TWO-FACTOR EXPERIMENT

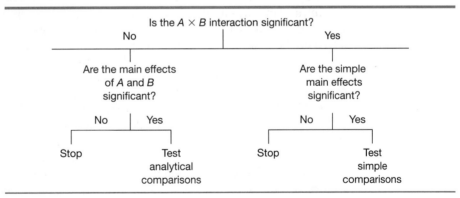

One of the many approaches psychologists have tried to use to understand depression is based on investigating the differences between the thought patterns of depressed and nondepressed people. You may remember that we touched briefly on this topic in Chapter 1. One aspect of this cognitive approach to depression deals with attributions, the causal explanations we use to try to account for our own behavior and the behavior of others. For example, depressed people exhibit a tendency to make attributions that are pessimistic, overgeneralized, and self-blaming (e.g., Myers, 1999). According to the cognitive approach, this tendency toward less optimistic thinking on the part of depressed people may be critically involved in causing the onset of depression, maintaining depression once it occurs, and alleviating depression by changing depressive thinking to be more optimistic. The study we will be using to illustrate the interpretation of the results of a complex design with an interaction represents one of the many experiments investigating the cognitive bases of depression.

Rodman and Burger (1985) investigated a particular phenomenon called the defensive attribution effect. In previous experiments, nondepressed participants read a description of an accident in which a person suffered mild or severe consequences. These nondepressed individuals attributed more responsibility to the perpetrator in the severe than in the mild accident condition. One interpretation of this phenomenon is that people do not want to attribute the cause of a severe accident to chance. If they did attribute the accident to chance, they would be increasing the perceived possibility that they themselves could be involved in a severe accident. Their attribution of greater responsibility to the perpetrator in the severe accident is a defensive attribution, allowing them to perceive themselves as protected against a likelihood of future severe accidents. Rodman and Burger reasoned that depressed people might be less likely to show this type of defensive attribution effect because their negative thinking would lead them to be less self-protective. Stated more formally, they tested the hypothesis that the defensive-attribution effect would decrease as a person's level of depression increased.

Rodman and Burger tested 56 college students in a 2 × 3 design. The first independent variable was the severity of the described accident (severe and nonsevere), and this was manipulated using the random groups design. The natural groups design was used for the second independent variable; students were selected on the basis of their scores on a paper-and-pencil test of depression to represent three groups: nondepressed, slightly depressed, and mildly depressed individuals. The dependent variable was a single item on a longer questionnaire that asked students to divide 100% among four potential sources of responsibility: each of the three drivers in the accident and uncontrollable "circumstances." The defensive-attribution effect would be reflected in a larger value assigned to uncontrollable circumstances for the nonsevere than for the severe accident. (Remember that it is protective to avoid making attributions to uncontrollable circumstances for severe accidents.) The mean percentage values for this uncontrollable factor for each of the six conditions are presented in Table 8.5.

As Rodman and Burger had predicted, there was an interaction between the two independent variables: as degree of depression increases, the differences between the percentage values for severe and nonsevere accidents change. (You may wish to use the subtraction method to see this.) Nondepressed students show the defensive-attribution effect and mildly depressed students do not. Analysis of these results using analysis of variance confirmed that the interaction was statistically significant.

**TABLE 8.5**   MEAN PERCENTAGE OF RESPONSIBILITY ATTRIBUTED TO UNCONTROLLABLE
CIRCUMSTANCES

| Type of Accident | Level of Depression | | |
|---|---|---|---|
| | Nondepressed | Slightly depressed | Mildly depressed |
| Severe | 7.00 (9.2) | 14.00 (16.1) | 16.90 (16.0) |
| Nonsevere | 30.50 (22.2) | 16.50 (12.7) | 3.75 (3.5) |

*Note:* Standard deviations appear in parentheses. Adapted from Rodman and Burger (1985).

Once we have confirmed that there is an interaction of two independent variables, we must locate more precisely the source of that interaction. As outlined in Table 8.4, there are statistical tests specifically designed for tracing the source of a significant interaction. These tests are called simple main effects and simple comparisons (see Keppel, 1991).

A **simple main effect** is the effect of one independent variable at one level of a second independent variable. In fact, one definition of an interaction is that the simple main effects across levels are different. We can illustrate the use of simple main effects by returning to the results of the Rodman and Burger experiment. There are five simple main effects in Table 8.5: the effect of the type of accident at each of the three levels of depression and the effect of the degree of depression at each of the two types of accidents. Rodman and Burger predicted that the defensive-attribution effect (the difference between the means for severe and nonsevere accidents) would decrease as severity of depression increased. Therefore, they chose to test the simple main effects of type of accident at each of the three levels of depression. They found, as predicted, that the simple main effect of type of accident was statistically significant for nondepressed students, but the simple main effects of type of accident for the slightly depressed and for the mildly depressed students were not statistically significant.

Two of the simple main effects in the Rodman and Burger (1985) study each involve three means. One can also examine how nondepressed, slightly depressed, and mildly depressed students differed in their attributions for severe accidents and how these three groups differed in their attributions for nonsevere accidents. That is, if statistical analysis reveals a significant simple main effect, then one concludes that there is a difference among the means (e.g., among the three groups for severe accidents). The next step, then, is to conduct *simple comparisons*, which are analytical comparisons that can be used to analyze simple main effects more fully (see Keppel, 1991). That is, once a simple main effect involving more than two levels of a variable has been shown to be statistically significant, simple comparisons can be done to determine the nature of the differences among the levels. In this procedure, means within the simple main effect are compared two at a time in order to identify the source of differences among levels. As you can see, simple comparisons only make sense when there is a simple main effect for an independent variable with three or more levels.

With two levels, a simple main effect compares the difference between the two means and no additional comparisons are necessary.

Once an interaction has been thoroughly analyzed, researchers can also examine the main effects of each independent variable. As we mentioned earlier in this chapter, however, the main effects are of much less interest when we know that an interaction is statistically significant. For instance, once we know that the effect of the type of accident varies depending on the level of depression, we have not added much when we learn that, overall, the nonsevere accident led to a higher mean percentage of responsibility attributed to uncontrollable circumstances than did the severe accident. Nonetheless, there are experiments in which the interaction and the main effects are all of interest. (Rosnow and Rosenthal [1995] describe additional procedures that can help you gain further understanding in analyzing and interpreting interactions and main effects.)

## Analysis with No Interaction

- If an omnibus analysis of variance indicates the interaction between independent variables is not statistically significant, the next step is to determine whether the main effects of the variables are statistically significant.
- The source of a statistically significant main effect can be specified more precisely by performing analytical comparisons that compare means two at a time.

Dittmar, Berch, and Warm (1982) used a 3 × 3 design to test whether people who are deaf perform better on a visual-vigilance task than people who can hear. A visual-vigilance task requires a person to detect intermittent visual signals such as blips on a radar screen for a long period of time. Dittmar et al. expected that deaf people would have an advantage on such a task because their deafness would keep them from being distracted. The deaf people who participated were offered a prize if their vigilance performance was the best in their group. To assess the possible effect of the prize as an incentive, two additional groups of hearing people were tested, one offered a prize and one not. These three groups represent the levels of the first independent variable in the experiment. The participants were all tested in a 45-minute session divided into three continuous 15-minute periods, and these three periods were the levels of the second independent variable. Note that this is a mixed factorial design in that the first independent variable is an independent groups variable and the second is a repeated measures variable.

The mean percentage of correct detections across the three periods for the three different groups of participants is presented in Table 8.6. The same data are depicted graphically in Figure 8.9. The interaction, or more accurately the lack of an interaction, can best be seen in Figure 8.9. Although the three lines in the figure are not perfectly parallel, the mean percentage of correct detections appears to decrease in all three groups at approximately the same rate. That there was *not* a statistically significant interaction is confirmed by the results of

**TABLE 8.6** MEAN PERCENTAGE OF CORRECT DETECTIONS ACROSS THREE PERIODS OF A VIGILANCE TASK FOR DEAF AND HEARING PARTICIPANTS

| | Period | | |
| Group | 1 | 2 | 3 |
| --- | --- | --- | --- |
| Deaf | 95 | 85 | 78 |
| Hearing—Prize | 93 | 82 | 70 |
| Hearing—No Prize | 93 | 74 | 68 |

Adapted from Dittmar et al. (1982).

**FIGURE 8.9** Results of a 3 × 3 complex design in which there was no interaction effect but there were two main effects. (Adapted from Dittmar et al., 1982.)

the analysis of variance. As you have learned, nonparallel lines in a graph may *suggest* an interaction, but alone they are not sufficient evidence that an interaction effect is present. Like any observed difference among sample means, we must examine the results of our inferential statistical test before deciding that more than simply error variation is present.

The guidelines for the analysis of a complex design listed in Table 8.4 suggest that, when the interaction effect is not statistically significant, the next step is to examine the main effects of each independent variable. This can be done most easily by referring to the data in Table 8.6. By collapsing (averaging) across the three vigilance periods, we can obtain the mean detection rates for the main effect of the group variable. These means are 86.0, 81.7, and 78.3 for the Deaf, Hearing—Prize, and Hearing—No Prize groups, respectively. The overall analysis of the group main effect was statistically significant. As indicated in Table 8.4, the source of a statistically significant main effect can be specified more precisely by performing analytical comparisons (see Chapter 6 and Appendix A). For example, a comparison of performance in the Hearing—Prize and Hearing—No Prize groups (81.7 and 78.3) was not statistically significant, indicating that the presence of an incentive did not produce a difference between these two groups. However, the average performance of the two groups of hearing participants (80.0) was significantly lower than the performance of the deaf participants (86.0). These two analytical comparisons allow us to confirm that deaf participants were better at the vigilance task than hearing participants and that the offer of a prize did not affect the vigilance performance.

A similar approach would be followed in assessing the main effect of the period variable. By collapsing across the three groups of participants, we obtain the means 93.7 (first period), 80.3 (second period), and 72.0 (third period) for the main effect of the period variable. The main effect of this variable was statistically significant, and visual inspection of the means reveals that performance decreased, on the average, over time. Analytical comparisons could then be used to determine whether the decreases over each successive period (93.7 to 80.3 and 80.3 to 72.0) were significant. The analysis of Dittmar et al.'s vigilance experiment illustrates that much can be learned from a complex design even when there is no interaction.

## INTERPRETING INTERACTIONS

### Interactions and Theory Testing

- Theories frequently predict that two or more independent variables interact to influence behavior; therefore, complex designs are needed to test theories.

In Chapter 1 we described the critical role that theories play in the scientific method. In Chapter 6 we described how experiments are used to test hypotheses derived from psychological theories. Complex designs greatly enhance the researcher's ability to test theories because of the possibility in complex designs to test for both main effects and interactions.

For instance, the optimal arousal theory of motivation predicts that performance will be best when our arousal level is moderate—neither too low nor too high. If you have ever had to perform in either a highly competitive athletic or artistic event (or even a class exam), you have some sense of what is meant by optimal arousal. Your performance is not likely to be at its best if your arousal level is too low (you don't care how well you do) or too high (you are scared out of your wits). The optimal arousal theory further predicts that the level of arousal that is best depends on the complexity of the task to be performed. Specifically, the theory predicts that higher arousal levels will lead to better performance on simple or well-learned tasks, but lower arousal levels will lead to better performance on complex tasks. For example, you would probably be able to do simple arithmetic problems at a high arousal level, but the same arousal level would probably be disastrous if you were solving differential equations. Our focus for now is not on the details of optimal arousal theory but on the use of complex designs to test predictions derived from such a theory.

If we were to test the prediction that optimal arousal varied with task complexity, we would need to manipulate two independent variables, each with at least two levels. For example, if our experiment included arousal level (high or low) and task complexity (simple or complex) we would have four conditions.

| | Arousal Level | |
| --- | --- | --- |
| Task Complexity | High | Low |
| Simple | 50 | 35 |
| Complex | 10 | 25 |

The values of the dependent variable entered in the body of our table are the mean number of problems completed correctly in each of the four conditions. As you can see, the effect of arousal level on performance depended on the level of task complexity—an interaction occurred. (You may want to use the subtraction method, or perhaps graph the results, in order to "see" the interaction.) For the simple task, high arousal led to better performance; however, for the complex task, low arousal led to better performance. This hypothetical but reasonable outcome supports the prediction derived from optimal arousal theory. The example also illustrates how interactions allow us to make more sophisticated tests of psychological theories.

## Interactions and Contradictory Findings

- By testing for interactions between independent variables, often in the form of partial replications, researchers can identify reasons for contradictory findings in previous studies.
- Researchers manipulate an independent variable that is hypothesized to account for contradictory findings.

When only one independent variable is manipulated in an experiment, it is essential that all other potential independent variables be controlled by holding them constant or by balancing them across conditions (see Chapter 6). A problem can arise, however, if two researchers choose to hold the same potential independent variable constant at different levels in their respective experiments. For example, two memory researchers might be studying the relative effectiveness of two different learning strategies (A and B). These two strategies would represent the levels of the manipulated independent variable in both experiments. One potential independent variable that would clearly need to be controlled in these experiments is the difficulty of the material to be learned. The first researcher might decide to control the level of difficulty of the material by giving students in both conditions relatively easy textbook passages to learn. The second researcher, who is equally concerned with the problem of controlling the difficulty of the material, might decide to give students in both conditions relatively hard textbook passages to learn. It would not be surprising if these two researchers obtained different results. One such possible outcome is illustrated in the following diagram:

| Passage Difficulty | Learning Strategy | |
| --- | --- | --- |
| | A | B |
| Easy (Researcher 1) | 50 | 50 |
| Hard (Researcher 2) | 25 | 10 |

The first researcher found that the two learning strategies are equally effective, while the second researcher found that strategy A is more effective than strategy B! Why couldn't these two researchers replicate each other's findings?

At first, we might try to account for the different outcomes in the two experiments by focusing on the difficulty of the textbook passages. We could argue that the two strategies are equally effective for learning easy textbook passages, but strategy A is better for learning hard passages. This argument would not be convincing, however, unless the two types of passages represented the only way that the two experiments differed. This seems highly unlikely. For example, the passages may very well have been studied for different lengths of time in the two experiments, the passages were probably on different topics, and the experimenters and participants in the two experiments were undoubtedly different. Clearly, the difficulty of the passages is not the only factor that could be responsible for the different effects of the strategy variable in the two experiments.

The best way to identify which factor is responsible for the different findings in the two experiments is to use a complex design in which you manipulate the factor you think is responsible along with the strategy variable in the *same* experiment. The use of a complex design to resolve discrepant findings follows a logic similar to the logic of doing a partial replication to establish the external validity of a finding (see Chapter 6). In both cases, you are examining whether the effect of the independent variable of interest depends upon a second independent variable; in this case, the variable of interest is the learning strategy (A or B), and the second independent variable is the difficulty of the passage. In an experiment in which the strategy variable and the passage-difficulty variable were both manipulated, there would be four conditions in a complex design: Strategy A—Easy Passage; Strategy A—Hard Passage; Strategy B—Easy Passage; and Strategy B—Hard Passage. By factorially combining the two independent variables, both easy and hard passages are tested using both learning strategies. Does the effect of learning strategy depend on the difficulty of the material?

Two possible outcomes of such an experiment are shown in the following diagram. The results outlined in Outcome 1 are the same as those observed for the two separate experiments when only the strategy variable was manipulated. That is, the strategies are equally effective for easy material, and strategy A is better than B for hard material. If you were to obtain this interaction, you could be confident that the difficulty of the text was responsible for the different effects of the strategy variable in the two original experiments.

| Passage Difficulty | Outcome 1 Strategy | | Outcome 2 Strategy | |
|---|---|---|---|---|
| | A | B | A | B |
| Easy | 50 | 50 | 50 | 50 |
| Hard | 25 | 10 | 15 | 15 |

The situation would be very different, however, if you were to obtain results in your new experiment like those displayed in Outcome 2. In Outcome 2, the strategy variable had no effect when tested using either the easy or the hard text material. Because the strategy variable has the same effect with both types of material, it would logically follow that differences in degree of difficulty between the materials in the two original experiments cannot be responsible for the different effects of strategy in those experiments. You must select another variable that you "suspect" and manipulate it along with the strategy variable. Both trial and error and the guidance of theory are involved in the selection of the variable. The process can be a painstaking one, but complex designs are extremely useful in tracking down the reasons for the seemingly contradictory finding that the same independent variable has had different effects in two different experiments.

## Interactions and External Validity

- When no interaction occurs in a complex design, the effects of each independent variable can be generalized across the levels of the other independent variable; thus, external validity of the independent variables increases.
- The presence of an interaction limits the external validity of a finding by specifying the conditions in which an effect of an independent variable occurs.

In Chapter 6 we discussed at some length the procedures for establishing the external validity of a research finding when an experiment involves only one independent variable. We noted at that time that partial replication was the primary means by which we establish external validity—that is, the extent to which our research findings may be generalized. We can now examine the role of complex designs in establishing the external validity of a finding. As you might have suspected, the presence or absence of an interaction is critical in determining the external validity of the findings in a complex design.

When no interaction occurs in a complex design, we know that the effects of each independent variable can be generalized across the levels of the other independent variable. For instance, the Dittmar et al. (1982) study that we just described showed that detection performance declined across three 15-minute vigilance periods, but the decline occurred at approximately the same rate for hearing and deaf participants. That is, there was no interaction of the hearing variable (hearing or deaf) and the period variable. Thus, declining performance in a vigilance task can be generalized to both hearing and deaf people.

Of course, we cannot generalize our findings beyond the boundaries or conditions that were included in the experiment. For example, the absence of an interaction between the hearing variable and periods in the vigilance task does not allow us to conclude that detection performance would decline at the same rate if young children or trained observers were tested. Similarly, we do not know whether the same decline across periods would occur if there were short breaks after each observation period. We must also remember that the absence of an interaction involves problems associated with the failure to reject the null hypothesis, such as the sensitivity of the experiment to detect any interaction that might be present (see Chapters 6 and 7). In other words, not finding a statistically significant interaction does not necessarily mean that an interaction is not really present; we may not have performed an experiment with sufficient sensitivity and power to detect it.

As we have seen, the absence of an interaction increases the external validity of the effects of each independent variable in the experiment. Perhaps more important, the presence of an interaction identifies limits for the external validity of a finding. For example, when they tested young adults, May et al. (1993) found that there was little effect of time of day on recognition memory performance. However, there was a substantial effect of the time of day when older adults were tested. This interaction clearly sets limits on the external validity of the effect that time of day has on memory performance. Given this finding, the best way to respond to someone's query regarding the general effect that time of testing has on memory is to say "it depends." In this case, it depends on the age of the person being tested. The presence of the interaction limits external validity but also specifies what those limits are.

## Interactions and Relevant Independent Variables

- Relevant independent variables are variables that influence behavior.
- An independent variable can be a relevant variable either directly (a main effect) or by interacting with another independent variable to influence behavior.
- Researchers should be cautious about identifying an independent variable as irrelevant.

One of the primary tasks facing researchers who use the experimental method is identifying relevant and irrelevant independent variables. A **relevant independent variable** is one that has been shown to influence behavior; an irrelevant independent variable is one that has been shown not to influence behavior. Distinguishing between factors that affect behavior and those that do not is essential for developing adequate theories to explain behavior and for designing effective interventions to deal with problems in applied settings such as schools, hospitals, and factories (see Chapters 9 and 10).

If independent variables did not interact with one another, the task of identifying relevant independent variables would be a long one, but not a particularly challenging one. Each independent variable would simply be manipulated across a wide range of levels in separate single-factor experiments. The variables would be classified as either relevant or irrelevant depending on whether they produced a significant difference in the dependent variable. Independent variables do interact, however, and we must adjust our definition of relevant and irrelevant independent variables accordingly.

Consider the following example. Thousands of children in the United States receive drug treatment for hyperactivity every year. A reasonable question is whether dosage of the drugs is a relevant independent variable in determining the effectiveness of treatment. A hypothetical but typical experiment that could be done to address this question might include two dose levels (low and high) and three types of tasks (easy, moderate, and difficult). One possible outcome of such an experiment is summarized in the following table, with the dependent variable being the percent correct performance in each condition.

| | Dose Level | | |
| Type of Task | Low | High | Overall Mean |
| --- | --- | --- | --- |
| Easy | 75 | 90 | 82.5 |
| Moderate | 70 | 70 | 70.0 |
| Difficult | 65 | 50 | 57.5 |
| Overall Mean | 70 | 70 | |

The overall means for the main effect of dose level are identical (70), and this information could mistakenly be used to argue that dose level was an irrelevant independent variable because it had no main effect on children's performance. By now you recognize, however, that the dose level produced different effects depending on the difficulty of the task. For difficult tasks a low dose is better, for moderate tasks there is no effect of dose level, and for easy tasks a high dose is better. Dose level is a relevant independent variable because it interacts with the difficulty variable. In general, *a relevant independent variable is one that influences behavior directly (results in a main effect) or produces an interaction when studied in combination with a second independent variable.*

In general, be cautious about declaring an independent variable irrelevant. First, if an independent variable is shown to have no effect in an experiment, one cannot assume that this variable wouldn't have an effect if different levels of the independent variable had been tested. Second, if an independent variable has no effect in a single-factor experiment, this doesn't mean that it won't interact with another independent variable when used in a complex design. Third, as you are no doubt beginning to appreciate, null-hypothesis testing is limited in what it can tell us. The absence of a statistically significant effect may or may not mean that the effect is not present. Minimally, we would want to consider the power of our experiment before deciding that we have identified an irrelevant variable. (See Appendix A for more discussion about power analysis.) For now, it is best if you avoid being dogmatic about identifying any independent variable as irrelevant.

## Interactions and Ceiling and Floor Effects

• When participants' performance reaches a maximum (ceiling) or a minimum (floor) in one or more conditions of an experiment, results for an interaction are uninterpretable.

Consider the results of a 3 × 2 experiment investigating the effects of increasing amounts of practice on performance during a physical-fitness test. There were six groups of participants in this plausible but hypothetical experiment. Participants were first given either 10, 30, or 60 minutes to practice, doing either easy or hard exercises. Then they took a fitness test using easy or hard exercises (the same they had practiced). The dependent variable was the percentage of exercises that each participant was able to complete in a 15-minute test period. Results of the experiment are presented in Figure 8.10.

The pattern of results in Figure 8.10 looks like a classic interaction; the effect of the practice time variable differed for the easy and hard exercises. Increasing practice time improved test performance for the hard exercises, but performance leveled off after 30 minutes of practice with the easy exercises. If a standard analysis of variance were applied to these data, the interaction effect would very likely be statistically significant. Unfortunately, this interaction would be essentially uninterpretable. For those groups given practice with the easy exercises, performance reached the maximum level after 30 minutes of practice, so

**FIGURE 8.10**    Illustration of a ceiling effect.

no improvement beyond this point could be shown in the 60-minute group. Even if the participants given 60 minutes of practice had further benefited from the extra practice, the experimenter could not measure this improvement on the chosen dependent variable.

The preceding experiment illustrates the general measurement problem referred to as a **ceiling effect.** Whenever performance reaches a maximum in any condition of an experiment, there is danger of a ceiling effect. The corresponding name given to this problem when performance reaches a minimum (e.g., zero errors on a test) is a **floor effect.** In general, one can avoid ceiling and floor effects by selecting dependent variables that allow ample "room" for performance differences to be measured across conditions. For example, in the fitness experiment it would have been better to test participants with a greater number of exercises than anyone could be expected to complete in the time allotted for the test. The mean number of exercises completed in each condition could then be used to assess the effects of the two independent variables without the danger of a ceiling effect.

## Interactions and the Natural Groups Design

- Researchers use complex designs to make causal inferences about natural groups variables when they test a theory for *why* natural groups differ.
- Three steps for making a causal inference involving a natural groups variable are to state a theory for why group differences exist, manipulate an independent variable that should demonstrate the theorized process, and test whether the hypothesized interaction occurs between the manipulated independent variable and natural groups variable.

The natural groups design, which we described briefly in Chapter 6, is one of the most popular research designs in psychology. Groups of people are formed by selecting individuals who differ on some characteristic such as gender, age, introversion-extraversion, or aggressiveness. Researchers then look for systematic relationships between these individual differences variables and other aspects of behavior. The natural groups design is an effective one for establishing correlations between individuals' characteristics and their performance. As we also noted in Chapter 6, however, the natural groups design is perhaps the most challenging design when it comes to drawing conclusions about the causes of behavior.

The difficulty in interpreting the natural groups design arises when we try to conclude that differences in performance are caused by the characteristics of the people we used to define the groups. For instance, consider an experiment in which participants are selected because of their musical training. One group of participants includes people with 10 or more years of formal musical training, and one group includes people with no formal training. Both groups are tested on their ability to remember the musical notation for simple 10-note melodies. Not surprisingly, the results of these tests show that those with musical training perform far better than those without such training.

We can conclude on the basis of these results that memory for simple melodies varies with (is correlated with) amount of musical training. But we cannot conclude that musical training *causes* superior memory performance. Why not? There are probably many additional ways in which people with 10 years of musical training differ from those without such training. The groups may differ in amount and type of general education, family background, socioeconomic status, and amount and type of experience they have had listening to music. Also, those with musical training may have generally better memories than those without such training, and their superior memory for simple melodies may reflect this general memory ability. Finally, those who sought out musical training may have done so because they had a special aptitude for music. Accordingly, they might have done better on the memory task even if they had not had any musical training. In short, there are many possible causes other than individual differences in musical training for the difference in memory performance that was observed.

There is a potential solution to the problem of drawing causal inferences based on the natural groups design (Underwood & Shaughnessy, 1975). The key to this solution is to develop a theory regarding the critical individual difference variable. For example, Halpern and Bower (1982) were interested in how memory for musical notation differs between musicians and nonmusicians. Halpern and Bower developed a theory of how musical training would influence the cognitive processing of musical notation by those who had such training. Their theory was based on a memory concept called "chunking." You can get some sense of the memory advantage provided by chunking if you imagine trying to memorize the following strings of 15 letters: IBMTWASOSUSAFBI. Chunking helps memory by changing the same string of letters to a series of five more easily remembered chunks: IBM-TWA-SOS-USA-FBI.

Halpern and Bower theorized that musical training led musicians to "chunk" musical notation into meaningful musical units, thereby reducing the amount of information they needed to remember in order to reproduce the notation for a simple melody. Furthermore, if this process were responsible for the difference between the memory performance of musicians and nonmusicians, then the difference should be greater for melodies with good musical structure than for those with poor musical structure. Halpern and Bower manipulated the independent variable of musical structure to test their theory. To do this, they used three different types of melodies to test their groups of musicians and nonmusicians. They prepared sets of simple melodies whose notations had similar visual structures but that were either good, bad, or random in musical structure. The critical test was whether they would obtain an interaction of the two independent variables. Specifically, they expected that the difference in memory performance between musicians and nonmusicians would be largest for the melodies exhibiting good structure, next largest for the melodies exhibiting bad structure, and smallest for the random melodies. The results of Halpern and Bower's experiment conformed exactly to these expectations.

The obtained interaction allowed Halpern and Bower to rule out many alternative hypotheses for the difference in memory performance between musicians and nonmusicians. Such characteristics as amount and type of general education, socioeconomic status, and family background are not likely to explain why there is a systematic relationship between the structure of the melodies and the size of the difference in memory performance between musicians and nonmusicians. The interaction makes such simple correlational explanations much less plausible.

There are several steps that the investigator must take in carrying out the general procedure for drawing causal inferences based on the natural groups design.

**Step 1: State Your Theory**   The first step is to develop a theory explaining why a difference should occur in the performance of groups that have been differentiated on the basis of an individual differences variable. Halpern and Bower theorized that musicians and nonmusicians differed in musical performance because of the way that these groups cognitively organize ("chunk") melodies.

**Step 2: Identify a Relevant Manipulated Variable**   The second step is to select an independent variable that can be manipulated and that is presumed to influence the likelihood that this theoretical process will occur. Halpern and Bower suggested that type of musical structure was a variable associated with ease of chunking.

**Step 3: Look for an Interaction**   The most critical aspect of the recommended approach is to strive to produce an interaction between the manipulated variable and the individual differences variable. Thus, the relevant manipulated independent variable is applied to both natural groups. Halpern and Bower sought an interaction between the individual differences variable (musician vs. nonmusician) and the manipulated variable (type of musical structure) in a $2 \times 3$ complex design. (The approach can be strengthened even further by testing predictions of interactions of three independent variables: two manipulated independent variables and the individual differences variable—see, for example, Anderson & Revelle [1982].)

## SUMMARY

A complex design is one in which two or more independent variables are studied in the same experiment. A complex design involving two independent variables allows one to determine the overall effect of each independent variable (the main effect of each variable). More important, complex designs can be used to reveal the interaction of two independent variables. Interactions occur when the effect of each independent variable depends on the level of the other independent variable.

The simplest possible complex design is the $2 \times 2$ design, in which two independent variables are both studied at two levels. The analytical power of complex designs increases when additional levels of one or both of the independent variables are included in the design, yielding designs such as the 3 × 2, the 3 × 3, the 4 × 2, the 4 × 3, and so on. Additional independent variables can also be included to yield designs such as the 2 × 2 × 2, the 3 × 3 × 3, and so on. Experiments involving three independent variables are remarkably efficient. They allow us to determine the main effects of each of the three variables, the three two-way interactions, and the simultaneous interaction of all three variables.

When two independent variables are studied in a complex design, three potential sources of systematic variation can be interpreted. Each independent variable can produce a significant main effect, and the two independent variables can combine to produce a significant interaction. Interactions can be initially identified by using the subtraction method when the descriptive statistics are reported in a table, or by the presence of nonparallel lines when the results appear in a line graph. If the interaction does prove to be statistically significant (using an analysis of variance), we can interpret the results further by examining simple main effects and simple comparisons. When no interaction arises, we interpret the main effects of each independent variable, using analytical comparisons when necessary.

Complex designs play a critical role in the testing of predictions derived from psychological theories. Complex designs are also essential to resolve contradictions that arise when two experiments involving the same independent variable result in different findings. Investigators can trace the source of the contradictory findings by using a complex design in which both the original independent variable and the independent variable that is presumed to be responsible for the discrepant findings are manipulated in the same experiment.

When a complex design is used and no interaction occurs, we know that the effects of each independent variable can be generalized across the levels of the other independent variable(s). When an interaction does occur, however, limits on the external validity of a finding can be clearly specified. The possibility of interactions requires that we expand the definition of a relevant independent variable to include those that influence behavior directly (produce main effects) and those that produce an interaction when studied in combination with another independent variable.

Interactions that may arise because of measurement problems such as ceiling or floor effects must not be confused with interactions that reflect the true combined effect of two independent variables. Interactions can also be most helpful in solving the problem of drawing causal inferences based on the natural groups design.

## KEY CONCEPTS

complex designs  
interaction  
main effect

simple main effect  
relevant independent variable  
ceiling and floor effects

## REVIEW QUESTIONS

1 Use the Hass et al. cross-racial evaluation experiment to illustrate that there is one possible interaction in a 2 × 2 design but that there are two possible ways to describe the interaction.

2 Describe the method you would use to decide whether an interaction was present in a table showing the results of a 2 × 2 complex design.

3 Describe the pattern in a line graph that indicates the presence of an interaction in a complex design.

4 Outline the steps in the analysis plan for a complex design with two independent variables when there is an interaction and when there is not an interaction.

5 Explain how a complex design can be used to resolve contradictions that arise when two researchers obtain different results after manipulating the same independent variable in their respective single-factor experiments.

6 Use an example to illustrate how a complex design can be used to test predictions derived from a psychological theory.

7 How is the external validity of the findings in a complex design influenced by the presence or absence of an interaction?

8 What expansion in the definition of a relevant independent variable is required by the use of complex designs?

9 What potential solution is there for the problem of drawing causal inferences on the basis of the natural groups design?

## CHALLENGE QUESTIONS

1 Consider an experiment in which two independent variables have been manipulated. Variable *A* has been manipulated at three levels, and Variable *B* has been manipulated at two levels.

   **A** Draw a graph showing an effect of Variable *B*, no effect of Variable *A*, and no interaction between the two variables.

   **B** Draw a graph showing no effect of Variable *A*, no effect of Variable *B*, but an interaction between the two variables.

   **C** Draw a graph showing an effect of Variable *A*, an effect of Variable *B*, and no interaction between the *A* and *B* variables.

2 A researcher has used a complex design to study the effects of training (untrained and trained) and problem difficulty (easy and hard) on participants' problem-solving ability. The researcher tested a total of 80 participants, with 20 randomly assigned to each of the four groups resulting from the factorial combination of the two independent variables. The data presented below represent the percentage of the problems that participants solved in each of the four conditions.

| | Training | |
|---|---|---|
| Problem Difficulty | Untrained | Trained |
| Easy | 90 | 95 |
| Hard | 30 | 60 |

**A**   Is there evidence of a possible interaction in this experiment?

**B**   What aspect of the results of this experiment would lead you to be hesitant to interpret an interaction if one were present in this experiment?

**C**   How could the researcher modify the experiment so as to be able to interpret an interaction if it should occur?

**3** A psychologist is interested in whether older people suffer a deficit with respect to their reaction time in processing complex visual patterns. He selects a random sample of 65-year-old people and another random sample of young adults (such as college students). He tests both groups of 50 people in the same reaction time task. He presents a simple figure to each participant, then a complex pattern, and asks the participant to indicate as quickly as possible whether the simple figure is present in the complex pattern. Participants are timed only for their reaction to the complex patterns. This test is called an embedded figures test. As he had expected, the mean reaction time for the older adults was markedly longer than that for the young adults. By any standard the results were statistically significant.

**A**   Explain what minimal set of conditions the psychologist would have to include in his experiment before he could conclude that older adults suffered a deficit in their processing of complex visual patterns. That is, state what additional reaction time test must be given to both groups. Finally, describe an outcome of the test you propose that would support his position and one that would lead you to question his conclusion.

**B**   Recognizing that his original study is flawed, the psychologist tries to use post hoc matching to try to equate his two groups. He decides to match on general health (i.e., the better your general health, the faster your reaction time). Although he cannot get an exact matching across groups he does find that when he looks only at the 15 healthiest older adults, their reaction times are only slightly longer than the mean for the college students. Explain how this outcome would change the psychologist's conclusion concerning the effect of age on reaction time. Could the psychologist reach the general conclusion that older adults do not suffer a deficit in reaction time in this task? Why or why not?

## Answer to Challenge Question 1

# Applied Research

# 9

# *Single-Case Research Designs*

## CHAPTER OUTLINE

## Overview

What do Sigmund Freud and B. F. Skinner have in common? They are, of course, among the best-known psychologists of the 20th century. However, having made this point, you may find it difficult to identify significant commonalities between these two psychologists. Freud introduced psychoanalysis. If we were to use the psychoanalyst's technique of free association, the mention of Freud would likely bring to mind concepts such as unconscious motives, defense mechanisms, and Freudian slips. Skinner developed the experimental analysis of behavior. Associations to Skinner's name are likely to include terms like behaviorism, reinforcement, and *Walden Two*. Interestingly, Freud and Skinner did have something in common: They based their research on the study of single subjects. And there the similarity ends!

Thus far in this book, we have emphasized *group methodology*—research designed to examine the average performance of one or more groups of subjects. This was particularly evident in the last few chapters, in which experimental methods were examined. The most common research design in psychological research is one involving many subjects, whose behavior is observed following one or more experimental treatments. A decision about the effectiveness of an independent variable is made when other potential independent variables have been controlled either within or between groups of subjects. Group methodology was emphasized when we discussed various kinds of independent groups designs in Chapter 6.

In this chapter we introduce an alternative methodology. The distinctive characteristic of this approach is its emphasis on a single subject or, at most, a few subjects (see, for example, Kratochwill & Levin, 1992). The approach is sometimes called "small *n* research." We use the name *single-case research designs* to identify this kind of psychological research. Single-case designs have been used since scientific psychology began in the 19th century. Psychophysical methods had their origin in the work of Gustav Fechner and were described in his 1860 book, *Elemente der Psychophysik*. Fechner, and countless other psychophysicists since, relied on data obtained through experiments with one or two individuals. You can find examples of single-case psychophysical experiments in journals such as *Perception & Psychophysics*.

Cognitive psychologists also have relied on single-case research designs. Most students of psychology know that Hermann Ebbinghaus initiated the scientific study of human memory with the publication, in 1885, of his monograph on memory. Ebbinghaus was both participant and experimenter; over a period of many months he learned and then attempted to relearn hundreds of series of nonsense syllables. His data provided psychologists with the first systematic evidence of forgetting over time (see, for example, Zechmeister & Nyberg, 1982). Closer to the present, Linton (1978) examined the retention of everyday events over a 6-year period by testing a single participant: herself. The study of expert performance, whether it be that of a ballet dancer, chess player, or musician, also relies heavily on small *n* research (e.g., Ericsson & Charness, 1994). Ericsson,

Chase, and Faloon (1980) studied the development of exceptional memory performance in a single undergraduate with average intelligence. The student practiced remembering sequences of random digits presented to him at the rate of one digit per second. Like most of us, he initially could remember only about seven digits, which is a typical adult "memory span" for digits. After more than 200 hours of practice, however, the student's memory span increased to nearly 80 digits! Single-case studies appear regularly in psychology journals, dealing with issues ranging from cognitive therapy for Vietnam veterans (Kubany, 1997) to the study of brain processes in amnesic patients (Gabrieli, Fleischman, Keane, Reminger, & Morrell, 1995).

In this chapter we discuss two specific single-case research methodologies. The first is the case study method. This approach, used by Freud and other psychoanalysts, is frequently associated with the field of clinical psychology, but as you will see, psychologists from other branches of psychology also make use of this important method. For example, Ruth Campbell's book *Mental Lives* (1992) is an interesting collection of case studies illustrating various aspects of human cognition. And the neurologist Oliver Sacks (1985, 1995) has captivated millions with his vivid descriptions of individuals with minds gone awry. Case studies are frequently the source of valuable hypotheses about behavior and can be an important complement to more rigorously controlled approaches to understanding behavior. Both the advantages and the disadvantages of the case study method will be reviewed.

The second single-case methodology we discuss is derived from Skinner's experimental analysis of behavior. Techniques derived from laboratory studies of animal and human behavior have been found to be effective in managing behavior in numerous applied situations, including schools, the home, hospitals, and businesses. Single-case experimental designs, also frequently called "$N = 1$ experimental designs," are characteristic of the approach called *applied behavior analysis*. We examine the rationale behind this approach and provide specific illustrations of the more common $N = 1$ experimental designs. These experimental designs represent a special case of the repeated measures design introduced in Chapter 7.

## THE CASE STUDY METHOD

### Characteristics

- Case studies, intensive descriptions and analyses of individuals, lack the degree of control found in $N = 1$ experimental designs.
- Case studies are a source of hypotheses and ideas about normal and abnormal behavior.

A **case study** is an intensive description and analysis of a single individual. Case studies frequently make use of qualitative data, but this is not always the case (e.g., Smith, Harré, & Van Langenhove, 1995). Data may be obtained from several different sources, including naturalistic observation (Chapter 3), interviews and psychological tests (Chapter 4), and even archival records (Chapter 5). A case study occasionally describes the application and results of a particular treatment, as, for example, when a new therapeutic technique is used to treat an emotionally disabled person. However, in the context of a case study, treatment variables are rarely varied systematically in an effort to control extraneous variables, and several different treatments are often applied simultaneously. Thus, case studies differ from $N = 1$ experimental designs in the degree to which variables are controlled (see, for example, Kazdin, 1998). The case study method has been used by child psychologists, memory researchers, and animal behaviorists, as well as by researchers in fields such as anthropology, criminology, neurology, and sociology.

In actual practice, the form and content of case studies are extremely varied. Published case studies may be only a few printed pages long or may fill a book. Kirsch (1978) described an attempt to implement "self-management training" with a woman experiencing low self-confidence and social inhibition. The case study, describing her treatment during nine therapy sessions and a 5-month follow-up, was presented in just four pages of one issue of the journal *Psychotherapy: Theory, Research and Practice*. In another case study, the personality psychologist Gordon W. Allport described the relationship between a mother and son as revealed in 301 letters that the mother wrote to friends. First reported in two consecutive issues of the *Journal of Abnormal and Social Psychology* (1946, Vol. 41, Nos. 3 and 4), this classic case study was published in 1965 as a 223-page book under the title *Letters from Jenny*.

Campbell's edited book, *Mental Lives* (1992), contains case studies of 15 individuals "with something 'abnormal' in the way they think, perceive, read, speak or remember" (p. 2). The focus of the book, however, is on what these cases reveal about *normal* cognitive functioning. For instance, Riddoch and Humphreys (1992) introduce us to Dennis, a 47-year-old man who experienced severe head trauma from a fall from a ladder. Dennis subsequently had difficulty recognizing familiar people (his own family) as well as common objects when he *saw* them (although his sight was good enough to watch TV); however, he could recognize people when he *heard* them speak and could identify common objects when he *touched* them. The authors of this case study use Dennis's experiences to teach us how visual recognition depends on stored knowledge. Emphasizing what we learn about normal behavior by examining unusual abnormal behaviors is, according to Campbell, what differentiates the case studies revealed in *Mental Lives* from those in other collections, such as those of Oliver Sacks. Sacks's collections of case studies focus mainly on detailed descriptions of individuals with peculiar, and rather fascinating, brain disorders. One of Sacks's best-known books is *The Man Who Mistook His Wife for a Hat* (1985). In it, as the title indicates, we are introduced to a man who quite literally, when searching for his hat, seized his wife's head, tried to lift it off and put it on. These "clinical tales," as Sacks calls them, not only provide insights into the relationship between mind and brain, but also reveal how individuals adapt, cope, and succeed when faced with profound neurological deficits. As you can see, case studies serve many important purposes.

Many aspects of the case study method make it a unique means of studying behavior. It differs somewhat from more experimental approaches in terms of its goals, the methods used, and the types of information obtained (Kazdin, 1998). For example, the case study method is often characterized as "exploratory" in nature and a source of hypotheses and ideas about behavior (Bolgar, 1965). Experimental approaches, on the other hand, are frequently viewed as opportunities to test specific hypotheses. The case study method has sometimes been viewed as antagonistic to more controlled methods of investigation. A more appropriate perspective is suggested by Kazdin (1998), who sees the case study method as interrelated with and complementary to other research methods in psychology. For instance, *Mental Lives* shows how case studies of abnormal lives can complement nomothetic studies of "normal" lives.

The case study method offers both advantages and disadvantages to the research psychologist (see, for example, Bolgar, 1965; Hersen & Barlow, 1976; Kazdin, 1998). Before reviewing its advantages and disadvantages, however, let us illustrate the method with a summary of an actual case study reported by Kirsch (1978), which was mentioned earlier. It is important that you read this slightly abbreviated version of a case study carefully because we will make reference to it when discussing the advantages and disadvantages of the methodology.

## CAN CLIENTS BE THEIR OWN THERAPISTS? A CASE STUDY ILLUSTRATION

This article reports on the use of Self-Management Training (SMT), a therapeutic strategy which capitalizes on the advantages of brief therapies, while at the same time reducing the danger of leaving too many tasks not fully accomplished. . . . The essence of this approach involves teaching the client how to be his or her own behavior therapist. The client is taught how to assess problems along behavioral dimensions and to develop specific tactics, based on existing treatment techniques, for overcoming problems. As this process occurs, the traditional client-therapist relationship is altered considerably. The client takes on the dual role of client and therapist, while the therapist takes on the role of supervisor.

### The Case of Susan

Susan, a 28-year-old married woman, entered therapy complaining that she suffered from a deficient memory, low intelligence, and lack of self-confidence. The presumed deficiencies "caused" her to be inhibited in a number of social situations. She was unable to engage in discussions about films, plays, books, or magazine articles "because" she could not remember them well enough. She often felt that she could not understand what was being said in a conversation and that this was due to her low intelligence. She attempted to hide her lack of comprehension by adopting a passive role in these interactions and was fearful lest she be discovered by being asked for more of a response. She did not trust her own opinions and, indeed, sometimes doubted whether she had any. She felt dependent on others to provide opinions for her to adopt.

Administering a Wechsler Adult Intelligence Scale (WAIS), I found her to have a verbal IQ of about 120, hardly a subnormal score. Her digit span (scale score = 12, raw score = 13) indicated that at least her short-term memory was not deficient. The test confirmed what I had already surmised from talking with her: that there was nothing wrong with her level of intelligence or her memory. After discussing this conclusion, I suggested that we investigate in greater detail what kinds of things she would be able to do if she felt that her memory, intelligence, and level of self-confidence were sufficiently high. In this way, we were able to agree upon a list of behavioral goals, which included such tasks as stating an opinion, asking for clarification, admitting ignorance of certain facts, etc. During therapy sessions, I guided Susan through overt and covert rehearsals of anxiety-arousing situations . . . structured homework assignments which constituted successive approximations of her behavioral goals, and had her keep records of her progress. In addition, we discussed negative statements which she was making to herself and which were not warranted by the available data (e.g., "I'm stupid"). I suggested that whenever she noticed herself making a statement of this sort, she counter it by intentionally saying more appropriate, positive statements to herself (e.g., "I'm not stupid—there is no logical reason to think that I am").

During the fifth session of therapy, Susan reported the successful completion of a presumably difficult homework assignment. Not only had she found it easy to accomplish, but, she reported, it had not aroused any anxiety, even on the first trial. . . . It was at this point that the nature of the therapeutic relationship was altered. During future sessions, Susan rated her progress during the week, determined what the next step should be, and devised her own homework assignments. My role became that of a supervisor of a student therapist, reinforcing her successes and drawing attention to factors which she might be overlooking.

After the ninth therapy session, direct treatment was discontinued. During the following month, I contacted Susan twice by phone. She reported feeling confident in her ability to achieve her goals. In particular, she reported feeling a new sense of control over her life. My own impressions are that she had successfully adopted a behavioral problem-solving method of assessment and had become fairly adept at devising strategies for accomplishing her goals.

**Follow-up**

Five months after termination of treatment, I contacted Susan and requested information on her progress. She reported that she talked more than she used to in social situations, was feeling more comfortable doing things on her own (i.e., without her husband), and that, in general, she no longer felt that she was stupid. She summarized by saying: "I feel that I'm a whole step or level above where I was."

I also asked her which, if any, of the techniques we had used in therapy she was continuing to use on her own. . . . Finally, she reported that on at least three separate occasions during the five-month period following termination of treatment, she had told another person: "I don't understand that—will you explain it to me?" This was a response which she had previously felt she was not capable of making, as it might expose her "stupidity" to the other person.

Three months after the follow-up interview, I received an unsolicited letter from Susan (I had moved out of state during that time), in which she reminded me that "one of [her] imaginary exercises was walking into a folk dancing class and feeling comfortable; well, it finally worked."*

* Source: Kirsch, I. (1978). Teaching clients to be their own therapists: A case-study illustration. *Psychotherapy: Theory, Research, and Practice, 15,* 302–305. (Reprinted by permission.)

## Advantages of the Case Study Method

- Case studies provide new ideas and hypotheses, opportunities to develop new clinical techniques, and a chance to study rare phenomena.
- Scientific theories can be challenged when the behavior of a single case contradicts theoretical principles or claims, and theories can receive tentative support using evidence from case studies.
- Idiographic research (the study of individuals to identify what is unique) complements nomothetic research (the study of groups to identify what is typical).

**Sources of Ideas About Behavior**   The "power" of the case study method, according to Bolgar (1965), "lies in its ability to open the way for discoveries" (p. 30). It acts as a breeding ground for hypotheses that may subsequently be pursued with more rigorous methodologies. This aspect of the case study method was acknowledged by Kirsch (1978) in discussing the successful psychotherapy with the women named Susan. He stated that the "conclusions [of this study] share the limitations of any inferences drawn from case study material. At this point they should be viewed as tentative. It is hoped that the utility of [this technique] will be established by more controlled research" (p. 305). The case study method is a natural starting point for a researcher who is entering an area of study about which relatively little is known. In psychology, the development of psychoanalytic theory stands as a classic example of hypothesis formation based on the case study method.

**Opportunity for Clinical Innovation**    The case study method provides an opportunity to "try out" new therapeutic techniques or to attempt unique applications of existing techniques. In this way it offers an opportunity for clinical innovation. The use of self-management training (SMT) in psychotherapy changes the typical client-therapist relationship. The approach is based on teaching clients to be their own therapists—in other words, to identify problems and design behavioral techniques for dealing with them. The client is both client and therapist, while the therapist acts as supervisor. In a similar vein, Kubany (1997) reported the effect of a "marathon" 1-day cognitive therapy session with a Vietnam War veteran suffering from multiple sources of combat-related guilt. Therapy of this kind generally occurs over many hour-long sessions, but the fact that this intensive session appeared to be successful suggests a new way to conduct this type of clinical intervention.

**Method to Study Rare Phenomena**    Certain events appear so infrequently in nature that it is possible to describe them only through the intensive study of single cases. Many of the cases described in *Mental Lives* and in books by Oliver Sacks, for example, describe individuals with rare brain disorders. Other examples are found in the vivid case studies of so-called "feral children." These are children abandoned at an early stage who developed without significant human contact while living in the wild. Among the most celebrated case studies of a feral child is that of the "Wild Boy of Aveyron" (see, for example, *The Forbidden Experiment: The Story of the Wild Boy of Aveyron* [Shattuck, 1994]). Victor, as he came to be called, was captured in 1800 in the Aveyron district of France. Someone may have tried to kill him (as evidenced by the knife wound on his neck) and then abandoned him (perhaps had left him for dead) in the woods when he was about 5 years old. When he was captured, at about age 11 or 12, he was described as follows:

> He was human in bodily form and walked erect. Everything else about him suggested an animal. He was naked except for the tatters of a shirt and showed no modesty, no awareness of himself as a human person related in any way to the people who captured him. He could not speak and made only weird meaningless cries. (Shattuck, 1994, p. 5)

To many, Victor provided an opportunity to test what were then (and still are today) burning hypotheses about human nature. How are we different from animals? How do people learn language? What is "natural" and what is "cultural"? The story of Victor's reintroduction to society and his steps toward "humanity," under the tutelage of a devoted medical doctor and governess, in no way provides definitive answers to such abstract questions. Rather, in one author's view, this story "obliges us to reflect on how to live with those unsolved questions" (Shattuck, 1994, p. 182). Such can be the power of the case study.

**FIGURE 9.1** Only surviving picture of the "Wild Boy of Aveyron."

**Challenge to Theoretical Assumptions**    A theory that all Martians have three heads would quickly collapse if a reliable observer spotted a Martian with only two heads. The case study method can often advance scientific thinking by providing a "counterinstance": a single case that violates a general proposition or universally accepted principle (Kazdin, 1998). Consider, for example, the theory that human language development depends on exposure to normal language during a *critical period*, from about 2 years of age to puberty (suggested by Lenneberg, 1967). A human child deprived of language exposure during this period would, then, not be expected to acquire language. Of course, depriving a child of language experience for purposes of testing this hypothesis would be immoral. Yet, there are "nature's experiments." You see why Shattuck's story of the Wild Boy of Aveyron was titled "The Forbidden Experiment." What was Victor capable of learning after such deprivation? Interest in Victor was stimulated by age-old theories about language development similar to the critical period theory. So, too, was interest in "Genie," a child discovered more recently (in 1970). Genie had been cruelly isolated from most human contact and normal language from about the age of 2 to age 13 (Curtiss, 1977). The circumstances surrounding Genie's imprisonment and abuse, as well as the attempts by psychologists and linguists to rehabilitate her, were chronicled by Rymer (1993). The scientists who surrounded her saw an opportunity to observe the results of a test (the forbidden one) of a critical period theory of language development:

> At best, Genie could have provided a flawed endorsement of Lenneberg's theory. But she was capable of a ringing refutation. If Genie could not learn language, her failure would be attributed ambiguously—either to the truth of the critical-period hypothesis or to her emotional problems. If Genie did learn language in spite of all that had happened to her, how much stronger the rebuttal! (Rymer, 1993, pp. 121–122)

According to the psychologist most closely associated with Genie's language training, Genie showed some language development but it was never completely normal. Thus, a "weak" version of Lenneberg's theory, namely, that *normal* language development would not appear after puberty without exposure during the critical period, "cannot be dismissed" by Genie's case study (Curtiss, 1977, p. 209).

**Tentative Support for a Psychological Theory**    Few researchers would accept the results of a case study as conclusive evidence for a particular hypothesis (see the discussion of disadvantages of the case study method that follows). The results of a case study generally must be viewed as tentative and must await investigation via more carefully controlled procedures before they are accepted by the scientific community. Nevertheless, the outcome of a case study can sometimes provide important evidence in support of a psychological theory, as we just saw occurred in the case of Genie and the weak version of Lenneberg's critical period theory. As another illustration, we can take an example from the memory literature.

In 1968, Atkinson and Shiffrin proposed a model of human memory that was to have considerable influence on research in this field. The model, which was based on principles of information processing, described both a short-term memory (STM) system and a long-term memory (LTM) system. Human memory, in other words, should be thought of as containing at least two structures, each with different characteristics and functions. STM was identified with "working memory" and represented the locus of conscious rehearsal and elaboration of information. It was the kind of memory we might use when looking up a telephone number and "holding" it until we had dialed it correctly. Information in LTM did not have to be actively processed in order to be remembered; rather, information in this memory system was stored on a relatively permanent basis, from whence it could be retrieved and brought into conscious memory (into STM).

Although results of numerous experiments provided evidence for this dual nature of our memory, Atkinson and Shiffrin considered the results of several case studies as "perhaps the most convincing demonstrations of a dichotomy in the memory system" (p. 97). These case studies involved patients who had been treated for epilepsy via surgical removal of parts of the brain within the temporal lobes, including a subcortical structure known as the hippocampus. Of particular importance to Atkinson and Shiffrin's theory was the case study of a patient known as H. M. (see Hilts, 1995; Scoville & Milner, 1957). Following the brain operation, H. M. was found to have a disturbing memory deficit. Although he could carry on a normal conversation and remember events for a short period of time, H. M. apparently could not put new information into long-term memory. He could not remember day-to-day events. He was able to read the same magazine over and over again without finding its contents familiar. It looked as though H. M. had an intact short-term memory system but could not get information into a long-term memory system. Subsequent testing of H. M. and patients with similar memory deficits revealed that the nature of this memory problem is more complex than originally suggested (see Zechmeister & Nyberg, 1982), but the case study of H. M. continues to be important whenever theories of human memory are discussed (for example, see Schacter, 1996).

Complement to the Nomothetic Study of Behavior    As we noted in Chapter 1, psychology is largely a **nomothetic** discipline. This means that psychology (like science in general) seeks to establish broad generalizations, "universal laws" that will apply to a wide population of organisms. As a consequence, psychological research is often characterized by studies that involve large numbers of subjects and that seek to determine the "average" or typical performance of a group. This average may or may not represent the value of any one individual in the group. Rather, a researcher hopes to be able to predict, on the basis of this mean performance, what organisms will be like "in general."

Some psychologists, notably Allport (1961), argue that a nomothetic approach is inadequate—that the individual is more than what can be represented by the collection of average values on various dimensions. Allport argues that the individual is both unique and lawful (operates in accordance with internally consistent principles) and that the study of the individual, called **idiographic** research, is an important goal (see also Smith et al., 1995). The need for an idiographic approach can be illustrated by the task confronting the clinical psychologist. As Allport points out, the clinician's goal "is not to predict the aggregate, but to foretell 'what any one man [sic] will do.' In reaching this ideal, actuarial predictions may sometimes help, universal and group norms are useful, but they do not go the whole distance" (p. 21). Allport suggests that our approach to understanding human nature should be neither exclusively nomothetic nor exclusively idiographic but should represent an "equilibrium" between the two. At the very least the idiographic approach, as represented by the case study method, permits the kind of detailed observation that has the power to reveal various nuances and subtleties of behavior that a "group" approach may miss. And, as you have seen, case studies have the ability to teach us about typical or average behavior by studying what is not average and is atypical.

## Disadvantages of the Case Study Method

- Because extraneous variables are not controlled and several "treatments" may be applied simultaneously in case studies, researchers are unable to make valid causal inferences using this method.
- Observer bias and biases in data collection can lead to incorrect interpretations of case study outcomes.
- Whether results from a case study may be generalized depends on the variability within the population from which the case was selected; some characteristics (e.g., personality) vary more across individuals than others (e.g., visual system).

**Difficulty of Drawing Cause-Effect Conclusions**   You are well aware by now that one of the goals of science is to discover the causes of phenomena—to reveal in an unambiguous manner the specific factors that produce a particular event. However, cause-effect conclusions can rarely be drawn on the basis of results that are obtained from the case study method. The major limitation of the case study method in this regard is its failure to control extraneous variables. Numerous plausible hypotheses are generally present to "explain" behavior change.

Consider, for instance, the treatment of Susan through SMT reported by Kirsch (1978). Although Susan apparently benefited from the SMT therapy, can we be sure that this particular factor accounted for her improvement? Many illnesses and certainly numerous emotional disorders are known to subside spontaneously. That is, over the course of time a certain number of people generally report a decrease in symptoms and an overall improvement even without treatment. The case study method generally does not permit one to dismiss the hypothesis that improvement would have been observed even if the specific treatment had never been administered. In addition, numerous aspects of the situation may be responsible for Susan's improvement. Her care was in the hands of a "clinical psychologist" who assured her that she should not trust her own feelings and discussed with her the reasons for these feelings. The "insight" provided by a professional therapist may be sufficient to change Susan's attitudes toward herself. The therapist also asked Susan, as part of her therapy, to rehearse anxiety-arousing situations covertly and overtly. This technique is similar to rehearsal desensitization, which may be an effective therapeutic treatment in itself (see Rimm & Masters, 1979).

The fact that several "treatments" were used simultaneously makes it difficult to argue conclusively that the SMT therapy "caused" Susan's improvement. As we have seen, Kirsch himself was sensitive to the limitations of his results and suggested that the inferences drawn from his study should be considered tentative until they were investigated more rigorously.

The case studies associated with feral children such as Victor, and abused and deprived children such as Genie, illustrate well the difficulty with isolating causal factors. We can only try to imagine the kinds of terror experienced by a child left alone in the woods year after year or of that experienced by a child who is isolated and physically abused by an emotionally disturbed parent. How much of the failure to acquire normal language is the result of such emotional disturbance? What else don't we know about these children? One story which circulated about Victor, for example, was that he had been abandoned by parents at about the age of 5 because he had not shown normal language development by that age (Shattuck, 1994). Did Victor have difficulty learning language *before* he was deprived of human contact? Genie had been severely ill at age 14 months and an attending physician had commented that she showed signs of retardation (Curtiss, 1977). Was Genie destined to be developmentally delayed even without the horrible isolation she experienced? The data from case studies frequently leave us wondering about causal events.

**Sources of Bias in Interpretation**  The "outcome" of a case study often depends on inferences drawn by a researcher who is both participant and observer (see Bolgar, 1965). A therapist is an observer but is also certainly a participant in the therapeutic process. Problems of observer bias can arise in the context of the case study as they do in other types of observation (see Chapter 3). In the absence of independent measures, the outcome of a case study may be based mainly on the "impressions" of the observer (see Hersen & Barlow, 1976). Kirsch (1978) described the patient Susan's "feelings" about her ability to achieve her goals and told how she reported a "sense of control" over her life. He stated that his "impressions are that she successfully adopted a behavioral problem-solving method of assessment and had become fairly adept at devising strategies for accomplishing her goals" (p. 304). Interpretation of an outcome solely on the basis of the subjective impressions of the observer can be seen as a serious weakness in the case study method.

**Possible Biases in Data Collection**  The material of a case study often includes several kinds of information, some of it obtained from personal documents and psychological tests. Each of these sources of information must be carefully examined for possible biases. Archival records, as we described in Chapter 5, are open to several sources of bias. Further, when information is based on self-reports, there is always the possibility of distortion or falsification. Such was a possibility (although not necessarily a significant one) in the case of Susan's treatment. We have no way of knowing whether the patient's self-reports of improvement were exaggerated or even false.

Reports of even the most intelligent and well-intentioned individuals are susceptible to biases and reconstructions, especially when memory for remote events is concerned. Consider the following excerpt from a self-analysis by the well-known personality psychologist Alfred Adler (1973, pp. 179–180):

> Shortly after I went to a board[ing] school. I remember that the path to the school led over a cemetery. I was frightened every time and was exceedingly put out at beholding the other children pass the cemetery without paying the least attention to it, while every step I took was accompanied by a feeling of fear and horror. Apart from the extreme discomfort occasioned by this fear I was also annoyed at the idea of being less courageous than the others. One day I made up my mind to put an end to this fear of death. Again (as on my first resolve), *I decided upon a treatment of hardening* (Proximity of death!). I stayed at some distance behind the others, placed my school-bag on the ground near the wall of the cemetery and ran across it a dozen times, until I felt that I had mastered the fear. After that, I believe, I passed along this path without any fear.
>
> Thirty years after that I met an old schoolmate and we exchanged childhood reminiscences of our school days. It happened to occur to me that the cemetery was no longer in existence and I asked him what had happened to it remembering the great uneasiness it had at one time caused me. Astonished, my former schoolmate who had lived longer in that neighborhood than I had, insisted that there never had been a cemetery on the way to our school. Then I realized that the story of the cemetery had been but a poetic dress for my longing to overcome the fear of death.

Problem of Generalizing from a Single Individual   As Bolgar (1965) has stated, "Much of the criticism leveled against the case study method of research is based on the accepted canon that it is impossible to generalize from one case" (p. 30). The ability to generalize from a single case depends on the degree of variability in the population from which the case was selected. Psychologists who study visual perception are often able to make wide generalizations based on the study of one individual. The assumption is that visual systems in humans are very similar and are related to the biological makeup of all humans. Thus, as we mentioned earlier, many psychophysicists perform experiments with only a "small *n*." When significant variability exists among individuals, as would be the case when measures are made of learning and memory, emotionality, or personality, it becomes impossible to claim that what is observed in one individual will hold for all individuals. In this situation researchers often use the "average" performance of a large group for their interpretation.

Even if we accept the validity of Kirsch's (1978) conclusion regarding the effectiveness of the SMT technique of psychotherapy, we do not know whether this particular treatment would be as successful for other individuals who might differ from the patient Susan in any of numerous ways, including intelligence, age, family background, and gender. Also consider the "marathon" treatment of the Vietnam veteran which we mentioned earlier. Kubany (1997) noted that the client whom he treated for war-related guilt "was highly motivated to work on his guilt issues" (p. 241), and this, among other reasons, made him "a particularly good candidate for therapy" (p. 241). Thus, the therapist acknowledged that definitive evidence for the generalizability of the effectiveness of this treatment must await more controlled studies "with many veterans" (p. 241).

## The Case Study Method: Final Comments

- When considering individuals' testimonials about the effectiveness of a particular treatment, we need to remember the limitations of the case study method.

Case studies sometimes offer "dramatic" demonstrations of "new" or "unusual" findings or provide evidence for "success" of a particular treatment. These reports are often highly persuasive (see Kazdin, 1998). Everyday examples are found in the media and in advertisements for various products. How many people who worry about their weight can resist the example of a formerly overweight individual who is shown to have lost considerable weight through "Treatment X." The persuasive value of case study examples are both an asset and a liability to the scientific community. Demonstrations of new or unusual findings based on a case study may lead scientists to rethink their original theoretical assumptions or may lead them into new and fruitful avenues of research. Learning techniques used by the French scientist, Itard, who worked with the feral child, Victor, are used today in special education classes and in Montessori schools (Shattuck, 1994). Genie's case study stimulated other studies of language in atypical children (Rymer, 1993).

Nevertheless, the results of case studies are often accepted by nonscientists with little regard for the limitations of such evidence. This is particularly likely when individuals are in a position to identify with the subject of the case study. A person who suffers from a life-threatening illness may see more than a ray of hope in the results of a dramatic "new cure" based on treatment of an individual with the same illness. If this treatment worked for this person, why wouldn't it work for me? For people who have (or think they have) few alternatives, this grasping at straws may not be totally unreasonable. However, too often people do not consider (perhaps they do not want to consider) the reasons why a particular treatment would *not* work for them. They fail, in other words, to recognize the limitations of the case study method. This may have unfortunate consequences. For example, during the early 1980s there was considerable controversy surrounding the supposed cancer-curing drug Laetrile (see Sun, 1981). Few respectable scientists or medical researchers considered this drug, which was made from apricot pits, to be beneficial in the treatment of cancer. Positive results, however, based on individual "case studies," were presented as evidence by advocates of the drug. Largely because of public (not scientific) pressure, the government carried out systematic tests of the drug under controlled conditions. No beneficial effect of the drug was found. As others have commented, by using Laetrile instead of traditional therapies, many patients may have postponed or interrupted valid courses of treatment and thus contributed to the spread of their cancer.

## Applied Behavior Analysis

- Single-case ($N = 1$) research is used in the experimental analysis of behavior.
- In operant conditioning, reinforcement and punishment are used to change behavior.
- In the experimental analysis of behavior, control is demonstrated when an individual's behavior changes systematically with the manipulation of an independent variable.
- Operant techniques are used in applied behavioral analysis, as in behavior modification and behavior therapy.

A particularly important form of behaviorism that emerged in the 1930s is that associated with B. F. Skinner. Skinner's approach is synonymous with what is called an *experimental analysis of behavior*. It presents a unique behavioral view of human nature that not only contains prescriptions for the way psychologists should do research but also has implications for the way society should be organized. Several of Skinner's books, including *Walden Two* and *Beyond Freedom and Dignity*, describe how the principles of behavior control that have been and will be derived from an experimental analysis of behavior can be put to work improving society.

*Operant conditioning* is the process by which behavior is modified by its consequences. Changes in behavior are usually measured in terms of frequency of responding, although other measures (such as duration or latency) may be used. Thus, rate of responding is a major dependent variable in operant conditioning. The task of the operant researcher is to relate changes in rate of responding to changes in the environment. Generally, an increase in rate of responding is brought about by a procedure known as reinforcement. The giving of "rewards" (such as praise, candy, flowers, ribbons, or high grades) following a response is one way to increase the subject's rate of responding. Decreases in rate of responding are brought about by a procedure known as punishment. One way to punish an organism is to follow a response with an aversive (noxious) event. The laboratory rat that is shocked when it presses a bar will soon stop bar pressing. Another way to use punishment is, following a response, to remove something that an organism would normally want. The parent who takes away the keys to the family car after a teenager gets a traffic ticket and the teacher who denies recess privileges to students who misbehave are using this form of punishment.

In conducting the experimental analysis of behavior, experimenters frequently make observations of single subjects. As we said earlier, it is often the case in the experimental analysis of behavior (unlike the group methodologies discussed in previous chapters) that $N = 1$. Experimental control is demonstrated by arranging experimental conditions such that the individual's behavior changes systematically with the manipulation of an independent variable. As Skinner (1966, p. 21) commented,

> instead of studying a thousand rats for one hour each, or a hundred rats for ten hours each, the investigator is likely to study one rat for a thousand hours. The procedure is not only appropriate to an enterprise which recognizes individuality, it is at least equally efficient in its use of equipment and of the investigator's time and energy. The ultimate test of uniformity or reproducibility is not to be found in the methods used but in the degree of control achieved, a test which the experimental analysis of behavior usually passes easily.

There is a minimum of statistical analysis. Conclusions regarding the effect of an experimental variable are made by visually inspecting the behavioral record in order to observe whether behavior changes systematically with the introduction and withdrawal of the experimental treatment.

In *applied behavior analysis*, the methods that are developed within an experimental analysis of behavior are applied to socially relevant problems. These applications are frequently referred to as **behavior modification** but when applied to clinical populations the term **behavior therapy** is preferred (Wilson, 1978). Behavior therapy is seen by many as a more effective approach to clinical treatment than that based on a psychodynamic model of therapy. Therapists who use a psychodynamic model "seek to help people gain insight into the unconscious roots of problems and work through newly resurrected feelings" (Myers, 1998, p. 490). Therapies based on Freud's psychoanalytic theory are particularly representative of this approach. In contrast, behavior therapy focuses on observable behavior rather than hypothesized unconscious forces. For example, self-stimulatory behaviors (e.g., prolonged body rocking, gazing at lights, or spinning) that often characterize so-called autistic children may be conceptualized as operant behaviors. In this way, clinicians and teachers may be able to control their frequency of occurrence by using behavior modification techniques (see Lovaas, Newsom, & Hickman, 1987). Numerous studies have been published showing how operant techniques can be employed successfully to change the behavior of psychotic individuals, normal and mentally impaired children and adults, individuals diagnosed as schizophrenic, stutterers, psychiatric patients, and many others. Behavior-analytic approaches have also been successfully used by school psychologists in educational settings (see Kratochwill & Martens, 1994). A primary source for these published studies is the *Journal of Applied Behavior Analysis*.

## SINGLE-CASE ($N = 1$) EXPERIMENTAL DESIGNS

- Researchers manipulate an independent variable in single-case experiments; therefore, these designs allow more rigorous control than case studies.
- There are several circumstances when single-case experiments may be preferred over multiple-group methods.
- In single-case experiments, baseline observations are first recorded to describe what an individual's behavior is like (and predicted to be like in the future) without treatment.
- Baseline behavior and behavior following the intervention are compared using visual inspection of recorded observations.

The use of a single subject, which we have seen is often characteristic of the experimental analysis of behavior, is also a hallmark of applied behavior analysis. The **single-case experiment,** as its name suggests, typically focuses on an examination of behavior change in one individual. This methodology can be extended, however, to treatments applied to single groups of individuals as well (Kazdin, 1998). Single-case experiments differ from the traditional case study method in that they contrast conditions within an individual whose behavior is being continuously monitored. That is, the independent variable of interest is manipulated systematically for each individual. Consequently, single-case experimental designs are an important alternative to the relatively uncontrolled case study method (Kazdin, 1982).

For certain kinds of applied research, $N = 1$ experimental designs may be more appropriate than designs based on multiple-group methodology (see Hersen & Barlow, 1976). This is likely to be true when research is directed toward changing the behavior of a specific individual. For example, the average response of a group of subjects will not necessarily be the same as the response of any one individual in the group. Therefore, the outcome of a group experiment may lead to recommendations about what treatments "in general" should be applied to modify behavior, but it is not possible to say what the effect of that treatment will be on any particular individual. As Kazdin (1982) commented, "Perhaps the most obvious advantage [of single-case experimental designs] is that the methodology allows investigation of the individual client and experimental evaluation of treatment for the client" (p. 482).

Another disadvantage of multiple-group methodology, particularly in the context of clinical research, is that ethical problems arise when a potentially beneficial treatment is withheld from individuals in order to provide a control group that satisfies the requirements of internal validity. Because single-case experimental designs contrast conditions of "No Treatment" and "Treatment" within the same individual, this problem can be avoided. Moreover, investigators doing clinical research often find it difficult to gain access to enough clients to do a group experiment. For instance, a clinician may be able to identify from a list of clients only a few individuals experiencing claustrophobia (excessive fear of enclosed spaces). The single-case experiment provides a practical solution to the problem of investigating cause-effect conclusions when only a few participants are available.

The first stage of a single-case experiment is usually an observation stage, or **baseline stage.** During this stage a record is made of the individual's behavior prior to any intervention. A typical measure is frequency of behavior per some unit of time, such as a day, an hour, or another recording interval. An applied researcher might record the number of times during a 10-minute interview that an excessively shy child makes eye contact, the number of headaches reported each week by a depressed migraine sufferer, or the number of verbal pauses per minute made by a chronic stutterer. The baseline record provides a description of behavior before treatment is provided and, most importantly, offers a prediction of what behavior will be like in the future without treatment (Kazdin, 1998). Of course, unless behavior is actually monitored we don't know for sure what future behavior will be like, but by taking baseline measures we can predict what the future holds. Figure 9.2 illustrates this function of the baseline record.

Once behavior is shown to be relatively stable—that is, it exhibits little fluctuation between recording intervals—an intervention (treatment) is introduced. Behavior immediately following an intervention is contrasted with that seen during baseline performance. The effect of a behavioral intervention is typically evaluated by visual inspection of the behavioral record. How did behavior change, in other words, following the experimental treatment? Keep in mind that we predicted what behavior would be like without treatment (see, for example, Figure 9.2). Traditionally, tests of statistical significance have not been used, although there is some controversy surrounding this aspect of single-case methodology (Kratochwill & Brody, 1978). Later in this chapter we will discuss some of the problems that arise when visual inspection is used to determine whether a treatment was effective (see also Kazdin, 1998).

Although there are numerous design possibilities for the researcher who uses a single-case experimental design (Hersen & Barlow, 1976; Kazdin, 1980), the most commonly employed are the ABAB and multiple-baseline designs (Kazdin, 1998).

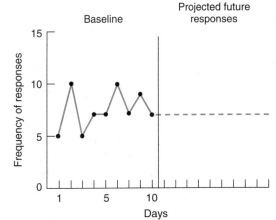

**FIGURE 9.2** Hypothetical example of baseline observations for the frequency of responses. Data in baseline stage (solid line) are used to predict the likely rate of responses in the future if treatment is not implemented (dashed line). (Adapted from Kazdin, 1998, p. 209.)

## Specific Experimental Designs

- In the ABAB design, baseline (A) and treatment (B) stages are alternated to determine the effect of treatment on behavior.
- Researchers conclude that treatment causes behavior change when behavior changes systematically with the introduction and withdrawal of treatment.
- Interpreting the causal effect of the treatment is difficult in the ABAB design if behavior does not reverse to baseline levels when treatment is withdrawn.
- Ethical considerations may prevent psychologists from using the ABAB design.
- In multiple-baseline designs, a treatment effect is shown when behaviors in more than one baseline change only following the introduction of a treatment.
- Multiple baselines may be observed across individuals, behaviors, or situations.
- Interpreting the causal effect of treatment is difficult in multiple-baseline designs when changes are seen in a baseline *before* an experimental intervention; this can occur when treatment effects generalize.

The ABAB Design   The **ABAB design** seeks to confirm a treatment effect by demonstrating that behavior changes systematically with alternating conditions of No Treatment and Treatment. An initial baseline stage (A) is followed by a treatment stage (B), next by a return to baseline (A), and then by another treatment stage (B). Because treatment is removed during the second A stage, and any improvement in behavior is likely to be reversed at this point, this design is also called a *reversal design*. The researcher using the ABAB design observes whether behavior changes immediately upon introduction of a treatment variable (first B), whether behavior reverses when treatment is withdrawn (second A), and whether behavior improves again when treatment is reintroduced (second B). When variations in behavior follow the introduction and withdrawal of treatment in this way, there is considerable evidence supporting the conclusion that the treatment caused behavior change.

Horton (1987) used an ABAB design to assess the effects of facial screening on the maladaptive behavior of a severely mentally impaired 8-year-old girl. Facial screening is a mildly aversive technique involving the application of a face cover (e.g., a soft cloth) when an undesirable behavior occurs. Previous research had shown this technique to be effective in reducing the frequency of self-injurious behaviors such as face slapping. Horton sought to determine whether it would reduce the frequency of spoon banging by a young child at mealtime. The spoon banging prevented the girl from dining with her classmates at the school for exceptional children that she attended. The banging was disruptive not only because of the noise but because it often led her to fling food on the floor or resulted in her dropping the spoon on the floor.

A clear definition of spoon banging was made to distinguish it from normal scooping motions. Then, a paraprofessional was trained to make observations and to administer the treatment. A frequency count was used to assess the magnitude of spoon banging within each 15-minute eating session. During the initial, or baseline, period the paraprofessional recorded frequency and, with each occurrence of the response, said "no bang," gently grasped the girl's wrist, and returned her hand to her dish. The procedure was videotaped, and an independent observer viewed the films and recorded frequency as a reliability check. Interobserver reliability was approximately 96%. The baseline stage was conducted for 16 days.

The first treatment period began on Day 17 and lasted for 16 days. Each time spoon banging was observed, the paraprofessional continued to give the corrective feedback of "no bang" and returned the girl's hand to her dish. However, the paraprofessional now also pulled a terry-cloth bib over the girl's entire face for 5 seconds. Release from facial screening was contingent on the participant's not banging for 5 seconds. The first treatment phase was followed by a second baseline period and another treatment phase. Posttreatment observations were also made at 6, 10, 15, and 19 months.

Figure 9.3 shows changes in the frequency of the mentally impaired girl's spoon-banging behavior as a function of alternating baseline and treatment phases. Facial screening was not only effective in reducing this behavior during treatment phases, follow-up observations revealed that the target behavior was still absent months later. Following the final treatment phase, the girl no longer required direct supervision during mealtime at either school or home and was permitted to eat with her peers. The facial-screening technique was a successful procedure for controlling the maladaptive behavior of the young child when other, less intrusive procedures had failed. Because only one treatment was administered, and because visual inspection revealed that behavior changed systematically with the introduction and withdrawal of treatment, it can be

**FIGURE 9.3**   Frequency of spoon-banging responses across baseline, treatment, and follow-up phases of study. (Adapted from Horton, 1987.)

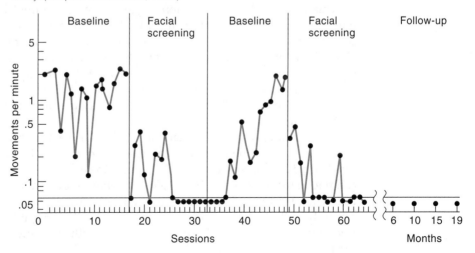

concluded that application of an aversive stimulus was responsible for eliminating spoon banging.

**Methodological Issues Associated with ABAB Designs**   A major methodological problem that sometimes arises in the context of an ABAB procedure can be illustrated by looking again at the results of the Horton (1987) study shown in Figure 9.3. In the second baseline stage, when application of the facial screening was withdrawn, spoon banging increased in frequency. That is, the improvement observed under the preceding treatment stage was reversed. What if spoon-banging behavior remained low even when the treatment was withdrawn? What can be concluded? If behavior in a second baseline stage does not revert to what it was during the initial baseline period, then serious problems of interpretation arise.

One reason why improvement in behavior may not reverse is that the behavior that is the focus of treatment would not logically be expected to become worse once improvement was observed. This might be the case if treatment involved training an individual in a new skill, such as tying one's shoes or commuting successfully to a job. Once the skill is acquired, it cannot reasonably be expected to be unlearned. The solution to this problem is one of foresight. That is, the ABAB design should not be used when the target behavior could not logically be expected to show reversal when treatment is withdrawn.

Given that the experienced researcher is likely to avoid using an ABAB design in situations wherein behavior would not be expected to reverse, the failure to observe a reversal of performance is probably due to one of two factors. One possibility is that a variable other than the treatment variable was responsible for the improvement in behavior in the first shift from baseline to treatment stages. For example, the individual may receive increased attention from staff or friends during treatment. This increased attention—rather than the treatment—may produce an improvement in behavior. If the attention persists even though the specific treatment is withdrawn, the behavior change is likely to persist as well. This explanation suggests a "confounding" between the treatment variable and some other, uncontrolled factor. On the other hand, it is also possible that, although the treatment caused behavior to improve, other variables "took over" to control the new behavior. Again, we might consider attention as a variable having an effect on behavior. When family and friends witness a change in behavior, they may pay increased attention to the individual. Positive reinforcement in the form of attention may maintain the behavior change that was initiated by the treatment.

In either case, when improvement in behavior does not reverse, it is not clear whether the experimental treatment or some other factor led to the initial behavior change; consequently, a causal claim for the effectiveness of the intervention can not be made (Kazdin, 1980, 1998). If behavior does not revert back to baseline when treatment is withdrawn, the researcher must examine the situation carefully with the hope of identifying variables that might be confounding the treatment variable or replicate the procedure with the same subject or with different subjects (Hersen & Barlow, 1976).

From an applied researcher's point of view, in some situations there is also an ethical problem in using the ABAB design. As you might imagine, the withdrawal of a beneficial treatment may not be justified in all cases. For example, although spoon-banging behavior would not be considered life-threatening or exceptionally debilitating, other kinds of behavior might be, and it would not be ethical in these cases to remove or even suspend treatment once a positive effect was observed. Some autistic children exhibit self-injurious behaviors such as head banging or face slapping. If a clinical researcher succeeded in reducing the frequency of such behavior, it would be unethical to withdraw treatment to meet the requirements of the ABAB design. Fortunately, there are other single-case experimental designs that do not involve withdrawal of treatment and that may be appropriate in such situations.

The Multiple-Baseline Design     The multiple-baseline design demonstrates the effect of a treatment by showing that behaviors in more than one baseline change following the introduction of a treatment. There are several variations on the multiple-baseline design, depending on whether multiple baselines are established for different individuals, for different behaviors in the same individual, or for the same individual in different situations. In each case, the conclusion that an experimental variable produced a reliable effect rests on the demonstration that behavior changed only when the experimental variable was introduced. Although they sound complex, multiple-baseline designs are frequently used and easily understood. Let us refer to a specific example of each type from the applied research literature.

A **multiple-baseline design across individuals** is a procedure wherein more than one individual is observed simultaneously. Specifically, baselines are first established for different individuals. When the behavior of each individual has stabilized, an intervention is introduced for one individual, then for another individual, later for another, and so on. That is, the experimental treatment is introduced at a different time for each participant. If the treatment is responsible for changing behavior, then an effect in the behavioral record will be seen immediately following the application of the treatment in each individual.

An interesting example of the use of a multiple-baseline design across individuals comes from the field of sports psychology. This subdiscipline involves the application of psychological principles to the improvement of recreation and sports (see, for example, Browne & Mahoney, 1984). Specifically, the researchers investigated the effect that a coaching method based on several behavioral techniques had on the acquisition of specific football, tennis, and gymnastic skills (see Allison & Ayllon, 1980). To evaluate this new behavioral coaching method, they used a multiple-baseline design. Although their investigation was successful in each sport, we will examine the effects of behavioral coaching only as it was applied to the acquisition of a football skill.

The participants in this experiment were second-string members of a city-wide football program chosen because they "completely lacked fundamental football skills" (Allison & Ayllon, 1980, p. 299). The skill to be acquired was blocking, which was defined operationally in terms of eight elements, ranging from the body's first being behind the line of scrimmage to maintaining body contact until the whistle was blown. Behavioral coaching involved specific procedures implemented by the team coach. The procedures included systematic verbal feedback, positive and negative reinforcement, and several other behavioral techniques. The experimenter first established baselines for several different members of the football team under "standard coaching" conditions. In this procedure, the coach used verbal instructions, provided occasional modeling or verbal approval, and, when execution was incorrect, "loudly informed the player and, at times, commented on the player's stupidity, lack of courage, awareness, or even worse" (p. 300). In short, an all-too-typical example of negative coaching behavior.

The experimenter and a second, reliability observer made observations of the frequency of correct blocks made in sets of 10 trials. Behavioral coaching was begun, in accordance with the multiple-baseline design, at different times for various football players. Results of this intervention are shown in Figure 9.4. Across four individuals, behavioral coaching was shown to be effective in increasing the frequency of correctly executed blocks. Observer agreement on blocking performance ranged from 84% to 94%, indicating that the observation of behavior was reliable. The skill execution changed for each player at the point where behavioral coaching was introduced. Thus it can be argued that this method *caused* the change in each player's performance.

When two or more baselines are established by observing different behaviors in the *same* individual, the design is called a **multiple-baseline design across behaviors.** A treatment is directed first at one behavior, then at another, and so on. A causal relationship between treatment and behavior is assumed if each behavior responds directly to treatment. For example, Gena, Krantz, McClannahan, and Poulson (1996) taught different appropriate affective behaviors to several youths with autism. As the researchers noted, children with autism often show inappropriate affective behaviors, which serve to limit their opportunities to communicate effectively with others and to develop interpersonal relationships. Treatment included verbal praise and tokens (exchangeable for rewards) delivered contingent on appropriate affective responses in three or four different behavior categories. Target behaviors were selected from the following: showing appreciation, talking about favorite things, laughing about absurdities, showing sympathy, indicating dislike. An inspection of the behavioral record showed for each child that the different affective behaviors changed immediately after introduction of the intervention.

The third major variation on the multiple-baseline design is that across situations. In a **multiple-baseline design across situations,** baselines are established for an individual's behavior in different situations. For example, a researcher might establish baselines showing frequency of a target behavior in the clinic and frequency of this same behavior in the home. As with other variations of this design, the treatment is applied at different times and the behavioral records are examined to determine whether behavior changes systematically with the introduction of treatment.

**FIGURE 9.4** Multiple baselines showing percentage of football blocks executed correctly by four players as a function of standard coaching and behavioral coaching. (From Allison & Ayllon, 1980.)

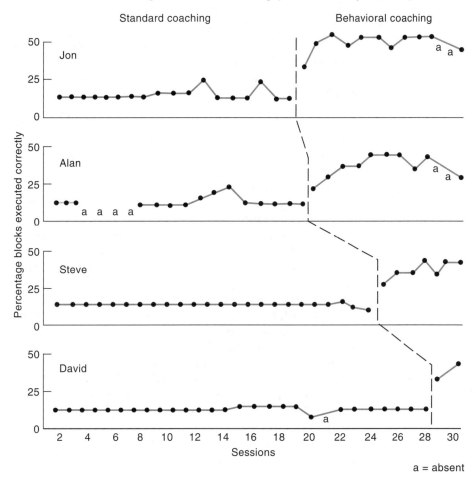

a = absent

In a study of verbal interaction among institutionalized mentally impaired persons, a multiple-baseline design across situations demonstrated that changes in the way meals were served influenced the frequency of mealtime language (VanBiervliet, Spangler, & Marshall, 1981). The investigators suggested that the typical institutional method of serving meals does not encourage peer interaction and that an alternative procedure, serving "family style," would increase verbal interactions. Baselines for frequency of verbalizations of five residents were made for three different situations (actually, three meals)—dinner, lunch, and breakfast. Behavior change was assessed in two ways: (a) by averaging the number of vocalizations made by the five residents, and (b) by examining individual behavioral records. Both measures showed that frequency of verbal behavior increased at each meal following the change in the way meals were served.

## Methodological Issues Associated with Multiple-Baseline Designs

- How many baselines are needed?

Often the first question to arise when one is doing a multiple-baseline experiment is "How many baselines do I need?" As with many other aspects of single-case methodology, there are no hard-and-fast rules. The bare minimum is clearly two baselines, but this is generally considered inadequate. Three to four baselines are recommended (Hersen & Barlow, 1976).

- What if behavior changes *before* the intervention?

A convincing demonstration of a treatment's effectiveness rests on the observation that behavior changes immediately after the treatment or intervention is introduced. Thus, problems arise when changes are seen in a baseline *before* an experimental intervention. This may occur in any of the types of multiple-baseline designs we have considered, and the reasons are not always clear. When changes in baseline performance occur prior to an experimental intervention, it is often difficult to draw a conclusion about the efficacy of the experimental treatment. However, the multiple-baseline design can still be interpreted with some confidence when preintervention changes appear in only one of several baselines that are being recorded—so long as plausible explanations for the baseline change, explanations based on procedural or situational variables, are available. For instance, Kazdin and Erickson (1975) used a multiple-baseline design across subjects to help severely mentally impaired individuals respond to instructions. Participants who followed instructions were reinforced with candy-coated cereal and praise, and this intervention was introduced in each of four small groups at different points in time. Performance changed directly with the application of the positive reinforcement procedure in three groups, but not in the fourth. In this group, which had the longest baseline, behavior gradually improved prior to the intervention. The researchers reasonably suggested that this occurred because individuals in this group saw other patients comply with instructions and then imitated the treated participants' behavior.

- What if the treatment generalizes to other behaviors or situations?

Another problem sometimes seen in multiple-baseline designs occurs when changes in one behavior generalize to other behaviors or situations. For example, when researchers successfully increased the degree of verbal interaction of mentally impaired persons at a dinner meal, we might not have been totally surprised if the residents increased their amount of talking at other meals. Once behavior at dinner was changed, at other meals the sight of food being served or the act of sitting down beside an acquaintance might prompt an increased level of verbal interaction. Such generalization effects were not seen, however, so the effect of the mealtime intervention was clearly demonstrated (see VanBiervliet et al., 1981).

To circumvent possible problems of generalization, we must again bring foresight to bear. If altering the behavior of one individual is likely to affect the behaviors of others, if behavior in one situation is likely to influence behavior in another situation, or if changing one type of behavior is likely to affect other behaviors, then multiple-baseline designs may need to be modified or perhaps abandoned altogether (Kazdin, 1980, 1998). As we have noted, unless behavior improves directly following an experimental intervention, concluding that the treatment variable was effective is problematic. Unfortunately, anticipating when changes will occur simultaneously in more than one baseline is not always easy, but these problems appear to be relatively infrequent exceptions to the effects usually seen in a multiple-baseline design (Kazdin, 1998).

## Problems and Limitations Common to All Single-Case Designs

- Interpreting the effect of a treatment can be difficult if the baseline stage shows excessive variability or increasing or decreasing trends in behavior.
- The problem of low external validity with single-case experiments can be reduced by testing small groups of individuals.
- Although psychologists can compare treatment and no-treatment conditions in single-case experiments, they cannot easily examine interactions among variables using this method.

**Problems with Baseline Records** It is difficult to evaluate the effects of an intervention when there are increasing or decreasing baseline trends or excessive variability in behavioral records. An ideal baseline record and response to an intervention are shown in panel A of Figure 9.5. Behavior during baseline is very stable, and behavior changes immediately following the introduction of treatment. If this were the outcome of the first stages of either an ABAB or a multiple-baseline design, we would be headed in the direction of showing that our treatment is effective in modifying behavior. However, consider the baseline and

**FIGURE 9.5** Examples of behavioral records showing possible relationships between baseline and intervention phases of a behavior modification program.

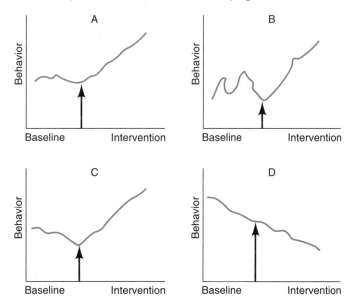

treatment stages shown in panel B of Figure 9.5. The baseline shows extreme variability, and, although the desired behavior appears to increase in frequency following an intervention, it is difficult to know whether the treatment produced the change or behavior just happened to be on the upswing. In this case it would be hard to decide whether our intervention successfully increased behavior.

There are several approaches to the problem of excessive baseline variability. One approach is to look for variables in the situation that might be producing the variability and could be removed. The presence of a particular staff member, for instance, might be causing changes in the behavior of a psychiatric patient. Another approach is to "wait it out"—to continue taking baseline measures until behavior stabilizes. It is, of course, not possible to predict when and if this might occur, but introducing an intervention before behavior has stabilized would jeopardize a clear interpretation of the experimental outcome. Another approach is to average data points. By charting a behavioral record using averages of several points, we can sometimes reduce the "appearance" of variability (Kazdin, 1978).

Another problem arises when the baseline record shows an increasing or a decreasing trend. In panel C of Figure 9.5, we see how behavior might change following an intervention when the initial baseline stage was characterized by a reduction in frequency of behavior. If the goal of the intervention was to increase frequency of behavior, the change described in panel C offers little problem of interpretation. An intervention that reversed the decreasing trend can be taken as evidence that the treatment was effective. However, should the goal of intervention be to reduce frequency of behavior, it would be difficult to know whether the decrease in frequency of behavior following the intervention is due to the intervention or to continuation of the baseline trend. This situation is illustrated in panel D. Here we see a decreasing trend in the baseline stage and continued reduction of frequency in the treatment stage. It is difficult in this case to know whether the experimental treatment had an effect. Generally speaking, when an intervention is expected to have an effect in the same direction as a baseline trend, the effect must be very marked in order to conclude that behavior was modified by the application of a treatment (Kazdin, 1978). Moreover, because a treatment effect in a single-case design is usually judged by visually inspecting the behavioral record, it is often difficult to say what constitutes a "marked" change in the behavioral record (see, for example, Parsonson & Baer, 1992). In such cases other means of evaluation should be employed, such as obtaining comparisons with "normal" individuals or asking for subjective evaluations from others familiar with the individual.

Questions of External Validity　When an effect is demonstrated using an $N = 1$ design, a frequent criticism is that external validity is limited. In other words, the $N = 1$ experiment appears to have the same limitation as the traditional case study method. Because each person is unique, it can be argued that there is no way of knowing whether the effect of a particular intervention will generalize to other individuals. There are several reasons why this problem may not be as serious as it seems. First, the types of intervention used in single-case studies are often potent ones and frequently produce dramatic and sizable changes in behavior (Kazdin, 1978). Consequently, these types of treatments are often found to generalize to other individuals. Other evidence for the generality of effects based on single-case studies comes from the use of multiple-baseline designs. A multiple-baseline design across subjects, for example, is often able to show that a particular intervention was successful in modifying the behavior of *several* individuals. Similarly, multiple baselines across situations and behaviors attest to the external validity of a treatment effect.

A treatment effect can also be shown to generalize to other individuals when a "single group" of subjects is used in a single-case experiment. As was mentioned before, the procedures associated with single-case designs are sometimes used with small groups of individuals as well. We have already seen two examples of this. VanBiervliet et al. (1981) showed that changes in a mealtime procedure were effective in increasing the average frequency of verbalizations of five mentally impaired individuals who were treated simultaneously. Similarly, Kazdin and Erickson (1975) found that positive reinforcement improved responsiveness to instructions in small groups of mentally impaired individuals. In both experiments, the researchers were able to demonstrate that an experimental treatment was, on average, effective for a small group of participants as well as for individuals in the group. In other words, an effect was replicated several times across members of a group each time an experimental manipulation was introduced. Such studies offer impressive evidence for both internal and external validity.

**Interaction Effects**   One limitation of the $N = 1$ methodology is not easily dismissed, and it illustrates again the lesson that no one research methodology is able to provide all the answers to questions that psychologists ask. The $N = 1$ experiment is not always appropriate for examining the effect of interactions among variables. For instance, although a single-case design can provide evidence of the effect of one variable (a main effect) by showing, for example, that behavior changes between conditions of No Treatment and Treatment, it is difficult to examine adequately the differential effect of combinations of various treatments and individual differences variables (Kazdin, 1998). In this situation, a large group design is often most appropriate (see especially Chapter 8). The experienced research psychologist realizes that there are problems and limitations associated with most methodologies. The methodology best suited to answering a particular question should be used. And, as we have stated previously, when possible, multimethod approaches to data collection are recommended.

## Ethical Issues in Single-Case Designs

- Psychologists are sometimes faced with the ethical dilemma of removing an apparently effective treatment in order to demonstrate its efficacy.
- Psychologists must carefully consider the risk/benefit ratio when behavior modification treatments involve punishment.

Two particularly salient ethical issues associated with single-case research should be mentioned. One of these we have already discussed briefly, namely, the withholding of an effective treatment as is required in the ABAB design. Ethical issues arise when treatments aimed at reducing painful or harmful events are shown to improve behavior (e.g., in the first, or treatment stage of an ABAB design) and then are withdrawn (in the second baseline stage) to provide more conclusive evidence of the treatment's efficacy. As you saw, one solution is to change research designs and use a multiple-baseline design in which treatments need not be withheld. This would be an appropriate and obvious strategy in many situations, especially if previous research has demonstrated a treatment's worth and the behavior being modified is clearly harmful. In some situations, however, whether a treatment will be effective is clearly an unanswered question (after all, we do research to find out if a treatment *will* work!) and the benefits of the treatment may not be entirely clear.

Consider, for example, research aimed at increasing the use of designated drivers to reduce alcohol-related driving accidents (see Brigham, Meier, & Goodner, 1995). Researchers used an ABAB design in which the treatment involved placing posters and table signs offering free nonalcoholic drinks to designated drivers at a bar frequented by college students. The dependent measure was the number of persons on a given weekend evening who registered with the bartender as designated drivers. Visual inspection of the graphed results revealed a clear effect of the prompts and free nonalcoholic drinks during the first treatment stage, then a reversal to baseline frequency when the prompts and drink offer were withdrawn, and finally, an increase in frequency again when the prompts and soft beverages were reinstated. Thus, we can suggest that drivers leaving the bar were "safer" when the signs were in evidence. Should an alternative design have been used to avoid the reversal during the second baseline stage?

Another ethical problem sometimes associated with single-case research concerns the nature of the treatment. Behavior modification using a noxious or aversive treatment is one example. Lovaas, for example, has used "aversives" such as mild electric shock with autistic and schizophrenic children in order to develop appropriate social responses (e.g., Lovaas, 1993; Lovaas, Schaeffer, & Simmons, 1965). This research has generated considerable controversy despite the fact that the aversive treatments were used only when other methods had failed and the alternative appeared even more injurious. That is, the success of these treatments apparently saved some individuals from permanent institutionalization and little hope of successful therapeutic intervention. This type of research clearly illustrates the often difficult nature of ethical decision making. Is the risk to the participant outweighed by the benefit of the treatment? It is interesting to note that the French doctor, Itard, who tried to rehabilitate the "wild boy" of Aveyron faced a similar vexing ethical dilemma (see Shattuck, 1994). At one point during training the boy became so frustrated and upset that he threw tantrums, biting the mantelpiece, tossing burning coals around the room, even losing consciousness. When this behavior was continually repeated the doctor had to decide whether to halt training or try somehow to control the tantrums. Itard decided on a most unconventional, but, as it turns out, highly effective

**FIGURE 9.6**   Research using an ABAB design revealed that offering free nonalcoholic drinks to designated drivers increased the frequency with which people registered with the bartender as designated drivers (Brigham, Meier, & Goodner, 1995).

treatment: He forcibly held the boy (who was afraid of heights) out the fifth-floor window. The boy was clearly scared and apparently cried for the first time, but training was able to proceed. Determining whether a treatment is justified requires careful consideration of all relevant factors and, as we noted in Chapter 2, consultation with knowledgeable others when the risk/benefit ratio is not easily calculated. Of course, these questions must be raised whenever research involves a potentially harmful treatment, and is not just associated with the use of single-case designs.

## SUMMARY

Two important single-case research designs are the case study and the single-case experiment, or $N = 1$ design. The case study method can be an important source of hypotheses about behavior, can provide an opportunity for clinical innovation (e.g., trying out new approaches to therapy), can permit the intensive study of rare phenomena, can challenge theoretical assumptions, and can provide tentative support for a psychological theory. The intensive study of individuals that is the hallmark of the case study method is called idiographic research, and it can be viewed as complementary to the nomothetic inquiry (seeking general laws or principles) that is also characteristic of psychology. Problems arise when the case study method is used to draw cause-effect conclusions, or when biases in the collection of, or interpretation of, data are not identified. The case study method also suffers from a lack of generalizability. How do we generalize on the basis of studying a single individual? Moreover, the "dramatic" results obtained from some case studies, though they may give scientific investigators important insights, are frequently accepted as valid by nonscientists who are not aware of the limitations of this method.

Behaviorism is an approach to the study of psychology that emphasizes the study of observable behavior under strictly controlled conditions. The behaviorism of B. F. Skinner is called the experimental analysis of behavior. Applied behavior analysis seeks to apply principles derived from an experimental analysis of behavior to socially relevant problems. The major methodology of this approach is the single-case experiment, or $N = 1$ design. Although there are many kinds of $N = 1$ designs, the most common are the ABAB design and the multiple-baseline design.

An ABAB design, or reversal design, allows a researcher to confirm a treatment effect by showing that behavior changes systematically with conditions of No Treatment (baseline) and Treatment. Methodological problems arise in this design when behavior that changed during the first treatment (B) stage does not reverse when treatment is withdrawn during the second baseline (A) stage. When this occurs, it is difficult to establish that the treatment, rather than some other factor, was responsible for the initial change. One may encounter ethical problems when using the ABAB design if a treatment that has been shown to be beneficial is withdrawn during the second baseline stage.

A multiple-baseline design demonstrates the effectiveness of a treatment by showing that behaviors across more than one baseline change as a consequence of the introduction of a treatment. Baselines are first established across different individuals, across behaviors in the same individual, or across situations. Methodological problems arise when behavior does not change immediately with the introduction of a treatment or when a treatment effect generalizes to other individuals, other behaviors, or other situations.

Problems of increasing or decreasing baselines, as well as excessive baseline variability, sometimes make it difficult to interpret the outcome of single-case designs. The problem of excessive baseline variability can be approached by seeking out and removing sources of variability, by extending the time during which baseline observations are made, or by averaging data points to remove the "appearance" of variability. Increasing or decreasing baselines may require the researcher to obtain other kinds of evidence for the effectiveness of a treatment—for example, measures of social comparison or subjective evaluation.

Finally, the $N = 1$ design is often criticized for its lack of external validity. However, because treatments typically produce substantial changes in behavior, these changes can often be easily replicated in different individuals. The use of single "groups" of subjects can also provide immediate evidence of generality across subjects. Treatments that are clearly aversive to the participants should only be used after careful consideration of the ethical implications, including the risk/benefit ratio.

The fact that the $N = 1$ design usually is not appropriate for testing the possible interactions of variables highlights the importance of selecting the research methodology that is most relevant for answering the particular question under investigation.

## KEY CONCEPTS

case study
nomothetic approach
idiographic approach
behavior modification/
    behavior therapy
single-case experiment

baseline stage
ABAB design
multiple-baseline design (across
    individuals, across behaviors,
    across situations)

## REVIEW QUESTIONS

1 Cite and give an example of the advantages of the case study method.
2 Distinguish between a nomothetic and an idiographic approach to research.
3 Cite and give an example of the disadvantages of the case study method.
4 What is the major limitation of the case study method in drawing cause-effect conclusions?
5 Under what conditions might a single-case ($N = 1$) design be more appropriate than a multiple-group design?
6 Distinguish between baseline and intervention stages of a single-case ($N = 1$) experimental design.
7 Why is an ABAB design also called a reversal design?
8 What major methodological problems are specifically associated with an ABAB design?
9 Outline the general rationale behind all the major forms of multiple-baseline designs.
10 What major methodological problems are specifically associated with multiple-baseline designs?
11 What major methodological problems are inherent in all single-case ($N = 1$) experimental designs?
12 How would you respond to the frequent criticism that single-case ($N = 1$) experimental designs lack external validity?
13 What types of research questions are not easily answered using single-case ($N = 1$) experimental designs?

## Challenge Questions

1 A case study showing how "mud therapy" was successful in treating an individual exhibiting excessive anxiety was reported in a popular magazine. The patient's symptoms included having trouble sleeping, loss of appetite, extreme nervousness when in groups of people, and general feelings of arousal that led the individual always to feel "on edge" and fearful. The California therapist who administered the mud therapy was known for this treatment, having appeared on several TV talk shows. He first taught the patient a deep relaxation technique and a "secret word" to repeat over and over in order to block out all disturbing thoughts. Then the patient was asked to lie submerged for two hours each day in a special wooden "calm tub" filled with mud. During this time the patient was to practice the relaxation exercises and to concentrate on repeating the secret word whenever the least bit of anxiety was experienced. The therapy was very costly, but after six weeks the patient reported to the therapist that he no longer had the same feelings of anxiety that he had had before. The therapist pronounced him cured and attributed the success of the treatment to immersion in the calming mud. The conclusion drawn by the author of the magazine article describing this therapy was that "it is a treatment that many people could benefit from." On the basis of your knowledge of the limitations of the case study method, answer the following questions:

   A   What possible sources of bias were there in the study?
   B   What alternative explanations can you suggest for the successful treatment?
   C   What problem arises from studying only one individual?

2 A 5-year-old child frequently gets skin rashes, and the mother has been told by her family doctor that the problem is due to "something" that the child eats. The doctor suggests that she "watch carefully" what the child eats. The mother decides to approach this problem by recording each day whether the child has a rash and what the child has eaten the day before. She hopes to find some relationship between eating a particular food and the presence or absence of the rash. Although this approach might help discover a relationship between eating certain foods and the appearance of the rash, a better approach might be one based on the logic and procedures associated with $N = 1$ designs. Explain how the mother might use such an alternative approach. Be specific and point to possible problems that may arise in this application of behavioral methodology.

3 During the summer months you find employment in a camp for mildly mentally impaired children. As a counselor you are asked to supervise a small group of children, as well as to look for ways to improve their attention to various camp activities that take place indoors (e.g., craft making and sewing). You decide to explore the possibility of using a system of rewards (M&M candies) for "time on task." You realize that the camp director will want evidence of the effectiveness of your intervention strategy as well as some assurance that it will work with other children in the camp. Therefore you are to:

   A   Plan an intervention strategy based on operant principles that has as its goal an increase in the time children spend on a camp activity.
   B   Explain what behavioral records you will need to keep and how you will determine whether your intervention has produced a change in the children's behavior. You will need, for example, to specify exactly when and how you will

measure behavior, as well as to justify your use of a particular design to carry out your "experiment."

   **C**  Describe the argument you will use to convince the director that your intervention strategy (assuming that it works) will work with other, similar children.

**4**  A schoolteacher asks your help in planning a behavioral intervention that will help manage the behavior of a problem child in his classroom. The child does not stay at her desk when asked to do so, does not remain quiet during "quiet times," and exhibits other behaviors that disrupt the teaching environment. Explain specifically how a positive reinforcer, such as candy or small toys, might be used as part of a multiple-baseline across behaviors design to improve the child's behavior.

## Answer to Challenge Question 1

   **A**  One source of bias in this case study was that the same individual served as therapist and as researcher with the commensurate problems of observer bias. A second source of bias is that the therapist based his conclusion solely on the self-reports of the patient.

   **B**  The successful treatment may have resulted from the relaxation technique alone; the use of the "secret word" in the face of anxiety; attention the patient received from the therapist; or even the high cost of the treatment.

   **C**  The major problem that arises from studying one individual is a potential lack of external validity.

# Quasi-Experimental Designs and Program Evaluation

## CHAPTER OUTLINE

## OVERVIEW

In the most general sense, an experiment is a test; it is a procedure used to find out something not presently known. In this sense we experiment when we add new ingredients to a chili recipe in order to see whether they improve its taste. We experiment with new ways to catch fish by changing the lures we use. We experiment when we take a different route to our job in order to find a faster way to commute. As you no doubt recognize, however, these kinds of informal "experiments" are much different from those experiments typically carried out in the conduct of psychological research. Experimental methods, unlike other research techniques such as observation and surveys, are viewed as the most efficient way to determine causation. But determining causation is not always easy, and in the last few chapters you were introduced to the complexity of the task facing the researcher who seeks to understand a phenomenon by discovering what caused it.

In this chapter we continue our discussion of experimental methods, but we focus on experiments as they are conducted in natural settings. You will see that the task of drawing cause-effect conclusions often becomes even more difficult, and that new problems arise, when an investigator leaves the confines of the laboratory to experiment in natural settings.

There are many reasons why experiments are carried out in natural settings. One important reason (mentioned in Chapter 6) for these "field experiments" is to test the external validity of a laboratory finding. We seek to find out if a treatment effect observed in the laboratory works in a similar way in another setting. Other reasons for experimenting in natural settings are more practical in that they are likely to be associated with attempts to improve conditions under which people live and work. The government may experiment with a new tax system or a new method of job training for the economically disadvantaged. Schools may experiment by changing lunch programs, after-school care, or curricula. A business may experiment with new product designs, methods of delivering employee benefits, or flexible work hours. In these cases, as is true in the laboratory, it is important to determine whether the "treatment" caused a change. Did a change in the way patients are admitted to a hospital emergency room cause patients to be treated more quickly and efficiently? Did a college energy conservation program cause a decrease in energy consumption? Knowing whether a treatment was effective permits us to make important decisions about continuing the treatment, about spending additional money, about investing more time and effort, or about changing the present situation on the basis of our knowledge of the results. Research that seeks to determine the effectiveness of changes made by institutions, government agencies, and other units of society is one goal of the discipline of *program evaluation*.

In this chapter we discuss the problems of conducting experiments in natural settings. We describe obstacles to doing true experiments in such settings, and we discuss ways of overcoming these obstacles so that true experiments are done whenever possible. Nevertheless, true experiments are sometimes not feasible outside the laboratory. In these cases, experimental procedures that only approximate the conditions of laboratory experiments must be considered. We discuss several of these quasi-experimental techniques. Problems with quasi-experimentation make us realize the value of true experiments, so we briefly consider alternatives to quasi-experiments in natural settings. One such alternative is the extension of single-case experimental designs (which we discussed in Chapter 9) to research in natural settings. We conclude the chapter by providing a brief introduction to the logic, procedures, and limitations of program evaluation.

## DIFFERENCES BETWEEN LABORATORY EXPERIMENTS AND EXPERIMENTS IN NATURAL SETTINGS

- Experiments conducted in a laboratory setting differ from experiments conducted in a natural setting in terms of control, external validity, goals, and consequences.
- Researchers usually have less control over experimental conditions in natural settings than in laboratories.
- As control decreases, researchers' ability to make causal inferences also decreases.
- Research is conducted in natural settings to establish the external validity of findings from laboratory studies.
- Basic research is carried out with the goal of understanding a phenomenon, whereas applied research is usually done with the goal of improving the present situation.
- Research conducted in natural settings tends to have greater impact on the lives of more individuals than research conducted in laboratories.

There are some important considerations to keep in mind as we discuss experimentation in natural settings. Experimentation outside the confines of the psychology laboratory is likely to differ from laboratory research in a number of significant ways. Not every experiment in a natural setting differs from laboratory experiments in all of these ways, of course. But if you are thinking of doing research in a natural setting, we urge you to consider the following critical issues.

### Control

More than anything else, the scientist is concerned with control. Only by controlling those factors that are assumed to influence a phenomenon can one make a decision about what caused it. As you have seen in previous chapters, control takes several forms. The random assignment of participants to conditions of an experiment is a method of control used to balance participant characteristics in treatment and no-treatment conditions. Other factors that are likely to influence a phenomenon may be controlled by holding them constant. In a natural setting, a researcher may not always have the same degree of control over conditions of an experiment or over assignment of participants as in a laboratory. A field experiment may have to be conducted according to the availability of participants or at the discretion of an administrator or government official. Natural settings place various restrictions on an experiment that limit the researcher's control. It is even possible that an investigator may not directly participate in the planning and conduct of the "experiment" but may be asked afterward whether a treatment "worked." This kind of situation is clearly the most difficult because important factors may not have been considered in planning or executing the intervention.

As an illustration, consider the following situation. As you saw in Chapter 1, many people frequently are too willing to believe in paranormal phenomena, including ESP and the claims of so-called "psychics." These beliefs may be due to deficiencies in human reasoning and in science education (e.g., Singer & Benassi, 1981). One response has been the creation of "critical thinking" and "science vs. pseudoscience" courses at the college level (e.g., Morier & Keeports, 1994). A reasonable question is, Do such courses "work"? That is, do students who take these courses acquire a more critical view of paranormal phenomena? The treatment in this case is exposure to the material and ideas presented in the course. The dependent variable might be responses to a questionnaire asking about belief in paranormal phenomena and the occult. We would like to know whether or not such courses "cause" a change in people's views of these ideas and events. However, you no doubt can see problems with this "experiment." Students are most likely not randomly assigned to take such a course. Are the students taking such a course already critical about paranormal claims, or did they take the course because of their interest and belief in paranormal phenomena? With whom do we compare the students in the course? Are there possible changes in students' views over time *that might occur independently of the course* and that need to be taken into account? What other events are not controlled in such a situation that might influence people's attitudes toward paranormal phenomena? In order to find out whether the treatment worked, a researcher faces a host of problems that arise due to the lack of control over the situation. Later, we will describe results of a published study that sought to answer this question: Can students be taught to be more critical of paranormal phenomena?

## External Validity

Field experiments are sometimes conducted with the goal of establishing the external validity of a laboratory finding. The "artificial" environment of the psychology laboratory, which increases the internal validity of research because of the high degree of control, often decreases the external validity of the findings. Experiments in natural settings may therefore need to be conducted in order to generalize results beyond the laboratory situation.

On the other hand, as you saw in Chapter 6, the external validity of a laboratory experiment may not be all that important (e.g., Mook, 1983). This may be particularly true when an experiment is done simply to test a specific psychological theory. In contrast, the external validity of research done in natural settings is often very important because the focus of such research is frequently on a treatment's general effectiveness. This is especially true when social experimentation serves as the basis for large-scale social changes, such as trying out new ways to curb drunk driving or new procedures for registering voters.

If the results of a field experiment are to be used to plan further interventions or to implement similar programs in other locations or different regions of the country, then it is vital to know to what extent the treatment and results can be generalized. For example, legislators may wish to generalize to a different state certain procedures that have been shown to produce an increase in voter registration in one state. A method to increase employee morale that succeeded in one branch of a company may be considered by company officials for all branches of the company. Will the results of a reading program that is judged to be beneficial at one grade level in one school generalize to other grade levels, other schools, or situations where it is implemented by different personnel? Does a course found to improve students' critical thinking skills at one college also "work" at other colleges? These are, of course, all questions of external validity.

## Goals

Experimentation in natural settings often has different goals from laboratory research. One major difference are the goals associated with basic and applied research. **Basic research** is often carried out with the single goal of understanding a phenomenon, of determining how "nature" works. It may be done to gain knowledge merely for knowledge's sake. **Applied research** is also directed toward discovering the reasons for a phenomenon, but it is likely to be done only when knowing the reasons for an event will lead to changes that will modify or improve the present situation. Experimentation in natural settings, therefore, is more likely to have practical goals. As you saw above, this is one reason why questions of external validity are more important for field experiments than they are for laboratory experiments.

## Consequences

Sometimes experiments are conducted that have far-reaching impact on communities and society, affecting large numbers of people. For example, during the 1970s the U.S. government experimented with the "new town" concept. Thirteen new towns were created under government sponsorship. Beginning from scratch, designers tried to avoid all the problems of older unplanned urban communities. Towns such as Columbia, Maryland, and Reston, Virginia, are examples. Another example of an experiment by the U.S. government was a program designed to aid prisoners following release from incarceration (see Berk, Boruch, Chambers, Rossi, & Witte, 1987). Individuals released from prison often have little in the way of resources to help them begin a new life, and they frequently have difficulty finding jobs. This economic hardship can contribute to new crime. The program involved random assignment of ex-prisoners to groups that either received financial assistance on leaving prison or did not receive financial assistance. The program targeted as participants about 2,000 ex-prisoners in Texas and Georgia.

Clearly, these examples of society's "experiments," as well as those we might imagine being carried out on a smaller scale in natural settings (such as those conducted in schools or businesses), are likely to have consequences of greater immediate impact than those of laboratory research. Consider that the Head Start program for disadvantaged children and the *Sesame Street* television show were social experiments designed to improve the education of literally hundreds of thousands of children across the nation. Experiments in businesses may be carried out with the eventual goal of reducing the number of employees or in other ways affecting the quality of employees' lives. Moreover, as is true of all experiments, the consequences are not always those that were anticipated. Although a few planned communities worked, others did not, and planners and builders went bankrupt (see *Time,* October 16, 1978, p. 84). Although the prison release program produced some identifiable positive results, it was also found to be responsible for an *increase* in crime, apparently due to the ex-prisoners' freedom from having to work (see Berk et al., 1987).

In order to draw meaningful conclusions about the effects of these experiments, we must consider the design and implementation of these "treatments" and to do the best we can to assess as clearly as possible whether the treatments

**FIGURE 10.1**    As a social experiment, *Sesame Street* was designed to improve the education of hundreds of thousands of children.

worked. This is especially important because, as we have seen, the consequences of such experiments frequently are so great in terms of money spent and the number of people whose lives are affected. By contrast, the consequences of a laboratory experiment are likely to be minimal. They may directly affect only the lives of a few researchers and of those relatively few participants recruited to participate.

## TRUE EXPERIMENTS

### Characteristics of True Experiments

- In true experiments, researchers manipulate an independent variable with treatment and comparison condition(s) and exercise a high degree of control (especially through random assignment to conditions).

Although many everyday activities (such as altering the ingredients of a recipe) might be called experiments, we would not consider them "true" experiments in the sense in which experimentation has been discussed in this textbook. Analogously, many "social experiments" carried out by the government (such as the "new town" concept) and those that are conducted by company officials or educational administrators are also not true experiments. *A true experiment is one that leads to an unambiguous outcome regarding what caused an event.*

True experiments exhibit three important characteristics:

**1** In a true experiment some type of intervention or treatment is implemented.

**2** True experiments are marked by the high degree of control that an experimenter has over the arrangement of experimental conditions, assignment of participants, systematic manipulation of independent variables, and choice of dependent variables. The ability to assign participants randomly to experimental conditions is often seen as the most critical defining characteristic of the true experiment (Judd et al., 1991).

**3** Finally, true experiments are characterized by an appropriate comparison. Indeed, the experimenter exerts control over a situation principally in order to establish a proper comparison to evaluate the effectiveness of a treatment. In the simplest of experimental situations, this comparison is one between two groups that are treated exactly alike except for the variable of interest.

When the conditions of a true experiment are met, any differences in a dependent variable that arise can logically be assigned to the differences between levels of the independent variable.

### Obstacles to Conducting True Experiments in Natural Settings

- Researchers may experience difficulty gaining access to participants and permission to conduct true experiments in natural settings.
- Although random assignment is viewed by some as unfair because it may deprive individuals from a new treatment, it is still the best way and fairest way to determine if a new treatment is effective.

Experimental research is an effective tool for solving problems and answering questions. Nevertheless, two major obstacles often arise when we try to carry out experiments in natural settings. The first problem is obtaining permission to do the research from individuals in positions of authority. Unless they believe that the research will be useful, school board presidents and government and business leaders are unlikely to support research financially or otherwise.

The second, and often more pressing, obstacle to doing experiments in natural settings is the problem of access to participants. This problem can prove especially troublesome if participants are to be randomly assigned to either a treatment group or a comparison group.

Random assignment to conditions appears unfair at first—after all, random assignment requires that a potentially beneficial treatment be withheld from at least some participants. Suppose that a new approach to the teaching of foreign languages was to be tested at your college or university. Suppose further that, when you went to register for your next semester's classes, you were told that you would be randomly assigned to one of two sections taught at the time you selected—one section involving the old method and one involving the new method. How would you react? Your knowledge of research methods tells you that the two methods must be administered to comparable groups of students and that random assignment is the best way to ensure such comparability. Nonetheless, you might be tempted to feel that random assignment is not fair, especially if you are assigned to the section using the old (old-fashioned?) method. Let's take a closer look at the fairness of random assignment.

If those responsible for selecting the method of foreign language instruction already knew that the new method was more effective than the old method at schools such as yours, there would be little justification for testing the method again. Under such circumstances we would agree that withholding the new method from students in the control group would be unjust. If we do not know whether the new method is better, however, any approach other than conducting a true experiment will leave us in doubt about the new method's effectiveness. Random assignment to treatments—call it a "lottery" if you prefer—may be the fairest procedure for assigning students to sections. The old method of instruction, after all, was considered effective before the development of the new method. If the new method proves less effective, random assignment will have actually "protected" the control participants from receiving an ineffective treatment.

There are ways to offer a potentially effective treatment to all participants while still maintaining comparable groups. One way is to alternate treatments. For example, Atkinson (1968) randomly assigned students to receive computer-assisted instruction in either English or math (the "treatment") and then tested both groups in English and math. Each group served as a control for the other on the test for which its members had not received computer-assisted instruction. After completing the experiment, both groups could then be given computer-assisted instruction in the subject matter to which they had not been previously exposed. Thus, all participants received all potentially beneficial treatments.

Establishing a proper control group is also possible if there is more demand for a service than an agency can meet. People who are waiting to receive the service can become a "waiting list" control group. It is essential, however, that people be assigned to the waiting list randomly. People who are "first in line" are no doubt different on important dimensions from those who arrive last (e.g., more eager for treatment). Random assignment is necessary to distribute these characteristics in an unbiased way between treatment and comparison groups.

There will always be circumstances in which random assignment simply cannot be used. For example, in clinical trials involving tests of new medical treatments, it may be extremely difficult to get patients to agree to be randomly assigned to either the treatment group or the control group. As you will see, quasi-experimental designs can be used in these situations. The logic and procedures for these quasi-experimental designs will be described later in this chapter.

## Threats to Internal Validity Controlled by True Experiments

- Threats to internal validity are confoundings that serve as plausible alternative explanations for a research finding.
- The major classes of threats to internal validity include history, maturation, testing, instrumentation, regression, selection, subject mortality, and interactions with selection.

One way to evaluate an experiment is to determine what kinds of alternative explanations for a phenomenon have been controlled. Prior to doing an experiment, we might look to see what major classes of possible explanations are ruled out by our experimental procedure. Only by eliminating all possible alternative explanations can we arrive at a definite conclusion about cause and effect. In previous chapters, we referred to various uncontrolled factors that threaten the internal validity of an experiment as confounding factors (they are also called confounds). Several types of confounds were identified in earlier chapters (see especially Chapter 6). We will now list eight classes of confounds, using the terminology of Campbell and Stanley (1966; see also Cook & Campbell, 1979). You have already been introduced to some of these **threats to internal validity;** others will be new. After reviewing the major classes of confounds, we will be able to judge the extent to which various experimental procedures control for these kinds of alternative explanations of a treatment effect.

History   The occurrence of an event other than the treatment can threaten internal validity if it produces changes in the research participants' behavior. A true experiment requires that participants in the experimental group and in the control group be treated the same (have the same history of experiences while in the experiment) except for the treatment. In the laboratory, this is usually accomplished by balancing or holding conditions constant. For example, the same experimenter might be asked to test people in all conditions of an experiment. If different experimenters were to test experimental and control participants, we would confound the possible effect due to the experimenter and that of the treatment. That is, the "history" of the two groups in the experiment would differ if different experimenters were used for each group. When doing experiments in natural settings, the researcher may not always be able to exercise the degree of control associated with laboratory settings, so confounding due to history can be a threat to internal validity. For example, suppose that you set out to test whether a college-level critical thinking course did, in fact, change students' thinking. And suppose further that your test was simply to examine students' performance on a critical thinking test at the beginning of the critical thinking course and then again at the end of the course. History would be a threat to internal validity if events other than the treatment (i.e., the critical thinking course) occurred that might improve the critical thinking abilities of the students. For example, suppose that many students taking this course also took it upon themselves to view a video designed to teaching critical thinking that wasn't required for the course, and also purchased extra books and pamphlets to help them think more critically. This particular history of experiences would confound the treatment.

Maturation  Participants in an experiment necessarily change as a function of time. They grow older, become more experienced, and so forth. Change associated with the passage of time per se is called maturation. For example, suppose a researcher is interested in assessing children's learning over a school year using a new teaching technique. Without a proper comparison a researcher might attribute the changes in performance between a pretest and a posttest of a group of schoolchildren to the effect of the teaching intervention when, in reality, the changes were simply due to the normal processes of maturation.

Testing  Taking a test generally has an effect on subsequent testing. Consider, for example, the fact that many students often improve from the initial test in a course to the second test. The familiarity with the testing procedure and with the instructor's expectations that they gain during the first test affects their performance on the second test. Likewise, in the context of a psychology experiment in which more than one test is given (e.g., in a pretest-posttest design), testing is a threat to internal validity if the effect of a treatment cannot be separated from the effect of testing. Can you see how an attempt to assess the effect of a critical thinking course would be problematic if the assessment is simply the same students' scores on a pretest and a posttest?

Instrumentation  It is possible that changes over time take place not only in the participants of an experiment (e.g., maturation or increased familiarity with testing), but also in the instruments used to measure the participants' performance. This is most clearly a possibility when human observers are used to assess behavior. As you learned in previous chapters (see especially Chapter 3), observer bias can result from fatigue, expectations, and other characteristics of observers. For example, as a researcher becomes more experienced in making observations, there is likely to be a change in the quality of the observations that she or he makes. Unless controlled for, these changes in instrumentation can threaten internal validity by providing alternative explanations for differences in behavior between one observation period and another. Mechanical instruments also may change with repeated use. A researcher known to the authors once found that a machine used to present material in a learning experiment was not working the same at the end of the experiment as it was at the beginning. Measures made near the end of the experiment differed from those made at the beginning of the experiment. Thus, what looked like a learning effect was really just a change in the instruments used to measure learning.

Regression   Statistical **regression** is always a problem when individuals have been selected to participate in an experiment because of their "extreme" scores. As summarized by Cook and Campbell (1979, pp. 52–53), statistical regression

> (1) operates to increase obtained pretest-posttest gain scores among low pretest scores, since this group's pretest scores are more likely to have been depressed by error; (2) operates to decrease obtained change scores among persons with high pretest scores since their pretest scores are likely to have been inflated by error; and (3) does not affect obtained change scores among scorers at the center of the pretest distribution since the group is likely to contain as many units whose pretest scores are inflated by error as units whose pretest scores are deflated by it. Regression is always to the population mean of a group.

In other words, a very, very bad performance, or a very, very good performance (both of which we have all experienced), is likely to be followed by a performance that is not quite so bad, or not quite so good, respectively. Consider, for instance, your best ever performance on a classroom examination. What did it take to "nail" this test? It took no doubt a lot of hard work. But it is also likely that luck was involved. Everything has to work just right to produce an extremely good performance. If we are talking about an exam, then it is likely that the material tested was that which you just happened to study the hardest, or the test format was one you particularly like, or it came at a time when you were feeling particularly confident, and so forth (or all of these and more). Particularly good performances are, as Cook and Campbell (1979) stated, "extreme" because they are inflated (over our usual or typical performance) by chance (error). Similarly, an especially bad test performance is likely to have occurred because of some bad luck. When tested again (following either a very good or a very bad performance), it is just not likely that chance factors will "gang up" the same way to give us that super (inflated) score or that very poor (depressed) score. We will, as Cook and Campbell suggest, likely see a performance closer to the average of our overall scores.

Now, consider an attempt to raise the academic performance of a group of college students who have performed very poorly during their first semester of college (the "pretest"). Of course, participants are selected *because of their extreme performance* (in this case, extremely poor performance). Let us assume that a treatment (e.g., a 10-hour study skills workshop) is then applied. Statistical regression is a threat to internal validity since we would expect these students to perform slightly better after the second semester (the "posttest") *without any treatment* simply due to statistical regression. An unknowing researcher may mistakenly confuse this "regression effect" with a "treatment effect." Consider people who sign up to be treated first in a psychotherapy program. Are these individuals seeking treatment early because their symptoms are particularly bad at this time? If so, do you see how these people might show signs of improvement over their pretherapy screening when tested later, whether or not they received therapy?

Selection   When, from the outset of a study, differences exist between the kinds of individuals in one group and those in another group in the experiment, there is a confounding due to selection. That is, the people who are in the treatment group may differ from people in the comparison group in many ways *other* than their group assignment. In the laboratory, this threat to internal validity is generally handled by balancing participant characteristics through random assignment. When one is doing experiments in natural settings, there are often many obstacles to randomization of participants to treatment and comparison conditions. These obstacles prevent doing a true experiment and hence present a possible confound due to selection.

Subject Mortality   When participants are lost from an experiment, there is a threat to internal validity. (Possible reasons for participant loss were discussed in Chapter 6.) The threat to internal validity rests on the assumption that participant loss (attrition) changes the nature of a group from that established prior to the introduction of the treatment—for example, by destroying the equivalence of groups that had been established through randomization. This might occur, for instance, if an experimental task is very difficult and causes some experimental participants to become frustrated and to drop out of the experiment. Participants who are left in the experimental group will differ from those who dropped out (and possibly from those in a control group) if for no other reason than that they were able to do the task (or at least stuck it out).

Interactions with Selection   Several of the foregoing threats to internal validity can be a source of additional concern because they can interact with characteristics of groups of individuals selected for an experiment. Specifically, when comparable groups are not formed by random assignment, there are possible problems due to interactions between (1) selection and history, (2) selection and maturation, and (3) selection and instrumentation. Basically, this means that one or more groups of participants respond differently to effects associated with history, maturation, or instrumentation. For example, if groups of participants in an experiment mature at different rates, then differences between groups in the form of changes from pretest to posttest may be due to an interaction of selection and maturation rather than to any treatment. Such might be the case if first-year students in college who served as an experimental group were compared with sophomores who served as a control group. Changes in students that occur during their first year (as students gain familiarity with the college environment) might be presumed to be greater than such changes that occur during the second or sophomore year. These differences in maturation rates might explain any observed differences between the experimental and control groups, rather than any experimental intervention.

An interaction of selection and history results when events occurring in time have a different effect on one group of participants than on another. This is particularly a problem when intact groups are compared. Perhaps due to events that are peculiar to one group's situation, an event may have more of an impact on that group than on another. Consider, for example, research involving an investigation of the effectiveness of an AIDS awareness campaign involving two college campuses (one treatment and one control). Nationwide media attention to this problem might reasonably be assumed to affect students on both campuses equally. However, if a prominent student with AIDS died at one college during this period, and the story was featured in the college newspaper, we would assume that students at this student's college would be affected differently from those at the other. In terms of assessing the effect of an AIDS awareness campaign, this situation would represent an interaction of selection and history.

Finally, an interaction of selection and instrumentation might occur if a test instrument is relatively more sensitive to changes in one group's performance than to changes in another's. This occurs, for instance, when ceiling or floor effects are present. Such is the case when a group scores initially so low on an instrument (*floor effect*), that any further drop in scores cannot be reliably measured, or so high (*ceiling effect*) that any more gain cannot be assessed. As you can imagine, a confound would be present if an experimental group showed relatively no change (due to floor or ceiling effects), while a control group changed reliably because its mean performance was initially near the middle of the measurement scale.

A true experiment controls all these threats to internal validity. Quasi-experiments can be viewed as compromises between the general aim of gaining valid knowledge regarding the effectiveness of a treatment and the realization that true experiments (and hence control of the major factors threatening internal validity) are not always possible. As Campbell (1969) emphasizes, so-called true experiments should be conducted when possible, but if they are not feasible, quasi-experiments should be conducted. "We must do the best we can with what is available to us" (p. 411).

## Problems That Even True Experiments May Not Eliminate

- Threats to internal validity that can occur in any study include contamination, experimenter expectancy effects, and the Hawthorne effect.
- Contamination occurs when information about the experiment is communicated between groups of participants, which may lead to resentment, rivalry, or diffusion of treatment.

- Threats to external validity occur when treatment effects may not be generalized beyond the particular people, setting, and time of the experiment.
- The Hawthorne effect occurs when people's behavior changes simply because they believe someone (e.g., researchers, persons in authority) is interested in them.

Before considering specific quasi-experimental procedures, we should point out that even true experiments may not control for all possible factors that might cloud the interpretation of an experimental result. Although major threats to internal validity are typically eliminated by the true experiment, there are some additional threats that the investigator must guard against, particularly when working in natural settings. We will use the term *contamination* to describe one general class of threats to internal validity. **Contamination** occurs when there is communication of information about the experiment between groups of participants. The result of this communication can be (1) *resentment* on the part of individuals receiving less desirable treatments, (2) *rivalry* among groups receiving different treatments, or (3) a general *diffusion of treatments* across the groups (see Cook & Campbell, 1979).

Consider a situation in which individuals have been randomly assigned to a control group. Further, assume that information is obtained by participants in this group indicating that "other" participants are receiving a treatment that appears to be beneficial. What do you think might be the reaction of the control participants? One possibility is resentment and demoralization. As Cook and Campbell explain, in an industrial setting the person receiving the less desirable treatment may retaliate by lowering productivity. In an educational setting teachers or students might "lose heart" or become angry. This effect of "leaked" information about a treatment may make a treatment look better than it ordinarily would because of the lowered performance of the control group that is demoralized.

Another possible effect that may occur when a control group learns about another group's good fortune is to generate a spirit of competition. That is, a control group might become motivated to reduce the expected difference between itself and the treatment group. As Cook and Campbell point out, this may be likely when intact groups (such as departments, work crews, branch offices, and the like) are assigned to various conditions. Realizing that another group will look better depending on how much it distinguishes itself from the control group, participants comprising the control group may be motivated to "try harder" so as not to look bad by comparison. Cook and Campbell call this problem compensatory rivalry. Like other contamination effects, it can potentially affect any experiment, but it can be of particular concern when experiments are done in natural settings.

Yet another possible effect of contamination is diffusion of treatments. According to Cook and Campbell, this occurs when participants in a control group use information given to others to help them change their own behavior. For example, control participants may use the information given to participants in the treatment group to imitate the behavior of individuals who were given the treatment. Of course, this reduces the differences between the treated and untreated groups and affects the internal validity of the experiment.

In addition to problems resulting from contamination, true experiments can be weakened by threats to external validity. As you have learned in previous chapters, the extent to which we can generalize across persons, settings, and times depends mainly on how representative our sample is of the persons, settings, and times to which we want to generalize. Representativeness is normally achieved through random sampling. However, because random sampling is used so infrequently, we can rarely say that our sample of participants, or the situation in which we are making observations, or the times during which we test individuals, are representative samples of all persons, settings, or times. Therefore, the investigator must be aware of possible interactions between the independent variable of an experiment and the type of individual, setting, or time of the experiment. Is a difference between an experimental group and a control group that is found when only volunteers are used, when the setting is an inner-city school, or when the experiment is conducted in the winter, also likely to be found when nonvolunteers are tested, when a suburban school is the setting, or when the experiment is performed in the spring of the year?

Cook and Campbell describe several approaches to evaluating threats to external validity, the foremost being determination of the representativeness of the sample. However, they point out that in the last analysis the best test of external validity is replication (see Chapter 6). External validity is an empirical question that is best answered through repetition of the experiment with different types of participants, in different settings, and at different times. Occasionally these replications can be "built into" an experiment—for example, by selecting more than one group to participate. Testing both schoolchildren from a lower socioeconomic group and a higher socioeconomic group in an experiment designed to determine the effectiveness of a new educational program would provide evidence of the generality of the treatment's effectiveness across these two socioeconomic groups.

Finally, true experiments do not always protect the experimenter from threats due to experimenter expectancy effects or to a "Hawthorne effect." Effects due to experimenter expectancies were discussed in earlier chapters. They occur when the experimenter unintentionally influences the results. Systematic errors in interpretation or mistakes in recording data can be the result of experimenter expectancy effects. Various ways to control experimenter or observer effects were outlined in Chapters 3 and 6 (e.g., using a double-blind procedure). The **Hawthorne effect** refers to changes in persons' behavior brought about by the interest that "significant others" show in them. The effect was named after events occurring at the Hawthorne plant of the Western Electric Company in Cicero, Illinois, near Chicago, between 1924 and 1932 (Roethlisberger, 1977). Studies were conducted to examine the relationship between productivity and conditions of the workplace. In one experiment, worker output was examined as a function of variation in the amount of lighting (illumination level) in the plant. Results revealed that *both* experimental and control groups increased their productivity during the study. Although there is some controversy surrounding the exact factors responsible for this effect (e.g., Parsons, 1974), a Hawthorne effect generally refers to behavior change resulting from participants' awareness that someone is interested in them.

As one example of the Hawthorne effect, consider a study in which prisoners are chosen to participate in research examining the relationship between changes in prison-cell conditions and attitudes toward prison life. If positive changes in prisoners' attitudes are obtained, the results could be due to the actual changes in cell conditions that were made, or they could be due to an increase in morale because prisoners saw the prison administration as expressing concern for them. The psychology investigator must be conscious of the fact that changes in participants' behavior may be at least partially due to their awareness of the fact that others are interested in them. Thus, you can see that a Hawthorne effect represents a specific kind of reactivity (i.e., an awareness that one is being observed), which we discussed in previous chapters (especially Chapter 3).

## QUASI-EXPERIMENTS

- Quasi-experiments provide an important alternative when true experiments are not possible.
- Quasi-experiments lack the degree of control found in true experiments; most notably, quasi-experiments typically lack random assignment.
- Researchers must seek additional evidence to eliminate threats to internal validity when they do quasi-experiments rather than true experiments.
- The one-group pretest-posttest design is called a preexperimental design or a bad experiment because it has so little internal validity.

A dictionary will tell you that one definition of the prefix *quasi-* is "resembling." A quasi-government, for example, is one resembling, but not actually the same as, a true government. Similarly, **quasi-experiments** involve procedures that resemble those that are characteristic of true experiments. Generally speaking, quasi-experiments include some type of intervention or treatment and they provide a comparison, but they lack the degree of control found in true experiments. Just as randomization is the hallmark of true experiments, so *lack of randomization* is the hallmark of quasi-experiments. As Campbell and Stanley (1966, p. 34) explain,

> there are many natural social settings in which the research person can introduce something like experimental design into [the] scheduling of data collection procedures (e.g., the when and to whom of measurement), even though [the researcher] lacks the full control over the scheduling of experimental stimuli (the when and to whom of exposure and the ability to randomize exposures) which makes a true experiment possible. Collectively, such situations can be regarded as quasi-experimental designs.

Quasi-experiments are recommended when true experiments are not feasible. Some knowledge about the effectiveness of a treatment is more desirable than none. The list of possible confounds provided by Campbell and Stanley (1966; Cook & Campbell, 1979), which we reviewed earlier, can be used as a checklist in deciding just how good that knowledge is. Moreover, although a particular experimental procedure may not control for one or more possible types of confounds, the investigator must be prepared to look for additional kinds of evidence that might rule out a confound that is not specifically controlled by an experimental procedure. For example, suppose that a quasi-experiment explicitly controls for only six of the eight major classes of confounds that are eliminated by a true experiment. It may be possible, on the basis of supplementary data or through evidence offered by a logical analysis of the situation, to rule out the remaining two classes of explanations as implausible. In this case a strong argument can be made for the internal validity of the research design, even though a true experiment was not performed. What is important is that the researcher recognize the specific shortcomings of quasi-experimental procedures and be prepared to address these shortcomings through whatever evidence or logic is available.

With full knowledge of their limitations, then, we present the following information about specific quasi-experimental designs so that you will understand the routes remaining open to an investigator when the path to a true experiment is hopelessly blocked. At the same time, this presentation should help you appreciate the clarity of inference provided by the true experiment. Following a discussion of specific quasi-experimental designs, we look at an alternative to quasi-experimentation—the extension of single-case experimentation to research in natural settings. You may also want to refer to the previous discussion of obstacles to true experiments in natural settings. *The difference between the power of the true experiment and that of the quasi-experiment is such that, before facing the problems of interpretation that result from quasi-experimental procedures, the researcher should make every effort possible to approximate the conditions of a true experiment.*

Perhaps the most serious limitation on experimentation in natural settings is that the experimenter is frequently unable to assign participants randomly to conditions. This occurs, for instance, when an intact group is singled out for treatment and when administrative decisions or practical considerations prevent randomly assigning participants. Children in one classroom or school and workers at a particular plant are examples of groups that might be treated in the absence of any random assignment of individuals to conditions. If we assume that behavior of a group is measured both before and after treatment, such an "experiment" can be described as follows:

$$O_1 \times O_2$$

where $O_1$ refers to the first observation of a group, or pretest, $\times$ indicates a treatment, and $O_2$ refers to the second observation, or posttest.

Campbell and Stanley (1966) call this particular design the "one-group pretest-posttest design." Although it is sometimes used in psychological research, the design has very little internal validity. You should be able to see, for instance, that this design does not control for many factors that can threaten the internal validity of a study. For example, should a difference between pretest and posttest measures be found, how do we know that this difference was not due to some event other than the treatment (*history threat*), that it was not due to the fact that participants benefited from initial testing (*testing threat*), or that it didn't occur simply because the group of participants changed over time (*maturation threat*)? This particular design has so little going for it in terms of allowing cause-and-effect inferences that it is sometimes referred to as a "preexperimental design," or one that serves as a "bad experiment" to illustrate possible confounds (see Campbell & Stanley, 1966).

## The Nonequivalent Control Group Design

- In the nonequivalent control group design, a treatment group and a comparison group are compared using pretest and posttest measures.
- If the two groups are similar in their pretest scores prior to treatment but differ in their posttest scores following treatment, researchers can more confidently make a claim about the effect of treatment.
- Threats to internal validity due to history, maturation, testing, instrumentation, and regression can be eliminated in a nonequivalent control group design.

The one-group pretest-posttest design can be modified to create a quasi-experimental design with greatly superior internal validity if two conditions are met: (1) there exists a group "like" the treatment group that can serve as a comparison group and (2) there is an opportunity to obtain pretest and posttest measures from individuals in *both* the treatment and the comparison groups. Because a comparison group is selected on bases other than random assignment, it cannot be assumed that individuals in the treatment and control groups are equivalent on all important characteristics (a selection threat arises). Therefore it is essential that a pretest be given to both groups to assess their similarity on the dependent measure. Campbell and Stanley (1966) call this quasi-experimental procedure a **nonequivalent control group design.** It can be outlined as follows:

$$O_1 \times O_2$$
$$\text{-----------}$$
$$O_1 \quad O_2$$

The dashed line indicates that the treatment and comparison groups were not formed by assigning participants randomly to conditions.

By adding a comparison group, threats to internal validity due to history, maturation, testing, instrumentation, and regression may be eliminated. A brief look at the logic of experimental design will help show why this occurs. We wish to begin a study with two similar groups; then one group receives the treatment and the other does not. If the two groups' posttest scores differ following treatment, we first must rule out alternative explanations before we can claim that treatment caused the difference. If the groups are truly comparable, and both groups have similar experiences, then we can assume that history, maturation, testing, instrumentation, and regression effects occur to *both* groups equally. Thus, we may assume that both groups change naturally at the same rate (maturation), experience the same effect of multiple testing, or are exposed to the same external events (history). If these effects are experienced in the *same* way by both groups, they cannot possibly be used to account for group *differences* on posttest measures. Therefore, they no longer are threats to internal validity. Thus, researchers can gain a tremendous advantage in their ability to make causal claims simply by adding a comparison group. However, these causal claims also depend on forming comparable groups at the start of the study, which then have comparable experiences, except for the treatment. Because this is difficult to realize in practice, as we'll see, threats to internal validity due to interactions with selection typically are not eliminated in this design.

A nonequivalent control group design was used by Morier and Keeports (1994) to assess the effectiveness of a college course designed to introduce students to the scientific method and to the "faulty, and often fraudulent, methods of pseudosciences" (p. 443). We referred to this situation and experiment earlier when we discussed the problems of control often found in natural settings. The situation met the requirements we just outlined for a nonequivalent control group design. There existed a group "like" the treatment group and it was possible to obtain both pretest and posttest measures from both groups. The investigators chose students enrolled in a "Psychology and Law" course at the same college to serve as a comparison group. Both courses were seminars and enrolled primarily nonscience majors. Students completed a questionnaire designed to measure belief in paranormal phenomena at the beginning of their respective courses and at the end. Although the two groups of students did not differ in their beliefs at the beginning of the courses, at the end of the semester the students in the "Science and Pseudoscience" course (the treatment group) scored significantly lower in their beliefs about paranormal phenomena than did the students in the "Psychology and Law" course (the comparison group). The researchers suggested that the course worked to reduce belief in paranormal phenomena because it explicitly confronted claims of the pseudosciences in the classroom.

As you approach the end of a course on research methods in psychology, you might appreciate learning about the results of another quasi-experimental study. This one examined the effect of taking a research methods course on reasoning about real-life events (VanderStoep & Shaughnessy, 1997), and it, too, used a nonequivalent control group design. Students enrolled in two sections of a research methods course (and who just happened to be using an edition of this textbook!) were compared with students in two sections of a developmental psychology course on their performance on a test emphasizing methodological reasoning about everyday events. Students in both kinds of classes were administered tests at the beginning and at the end of the semester. Results revealed that research methods students showed greater improvement than did students in the control group. Taking a research methods course improved students' ability to think critically about real-life events.

With that bit of encouraging news in mind, let us now examine in detail another study using a nonequivalent control group design. This will give us the opportunity to review both the specific strengths and weaknesses of this quasi-experimental procedure.

## Nonequivalent Control Group Design: The Langer and Rodin Study

- Quasi-experiments often assess the overall effectiveness of a treatment that has many components; follow-up research may then determine which components are critical for achieving the treatment effect.

Langer and Rodin (1976) hypothesized that environmental changes associated with old age contribute, in part, to feelings of loss, inadequacy, and low self-esteem among the elderly. Of particular importance is the change that occurs when elderly persons move into a nursing home. Although they usually care for the elderly quite adequately in physical terms, nursing homes often provide what Langer and Rodin call a "virtually decision-free" environment. The elderly are no longer called on to make even the simplest decisions, such as what time to get up, whom to visit, what movie to watch, and the like. In a nursing home, many or most of these everyday decisions are made for the elderly, leaving them with little personal responsibility and choice.

To test the hypothesis that the lack of opportunity to make personal decisions contributes to the psychological and even the physical debilitation sometimes seen in the elderly, Langer and Rodin carried out a quasi-experiment in a Connecticut nursing home. The independent variable was the type of communication given to two groups of nursing-home residents. One group was given a communication stressing the many decisions that the patients needed to make regarding how their rooms were arranged, visiting, care of plants, movie selection, and so forth. These residents were also given a small plant as a gift (if they decided to accept it) and told to take care of it as they wished. This was the *responsibility-induced condition*. The second group of residents, the comparison group, was also called together for a meeting, but the communication given to this group stressed the staff's responsibility for them. These residents also received a plant as a gift (whether they chose to have one or not) and were told that the nurses would water and care for the plants for them.

Residents of the nursing home had been assigned to a particular floor and room on the basis of availability, and some residents had been there for a long time. As a consequence, randomly assigning residents to the two communication groups was impractical—and probably undesirable from the administration's point of view. Therefore the two communications were given to residents on two different floors of the nursing home. These floors were chosen, in the words of

**FIGURE 10.2**    Langer and Rodin (1976) used a nonequivalent control group design to study the effect of two different types of communication on the behavior of nursing-home residents. A major difference in the two types of communication involved the offer, and subsequent care, of a small plant (see text).

the authors, "because of similarity in the residents' physical and psychological health and prior socioeconomic status, as determined from evaluations made by the home's director, head nurses, and social worker" (Langer & Rodin, p. 193). The floors were randomly assigned to one of the two treatments. In addition, questionnaires were given to residents 1 week before and 3 weeks after the communications. The questionnaires contained items that related to "how much control they felt over general events in their lives and how happy and active they felt" (p. 194). Furthermore, staff members on each floor were asked to rate the residents, before and after the experimental communications, on such traits as alertness, sociability, and activity. The investigators also included a clever posttest measure of social interest by holding a competition that asked participants to guess the number of jelly beans in a large jar. Residents entered the contest if they wished by simply filling out a piece of paper giving their estimate and name. Thus, there were a number of dependent variables to assess the residents' perceptions of control, happiness, activity, interest level, and so forth.

The Langer and Rodin study nicely illustrates the procedures of a nonequivalent control group design. Moreover, differences between pretest and posttest measures showed that the residents in the responsibility-induced group were generally happier, more active, and more alert following the treatment than were residents in the comparison group. Behavioral measures such as frequency of movie attendance also favored the responsibility-induced group, and, although 10 residents from this group entered the jelly-bean contest, only 1 resident from the comparison group participated! The investigators point to possible practical implications of these findings. Specifically, they suggest that some of the negative consequences of aging can be reduced or reversed by giving the aged the opportunity to make personal decisions and to feel competent.

Before turning to the specific weaknesses associated with this design, let us call your attention to another feature of the Langer and Rodin study, one that characterizes many experiments in natural settings. The treatment in the Langer and Rodin study actually had several components. For example, residents were encouraged by the staff to make decisions about a number of different things (e.g., movies, rooms, etc.) and they were offered a plant to take care of. The experiment evaluated, however, the treatment "package." That is, the effectiveness of the overall treatment was assessed and not individual components of the treatment. We only know (or at least we assume based on the evidence) that the treatment with all its components worked; we don't necessarily know whether the treatment would work with fewer components or whether one component is more critical than the other. In the same vein, consider the results of the course confronting the claims of pseudosciences that we mentioned earlier (Morier & Keeports, 1994). There, too, investigators obtained evidence for the effectiveness of the treatment (the college course). Again, however, there were many components to the treatment: examples of legitimate scientific methods, introduction to logical fallacies and aspects of critical thinking, exposure to instructors skeptical of these claims, guest lecturers (including a magician posing as a psychic who then revealed himself as a fake). Again, the results of the experiment do not tell us about the effectiveness of these individual components.

Research in natural settings is often characterized by treatments with many components. Moreover, the initial goal of such research is often to assess the overall effect of the treatment "package." Finding evidence for an overall treatment effect, therefore, may be only the first stage in a research program if we want to identify the critical elements of a treatment. There may be practical as well as theoretical benefits to such identification. On practical grounds, should research reveal that only some of the treatment's features are critical to the effect, then perhaps the less critical features could be dropped. This may make the treatment more cost effective and more likely to be adopted and carried out. From a theoretical standpoint, it is important to determine whether components of the treatment specified by the theory as being critical are, indeed, the critical components. When you hear about research showing an overall treatment effect you might think about how additional research could reveal what specific components are critical to the treatment's effect.

## Sources of Invalidity in the Nonequivalent Control Group Design

- To interpret the findings in quasi-experimental designs, researchers examine the study to determine if any threats to internal validity are present.
- The threats to internal validity that must be considered when using the nonequivalent control group design include interactions with selection, differential regression, observer bias, contamination, and Hawthorne effects.

- Although groups may be comparable on a pretest measure, this does not ensure that the groups are comparable in all possible ways that are relevant to the study outcome.

According to Cook and Campbell (1979), the nonequivalent control group design generally controls for all major classes of potential threats to internal validity except those due to interactions of (1) selection and maturation, (2) selection and history, (3) selection and instrumentation, and (4) those due to differential statistical regression. We will explore how each of these potential sources of invalidity might pose problems in an effort to interpret the results of the Langer and Rodin study. Then we will explain what evidence or argument the authors offered in defense of their interpretation, which was that the differential responsibility-induced communication *caused* the differences in posttest behavior between the two groups of residents. We will also examine how experimenter bias and problems of contamination were controlled, and we will comment briefly on problems of external validity inherent in the nonequivalent control group design.

First, it should be mentioned that Langer and Rodin found that the residents in the two experimental groups did not differ significantly on the pretest measures. Because the residents were not randomly assigned to conditions, it might not have been surprising to find a difference between the two groups before the treatment was introduced. Moreover, it is important to recognize that, even when pretest scores show no difference between groups, as Langer and Rodin reported, one cannot assume that the groups are "equivalent" (Campbell & Stanley, 1966). Why this is so will become apparent in the discussion that follows.

Interaction Between Selection and Maturation   An interaction between selection and maturation occurs when individuals in one group grow more experienced, more tired, or more bored at a faster rate than individuals in another group (Cook & Campbell, 1979). Campbell and Stanley (1966) illustrate this problem by describing a nonequivalent control group design using psychotherapy patients as a treatment group and individuals not in therapy as a comparison group. The psychotherapy patients would normally be expected to show some improvement without the treatment (called spontaneous remission), a change that could be falsely interpreted (given no change in the comparison group) as a treatment effect. Whenever the treatment group consists of individuals who are brighter or more competent than those in the comparison group, differences in rate of maturation may be a confounding factor.

An interaction of selection and maturation is more likely to be an actual source of invalidity (as are other sources) when the treatment group is self-selected (the members deliberately sought out exposure to the treatment) and when the comparison group is from a different population from the treatment group (Campbell & Stanley, 1966). This occurs when a particular group is singled out for treatment in order to determine whether behavior will improve as a function of the treatment. The example of psychotherapy patients who are compared with individuals not in therapy, which was mentioned earlier, is an example.

Before examining whether a selection and maturation interaction poses a problem for the Langer and Rodin study, we need to call your attention to another aspect of this issue. It is important to emphasize that, even when *pretest* scores are the same on the average for the treatment and control groups, we cannot conclude the groups are equivalent (comparable). This is true for two reasons. First, the pretest is likely to measure respondents on only one measure, or at best on a few measures. The mere fact that individuals do not differ on one measure does not mean they don't differ on other measures that are relevant to their behavior in this situation. Second, the natural growth rate of two groups from different populations might be different, but the pretest may have been taken at a time when both groups happened to be about the same. This problem is illustrated in Figure 10.3. The normal rate of change is greater in Group A than in Group B, but the pretest is likely to show that the groups do not differ. On the other hand, and again because of the differential growth rate, the groups would probably show a difference at the posttest that could be mistaken for a treatment effect. Langer and Rodin selected their groups (but not individuals) randomly from the same population of individuals. Consequently, their design more closely approaches a true experiment than it would if individuals in the two groups came from different populations (Campbell & Stanley, 1966), as would be the case if residents in a nursing home were compared with those attending a sheltered workshop program for the elderly.

Is there any reason to suspect an interaction of selection and maturation in the Langer and Rodin study? For instance, would residents on the treatment floor be expected to change naturally at a faster rate than patients on the no-treatment floor? Several kinds of evidence suggest that this would not be the case. First, the procedure of assigning residents to floors was basically random, and floors were selected randomly for treatment and no treatment. The authors also point out that various measures showed that the residents of the two floors were, on the average, equivalent in socioeconomic status and length of time at the nursing home. Finally, although it is not sufficient evidence in itself, residents on the two floors did not differ on the pretest measures. There is little in the Langer and Rodin study to suggest a confound due to an interaction of selection and maturation.

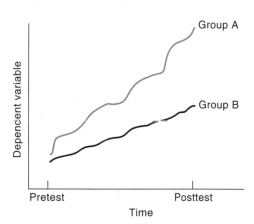

**FIGURE 10.3** Possible differential growth rates for two groups (A and B) in the absence of treatment.

Interaction Between Selection and History   Another type of confound that is not controlled in the nonequivalent control group design is the interaction between selection and history. Cook and Campbell (1979) refer to this problem as *local history effects*. This problem arises when an event other than the treatment affects one group and not the other. Local history, for example, could be a problem in the Langer and Rodin study if an event affecting the residents' happiness and alertness occurred on one floor of the nursing home but not on the other. You can probably imagine a number of possibilities. A change in nursing staff on one floor, for instance, might bring about either an increase or a decrease in residents' morale, depending on the nature of the change and the relationship between the behavior of a new nurse and that of an old one. Problems of local history become more problematic the more the locations or settings of the individuals in the treatment and comparison groups differ. Langer and Rodin do not specifically address the problem of local history.

Interaction Between Selection and Instrumentation   An interaction of selection and instrumentation occurs when changes in a measuring instrument are more likely to be detected in one group than they are in another. Floor or ceiling effects, for instance, could make it difficult to detect behavior change from pretest to posttest. If this is more of a problem in one group than in another, an interaction of selection and instrumentation is present. Cook and Campbell point out that this confound is likely to be more of a problem the greater the nonequivalence of the groups. Because Langer and Rodin's groups did not differ on the pretest, and because performance of the groups did not suggest floor or ceiling effects on the measurement scales that were used, this confound seems implausible in their study.

Differential Statistical Regression   Finally, the nonequivalent control group design does not control for differential statistical regression (Cook & Campbell, 1979). As was noted earlier, this is especially a problem when one group has been singled out for treatment because of its poor performance on some measure. Whenever individuals are selected on the basis of extreme scores (the poorest readers, the workers with the lowest productivity, the patients with the most severe problems), regression toward the mean is to be expected. Changes in behavior from pretest to posttest that are due to regression may be mistakenly interpreted as a treatment effect if regression is more likely in the treatment group than in the control group. Because the groups in the Langer and Rodin study came from the same population and there is no evidence that one group's pretest scores were more extreme than another's, a problem of differential statistical regression is not plausible in their study.

Observer Bias and Contamination   It is worthwhile to consider how Langer and Rodin handled problems of observer bias and possible effects of contamination and to inquire whether a Hawthorne effect was present. If observers in their study had been aware of the experimental hypothesis, it is possible that they might inadvertently have rated residents as being better after the experimental communication than before. However, all the observers were kept unaware of the experimental hypothesis. Thus, observer bias appears to have been controlled. Langer and Rodin were aware of possible contamination effects. Residents in the control group might have become demoralized if they learned that residents on another floor were given more opportunity to make decisions. In this case, the use of different floors of the nursing home was advantageous; Langer and Rodin indicate that "there was not a great deal of communication between floors" (1976, p. 193). Thus, if one accepts Langer and Rodin's argument, contamination effects do not seem to be present, at least on a scale that would destroy the internal validity of the study.

**Hawthorne Effect**   A Hawthorne effect would be present in the Langer and Rodin study if residents on the treatment floor interpreted the responsibility-inducing communication as a form of special attention. Such an interpretation might lead residents on the treated floor to feel better about themselves. The changes in behavior Langer and Rodin observed could then be attributed to a change in morale due to a Hawthorne effect as easily as to the opportunity to make decisions and assume personal responsibility that was available to residents in the treatment group. It is difficult to rule out completely a Hawthorne effect in this study. According to the authors, however, "there was no difference in the amount of attention paid to the two groups" (p. 194). In fact, communications to both groups stressed that the staff cared for them and wanted them "to be happy." Thus, without additional evidence to the contrary, we can conclude that the changes in behavior Langer and Rodin observed were due to the effect of the independent variable and not to the effect of an extraneous variable that the investigators failed to control.

What should be apparent at this point is that for an investigator to decide, in the context of a particular experiment, whether an independent variable "worked," he or she must be something of a detective. Evidence for and against the interpretation that the treatment actually caused behavior to change must be systematically (and sometimes ingeniously) collected and carefully weighed. As Cook and Campbell (1979, pp. 55–56) explain:

> Estimating the internal validity of a relationship is a deductive process in which the investigator has to systematically think through how each of the internal validity threats may have influenced the data. Then, the investigator has to examine the data to test which relevant threats can be ruled out. In all of this process, the researcher has to be his or her own best critic, trenchantly examining all of the threats he or she can imagine. When all of the threats can plausibly be eliminated, it is possible to make confident conclusions about whether a relationship is probably causal. When all of them cannot, perhaps because the appropriate data are not available or because the data indicate that a particular threat may indeed have operated, then the investigator has to conclude that a demonstrated relationship between two variables may or may not be causal.

## The Issue of External Validity

- Similar to internal validity, the external validity of research findings must be critically examined.
- The best evidence for the external validity of research findings is replication with different populations, settings, and times.

We must make the same systematic inquiry into the external validity of an experiment that we did into its internal validity. What evidence is there that the particular pattern of results is restricted to a particular group of participants, setting, or time? For example, although Langer and Rodin suggest that certain changes be made in the way the elderly are cared for, we might question whether the effectiveness of the responsibility-inducing communication would hold for all elderly residents, for all types of nursing homes, and at different times. That the particular nursing home selected by Langer and Rodin was described as "rated by the state of Connecticut as being among the finest care units" (1976, p. 193) suggests that the residents, facilities, and staff there would be different from those found in other facilities. For instance, if residents at this particular nursing home were relatively more independent before coming to the home than residents at other homes (perhaps because of differences in socioeconomic status), then the changes experienced upon moving into a home might have had greater impact on them. Consequently, the opportunity to be more independent of staff might be more important to these residents relative to residents in other homes. Similarly, if staff members at this home were more competent than those at other homes, they might be more effective in communicating the experimental communications than would the staff members at other homes.

As we indicated earlier, in the last analysis, the investigator must be ready to replicate an experimental finding under different conditions in order to establish external validity. The deductive process applied to questions of internal validity must also be used to examine a study's external validity. Moreover, *we must be ready to live with the fact that one experiment is not likely to answer all questions about an experimental hypothesis.*

## Interrupted Time-Series Designs

- In a simple interrupted time-series design, researchers examine a series of observations both before and after a treatment.
- Evidence for treatment effects occurs when there are abrupt changes (discontinuities) in the time series data at the time treatment was implemented.
- The major threats to internal validity in the simple interrupted time series design are history effects and changes in measurement (instrumentation) that occur at the same time as the treatment.

In situations in which we can observe changes in a dependent variable for some time before and after a treatment is introduced, another quasi-experiment is possible. It is called a **simple interrupted time-series design** (Cook &

Campbell, 1979). The essence of this design is the availability of periodic measures before and after a treatment has been introduced. It can be outlined in the following way:

$$O_1 O_2 O_3 O_4 O_5 \times O_6 O_7 O_8 O_9 O_{10}$$

Situations such as this may arise when a new product has been introduced, a new social reform instituted, or a special advertising campaign begun. Campbell's (1969) analysis of the effect on traffic fatalities of a crackdown on speeding ordered by the Connecticut governor made use of an interrupted time-series design. Because statistics related to traffic accidents are regularly kept by state agencies, a wealth of archival data was available to yield pretreatment and posttreatment measures. Besides number of fatalities, Campbell looked at number of speeding violations, number of drivers having their licenses suspended, and other measures related to driving behavior. Figure 10.4 shows the percentage of suspensions of licenses for speeding (as a percentage of all license suspensions) before and after the crackdown. There is a clear discontinuity in the time graph that provides evidence for an effect of the treatment. Indeed, the discontinuity in the time series is the major evidence of an effect.

As Campbell points out, only abrupt changes in the time graph can be evaluated because gradual changes are indistinguishable from normal fluctuations over time. Unfortunately, changes often are not nearly so dramatic as those seen in Figure 10.4. In fact, Campbell's analysis of traffic fatalities over the same time period, while revealing evidence of an effect of the crackdown, did not show as abrupt a change as that associated with suspension of drivers' licenses (see Campbell, 1969, Figure 2).

A more typical outcome of an interrupted time-series design is illustrated by the findings of Ross and White (1987), who examined the effect of newspaper

**FIGURE 10.4**  Suspensions of licenses for speeding, as a percentage of all suspensions. (From Campbell, 1969.)

publicity on subsequent crime rates. In June 1984, a metropolitan newspaper instituted a policy of publishing the court results of people convicted of shoplifting, impaired driving, or failure to take a Breathalyzer test. The published information identified the individual by name and also furnished details of the incident. For instance, in the case of shoplifting, the item that the individual attempted to shoplift and its value were also noted. Ross and White sought to assess the impact of this publication policy on the frequency of similar offenses. They obtained data from several police and government agencies detailing the incidence of these crimes over a time period beginning several years before the new policy was instituted and continuing for approximately 18 months after the new policy was implemented. The number of shoplifting offenses during this period is shown in Figure 10.5. Visual inspection, confirmed by the results of statistical analyses, revealed an effect of the publication policy on incidence of shoplifting. Interestingly, the policy showed no effect on the incidence of drinking and driving or refusing the Breathalyzer test. The investigators suggested that being associated with shoplifting carries a greater social stigma than does driving under the influence of alcohol.

**FIGURE 10.5**   Shoplifting offenses between January 1980 and December 1985. (From Ross & White, 1987.)

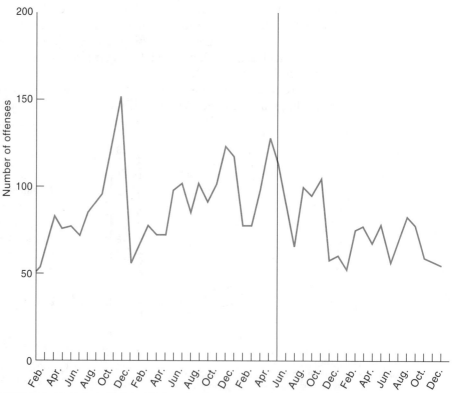

NOTE: Vertical line indicates start of publication policy.

Campbell and Stanley (1966) summarize the problem facing researchers using the simple interrupted time-series design: "The problem of internal validity boils down to the question of plausible competing hypotheses that offer likely alternate explanations of the shift in the time series other than the effect of $\times$" (p. 39). An effect of history is the main threat to internal validity in this type of design (Cook & Campbell, 1979). For instance, considering the results in Figure 10.5, is it possible that some factor other than newspaper publicity was responsible for the reduction in the frequency of shoplifting offenses?

Particularly threatening to the internal validity of the time-series design are influences of a cyclical nature, including seasonal variation (Cook & Campbell, 1979). For instance, when analyzing the effect of the Connecticut governor's crackdown on speeding, Campbell (1969) gathered data from neighboring states in order to rule out possible regional trends due to weather or the introduction of automotive safety features in order to strengthen his case for the effect of this particular social policy change.

Instrumentation must also be considered a threat to internal validity in the simple interrupted time-series design (Cook & Campbell, 1979). When new programs or new social policies are instituted, for example, there are often accompanying changes in the way records are kept or in the procedures used to collect information. A program intended to reduce crime may lead authorities to modify their definitions of particular crimes or to become more careful when observing and reporting criminal activities. Nevertheless, for an instrumentation threat to be plausible, it must be shown how changes in instrumentation could occur at exactly the time of the intervention (Campbell & Stanley, 1966). Ross and White (1987) showed that they were aware of possible influences due to instrumentation effects. They noted in their Method section that data collected more than 18 months after the newspaper's new policy went into effect were not comparable to prior data because the laws defining a shoplifting offense had been changed. Hence, data were collected only during the 18-month period immediately after the policy change.

Most other threats to internal validity are controlled in the simple interrupted time-series design. Problems of maturation, testing, and regression are pretty much eliminated by the presence of multiple observations both before and after treatment. None of these threats can be ruled out when only a single pretest and posttest measure is available, as in the single-group pretest-posttest design mentioned earlier. For example, an effect of maturation would not normally be expected to show a sharp discontinuity in the time series, although this might be possible in some situations (Campbell & Stanley, 1966). When only one pretest and one posttest observation are available, it is not possible to decide whether performance changes from pretest to posttest reflect a treatment effect or are simply due to maturational processes. The simple time-series design usually permits this decision to be made.

Threats to external validity in the simple interrupted time-series design must be examined carefully. It should be obvious that, if pretreatment observations of behavior are based on multiple tests, then an effect of the treatment may be restricted to those individuals who have had multiple test experiences. Moreover, because only a single group is generally tested, one that was not randomly selected, it is always possible that the results are limited to people with characteristics similar to those who took part in the experiment.

## Time Series with Nonequivalent Control Group

- In a time series with nonequivalent control group design, researchers make a series of observations before and after treatment for both a treatment group and a comparable comparison group.
- Archival data frequently provide the basis for time-series designs.

The interrupted time-series design can be enhanced greatly by including a control group. This procedure is identical to that followed in constructing a nonequivalent control group design, which we discussed previously. In this case the researcher must find a group that is comparable to the treatment group and that allows a similar opportunity for multiple observations before and after the time that the treatment is administered to the experimental group. This **time series with nonequivalent control group design** is outlined as follows:

$$\frac{O_1 O_2 O_3 O_4 O_5 \times O_6 O_7 O_8 O_9 O_{10}}{O_1 O_2 O_3 O_4 O_5 \quad O_6 O_7 O_8 O_9 O_{10}}$$

As before, a dashed line is used to indicate that the control group and the experimental group were not randomly assigned. This interrupted time series with nonequivalent control group permits one to control many threats due to history. As was mentioned earlier, Campbell (1969) used traffic fatality data obtained from neighboring states to provide a comparison with traffic fatality data following the crackdown on speeding in Connecticut. Although traffic fatalities in Connecticut showed a decline immediately following the crackdown, data from comparable states did not exhibit any such decline. This fact tends to rule out changes that might have been due to favorable weather conditions, improved automobile design, or other potentially positive factors.

Archival data, rather than direct observation, frequently provide the basis for time-series designs. For example, the extensive archival data in various fields of sport have furnished social psychologists with an opportunity to test the real-life implications of laboratory-based theories. In one study, researchers compiled statistics on baseball players who were traded in midseason to a new team (see Jackson, Buglione, & Glenwick, 1988). A quasi-experimental analysis revealed that the batting average of these players was higher when playing for the new club than for the old club, confirming a prediction made from a drive theory of social facilitation. The possibility that baseball players, regardless of whether they are traded, increase their batting average over the full-year season was ruled out as an alternative explanation for these findings by demonstrating that averages of a random sample of nontraded players did not show a similar rise.

A particularly good illustration of the interrupted time-series design is provided by McSweeney (1978), who analyzed the frequency of telephone calls asking for directory assistance following initiation of a charge for such calls. Directory assistance calls requesting information about phone numbers listed in standard directories cost the telephone company money, and they pay these expenses by charging more for other services. As McSweeney (1978) pointed out, an intervention that would effectively reduce the frequency of these unnecessary calls would benefit both the telephone company and the consumer.

In 1974, officials at Cincinnati Bell Telephone Company initiated charges for local directory assistance calls in excess of three per month. Subscribers were charged 20 cents for each additional call. Because the telephone company keeps extensive archival records, the effect of this intervention could be assessed using a time-series analysis. Furthermore, a simple time series could be expanded by seeking a comparison group. McSweeney chose to use as a control measure the long-distance directory assistance calls that were made from outside the Cincinnati area, for which no charge was made. Although the exact number of "participants" could not be known, it was estimated that the service charge for local directory assistance calls affected more than a million users. From data provided by Cincinnati Bell administrative records, McSweeney created the time-series graph shown in Figure 10.6. The frequency of local calls

**FIGURE 10.6**   Number of local and long-distance directory assistance calls placed per average business day before and after charges were introduced. (From McSweeney, 1978.)

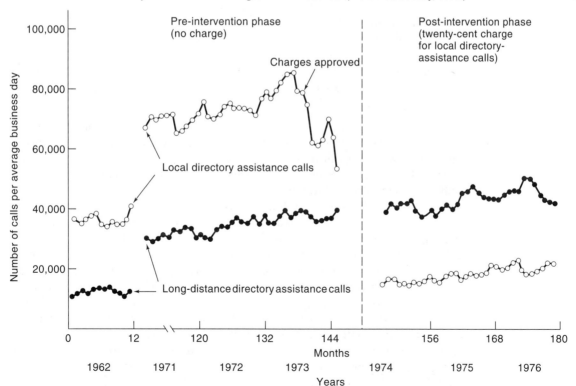

decreased dramatically after the charge was initiated; directory assistance calls from outside the area continued to increase gradually.

The time-series analysis revealed a small dip in frequency of local calls before the actual charges were levied. This was apparently in response to the announcement by telephone company officials of the upcoming cost to the user. McSweeney reasonably argued that this change was due to the fact that some individuals misunderstood the announcement in news reports and thought the charges were already being made. Others may simply have begun to change their calling habits in anticipation of the charges. The clear discontinuity in the time series associated with the treatment group, in conjunction with the absence of any decrease in calls by the comparison group, provides nearly incontrovertible evidence that the effect was due to the intervention made by the telephone company. A subsequent analysis showed that the decrease in local directory assistance calls resulted in an average savings of 65 cents on the telephone bill of each individual residential consumer.

## AN EXTENSION OF SINGLE-CASE DESIGNS TO RESEARCH IN NATURAL SETTINGS

### Rationale

- Both time-series designs and single-case experimental designs use observations before and after a treatment in order to make inferences about the effectiveness of the treatment.
- With both types of designs, researchers must consider history threats as a plausible alternative explanation for apparent treatment effects.
- Single-case experimental designs can be conducted as quasi-experiments when groups of individuals are tested using the ABAB design or multiple-baseline design.

You may have noticed a similarity between the simple time-series design and the single-case experimental designs discussed in Chapter 9. In both situations, observations made prior to a treatment represent a "baseline" that is compared with observations obtained after the treatment. If there is a clear discontinuity in the behavioral record following the application of a treatment, it is evidence for the effect of the treatment. Furthermore, for both types of design the major threat to internal validity is history. It is possible that some factor affecting the participants' behavior, other than the treatment, is responsible for the observed behavior change. However, the two types of design handle this threat differently.

When a simple time series is used, the investigator must search for historical factors (e.g., seasonal variation) that might explain a change in the behavioral record. The addition of a nonequivalent control group greatly enhances the internal validity of the time-series design but does not completely rule out a possible interaction with history or other threats, such as an interaction with instrumentation. Moreover, unless the discontinuity in the time-series record is abrupt and obvious, the investigator must consider the possibility that one of numerous subtle factors produced a change and must rely on sophisticated mathematical models to determine whether an effect is present (see, for example, McCain & McCleary, in Cook & Campbell, 1979). A single-case experimental design controls for effects due to history when changes in the behavioral record correspond systematically to the repeated introduction and withdrawal of an independent variable (as in an ABAB design) or to the staggered introduction of a treatment (as in a multiple-baseline design). Unless observed changes are very small, it may be possible to avoid using complex statistical procedures and to rely instead on visual inspection of the pattern of change associated with the sequential manipulation of a treatment.

Single-case experimental designs offer an alternative to quasi-experimental procedures when one is conducting research in natural settings (e.g., Horn & Heerboth, 1982). Although typically used to evaluate changes in a single participant, the single-case design strategy can be used for a group of individuals, such as a classroom singled out for treatment. Examples of single-case experimental designs using groups of participants are found in Chapter 9 (see, for instance, VanBiervliet et al., 1981). In some situations a *multiple-baseline design* can be employed (see Horn & Heerboth, 1982), as was done by Lyons and Ghezzi (1995) to evaluate the effect on the public's gambling behavior as a function of changes in state lottery games. Amount of dollars waged was measured in a multiple baseline "across states," Arizona and Oregon. To use an *ABAB design* the investigator must have control over the application and withdrawal of a treatment and an opportunity must be present for periodic observation both during no treatment (baseline) stages and during treatment stages. Clearly this is not always possible in natural settings.

Treatments are often initiated under the assumption that they will "work," and, unfortunately, their effects are often not evaluated. An energy conservation program, for example, is not likely to be applied, withdrawn, and then applied again in an attempt to measure its effectiveness. However, when control over the application and withdrawal of a treatment is feasible, a single-case ABAB design may be used to determine whether a treatment effect exists. The advantage to the researcher is a design whose internal validity is close to, if not the same as, that of a true experiment (see Horn & Heerboth, 1982). The following example illustrates the possibilities of using an ABAB design in natural settings.

## The ABAB Design

- When the ABAB design is used as a quasi-experiment, treatment is alternately introduced and withdrawn (baseline) for a group of individuals.
- The effect of treatment can be observed by comparing records for observations made during treatment and baseline periods.

Schnelle and his associates used a single-case methodology to evaluate the effect of police procedures on reducing crime rate (see, for example, Schnelle et al., 1978). In one study they sought evidence for the effect of a combined police car and helicopter patrol in reducing the frequency of home burglaries in a neighborhood of Nashville, Tennessee. The area was selected because police records showed it had a chronically high number of burglaries. (Even though this "group" was selected because it was extreme, do you see how the *chronic* nature of the burglaries neutralizes the problem of statistical regression?) The plan was to increase surveillance of the area by adding a helicopter patrol to the usual police car patrol. When the helicopter was used, the pilots were told to fly low enough to observe suspicious activity. Pilots were in radio contact with the police in the patrol car. The helicopter was flown between 9 A.M. and 5 P.M. (weather permitting), a time that coincides with most home burglaries.

An ABAB procedure was used. Following a baseline observation of frequency of home burglaries in the experimental area, the helicopter was introduced for a period of time, then withdrawn, and then introduced again. The addition of the helicopter was an experimental program by the Nashville police, so the helicopter was again removed following the second treatment stage, providing an additional (and final) baseline period.

Figure 10.7 shows daily frequency of home burglaries during baseline and treatment periods. Visual inspection of the behavioral record clearly shows that the frequency of burglaries decreased when the helicopter was added to the police surveillance and increased when no helicopter was present. Interestingly, a check of police records showed no displacement of burglary activity to surrounding neighborhoods. That is, when the frequency of burglaries dropped in the experimental area, there was no corresponding rise in these types of crime in nearby neighborhoods, which served as a type of comparison group. Note that the dependent variable in this example is frequency based on a group of individuals—in this case, residents in an approximately 6-square-mile area. Except for this change in the way behavior is assessed, the design strategy is exactly the same as might be used with a single individual.

**FIGURE 10.7**    Daily frequency of home burglaries. Arrows indicate the days the helicopter was prevented from flying. (From Schnelle et al., 1978.)

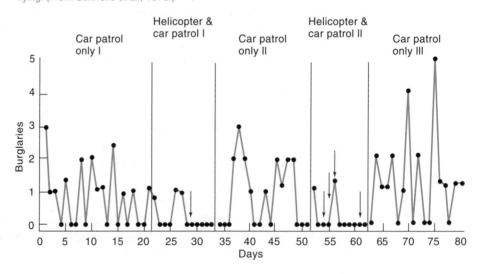

## PROGRAM EVALUATION

- Program evaluation is used to assess the effectiveness of human service organizations and provide feedback to administrators about their services.
- Program evaluators assess needs, process, outcome, and efficiency of social services.
- The relationship between basic research and applied research is reciprocal.
- Despite society's reluctance to use experiments, true experiments and quasi-experiments are the best approaches for evaluating social reforms.

Organizations that produce goods have a ready-made index of success. If a company is set up to make beach balls, its success is ultimately determined by its profits from the sale of beach balls. At least theoretically, the efficiency and effectiveness of the organization can be easily assessed by examining the company's financial ledgers. Increasingly, however, organizations of a different sort play a critical role in our society. Because these organizations typically provide services rather than goods, Posavac and Carey (1997) refer to them as *human service organizations*. For example, hospitals, schools, police departments, and government agencies provide a variety of services ranging from emergency room care to fire prevention inspections. Because profit making is not their goal, some other method must be found to distinguish between effective and ineffective agencies. One useful approach to assessing the effectiveness of human service organizations is the discipline of program evaluation.

Posavac and Carey (1997, p. 1) define **program evaluation** as a

> "collection of methods, skills, and sensitivities necessary to determine whether a human service is needed and likely to be used, whether it is sufficiently intense to meet the unmet need identified, whether the service is offered as planned, and whether the human service actually does help people in need without undesirable side effects."

You should see that there are several components in their definition, and we will take up each of these components in turn. However, before doing so, we wish to note, as these authors emphasize, that the basic goal of program evaluation is *providing feedback regarding human service activities*. Program evaluations are designed to provide feedback to the administrators of human service organizations in order to help them decide what services to provide to whom and how to provide them most effectively and efficiently. Program evaluation represents a hybrid discipline that draws on political science, sociology, economics, education, and psychology. We discuss program evaluation at the end of this chapter on research in natural settings because it represents perhaps the most large-scale application of the principles and methods we have been describing throughout this book.

According to Posavac and Carey (1997), the questions asked by program evaluators are about needs, process, outcome, and efficiency.

An assessment of *needs* seeks to determine the unmet needs of the people for whom an agency might provide a service. If a city government were to consider instituting a program of recreational activities for senior citizens in the community, for example, it would first want to determine whether senior citizens actually need or want such a program and, if they do, what kind of program would be most attractive to them. The methods of survey research are used extensively in studies designed to assess needs. Information obtained in this type of program evaluation is also used to help program planning.

Once a program has been set up, program evaluators may ask about the process that has been established. Programs are not always implemented the way they were planned, and it is essential to know what actually *is* being done when a program is implemented. If the planned activities were not being used by the senior citizens in a recreational program designed specifically for them, it might suggest that the program was inadequately implemented. An evaluation that provides answers to questions about *process*, that is, about how a program is actually being carried out, permits administrators to make adjustments in the delivery of services in order to strengthen the existing program (Posavac & Carey, 1997). Observational methods may be employed in such evaluations.

An evaluation of *outcome* is just that; it asks whether the program has been effective in meeting its stated goals. For example, do senior citizens now have access to more recreational activities, and are they pleased with these activities? Are these particular activities preferred over other activities? The outcome of a community-watch program designed to curb neighborhood crime might be evaluated by assessing whether there were actual decreases in burglaries and assaults following the implementation of the program.

Evaluators might also ask about the *efficiency* of the program, that is, about its cost. Choices often have to be made among possible services that a government or other institution is capable of delivering. Information about how successful a program is (outcome evaluation) and information about the program's cost (efficiency evaluation) are necessary if we want to make informed decisions about continuing the program, how to improve it, whether to try an alternative program, or to cut back on the program's services. These evaluations may use both experimental and quasi-experimental methods for research in natural settings. An evaluator may, for example, use a nonequivalent control group design to assess the effectiveness of a school reform program by comparing students' performance in two different school districts, one with the reform program and one without. It is also possible to use archival data like those described in Chapter 5 to carry out evaluations examining outcome and efficiency. For example, examining police records in order to document the frequency of various crimes is one way to assess the effectiveness of a community-watch program.

Earlier in this chapter we described differences between basic and applied research. Program evaluation is perhaps the extreme case of applied research. The purpose of program evaluation is practical, not theoretical. Nevertheless, even in the context of blatantly practical goals, a case can be made for a reciprocal relationship between basic and applied research. Writing in the *International Journal of Psychology*, Salomon (1987) argues that each domain of research serves the other in an ongoing circular way. Specifically, basic research provides us with certain abstractions (e.g., scientifically based principles) that express certain regularities in nature. When these principles are examined in the complex and "dirty" world where they supposedly apply, new complexities are recognized and new hypotheses are called for. These new complexities are then tested and evaluated before being tried out again in the real world. Salomon's model is illustrated in Figure 10.8.

Salomon points to the work of Ellen Langer as a concrete example of this circular relationship. She identified a decline in elderly people's health once they entered nursing homes (see Langer, 1989; Langer & Rodin, 1976, described in this chapter). These naturalistic observations led her to develop a theory of mindfulness, which she has tested under controlled experimental conditions and which has implications for more general theories of cognitive development and of education (see, for example, Langer, 1989, 1997; Langer & Piper, 1987). The theory provides a guide for her applied work—designing new models of nursing homes. Tests of the practical effects of changes in the care given by nursing homes on the residents' health and well-being will undoubtedly lead to modifications of her theory of mindfulness.

Perhaps the greatest difference between basic research and program evaluation lies in the political and social realities surrounding program evaluation. Governments at both local and national levels regularly propose, plan, and execute various types of social reforms. Tax relief programs, work incentive programs, educational reforms, police reforms, and medical care for senior citizens are just a few of the types of social reform programs that a government might

**FIGURE 10.8** Model illustrating reciprocal relationship between basic and applied research. (From Salomon, 1987, p. 444.)

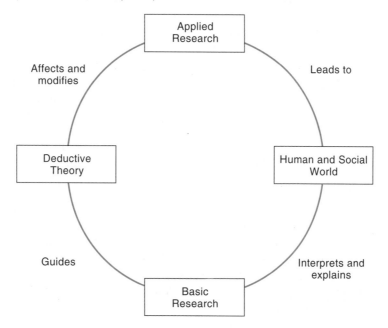

initiate. Unfortunately, as Donald Campbell (1969), a past president of the American Psychological Association, pointed out, the outcome of these social reforms often cannot be meaningfully evaluated. Did a change in police techniques lead to greater crime stoppage? Are more elderly people gaining access to public transportation after a reduction in fares? Does a work incentive program take more people off the unemployment rolls? The answers to such questions often cannot be found, said Campbell, because most social reforms are instituted in a political climate that is not ready for hardheaded evaluation. What public official, for instance, wants to be associated with a program that failed? As Campbell suggested, there is "safety under the cloak of ignorance" (pp. 409–410). Furthermore, many social reforms are begun under the assumption that they are certain to be successful. Otherwise why spend all that tax money? For many public administrators it is advantageous to leave that assumption in people's minds rather than face the truth about what happened.

Campbell (p. 409) put forth the argument that

> the United States and other modern nations should be ready for an experimental approach to social reform, an approach in which we try out new programs, in which we learn whether or not these programs are effective, and in which we retain, imitate, modify, or discard them on the basis of apparent effectiveness on the multiple imperfect criteria available.

Social scientists need to convince administrators to use true experiments, if at all possible, or quasi-experiments at the very least, when instituting new social programs. For example, a randomization procedure, perhaps based on public lottery, could be used to decide which group receives a pilot program or gains access to scarce resources. Groups not receiving the program or the available resources would become comparison groups. The effect of a social "treatment" could then be meaningfully evaluated. At present, decisions regarding who gets what are often influenced by particular interest groups—as the result of intense lobbying, for example—or made on the basis of political favoritism.

According to Campbell, the most significant change needed is for public officials to emphasize the importance of the problem rather than the importance of the solution. Instead of pushing for one certain cure-all (which, in most cases, has little opportunity for success), officials must be ready to execute reform in a manner that permits the clearest evaluation and must be prepared to try different solutions if the first one fails. Public officials must, in other words, be ready to use the experimental method to identify society's problems and to determine effective solutions.

Campbell's (1969) idea that social reforms and experimental methods be routinely brought together has had some impact on social policymakers, but it is still underutilized (see Berk et al., 1987). The reasons are some of the same ones initially identified by Campbell. Nevertheless, without social experimentation, especially that which makes use whenever possible of randomized field experiments, policymakers and the community at large may believe a treatment works when it doesn't or vice versa. Such incorrect decisions lead us to allocate money and resources to ineffective programs.

Not too many years ago, a show called "Scared Straight" was aired on national television. It described a juvenile education program implemented at Rahway State Prison in New Jersey. The program involved taking youthful offenders into a prison to meet with selected convicts from the inmate population. The goal was to inform juveniles about the reality of prison life and, thereby, the program leaders hoped, dissuade them from further illegal activity. Unsubstantiated claims were made for the effectiveness of the program, including some suggesting a success rate as high as 80% to 90% (see Locke, Johnson, Kirigin-Ramp, Atwater, & Gerrard, 1986). The Rahway program is just one of several similar programs around the country. But do these programs really work?

Several evaluation studies of the exposure-to-prison programs produced mixed results, including positive findings, findings of no difference between control and experimental participants, as well as results suggesting that the program may actually *increase* juvenile crime among some types of delinquents. There is a possibility that less hardened juvenile offenders may increase their criminal activity after meeting the prisoners. It has been suggested that because these less hardened offenders have recently begun a lifestyle wherein they are being recognized and reinforced by their peers for their toughness, this image is also reinforced by the tough image often projected by the prisoners. On the other hand, more frequent juvenile offenders, who have achieved a level of status among their peers for some period of time, may be more threatened by the prospects of prison life because it would mean loss of that status (see Locke et al., 1986).

Attempts to evaluate the effectiveness of this significant social program provide good examples of the difficulties inherent in evaluation research: the difficulty of randomly assigning participants, of getting administrators to cooperate with experimental procedures, and of dealing with loss of participants during the evaluation. Nevertheless, program evaluation based on sound experimental methodology offers policymakers at all levels (institution, community, city, state, federal) the information that can help them make more informed choices among possible treatments for social problems. Since resources inevitably are in short supply, it is critical that those that are available to help society be put to the best possible use.

Our hope is that your knowledge of research methods will allow you to participate knowledgeably and perhaps contribute constructively to the ongoing debate concerning the role of experimentation in society.

## SUMMARY

Experimentation in natural settings differs in many ways from experimentation in psychology laboratories. There are likely to be more problems in exerting experimental control in a natural setting, and establishing external validity or generalizing results is more often a key objective. The stated goals of the research and its possible consequences also differ when research is conducted in natural settings. Reasons for doing experiments in natural settings include testing the external validity of laboratory findings and assessing the effects of "treatments" aimed at improving conditions under which people work and live.

Campbell and others have argued that society must be willing to take an experimental approach to social reform—one that will allow the clearest evaluation of the effectiveness of new programs. In many situations (for instance, when available resources are scarce), true experiments involving randomization of individuals to treatment and no-treatment conditions are recommended. However, if a true experiment is not feasible, quasi-experimental procedures are the next best approach. Quasi-experiments differ from true experiments in that fewer plausible rival hypotheses for an experimental outcome are controlled. When specific threats to the internal validity of an experiment are not controlled, then the experimenter, by logically examining the situation and by collecting additional evidence, must seek to rule out these threats to internal validity.

A particularly strong quasi-experimental procedure is the nonequivalent control group design. This procedure generally controls for all major threats to internal validity except those associated with interactions of (1) selection and history, (2) selection and maturation, (3) selection and instrumentation, and (4) threats due to differential statistical regression. In addition to the major threats to internal validity, an experimenter must be sensitive to possible contamination resulting from communication between groups of participants. Problems of observer or experimenter bias, questions of external validity, and Hawthorne effects are potential problems in all experiments, whether conducted in the laboratory or in the field.

When it is possible to observe changes in a dependent measure before and after a treatment is administered, one can carry out a simple interrupted time-series design. The researcher using this design looks for an abrupt change in the time series that coincides with the introduction of the treatment. The major threat to internal validity in this design is history—some event other than the treatment may have been responsible for the change in the time series. Instrumentation also can be a problem, especially when the treatment represents a type of social reform that may lead to changes in the way records are kept or data collected. By including a control group that is as similar as possible to the experimental group, one can strengthen the internal validity of a simple time-series design. A time series with nonequivalent control group, for example, controls for many possible history threats.

In this chapter we also discussed how the logic and methodology associated with single-case experimental designs (see Chapter 9) can be applied to experimentation in natural settings. For instance, an ABAB design may be used when a researcher can control the application and withdrawal of a treatment. In such cases the internal validity of the experiment can approach that of a true experiment.

A particularly important goal of research in natural settings is program evaluation. Persons other than psychologists (such as educators, political scientists, and sociologists) are often involved in this process. Types of program evaluation include assessment of needs, process, outcome, and efficiency. Perhaps the most serious constraints on program evaluation are the political and social realities that surround it. The reluctance of public officials to seek an evaluation of social reforms is often an obstacle to be overcome. Nevertheless, social scientists have called on individuals who are knowledgeable about the procedures of program evaluation to make themselves available to those who are responsible for the delivery of human services. By answering this call, we may help change society in a way that will bring the most effective services to those most in need.

## KEY CONCEPTS

basic research
applied research
threats to internal validity
regression
contamination
Hawthorne effect
quasi-experiments

nonequivalent control group
  design
simple interrupted time-series
  design
time series with nonequivalent
  control group design
program evaluation

## REVIEW QUESTIONS

1  What special reasons are there for carrying out experiments in natural settings?
2  Explain how laboratory experiments and those in natural settings differ in control, external validity, goals, and consequences.
3  What are the three distinguishing characteristics of true experiments?
4  What obstacles arise in trying to carry out experiments in natural settings?
5  How can participants be randomly assigned to conditions while still giving all participants access to the experimental treatment?
6  How might participants in a control group respond when contamination occurs?
7  What do Cook and Campbell (1979) consider the best test of external validity?
8  Why is the use of a pretest critical in the nonequivalent control group design?
9  Cite one example of a threat to internal validity that is controlled in the nonequivalent control group design and two examples of threats that are not controlled.
10  Explain why we cannot conclude that the treatment and control groups in a nonequivalent control group design are equivalent even when the pretest scores are the same for both groups.
11  What is meant by a "local history effect" in the nonequivalent control group design?
12  What is the major evidence for an effect of the treatment in a simple interrupted time-series design?
13  Explain how the addition of a nonequivalent control group to a simple interrupted time-series design reduces the threat to the internal validity of the design.
14  How can single-case experimental designs be used to determine whether an effect is due to a treatment or to the threat to internal validity called *history?*
15  What are the four types of assessment typically addressed in program evaluation?

## CHALLENGE QUESTIONS

**1** A quasi-experiment was used to determine whether multi-media instruction is effective. Two sections of introductory psychology were taught by the same instructor. In one section (the treatment group) the instructor used multi-media instruction. In the other section the instructor covered the same material but did not use multi-media instruction. Students did not know when they registered for the course whether multi-media instruction would be used. The students were not randomly assigned to sections. Students' knowledge of the course material was assessed using two forms of a comprehensive introductory psychology test. The students in both sections were tested on the second day of class (the pretest) and at the final (the posttest) on different forms of the test. The comprehensive test can be considered a reliable and valid test that can be used to compare the effectiveness of the instruction in the two sections.

**A**  What quasi-experimental design is used in the study?

**B**  Comment critically on the fairness of random assignment if you were arguing in favor of doing a true experiment to test the effectiveness of multi-media instruction.

**C**  Identify and briefly describe one threat to the internal validity of this study if it had tested only the students who had received multi-media instruction.

**2** A psychologist published a book describing the effects of divorce on men, women, and children. She was interested in the effects of divorce that occurred 10 years after the divorce. She found that even 10 years after a divorce half of the women and one-third of the men were still intensely angry. Although half the men and women described themselves as happy, 25% of the women and 20% of the men remained unable to "get their lives back on track." In only 10% of the divorced families did both the former husbands and wives have happy, satisfying lives a decade later. Finally, more than half of the children of divorce entered adulthood as underachieving and self-deprecating men and women. These findings were based on a 15-year study of 60 divorced couples and their 131 children living in Marin County, California (an affluent suburban area including mostly well-educated people). Explain how the use of a quasi-experimental design would have been helpful in order to specify which of the reported results are due to the effects of divorce.

**3** The police force of a large city had to decide between two different approaches to keeping the officers on the force informed about the changes in laws. An enlightened administrator of this force decided to put the two approaches to test in a research study. She decided to use the random groups design and she assigned 30 officers randomly to each of the two programs for a period of 6 months. At the end of this time all the officers who successfully completed the training required under the two approaches were given a final test on their knowledge of the law. The 20 officers who completed Program A showed a reliably higher mean score on this test than did the 28 officers who completed Program B. The administrator wisely chose not to accept these results as decisive evidence of the effectiveness of the two programs. Using only the data reported in this problem, explain why she made this decision. Next, explain how her decision would have been different if 20 officers completed both programs (from the original 30 assigned to each) and there was still a sizable difference favoring Program A. Be sure to mention any limitations on the conclusions she could reach concerning the overall effectiveness of these programs.

4 A small undergraduate college with a new physical fitness center decided to introduce a health enhancement program for faculty and staff. The program is designed to take one semester to complete with three 1-hour sessions per week. Comment critically on each of the following questions regarding the evaluation of this program.

    **A** How might an evaluation of needs have played a role in planning the program?

    **B** What obstacles generally exist in real-world settings, and probably apply in this situation, that prevent the conduct of a true experiment to evaluate the outcome of the program? (Be sure to define the three characteristics of a true experiment.)

    **C** As an alternative to a true experiment, a nonequivalent control group design is proposed in which a group of faculty who did not participate in the program agree to take the performance tests before the program begins and after the program has ended. Explain why this nonequivalent control group design is superior to a pretest-posttest design in which only the program participants would be tested. State one threat to internal validity that is controlled in the nonequivalent control group design.

## Answer to Challenge Question 1

**A** The nonequivalent control group design was used in this study.

**B** Students may perceive random assignment to the two sections as unfair because they would not have a choice about which section they would take. If we do not know whether multi-media instruction is effective, however, then random assignment is the best and fairest method to determine whether multi-media instruction is effective.

**C** There are several threats to the internal validity of a pretest-posttest single group design. That is why it is referred to as a preexperimental design or a bad experiment. One possible threat in this study is maturation; that is, students are likely (we hope) to increase in knowledge of introductory psychology by the end of the course in which they are enrolled even if multi-media instruction had not been used. The nonequivalent control group design used in this study controls for this threat.

APPENDIX

A

# Data Analysis and Interpretation

## CHAPTER OUTLINE

# INTRODUCTION

The primary goal of data analysis is to determine whether our observations support a claim about behavior (Abelson, 1995). The claim may be that children of drug-addicted mothers exhibit more learning difficulties than those born to drug-free mothers, or that a program intended to prevent depression has worked. Whatever the claim, our case must be prepared with careful attention given to the quality of the evidence and to the way it is presented. When a quantitative research study is conducted, the evidence is primarily the numerical data we collected. To prepare a convincing argument, we need to know what to look for in these data, how to summarize that information, and how best to evaluate the information.

Data, of course, do not come out of thin air; we can assume results were obtained using a particular research methodology (e.g., observation, survey, experiment). If serious errors were made in the data collection stage, then there may be nothing we can do to "save" the data and it may be best to start again. Thus, we would like to assume that the data obtained for the analysis were generated after giving careful consideration to the statement of the research hypothesis (i.e., our tentative claim about behavior), the choice of a proper research design to test that hypothesis, selection of appropriate response measures, and assessment of statistical power. And, of course, we want to make sure that the data were collected in a manner that minimizes the contribution of demand characteristics, experimenter biases, confoundings, or other artifacts of the research situation. In short, we expect that a "good" research study was conducted, one that is internally and externally valid, sensitive, and reliable (see Chapter 6).

Consider what makes an experiment sensitive. A sensitive experiment is one that has a good chance of detecting the effect of an independent variable even if the effect is small. Several factors contribute to experimental sensitivity, including the number of extraneous variables held constant or balanced and the choice of research design. A concept related to experimental sensitivity is *statistical power* or the probability that we will reject a false null hypothesis. (Experimental sensitivity as well as the rationale and techniques associated with statistical power analysis were reviewed in Chapter 7.) Psychological research is frequently "underpowered." Too often research is done that has a high probability of missing a real effect; in other words, there is a high probability of making a Type II error (e.g., Cohen, 1990; Schmidt, 1996). *An assessment of the statistical power for your proposed study should always be part of a research plan.*

Power analysis begins by estimating the size of the effect you are seeking. This typically is done by calculating an effect size based on results of previous studies. We examine, in other words, the effect sizes other researchers obtained when studying the same or similar independent variables. Unfortunately, there is no one single measure of effect size used by researchers in all situations (see, for example, Kirk, 1996). One frequently reported measure of effect size, a standardized difference between means called *d*, was introduced in Chapter 6. Later in this appendix we discuss *d* as well as other popular measures of effect size.

Although power can be controlled in several different ways (see Chapter 7), the most common procedure is through adjustments of sample size. Consequently, once we estimate the size of the effect we are looking for (and choose an alpha level), we can consult "power tables," like the one at the end of this appendix, which identify the sample size needed to "see" (i.e., to obtain statistical significance for) that effect (see Tables A.5 and A.6). We will have more to say about power analyses later in this appendix.

## THE MULTIPLE STAGES OF DATA ANALYSIS

Trusting we have obtained data based on a sound research study with sufficient power, what should we do next?

There are three distinct stages of data analysis:

**I** *Getting to Know the Data:*  In the first stage we want to become familiar with the data. This is an exploratory or investigative stage (Tukey, 1977). We inspect the data carefully, get a feel for it, and even, as some have said, "make friends" with it (Hoaglin, Mosteller, & Tukey, 1991, p. 42). What is going on in this number set? Are there errors in the data? Do the data make sense or are there reasons for "suspecting fishiness" (Abelson, 1995, p. 78)? Visual displays of distributions of numbers are important at this stage. What do the data look like? Only when we have become familiar with the general features of the data, have checked for errors, and have assured ourselves that the data make sense, should we proceed to the second stage.

**II** *Summarizing the Data:*  In the second stage we seek to summarize the data in a meaningful way. The use of descriptive statistics and creation of graphical displays are important at this stage. How should the data be organized? Which ways of describing and summarizing the data are most informative? What happened in this study as a function of the factors of interest? What trends and patterns do we see? Which graphical display best reveals these trends and patterns? When the data are appropriately summarized, we are ready to move to the confirmation stage.

**III** *Confirming What the Data Tell Us:*  In the third stage we decide what the data tell us about behavior. Do the data provide confirmation of our tentative claim (research hypothesis) made at the beginning of the study? What *can* we claim based on the evidence? Sometimes we look for a categorical, yes-no, judgment, and act as judge and jury to render a verdict. Do we have evidence to convict? Yes or no: Is the effect real? At this stage we may use various statistical techniques to counter arguments that our results are simply "due to chance." Null-hypothesis testing, when appropriate, is performed at this stage of analysis. Our evaluation of the data, however, need not always lead us to a categorical judgment about the data (e.g., Schmidt, 1996). We don't, in other words, have to attempt a definitive statement about the "truth" of the results. Our claim about behavior may be based on an evaluation of the probable range of effect sizes for the variable of interest. What, in other words, is likely to happen when this variable is present? Confidence intervals are particularly recommended for this kind of evaluation (e.g., Cohen, 1995; Hunter, 1997; Loftus, 1996).

The confirmation process actually begins at the first or exploratory stage of data analysis, when we first get a feel for what our data are like. As we examine the general features of the data we start to appreciate what we found. In the summary stage we learn more about trends and patterns among the observations. This provides feedback that helps to confirm our hypotheses. The final step in data analysis is called the confirmation stage to emphasize that it is typically at this point when we come to a decision about what the data mean. Information obtained at each stage of data analysis, however, contributes to this confirmatory process (e.g., Tukey, 1977).

## THE ANALYSIS STORY

Making a convincing argument for a claim about behavior requires more than simply analyzing the data. A good argument requires a good story. A trial attorney, in order to win a case, must not only call a jury's attention to the facts of a case, but also must be able to weave those facts into a coherent and logical story. If the evidence points to the butler, then we want to know "why" the butler (and not the cook) might have done it. Abelson (1995, p. 13) makes a similar point regarding a research argument:

> High-quality evidence, embodying sizeable, well-articulated and general effects, is necessary for a statistical argument to have maximal persuasive impact, but it is not sufficient. Also vital are the attributes of the research story embodying the argument.

Consequently, when data analysis is completed, we must construct a coherent narrative that explains our findings, counters opposing interpretations, and justifies our conclusions. (Guidelines to help you construct an appropriate narrative to accompany your data analysis are found in Appendix C.)

## COMPUTER-ASSISTED DATA ANALYSIS

Today, most researchers have access to mainframe computers or microcomputers that include appropriate software to carry out the statistical analysis of data sets. This access to computers has led to a change in the approach taken to introduce students to statistical analysis. Stated simply, the availability of computer-assisted analyses has made knowing step-by-step computational procedures for complex analyses less important. Being able to set up and carry out an analysis using a statistical software package and being able to interpret the output have become essential skills that must be learned by researchers.

Carrying out statistical analyses using computer software requires two types of knowledge. First, the researcher must have a good knowledge of research design and statistics. Second, the researcher must be familiar with the requirements and capabilities of an appropriate statistical software package. Many software packages for statistical analysis are available for use both on mainframe computers and microcomputers. Some of the more popular ones are known by abbreviations like BMDP, SAS, SPSS, STATA, and SYSTAT. You may have access to one or more of these programs on the computers in your psychology department or at your campus computer center. Be sure to check with your instructor regarding the availability of these statistical packages on your campus. Should you decide to purchase a statistical software package for your personal computer, be sure to first obtain advice from an experienced researcher who is familiar with the characteristics of your computer and with the kinds of statistical analyses you want to perform.

In Chapters 6, 7, and 8 of this text we introduced various experimental designs and the logic of null-hypothesis testing and inferential statistics. This knowledge is essential if you wish to use computer-assisted analysis. A computer is not able to determine what research design you used or the rationale behind the use of that design (although some of the more user-friendly programs provide prompts to guide your thinking). To carry out computer-assisted data analysis, you must enter information such as the type of design that was used (e.g., random groups or repeated measures); the number of independent variables (e.g., single factor or multifactor); the number of levels of each independent variable; and the number of dependent variables and the level of measurement employed for each. You must also be able to articulate your research hypotheses and to plan appropriate statistical tests of your research hypotheses. For example, you should know what analytical comparisons you plan to do after performing an omnibus $F$-test. A computer will quickly and efficiently perform the computations necessary for obtaining descriptive and inferential statistics. To use the computer effectively as a research tool, however, you must give it specific directions regarding which inferential test you want it to do and which data are to be used in computing the test. Finally, when the computer has carried out the computations, you must be able to interpret correctly the output showing the results of the analysis.

## A RESEARCH EXAMPLE

How many words do you know? That is, what is the size of your vocabulary? You may have asked yourself this question as you prepared for college entrance exams such as the SAT or ACT, or perhaps it crossed your mind as you thought about preparing for professional school exams such as the LSAT or GRE, as all of these exams emphasize vocabulary knowledge. Surprisingly, estimating a person's vocabulary size is a complex task (e.g., Anglin, 1993; Lorge & Chall, 1963; Miller & Wakefield, 1993). Problems immediately arise, for instance, when we begin to think about what we mean by a "word." Is *play, played, playing,* one word or three? Are we interested in highly technical or scientific words, including six-syllable names of chemical compounds? What about made-up words, such as the name of your dog, Tootles, or the word you use to call your significant other? One rather straightforward approach is to ask how many words a person knows in a dictionary of the English language. But even here we run into difficulties because dictionaries vary in size and scope, and thus results will vary depending on the specific dictionary that was used to select a word sample. And, of course, estimates of vocabulary knowledge will vary depending on how knowledge is tested. Multiple-choice tests will reveal more knowledge than will tests requiring written definitions of words.

One of the authors of your textbook was interested in the question of vocabulary size and conducted a study examining the vocabulary size of college students and older adults (see Zechmeister, Chronis, Cull, D'Anna, & Healy, 1995). A stratified (by letter of the alphabet) random sample of 191 words was selected from a modest-sized dictionary of the English language. Then a multiple-choice test with five alternatives was prepared. The correct meaning of the word appeared along with four lures or distractors chosen to make discrimination of the correct meaning difficult. For example, respondents were asked to identify the meaning of the word *chivalry* among the following alternatives: a. *warfare,* b. *herb,* c. *bravery,* d. *lewdness,* e. *courtesy.* The random sample of dictionary words was presented in booklets to 26 college age students (mean age = 18.46) and 26 older adults (mean age = 76). On the basis of previous studies, the older adult group was expected to outperform the younger group on the test of vocabulary knowledge.

Data from this study of vocabulary size will be used to illustrate the three stages of data analysis.

## Stage 1. Getting to Know the Data

We want to begin by examining the general features of the data and edit or "clean" the data as necessary (Mosteller & Hoaglin, 1991). We check carefully for errors such as missing or impossible values (e.g., numbers outside the range of a given scale). Errors can arise because participants misuse a scale (e.g., by reversing the order of importance) or because someone entering data into a computer skips a number or transposes a digit. When typing a manuscript most of us rely on a "spellchecker" to catch our many typos and just plain misspellings. Unfortunately, there is no such device for detecting numerical errors that are entered into a computer. It is up to the researcher to make sure that data are clean prior to moving ahead.

Of particular importance is the detection of anomalies or what Abelson (1995) calls "klinkers." These are unusual or extreme values that don't appear to belong in the distribution of numbers. As we have seen, an anomaly sometimes signals an error in data recording, such as would be the case if the number 8 appears among data based on respondents' use of a 7-point scale, or if an IQ score of 10 was recorded in a sample of college student participants. Other anomalies are outliers. An *outlier* is an extreme number in an array; it just doesn't seem to "go with" the main body of data even though it may be within the realm of possible values. When doing a reaction-time study, for instance, where we expect most responses to be less than 1,500 ms, we might be surprised to see a reaction time of 4,000 ms. If nearly all of the other values in a large data set are less than 1,500, a value of 4,000 in the same data set certainly could be viewed as an outlier. Yet, such values are possible in reaction time studies when participants sneeze, absentmindedly look away from a display, or mistakenly think that data collection has halted and start to leave. A respondent completing a questionnaire may misread a question and submit a response that is far more extreme than any other response in our data set.

When anomalies appear in a data set we must decide whether they should be excluded from additional analyses. Those anomalies that clearly can be judged to be errors should be corrected or dropped from the data set, but, when doing so, a researcher must report their removal from the data analysis and explain, if possible, why the anomaly occurred. Consider a study by Haden (1998) which examined maternal styles of conversation with children. The researcher contacted 24 mothers who had one child about 70 months old and one child approximately 40 months old. The details of the study need not concern us except to note that homes of the participants were visited four times, with only a few days separating the experimental sessions. The researcher found that sessions three and four for one family were separated by 2 months instead of a few days. Scheduling difficulties with this family had caused the unintended longer interval between sessions. Further inspection during the initial data analysis stage revealed that this family's data consistently produced outliers. Haden (1998) decided not to include the data obtained from this family in further analyses and she explained in the "Participants" section of her published article the circumstances and rationale leading to her decision to exclude this family from her study.

In the first stage of data analysis we also want to look for ways to describe the distribution of scores meaningfully. What is the dispersion (variability) like? Are the data skewed or relatively normally distributed? One of the goals of this first stage of analysis is to determine whether the data require transformation prior to proceeding. Transforming data is a process of "re-expression" (Hoaglin, Mosteller, & Tukey, 1983). Examples of relatively simple transformations include those that express inches as feet, degrees Fahrenheit as Celsius, or number correct as percent correct. More sophisticated statistical transformations are also sometimes useful. (Information concerning the rationale and techniques for data transformation is found in many standard statistics textbooks. See also Emerson [1991].)

The best way to get a feel for a set of data is to construct a picture of it. An advantage of computer-aided data analysis is that we can quickly and easily plot data using various display options (e.g., frequency polygons, histograms) and just as easily incorporate changes of scale (e.g., inches to feet) to see how the data picture is altered. Minimally, by experimenting with different ways to visualize our data set we become more familiar with it. Which visual representation reveals the most about our data? What do we learn about our data when we compare plots with the axes defined differently? Is a polygon or histogram more informative? A picture is not only worth a proverbial 1,000 words, it also can quickly summarize 1,000 numbers. As we become more familiar with different pictures of our data, we learn that some pictures are better than others.

The data from the Zechmeister et al. (1995) vocabulary study represented the number of correct meanings identified out of a possible 191. Because participants without knowledge of the correct answer can be correct by chance on multiple-choice tests, a standard correction for guessing was applied to individual responses. However, two typographical errors appeared in the booklets given to the older adult group and so these items were deleted from further analysis. Also, examination of the test booklets revealed that several of the older participants omitted a page when working through the test booklet. Thus, the number of possible words was reduced for these individuals. Finally, the data were transformed to percentages to account for differences in the total number of possible responses among participants.

After cleaning the data set, the researchers obtained the following data in the first stage of the analysis. These data are expressed in terms of percentage correct multiple-choice performance for college students and older adults.

> **College** ($n$ = 26): 59, 31, 47, 43, 54, 42, 38, 44, 48, 57, 42, 48, 30, 41, 59, 23, 62, 27, 53, 51, 39, 38, 50, 58, 56, 45.
> **Elderly** ($n$ = 26): 70, 59, 68, 68, 57, 66, 78, 78, 64, 43, 53, 83, 74, 69, 59, 44, 73, 65, 32, 60, 54, 64, 82, 62, 62, 78.

A *stem-and-leaf display* is particularly useful for visualizing the general features of a data set and for detecting outliers (Tukey, 1977). A stem-and-leaf display obtains its name through the convention of using leading digits in a numerical array as "stems" and trailing digits as "leaves."

The following is a stem-and-leaf display for the college student data from our example vocabulary study:

|      |       |
|------|-------|
| 2*   | 3     |
| 2    | 7     |
| 3*   | 01    |
| 3    | 889   |
| 4*   | 12234 |
| 4    | 5788  |
| 5*   | 0134  |
| 5    | 67899 |
| 6*   | 2     |

The leading digits are the first or tens' digits (e.g., 2-, 3-, 4-,) and the trailing digits are just that, those that trail the leading or most significant digits; in this example the trailing digits are the units' or ones' digits (e.g., -5, -6, -8). The display is made by arranging the leading digits in a vertical array beginning with the smallest at the top. A leading digit is followed, in ascending order, by as many trailing digits as appear in the distribution. Each line in the display is a stem followed by its leaves (Tukey, 1977). For example, the stem 3 in the above display has three leaves, 8,8,9, indicating that the numbers 38, 38, and 39 appear in the distribution. By convention, when many numbers are displayed, or when the entire data set contains only a few leading digits, a leading digit followed by an asterisk is frequently used to indicate the first half of an interval (see Tukey, 1977). For example, 5* would be the stem for leaves 0,1,2,3, and 4 (i.e., numbers 50–54); the leading digit 5 (without the *) would be the stem for leaves 5,6,7,8,9 (i.e., numbers 55–59). In the above display, for instance, the stem 2* has one leaf, 3, and the stem 2 has one leaf, 7, corresponding to the numbers 23 and 27, respectively. Leading digits may also be greater than one. For example, if scores varied between 50 and 150, single leading digits would be used for number less than 100 (8-, 9-, etc.), and two leading digits for numbers greater than 100 (10-, 11-, 12-, etc.).

As you might see, a stem-and-leaf display is something of a histogram on its side. It has an advantage over a histogram, however, in that each value is displayed; thus, specific item information is not lost, as occurs when a histogram is formed using class intervals (Howell, 1997). The most important advantage of a stem-and-leaf display is that it can clearly reveal the shape of the distribution and the presence, if any, of outliers.

Look carefully at the stem-and-leaf display for the vocabulary data of the 26 college students. What do you see? Is the general shape of the distribution "normal" (i.e., symmetrical and "bell-shaped") or skewed (i.e., asymmetrical with scores trailing off in one direction)? Does there seem to be a lot of dispersion or do the numbers tend to "center" around a particular value? Are anomalous values present? We suggest that the stem-and-leaf display for these data reveals that the data are concentrated around the 40 and 50 percentages with the distribution somewhat negatively skewed (note how the "tail" trails off toward the low or negative end of the distribution). Outliers do not seem to be present (e.g., there are no single digit percentages or percentages beyond the 60s).

It can be particularly revealing to display two stem-and-leaf displays side-by-side when comparing two groups of data. Consider the display pictured below. The same stems are used with trailing digits in one distribution increasing from right to left (e.g., 997  5) and leaves in the other distribution ascending (on the same line) from left to right (e.g., 5  67899). This indicates that the first distribution had scores of 57, 59, and 59, and the second distribution had scores of 56, 57, 58, 59, and 59. Side-by-side stem-and-leaf displays might be meaningfully used, for instance, to compare responses to a questionnaire item when a researcher is comparing two groups that differ in socioeconomic status, age, gender, or in some other meaningful way.

A side-by-side stem-and-leaf display for the two conditions of the vocabulary study looks like this:

| Older Adults | | College Students |
|---:|:---:|:---|
|  | 2* | 3 |
|  | 2 | 7 |
| 2 | 3* | 01 |
|  | 3 | 889 |
| 43 | 4* | 12234 |
|  | 4 | 5788 |
| 43 | 5* | 0134 |
| 997 | 5 | 67899 |
| 44220 | 6* | 2 |
| 98865 | 6 |  |
| 430 | 7* |  |
| 888 | 7 |  |
| 32 | 8* |  |

Look at the display on the left, the one for the older participants. How would you characterize it? The data seem to be somewhat normally distributed, although an extreme score, an outlier, appears to be present. The "32" doesn't seem to belong with the rest of the data. (There are ways to operationalize outliers in terms of their distance from the middle of the distribution and some computer programs will do this automatically.) Without additional information about the nature of the respondent (e.g., amount of medication taken that day, or possible reading problems) the experimenters could find no reason to exclude this score from the study. The presence of this possible outlier necessarily increases the amount of variability present in this group relative to what it would be without this score. Nevertheless, we must acknowledge that some data sets are naturally going to be more variable than others. For example, the older adults in this study simply may represent a more heterogeneous group of individuals than those in the college student sample. (There is a moral here: Obtain as much relevant information about your participants as is conveniently possible at the time you collect data. An extreme score has to be treated as a true score unless you know the reason it is extreme is due to error or to circumstances unrelated to the study.)

Now look at what the side-by-side stem-and-leaf display reveals about both distributions. You should immediately see that scores in the groups overlap to some degree, but there are many more scores above 60 in the older group than in the college group. This "picture" of the data begins to confirm the idea that the older adults performed better overall than the college students on this test of vocabulary size.

Conclusion    In the first stage of data analysis—the process of getting to know our data—we should identify:

a  the nature and frequency of any errors in the data set, and, if errors were present, whether corrections could be made or data need to be dropped;

b  anomalous values, including outliers, and if they are present, what reasons there might be for the presence of these values and what should be done about them (retained or dropped);

c  the general features and shape of the distribution of numbers; and

d  alternate ways to more meaningfully express the data.

## Stage 2. Summarizing the Data

Data can be effectively summarized numerically, pictorially, or verbally. Good descriptions of data frequently use all three modes. In this appendix we will focus mainly on ways to summarize data numerically, that is, using descriptive statistics, although we do present some graphs. Information about drawing graphs to summarize data is also found in Appendix C. Verbal description of data also is a major topic of Appendix C (see especially guidelines for writing the results section of a research report).

The data from the vocabulary study will be summarized using measures of central tendency, dispersion, standard error of the mean, effect size, and power analysis.

Central Tendency   Measures of central tendency include the mean, median, and mode. These measures do just what their name implies: They indicate the score that the data tend to center around. The *mode* is the crudest measure of central tendency: It simply indicates the score in the frequency distribution that occurs most often. If two scores in the distribution occur with higher frequency than do other scores in the distribution, and if these two scores occur at different locations in the frequency distribution, this two-humped distribution is said to be *bimodal* (to have two modes).

The *median* is defined as the middle score in the frequency distribution. It is calculated by ranking all the scores from lowest to highest and identifying the value that splits the distribution into two halves, each half having the same number of values. The median is the best measure of central tendency when the distribution includes extreme scores because it is less influenced than is the mean by the extreme scores.

The *mean* is the most commonly reported measure of central tendency and is determined by dividing the sum of the scores by the number of scores contributing to that sum. The mean of a population is symbolized as $\mu$ (Greek letter mu); the mean of a sample is indicated by $M$ when reported in text, for example, in a results section. (The symbol $\overline{X}$ [read "X bar"] is typically used in statistical formulas.) The mean should always be reported as a measure of central tendency unless there are extreme scores in the distribution.

Measures of central tendency for the two groups in the vocabulary study are:

|  | College | Older Adult |
|---|---|---|
| Mean ($M$ or $\overline{X}$) | 45.58 | 64.04 |
| Median | 46.00 | 64.50 |
| Mode | 38,42,48,59 | 78 |

As you can see, the mean performance of the college group is much lower than the mean or average performance of the older adults. This confirms what we saw in the side-by-side stem-and-leaf display: The older group performed better overall on the average than did the college group. Note that the mean and median in each group are similar; thus, even though we identified an extreme score in the older sample when looking at the stem-and-leaf display, the presence of this score does not seem to have "thrown off" the mean as a measure of central tendency. There is more than one mode in the college data, each appearing twice; the most frequent score in the older group is 78, and it appeared only three times. As you can see, the mode is not particularly helpful in summarizing these small data sets.

Dispersion   Whenever you report a measure of central tendency, it should always be accompanied by an appropriate measure of dispersion (variability). Measures of central tendency indicate the center of a frequency distribution; measures of dispersion indicate the breadth or variability of the distribution.

The crudest measure of dispersion (the counterpart of the mode) is the range. The *range* is determined by subtracting the lowest score in the distribution from the highest score. For example, in a small distribution made up of the scores 1,3,5,7, the range would be equal to $7 - 1$, or 6.

The most commonly used measure of dispersion (the counterpart of the mean) is the standard deviation. The *standard deviation* tells you approximately how far on the average a score is from the mean. It is equal to the square root of the average squared deviations of scores in the distribution about the mean. The standard deviation is defined as:

$$\sqrt{\frac{\sum(X - \overline{X})^2}{n - 1}}$$

where:
$X$ = individual score
$\overline{X}$ = sample mean
$n$ = sample size
$\sum$ = "sum of"

For reasons that need not concern us here the average of the squared deviations about the mean involves division by $n - 1$ rather than $n$ so as to provide an unbiased estimate of the population standard deviation based on the sample. The standard deviation of a population is symbolized as $\sigma$ (Greek letter sigma); the standard deviation of a sample of scores is indicated as *SD* when appearing in text, but it is often symbolized as $s$ in statistical formulas. The variance, a measure of dispersion that is important in the calculation of various inferential statistics, is the square of the standard deviation, that is, $s^2$.

Measures of variability for the two vocabulary groups are:

|  | College | Older Adult |
|---|---|---|
| Range | 23–62 | 32–83 |
| Variance ($s^2$) | 109.45 | 150.44 |
| Standard Deviation (*SD* or *s*) | 10.46 | 12.27 |

Note that the stem-and-leaf display showed greater dispersion among the older adults; with the *SD* we have a number to reflect that observation.

Standard Error of the Mean   In doing inferential statistics, we use the sample mean as a point estimate of the population mean. That is, we use a single value ($\overline{X}$) to estimate (infer) the population mean ($\mu$). It is often helpful to be able to determine how much error there is in estimating $\mu$ on the basis of $\overline{X}$. The central limit theorem in mathematics tells us that if we draw an infinite number of samples of the same size and we compute $\overline{X}$ for each of these samples, the mean of these sample means ($\mu_{\overline{X}}$) will be equal to the population mean ($\mu$), and the standard deviation of the sample means ($\sigma_{\overline{X}}$) will be equal to the population standard deviation ($\sigma$) divided by the square root of the sample size ($\sqrt{n}$). The standard deviation of this theoretical sampling distribution of the mean is called the *standard error of the mean*. Typically, we do not know the standard deviation of this population so we estimate it on the basis of a sample using the formula:

$$s_{\overline{X}} = \frac{s}{\sqrt{n}}$$

Small values of $s_{\overline{X}}$ suggest that we have a good estimate of the population mean, and large values of $s_{\overline{X}}$ suggest that we have only a rough estimate of the population mean. The formula for the standard error of the mean indicates that our ability to estimate the population mean on the basis of a sample depends on the size of the sample (large samples lead to better estimates) and on the variability in the population from which the sample was drawn, as estimated by the sample standard deviation (the less variable the scores in a population, the better our estimate of the population mean will be). As we will show later, the standard error of the mean plays an important role in the construction of confidence intervals and is frequently displayed along with sample means in a figure summarizing results of a research study. It is symbolized as *SE* when reporting results in a research manuscript.

Effect Size   The concept of effect size was introduced in Chapter 6. Measures of effect size or what are more generally called measures of "effect magnitude" (see Kirk, 1996) are important because they provide information about the strength of the relationship between the independent variable and the dependent variable that is independent of sample size. In Chapter 6 we described an effect size measure called *d* which is useful when we have performed an experiment involving two groups. The measure *d* yields information about the size of the mean difference in standard deviation units. Expressing the mean difference in terms of the standard deviation permits effect sizes to be compared across studies using different units of measure. For example, an effect size from a study of vocabulary knowledge that compared college students and older adults on tests emphasizing discrimination of word meanings (i.e., multiple-choice tests) and an effect size from a study contrasting performance of two similar groups using recall of word definitions could be directly compared. Such comparisons form the bases of meta-analyses, which seek to summarize the effect of a particular independent variable across many different studies.

The effect size measure, *d*, defined as the difference between sample means divided by the common population standard deviation, is called Cohen's *d* after the late statistician Jacob Cohen (see Cohen, 1988, for more information about *d*).

$$\text{Cohen's } d = \frac{\overline{X}_1 - \overline{X}_2}{\sigma}$$

The population standard deviation ($\sigma$) is obtained by pooling the within group variability and dividing by the total number ($N$) of scores in both groups. A formula for the common *population* standard deviation using sample variances is:

$$\sigma = \sqrt{\frac{(n_1 - 1)s_1^2 + (n_2 - 1)s_2^2}{N}}$$

where:

$n_1$ = sample size of Group 1
$n_2$ = sample size of Group 2
$s_1^2$ = variance of Group 1
$s_2^2$ = variance of Group 2
$N = n_1 + n_2$

*Note:* Researchers define the standardized difference between means in slightly different ways (see, for example, Cohen, 1988; Kirk, 1996; Rosenthal, 1991). Dividing the pooled within group variability by $N - 2$ rather than $N$ in the above ratio produces a measure called Hedges's $g$ (Hedges, 1981). The denominator in Hedges's $g$, in other words, is the pooled *estimate* of the population standard deviation, which is equivalent to the square root of the mean square error in a between-group analysis of variance. As sample sizes increase, the difference between $d$ and $g$ decreases.

Fortunately there are equivalency formulas that permit easy translation from one definition of effect size to another (see Rosenthal & Rosnow, 1991). For example, Cohen's $d$ can be converted to Hedges's $g$ by the formula:

$$g = \frac{d}{\sqrt{\dfrac{N}{df}}}$$

where:

$N = n_1 + n_2$
$df = N - 2$

Inconsistencies in defining effects size based on a difference between means have led some researchers to suggest that an effect size using the correlation coefficient, $r$, be used (e.g., Rosenthal, 1991). Knowing $d$, we can obtain $r$ by the following:

$$r = \frac{d}{\sqrt{d^2 + 4}}$$

or directly from $t$, $r$ is defined as:

$$r = \sqrt{\frac{t^2}{(t^2 + df)}}$$

(see Rosenthal & Rosnow, 1991).

An advantage of $r$ is that it is interpreted in the same way that we interpret a linear correlation coefficient. When $r$ is used, small, medium, and large effect sizes correspond to .10, .30, and .50, respectively (Cohen, 1988).

Which measure of effect size to use is a decision left up to the investigator. But, given the differences in measures appearing in the psychology literature, *it is very important to identify in a research report precisely how a measure of effect size was calculated.*

An effect size for the vocabulary study using Cohen's *d* is:

$$d = \frac{\overline{X}_1 - \overline{X}_2}{\sigma} = \frac{64.04 - 45.58}{\sqrt{\dfrac{(26 - 1)(150.04) + (26 - 1)(109.45)}{52}}} = 1.65$$

To interpret the value of 1.65, we can use J. Cohen's (1992) classification of effect sizes of *d* = .20 for a small effect size, *d* = .50 for a medium effect size, and *d* = .80 for a large effect size. Because our value is larger than .80, we can conclude that the strength of the relationship between the independent and dependent variable is large. "Age," in other words, had a large effect on vocabulary knowledge.

Power Analysis    Knowing the effect size we can determine the statistical power of an analysis. Power, as you will recall, is the probability that a statistically significant effect will be obtained. Suppose that a previous study of vocabulary size contrasting younger and older adults produced an effect size of .50, a medium effect according to Cohen's (1988) rule of thumb. We can use the power tables created by Cohen (1988) to determine the number of participants needed in a test of mean differences to "see" an effect of size .50 with alpha = .05. (See Table A.5 at the end of this appendix.) The table identifies the power associated with various effect sizes as a function of sample size. Looking at the power table we see that the sample size (in *each* group) of a two group study would have to be about 64 to achieve power of .80 (for a two-tailed test). Looking for a medium effect size we would need a total of 128 participants to obtain statistical significance in 8 of 10 tries. Had Zechmeister et al. been looking for a medium effect, their vocabulary study would have been underpowered. As it turns out, anticipating a large effect size, a sample size of 26 was appropriate to obtain power = .80.

Conclusion    In the second, summary stage of data analysis, we should identify:

a  the central tendency (e.g., mean) of each condition or group in the study;
b  measures of dispersion (variability), such as the range and standard deviation, for each condition of the study;
c  the effect size for each of the major independent variables; and
d  how to best present pictorial summaries of the data (e.g., figure showing mean performance across conditions);

*Note:* Although a graph showing mean performance in the two groups of the vocabulary study could be drawn, a figure usually is not needed when only two group means are involved. Pictorial summaries become more important when summarizing the results of experiments with more than two groups.

## Stage 3. Confirming What the Data Tell Us

In the final stage of data analysis we evaluate the evidence for our claim about behavior. What, given these data, can we say about behavior? This stage is sometimes called confirmatory data analysis (e.g., Tukey, 1977). At this point we seek confirmation for what the data are telling us.

The traditional approach to confirmatory data analysis is null-hypothesis significance testing (NHST). It presently is the most common way of performing confirmatory data analysis. Nevertheless, criticisms of NHST have been persistent (e.g., Cohen, 1995; Loftus, 1991; 1996; Hunter, 1997; Schmidt, 1996), and for good reason. We psychologists have been misusing (and misinterpreting) it for decades, all the time ignoring warnings that we were doing so (e.g., Meehl, 1967). Some of the major misuses and misunderstandings associated with NHST were reviewed in Chapter 6. There are critics who suggest we discard NHST altogether (e.g., Hunter, 1997; Schmidt, 1996). Other experts, in what appears to be the majority view, suggest that we hang on to NHST but be cautious about its use (e.g., Abelson, 1995, 1997; Chow, 1988; Estes, 1997; Hagen, 1997; Muliak, Raju, & Harshman, 1997). Whatever the outcome of this debate within the psychology community, there is nearly universal agreement on the need (a) to understand exactly what it is that NHST can and cannot do, and (b) to increase our use of alternative methods of data analysis, especially the use of confidence intervals for effect sizes. Sometimes these alternative techniques will supplant NHST, at other times they will complement NHST.

The rationale both for NHST and for using confidence intervals was discussed in Chapter 6 and we strongly recommend that you review this information before proceeding. In what immediately follows we illustrate data analysis using traditional NHST, pointing out what we can and cannot say based on this form of data evaluation. Then, we will look at an evaluation of the same data based on an examination of confidence intervals for the effect size and contrast the information obtained from this evaluation with that provided by NHST. Finally, we will provide some recommendations for you to follow when evaluating evidence for a claim about behavior involving two means. The most common technique of confirmatory data analysis associated with studies involving more than two groups is the analysis of variance (ANOVA). The rationale for using an ANOVA and the interpretation of ANOVA results are discussed in the second half of this appendix.

## Confirmatory Analysis Using NHST

### Comparison Between Two Means

A $t$-test for independent groups was used to evaluate the difference between the mean percent multiple-choice performance of the college and older adult samples. We can define $t$ for independent groups as the difference between sample means divided by the standard error of the mean difference ($s_{\bar{X}_1-\bar{X}_2}$):

$$t = \frac{\bar{X}_1 - \bar{X}_2}{s_{\bar{X}_1-\bar{X}_2}} \qquad \text{where } s_{\bar{X}_1-\bar{X}_2} = \sqrt{\left[\frac{(n_1 - 1)s_1^2 + (n_2 - 1)s_2^2}{n_1 + n_2 - 2}\right]\left[\frac{1}{n_1} + \frac{1}{n_2}\right]}$$

The obtained *t* was 5.84. An alpha of .05 had been chosen prior to doing the analysis. Table A.3 shows critical values of *t* associated with various *df*. The obtained *t* of 5.84 is larger than the critical *t* value with 50 *df* (the *df* = N − 2) and, thus, the obtained *t* can be said to be statistically significant. Statistical software programs typically provide the actual probability of an obtained *t* as part of the output, thus circumventing the need to consult a table of *t* values. In fact, the *Publication Manual of the American Psychological Association* (1994) advises that the exact probability be reported. Thus, the result of the inferential statistics test can be summarized as follows:

$$t(50) = 5.84, p = .000.$$

(*Note:* When the exact probability is less than .001 [e.g., $p = .0004$], only the first three zeroes are reported.)

At this point it is important to understand what we learned using NHST and what we didn't learn. Some of the information presented below is also found in Chapter 6; other information may well be new to you. Examine each of the following statements closely and decide if the statement is warranted given the results of NHST reported above. To get feedback about your knowledge regarding the subtleties of NHST we suggest that you mark each statement true or false before reading the discussion that follows.

Based on the above results ($p = .000$), are the following statements true or false?

**1** The null hypothesis has a very low probability of being true. (That is, we can safely assume there is little chance, if any, that the difference between the population means equals zero.)

In many ways this is what we would like to say, but we can't (e.g., Cohen, 1995). The results of NHST tell us what the likelihood is of a difference of at least this size given that the null hypothesis of zero difference between means is assumed to be true. IF the null hypothesis is true and we obtain a result with $p < .05$ then we may conclude that the sample mean difference we obtained is an unlikely event given this assumption. This can be useful information (e.g., Abelson, 1997). Nevertheless, as we emphasized in Chapter 6, NHST tests our research hypothesis indirectly. We begin by assuming that the null hypothesis is true; the data do not tell us its probability of being true. Correct answer: False. *Bottom line:* Be careful when you claim what the outcome of NHST is really telling you.

**2** The results provide evidence of a scientifically important finding.

Statistical significance does not indicate the scientific importance of a study. Whether the results of a study are important to the scientific community will depend on the nature of the variable under study (the effects of some variables are simply more important than those of others), how sound is the study (statistically significant findings are easily produced by poorly done studies), and other criteria such as effect size (see, for example, Abelson, 1995). Correct answer: False. *Bottom line:* Statistical significance is not the same as scientific significance.

**3** The results are of practical importance. (For example, we might recommend that older adults rather than college students be hired in jobs requiring good vocabulary knowledge.)

The practical or clinical significance of a treatment effect depends on the external validity associated with the study, the size of the effect, and various practical considerations (including financial ones) associated with a treatment's implementation. A very large effect might be obtained as a part of a study that does not generalize well from the laboratory to the real world (i.e., has low external validity); thus, the results may be of little value to the applied psychologist. It is also possible that, given enough power, a small effect size will be statistically significant. Small effect sizes may not be practically important outside the laboratory. As you saw in Chapter 6, external validity is an empirical question. It is important to conduct a study under conditions similar to those in which the treatment will be used in order to see whether a finding is practically significant. We are not likely to carry out such an empirical test, however, if the effect size is small (although see Rosenthal [1990] and Prentice and Miller [1992] for some important exceptions). Finally, even a relatively large treatment effect might generalize well to real-world settings but never be applied because it is too costly, too difficult to implement, too controversial, or too similar in its effects to existing treatments. Correct answer: False. *Bottom line:* Remember that statistical significance (or effect size) is not the same as practical or clinical significance.

**4** The smaller the $p$ value, the larger the effect of the independent variable. (For example, because the actual probability of obtaining an effect in our example study was less than .001 we can assume that the magnitude of the effect is actually greater than if the probability had been .04.)

The $p$ value does not tell you about effect size (see, for example, Muliak et al., 1997; Schmidt, 1996). Not being aware of this fact, researchers sometimes (incorrectly) believe that a result significant at $p = .01$ level is more important (i.e., the effect is "greater") than a result significant "only" at $p = .05$ level. Thus, when reporting results, researchers have been known to say such things as "the difference is highly significant, $p < .001$" (see Schmidt, 1996, p. 125). It is just as wrong to think that the null hypothesis is less likely to be true when an outcome occurs with $p = .01$ than, for example, one that occurs with $p = .05$ (Muliak et al., 1997). The $p$ value tells you how likely is the outcome assuming the hypothesized value (usually zero) of your null hypothesis. It does not tell you the probability of the null hypothesis (see also discussion following statement 1). Correct answer: False. *Bottom line:* Do not confuse the $p$ value with the effect size or with the probability that the null hypothesis is true.

**5** The probability that the observed difference between the means reflects a real (true) mean difference in the populations is .95.

We cannot specify the exact probability for the difference between the means. The outcome of NHST reveals the probability of a difference this great by chance assuming the null hypothesis is true. It does not tell us about probabilities in the real world (e.g., Muliak et al., 1997). If results occur with a probability less than our chosen alpha level (e.g., .05), then, assuming the null hypothesis is true, all we can conclude is that the outcome is not likely to be a chance event in this situation (see also discussion following statement 1). Correct answer: False. *Bottom line:* Be sure you know what the outcome of NHST is really telling you.

**6** The probability of mistakenly saying that an effect is present, when the effect is not really present, is .05.

When learning about NHST (e.g., see Chapter 6) we were taught that making a so-called Type I error is equivalent to alpha (.05 in this case). Logically, to make this kind of error, the null hypothesis must be capable of being false. Yet, critics argue that the null hypothesis defined as zero difference is "always false" (e.g., Cohen, 1995, p. 1000) or, somewhat more conservatively is "rarely true" (Hunter, 1997, p. 5). If an effect is always, or nearly always, present (i.e., there is more than a zero difference), then we can't possibly (or at least hardly ever) make a mistake by claiming that an effect is there when it is not. Following this line of reasoning, the only error we are capable of making is a Type II error (see Hunter, 1997; Schmidt & Hunter, 1997), that is, saying a real effect is not there. This type of error, largely due to low statistical power of most psychological studies, typically is much greater than .05 (e.g., Cohen, 1990; Hunter, 1997; Schmidt & Hunter, 1997). On the other hand, as you perhaps can easily imagine, there is always a possibility that researchers will claim an effect to be present when in fact one is not present. Thus, we must leave open the possibility for a Type I error, at least on the conceptual level. False alarms do happen, although it does not seem reasonable given the arguments of the critics of NHST always to assign .05 as the probability of a Type I error. Let us just suggest that Type I errors do occur. Correct answer: False, if the null hypothesis is taken literally; true, if there really is a zero difference between the population means or if we believe that in some situations it is worth testing an effect against a hypothesis of no difference (see Abelson, 1997; Muliak et al., 1997). *Bottom line:* The most common error in psychological research using NHST is a Type II error; nevertheless, as researchers we must be alert to the fact that in some situations it may be important not to conclude an effect is present when it is not (i.e., a Type I error).

**7** If the results had *not* been statistically significant (i.e., $p > .05$), then we could correctly conclude that the null hypothesis is true.

By now you should recognize that this statement is false for two reasons. First, there is reason to believe that the null hypothesis is rarely, if ever, literally true. Second, we can always make a Type II error (and some experts, as we have seen, argue this is the only error we can make). Type II errors are likely when power is low, and low power has characterized many studies in the literature (see discussion following statement 6). Just because we did not obtain statistical significance does not mean that an effect is not present (e.g., Schmidt, 1996). In fact, one important reason for obtaining a measure of effect size is that we can compare the obtained effect with that found in other studies, whether or not the effect was statistically significant. This is the goal of meta-analysis (see Chapter 6). Correct answer: False. *Bottom line:* A nonsignificant finding does not tell us that an effect is absent. On the other hand, as we noted in Chapter 6, assuming that our study was conducted with sufficient power, a nonsignificant finding may indicate that an effect is so small that it isn't worth worrying about.

**8** The results show that the effect is "reliable" and, thus, repeating this study with the same number of participants would produce a statistically significant result in at least 95/100 tries.

Researchers sometimes mistakenly say that when a result occurs with $p < .05$ that "this outcome will be obtained 95/100 times if the study is repeated." This is simply not true. Statistical significance does not tell us about the probability of replicating the results. The best way to determine the likelihood of replicating a finding is to replicate it. On the other hand, measures of power estimate the probability of obtaining statistical significance if the same study was repeated (Schmidt, 1996). Thinking that a significant result is easily replicated sometimes leads researchers to conduct a replication with fewer participants (i.e., less power) and, consequently, to reduce the chance of finding statistical significance. Correct answer: False. *Bottom line:* The level of statistical significance (i.e., the $p$ value) does not tell us about the probability of replicating this result.

**9** Statistically significant results prove that the research hypothesis is correct. (For example, the data from the vocabulary study prove that older adults have greater vocabulary knowledge than do younger adults.)

NHST cannot prove that a research hypothesis is correct. A statistically significant result is (reasonably) sometimes said to "provide support for" or to "give evidence for" a hypothesis, but it cannot prove that the research hypothesis is correct. There are a couple of important reasons why. First, NHST is a game of probabilities; it provides answers in the form of likelihoods that are never 1.00 (e.g., $p$ greater or less than .05). There is always the possibility of error. If there is "proof" it is only "circumstantial" proof. As we have seen (see discussion following statement 1) the research hypothesis can only be tested indirectly by referring to the probability of these data given that the null hypothesis is true. If the probability that our results occurred by chance is very low (assuming a true null hypothesis), we may reason that the null hypothesis is really not true; this does not, however, mean our research hypothesis is true. As Schmidt and Hunter (1997, p. 59) remind us, researchers doing NHST "are focusing not on the actual scientific hypothesis of interest." Second, evidence for the effect of an independent variable is only as good as the methodology that produced the effect. The data used in NHST may or may not be from a study that is free of confounds or experimenter errors. It is possible that another factor was responsible for the observed effect. (For example, suppose that the older adults in the vocabulary study, but not the college students, had been recruited from a group of expert crossword puzzle players.) Evidence for a research hypothesis must be sought by examining the methodology of a study as well as considering the effect produced on the dependent variable. NHST tells us nothing about the soundness of a study's methodology. Correct answer: False. *Bottom line:* A statistically significant finding does not tell us the probability that our research hypothesis is correct.

**10** The size of the treatment effect is directly related to the size of the test statistic (e.g., the value of $t$). (That is, in the example study above we may assume that the effect of the independent variable given $t = 5.84$ is not as large as it would be if $t > 5.84$.)

The size of a test statistic, such as $t$ or $F$ (or the $p$ value; see discussion following statement 5) is not easily related to effect size. Test statistics are influenced by sample size; the same size effect of a variable will yield a larger test statistic if more participants are used. In fact, the development of effect size procedures was motivated by a desire to have a measure of the effect size that was independent of sample size (and, consequently, the size of our test statistic). Correct answer: False. *Bottom line:* Do not confuse the size of your test statistic (e.g., $t$ or $F$ values) with the size of the treatment effect.

## Summary of Confirmatory Analysis Based on NHST

Perhaps you can appreciate why researchers urge caution when interpreting results based on NHST. The knowledge gained from NHST is limited, to say the least. Even when a result is "statistically significant," we don't know if the null hypothesis is true or false (although some argue that it is always false). Unless we have calculated an effect size, we don't know the size of the treatment effect. We don't know how likely it is we will be able to replicate the result. The only thing we can say when a result is statistically significant is that *"given these data, and assuming the null hypothesis is true, this outcome is unlikely due to chance."* We have obtained evidence for the fact that there is a nonzero difference between the population means and it is likely to be in the direction that we observed. This information is sometimes useful. There are times when we do want to know what NHST tells us (e.g., Abelson, 1995, 1997; Chow, 1988; Estes, 1997; Rindskopf, 1997). We may use a statistically significant outcome, for instance, as evidence that, as Abelson (1997, p. 14) says, "something surprising and interesting has occurred," and, thus, the effect may be worth pursuing.

If a result is *not* statistically significant we may *not* conclude that the null hypothesis is true (it rarely, if ever, is literally true, and Type II errors are the most common errors in psychological studies). A nonsignificant result leaves us in a state of uncertainty regarding the direction of an effect. *When results are not statistically significant, the information obtained from NHST is greatly improved if we report the power of our study*. Power tells us how likely we are to "see" an effect that is there and is an estimate of the study's replicability. Because power tells us the probability of rejecting a false null hypothesis, we know how likely we are to miss a real effect. For instance, if a result is not significant and power is only .30, we know that a study with these characteristics detects an effect only 3 out of 10 times. Therefore, 7 of 10 times we do this study we will miss seeing the effect. In this case we may want to suspend judgment until the study can be redone with increased power.

Measures of effect size tell us "how big" an effect the independent variable had on the dependent variable. When included with the outcome of NHST, we know what happened in the study independently of sample size and *p* values. This information can be summarized with effect size information from other studies looking at the effect of the same independent variable as part of a meta-analysis. Effect sizes will vary from study to study; a meta-analysis summarizes the results of many studies to reveal a typical effect size for this independent variable. *As recommended by the APA Publication Manual (1994), you should consider reporting a measure of effect magnitude whenever you describe the results of a study using NHST.*

*Note:* Cohen's *d* can be calculated from the outcome of the independent groups *t*-test, according to the following formula:

$$d = \frac{2t}{\sqrt{df}} \qquad \text{(see Rosenthal \& Rosnow, 1991).}$$

**Final Statement of Results Based on NHST for Vocabulary Study**   We are now in a position to model a statement of results based on NHST that takes into account the information gained from all three stages of data analysis and the recommendations of the *Publication Manual of the American Psychological Association* (1994) regarding reporting results (see especially pp. 15–19 of the *Manual* and also Appendix C in this book).

> The mean performance on the multiple-choice vocabulary test for college students was 45.58 (*SD* = 10.46); the mean of the older group was 64.04 (*SD* = 12.27). This difference was statistically significant, $t(50) = 5.84, p = .000$. Older participants in this study had a greater vocabulary size than did the younger participants. The effect size based on Cohen's *d* was 1.65.

(If a figure was drawn showing the mean performance in the groups, then the statement of results should refer to the figure. See Appendix C.)

## CONFIRMATORY ANALYSIS USING CONFIDENCE INTERVALS

We illustrated the use of confidence intervals in Chapter 6 in the context of a simple, one-factor experiment. Confidence intervals provide an important supplement to the information obtained through NHST, and, at other times, may replace NHST entirely. Confidence intervals are calculated for a single population mean or population mean difference. We first review the use of confidence intervals for one population mean. Then we introduce confidence intervals for the difference between two population means. After reviewing the procedures and rationale for constructing confidence intervals, we apply them to the data obtained in the two-group vocabulary study used previously to discuss NHST. The data and summary statistics are exactly the same; only the confirmatory stage of analysis has changed.

## Construction of Confidence Interval for a Single Population Mean

Imagine you are having a physical examination at the campus health clinic. The technician reports that your pulse is 75 beats per minute. You are unlikely to be concerned that your heart is racing if you are also told the average pulse rate at rest for a person your age is 72 beats per minute. Your knowledge of the variability of pulse rates keeps you from being alarmed. In both physiological and psychological measurement we are often more interested in knowing a range of values that define a "normal" range than we are in specifying a single estimate of a population value. These normal ranges are based on the standard error of the mean and are called *confidence intervals*. In computing a confidence interval we specify a range of values within which we can have a certain degree of confidence that the population mean is included within the interval. As you may suspect, the larger the interval we specify, the greater our confidence that the mean will be included; but larger intervals give us less specific information about the exact value of the population mean. As a compromise, researchers have agreed that the 95% confidence interval and the 99% confidence interval will be used when an interval estimate of the population mean is desired. The confidence interval is centered about our point estimate of the mean ($\overline{X}$), and the boundaries of the 95% confidence interval can be calculated using the following formulas:

$$\text{Upper limit of 95\% confidence interval} = \overline{X} + [t(n-1)]_{\alpha=.05} [s_{\overline{X}}]$$
$$\text{Lower limit of 95\% confidence interval} = \overline{X} - [t(n-1)]_{\alpha=.05} [s_{\overline{X}}]$$

We have already described procedures for computing the sample mean ($\overline{X}$) and the standard error of the mean ($s_{\overline{X}}$). The unfamiliar symbols in the two equations for the limits of the 95% confidence interval are $[t(n-1)]$ and $\alpha = .05$. The level of significance, alpha (.05), may be familiar to you if you have studied the procedures for inferential statistics tests described in Chapter 6. In the case of confidence intervals, $\alpha = (1 - \text{level of confidence})$, expressed as a proportion. So, for the 95% confidence interval, $\alpha = 1 - .95 = .05$ and for the 99% confidence interval, $\alpha = 1 - .99 = .01$. The $t$ statistic included in the equation is defined by the number of degrees of freedom ($n - 1$), and the $t$ is determined by looking it up in Table A.3.

## Construction of Confidence Interval for Difference Between Population Means

The procedure and logic for constructing confidence intervals for a difference between means is similar to that for setting confidence intervals for a single mean. Because our interest is now in the difference between the population means (i.e., "the effect" of our independent variable) we substitute $\bar{X}_1 - \bar{X}_2$ for $\bar{X}$ and use the standard error of the mean difference rather than the standard error of the mean. To construct confidence intervals for the effect of our independent variable we use exactly the same information we used to carry out NHST for two means. The .95 confidence interval for the difference between two population means is defined as:

$$CI(.95) = (\bar{X}_1 - \bar{X}_2) \pm (t_{crit})(s_{\bar{X}_1 - \bar{X}_2})$$

where $t_{crit}$ is found in Table A.3 with $df = (n_1 + n_2 - 2)$ at alpha = .05

We are now in a position to calculate the confidence limits for the difference between the two means in our example vocabulary research study. The .95 confidence interval for the population mean difference is:

$$CI(.95) = 18.46 \pm (2.009)(3.16)$$

thus, upper limit = 18.46 + 6.35 = 24.81
lower limit = 18.46 − 6.35 = 12.11

We discuss the interpretation of confidence intervals in the context of the two group experiment or mean difference, but a similar interpretation also applies to the single sample case reviewed above. The following is what can be said based on these results.

**1** The odds are 95/100 that the obtained confidence interval contains the true population mean difference or effect size.

As Muliak et al. (1997) point out, the confidence interval either does or does not contain the true effect. A .95 probability associated with the confidence interval for an effect size refers to the probability of capturing the true effect size if we were to construct many confidence intervals based on different random samples of the same size. That is, confidence intervals around the sample mean difference tell us what happens if we were to repeat this experiment under the same conditions (e.g., Estes, 1997). In 95 of 100 replications we would expect to capture the true mean difference with our confidence intervals. Confidence intervals do not require us to decide one way or the other about the truth of some hypothesis and thus do not force errors upon us. Decision errors arise in the context of NHST when we decide to accept or reject a null hypothesis. Note that data evaluation based on confidence intervals emphasizes what is of most interest: the effect of our independent variable. Confidence intervals give us information regarding the likelihood of the effect size.

**2** The width of the confidence interval provides information about effect size.

Unlike NHST, by using confidence intervals we obtain information about the probable effect size of our independent variable. Obtained effect sizes vary from study to study as characteristics of samples and procedures differ. The confidence interval "specifies a probable range of magnitude for the effect size" (Abelson, 1997, p. 130). It says that the effect size likely could be as small as the value of the lower boundary and as large as the value of the upper boundary. Researchers are sometimes amazed to see just how large an interval is needed to specify an effect size with a high degree of confidence (e.g., Cohen, 1995). Thus, the smaller the width of the confidence interval the better job we have done at estimating the true effect size of our independent variable.

**3**  The size (width) of the confidence interval is directly related to sample size.

Interval size corresponds to power for NHST (e.g., Cohen, 1994; Loftus, 1996), and, like power, is affected by sample size. Increasing sample size will shrink the confidence interval. Note, however, that "$p$ values" do not change as obtained $p$ values do when increasing sample sizes using NHST. Confidence (e.g., .95) stays the same; what changes is the width of the interval to which our confidence refers. By increasing sample size we get a better idea of exactly what our effect looks like.

**4**  When establishing confidence intervals for a mean difference (as in this example), if the interval brackets zero, then we cannot say if an effect is present.

When a "zero" mean difference is a probable value for our effect, we must accept the possibility that an effect is not present. Confidence intervals give us a probable range for our effect. If zero is among the probable values, then we should admit our uncertainty regarding the direction of an effect (e.g., Abelson, 1997). Note the similarity of this situation to that when a nonsignificant result is found using NHST.

**5**  All the information obtained through NHST is found in confidence intervals.

Nothing is lost when constructing confidence intervals for an effect size; we get all the information found in NHST and more (e.g., Abelson, 1997; Cohen, 1994; Loftus, 1996; Schmidt & Hunter, 1997). As we saw above (see discussion following statement 2), when zero (mean difference) is in the interval, then we would fail to reject the null hypothesis were we using NHST. If we wish, we can use confidence intervals to make binary decisions as we do in NHST; all the information we need to make such a decision is present.

There are some things we should *not* say based on the use of confidence intervals. For example, we should not say:

**1**  The odds are 95/100 that the true mean difference lies in this interval.

At first blush this statement may seem to be identical to statement 1 on the previous page. It isn't. Keep in mind that the value in which we are interested is fixed, a constant; it is a population characteristic or parameter. As we noted previously, intervals are not fixed; they are characteristics of sample data. Intervals are constructed from sample means and measures of dispersion that are going to vary from experiment to experiment and consequently, so do confidence intervals. Howell (1997) provides a nice analogy to help understand how these facts relate to our interpretation of confidence intervals. He suggests we think of the parameter as a stake and confidence intervals as rings. From the sample data the researcher constructs rings of a specified width that are tossed at the stake. When using .95 confidence interval, the rings will encircle the stake 95% of the time and will miss it 5% of the time. "The confidence statement is a statement of the probability that the ring has been on target; it is *not* a statement of the probability that the target (parameter) landed in the ring" (Howell, 1997, p. 204).

**2** The results provide evidence of a scientifically important study.

Data analysis follows the design and conduct of a research study. It is only one part of the research story. For all the same reasons we mentioned when discussing NHST, an evaluation of the numerical data alone does not speak to a study's scientific importance.

**3** The results are of practical importance.

Again, data analysis by itself does not tell us whether a study has practical value. But, because confidence intervals yield estimates of the effect size, we have more information than we did following NHST (i.e., without effect size measures). There still may be issues of external validity or practical problems with applying a treatment in the real world, but confidence intervals for an effect size at least suggest the range of magnitude for probable effects we might expect under the conditions of our study.

## Summary of Confirmatory Analysis Based on Confidence Intervals

We are now in a position to model a statement of results for the analysis of mean performance in two groups based on confidence intervals for the effect of the independent variable in the vocabulary study.

> The mean performance on the multiple-choice vocabulary test for college students was 45.58 (*SD* = 10.46); the mean of the older group was 64.04 (*SD* = 12.27). Older participants in this study had a greater vocabulary size than did the younger participants (*SEM* = 3.16). There is a .95 probability that the obtained confidence interval, 12.11 − 24.81, contains the true population mean difference.

(Note that the confidence interval provides a range of effect sizes in terms of actual mean differences and not a standardized difference such as Cohen's *d*. The standard error of the mean (*SEM*) difference is given, although knowing the sample sizes, it may be calculated from the standard deviations of the groups. As a rule of thumb, the lower and upper .95 confidence limits are approximately 2 times the standard error of the mean. That is, 2 times 3.16 ± the mean difference approximates the .95 confidence limits.)

## COMPARISON OF TWO MEANS IN A REPEATED MEASURES DESIGN

Thus far we have considered experiments involving two independent groups of subjects. As you are aware, experiments can also be carried out by having each subject participate in each condition of the experiment or by "matching" subjects on some measure related to the dependent variable (e.g., IQ scores, weight, etc.). Such experiments are called matched pairs, within-subjects designs or repeated measures designs (see Chapter 7). The logic of NHST is the same in a repeated measures design as it is in an independent groups design. However, the *t*-test comparing two means takes on a different form in a repeated measures design. The *t*-test in this situation is typically called a direct-difference *t* or repeated measures (within-subjects) *t*. When each subject is in both conditions of the experiment *t* is defined as:

$$t = \frac{\bar{D}}{s_{\bar{D}}}$$   where   $\bar{D}$ = mean of difference scores or $\sum D / n$, and
$s_{\bar{D}}$ = standard error of difference scores, or

$$s_{\bar{D}} = \frac{s_D}{\sqrt{n}}$$   where   $s_D$ = standard deviation of difference scores, and
$n$ = number of difference scores (i.e., number of pairs of scores)

The numerator of the repeated measures *t* is the mean of the difference scores (called "D bar") and is algebraically equivalent to the difference between the sample means (i.e., $\bar{X}_1 - \bar{X}_2$). Statistical significance is determined by consulting a table of critical values of *t* with *df* = $n - 1$ (see Table A.3). In this case *n* refers to the number of participants or pairs of scores in the experiment. You interpret the obtained *t* as you would the *t* obtained in an independent groups design.

Procedures for assessing effect size in a matched groups or repeated measures design are somewhat more complex than those we reviewed for an independent groups design (see Cohen, 1988; and Rosenthal & Rosnow, 1991, for information pertaining to the calculation of *d* in these cases).

Confidence intervals, too, can be constructed for the population mean difference in a repeated measures design involving two conditions. As with the *t*-test, however, the underlying calculations change for this situation. The confidence interval for the difference between two means in a repeated measures design can be defined as:

$$CI = (\bar{X}_1 - \bar{X}_2) \pm (t_{\text{crit}})(s_{\bar{D}})$$

## RECOMMENDATIONS FOR COMPARING TWO MEANS

We offer the following recommendations when evaluating the data from a study looking at the difference between two means. First, keep in mind the final goal of data analysis: to make a case based on our observations for a claim about behavior. In order to make the best case possible you will want to explore various alternatives for data analysis. Don't fall into the trap of thinking that there is one and only one way to provide evidence for a claim about behavior. When there is a choice (and there almost always is), as recommended by the APA's Task Force on Statistical Inference (see Azar, 1997, p. 27), *use the simplest possible analysis.* Second, when using NHST be sure to understand its limitations and what the outcome of NHST allows you to say. Always consider reporting a measure of effect magnitude when using NHST, and, especially when a non-significant result is found, also a measure of power. Although there will be some situations when effect size information is not warranted—for example, when testing a theoretical prediction of direction only (e.g., Chow, 1988), these situations are relatively rare. In many research situations, and in nearly all applied situations, effect size information is an important, even necessary, complement to NHST. Finally, try to "break the habit" of relying solely on NHST and consider reporting confidence intervals for effect sizes in addition to, or even rather than, *p* values associated with *t* or *F*-tests. As we have seen, we get all the information found in NHST and *more.*

# DATA ANALYSIS INVOLVING MORE THAN TWO INDEPENDENT GROUPS

Thus far we have discussed the stages of data analysis in the context of a two-group experiment. We can think of a two-group experiment as representing two levels of one independent variable. What happens when we have more than two levels (groups) or, as is often the case in psychology, more than two independent variables? The most frequently used statistical procedure for analyzing results of psychology experiments involving more than two groups is the analysis of variance (ANOVA).

## Analysis of Variance (ANOVA)

An introduction to ANOVA was presented in Chapter 6. ANOVA is a special case of confirmatory data analysis examining statistical significance under the null hypothesis. Consequently, many of the problems associated with NHST reviewed earlier apply here as well. In the following sections we describe data analysis and interpretation of experiments using ANOVA. It is assumed that these analyses will be done using a computer (we did!), and thus emphasis will be on interpreting the output obtained from a typical statistical computer package. It should be noted that we consider only cases when all groups (or cells) in the experiment are the same size. We will also assume that the data in our illustrations have already passed through the first, exploratory stage of data analysis when data are inspected carefully, any anomalies are noted, and editing and cleaning have taken place as necessary. Prior to examining the ANOVA results, we summarize the results using major descriptive statistics. As we have emphasized, *appropriate summaries of the data should be performed before making any attempt to interpret the results of NHST.*

As we did when discussing data analysis of two-group experiments, we will point out ways to improve on the information obtained using NHST, especially through the use of effect size measures that complement results of NHST. The specific effect size measures used in multi-group experiments differ somewhat from those introduced in the context of analyzing results from two group experiments. We will also show how data from multi-group experiments might be evaluated using confidence intervals and what has been called the plot-plus-error-bar technique.

We consider four research designs: single-factor analysis of independent groups designs; single-factor analysis for repeated measures designs; two-factor analysis for independent groups designs; and two-factor analysis for mixed designs. *We recommend that, before proceeding, you read carefully the overview of the logic and rationale for ANOVA presented in Chapter 6, as well as the information found in Chapters 6, 7, or 8, that pertains to your specific research design.*

**Single-Factor Analysis of Variance for Independent Groups Designs**   The single-factor analysis of variance for independent groups designs is used to analyze the results of random groups and natural groups designs involving one independent variable with two or more levels. (The assumptions underlying the test strictly apply only to the random groups design.) The logic of this statistical test is described in Chapter 6.

The data in the following table represent the number of words correctly recalled (out of a possible 20) on a retention test in an experiment investigating memory training techniques. Five participants were randomly assigned to each of four groups (defined by the method of study that individuals were instructed to use to learn the words in preparation for the memory test). The control method involved no specific instructions, but in the three experimental groups participants were instructed to study by making up a story using the to-be-remembered words (story method), to use rhymes to remember the words (rhyme method), or to use visual imagery (imagery method). The independent variable being manipulated is instruction, and it can be symbolized by the letter "A." The levels of this independent variable can be differentiated by using the symbols, $a_1$, $a_2$, $a_3$, and $a_4$ for the four respective groups. The number of participants within each group is referred to as $n$; in this case, $n = 5$. The total number of individuals in the experiment is symbolized as $N$; in this case, $N = 20$. Finally, the number of groups is referred to as $a$; in this case, $a = 4$.

| | | | | Instruction (A) | | | | |
|---|---|---|---|---|---|---|---|---|
| Subject | Control $(a_1)$ | Subject | Story $(a_2)$ | Subject | Imagery $(a_3)$ | Subject | Rhymes $(a_4)$ |
| 1 | 12 | 6 | 15 | 11 | 16 | 16 | 14 |
| 2 | 10 | 7 | 14 | 12 | 16 | 17 | 14 |
| 3 | 9 | 8 | 13 | 13 | 13 | 18 | 15 |
| 4 | 11 | 9 | 12 | 14 | 12 | 19 | 12 |
| 5 | 8 | 10 | 12 | 15 | 15 | 20 | 12 |
| Mean | 10.0 | | 13.2 | | 14.4 | | 13.4 |
| Standard deviation | 1.6 | | 1.3 | | 1.8 | | 1.3 |
| Range | 8–12 | | 12–15 | | 12–16 | | 12–15 |

An important step in the analysis of any experiment is to set up a data matrix like the one here. The number of correct responses is listed for each person in each of the four groups with each participant identified with a unique subject number. In order to understand the results of an experiment it is essential to summarize the data prior to examining the outcome of the ANOVA. Below the data matrix the mean, range (minimum and maximum scores), and standard deviation are provided for each group.

Before examining the "significance" of an *F*-ratio, try to get an impression of what the summary statistics are telling you. Look to see if there is a visible "effect" of the independent variable; that is, see if there is substantial variation among the means. (Later, we will show you how to calculate an effect size.) By examining the ranges and standard deviations, get a sense of the variability in each group. (Remember, the less scores vary around their sample means the better the chance of seeing an effect that is present.) The range, or difference between the minimum and maximum values, is useful in identifying floor and ceiling effects. Is the variability among the groups similar? (We want the variation to be relatively homogeneous as wide discrepancies in within-group variability can create interpretation problems when using ANOVA. Many computer programs provide a test of "homogeneity of variance" along with the ANOVA output.)

Our examination of the summary statistics reveals that there appears to be systematic variation among the means; the largest difference is seen between the Control (10.0) and the Imagery Group (14.4). All the experimental means are larger than the Control mean. You will want to refer to the means as you "read" the ANOVA summary table. Note that the range is similar for all the groups; the standard deviations, too, are fairly similar. This attests to the homogeneity of variance among the groups. Moreover, an inspection of the highest scores in each group shows that ceiling effects are not a problem in this data set (as total possible was 20). With these facts in mind we can proceed to an examination of the results of our *F*-test.

Interpreting the ANOVA Summary Table   The ANOVA summary table for the omnibus *F*-test for the independent groups design described above is reported below. Remember that there were four groups of size $n = 5$ and, thus, overall $N = 20$.

ANALYSIS OF VARIANCE

| Source | Sum of Squares | df | Mean Square | F-Ratio | p |
|--------|---------------|-----|-------------|---------|-----|
| Group | 54.550 | 3 | 18.183 | 7.821 | 0.002 |
| Error | 37.22 | 16 | 2.325 | | |

It is critically important you know what the ANOVA summary table contains. In Chapter 6 we described in detail the typical contents of an ANOVA table for a single-factor design with independent groups and we recommend that you review that information before proceeding.

The probability for the *F*-ratio in this experiment of .002 appears in the far right column of the summary table. Since this probability is less than the conventional level of significance (.05), we can conclude that this *F*-ratio is statistically significant. The results of NHST using ANOVA would be summarized in your research report as follows:

$$F(3, 16) = 7.82, p = .002.$$

At this point we know that the omnibus *F*-test was statistically significant. In other words, these results, assuming the null hypothesis is true, are unlikely in this situation. Thus, we conclude that there was an overall effect of the independent variable of type of memory training in the experiment. This tells us that something happened in the experiment, but it does not specify exactly what happened. It does not, for instance, tell us the degree of relationship between the independent and dependent variable, and thus we should consider calculating an effect size for our independent variable.

## Calculating Effect Size for Independent Groups Designs

We mentioned earlier that the psychology literature contains many different measures of effect magnitude, which depend on the particular research design, test statistic, and other peculiarities of the research situation (e.g., Cohen, 1992; Kirk, 1996; Rosenthal & Rosnow, 1991). As we also noted, however, knowing one measure of effect magnitude we usually can translate it to another, comparable measure without too much difficulty. One measure, designed by J. Cohen, for independent groups is *f* (see Cohen, 1988). It a standardized measure of effect size not unlike *d*, which we saw was useful for assessing effect sizes in a two-group experiment. However, unlike *d*, which defines an effect in terms of the difference between two means, *f* defines an effect in terms of a measure of dispersal among group means. Both *d* and *f* express the effect relative to (i.e., "standardized" on) the within-population standard deviation. Consequently, *f* is defined as follows:

$$f = \frac{\sigma_m}{\sigma} \qquad \text{where} \quad \begin{aligned} \sigma_m &= \text{standard deviation of means} \\ \sigma &= \text{population standard deviation} \end{aligned}$$

Cohen has provided guidelines for interpreting *f*. Specifically, he suggests that small, medium, and large effects sizes correspond to *f* values of .10, .25, and .40. The calculation of *f* is not easily accomplished using the information found in the ANOVA summary table, but it can be obtained without too much difficulty from other measures of effect magnitude as we will show.

Another important class of effect magnitude measures that applies to experiments with more than two groups is based on measures of "strength of association" (Kirk, 1996). What these measures have in common is that they allow estimates of the proportion of total variance accounted for by the effect of the independent variable on the dependent variable. A popular strength of association measure is eta squared or $\eta^2$. It is easily calculated based on information found in the ANOVA summary table for the omnibus $F$-test (although many computer programs automatically provide eta squared as a measure of effect size). In this case, eta squared is defined as the Sum of Squares Between Groups divided by the Total Sum of Squares. In our example,

$$\text{eta squared} = \frac{SS_{\text{between}}}{SS_{\text{total}}} = \frac{54.55}{54.55 + 37.20} = .595$$

Eta squared can also be computed directly from the $F$-ratio for the Between Groups effect when the ANOVA table is not available (see Rosenthal & Rosnow, 1991, p. 441):

$$\text{eta squared} = \frac{F(df_{\text{effect}})}{F(df_{\text{effect}}) + (df_{\text{error}})}$$

or, in our example,

$$\text{eta squared} = \frac{(7.821)(3)}{(7.821)(3) + 16} = .595$$

Once eta squared is known, we can calculate $f$ according to the following formula (see Cohen, 1988):

$$f = \sqrt{\frac{\text{eta squared}}{1 - \text{eta squared}}}$$

or, in our example,

$$f = \sqrt{\frac{.595}{1 - .595}} = 1.21$$

We can thus conclude that memory training accounted for .595 of the total variance in the dependent variable and produced a standardized effect size, $f$, of 1.21. Based on Cohen's guidelines for interpreting $f$ (on previous page), it is apparent that memory training had a large effect on recall scores.

## Assessing Power for Independent Groups Designs

Once the effect size is known we can obtain an estimate of power for a specific sample size and degrees of freedom associated with the numerator (between groups effect) of the $F$-ratio. In our example, we set alpha at .05; the experiment was done with $n = 5$ and $df = 3$ for the between groups effect (number of groups − 1). The effect size, $f$, associated with our data set is very large (1.21), and there really is no good reason to conduct a power analysis for this large effect which was statistically significant.

Let us assume that the ANOVA in the example on page 443 yielded a nonsignificant $F$ and effect size was $f = .40$, a large effect. An important question to answer is: What was the power of our experiment? How likely were we to see an effect of this size given an alpha of .05, a sample size of $n = 5$, and $df = 3$ for our effect? Consulting the abbreviated power table, Table A.6, at the end of this appendix, we find that under these conditions power was .26. In other words, the probability of obtaining statistical significance in this situation was only .26. In only approximately one fourth of the tries under these conditions would we obtain a significant result. The experiment was clearly underpowered and it is unreasonable to make much of the fact that NHST did not reveal a significant result. To do so would ignore the very important fact that the effect of our independent variable was, in fact, large.

Although learning about power post hoc can be important, particularly when we obtain a nonsignificant outcome based on NHST, ideally *power analysis should be conducted prior to an experiment* in order to reveal the a priori (from the beginning) probability of finding a statistically significant effect. An experimenter who begins an experiment knowing that power is only .26 would appear to be wasting time and resources given that the odds of *not* finding a significant effect are .74. Let us assume, therefore, that the experiment has not been conducted and that the investigator examined the literature on memory training and found that a large effect was often obtained by previous researchers in this area. Let us further assume that the researcher wants power to be .80 in the experiment. Because power is typically increased by increasing sample size, we want to find out what the sample size should be in order to find a large effect with power $= .80$.

To find the sample size needed to see a large effect in 8 of 10 tries we use the power table to find $n$ with $df = 3$ under the effect size heading of .40. Table A.6 shows that to achieve power of .80 we would need 18 participants *in each condition* of the experiment. The researcher should take this information into consideration *before* doing the experiment.

## Analytical Comparisons

As we noted, knowing that "something happened" in a one-factor, multiple-group experiment is often not all that interesting. We generally do research, or at least we should, with more specific hypotheses in mind than "this variable will have an effect" on the dependent variable. Neither the results of the omnibus $F$, nor a measure of overall effect size, tell us which means are different from which other means. We can *not*, for instance, look at the four means in our experiment and judge that the "imagery" mean is significantly different from the "story" mean. The results of the omnibus $F$ simply tell us there is variation present that is larger than would be expected by chance in this situation.

One way to learn more about what happened in a multiple-group, single-factor experiment is to perform analytical comparisons (see Chapter 6). Analytical comparisons help specify the source of the overall effect of the independent variable. Typically, a small set of comparisons is required to locate the sources of systematic variation in a single-factor experiment. *Analytical comparisons focus on the particular differences of interest.*

We will illustrate the procedure for doing analytical comparisons by describing the analysis of only one comparison. We will use as our example the analytical comparison of the control group with the average of the three experimental groups to see if this is one source of systematic variation contributing to the overall effect of the memory training variable.

## Steps in Developing Coefficients for Analytical Comparison

**1** State hypothesis in words: Compare control method with average of three experimental methods.

**2** State null hypothesis for comparison:

$$\mu_{a_1} = \frac{\mu_{a_2} + \mu_{a_3} + \mu_{a_4}}{3}$$

**3** Set null hypothesis statement equal to zero:

$$\mu_{a_1} - \frac{\mu_{a_2} + \mu_{a_3} + \mu_{a_4}}{3} = 0$$

**4** Expand expression by taking minus sign inside brackets and isolating terms over common denominator:

$$\mu_{a_1} - \frac{\mu_{a_2}}{3} - \frac{\mu_{a_3}}{3} - \frac{\mu_{a_4}}{3} = 0$$

**5** Eliminate fractions by multiplying expression by common denominator:

$$3\mu_{a_1} - \mu_{a_2} - \mu_{a_3} - \mu_{a_4} = 0$$

**6** The coefficients for each group are the multipliers for each mean in this equation.

$$C_1 = +3$$
$$C_2 = -1$$
$$C_3 = -1$$
$$C_4 = -1$$

**7** Computation check: The coefficients for an analytical comparison must sum to zero.

**8** If a group is not included in a comparison, its coefficient is 0.

*F*-Test for Analytical Comparison    Once you have determined the coefficients for the analytical comparison you want to do, using the procedures described in the preceding section you are ready to run the program to compute the *F*-test for your comparison. Computer output for the analysis of the comparison of the control group to the average of the three experimental groups typically will resemble the following:

TEST OF HYPOTHESIS

| Source | SS | df | MS | F | p |
|---|---|---|---|---|---|
| Hypothesis | 50.417 | 1 | 50.417 | 21.685 | 0.000 |
| Error | 37.200 | 16 | 2.325 | | |

The format of the summary table is very similar to that for the single-factor analysis we described earlier. In fact, the source of variation labeled "Error" is exactly the same as for the omnibus *F*-test for this experiment. In general, the error term for analytical comparisons in an independent groups design is the same as the error term for the omnibus test. The source of variation being tested in this analysis is labeled "Hypothesis." It reflects the potential systematic variation due to the analytical comparison being tested. Since analytical comparisons reflect the contrast between two means, they always have only one degree of freedom. In this case, the contrast is between the mean for the control group and the mean of the three means in the experimental groups. The *F*-ratio for testing the effect of the analytical comparison (called Hypothesis in the summary table) is the ratio of the Mean Square (*MS*) for Hypothesis over the *MS* Error. The resulting *F* shown in the summary table is 21.685. The probability of this *F* (with 1 and 16 degrees of freedom) under the null hypothesis is less than 1 in 1,000. This probability is less than the conventional level of significance (.05), and so we conclude that this analytical comparison is statistically significant. A report of the outcome of the analytical comparison would be written: $F(1, 16) = 21.68, p = .000$.

The mean for the control group was 10.0, and the mean across the three experimental groups was 13.7. These means along with the statistically significant *F*-ratio lead to the conclusion that the three experimental groups recalled more words than did the control group. This conclusion based on the test of an analytical comparison is much more specific than the conclusion based on the omnibus test that something happened in the experiment. Because the analytical comparison contrasts performance between two groups, we can obtain a measure of effect size for this comparison using Cohen's *d* or eta squared ($\eta^2$). When two groups are compared, eta ($\eta$), or the square root of eta squared, is equivalent to *r*, a measure of effect size sometimes recommended in this situation (see Rosenthal & Rosnow, 1991). We interpret *r* as representing a small, medium, or large effect size when *r* is .10, .25, or .40, respectively (Cohen, 1992). In this example, eta squared = .57, and eta (and *r*) = .75. How would you interpret the effect size?

## Confidence Intervals for Independent Groups Design

As we saw in Chapter 6, the construction of confidence intervals can complement NHST and, at times, represent an alternative to NHST when performing confirmatory data analysis in an experiment involving more than two groups. The logic is similar to that which we outlined for the two-group designs described earlier in this appendix. Consider Figure A.1. We have plotted confidence intervals for each of the four means in our memory training experiment. When presenting confidence intervals for the four groups in our experiment we see immediately that we know more than the omnibus $F$-test revealed. Inspection of Figure A.1 reveals that the probable effect sizes for the three experimental groups do not overlap the confidence limits of the effect size for the control group. On the other hand, confidence intervals for the experimental groups do overlap; the probable (.95) effect sizes for the training groups are not all that different.

The calculation of confidence intervals for an independent groups design makes use of the error term for the omnibus $F$, that is, the $MS$ within groups (see Loftus & Masson, 1994). Remember that the $MS$ error is a pooled estimate of the sample variances. In our sample data set the $MS$ error was 2.325 (see ANOVA summary table). The formula for computing confidence intervals around the sample means is:

$$CI = \overline{X} \pm \left( \sqrt{\frac{MS_{\text{error}}}{n}} \right)(t_{\text{crit}})$$

where $n$ is sample size. The critical $t$ value at .05 is obtained from Table A.3 using the $df$ associated with the $MS$ error. In our example, the values are:

$$CI = \overline{X} \pm \left( \sqrt{\frac{2.325}{5}} \right)(2.12) = \overline{X} \pm 1.45$$

**FIGURE A.1**   Means and .95 confidence intervals for the memory training experiment.

*Note:* Each of the four means are substituted for $\overline{X}$ in the above formula to obtain a confidence interval for each group.

## Error Bars and Confidence Intervals

Researchers frequently plot the interval associated with the standard error of the mean rather than the confidence interval when describing mean results of an experiment. This technique is referred to as the *plot-plus-error-bar* technique (Loftus, 1993). The "bars" surrounding each mean indicate how much sampling error there is in estimating the population mean based on the sample mean. The smaller the error bar (i.e., the smaller the difference between the upper and lower bars), the better is our estimate of the population mean. Figure A.2 shows "error bars" based on 1 standard error of the mean for each of the four groups in our memory training experiment.

The bars surrounding the means in Figure A.2, based on plus or minus 1 standard error of the mean, differ from the bars revealing confidence limits (see Figure A.1) in a couple of important ways. First, comparing the bars in the two figures, A.1 and A.2, reveals that the bars are much smaller when drawn using 1 standard error of the mean. This is necessarily the case because .95 confidence limits are constructed by multiplying the standard error of the mean by the critical value of *t* for a two-tailed test at alpha = .05. Second, the interpretation of standard error bars and confidence limits differs (see, especially, Estes, 1997). As calculated from sample data, the standard error of the mean estimates the standard deviation of sample means around the population mean. If scores are normally distributed, approximately 68% of the scores will fall within plus or minus 1 standard deviation. The standard error of the mean thus provides a measure of dispersion (i.e., variability) around the population mean. It indicates approximately the average distance in the population a sample mean is from the population mean. The smaller the error bar the better is our estimate of the population mean. *We can consider error bars based on plus or minus 1 standard*

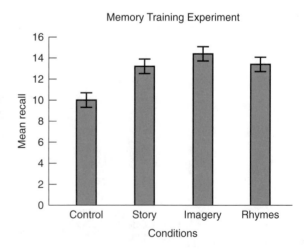

**FIGURE A.2**   Means plus error bars (±1 standard error of the mean) for the memory training experiment.

*error of the mean (see Figure A.2) as telling us how well our sample mean estimates the population mean.* Bars drawn using the standard error of the mean should *not* be interpreted to refer to the probability (e.g., .68) that replications will yield means within this interval (see Estes, 1997).

As we mentioned in an earlier section, confidence limits tell us the probability that this interval has captured the population parameter, in this case the population mean. We may assume that over replications of this experiment the population mean will fall 95 of 100 times within the particular interval we have constructed. We must always keep in mind the fact that the specific interval size changes with each replication due to variation in sampling. *We can consider bars drawn from confidence limits (see Figure A.1) as telling us how likely the population mean is to be within this range*, realizing that "this range" will vary from experiment to experiment. Like error bars, confidence limits give us information about the precision with which we have estimated the population mean (the smaller the interval the better is the estimate). Because, except for very small samples, .95 confidence intervals are approximately 2 times the standard error of the mean, it is not uncommon to see researchers construct plots based on 2 standard errors of the mean above and below the sample mean. This type of error bar permits you to say with (approximately) 95% confidence that the interval has captured the population mean.

You should note that the error bars in Figure A.2 are exactly the same size. This is because they (just like the confidence limits) were constructed using a "pooled" variance, specifically, the Mean Square within groups (error), from the independent groups ANOVA (see Estes, 1997). For our hypothetical data set, the Mean Square error is obtained from the ANOVA summary table. The formula for the standard error of the mean is thus calculated as:

$$\frac{\sqrt{MS_{error}}}{\sqrt{n}} \quad \text{where } n = \text{sample size}$$

As we advised you in Chapter 6, *be very careful when reviewing bar plots in the results sections of research reports.* Investigators (and the computer software programs they use) vary in their choice of bars to display and in the calculations on which the bars are based. We recommend that you display confidence limits rather than error bars whenever possible, but that in either case you *always explain to your research audience exactly how these intervals were constructed.*

## SINGLE-FACTOR ANALYSIS OF VARIANCE FOR REPEATED MEASURES DESIGNS

The results of experiments that involve repeated measures (within-subjects) comparisons with one independent variable manipulated at two or more levels are analyzed using a single-factor analysis of variance. The within-subjects designs involve the repeated testing of subjects, and so the analyses of the within-subjects designs are also called repeated measures analyses. The underlying logic and the interpretation of the repeated measures ANOVA are the same as for the independent groups designs.

One distinctive characteristic is the procedure used to prepare the data matrix for repeated measures designs. These procedures were illustrated in Chapter 7 using an example of a time-perception experiment involving the complete repeated measures design. The independent variable was interval length, and there were four levels: 12, 24, 36, and 48 seconds. The means (and standard deviations) of the median time estimates for each of five participants for the four intervals were 12.6 (2.19), 22.0 (8.60), 38.0 (18.23), and 39.4 (11.78) seconds. Note that median time estimates represented individual scores because medians are affected less than means by extreme scores that sometimes appear when time is the dependent measure. This represents an example of "re-expression" (transformation) of raw data prior to further analysis that results from the important first stage of data analysis when we become familiar with the characteristics of our data set.

The data from the time-perception experiment outlined in Chapter 7 were analyzed with a single-factor ANOVA for repeated measures designs. The outline of a typical computer output is reported below:

| Source | SS | df | MS | F | p |
|---|---|---|---|---|---|
| Interval | 2515.600 | 3 | 838.533 | 15.555 | 0.000 |
| Error | 646.900 | 12 | 53.908 | | |

The purpose of the analysis was to determine if the participants' estimates of the intervals changed with increasing interval length. Although the body of the ANOVA summary table looks pretty much like the one for the analysis of independent groups designs experiments, everything is not the same. The $F$-ratio is still made up of a numerator reflecting potential systematic variation and a denominator reflecting only error variation. As we described in Chapter 7, however, the error variation in the repeated measures designs is different from the error variation in the independent groups designs. In the repeated measures designs, error variation reflects the residual variation after the variation due to the independent variable and the variation due to subjects have been subtracted from the total variation in the analysis (see Chapter 7).

The Subjects Variation and the Total Variation do not always appear in the computer summary tables because neither is essential to computing the $F$-ratio for the independent variable. Thus we need to keep in mind that the sources of variation presented in the computer output may not represent all the sources of variation in the experiment.

When we examined the computer output for the data in our sample, we found that the probability associated with the obtained $F$-ratio of 15.55 was 0.000. Remember that when the probability of an obtained $F$ is so low that it is beyond three decimal places a computer typically presents the probability as 0.000. Thus, do not be worried that something appears fishy; the probability that these results occurred by chance in this situation is simply so low that it would take at least three zeros to express it. Obviously it must be less than the conventional level of significance of .05, so we conclude that the effect of the interval length variable was statistically significant. Participants' time estimates did change with increasing interval length.

The statistically significant *F*-test for the overall effect of interval length is an omnibus *F*-test. As was the case in the analysis of independent groups designs experiments, analytical comparisons can be used to identify the source of the effect of an independent variable more specifically. Unfortunately, in the repeated measures designs, the Residual Mean Square is not necessarily the best error term for analytical comparisons and it is recommended that a new error term be calculated for each comparison (see Keppel, 1991, pp. 356–358, for more specific guidelines regarding appropriate error terms for analytical comparisons in repeated measures designs). When an analytical comparison involves only two conditions of a repeated measures design, for example, comparing the mean performance in Condition 1 with the mean in Condition 4 (i.e., performance is not averaged across conditions), the analytical comparison is safely done using a *t*-test for repeated measures.

## Effect Size for Repeated Measures ANOVA

A common measure of effect size for the multiple-group repeated measures design, as it is for the independent groups design, is the strength of association measure, eta squared ($\eta^2$). It may be calculated from the Sums of Squares for the within-subjects effect and the Sums of Squares for the Residual or Error. In this situation,

$$\text{eta squared} = \frac{SS_{\text{effect}}}{SS_{\text{effect}} + SS_{\text{error}}} = \frac{2515.6}{2515.6 + 646.9} = .795$$

As mentioned previously, eta squared as a measure of effect size is the proportion of variance accounted for by the independent variable. However, it can be criticized when calculated with more than two conditions because its meaning is rather nonspecific (see Rosenthal & Rosnow, 1991). Like the omnibus *F*-test, it does not tell us exactly what we want to know. Whenever, possible, we will want to specify more clearly the source of an overall effect, and, as we saw, analytical comparisons with 1 *df* serve that purpose nicely. Eta squared is much more meaningful when there are only two conditions. As noted previously, in this case, eta($\eta$), or the square root of eta squared, is equivalent to the correlation coefficient *r*, and effect sizes may be assessed using the guidelines for *r*. A small, medium, and large effect size based on *r* corresponds to .10, .30, and .50 (Cohen, 1988).

## Using Confidence Intervals with Repeated Measures Designs

Figure A.3 shows confidence intervals around the means in the time-perception experiment. These intervals were constructed using the Mean Square error (Residual) in the omnibus ANOVA (see summary table on page 450) as

**FIGURE A.3**    Means and .95 confidence intervals for the time-perception experiment.

recommended by Loftus and Masson, 1994). Thus, calculation of the confidence interval was as follows:

$$CI = \bar{X} \pm \left( \sqrt{\frac{MS_{error}}{n}} \right)(t_{crit})$$

The interpretation of confidence intervals in the repeated measures design is analogous to that for the independent groups design, which we discussed above.

## TWO-FACTOR ANALYSIS OF VARIANCE FOR INDEPENDENT GROUPS DESIGNS

The two-factor analysis of variance for independent groups designs is used for the analysis of experiments in which each of two independent variables was manipulated at two or more levels. The logic of complex designs with two independent variables and the conceptual basis for the analysis of these experiments are described in Chapter 8. We will focus in this appendix on the computer-assisted analysis of a complex design that involves $F$-ratios for the main effect of A, the main effect of B, and the interaction effect, A $\times$ B. Our example will involve a significant A $\times$ B interaction, and so we will also illustrate the computations for a simple main effect. The two-factor analysis for independent groups is applicable to experiments in which both independent variables are manipulated using a random groups design, in which both independent variables represent the natural groups design, or in which one independent variable represents the natural groups design and the other represents the random groups design.

The data in the following table summarize the number of correct responses on a simple motor learning task as a function of two independent variables. The first independent variable was the hand the participant used to perform the task, and the two levels of this variable were the dominant and the nondominant hand. The second independent variable was the delay (in seconds) between successive trials on the task, and it was manipulated at three levels (0, 30, and 60 seconds). The hand variable will be referred to as A, with the dominant hand being $a_1$, and the nondominant hand being $a_2$. The delay variable will be referred to as B with the 0-second delay as $b_1$, the 30-second delay as $b_2$, and the 60-second delay as $b_3$. Five college students ($n = 5$) were randomly assigned to each of the six groups ($N = 30$) resulting from the factorial combination of the two independent variables.

HAND DOMINANCE (VARIABLE A) $\times$ DELAY INTERVAL (VARIABLE B)

| Dominant/0 sec | | Dominant/30 sec | | Dominant/60 sec | |
|---|---|---|---|---|---|
| Subject | $a_1b_1$ | Subject | $a_1b_2$ | Subject | $a_1b_3$ |
| 1 | 18 | 6 | 17 | 11 | 18 |
| 2 | 17 | 7 | 19 | 12 | 20 |
| 3 | 19 | 8 | 22 | 13 | 21 |
| 4 | 21 | 9 | 20 | 14 | 22 |
| 5 | 20 | 10 | 17 | 15 | 19 |
| M | 19.0 | | 19.0 | | 20.0 |
| SD | 1.58 | | 2.12 | | 1.58 |
| Range | 17–21 | | 17–22 | | 18.22 |

| Nondominant/0 sec | | Nondominant/30 sec | | Nondominant/60 sec | |
|---|---|---|---|---|---|
| Subject | $a_2b_1$ | Subject | $a_2b_2$ | Subject | $a_2b_3$ |
| 16 | 9 | 21 | 15 | 26 | 16 |
| 17 | 11 | 22 | 17 | 27 | 19 |
| 18 | 10 | 23 | 16 | 28 | 18 |
| 19 | 11 | 24 | 27 | 29 | 20 |
| 20 | 12 | 25 | 14 | 30 | 18 |
| M | 10.6 | | 15.8 | | 18.2 |
| SD | 1.14 | | 1.30 | | 1.48 |
| Range | 9–12 | | 14–17 | | 16–20 |

Summary data represent mean ($M$) values for the dependent variable, in this case, number of correct responses (abbreviated as Response). A measure of dispersion, the standard deviation ($SD$), for each condition is also presented. Another measure of dispersion, the range (minimum and maximum scores) is shown for each group. The minimum and maximum values are useful in identifying basement and ceiling effects (see Chapter 8) when the absolute minimum and maximum possible values in the experiment are known. It is good practice to examine the means carefully to make sure they correspond to the correct cells of the design matrix. It is very easy to make a mistake when identifying variables and levels in a complex design. You might, for instance, want to use a calculator to verify that the means of specific cells in the data matrix are labeled correctly in the computer output.

The standard deviation provides helpful information about the variation in each group. Looking across the six groups, we can see that the largest standard deviation was in the dominant hand/30-second delay group (2.12) and the smallest standard deviation was in the nondominant hand/0-second delay group (1.14). The small difference between these two values indicates that there was little difference in the amount of variation across the six groups in the experiment. The fact that the largest standard deviation in any group was just over two correct responses indicates that there was not much variation within any of the six groups. We are almost ready to examine the ANOVA summary table for our two-factor experiment to see if there were any statistically significant sources of variation.

The means for the six groups are used to describe what happened in the experiment. When a complex design is carried out, it will nearly always be the case that interpretation of the results is greatly aided by drawing a graph. We have drawn one such graph in Figure A.4 (see Chapter 8 and Appendix C for more information on drawing graphs). The pattern of means should be reviewed carefully before examining the ANOVA summary table. A figure, or minimally, a table of means, and the ANOVA summary table are the essential tools needed to interpret the results of a factorial experiment.

As we inspect the ANOVA summary table we want to keep in mind the results of our summary analyses. This will help us to know what to look for in the output and how to interpret what we find there. For example, first look at Figure A.4. Note that the figure indicates that there was little change in the number of correct responses as a function of delay for the dominant-hand groups. For the nondominant-hand groups, however, there was an apparent change across the three levels of delay. The presence of a possible interaction is most easily detected by examining the graph of the means. Examination of Figure A.4 reveals that the two lines representing dominant and nondominant

**FIGURE A.4**   Mean number of correct responses as a function of the delay between trials (in seconds) and hand used to perform motor task (dominant, nondominant).

hands diverge (are not parallel) across the three delay intervals. Descriptively, an interaction between the two independent variables is suggested.

With this pattern of results in mind, we can turn to the analysis-of-variance summary table.

ANALYSIS-OF-VARIANCE SUMMARY TABLE

| Source | Sum of Squares | df | Mean Square | F | p |
|---|---|---|---|---|---|
| Hand | 149.633 | 1 | 149.633 | 61.075 | 0.000 |
| Delay | 93.800 | 2 | 46.900 | 19.143 | 0.000 |
| Hand × Delay | 60.467 | 2 | 30.233 | 12.340 | 0.000 |
| Error | 58.800 | 24 | 2.450 | | |

The three $F$-ratios in a two-factor design take the same form as when the experiment involves a single independent-groups designs. The Mean Square Error is used as the denominator for all three $F$-tests. The Mean Square for each main effect and for the interaction are used as the numerators for three independent $F$-ratios. The three $F$-ratios appear in the summary table in the $F$ column. It is best to evaluate the $F$-ratio for the interaction first (see Chapter 8). Interactions allow us to determine whether the effect of one independent variable differs depending on the level of a second independent variable (see Chapter 8).

The obtained probability of less than 1 in 1,000 for the $F$ of 12.34 for the interaction is less than the conventional level of significance of .05. So, we can conclude that the interaction was statistically significant. A statistically significant interaction indicates that the effect of the delay variable was different as a function of which hand was used. This result confirms our impression of the pattern of mean performance seen in Figure A.4.

The pattern of means indicates the nature of the interaction. The delay variable had less of an effect on the groups using their dominant hand than on those using their nondominant hand. In the next section we will describe simple main effects, a type of analysis that can be used to specify the nature of an interaction even better. After examining the interaction effect, the two main effects should be examined. The $F$-ratio for the main effect of hand was 61.075, with a probability of less than one in a thousand. Because the probability is less than the conventional level of significance of .05, the main effect of hand was statistically significant. The means for this main effect can be obtained by averaging across the columns of the table, thereby computing a mean for the dominant hand of 19.3 and for the nondominant hand of 14.9. These means along with the statistically significant $F$-test indicate that those working with their dominant hand made more correct responses than those working with their nondominant hand. The $F$-ratio for the main effect of delay was 19.143, with a probability of less than 1 in 1,000. As was true for the main effect of hand, this probability is less than the conventional level of significance of .05, and thus the main effect of delay was statistically significant. The means for the main effect of delay are obtained by averaging across the rows of the table of means. These three means for the main effect of delay are 14.8, 17.4, and 19.1 for the 0-, 30-, and 60-second delays, respectively. These means and the accompanying statistically significant *F*-test for the main effect of delay indicate that the number of correct responses increased with increasing delay. Analytical comparisons could be used to specify the nature of the changes as a function of delay more precisely.

## Effect Sizes for Two-Factor Design with Independent Groups

A common measure of effect size for a complex design using ANOVA is eta squared ($\eta^2$), or proportion of variance accounted for, which was discussed earlier in the context of single-factor designs. In calculating eta squared, it is recommended that we focus only on the effect of interest (see Rosenthal & Rosnow, 1991). Specifically, eta squared can be defined as:

$$\text{eta squared} = \frac{SS_{\text{effect of interest}}}{SS_{\text{effect of interest}} + SS_{\text{within}}}$$

(see Rosenthal & Rosnow, 1991, p. 352).

Thus, eta squared is obtained for each of the three effects in our sample experiment by the following:

Factor A (Hand):

$$\text{eta squared} = \frac{149.633}{149.633 + 58.80} = .718$$

Factor B (Delay):

$$\text{eta squared} = \frac{93.80}{93.80 + 58.80} = .615$$

Interaction (A × B):

$$\text{eta squared} = \frac{60.467}{60.467 + 58.80} = .507$$

As noted above (and see Rosenthal & Rosnow, 1991), when the sums of squares for the effects are not available, eta squared can be computed using the following formula:

$$\text{eta squared} = \frac{F(df_{\text{effect}})}{F(df_{\text{effect}}) + (df_{\text{error}})}$$

## Illustration of Simple Main Effect

Simple main effects are used in the analysis of two-factor designs to identify more specifically the nature of statistically significant interactions (see Chapter 8). A simple main effect involves the overall effect of one independent variable at one level of a second independent variable. Statistical software packages vary as to whether they include the computation of simple main effects. We will illustrate the computation using calculations that can be done with a calculator. For these computations we will use the data for the three delay groups who used their non-dominant hand. These data are in the bottom half of the data matrix near the beginning of the section on the analysis of the two-factor design for independent groups. This simple main effect would be referred to as the effect of delay at the nondominant hand (or more generally, the effect of variable B at $a_2$). We will first present the computations and then briefly describe the interpretation of simple main effects.

Computing the simple main effect of B at $a_2$:

**1** Compute $SS_{B/a_2}$

$$= \frac{\left(\sum X_{a_2b_1}\right)^2 + \left(\sum X_{a_2b_2}\right)^2 + \left(\sum X_{a_2b_3}\right)^2}{n} - \frac{\left(\sum X_{a_2b_1} + \sum X_{a_2b_2} + \sum X_{a_2b_3}\right)^2}{(b)(n)}$$

$$= \frac{(53)^2 + (79)^2 + (91)^2}{5} - \frac{(53 + 79 + 91)^2}{(3)(5)}$$

$$= \frac{2{,}809 + 6{,}241 + 8{,}281}{5} - \frac{(223)^2}{15}$$

$$= \frac{17{,}331}{5} - \frac{49{,}729}{15}$$

$$= 3{,}477.20 - 3{,}315.27 = 150.93$$

**2** Compute $df_{B/a_2} = b - 1 = 3 - 1 = 2$

**3** Compute $MS_{B/a_2} = \dfrac{SS_{B/a_2}}{df_{B/a_2}} = \dfrac{150.93}{2} = 75.47$

**4** Compute $F(df_{B/a_2}, df_{WG}) = \dfrac{MS_{B/a_2}}{MS_{WG}} = \dfrac{75.47}{2.45} = 30.80$

The final computation of the F-ratio involved the use of the Mean Square Error (within groups) from the omnibus F-test. The computations for all the other values needed to compute a simple main effect are shown in the four steps we have outlined. As with any F-ratio, it is necessary to determine the probability of the F under the null hypothesis. The obtained $F(2, 24) = 30.8$ is associated with a probability of less than one in a thousand which is less than the conventional level of significance of .05. Thus, the simple main effect of delay at the level of nondominant hand was statistically significant. Although we will not illustrate the computations here, we did compute the simple main effect of delay for those persons using their dominant hand. The resulting $F(2, 24)$ was .68. An F-ratio less than 1 cannot be statistically significant so this nonsignificant simple main effect indicates that there was no statistically significant effect of delay when participants used their dominant hand. Together, the two simple main effects help us to specify the source of the statistically significant interaction of delay and hand dominance. As described in Chapter 8, the source of an interaction can be specified even more exactly by using simple comparisons to follow up statistically significant simple main effects.

## TWO-FACTOR ANALYSIS OF VARIANCE FOR A MIXED DESIGN

The two-factor analysis of variance for a mixed design is appropriate when one independent variable represents either the random groups or natural groups design and the second independent variable represents the repeated measures design. The first independent variable is called the between-subjects factor (here symbolized as A). The second independent variable is called the within-subjects factor (symbolized as B). The two-factor analysis for a mixed design is somewhat of a hybrid of the single-factor analysis for independent groups and the single-factor analysis for the repeated measures designs. This particular complex design was not discussed in Chapter 8 and, therefore, we will present it in some detail here.

The data presented in the following table represent the mean frequency judgments participants gave to four brief segments of popular songs. The participants listened to a tape including several songs; half the individuals did not expect the frequency judgment test (incidental group), and half did expect the test (intentional group). In addition, all participants judged songs that had been presented either one, two, or three times. Thus, the experiment was a 2 × 3 design in which instructions were manipulated in a random groups design with five people assigned to each of two groups and in which the presented frequency variable was manipulated in a complete repeated measures design. The following data matrix shows the mean frequency judgments at three levels of presentation frequency for each participant in each group, as well as summary statistics in the form of means, standard deviations, and ranges, for each condition.

| Group (A) | Subject | Presentation Frequency (B) 1 ($b_1$) | 2 ($b_2$) | 3 ($b_3$) |
|---|---|---|---|---|
| | 1 | 1.2 | 2.2 | 3.0 |
| | 2 | .8 | 2.0 | 3.2 |
| Incidental | 3 | 1.2 | 1.8 | 2.8 |
| Group ($a_1$) | 4 | 1.5 | 2.0 | 2.5 |
| | 5 | 1.2 | 2.5 | 3.2 |
| | *M* | 1.18 | 2.1 | 2.94 |
| | *SD* | .249 | .265 | .297 |
| | Range | .8–1.5 | 1.8–2.5 | 2.5–3.2 |
| | 6 | 1.2 | 1.5 | 2.0 |
| | 7 | 1.0 | 2.0 | 2.5 |
| Intentional | 8 | 1.0 | 1.2 | 3.2 |
| Group ($a_2$) | 9 | 1.2 | 2.2 | 2.8 |
| | 10 | 1.0 | 2.2 | 3.5 |
| | *M* | 1.08 | 1.82 | 2.80 |
| | *SD* | .110 | .449 | .587 |
| | Range | 1.0–1.2 | 1.2–2.2 | 2.0–3.5 |

As you should now be aware, it is important to appreciate the trends in the data before looking at the ANOVA summary table. For instance, note that the mean frequency judgments increase in each group as a function of the presented frequency. Interestingly, there is not that great of a difference between group means (i.e., incidental vs. intentional) within each frequency presentation condition.

An outline of typical computer output for a two-factor analysis of variance for a mixed design is presented below; however, be aware that some computer programs separate the output of a mixed design, showing first the output for the between-groups analysis and then the output for the within-subjects analysis (which included the interaction effect). You may find that you have to scroll the computer screen to get all of the information.

| Between Subjects | | | | | |
|---|---|---|---|---|---|
| Source | SS | df | MS | F | p |
| Group | 0.225 | 1 | 0.225 | 1.718 | 0.226 |
| Error | 1.049 | 8 | 0.131 | | |

| Within Subjects | | | | | |
|---|---|---|---|---|---|
| Source | SS | df | MS | F | p |
| Present | 15.149 | 2 | 7.574 | 58.640 | 0.000 |
| Present × Group | 0.045 | 2 | 0.022 | 0.173 | 0.843 |
| Error | 2.067 | 16 | 0.129 | | |

The summary table is divided into two parts. The Between Subjects section includes the $F$-ratio for the main effect of groups. The form of this part of the table is like that of a single-factor analysis for the independent-groups design. The Error listed in this section is the within-groups variation. The $F$-ratio for the effect of group was not statistically significant because the obtained probability of .226 was greater than the conventional level of statistical significance of .05.

The second part of the summary table is headed Within Subjects. It includes the main effect of the within-subjects variable of presentation frequency and the interaction of presentation frequency and group. In general, any effect including a within-subjects variable (main effect or interaction) must be tested with the residual error term used in the within-subjects design. The $F$-ratio for the interaction is less than 1 and so was not statistically significant. The main effect of presentation frequency, however, did result in a statistically significant $F$. (As was true in the analysis of the single-factor within-subjects design, your computer output may include additional information than that presented here.)

Interpreting the results of a two-factor analysis for a mixed design follows the logic for any complex design (see Chapter 8). That is, the interaction is examined first, and if the interaction is statistically significant, then simple main effects and simple comparisons are used to identify the source of the interaction. The main effects are then examined, and analytical comparisons can be used to analyze further statistically significant main effects of independent variables with more than two levels.

Care must be taken when analyzing a mixed design to use the appropriate error term for analyses beyond those listed in the summary table (i.e., simple main effects, simple comparisons, and analytical comparisons). For example, if a significant interaction is obtained, it is recommended that simple main effects be analyzed by treating each simple effect as a single-factor ANOVA at that level of the second independent variable. If, for instance, we had obtained a significant interaction between group and presentation frequency in our sample

## Statistical Tables

**TABLE A.1**   TABLE OF RANDOM NUMBERS*

| Col. Line | (1) | (2) | (3) | (4) | (5) | (6) | (7) | (8) | (9) | (10) | (11) | (12) | (13) | (14) |
|---|---|---|---|---|---|---|---|---|---|---|---|---|---|---|
| 1 | 10480 | 15011 | 01536 | 02011 | 81647 | 91646 | 69179 | 14194 | 62590 | 36207 | 20969 | 99570 | 91291 | 90700 |
| 2 | 22368 | 46573 | 25595 | 85393 | 30995 | 89198 | 27982 | 53402 | 93965 | 34095 | 52666 | 19174 | 39615 | 99505 |
| 3 | 24130 | 48360 | 22527 | 97265 | 76393 | 64809 | 15179 | 24830 | 49340 | 32081 | 30680 | 19655 | 63348 | 58629 |
| 4 | 42167 | 93093 | 06243 | 61680 | 07856 | 16376 | 39440 | 53537 | 71341 | 57004 | 00849 | 74917 | 97758 | 16379 |
| 5 | 37570 | 39975 | 81837 | 16656 | 06121 | 91782 | 60468 | 81305 | 49684 | 60672 | 14110 | 06927 | 01263 | 54613 |
| 6 | 77921 | 06907 | 11008 | 42751 | 27756 | 53498 | 18602 | 70659 | 90655 | 15053 | 21916 | 81825 | 44394 | 42880 |
| 7 | 99562 | 72905 | 56420 | 69994 | 98872 | 31016 | 71194 | 18738 | 44013 | 48840 | 63213 | 21069 | 10634 | 12952 |
| 8 | 96301 | 91977 | 65463 | 07972 | 18876 | 20922 | 94595 | 56869 | 69014 | 60045 | 18425 | 84903 | 42508 | 32307 |
| 9 | 89579 | 14342 | 63661 | 10281 | 17453 | 18103 | 57740 | 84378 | 25331 | 12566 | 58678 | 44947 | 05585 | 56941 |
| 10 | 85475 | 36857 | 53342 | 53988 | 53060 | 59533 | 38867 | 62300 | 08158 | 17983 | 16439 | 11458 | 18593 | 64952 |
| 11 | 28918 | 69578 | 88231 | 33276 | 70997 | 79936 | 56865 | 05859 | 90106 | 31595 | 01547 | 85590 | 91610 | 78188 |
| 12 | 63553 | 40961 | 48235 | 03427 | 49626 | 69445 | 18663 | 72695 | 52180 | 20847 | 12234 | 90511 | 33703 | 90322 |
| 13 | 09429 | 93969 | 52636 | 92737 | 88974 | 33488 | 36320 | 17617 | 30015 | 08272 | 84115 | 27156 | 30613 | 74952 |
| 14 | 10365 | 61129 | 87529 | 85689 | 48237 | 52267 | 67689 | 93394 | 01511 | 26358 | 85104 | 20285 | 29975 | 89868 |
| 15 | 07119 | 97336 | 71048 | 08178 | 77233 | 13916 | 47564 | 81506 | 97735 | 85977 | 29372 | 74461 | 28551 | 90707 |
| 16 | 51085 | 12765 | 51821 | 51259 | 77452 | 16308 | 60756 | 92144 | 49442 | 53900 | 70960 | 63990 | 75601 | 40719 |
| 17 | 02368 | 21382 | 52404 | 60268 | 89368 | 19885 | 55322 | 44819 | 01188 | 65255 | 64835 | 44919 | 05944 | 55157 |
| 18 | 01011 | 54092 | 33362 | 94904 | 31273 | 04146 | 18594 | 29852 | 71585 | 85030 | 51132 | 01915 | 92747 | 64951 |
| 19 | 52162 | 53916 | 46369 | 58586 | 23216 | 14513 | 83149 | 98736 | 23495 | 64350 | 94738 | 17752 | 35156 | 35749 |
| 20 | 07056 | 97628 | 33787 | 09998 | 42698 | 06691 | 76988 | 13602 | 51851 | 46104 | 88916 | 19509 | 25625 | 58104 |
| 21 | 48663 | 91245 | 85828 | 14346 | 09172 | 30168 | 90229 | 04734 | 59193 | 22178 | 30421 | 61666 | 99904 | 32812 |
| 22 | 54164 | 58492 | 22421 | 74103 | 47070 | 25306 | 76468 | 26384 | 58151 | 06646 | 21524 | 15227 | 96909 | 44592 |
| 23 | 32639 | 32363 | 05597 | 24200 | 13363 | 38005 | 94342 | 28728 | 35806 | 06912 | 17012 | 64161 | 18296 | 22851 |
| 24 | 29334 | 27001 | 87637 | 87308 | 58731 | 00256 | 45834 | 15298 | 46557 | 41135 | 10367 | 07684 | 36188 | 18510 |
| 25 | 02488 | 33062 | 28834 | 07351 | 19731 | 92420 | 60952 | 61280 | 50001 | 67658 | 32586 | 86679 | 50720 | 94953 |

*Source: Table of 105,000 Random Decimal Digits, Starement no. 4914, File no. 261-A-1, Interstate Commerce Commission, Washington, D.C. May 1949.

experiment, a simple main effect for the intentional group would involve carrying out a repeated measures ANOVA for only that group (see Keppel, 1991, for more information on these comparisons).

Effect size estimates in a mixed design also frequently make use of eta squared, that is, an estimate of proportion of variance accounted for by the independent variable. As in the independent groups design (see above), eta squared is defined as the *SS* effect divided by the *SS* Effect plus the *SS* Error for that effect.

| Col. Line | (1) | (2) | (3) | (4) | (5) | (6) | (7) | (8) | (9) | (10) | (11) | (12) | (13) | (14) |
|---|---|---|---|---|---|---|---|---|---|---|---|---|---|---|
| 26 | 81525 | 72295 | 04839 | 96423 | 24878 | 82651 | 66566 | 14778 | 76797 | 14780 | 13300 | 87074 | 79666 | 95725 |
| 27 | 29676 | 20591 | 68086 | 26432 | 46901 | 20849 | 89768 | 81536 | 86645 | 12659 | 92259 | 57102 | 80428 | 25280 |
| 28 | 00742 | 57392 | 39064 | 66432 | 84673 | 40027 | 32832 | 61362 | 98947 | 96067 | 64760 | 64584 | 96096 | 98253 |
| 29 | 05366 | 04213 | 25669 | 26422 | 44407 | 44048 | 37937 | 63904 | 45766 | 66134 | 75470 | 66520 | 34693 | 90449 |
| 30 | 91921 | 26418 | 64117 | 94305 | 26766 | 25940 | 39972 | 22209 | 71500 | 64568 | 91402 | 42416 | 07844 | 69618 |
| 31 | 00582 | 04711 | 87917 | 77341 | 42206 | 35126 | 74087 | 99547 | 81817 | 42607 | 43808 | 76655 | 62028 | 76630 |
| 32 | 00725 | 69884 | 62797 | 56170 | 86324 | 88072 | 76222 | 36086 | 84637 | 93161 | 76038 | 65855 | 77919 | 88006 |
| 33 | 69011 | 65795 | 95876 | 55293 | 18988 | 27354 | 26575 | 08625 | 40801 | 59920 | 29841 | 80150 | 12777 | 48501 |
| 34 | 25976 | 57948 | 29888 | 88604 | 67917 | 48708 | 18912 | 82271 | 65424 | 69774 | 33611 | 54262 | 85963 | 03547 |
| 35 | 09763 | 83473 | 93577 | 12908 | 30883 | 18317 | 28290 | 35797 | 05998 | 41688 | 34952 | 37888 | 38917 | 88050 |
| 36 | 91567 | 42595 | 27958 | 30134 | 04024 | 86385 | 29880 | 99730 | 55536 | 84855 | 29080 | 09250 | 79656 | 73211 |
| 37 | 17955 | 56349 | 90999 | 49127 | 20044 | 59931 | 06115 | 20542 | 18059 | 02008 | 73708 | 83517 | 36103 | 42791 |
| 38 | 46503 | 18584 | 18845 | 49618 | 02304 | 51038 | 20655 | 58727 | 28168 | 15475 | 56942 | 53389 | 20562 | 87338 |
| 39 | 92157 | 89634 | 94824 | 78171 | 84610 | 82834 | 09922 | 25417 | 44137 | 48413 | 25555 | 21246 | 35509 | 20468 |
| 40 | 14577 | 62765 | 35605 | 81263 | 39667 | 47358 | 56873 | 56307 | 61607 | 49518 | 89696 | 20103 | 77490 | 18062 |
| 41 | 98427 | 07523 | 33362 | 64270 | 01638 | 92477 | 66969 | 98420 | 04880 | 45585 | 46565 | 04102 | 46880 | 45709 |
| 42 | 34914 | 63976 | 88720 | 82765 | 34476 | 17032 | 87589 | 40836 | 32427 | 70002 | 70663 | 88863 | 77775 | 69348 |
| 43 | 70060 | 28277 | 39475 | 46473 | 23219 | 53416 | 94970 | 25832 | 69975 | 94884 | 19661 | 72828 | 00102 | 66794 |
| 44 | 53976 | 54914 | 06990 | 67245 | 68350 | 82948 | 11398 | 42878 | 80287 | 88267 | 47363 | 46634 | 06541 | 97809 |
| 45 | 76072 | 29515 | 40980 | 07391 | 58745 | 25774 | 22987 | 80059 | 39911 | 96189 | 41151 | 14222 | 60697 | 59583 |
| 46 | 90725 | 52210 | 83974 | 29992 | 65831 | 38857 | 50490 | 83765 | 55657 | 14361 | 31720 | 57375 | 56228 | 41546 |
| 47 | 64364 | 67412 | 33339 | 31926 | 14883 | 24413 | 59744 | 92351 | 97473 | 89286 | 35931 | 04110 | 23726 | 51900 |
| 48 | 08962 | 00358 | 31662 | 25388 | 61642 | 34072 | 81249 | 35648 | 56891 | 69352 | 48373 | 45578 | 78547 | 81788 |
| 49 | 95012 | 68379 | 93526 | 70765 | 10592 | 04542 | 76463 | 54328 | 02349 | 17247 | 28865 | 14777 | 62730 | 92277 |
| 50 | 15664 | 10493 | 20492 | 38391 | 91132 | 21999 | 59516 | 81652 | 27195 | 48223 | 46751 | 22923 | 32261 | 85653 |

**TABLE A.2**　VALUES OF *r* AT THE .05 AND .01 LEVELS OF SIGNIFICANCE*

| df | .05 | .01 | df | .05 | .01 | df | .05 | .01 |
|---|---|---|---|---|---|---|---|---|
| 1 | .997 | 1.000 | 16 | .468 | .590 | 35 | .325 | .418 |
| 2 | .950 | .990 | 17 | .456 | .575 | 40 | .304 | .393 |
| 3 | .878 | .959 | 18 | .444 | .561 | 45 | .288 | .372 |
| 4 | .811 | .917 | 19 | .433 | .549 | 50 | .273 | .354 |
| 5 | .754 | .874 | 20 | .423 | .537 | 60 | .250 | .325 |
| 6 | .707 | .834 | 21 | .413 | .526 | 70 | .232 | .302 |
| 7 | .666 | .798 | 22 | .404 | .515 | 80 | .217 | .283 |
| 8 | .632 | .765 | 23 | .396 | .505 | 90 | .205 | .267 |
| 9 | .602 | .735 | 24 | .388 | .496 | 100 | .195 | .254 |
| 10 | .576 | .708 | 25 | .381 | .487 | | | |
| 11 | .553 | .684 | 26 | .374 | .478 | | | |
| 12 | .532 | .661 | 27 | .367 | .470 | | | |
| 13 | .514 | .641 | 28 | .361 | .463 | | | |
| 14 | .497 | .623 | 29 | .355 | .456 | | | |
| 15 | .482 | .606 | 30 | .349 | .449 | | | |

*Adapted from Table VII of Fisher and Yates, *Statistical Tables for Biological, Agricultural, and Medical Research,* 6th ed., 1974. Published by Oliver and Boyd, Limited, Publishers, Edinburgh, by permission of the authors and publishers. Published by Longman Group Ltd., London.

**TABLE A.3**　SELECTED VALUES FROM THE *t* DISTRIBUTION*

*Instructions for use:* To find a value of *t*, locate the row in the left-hand column of the table corresponding to the number of degrees of freedom (*df*) associated with the standard error of the mean, and select the value of *t* listed for your choice of $\alpha$. The value given in the column labeled $\alpha = .05$ is used in the calculation of the 95% confidence interval, and the value given in the column labeled $\alpha = .01$ is used to calculate the 99% confidence interval.

| df | $\alpha = .05$ | $\alpha = .01$ | df | $\alpha = .05$ | $\alpha = .01$ |
|---|---|---|---|---|---|
| 1 | 12.71 | 63.66 | 18 | 2.10 | 2.88 |
| 2 | 4.30 | 9.92 | 19 | 2.09 | 2.86 |
| 3 | 3.18 | 5.84 | 20 | 2.09 | 2.84 |
| 4 | 2.78 | 4.60 | 21 | 2.08 | 2.83 |
| 5 | 2.57 | 4.03 | 22 | 2.07 | 2.82 |
| 6 | 2.45 | 3.71 | 23 | 2.07 | 2.81 |
| 7 | 2.36 | 3.50 | 24 | 2.06 | 2.80 |
| 8 | 2.31 | 3.36 | 25 | 2.06 | 2.79 |
| 9 | 2.26 | 3.25 | 26 | 2.06 | 2.78 |
| 10 | 2.23 | 3.17 | 27 | 2.05 | 2.77 |
| 11 | 2.20 | 3.11 | 28 | 2.05 | 2.76 |
| 12 | 2.18 | 3.06 | 29 | 2.04 | 2.76 |
| 13 | 2.16 | 3.01 | 30 | 2.04 | 2.75 |
| 14 | 2.14 | 2.98 | 40 | 2.02 | 2.70 |
| 15 | 2.13 | 2.95 | 60 | 2.00 | 2.66 |
| 16 | 2.12 | 2.92 | 120 | 1.98 | 2.62 |
| 17 | 2.11 | 2.90 | Infinity | 1.96 | 2.58 |

*This table is adapted from Table 12 in *Biometrika tables for statisticians,* vol. 1 (3d ed.), New York: Cambridge University Press, 1970, edited by E. S. Pearson and H. O. Hartley, by permission of the *Biometrika* Trustees.

**TABLE A.4**  CRITICAL VALUES OF THE *F*-DISTRIBUTION*

*Instructions for use:* To find the critical value of *F*, locate the cell in the table formed by the intersection of the row containing the degrees of freedom associated with the denominator of the *F*-ratio and the column containing the degrees of freedom associated with the numerator of the *F*-ratio. The numbers listed in boldface type are the critical values of *F* at $\alpha = .05$; the numbers listed in Roman type are the critical values of *F* at $\alpha = .01$. As an example, suppose we have adopted the 5% level of significance and wish to evaluate the significance of an *F* with $df_{num} = 2$ and $df_{denom} = 12$. From the table we find that the critical value of $F(2, 12) = 3.89$ at $\alpha = .05$. If the obtained value of *F* equals or exceeds this critical value, we will reject the null hypothesis; if the obtained value of *F* is smaller than this critical value, we will not reject the null hypothesis.

Degrees of freedom for denominator

| | | | | | | | Degrees of freedom for numerator | | | | | | | | | | | |
|---|---|---|---|---|---|---|---|---|---|---|---|---|---|---|---|---|---|---|
| | 1 | 2 | 3 | 4 | 5 | 6 | 7 | 8 | 9 | 10 | 12 | 15 | 20 | 24 | 30 | 40 | 60 | Infinity |
| **1** | **161** | **200** | **216** | **225** | **230** | **234** | **237** | **239** | **241** | **242** | **244** | **246** | **248** | **249** | **250** | **251** | **252** | **254** |
| | 4052 | 4999 | 5403 | 5625 | 5764 | 5859 | 5928 | 5981 | 6022 | 6056 | 6106 | 6157 | 6209 | 6235 | 6261 | 6287 | 6313 | 6366 |
| **2** | **18.5** | **19.0** | **19.2** | **19.2** | **19.3** | **19.3** | **19.4** | **19.4** | **19.4** | **19.4** | **19.4** | **19.4** | **19.4** | **19.4** | **19.5** | **19.5** | **19.5** | **19.5** |
| | 98.5 | 99.0 | 99.2 | 99.2 | 99.3 | 99.3 | 99.4 | 99.4 | 99.4 | 99.4 | 99.4 | 99.4 | 99.4 | 99.5 | 99.5 | 99.5 | 99.5 | 99.5 |
| **3** | **10.1** | **9.55** | **9.28** | **9.12** | **9.01** | **8.94** | **8.89** | **8.85** | **8.81** | **8.79** | **8.74** | **8.70** | **8.66** | **8.64** | **8.62** | **8.59** | **8.57** | **8.53** |
| | 34.1 | 30.8 | 29.5 | 28.7 | 28.2 | 27.9 | 27.7 | 27.5 | 27.4 | 27.2 | 27.0 | 26.9 | 26.7 | 26.6 | 26.5 | 26.4 | 26.3 | 26.1 |
| **4** | **7.71** | **6.94** | **6.59** | **6.39** | **6.26** | **6.16** | **6.09** | **6.04** | **6.00** | **5.96** | **5.91** | **5.86** | **5.80** | **5.77** | **5.75** | **5.72** | **5.69** | **5.63** |
| | 21.2 | 18.0 | 16.7 | 16.0 | 15.5 | 15.2 | 15.0 | 14.8 | 14.7 | 14.6 | 14.4 | 14.2 | 14.0 | 13.9 | 13.8 | 13.8 | 13.6 | 13.5 |
| **5** | **6.61** | **5.79** | **5.41** | **5.19** | **5.05** | **4.95** | **4.88** | **4.82** | **4.77** | **4.74** | **4.68** | **4.62** | **4.56** | **4.53** | **4.50** | **4.46** | **4.43** | **4.26** |
| | 16.3 | 13.3 | 12.1 | 11.4 | 11.0 | 10.7 | 10.5 | 10.3 | 10.2 | 10.0 | 9.89 | 9.72 | 9.55 | 9.47 | 9.38 | 9.29 | 9.20 | 9.02 |
| **6** | **5.99** | **5.14** | **4.76** | **4.53** | **4.39** | **4.28** | **4.21** | **4.15** | **4.10** | **4.06** | **4.00** | **3.94** | **3.87** | **3.84** | **3.81** | **3.77** | **3.74** | **3.67** |
| | 13.8 | 10.9 | 9.78 | 9.15 | 8.75 | 8.47 | 8.26 | 8.10 | 7.98 | 7.87 | 7.72 | 7.56 | 7.40 | 7.31 | 7.23 | 7.14 | 7.06 | 6.88 |
| **7** | **5.59** | **4.74** | **4.35** | **4.12** | **3.97** | **3.87** | **3.79** | **3.73** | **3.68** | **3.64** | **3.57** | **3.51** | **3.44** | **3.41** | **3.38** | **3.34** | **3.30** | **3.23** |
| | 12.2 | 9.55 | 8.45 | 7.85 | 7.46 | 7.19 | 6.99 | 6.84 | 6.72 | 6.62 | 6.47 | 6.31 | 6.16 | 6.07 | 5.99 | 5.91 | 5.82 | 5.65 |
| **8** | **5.32** | **4.46** | **4.07** | **3.84** | **3.69** | **3.58** | **3.50** | **3.44** | **3.39** | **3.35** | **3.28** | **3.22** | **3.15** | **3.12** | **3.08** | **3.04** | **3.01** | **2.93** |
| | 11.3 | 8.65 | 7.59 | 7.01 | 6.63 | 6.37 | 6.18 | 6.03 | 5.91 | 5.81 | 5.67 | 5.52 | 5.36 | 5.28 | 5.20 | 5.12 | 5.03 | 4.86 |
| **9** | **5.12** | **4.26** | **3.86** | **3.63** | **3.48** | **3.37** | **3.29** | **3.23** | **3.18** | **3.14** | **3.07** | **3.01** | **2.94** | **2.90** | **2.86** | **2.83** | **2.79** | **2.71** |
| | 10.6 | 8.02 | 6.99 | 6.42 | 6.06 | 5.80 | 5.61 | 5.47 | 5.35 | 5.26 | 5.11 | 4.96 | 4.81 | 4.73 | 4.65 | 4.57 | 4.48 | 4.31 |
| **10** | **4.96** | **4.10** | **3.71** | **3.48** | **3.33** | **3.22** | **3.14** | **3.07** | **3.02** | **2.98** | **2.91** | **2.85** | **2.77** | **2.74** | **2.70** | **2.66** | **2.62** | **2.54** |
| | 10.0 | 7.56 | 6.55 | 5.99 | 5.64 | 5.39 | 5.20 | 5.06 | 4.94 | 4.85 | 4.71 | 4.56 | 4.41 | 4.33 | 4.25 | 4.17 | 4.08 | 3.91 |
| **11** | **4.84** | **3.98** | **3.59** | **3.36** | **3.20** | **3.09** | **3.01** | **2.95** | **2.90** | **2.85** | **2.79** | **2.72** | **2.65** | **2.61** | **2.57** | **2.53** | **2.49** | **2.40** |
| | 9.65 | 7.21 | 6.22 | 5.67 | 5.32 | 5.07 | 4.89 | 4.74 | 4.63 | 4.54 | 4.40 | 4.25 | 4.10 | 4.02 | 3.94 | 3.86 | 3.78 | 3.60 |
| **12** | **4.75** | **3.89** | **3.49** | **3.26** | **3.11** | **3.00** | **2.91** | **2.85** | **2.80** | **2.75** | **2.69** | **2.62** | **2.54** | **2.51** | **2.47** | **2.43** | **2.38** | **2.30** |
| | 9.33 | 6.93 | 5.95 | 5.41 | 5.06 | 4.82 | 4.64 | 4.50 | 4.39 | 4.30 | 4.16 | 4.01 | 3.86 | 3.78 | 3.70 | 3.62 | 3.54 | 3.36 |
| **13** | **4.67** | **3.81** | **3.41** | **3.18** | **3.03** | **2.92** | **2.83** | **2.77** | **2.71** | **2.67** | **2.60** | **2.53** | **2.46** | **2.42** | **2.38** | **2.34** | **2.30** | **2.21** |
| | 9.07 | 6.70 | 5.74 | 5.21 | 4.86 | 4.62 | 4.44 | 4.30 | 4.19 | 4.10 | 3.96 | 3.82 | 3.66 | 3.59 | 3.51 | 3.43 | 3.34 | 3.17 |
| **14** | **4.60** | **3.74** | **3.34** | **3.11** | **2.96** | **2.85** | **2.76** | **2.70** | **2.65** | **2.60** | **2.53** | **2.46** | **2.39** | **2.35** | **2.31** | **2.27** | **2.22** | **2.13** |
| | 8.86 | 6.51 | 5.56 | 5.04 | 4.69 | 4.46 | 4.28 | 4.14 | 4.03 | 3.94 | 3.80 | 3.66 | 3.51 | 3.43 | 3.35 | 3.27 | 3.18 | 3.00 |
| **15** | **4.54** | **3.68** | **3.29** | **3.06** | **2.90** | **2.79** | **2.71** | **2.64** | **2.59** | **2.54** | **2.48** | **2.40** | **2.33** | **2.29** | **2.25** | **2.20** | **2.16** | **2.07** |
| | 8.68 | 6.36 | 5.42 | 4.89 | 4.56 | 4.32 | 4.14 | 4.00 | 3.89 | 3.80 | 3.67 | 3.52 | 3.37 | 3.29 | 3.21 | 3.13 | 3.05 | 2.87 |
| **16** | **4.49** | **3.63** | **3.24** | **3.01** | **2.85** | **2.74** | **2.66** | **2.59** | **2.54** | **2.49** | **2.42** | **2.35** | **2.28** | **2.24** | **2.19** | **2.15** | **2.11** | **2.01** |
| | 8.53 | 6.23 | 5.29 | 4.77 | 4.44 | 4.20 | 4.03 | 3.89 | 3.78 | 3.69 | 3.55 | 3.41 | 3.26 | 3.18 | 3.10 | 3.02 | 2.93 | 2.75 |
| **17** | **4.45** | **3.59** | **3.20** | **2.96** | **2.81** | **2.70** | **2.61** | **2.55** | **2.49** | **2.45** | **2.38** | **2.31** | **2.23** | **2.19** | **2.15** | **2.10** | **2.06** | **1.96** |
| | 8.40 | 6.11 | 5.18 | 4.67 | 4.34 | 4.10 | 3.93 | 3.79 | 3.68 | 3.59 | 3.46 | 3.31 | 3.16 | 3.08 | 3.00 | 2.92 | 2.83 | 2.65 |
| **18** | **4.41** | **3.55** | **3.16** | **2.93** | **2.77** | **2.66** | **2.58** | **2.51** | **2.46** | **2.41** | **2.34** | **2.27** | **2.19** | **2.15** | **2.11** | **2.06** | **2.02** | **1.92** |
| | 8.29 | 6.01 | 5.09 | 4.58 | 4.25 | 4.01 | 3.84 | 3.71 | 3.60 | 3.51 | 3.37 | 3.23 | 3.08 | 3.00 | 2.92 | 2.84 | 2.75 | 2.57 |
| **19** | **4.38** | **3.52** | **3.13** | **2.90** | **2.74** | **2.63** | **2.54** | **2.48** | **2.42** | **2.38** | **2.31** | **2.23** | **2.16** | **2.11** | **2.07** | **2.03** | **1.98** | **1.88** |
| | 8.18 | 5.93 | 5.01 | 4.50 | 4.17 | 3.94 | 3.77 | 3.63 | 3.52 | 3.43 | 3.30 | 3.15 | 3.00 | 2.92 | 2.84 | 2.76 | 2.67 | 2.49 |
| **20** | **4.35** | **3.49** | **3.10** | **2.87** | **2.71** | **2.60** | **2.51** | **2.45** | **2.39** | **2.35** | **2.28** | **2.20** | **2.12** | **2.08** | **2.04** | **1.99** | **1.95** | **1.84** |
| | 8.10 | 5.85 | 4.94 | 4.43 | 4.10 | 3.87 | 3.70 | 3.56 | 3.46 | 3.37 | 3.23 | 3.09 | 2.94 | 2.86 | 2.78 | 2.69 | 2.61 | 2.42 |
| **22** | **4.30** | **3.44** | **3.05** | **2.82** | **2.66** | **2.55** | **2.46** | **2.40** | **2.34** | **2.30** | **2.23** | **2.15** | **2.07** | **2.03** | **1.98** | **1.94** | **1.89** | **1.78** |
| | 7.95 | 5.72 | 4.82 | 4.31 | 3.99 | 3.76 | 3.59 | 3.45 | 3.35 | 3.26 | 3.12 | 2.98 | 2.83 | 2.75 | 2.67 | 2.58 | 2.50 | 2.31 |
| **24** | **4.26** | **3.40** | **3.01** | **2.78** | **2.62** | **2.51** | **2.42** | **2.36** | **2.30** | **2.25** | **2.18** | **2.11** | **2.03** | **1.98** | **1.94** | **1.89** | **1.84** | **1.73** |
| | 7.82 | 5.61 | 4.72 | 4.22 | 3.90 | 3.67 | 3.50 | 3.36 | 3.26 | 3.17 | 3.03 | 2.89 | 2.74 | 2.66 | 2.58 | 2.49 | 2.40 | 2.21 |

(continued)

**TABLE A.4**   CRITICAL VALUES OF THE *F*-DISTRIBUTION* (*Concluded*)

| | | | | | | Degrees of freedom for numerator | | | | | | | | | | | | | |
|---|---|---|---|---|---|---|---|---|---|---|---|---|---|---|---|---|---|---|---|
| | | 1 | 2 | 3 | 4 | 5 | 6 | 7 | 8 | 9 | 10 | 12 | 15 | 20 | 24 | 30 | 40 | 60 | Infinity |
| | 26 | 4.23 | 3.37 | 2.98 | 2.74 | 2.59 | 2.47 | 2.39 | 2.32 | 2.27 | 2.22 | 2.15 | 2.07 | 1.99 | 1.95 | 1.90 | 1.85 | 1.80 | 1.69 |
| | | 7.72 | 5.53 | 4.64 | 4.14 | 3.82 | 3.59 | 3.42 | 3.29 | 3.18 | 3.09 | 2.96 | 2.81 | 2.66 | 2.58 | 2.50 | 2.42 | 2.33 | 2.13 |
| | 28 | 4.20 | 3.34 | 2.95 | 2.71 | 2.56 | 2.45 | 2.36 | 2.29 | 2.24 | 2.19 | 2.12 | 2.04 | 1.96 | 1.91 | 1.87 | 1.82 | 1.77 | 1.65 |
| | | 7.64 | 5.45 | 4.57 | 4.07 | 3.75 | 3.53 | 3.36 | 3.23 | 3.12 | 3.03 | 2.90 | 2.75 | 2.60 | 2.52 | 2.44 | 2.35 | 2.26 | 2.06 |
| Degrees of freedom for denominator | 30 | 4.17 | 3.32 | 2.92 | 2.69 | 2.53 | 2.42 | 2.33 | 2.27 | 2.21 | 2.16 | 2.09 | 2.01 | 1.93 | 1.89 | 1.84 | 1.79 | 1.74 | 1.62 |
| | | 7.56 | 5.39 | 4.51 | 4.02 | 3.70 | 3.47 | 3.30 | 3.17 | 3.07 | 2.98 | 2.84 | 2.70 | 2.55 | 2.47 | 2.39 | 2.30 | 2.21 | 2.01 |
| | 40 | 4.08 | 3.23 | 2.84 | 2.61 | 2.45 | 2.34 | 2.25 | 2.18 | 2.12 | 2.08 | 2.00 | 1.92 | 1.84 | 1.79 | 1.74 | 1.69 | 1.64 | 1.51 |
| | | 7.31 | 5.18 | 4.31 | 3.83 | 3.51 | 3.29 | 3.12 | 2.99 | 2.89 | 2.80 | 2.66 | 2.52 | 2.37 | 2.29 | 2.20 | 2.11 | 2.02 | 1.80 |
| | 60 | 4.00 | 3.15 | 2.76 | 2.53 | 2.37 | 2.25 | 2.17 | 2.10 | 2.04 | 1.99 | 1.92 | 1.84 | 1.75 | 1.7 | 1.65 | 1.59 | 1.53 | 1.39 |
| | | 7.06 | 4.98 | 4.13 | 3.65 | 3.34 | 3.12 | 2.95 | 2.82 | 2.72 | 2.63 | 2.50 | 2.35 | 2.20 | 2.12 | 2.03 | 1.94 | 1.84 | 1.60 |
| | 120 | 3.92 | 3.07 | 2.68 | 2.45 | 2.29 | 2.17 | 2.09 | 2.02 | 1.96 | 1.91 | 1.83 | 1.75 | 1.66 | 1.61 | 1.55 | 1.50 | 1.43 | 1.25 |
| | | 6.85 | 4.79 | 3.95 | 3.48 | 3.17 | 2.96 | 2.79 | 2.66 | 2.56 | 2.47 | 2.34 | 2.19 | 2.03 | 1.95 | 1.86 | 1.76 | 1.66 | 1.38 |
| | INFINITY | 3.84 | 3.00 | 2.60 | 2.37 | 2.21 | 2.10 | 2.01 | 1.94 | 1.88 | 1.83 | 1.75 | 1.67 | 1.57 | 1.52 | 1.46 | 1.39 | 1.32 | 1.00 |
| | | 6.63 | 4.61 | 3.78 | 3.32 | 3.02 | 2.80 | 2.64 | 2.51 | 2.41 | 2.32 | 2.18 | 2.04 | 1.88 | 1.79 | 1.70 | 1.59 | 1.47 | 1.00 |

*This table is abridged from Table 18 in *Biometrika tables for statisticians,* vol. 1 (3d ed.), New York: Cambridge University Press, 1970, edited by E. S. Pearson and H. O. Hartley, by permission of the *Biometrika* Trustees.

**TABLE A.5**   POWER TABLE FOR COMPARISON BETWEEN TWO MEANS (INDEPENDENT GROUPS) WITH ALPHA = .05 (TWO-TAILED TEST)

*Note:* The table shows the power associated with various effect sizes (.10–1.00) as a function of sample size for an independent groups *t*-test ($\alpha$ = .05, two-tailed test). Effect size is based on Cohen's *d*. The table may be used to assess power post hoc, that is, after a study has been completed. For example, when *n* = 20 in *each group* and the effect size is medium (.50), power is .33. (Decimal points have been omitted in table.) For the same sample size and a large effect size (.80), power is .69. The table may also be used in planning an experiment. Suppose that an examination of the literature suggests that the effect you are looking for is about .60, slightly greater than a medium effect size according to Cohen's (1988) rule of thumb. What sample size in needed to see this effect with power =.80? Looking at the column for this size effect (.60), you will see that power increases as sample size increases until .84 power is achieved when sample size is 50. To obtain power =.80 we can estimate that sample size should be about 45 (by interpolating between sample size 40 and 50). What sample size is needed to see this effect with power = .70? You should see that sample size must be 35 in each group to achieve power =.70. (Based on Cohen, 1988, pp. 36–37.)

| | | | | Effect Size (d) | | | | | |
|---|---|---|---|---|---|---|---|---|---|
| | | (Small) | | | (Medium) | | | (Large) | |
| *n* | .10 | .20 | .30 | .40 | .50 | .60 | .70 | .80 | 1.00 |
| 10 | 06 | 07 | 10 | 13 | 18 | 24 | 31 | 39 | 56 |
| 15 | 06 | 08 | 12 | 18 | 26 | 35 | 45 | 56 | 75 |
| 20 | 06 | 09 | 15 | 23 | 33 | 45 | 58 | 69 | 87 |
| 25 | 06 | 11 | 18 | 28 | 41 | 55 | 68 | 79 | 93 |
| 30 | 07 | 12 | 21 | 33 | 47 | 55 | 68 | 79 | 93 |
| 35 | 07 | 13 | 23 | 38 | 54 | 70 | 82 | 91 | 98 |
| 40 | 07 | 14 | 26 | 42 | 60 | 75 | 87 | 94 | 99 |
| 50 | 08 | 17 | 32 | 50 | 70 | 84 | 93 | 98 | * |
| 60 | 08 | 19 | 37 | 58 | 77 | 90 | 97 | 99 | * |
| 80 | 10 | 24 | 47 | 71 | 88 | 96 | 99 | * | * |
| 100 | 11 | 29 | 56 | 80 | 94 | 99 | * | * | * |

**TABLE A.6** POWER TABLE FOR ANALYSIS OF VARIANCE FOR INDEPENDENT GROUPS WITH ALPHA = .05

*Note:* The table shows the power associated with various effect sizes (.05–.50) as a function of sample size in each group in an independent groups design. Effect size is assessed using Cohen's *f* (see Appendix A text). Power is summarized separately for an experiment with independent groups of 2, 3, 4, and 5. The table may be used to assess power post hoc, after a study is completed. For example, assume that an experiment was conducted with 3 groups (*n* = 30) and an analysis of variance performed on the data. Assume further that the effect size based on *f* was .40, a large effect according to Cohen's (1988) rule of thumb. What was the power associated with this test? Looking at that portion of the table that reveals power values for 3 groups (*df* = 2), and under the column .40, you can see that power = .93 when sample size is 30. (Decimal points have been omitted in the table.) The table also may be used to plan an experiment by determining the sample size needed to see an effect of a specific magnitude. Suppose that a review of previous studies revealed that on the average an effect size of .30 was obtained for the variable of interest. What sample size would be needed in a 4 group experiment to see an effect of this size with power = .80? Looking at the power values for an independent groups experiment with 4 groups, and under the effect size column .30, you will see that power increases as sample size increases and is .84 when sample size is 30. Power is .76 when *n* = 25; thus we can interpolate to estimate that sample size should be about 28 to achieve power = .80. If the effect size we are seeking is .10, a small effect size according to Cohen, you can see that power is only .22 even when sample size is 60. (Based on Cohen, 1988, pp. 311–318.)

2 Groups (*df* = 1)

| | | | Effect Size (*f*) | | | | | | |
|---|---|---|---|---|---|---|---|---|---|
| | | (Small) | | | (Medium) | | | (Large) | |
| *n* | .05 | .10 | .15 | .20 | .25 | .30 | .35 | .40 | .50 |
| 5 | 05 | 06 | 07 | 08 | 11 | 13 | 16 | 20 | 29 |
| 10 | 05 | 07 | 09 | 13 | 18 | 25 | 32 | 40 | 57 |
| 15 | 06 | 08 | 12 | 18 | 26 | 36 | 47 | 57 | 76 |
| 20 | 06 | 09 | 15 | 23 | 34 | 46 | 59 | 70 | 88 |
| 25 | 06 | 10 | 18 | 29 | 42 | 56 | 69 | 80 | 94 |
| 30 | 06 | 11 | 21 | 34 | 49 | 64 | 77 | 87 | 97 |
| 35 | 07 | 12 | 24 | 39 | 55 | 71 | 83 | 92 | 99 |
| 40 | 07 | 14 | 27 | 43 | 61 | 77 | 88 | 95 | 99 |
| 50 | 07 | 16 | 32 | 52 | 71 | 85 | 94 | 98 | * |
| 60 | 08 | 19 | 38 | 60 | 79 | 91 | 97 | 99 | * |

3 Groups (*df* = 2)

| | | | Effect Size (*f*) | | | | | | |
|---|---|---|---|---|---|---|---|---|---|
| | | (Small) | | | (Medium) | | | (Large) | |
| *n* | .05 | .10 | .15 | .20 | .25 | .30 | .35 | .40 | .50 |
| 5 | 05 | 06 | 07 | 09 | 11 | 14 | 17 | 22 | 32 |
| 10 | 05 | 07 | 10 | 14 | 20 | 27 | 35 | 45 | 64 |
| 15 | 06 | 08 | 13 | 20 | 29 | 40 | 52 | 64 | 84 |
| 20 | 06 | 09 | 16 | 26 | 38 | 52 | 66 | 78 | 93 |
| 25 | 06 | 10 | 19 | 32 | 47 | 63 | 77 | 87 | 98 |
| 30 | 06 | 12 | 22 | 37 | 55 | 71 | 85 | 93 | 99 |
| 35 | 07 | 13 | 26 | 43 | 62 | 79 | 90 | 96 | * |
| 40 | 07 | 15 | 29 | 48 | 68 | 84 | 94 | 98 | * |
| 50 | 08 | 18 | 36 | 58 | 79 | 92 | 98 | 99 | * |
| 60 | 08 | 21 | 42 | 67 | 86 | 96 | 99 | * | * |

*(continued)*

**TABLE A.6**   POWER TABLE FOR ANALYSIS OF VARIANCE FOR INDEPENDENT GROUPS WITH ALPHA = .05
(*Concluded*)

4 Groups (*df* = 3)

| | | | | | Effect Size (*f*) | | | | |
|---|---|---|---|---|---|---|---|---|---|
| | | (Small) | | | | (Medium) | | | (Large) | |
| *n* | .05 | .10 | .15 | .20 | .25 | .30 | .35 | .40 | .50 |
| 5 | 05 | 06 | 07 | 09 | 12 | 16 | 21 | 26 | 40 |
| 10 | 06 | 07 | 10 | 16 | 23 | 33 | 44 | 56 | 78 |
| 15 | 06 | 09 | 14 | 23 | 36 | 50 | 65 | 78 | 94 |
| 20 | 06 | 10 | 18 | 31 | 47 | 65 | 79 | 90 | 99 |
| 25 | 06 | 12 | 23 | 39 | 58 | 76 | 89 | 96 | * |
| 30 | 07 | 13 | 27 | 46 | 67 | 84 | 94 | 98 | * |
| 35 | 07 | 15 | 31 | 54 | 75 | 90 | 97 | 99 | * |
| 40 | 07 | 17 | 36 | 60 | 81 | 94 | 99 | * | * |
| 50 | 08 | 19 | 40 | 65 | 85 | 96 | 99 | * | * |
| 60 | 09 | 22 | 47 | 74 | 91 | 98 | * | * | * |

5 Groups (*df* = 4)

| | | | | | Effect Size (*f*) | | | | |
|---|---|---|---|---|---|---|---|---|---|
| | | (Small) | | | | (Medium) | | | (Large) | |
| *n* | .05 | .10 | .15 | .20 | .25 | .30 | .35 | .40 | .50 |
| 5 | 05 | 06 | 07 | 10 | 13 | 17 | 22 | 29 | 44 |
| 10 | 06 | 07 | 11 | 17 | 25 | 36 | 48 | 61 | 83 |
| 15 | 06 | 09 | 15 | 25 | 39 | 55 | 70 | 82 | 96 |
| 20 | 06 | 11 | 20 | 34 | 52 | 70 | 84 | 93 | 99 |
| 25 | 07 | 12 | 24 | 43 | 63 | 81 | 92 | 98 | * |
| 30 | 07 | 14 | 29 | 51 | 73 | 88 | 96 | 99 | * |
| 35 | 07 | 16 | 34 | 65 | 80 | 93 | 98 | * | * |
| 40 | 08 | 18 | 39 | 68 | 86 | 96 | 99 | * | * |
| 50 | 08 | 21 | 44 | 71 | 90 | 98 | * | * | * |
| 60 | 09 | 24 | 52 | 80 | 95 | 99 | * | * | * |

*Indicates that power is greater than .995.

APPENDIX

# B

# *Questionnaire Construction*

## INTRODUCTION

In Chapter 4 we discussed procedures for administering a survey without describing in detail the nature of the most common survey research instrument: the questionnaire. Even if the sample used was perfectly representative, the response rate was 100%, and the research design was elegantly planned and perfectly executed, the results of a survey will be useless if the questionnaire was poorly constructed. Although there is no substitute for experience when it comes to preparing a good questionnaire, there are a few general principles of sound questionnaire construction with which you should be familiar before you do your first survey. In this appendix we describe six basic steps in preparing a questionnaire and then offer some more specific guidelines for writing and administering individual questions. This material will be most useful should you decide to make use of a questionnaire as part of a research project you are doing.

## STEPS IN PREPARING A QUESTIONNAIRE

We can suggest six basic steps in preparing a questionnaire:

1 Decide what information should be sought.
2 Decide what type of questionnaire should be used.
3 Write a first draft of the questionnaire.
4 Reexamine and revise the questionnaire.
5 Pretest the questionnaire.
6 Edit the questionnaire and specify the procedures for its use.

Step 1    The warning "Watch out for that first step!" is appropriate here. *The first step in questionnaire construction—deciding what information is to be sought— should actually be the first step in planning the survey as a whole.* This decision, of course, determines the nature of the questions to be included in the questionnaire. It is important to project the likely results of the survey if the proposed questionnaire is used and then to decide whether these "findings" will answer the questions the study is intended to address. Surveys are frequently done under considerable time pressure, and inexperienced researchers are especially prone to impatience. Just remember that a poorly conceived questionnaire takes just as much time and effort to administer and analyze as does a well-conceived questionnaire. The difference is that a well-constructed questionnaire leads to interpretable results. The best that can be said for a poorly designed one is that it is a good way to learn how important careful deliberation is in the planning stages.

Step 2    *Once the information to be sought from respondents has been clearly specified, the next step is to decide on the type of questionnaire to be used.* For example, will it be self-administered, or will trained interviewers be using it? This decision is determined primarily by the survey method that has been selected. For instance, if a telephone survey is to be done, trained interviewers will be needed. In designing the questionnaire, one should also consider using items that have been prepared by other researchers. For example, there is no reason to develop your own instrument to assess racial prejudice if a reliable and valid one is already available. Besides, if you use items from a questionnaire that has already been used, you can compare your results directly with those of earlier studies.

**Step 3**  *If you decide that no available instrument suits your needs, you will have to take the third step and write a first draft of your own questionnaire.* Guidelines concerning the format and ordering of questions, as well as suggestions for wording questions effectively, will be presented in later sections of this appendix.

**Step 4**  *The fourth step in questionnaire construction—reexamining and rewriting—is an essential one.* Questions that appear objective and unambiguous to you may strike others as slanted and ambiguous. It is most helpful to have your questionnaire reviewed by experts, both those who have knowledge of survey research methods and those with expertise in the area on which your study is focused. For example, if you are doing a survey of students' attitudes toward the campus food service, it would be advisable to have your questionnaire reviewed by the campus food service director. When you are dealing with a controversial topic, it is especially important to have representatives of both sides of the issue screen your questions for possible bias. Sometimes no one particular wording can be agreed on by all. In such cases, the *split-ballot technique* is helpful. In this technique, different wordings of the same questions are used for equivalent samples of respondents. The effect of the wording can be directly examined by comparing responses made in these two (or more) samples. For example, Schuman and Bobo (1988) used the split-ballot technique to embed randomized experiments within their survey design. Their overall objective was to examine the opposition of Whites to the rights of Blacks to open housing. They used the split-ballot technique to assign subgroups within their samples randomly to different versions of questions. Comparing the responses of these subgroups led to the identification of factors that affect attitudes toward open housing, factors such as people's general resistance to government coercion.

**Step 5**  *By far the most critical step in the development of a sound questionnaire is Step 5, the pretest.* A pretest involves actually administering the questionnaire to a small sample of respondents under conditions as much as possible like those to be used in the final administration of the survey. Pretest respondents must also be typical of those to be included in the final sample; it makes little sense to pretest a survey of nursing home residents by administering the questionnaire to college students. There is one way, however, in which a pretest does differ from the final administration of the survey. Respondents should be interviewed at length regarding their reactions to individual questions and to the questionnaire as a whole. This provides information about potentially ambiguous or offensive items.

The pretest should also serve as a "dress rehearsal" for interviewers, who should be closely supervised during this stage to ensure that they understand and adhere to the proper procedures for administering the questionnaire. If major changes have to be made as a result of problems arising during the pretest, a second pretest may be needed to determine whether these changes solved the problems originally encountered.

Step 6    *After pretesting is completed, the final step is to edit the questionnaire and specify the procedures to be followed in its final administration.*

In the next two sections, we return to two issues pertinent to the third step in preparing a questionnaire: writing a first draft. We will consider two sets of guidelines: one for writing questions and one for the general format of a questionnaire.

## GUIDELINES FOR THE EFFECTIVE WORDING OF QUESTIONS

Lawyers have long known that how a question is phrased has great impact on how that question is answered. Survey researchers need to be equally conscious of this principle. This point is illustrated in a survey Loftus (1979) conducted for the manufacturer of a leading headache remedy. She found that people reported having more headaches when they were asked "Do you get headaches frequently and, if so, how often?" than when they were asked "Do you get headaches occasionally and, if so, how often?" Unfortunately, the extent of the influence of the wording of questions in a given survey can almost never be determined precisely.

For instance, Clark and Schober (1992) suggest that survey respondents typically make what they call the "interpretability presumption," namely, that "each question means what it is obvious to me here and now that it means" (p. 27). This presumption on the part of the respondent, as they point out, has some important consequences. For instance, when a question includes a vague word, respondents often assume that the surveyor meant something very specific by this word. But because the word *is* vague, respondents produce various interpretations according to their individual biases and ideas of "what it is obvious to me." Thus, words like "few" or "usually," or terms such as "energy crisis," may be interpreted differently by different individuals. Respondents also tend to assume that a word is used in the way it is typically used in their subculture or culture. Clark and Schober (1992) cite as an example a surveyor who wanted to ask Mexican residents in the Yucatan the question, "How many children do you have?" When translated into Spanish, the surveyor used the word *niños* for children, but villagers in this area of Mexico treated *niños* as including living children and children who have died. The interpretability presumption may also lead respondents to assume that if the researcher asks a question, then it is one that the respondent can answer. Thus, respondents will often willingly give answers to questions that have no (valid) answers! For example, when asked to give opinions about nationalities that didn't exist, respondents nevertheless gave opinions.

Clark and Schober (1992) summarize well the problem of question wording facing survey researchers: "Surveyors cannot possibly write perfect questions, self-evident to each respondent, that never need clarification. And because they cannot, the answers will often be surprising" (p. 29).

The problem of question wording is clearer than the solution. Schuman and Scott (1987) argue that investigators should realize the limitations on assessing, in an absolute sense, people's opinions or attitudes based on any one set of questions. They encourage researchers to emphasize participants' responses to the same set of questions over time. At a minimum, *the exact wording of critical questions should always be reported along with the data describing respondents' answers.* The problem of the potential influence of the wording of questions is yet another illustration of why a multimethod approach is so essential in investigating behavior.

There are certain guidelines to follow to minimize problems arising from the phrasing of survey questions. These guidelines can be applied to *free-response* (open-ended) questions and to *closed* (multiple-choice) questions. Free-response questions, like the essay questions on a classroom test, merely specify the area to be addressed in a response. For example, the question "What are your views on the legalizing of abortion?" is a free-response question. By contrast, closed questions provide specific response alternatives. "Is police protection very good, fairly good, neither good nor bad, not very good, or not good at all?" is a closed question about the quality of police protection in a community.

The advantages of free-response questions are that they can be written more quickly and that they offer the respondent greater flexibility. However, these advantages are often more than offset by the difficulties that arise in recording and scoring responses to free-response questions. For example, extensive coding is frequently necessary before rambling responses to free-response questions can be summarized succinctly. Closed questions, on the other hand, are more difficult to write, but they can be answered more easily and quickly and fewer scoring problems arise. It is also much easier to summarize responses to closed questions because the answers are readily comparable across respondents. A major disadvantage of closed questions is that they reduce expressiveness and spontaneity. Further, the possibility exists that the respondent will have to choose a less than preferred response because no presented alternative really captures his or her views. Hence, the responses obtained may not accurately reflect the respondent's opinion.

Newcomb, Koenig, Flacks, and Warwick (1967) used both free-response and closed questions in a survey of students' attitudes. Their survey was done in two stages. In the first stage, student respondents were asked a series of free-response questions about how their lives had changed as a result of attending college. The trained interviewers used probes extensively and effectively in this stage. A self-administered questionnaire was then developed for the second stage of the survey. During this second stage, a different sample of students rated how much they had changed in each of a number of areas. The researchers wrote closed questions for the second stage of the survey using specific areas of change that had been indicated in the answers to the original set of free-response questions. This survey illustrates the complementary strengths of free-response and closed questions. The findings of the survey showed that one area in which change did occur was in the students' political views. What is more, these changes were shown to persist well after the students had left college.

Closed questions frequently include a scale which is used to measure the degree or amount of response to the question. A typical 5-point, Likert-type scale would include the categories "strongly agree," "agree," "neutral," "disagree," and "strongly disagree" (see Chapter 4 for more information on scaling methods). Alternatively, degree of response can be measured by asking respondents to rank several alternatives from "most preferred" to "least preferred." Rank-order scaling has the advantage that it forces the respondent to make discriminations among alternatives. Rank-order scaling is sensitive in measuring differences that respondents can detect.

The disadvantage of rank-order scaling is that it is not informative about the absolute judgment of any one alternative. For example, respondents could rank the beauty of 15 photographs even if they judged all the photographs to be ugly; they could reliably identify the least ugly (most beautiful) of the group even if they judged them all to be ugly. If they were asked to use Likert-type scales to rate the beauty of the photographs, it would be possible to measure the absolute level of rated beauty of each photograph. It would also be possible to interpret the relative distances between the ratings for different photographs, something that is not possible with rank-order scaling. (The winner and runner-up in a race can be decided in a photo finish or "by a mile," and the winner will still be first and the runner-up second.) The ability to obtain absolute judgments and to interpret distances between ratings are the primary advantages of Likert-type rating scales. The major disadvantage is that respondents may fail to make discriminations that they are capable of making. They may, for example, give the same rating of beauty to all the photographs. In general, rank-order scaling is preferred if the researcher is interested in relative preferences; rating scales are preferred if the researcher is interested in the absolute level of the respondents' reactions (e.g., the frequency with which items are rated as "poor," or the overall average rating for a stimulus event).

Regardless of the type of question used, the *vocabulary should be simple, direct, and familiar to all respondents. Questions should be as clear and specific as possible. Double-barreled questions should be avoided.* An example of a double-barreled question is: "Have you suffered from headaches and nausea recently?" A person may respond "no" if both symptoms have not occurred at exactly the same time or may respond "yes" if either symptom has occurred. The solution to the problem of double-barreled questions is a simple one—rewrite them as separate questions. *Survey questions should be as short as possible without sacrificing the clarity of the questions' meaning.* Twenty or fewer words should suffice for most survey questions. *Each question should be carefully edited for readability and should be phrased in such a way that all conditional information precedes the key idea.* For example, it would be better to ask, "If you were forced to leave your present job, what type of work would you seek?" than to ask, "What type of work would you seek if you were forced to leave your present job?"

*Leading or loaded questions should also be avoided in a questionnaire. Leading questions* take the form "Most people favor the use of nuclear energy. What do you think?" To avoid bias, it is better to mention all possible perspectives or to mention none. A survey question about attitudes toward nuclear energy could read either "Some people favor the use of nuclear energy, some people oppose the use of nuclear energy, and some people have no opinion one way or the other. What do you think?" or "What do you think about the use of nuclear energy?" *Loaded questions* are questions that contain emotion-laden words. For example, terms such as *radical* and *racist* should be avoided. To guard against loaded questions, it is best to have your questionnaire reviewed by individuals representing a range of social and political perspectives.

In summary, good questionnaire items should:

- include vocabulary that is simple, direct, and familiar to all respondents;
- be clear and specific;
- *not* involve leading, loaded, or double-barreled questions;
- be as short as possible (20 or fewer words);
- include all conditional information prior to the key idea; and
- be edited for readability.

## GUIDELINES FOR THE GENERAL FORMAT OF A QUESTIONNAIRE

Two aspects of the general format should be considered in constructing the final copy of a questionnaire: the design or layout of the questionnaire, and the ordering of questions.

### Questionnaire Design

An effort should be made to make the design of the questionnaire attractive, but the emphasis should be on making it as easy as possible to use.

A section of a questionnaire designed for personal or phone interviews is shown in Table B.1. This questionnaire was used by trained interviewers in a survey done by the Institute for Social Research at the University of Michigan. The aim of the survey was to examine the quality of American life (Campbell, Converse, & Rodgers, 1975). Several characteristics of this questionnaire are noteworthy. Each question is identified with a letter indicating the section of the questionnaire and a number specifying the individual question. This is done to facilitate later scoring and analysis of responses. The arrangement of the questions on each page is compact, but the structure is designed to make it easy to read the questions and to record responses. Whenever possible, questions with the same response format appear together. When closed questions are asked, a note is included to remind the interviewer to give the respondent a card listing the response alternatives so that the respondent can concentrate on the question and not on remembering the alternatives. At the beginning of the first question,

**TABLE B.1**   SAMPLE QUESTIONNAIRE FORMAT FOR PERSONAL OR PHONE INTERVIEW

*Section A: City and Neighborhood*

A1 In this study we are interested in measuring the quality of life of people in this country—that is, the things people like and dislike about their homes, cities, neighborhoods, jobs, and so on. The first question is: How long have you lived in (INSERT NAME OF COMMUNITY, OR OF COUNTY IF RURAL)? _____. (IF *LESS* THAN TWO YEARS, GET NUMBER OF MONTHS.)
_____ YEARS _____ MONTHS, OR SINCE_____

A2 And how long have you lived here in this (house/apartment)? (IF *LESS* THAN TWO YEARS, GET NUMBER OF MONTHS.)
_____ YEARS _____ MONTHS, OR SINCE_____

A3 I'd like to ask how satisfied you are with some of the main public services you are supposed to receive. (Hand R CARD 1, YELLOW) Please tell me how you feel about each thing I mention, using one of the answers on this card. First, how about the way streets and roads are kept up around here. Would you say this service is *very good, fairly good, neither good nor bad, not very good, or not good at all?*

| 1. VERY GOOD | 2. FAIRLY GOOD | 3. NEITHER GOOD NOR BAD | 4. NOT VERY GOOD | 5. NOT GOOD AT ALL |
|---|---|---|---|---|

A4 How do you feel about the quality of the *public* schools that the children from around here go to—would you say it is *very good, fairly good, neither good nor bad, not very good, or not good at all?* [DK is don't know.]

| 1. VERY GOOD | 2. FAIRLY GOOD | 3. NEITHER GOOD NOR BAD | 4. NOT VERY GOOD | 5. NOT GOOD AT ALL | 8. DK |
|---|---|---|---|---|---|

IF R LIVES IN A CITY, TOWN, OR VILLAGE, ASK A5 AND A6: IF RURAL, TURN TO A7

A5 How good is garbage collection in this neighborhood? Is it *very good, fairly good, neither good nor bad, not very good, or not good at all?* [DK is don't know.]

| 1. VERY GOOD | 2. FAIRLY GOOD | 3. NEITHER GOOD NOR BAD | 4. NOT VERY GOOD | 5. NOT GOOD AT ALL | 8. DK |
|---|---|---|---|---|---|

A6 What about the parks and playgrounds for children in this neighborhood? Are they *very good, fairly good, neither good nor bad, not very good, or not good at all?* [DK is don't know.]

| 1. VERY GOOD | 2. FAIRLY GOOD | 3. NEITHER GOOD NOR BAD | 4. NOT VERY GOOD | 5. NOT GOOD AT ALL | 8. DK |
|---|---|---|---|---|---|

ASK EVERYBODY:

A7 How about police protection around here. Is it *very good, fairly good, neither good nor bad, not very good, or not good at all?* [DK is don't know.]

| 1. VERY GOOD | 2. FAIRLY GOOD | 3. NEITHER GOOD NOR BAD | 4. NOT VERY GOOD | 5. NOT GOOD AT ALL | 8. DK |
|---|---|---|---|---|---|

the respondent is given a brief rationale for the study as a whole, but this preamble is kept short so as to require as little of the respondent's time as possible.

The format of a questionnaire that is meant to be self-administered must be somewhat different. The first section of a self-administered questionnaire distributed to passengers on Amtrak trains is shown in Table B.2. The items are arranged in a clear and uncluttered manner, and the order of the questions is clearly indicated by the large boldface numbers. Each item is short and direct, and the instructions for each question are simple. The small numbers next to each blank are used to computer-code the responses. The numbers in parentheses indicate column numbers in a computer file, and the other numbers are the ones to be entered if the respondent checks that blank. Such prior coding saves time when the data are to be analyzed and helps reduce the number of errors in data entry. In designing a self-administered questionnaire, one should make every effort to make it visually appealing; visual appeal increases the response rate. It is most important that the questions be self-explanatory and that respondents be able to complete the questionnaire quickly and correctly.

## Ordering of Questions

A crucial issue in deciding the order of the questions in a survey is which question or questions to ask first. The first few questions set the tone for the rest of the questionnaire and determine how willingly and conscientiously respondents will work on subsequent questions.

- Begin self-administered questionnaires with the most interesting set of questions in order to capture the respondent's attention. (Demographic data should be obtained at the end of a self-administered questionnaire.)
- In surveys involving personal or telephone interviews, on the other hand, demographic questions are frequently asked at the beginning because they are easy for the respondent to answer and thus bolster the respondent's confidence. They also allow time for the interviewer to establish rapport before asking questions about more sensitive matters.

The order in which particular questions are asked can have dramatic effects, as illustrated in a study by Schuman, Presser, and Ludwig (1981). They found differential responding depending on the order of two questions concerning abortion, one general and one specific. The general question was "Do you think it should be possible for a pregnant woman to obtain a legal abortion if she is married and does not want any more children?" The more specific question was "Do you think it should be possible for a pregnant woman to obtain a legal abortion if there is a strong chance of a serious defect in the baby?" When the general question was asked first, 60.7% of respondents said "yes," but when the general question followed the specific question, only 48.1% of respondents said "yes." The corresponding values for the specific question were 84% and 83% agreement in the first and second positions, respectively. The generally accepted method for dealing with this problem is to use *funnel questions*, which

**TABLE B.2** SAMPLE FORMAT FOR SELF-ADMINISTERED QUESTIONNAIRE

**Illinois Department of Transportation**
Survey of Amtrak Passengers

Dear Amtrak Passenger:

The Illinois Department of Transportation is conducting a study of rail passenger service on the Chicago-St. Louis corridor to determine what improvements should be made to upgrade service on this route. This survey is designed to identify the preferences and travel needs of passengers on Amtrak trains. Your cooperation in filling out this questionnaire will be greatly appreciated.

A Department representative will collect the survey when you have finished. If you leave your seat before the representative returns, kindly leave the questionnaire on your seat. If you have filled out this survey previously, please take a few minutes to answer questions 1 through 7 and 21 through 26.

Have an enjoyable trip and thank you for your cooperation.

**1** Please check the station where you boarded this train and the station where you will get off.

| Station | Boarded | Will Get Off |
|---|---|---|
| Chicago | ___ 01 (1–6) | ___ 01(7–8) |
| Joliet | ___ 02 | ___ 02 |
| Pontiac | ___ 03 | ___ 03 |
| Bloomington | ___ 04 | ___ 04 |
| Lincoln | ___ 05 | ___ 05 |
| Springfield | ___ 06 | ___ 06 |
| Carlinville | ___ 07 | ___ 07 |
| Alton | ___ 08 | ___ 08 |
| St. Louis | ___ 09 | ___ 09 |
| Points in Missouri | ___ 10 | ___ 10 |
| Points in Arkansas | ___ 11 | ___ 11 |
| Points in Texas | ___ 12 | ___ 12 |

**2** Please indicate how you reached the station to board this train and how you will reach your next destination after you get off this train. (Check as many as apply.)

| | To Station Where You Got On | From Station Where You Will Get off |
|---|---|---|
| Automobile | ___ 01 (9–11) | ___ 01(12–14) |
| Taxi | ___ 02 | ___ 02 |
| City Bus | ___ 03 | ___ 03 |
| Airline | ___ 04 | ___ 04 |
| Commuter Train | ___ 05 | ___ 05 |
| Amtrak Train | ___ 06 | ___ 06 |
| Amtrak Shuttle | ___ 07 | ___ 07 |
| Intercity Bus | ___ 08 | ___ 08 |
| Walker | ___ 09 | ___ 09 |
| Other | ___ 10 | ___ 10 |

**3** Is your car parked at or near an Amtrak Station during this trip?

Yes ___ 15.1    No ___ 15.2

**4** What is the zip code of the place you left to get to this train? (If zip code is unknown, the city and a nearby major street intersection will be sufficient.)

Zip Code $\underline{\quad\quad\quad\quad\quad}$
$\phantom{Zip Code}$ $_{16\ \ 17\ \ 18\ \ 19\ \ 20}$

OR: City _____

Street

Intersection _____

_____

**5** What is the zip code (or city and nearby street intersection) of the place where you will be going upon leaving this train?

Zip Code $\underline{\quad\quad\quad\quad\quad}$
$\phantom{Zip Code}$ $_{21\ \ 22\ \ 23\ \ 24\ \ 25}$

OR: City _____

Street

Intersection _____

_____

**6** Which one of the following best describes the main purpose of this trip? (Mark only one)

26-1 ___ Business or work

2 ___ Vacation or recreation

3 ___ Travel to or from school

4 ___ Personal business

5 ___ Shopping

6 ___ Visit family or friends

7 ___ Entertainment/Spectator sport

8 ___ Other (Please specify) _____

**7** How long before the departure time of this train did you leave for the station?

27-1 ___ 10–15 minutes

2 ___ 16–30 minutes

3 ___ 31–45 minutes

4 ___ 46–60 minutes

5 ___ more than 1 hour

means proceeding from the most general to the most specific when ordering the questions pertaining to a given topic.

Problems resulting from the order of questions can also arise when several questions on the same topic are asked, all at the same level of specificity. For example, we might ask a series of questions regarding a person's views about several minority groups. Our interest might be in how the person's responses differ for the different minority groups. But responses could also be affected by the sequence in which the various questions were asked within each of the minority groups. A person's reaction to one question, for example, might influence how the next question is interpreted. Effects due to the order in which such questions are asked can be handled in one of two ways. The first technique is to use exactly the same order for all samples to be compared, thus holding the effect of order constant. This technique does not allow us to determine what the effects of order were. Alternatively, many different orders of the questions might be used within each of the samples to be compared, thus neutralizing the effect of order. This problem of dealing with order effects is discussed much more fully in Chapter 7.

The final aspect of the ordering of survey questions that we will consider is the use of *filter questions*—general questions asked of respondents to find out whether they need to be asked more specific questions. For example, the question "Do you own a car?" might precede a series of questions about the costs of maintaining a car. In this instance, the respondents would answer the specific questions only if their response to the general question was "yes." If that answer was "no," the interviewer would not ask the specific questions (in a self-administered questionnaire, the respondent would be instructed to skip that section). When the filter questions involve objective information (e.g., "Are you over 65?"), their use is relatively straightforward. Caution must be exercised, however, in using behavioral or attitudinal questions as filter questions. Smith (1981) first asked respondents whether they approved of hitting another person in "any situations you can imagine." Logically, a negative response to this most general question should imply a negative response to any more specific questions. Nonetheless, over 80% of the people who responded "no" to the general question then reported that they approved of hitting another person in specific situations, such as in self-defense. Although findings such as this suggest that filter questions should be used cautiously, the need to demand as little of the respondent's time as possible makes filter questions an essential tool in the design of effective questionnaires.

## ENHANCING RESPONSE RATE IN A MAIL SURVEY

In addition to providing a well-designed questionnaire that is attractive (visually appealing), as well as easy to understand and complete, a survey researcher should consider the following procedures to enhance response rate in a mail survey:

- Include a letter summarizing the purpose of the survey, explaining the basis on which the respondents were selected, and assuring the respondents of confidentiality.

- Include a postage-paid return envelope along with the questionnaire.
- Mail a follow-up questionnaire. (And perhaps consider more than one follow-up mailing.)

As questionnaires are returned, the researcher should plot a cumulative response rate graph. Numbering the returned questionnaires in the order received allows researchers to make comparisons such as that between early and late respondents. Plateaus in the cumulative response rate graph indicate that a follow-up mailing should be sent. To obtain a high response rate, it is often necessary to send three mailings. These should be spaced about 2 to 3 weeks apart or when a plateau appears on the cumulative response rate graph. Because the original copy is likely to have been lost, a new copy of the questionnaire should be sent with each mailing.

APPENDIX

C

# Communication in Psychology

## CHAPTER OUTLINE

# INTRODUCTION

Scientific research is a public activity. A clever hypothesis, an elegant research design, meticulous data collection procedures, reliable results, and an insightful theoretical interpretation of the findings are not useful to the scientific community unless they are made public. As one writer suggests most emphatically, "Until its results have gone through the painful process of publication, preferably in a refereed journal of high standards, scientific research is just play. Publication is an indispensable part of science" (Bartholomew, 1982, p. 233). Bartholomew (1982) expresses a preference for a "refereed" journal because refereed journals involve the process of peer review. Submitted manuscripts are reviewed by other researchers ("peers") who are experts in the specific field of research addressed in the paper under review. These peer reviewers decide whether the research is methodologically sound and whether it makes a substantive contribution to the discipline of psychology. These reviews are then submitted to a senior researcher who serves as editor of the journal. It is the editor's job to decide which papers warrant publication. Peer review is the primary method of quality control for published psychological research.

There are many journals in which psychologists can publish their research. *Memory & Cognition, Child Development, Journal of Personality and Social Psychology*, and *Journal of Clinical and Consulting Psychology* are but a few of the many psychology journals. As we mentioned, editors of these journals make the final decisions about which manuscripts will be published. Their decisions are based on (a) the quality of the research and (b) the effectiveness of its presentation in the written manuscript, as assessed by the editor and the peer reviewers. Thus both content and style are important. Editors seek the best research, clearly described. The editors of the 25 primary journals of the American Psychological Association reviewed about 6,000 manuscript submissions per year in the 1990s. Journal editors set rigorous standards; *only about one of every four submitted manuscripts is accepted for publication* (American Psychological Association, 1998).

Editorial review and the publication process can take a long time. A year or more may elapse between when a paper is submitted and when it finally appears in the journal. The review of the manuscript can take three to six months before a decision whether to accept the paper is made. Another seven to eight months is required for the publication process between the time the paper is accepted and when it is actually published in the journal. To provide a more timely means of reporting research findings, professional societies such as the American Psychological Association, the American Psychological Society, the Psychonomic Society, the Society for Research in Child Development, and regional societies such as the Eastern, Midwestern, Southeastern, and Western Psychological Associations sponsor conferences at which researchers give brief oral presentations or present posters describing their recent work. Such conferences provide an opportunity for timely discussion and debate among investigators interested in the same research questions. Research that is "in press" (i.e., waiting completion of the publication process) may be discussed, thus giving conference attendees a preview of important, but yet-to-be-published, research findings.

Researchers often must obtain financial support in the form of a grant from a government or private agency in order to carry out their research. Grants are awarded on the basis of a competitive review of research proposals. Research proposals also typically are required of graduate students when preparing a master's thesis or dissertation. A faculty committee then reviews the proposal before the thesis or dissertation research is begun. So, too, undergraduate students often are required to prepare a research proposal as part of a research methods or laboratory class in psychology. Finally, researchers at all levels will find that research proposals are required by IRBs in order to assess the ethical nature of proposed research at an institution (see Chapter 2). Research proposals require a slightly different style and format from a journal article that reports results of a completed study. We provide suggestions for preparing a research proposal later in this appendix.

What do journal articles, oral presentations, and research proposals have to do with you? If you attend graduate school in psychology, you will probably have to describe your research using all three of these types of scientific communication. Even if you do not pursue a professional career in psychology, the principles of good written and oral research reports are applicable to a wide variety of employment situations. For example, a memo to your department manager describing the outcome of a recent sale may have much the same content and format as a short journal article. Of more immediate concern, you may have to prepare a research proposal and write or deliver a research report in your research methods course. This appendix will help you do these things well.

The primary source for scientific writing in psychology is the fourth edition of the *Publication Manual* (1994) of the American Psychological Association. Editors and authors use this manual to ensure a consistent style across the many different journals in psychology. It includes chapters on the content and organization of a manuscript; the expression of ideas; APA editorial style; manuscript preparation; manuscript acceptance and production; and APA journals. The publication manual also includes information about ethical issues in scientific writing (see our discussion of this in Chapter 2) and instructions for submitting manuscripts in electronic form.

Throughout this appendix we have drawn heavily on the *Publication Manual* (1994).[1] This appendix is intended to help you complete successfully the writing you are likely to be doing in your research methods course. It is not intended as a substitute for the *Publication Manual* (1994). If advanced study in psychology is in your future, we recommend that you add the *Publication Manual* (1994) to your personal library. Another resource available from APA that you might find helpful is Gelfand, H., & Walker, C. J. (1994). *Mastering APA style: Student's workbook and training guide.* (You can order both from the American Psychological Association, 750 First Street, N.E., Washington, DC 20002-4242.) If you have reached that exciting point in the research process when you are preparing a manuscript for submission to a scientific journal, we urge you to read a brief article written by Robert J. Sternberg (1992), which was published in the monthly newsletter of the American Psychological Society, the *APS Observer.* Its title says it all: "How to Win Acceptances by Psychology Journals: 21 Tips for Better Writing."

Formal communication among researchers through journal articles and convention presentations is not sufficient to sustain the collaborative nature of science. Informal communication is vital to doing research. Research ideas are often formulated in research team meetings or in informal conversations with colleagues. Increasingly, researchers are collaborating at a distance using one of today's most exciting developments in scientific communication, the Internet and the World Wide Web (WWW). Researchers use electronic mail to discuss their research and access electronic databases through the Internet that make their research more efficient and more extensive. We describe some of the research-related features of the Internet in the next section.

## THE INTERNET AND RESEARCH

— A researcher posts a questionnaire on the Internet . . .
— Clinical psychology graduate students participate in group discussions about managed health care with other graduate students on the Internet . . .
— Researchers working on the problem of alcohol abuse search databases on the Internet for statistics related to alcohol use and treatment . . .
— An undergraduate student obtains background information for a class project by e-mailing the author of a published study . . .
— Having completed the data collection phase of a psychology study, researchers prepare an article for publication in an electronic journal . . .

Access to the Internet has already become an indispensable tool for research psychologists. Although mainly used for communication via electronic mail (e-mail), the Internet also serves students and professional psychologists in many other important ways, including as a vehicle for conducting original research (see, for example, Azar, 1994b; 1994c; Kardas & Milford, 1996; Kelley-Milburn & Milburn, 1995). We describe here a few of the more important ways that the Internet is used by psychologists.

*E-mail* is, for many researchers, their primary means of communication with colleagues, journal editors, research collaborators, directors of granting agencies, and other professionals. Authors of published journal articles now typically list their e-mail addresses along with their regular mailing address. Have a question about an article you just read? Ask the author by sending an e-mail message. E-mailing is simple, efficient, and convenient. The authors of your textbook, for example, can be reached via e-mail by sending a message via Internet to:

John J. Shaughnessy (Hope College) at shaughnessy@hope.edu
Eugene B. Zechmeister (Loyola University of Chicago) at ezechme@luc.edu
Jeanne S. Zechmeister (Loyola University of Chicago) at jzechme@luc.edu

There is also a home page on the WWW dedicated to this textbook, which can be accessed for information about the authors, changes in editions, additional resources for doing psychological research, and errors or omissions in the current edition, publisher's address, ordering information, etc. Visit our page at www.mhhe.com/shaughnessy.

*Discussion groups*, called "Listservs," allow interested individuals to communicate with each other about various psychological issues. The group consists of a "list" of "subscribers" who wish to contribute to an ongoing discussion. List members are immediately "served" any message posted by a subscriber. (If the Listserv is large, the number of messages accumulating in your mailbox can be rather large. As a consequence, unless regularly attended to and edited, you may find your abilities to keep up with new information seriously challenged.) Listservs on the Internet focus on a wide variety of topics, including addiction, religion, and women's studies. The APA plans to create as many as 500 special-interest groups to link researchers around the world (Azar, 1995). Some Listservs are open to anyone who wishes to take part in the discussion, or who even just want to "lurk" (only passively participate), as many people do who follow the discussion "threads" (a group of messages focusing on a specific idea or issue). Other Listservs are open only to individuals with certain credentials (e.g., members of a particular APA division).

Of particular interest to graduate students in psychology are two discussion groups set up by and for graduate students. These forums allow graduate students to share information about graduate programs, research projects, as well as about postdoctoral and career opportunities. One discussion group, APSSCNET, is sponsored by the Student Caucus of APS (see Fiore, 1994). APA also sponsors discussion groups for students, which can be accessed through their web site (see next page).

*Databases* on the Internet are just that: collections of information (data) available via an electronic hookup. Databases related to medicine, alcoholism, and opinion polls are available, to mention but a few (see Kelley-Milburn & Milburn, 1995). Many databases are reached by using a TELNET command. TELNET allows you to connect your computer to a remote site. By following the rules laid out for you when you access a site, you can carry out searches and even download information to your own computer (see Kardas & Milford, 1996, for more information on using TELNET commands).

*Electronic journals* are here and more are on their way. Electronic journals such as *Psycholoquy*, *Psyche*, and *Prevention and Treatment* are examples. Subscribers receive articles in their electronic mailboxes to peruse and even to comment on should they have the expertise. Articles submitted to electronic journals for publication are professionally reviewed in the same manner as manuscripts submitted to print journals, but, of course it is all done via the Internet.

*Original research* can also be done electronically (see, for example, Kiesler, Walsh, & Sproull, 1992; and Smith & Leigh, 1997). Surveys, for example, can be conducted of individuals tied to a specific network or discussion group (Listserv) (see Schmidt, 1997, and also Chapter 4). Respondents usually have the option of replying electronically or printing a copy of the questionnaire and mailing the completed form to the survey administrator. As more and more people become connected to the Internet through commercial providers, there exists the potential for administering "treatments" electronically. Kiesler et al., for instance, describe a smoking cessation study carried out with CompuServe users. The University of Mississippi hosts a web site, PsychExps, where teachers and researchers can post experiments that can be accessed by students in psychology lab classes from around the world (see Bourke, 1998).

Where to begin? With all of the electronic resources now available, it's often hard to know where to begin. Internet service providers are commonly available at most universities and colleges. For those without this advantage, commercial services such as America Online, AT&T World Net, Earth Link, and MSN Premier provide access for a fee.

How useful you will find the Internet in planning and conducting research will depend both on your specific needs and on your level of expertise at accessing the Internet. If you are already experienced at using psychology-related information on the Internet, then there isn't much we can tell you. You are already on the cutting edge of what will be the main vehicle for information exchange at the beginning of the 21st century.

Both novices on the Web as well as experienced surfers can find a wealth of psychology-related information at the home pages of the American Psychological Association and American Psychological Society. These pages provide hyperlinks (Internet connections) to many other psychology-related sites and even permit you to be a participant "online" in a psychology experiment or survey.

To access APA via the Web: http://www.apa.org
To access APS via the Web: http://www.psychologicalscience.org

## GUIDELINES FOR EFFECTIVE WRITING

Learning to write well is like learning to swim, drive a car, or play the piano. Improvement is unlikely to result solely from reading about how the activity is to be done. (Although listening to experts is an important place to begin. See, for example, the "21 Tips for Better Writing" by Sternberg [1992], which we mentioned earlier.) A person learns to write well by writing and then getting critical feedback from writing "coaches" (teachers, friends, editors). Lee Cronbach (1992), author of several of the most widely cited articles in the *Psychological*

*Bulletin*, writes:

> My advice must be like the legendary recipe for jugged hare, which begins, "First catch your hare." First, have a message worth delivering. Beyond that, it is care in writing that counts. . . . Rework any sentence that lacks flow or cadence, any sentence in which first-glance reading misplaces the emphasis, and any sentence in which comprehension comes less than instantly to that most knowledgeable of readers, the writer of the sentence. At best, technical writing can aspire to literary virtues—a change of pace from abstract thesis to memorable example, from brisk to easeful, from matter-of-fact to poetic. (p. 391)

Professional writer Jack Ridl provides the first maxim for effective writing: "Write, not assuming that you will be understood, but trying to avoid being misunderstood." Good writing, like good driving, is best done defensively. Assume that whatever can be misunderstood will be! To avoid these writing accidents, we offer the following tips to consider *before* you begin writing.

- KNOW YOUR AUDIENCE. If you assume your readers know more than they actually do, you will leave them confused. If you underestimate your readers, you risk boring them with unnecessary details. Either risk increases the likelihood that what you have written will not be read. But if you must err, it is better to underestimate your readers. For example, when you prepare a research report in a psychology class you might reasonably assume that your intended audience is your instructor. Writing for your instructor might lead you to leave a lot out of your paper because, after all, you assume your instructor knows all that anyway. It would probably be better to consider students in another section of your research methods course as your audience. This might result in your including more detail than necessary, but it will be easier for your instructor to help you learn to "edit out" the nonessential material than to "edit in" essential material that you have omitted. Whatever audience you choose, make the selection before you begin to write, and keep that audience in mind every step of the way.
- IDENTIFY YOUR PURPOSE. The principal purposes of a journal article are to describe and to convince. You want first to describe what you have done and what you have found, and second to convince the reader that your interpretation of these results is an appropriate one. Journal articles fall within the general category of expository writing. *Webster's Dictionary* defines exposition as "discourse designed to convey information or explain what is difficult to understand." The foundation of good expository writing is clarity of thought and expression.
- WRITE CLEARLY. The *Publication Manual* (1994) clearly outlines the road to clarity:

> You can achieve clear communication, which is the prime objective of scientific reporting, by presenting ideas in an orderly manner and by expressing yourself smoothly and precisely. By developing ideas clearly and logically and leading readers smoothly from thought to thought, you make the task of reading an agreeable one. (p. 23)

The *Publication Manual* cites three avenues to clarity:

**1** economy of expression,
**2** precision, and
**3** adherence to grammatical rules.

- BE CONCISE. Economy of expression can best be achieved by saying only what needs to be said. Short words and short sentences are easier for readers to understand. Wordiness can best be eliminated by editing your own writing across successive drafts and asking others to edit drafts of your paper.
- BE PRECISE. Precision in using language means choosing the right word for what you want to say. The *Publication Manual* (1994) contains sage advice regarding precision of expression:

  > Make certain that every word means exactly what you intend it to mean. Sooner or later most authors discover a discrepancy between their accepted meaning of a term and its dictionary definition. In informal style, for example, *feel* broadly substitutes for *think* or *believe,* but such latitude is not acceptable in scientific style. (p. 28)

- FOLLOW GRAMMATICAL RULES. Adherence to grammatical rules is absolutely necessary for good writing because failure to do so distracts the reader and can introduce ambiguity. It also makes you, the writer, look bad, and, as a consequence, can serve to weaken your credibility (and your argument) with your reader. Economy of expression, precision, and adherence to grammatical rules do not guarantee effective writing. They do, however, greatly increase the likelihood that your writing will be effective.
- WRITE FAIRLY. As a writer you should also strive to choose words and use constructions that acknowledge people fairly and objectively. The American Psychological Association has developed guidelines (*Publication Manual,* 1994) regarding bias in the language authors use:

  > As a publisher, APA accepts authors' word choices unless those choices are inaccurate, unclear, or ungrammatical. As an organization, APA is committed both to science and to the fair treatment of individuals and groups, and policy requires authors of APA publications to avoid perpetuating demeaning attitudes and biased assumptions about people in their writing. Constructions that might imply bias against persons on the basis of gender, sexual orientation, racial or ethnic group, disability, or age should be avoided. Scientific writing should be free of implied or irrelevant evaluation of the group or groups being studied. (p. 46)

The *Publication Manual* (1994) describes several guidelines to achieve unbiased communication:

**1** Describe the person or persons at the appropriate level of specificity. For example, the phrase *men and women* is more accurate than the generic term *man* when referring to all human beings. "Chinese Americans" or "Mexican Americans" would be a more specific reference for participants in a study than would be Asian Americans or Hispanic Americans.

**2** Be sensitive to the labels we use to refer to people, for example, terms we use to refer to people's racial or ethnic identity. One of the best ways to follow this guideline is to avoid labeling people whenever possible. A label that is perceived by the labeled group as pejorative should never be used. In trying to follow this guideline it is important to remember that preferences for labeling groups of individuals change with time and that people within a group disagree about what label is preferred.

**3** "Write about the people in your study in a way that acknowledges their participation" (p. 49). One way to accomplish this is to describe the people who participated in your study using more descriptive terms such as *college students* or *children* rather than the more impersonal term, *subjects*. Active voice is better than passive voice in acknowledging participation—"the students completed the survey" is preferred over "the survey was administered to the students." The *Publication Manual* (1994) includes several good applications and illustrations of these guidelines to the labeling of persons based on their gender, sexual orientation, racial and ethnic identity, disabilities, and age.

- WRITE AN INTERESTING REPORT. The *Publication Manual* provides useful advice about the overall tone of scientific writing:

  > Although scientific writing differs in form from literary writing, it need not and should not lack style or be dull. In describing your research, present the ideas and findings directly, but aim for an interesting and compelling manner that reflects your involvement with the problem. (p. 6)

  One way to try to achieve an appropriate tone in writing your research reports is to strive to tell a good story about your research. Good research makes for good stories; and well-told stories are good for advancing research.

## STRUCTURE OF A RESEARCH REPORT

The structure of a research report serves two major purposes. First, the structure provides an organization that the author can use to present a clear description of the research and a convincing interpretation of the findings. In this sense, the structure of a research report parallels the structure of a Shakespearean play. In a Shakespearean play, both the playwright and the audience share certain expectations about what should occur in each act as the play unfolds. For example "the stage is set" in the first act, and the climax can be expected in the third act. Similarly, in a research report both author and reader share expectations about the content of each section of the report. Similar to a play, the reader of a research report can expect to find specific information in each section. If you want to know how an experiment was done, you would look in the Method section; if you want information about the statistics used in the study, you would refer to the Results section. The structure is not intended to shackle the playwright or the author. It simply provides a vehicle to make it easier for the audience to focus on the particular point being made in the play or the research report.

A research report consists of the following sections:

Title Page
Abstract
Introduction
Method          ⎫   Body of
Results         ⎬   report
Discussion      ⎭
References
Appendixes
Author Note
Footnotes

The body of the report is made up of four sections: Introduction, Method, Results, and Discussion (the four acts of the "play"). The title page and the abstract are like the playbill you see before the play itself begins, and the References, Footnotes, and Appendixes are analogous to the credits. In this appendix we will provide descriptions of the content and format of each of these sections; more complete descriptions are provided in the *Publication Manual* (1994). Neither this appendix nor the *Publication Manual* will suffice for teaching you how to write a research report. The best preparation for that is to read journal articles reporting research in an area of psychology that interests you. Ultimately, however, you will develop the skills for writing research reports only by actually writing them.

## Title Page

The first page of a research report is the title page. It indicates what the research is about (i.e., the title), who did the research (i.e., the authors), where the research was done (i.e., authors' affiliation), and a brief heading to indicate to readers what the article is about (the "running head"). An illustration of a correctly typed title page and succeeding pages of a research report is presented in the sample paper at the end of this appendix. The sample paper includes notes to highlight several important aspects of the final typed draft of a research report.

The title is perhaps the most critical aspect of your paper because it is the part that is most likely to be read! The title should clearly indicate what the central topic of your paper is. In the words of the *Publication Manual*:

> A title should summarize the main idea of the paper simply and, if possible, with style. It should be a concise statement of the main topic and should identify the actual variables or theoretical issues under investigation and the relation between them.
>
> Titles are commonly indexed and compiled in numerous reference works. Therefore, avoid words that serve no useful purpose; they increase length and can mislead indexers. For example, the words *method* and *results* do not normally appear in a title, nor should such redundancies as "A Study of" or "An Experimental Investigation of" begin a title. (p. 7)

The byline for a research report includes the name(s) of the author(s) and the institution with which each author is affiliated. We discussed the criteria for authorship in Chapter 2; only those who meet these criteria should be listed as authors of a research report. Others who contributed to the research are acknowledged in an author note. The preferred form for an author's name is first name, middle initial, and last name.

The *Publication Manual* provides a succinct statement describing the last component of a title page, the running head: "The running head is an abbreviated title that is printed at the top of the pages of a published article to identify the article for readers" (p. 8). The running head should not exceed 50 characters, and it should appear on the title page typed in all uppercase letters one double-spaced line below the first line that includes the page 1 and the manuscript page heading (see sample paper). Note that the running head is *not* the same as the manuscript page heading that appears on every manuscript page. The running head appears once and only once in your manuscript, on the title page.

## TIPS ON WRITING A TITLE

A common format for the title of a research report is "[The Dependent Variable(s)] as a Function of [the Independent Variable(s)]." For example, "Anagram Solution Time as a Function of Problem Difficulty" would be a good title. The title must not only be informative, but it should also be brief; the recommended length is 10 to 12 words. Most important of all, be sure your title describes as specifically as possible the content of your research.

## Abstract

The second page of the report, the abstract, appears under that single word, which is typed as a centered heading (see sample paper). The abstract is a one-paragraph summary of the content and purpose of the research report. The abstract should be 100 to 120 words long (about 10 double-spaced typewritten lines). The abstract should identify four elements of your research:

**a** the problem under investigation;
**b** the experimental method, including tests and apparatus that were used, data gathering procedures, and pertinent characteristics of participants;
**c** the findings; and
**d** the conclusions and implications of the findings.

The abstract, in other words, should highlight the critical points made in the Introduction, Method, Results, and Discussion sections of the research report.

A well-written abstract can have a big influence on whether the rest of a journal article will be read. Abstracts are used by information services to index and retrieve articles. The fate of an article based on a reader's reaction to its abstract is well described in the *Publication Manual*,

Most people will have their first contact with an article by seeing just the abstract, usually on a computer screen with several other abstracts, as they are doing a literature search through an electronic abstract-retrieval system. Readers frequently decide on the basis of the abstract whether to read the entire article; this is true whether the reader is at a computer or is thumbing through a journal. The abstract needs to be dense with information but also readable, well organized, brief, and self-contained. Also, embedding many key words in your abstract will enhance the user's ability to find it. (p. 8)

### TIPS ON WRITING AN ABSTRACT

Writing a good abstract is challenging. The best way to meet this challenge is to write it last. By writing the abstract after you have written the rest of the report you will be able to *abstract*, or paraphrase, your own words more easily.

## Introduction

**Objectives for the Introduction**   The title of your report appears at the top of the third page as a centered heading, and then the first paragraph of the Introduction section begins immediately (see sample paper). The introduction serves three primary objectives:

1  to introduce the problem being studied;
2  to summarize briefly the relevant background literature that led you to the present research problem and approach; and
3  to state the purpose and rationale of the present study with a logical development of the predictions or hypotheses guiding the research.

The order in which these objectives are met in any given report may vary, but the order in which we described them here is the most common one. All three of these objectives share a common purpose: to give the reader a firm sense of what you are doing and why you are doing it.

The second objective, that of summarizing related research studies, is not to provide an exhaustive literature review. Instead, care should be taken to select the most pertinent studies to develop the rationale of your experiment. In summarizing these selected studies, you should emphasize whatever details of the earlier work will best help the reader understand what you have done and why. You must acknowledge the contributions of other researchers to your understanding of the problem. Of course, if you quote directly from another person's work, you must use quotation marks (see Chapter 2 for advice about citing others' work).

More commonly, however, reference is made to the work of other researchers in one of two ways. Either you refer to the authors of the article you are citing by their last names, with the year in which the paper was published appearing in parentheses immediately after the names, or you make a general reference to their work and follow it with both the names and the year of publication in parentheses. For example, if you were citing a study by David G. Myers and Jane R. Dickie that was published in 1996, you would write either "Myers and

Dickie (1996) found . . ." or "Recent research (Myers & Dickie, 1996) showed that . . ." Complete bibliographical information on Myers and Dickie's paper, including the journal title, volume number, and specific pages, would appear in the References section. Footnotes are not used to cite references in a research report in psychology.

You should include in your paper only those references that you have actually read. If you read a paper by Barney (1993) in which the research of Ludwig (1990) is described, you should not cite the Ludwig paper unless you have actually read that paper. Instead, you should use some form such as "Ludwig (1990), as reported by Barney (1993), found that . . ." You should use this approach for two reasons. The first and most obvious one is that you should accurately report what you have read. If this appeal to scholarly integrity does not suffice, you should recognize the risk you are taking. If Barney (1993) has misreported the work of Ludwig (1990) and you repeat this misrepresentation, you are equally subject to criticism. The general rule is simple: Cite only what you have read. (See also Chapter 2.)

TIPS ON WRITING THE INTRODUCTION

In order to write an effective introduction, be sure you can answer the following four questions *before* beginning to write:

- "What is the point of the study?
- How do the hypothesis and the experimental design relate to the problem?
- What are the theoretical implications of the study, and how does the study relate to previous work in the area?
- What are the theoretical propositions tested, and how were they derived?" (*Publication Manual*, p. 11).

Searching the Psychological Literature    In the long run, the best way to develop ideas for research and to become familiar with the relevant literature is to read the journals in your area of interest on a regular basis. If you are just beginning to do research in psychology, you may not have had a chance to read the research literature widely or to have settled on a principal area of interest in psychology. Or, even if experienced, you may wish to explore a new area of psychology, one found in a literature different than you are used to reading. For example, you may have an idea for an experiment and you may wonder whether the experiment has already been done. Or you may have read an article describing an experiment on which you would like to base an experiment, and you may be interested in finding other studies related to this topic. Whatever the case, there likely will come a time when you need to search the psychological literature. Resources for searching the psychological literature are available to help you answer these types of questions.

Modern methods of searching the psychological literature are built on *Psychological Abstracts*. The American Psychological Association has published

*Psychological Abstracts* since 1927. The abstracts, taken from over 1,000 national and international periodicals, are published monthly in the *Psychological Abstracts*. These abstracts are organized under 16 general categories, such as "Physical and Psychological Disorders." In the printed version of *Psychological Abstracts*, abstracts are arranged alphabetically under each category by the first author's last name, and the abstracts are numbered consecutively in one or two volumes each year. Searching *Psychological Abstracts* was often a time-consuming and cumbersome task before it became possible to use computers to search the psychological literature. Electronic databases have made the task of searching the psychological literature much less labor intensive.

PsycLIT is the CD-ROM version of *Psychological Abstracts*. PsycLIT includes *Psychological Abstracts* going back more than 25 years and is updated quarterly. One of the greatest advantages of PsycLIT is that it can be used so easily following only brief instruction. PsychINFO is the online version of PsycLIT. Other online databases that permit electronic searching are *FirstSearch* and *InfoTrac 2000*. Check with your local library staff to find out what online services are available to you. Joswick (1994) provides recommendations for electronic searches for those who want to move beyond the basics.

To illustrate the use of electronic databases to search the psychological literature, we describe a computer-assisted search done by one of our undergraduate students. The student was interested in conducting a survey to determine the incidence of rapes and other sexual assaults on dates (i.e., "date rape"). She came across a few references to this topic in her general reading in the area of women's studies, and then wanted to make a more systematic search of the psychological literature. A reference librarian helped her make a search of PsycLIT and the electronic database that included the *Social Science Citation Index*. The *Social Science Citation Index* records the reference history of an article. That is, once an article has been published, the citation index searches the references sections of all future articles in that area and notes whenever the original article is cited. The citation index can be used to determine how many times a given article has been cited or to identify the specific articles in which the original article is cited.

The student used a keyword search on PsycLIT and she had a chapter on rape by Klemmack and Klemmack (1976) to serve as the basis of her search of the *Social Science Citation Index*. An electronic database makes it possible to scan the titles and abstracts of articles in the database and to identify all those that contain particular keywords. The most effective approach to this type of search is to have intersecting keywords, both of which need to be present before the computer will "flag" an article. For example, the student used the keyword RAPE and the letter string DAT to guide her search. She chose the letter string DAT in order to catch such variants as DATE, DATES, and DATING. This intersection led to the identification of 75 references, 73 of which were written in English. The student also obtained 11 additional references that had cited the Klemmack and Klemmack (1976) paper when she did a computer search of the *Social Science Citation Index* database.

The major advantage of searching electronic databases is that they provide quick access to large amounts of information. The student completed both searches in less than half an hour. There are a few disadvantages. One disadvantage is that the quality of the search greatly influences the likelihood that you will obtain all the relevant references. When it comes to electronic databases, what you search is what you get. Estimates are that 30% to 50% of all users miss pertinent information in their search (Joswick, 1994). After searching such vast databases we may become unduly confident that we have identified "all that there is on the subject." These two potential problems are not problems with the *use* of electronic databases but with the *users* of electronic databases. Another possible disadvantage is that many of the references the computer locates do not prove useful. For example, the student obtained one reference on rape among mallard ducks on specific chronological dates. Keywords can also prove tricky. The string DAT identified all studies using the word DATA, so a number of the student's references provided data about rape—but not solely in the context of dating. When they are used properly, the advantages of searching the psychological literature with electronic databases like PsycLIT and PsychINFO far outweigh their disadvantages.

## Method

The second major section of the body of a research report is the Method section. The Method section is usually identified by a centered heading ("Method") with a double space separating it from the preceding and following text (see sample paper). The Method section follows right after the introduction. The introduction has provided a broad outline of the research you have done; the method fills in the nitty-gritty details. The *Publication Manual* presents a straightforward description of the goals of the Method section:

> The Method section describes in detail how the study was conducted. Such a description enables the reader to evaluate the appropriateness of your methods and the reliability and the validity of your results. It also permits experienced investigators to replicate the study if they so desire. (p. 12)

Writing a good Method section can be difficult. It sounds easy because all you have to do is describe exactly what you have done. But if you want to get a sense of how challenging this can be, just try to write a clear and interesting paragraph describing how to tie your shoelaces.

### Tips on Writing the Method Section

The key to writing a good Method section is organization. Fortunately, the structure of this section is so consistent across research reports that a few basic subsections provide the pattern of organization you need for most research reports. Before describing the content of these subsections, however, we must address the question that students writing their first research report ask most frequently: "How much detail should I include?" The quality of your paper will be adversely affected if you include either too much or too little detail. The rule stated in the *Publication Manual* seems simple enough: "Include in these subsections only the information essential to comprehend and replicate the study" (p. 13). As we have said before, the best way to learn how to follow this rule is to read the Method sections of journal articles and to write your own research reports. Be sure to get feedback from your instructor concerning the appropriate level of detail for your research reports.

The three most common subsections of the Method section are participants, materials (apparatus), and procedure. Each of these subsections is introduced by an underlined subheading that usually begins at the left margin (see sample paper). The *Publication Manual* (p. 13) aptly summarizes the purpose and the content of the *participants* subsection.

Appropriate identification of research participants and clientele is critical to the science and practice of psychology, particularly for assessing the results (making comparisons across groups), generalizing the findings, and making comparisons in replications, literature reviews, or secondary data analyses.

When humans are the participants, report the procedures for selecting and assigning them and the agreements and payments made. Report major demographic characteristics such as sex and age. When a particular demographic characteristic is an experimental variable or is important for the interpretation of results, describe the group specifically—for example, in terms of racial and ethnic designation, national origin, level of education, health status, and language preference and use.

For nonhuman animal subjects, report the genus, species, and strain number or other specific identification, such as the name and location of the supplier and the stock designation.

Give the total number of subjects and the number assigned to each experimental condition. If any did not complete the experiment, state how many and explain why they did not continue. (pp. 13–14)

The *apparatus* or *materials* subsection is not always included in a research report. If the only equipment you used is paper, pencils, and a stopwatch, it is better to include this information in the procedure subsection than in a separate apparatus section. On the other hand, if the apparatus or materials played a central role in the study, a separate subsection is useful. If complex or custom-made equipment has been used, a diagram or drawing is helpful for both the reader and the writer of an apparatus subsection. In general, the label *Apparatus* is used when mechanical equipment is described. The label *Materials* is used when less mechanical instruments, such as a paper-and-pencil questionnaire, have been constructed or used. If you use equipment or materials developed by another investigator, you should cite the work of that investigator, but you should also include the general characteristics of the materials in your own report.

The *procedure* subsection is the most critical component of the Method section. In this subsection you describe what happened from the beginning to the end of the sessions in which you tested your participants. As the previous sentence implies, the organization of the procedure subsection is usually chronological. You should begin writing this subsection by outlining the important steps in testing participants in each group of your study. Next you can either describe the procedure for each group in turn or describe the procedures common to all groups and then point out the distinguishing features of each group. Whichever organization you choose (you may not learn which works best until you have tried to write both), it is best to begin writing only after you have prepared a checklist of the important features of your procedure. The instructions given to participants should be presented in paraphrase form unless they define an experimental manipulation, in which case they should be reported verbatim. The *Publication Manual* recommends that the Method section, and especially the procedure subsection, "should tell the reader what you did and how you did it in sufficient detail so that a reader could reasonably replicate your study" (pp. 14–15).

## Results

The centered heading "Results" introduces this third major section of the body of a research report (see sample paper). Like the third act of a dramatic play, the Results section contains the climax of the research report—the actual findings of the study. For many students, though, the excitement of describing the climax is blunted by concern about the necessity of reporting statistical information in the Results section. The best way to alleviate this concern, of course, is to develop the same command of statistical concepts that you have of other concepts. While you are acquiring this mastery of statistics, however, you need a way to deal effectively with the problem of presenting statistical information. One solution to this problem is to adopt a simple organizational structure to guide your writing of the Results section.

You should use your Results section to answer the questions you raised in your introduction. However, the guiding principle in the Results section is to "stick to the facts, just the facts." You will have the opportunity to move beyond just the facts when you get to the Discussion.

### Reporting Statistics

The *Publication Manual* provides an excellent overview of the objectives of a Results section:

> The Results section summarizes the data collected and the statistical treatment of them. First, briefly state the main results or findings. Discussing the implications of the results is not appropriate here. Mention all relevant results, including those that run counter to the hypothesis. Do not include individual raw scores or raw data, with the exception, for example, of single-case designs or illustrative samples. (p. 15)

One way to meet these objectives is to use an organizational structure that is typical of paragraphs in the Results section. This structure is outlined in Table C.1, and an illustration of a paragraph from the Results section of a published article appears after the table.

**TABLE C.1**   STRUCTURE OF A TYPICAL PARAGRAPH IN THE RESULTS SECTION

1. State the purpose of the analysis.
2. Identify the descriptive statistic to be used to summarize results.
3. Present a summary of this descriptive statistic across conditions in the text itself, in a table, or in a figure.
4. If a table or figure is used, point out the major findings on which the reader should focus.
5. Present the reasons for, and the results of, inferential statistics tests.
6. State the conclusion that follows from each test, but do not discuss implications. These belong in the discussion section.

---

### Sample paragraph

To examine retention as a function of instructions given at the time of study, the number of words recalled by each participant in each instruction condition was determined. Words were scored as correct only if they matched a word that had appeared on the target list. Thus, synonyms were not counted as correct; misspelled words were accepted if the spelling was sufficiently similar to a target item that it could be reasonably concluded that the intended word had actually appeared on the list. Mean numbers of words recalled were 15.6, 15.2, and 10.1 in the bizarre imagery condition, the standard imagery condition, and the control condition, respectively. Overall, mean recall differed significantly among the conditions, $F(2, 72) = 64.84$, $MSE = 0.44$, $p = .0001$, eta squared $= .64$. Two analytical comparisons were performed to determine the source of this effect. These tests revealed that the two groups given imagery instructions when averaged together differed significantly from the control condition, $F(1, 72) = 44.62$, $p = .0001$; the effect size ($d$) for this comparison was 1.57. However, the two imagery conditions did not differ significantly from each other, $F(1, 72) = 1.66$, $p = .20$. In conclusion, retention by participants instructed to use imagery was higher than that by participants given no specific study instructions, but retention did not differ for the two types of imagery instructions.

---

### TIPS ON WRITING A GOOD RESULTS SECTION

We suggest you follow these steps when writing your results section.

- *Step 1.* A Results section paragraph begins by stating the purpose of the analysis. The reason(s) for doing an analysis should be stated succinctly; often, no more than a phrase is necessary. In the sample paragraph, for example, the purpose of the analysis is, "to examine retention as a function of the instructions given at the time of study." There are two reasons for making the purpose for each analysis explicit. It helps your reader follow the logic of your analysis plan. And, perhaps more importantly, it ensures that you will never try to report an analysis whose purpose you do not understand.
- *Step 2.* The second step in writing a Results section paragraph is to identify the descriptive statistic that will be used to summarize the results for a given dependent variable. For example, you might use the mean numbers of words recalled, as in the sample paragraph. Other possible descriptive statistics that could be used to summarize the results in each condition of your experiment are the median reaction time or the cumulative number of responses per minute.

• *Step 3.* The third step is to present a summary of this descriptive statistic across conditions. Whenever possible, measures of central tendency should be accompanied by corresponding measures of variability. If there are only two or three conditions in your experiment, this summary can be presented in the text itself. For instance, you could summarize the results of a two-group study by saying, "The mean number of correct responses for the experimental group was 10.5 ($SD$ = 2.1), whereas that for the control group was 5.2 ($SD$ = 1.8)." More commonly, however, you will have more data to summarize and you will need to present your findings in either a table or a figure (graph). We will describe the procedures for constructing tables and figures later in this section. The *Publication Manual* gives good advice regarding the use of tables and figures:

> To report the data, choose the medium that presents them clearly and economically. Tables provide exact values and can efficiently illustrate main effects. Figures of professional quality attract the reader's eye and best illustrate interactions and general comparisons, but they are not quite as precise as tables.
>
> Summarizing the results and the analysis in tables or figures instead of text may be helpful; for example, a table may enhance the readability of complex sets of analysis of variance results. Avoid repeating the same data in several places and using tables for data that can be easily presented in a few sentences in the text. (p. 15)

• *Step 4.* We should not expect a table or figure to be self-sufficient. Your reader will need help to gain as much information as possible from a table or figure. You are in the best position to offer this assistance because you are the person most familiar with your results. You should direct your reader's attention to the highlights of the data in the table or figure, focusing especially on those aspects of the results that are consistent (or discrepant) with the hypotheses you proposed in the introduction. Usually the same data are not reported in both a table and a figure. Tables provide a more precise description of the results, but figures make it easier to see trends or patterns in the data. Whichever you choose, be sure to highlight in the text itself the critical results that the table or figure reveals.

• *Step 5.* The fifth step in writing a paragraph of the Results section is to present the results of inferential statistical tests. Three pieces of information should always be reported with any inferential statistics test: the name of the test (usually indicated by a symbol such as *t*, *r*, or *F*); the degrees of freedom for the test (presented in parentheses after the test is identified); and the value of the test statistic that you obtained. Three additional pieces of information are useful in reporting the results of an inferential test: the exact probability of the test under the assumption that the null hypothesis is true, the estimate of error variation for that test, and a measure of effect size (see Chapter 6 and Appendix A for information on effect sizes). For instance, you might see "The overall effect of the drug variable was statistically significant, $F(3, 64) = 7.15, p = .0005, MSE = 2.4$. The effect size ($d$) was .85." (When you write the Results section, you should assume that your reader has a basic knowledge of inferential statistics. Therefore, you do not need to refer to concepts such as the null hypothesis or mention whether your obtained probability is less than your chosen alpha level. All that is required is that you use the term "statistically significant" correctly.)

- *Concluding Step.* The final step in writing a paragraph in the Results section is to state a brief conclusion that follows from each test you report. This is accomplished by referring to the descriptive statistics on which the inferential test is based. For example, if the mean number correct in the experimental group is 10, that in the control group is 5, and this difference is statistically significant, an appropriate concluding statement would be "The control group did worse than the experimental group." In this simple example the conclusion may seem obvious, but appropriate concluding statements are essential in more complex analyses. It is not enough to string together a series of inferential statistical tests with appropriate commentary on the statistical significance of each test, and then never report the descriptive statistics or any conclusion. It is almost useless for your readers to know that an independent variable has had a statistically significant effect if you have failed to describe the nature of that effect. Descriptive statistics are essential in providing such a description.

Each paragraph of the Results section follows the structure outlined in Table C.1. The idea is not to overload your reader with statistics. The challenge is to select those findings that are most critical, being sure to report all the data pertinent to the questions raised in your introduction. Before concluding our discussion of the Results section, we will briefly describe the basic procedures for constructing tables and figures, two key tools in reporting results effectively.

Presenting Data in Tables    Tables are an effective and efficient means for presenting large amounts of data in concise form. The table should supplement and not duplicate information in the text of the paper, but it should be well integrated into the text. The tables in your paper should be numbered consecutively (Arabic numerals are used to number tables) so that they can be referred to easily in the text by their numbers. Each table should also have a brief explanatory title, and the columns and rows of the table should be labeled clearly. The data entries in the table should all be reported to the same degree of precision (i.e., all values should have the same number of decimal places), and the values should be consistently aligned with the corresponding row and column headings. An appropriately constructed table appears in the sample manuscript at the end of this appendix. When manuscripts are submitted for publication, each table is typed on a separate page and appears at the end of the paper after the references and footnotes sections.

Presenting Data in Figures   Figures, like tables, are a concise way to present large amounts of information. A figure has two principal axes: the horizontal axis, or *x*-axis, and the vertical axis, or *y*-axis. Typically, the levels of the independent variable are plotted on the *x*-axis and those of the dependent variable are plotted on the *y*-axis. When there are two or more independent variables, the levels of the second and succeeding independent variables serve as labels for the data within the figure or are indicated in a figure legend. In Figure C.1 the values of the dependent variable (mean number recalled) are plotted on the *y*-axis, the levels of one independent variable (serial position) are indicated on the *x*-axis. The levels of the second independent variable (Cued [C] or NonCued [NC]) label the data within the figures, and the levels of the third independent variable (instructions) serve as the headings for each of the two separate panels of the figure.

There are alternative ways to construct useful graphic presentations. All figures must include certain features, however. The *x*- and *y*-axes must be clearly labeled, with each label printed next to the corresponding axis. Selected points (called grid points) on each axis must be identified with labeled grid marks, and the grid labels are always printed horizontally. The grid scale for the *x*- and *y*-axes should be chosen such that the plotted data are legible and span the entire illustration. When a manuscript is submitted for publication, each figure

**FIGURE C.1**   Mean number of words recalled (of a possible ten) as a function of serial position within blocks, cuing (C = Cued; NC = Noncued),  and instructional condition.

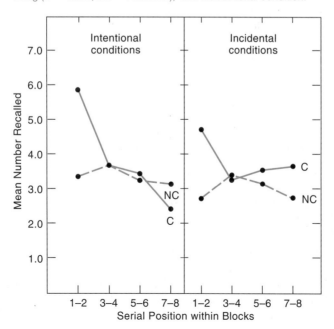

**FIGURE C.2**    Proportion recognition errors made by two groups of college students after rating verbal items for either familiarity or meaning. The items were nonwords (NW) and words appearing less than one time, one through ten times and more than forty times per million in the Thorndike-Lorge count.

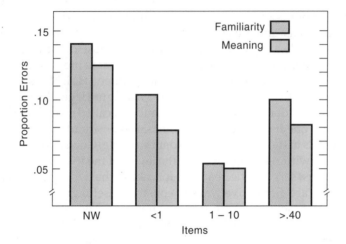

appears on a separate page but the figure captions do not appear on the figures themselves. They are presented on a separate page under the centered heading "Figure Captions." This page follows the tables at the end of the manuscript but precedes the figures, which are then presented in order (see sample paper).

Two general types of figures are commonly used in psychology: bar graphs and line graphs. A bar graph is often used when the independent variable plotted on the *x*-axis is a nominal-scale variable. For example, if you were plotting the mean GPA (dependent variable) of students enrolled in different academic majors (independent variable), you could use a bar graph. An illustration of a bar graph is presented in Figure C.2. The most common type of figure is the line graph shown in Figure C.1.

## Discussion

The fourth section of the body of your report, the discussion, begins with a centered heading (see sample paper). The Discussion section, unlike the Results sections, contains "more than just the facts." In the words of the *Publication Manual:*

> After presenting the results, you are in a position to evaluate and interpret their implications, especially with respect to your original hypothesis. You are free to examine, interpret, and qualify the results, as well as to draw inferences from them. (p. 18)

(*Note:* For some research reports, when the results are relatively brief and discussion is straightforward and also not very lengthy, the two sections can be combined in a Results and Discussion section.)

The discussion begins with a succinct statement of the essential findings. You should give particular attention to how your findings support or refute your original hypotheses. You do not repeat the descriptive statistics in this summary, nor do you necessarily refer to the statistical significance of the findings. The *Publication Manual* provides good advice about what to do and not to do after the succinct summary of the findings:

> Similarities and differences between your results and the work of others should clarify and confirm your conclusions. Do not, however, simply reformulate and repeat points already made; each new statement should contribute to your position and to the reader's understanding of the problem. You may remark on certain shortcomings of the study, but do not dwell on every flaw. Negative results should be accepted as such without an undue attempt to explain them away. (pp. 18–19)

The discussion is written in a tone and style consistent with the introduction. Be careful, however, to keep the statements you make in the discussion consistent with the data reported in the results. For instance, you should not report that one group did better than another if the comparison between these groups was not statistically significant—at least not without some qualification of what you mean by "better."

As just noted from the *Publication Manual*, the discussion includes a description of how your findings relate to the relevant literature, most of which you will have cited in the introduction. If your results are not consistent with your original hypotheses, you should suggest an explanation for these discrepancies. Such post hoc (after-the-fact) explanations should be considered tentative at best. If the reasons for your results are unclear, you should not hesitate to say so. It sometimes is necessary and helpful to include a paragraph describing limitations or problems in the research. As noted in the *Publication Manual*, however, "do not dwell compulsively on every flaw." Do try to anticipate criticisms of your study that others might make.

If appropriate, conclude the discussion by proposing additional research that should be done on the problem you are investigating. Avoid cliches such as "Additional research on this problem is needed before definitive conclusions can be reached." Instead, be specific about what research should be done and why it needs to be done. That is, be sure to explain what the new research should reveal that we do not already know. The reader will not learn much if you say, "It would be interesting to do this experiment with younger participants." The reader can learn much more if you explain how you would expect the results to differ with younger participants and what you would conclude if the results of the proposed experiment were to turn out as expected. Remember, the watchword in proposing new research is to be specific. Your emphasis when writing your report should definitely be on quality, not quantity.

### TIPS ON WRITING THE DISCUSSION SECTION

Again, the *Publication Manual* gives good advice for authors beginning to write their Discussion section:

"In general, be guided by the following questions:

- What have I contributed here?
- How has my study helped to resolve the original problem?
- What conclusions and theoretical implications can I draw from my study?

The responses to these questions are the core of your contribution, and readers have a right to clear, unambiguous, and direct answers" (p. 19).

## References

We have already described the procedure for citing references within the body of a research report by using the name(s) of the author(s) and the date of publication. The References section, which appears with a centered heading on a separate page after the discussion (see sample paper), includes the complete citation for each reference. "Just as data in the paper support interpretations and conclusions, so reference citations document statements made about the literature" (*Publication Manual*, p. 20).

There are three types of references that will cover almost all those needed for most research reports: journal articles, books, and chapters in edited books. In addition, with the availability of information on the Internet, there is a need to cite appropriately an Internet source. The format for each of these reference types is illustrated in Table C.2. As this table shows, the first line of each reference is indented. The journal article reference includes the authors, the year of

**TABLE C.2**    ILLUSTRATION OF FORMAT OF REFERENCE CITATIONS

| Journal article |
| --- |
| Loftus, E. F., & Burns, T. E. (1982). Mental shock can produce retrograde amnesia. Memory & Cognition, *10*, 318–323. |

| Book |
| --- |
| Posavac, E. J., & Carey, R. G. (1992). Program evaluation (4th ed.). Englewood Cliffs, NJ: Prentice Hall. |

| Chapter in an edited book |
| --- |
| Weiss, J. M. (1977). Psychological and behavioral influences on gastrointestinal lesions in animal models. In J. D. Maser & M. E. P. Seligman (Eds.), Psychopathology: Experimental models (pp. 232–269). San Francisco: W. H. Freeman. |

| Article in electronic journal |
| --- |
| Kirsch, I., & Sapirstein, G. (1998). Listening to prozac but hearing placebo: A meta-analysis of antidepressant medication. Prevention and Treatment [On-line serial], *1*. Available: journals.apa.org/prevention/volume1/pre0010002a.html. |

publication, the title of the article, the name of the journal, the volume number, and the page numbers. The book citation includes the authors, the copyright date, the title, the city in which the book was published, and the publisher. The reference for a chapter in an edited volume includes the author of the chapter, the date, the chapter title, the editors of the book, the title of the book, the page numbers of the chapter, the city of publication, and the publisher. The citation to an electronic journal identifies the specific Internet address.

When citing information from the Internet, especially Web sites, it is critical that you give the reader the specific information required to locate the electronic source. Be aware, however, that Internet addresses change regularly, as does the information that is found in them. It is recommended (e.g., Harnack & Kleppinger, 1997) that you indicate the date you accessed a Web site, for example in parentheses following the citation.

You can save your readers much aggravation if you follow the reference formats closely and proofread your reference list carefully. The references are listed in alphabetical order by the last name of the first author of each article. If there are two articles by the same author(s), they are arranged in ascending order by year of publication.

## Appendixes

Appendixes are rare in published research articles, but they are a bit more common in students' research reports. When they are intended for a published article, each appendix begins on a separate manuscript page and they appear at the end of the paper following the references. (*Note:* Instructors may require you to submit an appendix including your raw data, the worksheets for a statistical analysis, or the computer printout of the analyses. The appendix can also be used to provide a verbatim copy of the instructions to participants or a list of the specific materials used in an experiment.) Each appendix is identified by letter (A, B, C, and so on), and any reference to the appendix in the body of the text is made using this letter. For instance, you might write, "The complete instructions can be found in Appendix A."

## Author Note

The *Publication Manual* provides a concise description of the contents of an author note:

> The author note (a) identifies the departmental affiliation of each author, (b) identifies sources of financial support, (c) provides a forum for authors to acknowledge colleagues' professional contributions to the study and personal assistance, and (d) tells whom the interested reader may contact for further information concerning the article. (p. 21)

The author note appears on a separate page under the centered heading "Author Note" immediately after the References section (or after the appendixes, if there are any).

## Footnotes

Because they are not used for citing references, footnotes are rare in journal articles and even more rare in students' research reports. When footnotes appear in the text they are of two types: content footnotes and copyright permission footnotes. Content footnotes supplement or expand upon the text material. Copyright permission footnotes acknowledge the source of quotations. Footnotes (of both kinds) are numbered consecutively in the text. In the typed manuscript, footnotes appear on a separate page following the references section under the centered heading "Footnotes."

## Order of Manuscript Pages

The pages of your research report should be numbered consecutively in the following order:

Title Page
Abstract
Text (introduction, method, results, discussion)
References (start on a separate page)
*Appendixes (start each on a separate page)
Author note (start on a separate page)
*Footnotes (list together, starting on a separate page)
Tables (start each on a separate page)
Figure Captions (list together, starting on a separate page)
Figures (place each on a separate page).

*Appear only infrequently in journal articles.

## ORAL PRESENTATIONS

Research psychologists regularly attend professional conventions at which they present brief oral descriptions of their research. Similarly, students may give oral presentations of their research either in class or at a department research symposium involving students from a number of different classes or at undergraduate research conferences. All of these settings share one characteristic—the time allowed for the presentation is usually no more than 10 to 15 minutes. In this length of time it is impossible to provide the detailed description that is included in a journal article. In general, as noted in the *Publication Manual*, "Material delivered verbally should differ from written material in its level of detail, organization, and presentation" (p. 339). To reach your audience the *Publication Manual* recommends that you:

> Omit most of the details of scientific procedures, because a listener cannot follow the same level of detail as a reader can. The audience wants to know (a) what you studied and why, (b) how you went about the research (give a general orientation), (c) what you discovered, and (d) the implications of your results. A verbal

presentation should create awareness about a topic and stimulate interest in it; colleagues can retrieve the details from a written paper, copies of which you may want to have available. (p. 339)

A colleague of ours in the biology department has developed five principles that he distributes to his cell physiology students to help them prepare the oral presentation required in his class. Like all good maxims these five sound simple enough, but they are all too frequently ignored even by experienced researchers.

### FIVE PRINCIPLES FOR EFFECTIVE ORAL PRESENTATIONS

- AVOID THE TEMPTATION TO TELL EVERYTHING YOU KNOW IN 10 MINUTES. This temptation can best be avoided by limiting your presentation to one or two main points. What are the important "take home messages"? The brief time available for an oral presentation is barely sufficient to allow you to present the evidence supporting these main points. There simply will not be time to discuss any side issues.
- CULTIVATE A GOOD PLATFORM PRESENCE. This can best be achieved by developing public speaking skills. Most people need a written copy of their presentation in front of them while they are presenting, but your presentation will be more effective if you can appear not to be reading. Many people speak too quickly in front of an audience, particularly if they are reading; it is best to use simple, direct sentences presented at a moderate rate. Most important, speak loudly and clearly.
- USE EFFECTIVE VISUAL AIDS. The use of effective visual aids can help your listeners follow your presentation. Slides, overhead transparencies, and electronic presentations must be distinct enough to be seen clearly at a distance. The successful use of audiovisual aids is a skill and it can be improved with practice. Be sure that whatever visual aids you use are as close to self-explanatory as you can make them.
- LEAVE TIME FOR QUESTIONS. You need to keep in mind the fourth principle, leaving time for questions, because most professional conferences and classroom presentations will require that you reserve time for questions. Although questions from the audience can be somewhat intimidating, the opportunity for questions gives your listeners a chance to become actively involved in your presentation.
- PRACTICE YOUR TALK BEFORE A CRITICAL AUDIENCE BEFORE YOU GIVE IT. This final principle is perhaps the most important. Practicing your talk before an audience is more beneficial than simply rehearsing the talk over and over by yourself. Such private rehearsal is a good way to prepare for your "dress rehearsal," but it is no substitute for practicing before others.

These five principles provide a good coaching manual for oral presentations. The best way to develop this skill, however, is to deliver as many oral presentations as possible under "game conditions." Practice may not make perfect, but it is the best route we know to improvement.

## RESEARCH PROPOSALS

In the last section of this appendix we discuss writing again—but this time the writing of research proposals. As we mentioned at the beginning of this appendix, researchers must often seek financial support for their research by submitting grant proposals to private or government agencies. Students in research methods classes are also sometimes required to submit proposals describing research they might do. Even if a written proposal is not required, only a foolhardy researcher would tackle a research project without careful prior consideration of related literature, possible practical problems, workable statistical analyses of the data, and eventual interpretation of the expected results. Without a carefully constructed plan for the research, the unprepared investigator is likely to produce an unworkable, unanalyzable, or uninterpretable piece of research.

The purpose of a research proposal is to ensure a workable experimental design that, when implemented, will result in an interpretable empirical finding of significant scientific merit. No research proposal, no matter how carefully prepared, can guarantee important results. Researchers learn early in their careers about Murphy's Law. In essence, Murphy's Law states that "anything that can go wrong will go wrong." Nonetheless, it is worthwhile to develop a research proposal, if only to avoid the research problems that are avoidable.

A written research proposal follows the general format of a journal article, but the headings of the various sections are slightly different. The proposal should include the following main sections:

Introduction
Method
Expected Results and Statistical Treatment
References
Appendix
Information for Institutional Review Board

An abstract is not included in a research proposal. The introduction of a research proposal is likely to include a more extensive review of the relevant literature than is required for a journal article. The statement of the research problem and the logical development of hypotheses in a research proposal are the same as required in a journal article. Similarly, the Method section in the proposal should be as close as possible to the one that will accompany the finished research. Thus our remarks about the format and content of the Method section of a research report apply equally to the writing of a proposal.

The section of the proposal entitled "Expected Results and Statistical Treatment" should include a brief discussion of the anticipated results of the research. In most cases the exact nature of the results will not be known. Nevertheless, you will always have some idea (in the form of a hypothesis or prediction) of the outcome of the research. The Expected Results section may include tables or figures of the results as you expect (hope) that they will come out. The results that are most important to the project should be highlighted. A statistical analysis plan for the proposed results should be in this section. For example, if you are proposing a complex design, you would need to indicate which effects you will be testing and what inferential test you will use for these tests. Reasonable alternatives to the expected results should also be mentioned, as well as possible problems of interpretation that will arise if the results deviate from the research hypothesis. Implications of the expected results (should they be obtained) often conclude a research proposal.

The References section should be in exactly the same form as the one you would submit with the final report. An appendix should complete the research proposal and should include a list of all materials that will be used in doing the experiment. In most cases this will mean that a copy of the instructions to participants will be included, as well as the type of apparatus used, a list of stimulus materials or a description of the stimuli, and so on. To repeat, all materials should be listed. For example, if you are doing a study involving students' memory for lists of words, the following must be included in the appendix: actual lists with randomizations made, type of apparatus used for presentation, instructions to participants for all conditions, and randomizations of conditions.

Finally, a research proposal should include material to be submitted to an Institutional Review Board (IRB) or similar committee designed to review the ethics of the proposed research (see Chapter 2).

## A SAMPLE RESEARCH REPORT

First few words of title
appear before page number.

5 spaces

Running head: FALSE MEMORIES

False Recall    1

Type flush
with left
margin.

Type running
head all in caps.

Number pages
consecutively,
beginning with
title page.

False Recall and Recognition of List Items Following Delay

Jeanne S. Zechmeister and Eugene B. Zechmeister

Loyola University of Chicago

Use upper and lower case for title,
name, and affiliation
(centered).

Note:
Use one-inch margins at the top,
bottom, right, and left of all pages.

*Center, do not underline.*

↓

False Recall    2

Abstract

*No paragraph indentation for abstract.*

Whether false memories persist over a delay was investigated using H. L. Roediger and K. B. McDermott's (1995) false memory procedure. College students (N = 19) studied 12 15-item lists and either recalled items immediately or following a 90-s delay. A first recognition test immediately followed recall of lists; a second test occurred 2 days later. The proportion of correctly recalled list items decreased with the 90-s delay, whereas the proportion of falsely recalled critical items increased. The overall proportion of items recognized as "old" was greater for false critical items than for correct list items, but both false recognition and correct recognition decreased over the 2-day period. These findings are compared to other studies that examined false memories following delays.

*Abstract should be a single paragraph with no more than 960 characters, including punctuation and spaces (about 120 words).*

*Note:*
*Double-space between all lines of the manuscript. There should be no more than 27 lines of text on each page.*
*When using a word processor, use left justification only (not full). Do not use italic and bold fonts, and use one font size throughout the manuscript.*

Leave one space at end of all sentences, and after all commas, colons, and semi-colons.

Identify all authors (surnames only) the first time you cite a source (five or fewer authors).

List multiple sources in alphabetical order, separated by a semi-colon.

Indent every paragraph five to seven spaces (consistently).

Abbreviated terms are first spelled out, followed by the abbreviation in parentheses.

Title appears centered on page 3, with first letter of major words in caps.

False Recall    3

False Recall and Recognition of List Items Following Delay

Roediger and McDermott (1995) captured the attention of memory researchers by reminding us of the importance of examining participants' errors in recall and that these errors can sometimes be quite predictable. Moreover, these "false memories" are relevant to ongoing debates about false memories that may occur in more natural settings (e.g., clinics, courtrooms). Roediger and McDermott, and many others, have demonstrated that false memories are easily created and that participants' phenomenological experience of these memories mimics their memories for actual events (e.g., Mather, Henkel, & Johnson, 1997; Norman & Schacter, 1997; Payne, Elie, Blackwell, & Neuschatz, 1996). The purpose of the present study was to replicate Roediger and McDermott's (1995) findings and to extend their findings by examining the persistence of false memories following delays. If false memories persist following delays, important implications exist regarding courtroom testimony and recovered memories in therapy. For example, memory retrieval in these cases follows varying periods of delay and the accuracy of these memories may thus be questioned.

In this false memory paradigm word lists are constructed such that each word is highly associated with a critical, not-presented word. For example, participants may hear the words bed, rest, awake, tired, dream, etc., but never the critical word, sleep. False recall and recognition for the word sleep is quite high. Underwood (1965) proposed that an implicit associative response (IAR) occurs when participants study an associated word. For example, when participants hear "bed" they may think of "sleep" (the IAR). With the next word, "rest," they again may experience "sleep" as an IAR, and so on. When their memory is tested participants may have difficulty discriminating the

False Recall    4

Use Latin abbreviations (such as *e.g.* and *i.e.*) only in parentheses.

Use numbers to express amounts 10 and above, and when numbers are grouped with numbers 10 and above.

An "s" (with no period) is the abbreviation for second.

Use number for units of time or measure.

Note: Use past tense to describe the study.

Flush with left margin, underlined, only first letter in caps.

Always use words to express numbers that begin a sentence.

IAR from the presented items, resulting in false recall or recognition. An alternative account relies on the extent to which the lists of associated words activate a schema for the words (e.g., a "sleep" schema). According to this account, recall after a delay may be based on memory for the schema rather than the actual list presentation.

In the present study participants listened to 12 lists comprised of 15 words that were associated to a critical, not-presented word. Participants were randomly assigned to recall 4 of the 12 lists in either an immediate-recall condition or following a 90-s delay in a single trial of free recall. When not recalling words (and during the 90-s delays) participants completed distractor tasks consisting of math problems. Additionally, two recognition tests were administered. The first recognition test followed the presentation and recall of the 15 lists; the second was 2 days later.

We hypothesized that the proportions of correct recall and false recall would not differ in the immediate-recall condition because of participants' inability to differentiate their memory for the presented words from the IARs generated for the critical items. In the delayed-recall condition, we expected the proportion of false items recalled to be greater than the proportion of correct items recalled because of participants' activation of a schema for the list to aid recall. This activation was assumed to lead to recall of the highly associated, critical item. Furthermore, we anticipated that correct recall would decrease over time but false recall would increase with the delay. Similar predictions were made for participants' recognition of correct list items and false critical items.

Method    Center, no underline, only the first letter in caps.

Participants

Nineteen students (16 women, 3 men) from a research methods in psychology

Note: Method, Results, and Discussion sections do not begin on new page (unless coincidentally).

*Note: "Data" is plural.*

*Indented, underlined paragraph heading, followed by a period. Only first letter of first word in caps.*

*Use words to express numbers less than 10.*

*The word "participants" is preferred over "subjects."*

False Recall    5

class at Loyola University of Chicago participated as part of a class project. Data for one student were omitted from all analyses because the student attempted recall for the wrong lists; recognition data for two students were omitted from analyses because they missed the second class session in which the experiment was conducted.

Materials

Word lists. We used 12 15-item word lists from Roediger and McDermott's (1995) study. They constructed 24 lists by selecting 15 words that were highly associated with a critical word that was not presented. Words were ordered such that the strongest associates were presented first, followed by more weakly associated words. For example, the list for the critical word, needle, was thread, pin, eye, sewing, sharp, point, prick, thimble, haystack, thorn, hurt, injection, syringe, cloth, and knitting. Six lists in the present study were identified by Roediger and McDermott as having a high likelihood of creating false memories (identified by the critical item): chair, mountain, needle, rough, sleep, sweet. The other six lists used in the present study for recall were randomly selected from their remaining lists (identified by the critical item): bread, cold, doctor, foot, music, slow .

Participants recalled words from 4 of the 12 lists in a single trial of free recall. In order to rule out the possibility that proportions of correct and false recall would be determined by the particular lists used for the recall task, the four recall lists were counterbalanced. The 12 lists were randomly divided into three sets of four lists, with the provision that two lists in each set have high likelihoods for creating false memories. Participants were randomly assigned to recall words for four lists. Seven participants recalled the chair, bread, slow, and sleep lists; seven participants recalled the needle,

False Recall    6

foot, doctor, and rough lists, and four participants recalled the sweet, music, cold, and mountain lists.

    Distractor task. Participants completed a distractor task consisting of math problems when not recalling words and during the 90-s delay. We generated 20 pages of math problems. Each page had six complex math problems involving addition, subtraction, multiplication, and division.

    Recall packets. We created six different packets to manipulate the recall condition (immediate, delayed) and counterbalance the lists used for recall. Four pages presented recall instructions based on those used by Roediger and McDermott (1995): "Please write down as many words from the list that you remember. A good strategy is to write down the last few items first, then the rest of the words in any order." Twenty pages had math problems. Between each page was a colored sheet of paper, which masked the participants' next task (recall or math problems). The order of the 24 pages depended on whether participants were in the immediate- or delayed-recall condition and which list set participants were assigned to recall. For example, the "music" list was presented first. Following the presentation of the list, participants assigned to recall the music list in the immediate condition opened their packet to a page with recall instructions; all other participants opened their packet to a page of math problems. After 90 s, a tone signaled participants to turn to the next white page (following the colored sheet). If assigned to recall the music list in the delayed-recall condition, participants' next sheet had recall instructions; all other participants received math problems. This sequence was followed for the remaining 11 word lists.

    Recognition tests. Participants completed two different recognition tests, the first

*Place periods or commas within quotation marks.*

False Recall    7

followed the presentation and recall of lists (immediate), the second was 2 days later

(delayed). Because three list sets were used for recall (to counterbalance recall lists

across participants), we created three versions of the first recognition test (session 1)

and three versions of the second recognition test (session 2). Following Roediger and

McDermott's terminology, recognition-test items that were presented during the recall

portion of the study are referred to as "studied," and new distractor items are referred to

as "not studied." Each 72-item recognition test consisted of six different types of items:

10 Studied/Recalled items (5 each from two of the four lists participants were asked to

recall); 2 corresponding critical items for these lists; 20 Studied/Not Recalled items (5

each from four of the eight lists participants did not recall); 4 corresponding critical

items for these lists; 30 Not Studied Distractor items (5 each from six lists that were not

presented); and 6 corresponding critical items for the distractor lists (these lists also

were from Roediger & McDermott, 1995). The five items selected from the word lists for

each recognition test were the first, third, fifth, seventh, and ninth words. The 72 words

on each list were randomly ordered. Participants made recognition judgments using a

4-point scale (1 = <u>sure new</u>, 2 = <u>probably new</u>, 3 = <u>probably old</u>, and 4 = <u>sure old</u>).

Procedure

A 2 (condition) X 2 (memory type) mixed factorial design was used for the recall

portion of the experiment. Students were randomly assigned to either the immediate-

recall condition or the delayed-recall condition; thus, the condition variable was

manipulated as a random groups design. Memory type was a repeated measures

variable with two levels: correct and false memory. The recognition portion of the

experiment was a repeated measures independent variable. Participants completed the

*A comma separates authors' surnames and year of publication when citation is within parentheses.*

*Use ampersand to indicate "and" for references within parentheses.*

*Underline the anchors of a scale.*

*Numbers are used to indicate the levels of a design. Include one space to left and right of multiplication sign.*

False Recall    8

"min" (without a period) is the abbreviation for minute.

first recognition test immediately following the presentation and recall of word lists and completed the delayed recognition test 2 days later. The dependent variables were proportion of correct and false recall and proportion of correct and false recognition.

The experiment was conducted during two scheduled class periods. In the first session, lasting 50 min, the experimenter gave students a consent form and a packet that corresponded to their condition when they entered the class (students were randomly assigned to conditions prior to their arrival). A participant number appeared on top of the packet. Instructions requested students not to open their packet. After students read and signed their consent form, they listened to tape-recorded instructions for the study. Following this, the experimenter stopped the tape recorder and asked if there were any questions. Tape-recorded word lists were then presented. The random order of the lists was as follows (identified by the critical item): music, needle, sleep, doctor, slow, mountain, rough, bread, sweet, cold, chair, and foot. Words were presented at the rate of approximately one word every 1½ s. Following the list presentation, participants heard a tone informing them to turn to the next white page. They then either recalled list items or completed math problems for 90 s. A tone then signaled participants to turn to the next white page. This page instructed them to recall the list items or complete math problems.  This procedure was followed for all 12 lists.

After the study and recall phase of the experiment, the experimenter distributed the first recognition test and asked participants to record their participant number on the top of the recognition test. After completing the recognition test, participants were asked to write their participant number in their notebook; they were then dismissed. At the beginning of the next class session (2 days later), participants reported their number

Note: Words are not hyphenated at the end of a line.

*Note: Always double-space. Do not insert extra spaces between sections.*

*Center, no underline.*

and they were given the corresponding second recognition test. Each recognition test took approximately 5 min to complete. The instructor then fully debriefed participants regarding the purpose of the experiment.

Results

Results are presented first for participants' recall and then for their recognition of list items. The dependent variables were proportion of correct recall/recognition and proportion of false recall/recognition. Proportion of correct recall was determined by counting the number of words participants correctly recalled and dividing by 60 (the total number of list items they were asked to recall). Proportion of false recall was determined by counting the number of critical items falsely recalled and dividing by 4 (the total number of critical items for the four lists participants recalled).

Similar proportions were computed for recognition data. For ease of comparisons, participants' recognition responses were collapsed such that ratings of 1 or 2 indicated judgments that the word was "new" (i.e., not presented during the recall portion of the study), and ratings of 3 or 4 indicated the word was "old" (i.e., presented during the recall portion). The number of items judged "old" for each type of word (e.g., studied, recalled; not studied distractor) was counted and divided by the total number of words of that type presented on the recognition test.

Recall

Mean proportions for correct and false recall were entered into a 2 (condition) X 2 (memory type) mixed-design analysis of variance (ANOVA). Across the two recall conditions the proportion of falsely recalled critical items ($M$ = .60, $SD$ = .23) tended to be greater than the proportion of correctly recalled list items ($M$ = .48, $SD$ = .12), $F$(1,

*$M$ is the abbreviation for arithmetic mean.*

*$SD$ is the abbreviation for standard deviation.*

MSE is the abbreviation for Mean Square Error.

Underline all statistical terms.

Do not capitalize names of conditions.

Footnotes appear on a separate page near end of manuscript (not at bottom of the page).

Do not abbreviate "Figure." Figure caption and figure appear on separate pages at end of manuscript.

Degrees of freedom for statistical tests are reported in parentheses (with no space after statistical term).

16) = 4.38, $p$ = .053 (MSE = .03, effect size $r$ = .47).[1] The observed power to detect this

large effect with the small sample size ($n$ = 9 per condition), at alpha = .05, was

estimated to be only .50. The main effect of condition was not significant, $F$(1, 16) = .10,

$p$ > .05 (MSE = .02, $r$ = .10, power = .06). As predicted, however, recall condition and

memory type interacted to influence participants' recall, $F$(1, 16) = 9.50, $p$ < .01 (MSE =

.03, $r$ = .61). Simple main effects analyses revealed that recall differed in the

immediate- and delayed-recall conditions in the predicted direction (see Figure 1).

Participants in the immediate-recall condition did not differ in their proportions of correct

recall and false recall, $F$(1, 8) = .41, $p$ > .05 (MSE = .036, $r$ = .22, power = .09);

however, participants in the delayed-recall condition were more likely to recall a greater

proportion of false critical items than correct list items, $F$(1, 8) = 16.57, $p$ < .005 (MSE =

.024, $r$ = .82).[2]

A second set of simple main effects analyses examined the effect of delay for

each type of recall. As expected, the proportion of correctly recalled list items

decreased following delay and the proportion of false recall increased following delay

(see Figure 1). For correct list items, participants in the delayed-recall condition recalled

fewer items than participants who recalled list items immediately, $F$(1, 16) = 15.42, $p$ <

.005 (MSE = .008). The effect size ($r$) was .70, indicating a very large effect of

immediate- vs. delayed-recall on participants' correct recall (see Cohen, 1988). In

contrast, the proportion of falsely recalled critical items increased following the 90-s

delay relative to the immediate-recall condition, $F$(1, 16) = 3.77, $p$ = .07. The effect size

($r$) was .44; however, the estimated power to detect this large effect was only .45 (alpha

= .05).

*Table appears on separate page near end of manuscript.*

*Note use of spaces and punctuation when typing statistics.*

*Variable names in caps when they appear with a multiplication sign.*

<u>Recognition</u>

Across two testing sessions separated by 2 days, we examined the proportion of items recognized as "old" as a function of whether items were correct list items or false critical items and whether the items were recalled (vs. not recalled) during the recall portion of the experiment (see Table 1).[3] Distractor items were excluded from the analyses because the proportion of these items judged "old" was generally low across item type and sessions, $\underline{M}$ = .18 ($\underline{SD}$ = .12). Main effects were observed for the time, memory type, and recalled/not recalled variables. As expected, memory for the items decreased over the 2-day period, as the proportion of all items recognized as "old" decreased at Time 2 ($\underline{M}$ = .71, $\underline{SD}$ = .14) relative to Time 1 ($\underline{M}$ = .87, $\underline{SD}$ = .11), $\underline{F}$(1, 14) = 16.40, $\underline{p}$ < .005 ($\underline{MSE}$ = .04, $\underline{r}$ = .73). Additionally, the main effect of memory type indicated that participants rated a higher proportion of false critical items "old" ($\underline{M}$ = .85, $\underline{SD}$ = .11) than correct list items ($\underline{M}$ = .73, $\underline{SD}$ = .13), $\underline{F}$(1, 14) = 14.72, $\underline{p}$ < .005 ($\underline{MSE}$ = .026, $\underline{r}$ = .71). Thus, in terms of proportions, false recognition was greater than correct recognition at Time 1 and Time 2. Finally, the proportion of items judged "old" was greater for lists participants were asked to recall ($\underline{M}$ = .87, $\underline{SD}$ = .09) relative to lists they did not recall ($\underline{M}$ = .71, $\underline{SD}$ = .14), $\underline{F}$(1, 14) = 23.57, $\underline{p}$ < .001 ($\underline{MSE}$ = .032, $\underline{r}$ =.79). This is the "testing effect" identified by Roediger and McDermott (1995), in which rehearsal during the recall portion of the experiment increases subsequent recognition.

There was also a Time X Recalled/Not Recalled interaction, $\underline{F}$(1, 14) = 7.49, $\underline{p}$ < .05 ($\underline{MSE}$ = .024, $\underline{r}$ = .59). This interaction indicated that recognition of words for recalled lists was slightly higher at Time 1 ($\underline{M}$ = .90, $\underline{SD}$ = .07) relative to Time 2 ($\underline{M}$ = .83, $\underline{SD}$ = .16), $\underline{F}$(1, 15) = 3.22, $\underline{p}$ < .10 ($\underline{MSE}$ = .013, $\underline{r}$ = .42, power = .39). In contrast,

*Capitalize nouns that are followed by a number.*

False Recall    12

recognition of words from not-recalled lists dropped significantly at Time 2 (M = .60, SD = .18) relative to Time 1 (M = .83, SD = .18), F(1, 15) = 18.63, p < .005 (MSE = .023, r = .74). Thus, rehearsal of the lists (through recall) increased the proportion of correct items and false critical items recognized as "old" even after a 2-day period, relative to lists that were not rehearsed.

As noted above, we observed differential effects of delay on the proportion recall of correct list items and false critical items. However, a similar effect was not observed for recognition data, as the Time X Memory Type interaction was not statistically significant, F(1, 14) = .028, p > .05 (MSE = .014). The effect size, r, for this interaction was quite small (.04, power = .05). Thus, the 2-day delay between the recognition tests resulted in similar decreases in the proportions of correct list items and false critical items that were recognized as "old."

*Note: Make sure you use the "greater than" or "less than" sign correctly.*

*Center, no underline.*

Discussion

Participants recalled list items in a single trial of free recall immediately after list presentation or following a 90-s filled delay. The proportion of correctly recalled list items decreased as a function of delay, but the proportion of false critical items recalled increased following the 90-s delay. Participants' recognition of correct list items and false critical items was tested following a 2-day delay. In terms of proportions, false recognition of critical items was greater than correct recognition of list items at Time 1 and Time 2, but recognition for both types of items decreased over the 2-day period. A testing effect occurred such that correct and false recognition were greater for lists participants had attempted recall relative to lists not recalled. The effects of rehearsal persisted over the 2-day period. In general, delay produced large effect sizes for both

*Year of publication in parentheses after author's surname.*

*Do not use contractions such as "wasn't."*

*Year of publication is not repeated within a paragraph if it is clear that the same study is being described.*

*Year of publication appears in parentheses even when reference has appeared previously in manuscript.*

*Use "et al." following surname of first author for work with three or more authors.*
*Note: First citation to this work lists all authors (see p. 3).*

recall and recognition.

McDermott (1996) used a 30-s filled delay to examine the effects of delay on participants' recall of correct list items and false critical items. Although she observed a decrease in correct recall following delay, her participants' false recall of critical items was not affected by delay. In contrast, we observed an increase in the proportion of false critical items recalled following a 90-s delay. One reason for this discrepancy may be derived from our differing findings for correct list recall. In McDermott's study the proportion of correct list items recalled following a 30-s delay was .50; in our study, the proportion of correct recall following a 90-s delay was .39. To the extent that a longer delay increased participants' forgetting of correct list items in our study, they may have had to rely more on schema-based recall, which we hypothesized to increase the occurrence of false memories. Alternatively, discrimination between IARs and memory for list items may become more difficult with longer delays. As a result, greater proportions of false recall would be expected (as was observed). This explanation is corroborated by McDermott's findings that after a 2-day delay, the proportion of falsely recalled critical items was greater than the proportion of correctly recalled items (similar to our findings for recognition). Thus, in both studies, participants demonstrated high levels of false recall that persisted over time.

Payne et al. (1996) examined participants' recognition memory for correct list items and false critical items in immediate (2 min) and delayed (24 hr) conditions. Similar to our recognition data, Payne et al. observed that false critical items were recognized with higher likelihood at both testing sessions than correct list items. However, they also observed an interaction between item type (correct, false) and

False Recall    14

*"hr" (with no period) is the abbreviation for hour.*

retention (immediate, delayed) for their recognition data that we did not. They observed more forgetting for correct list items than false critical items over the 24-hr period, whereas over our 2-day period we observed similar decreases for correct list items and false critical items. Differences in the retention interval (24 vs. 48 hr), the number of word lists (16 vs. 12), or other procedural differences may account for this discrepancy.

The findings of this study and those of other recent studies indicate that false memories are frequent and persist following delays. Moreover, there is accumulating evidence to suggest that false memories for highly associated information may exceed correct memory over time. These data are limited to individuals' recall for highly associated list items. Important areas for future research include false memories for natural categories such as people and events. Also, it is not clear to what extent individuals' emotions may affect correct and false recall. This question is particularly relevant to the issue of false memory in the emotionally charged situations of eyewitness testimony and therapy.

*Note: References section begins on a new page immediately after the Discussion section.*

Underline titles of books. Only first letter of first word and word following a colon in caps.

Publisher of book.

Use ampersand before last author's name.

First letter of questionnaire names in caps.

Use initials for first and middle names.

Period after year of publication (in parentheses).

Page numbers.

Use lower case for titles of articles and book chapters (except first word and word after a colon).

Underline journal name and volume number. Capitalize first letter of major words in journal name. Use comma after journal name and volume number.

Indent first line of each reference (same as paragraph).

Center, no underline.

False Recall   15

References

Cohen, J. (1988). <u>Statistical power analysis for behavioral sciences</u> (2nd ed.). New York: Academic Press.

Keppel, G. (1991). <u>Design and analysis: A researcher's handbook</u> (3rd ed.). Englewood Cliffs, NJ: Prentice-Hall.

Mather, M., Henkel, L. A., & Johnson, M. J. (1997). Evaluating characteristics of false memories: Remember/know judgments and Memory Characteristics Questionnaire compared. <u>Memory & Cognition, 25,</u> 826-837.

McDermott, K. B. (1996). The persistence of false memories in list recall. <u>Journal of Memory and Language, 35,</u> 212-230.

Norman, K., & Schacter, D. L. (1997). False recognition in younger and older adults: Exploring the characteristics of illusory memories. <u>Memory & Cognition, 25,</u> 838-848.   Separate authors' names with a comma.

Payne, D. G., Elie, C. J., Blackwell, J. M., & Neuschatz, J. S. (1996). Memory illusions: Recalling, recognizing, and recollecting events that never occurred. <u>Journal of Memory and Language, 35,</u> 261-285.

Roediger, H. L., & McDermott, K. B. (1995). Creating false memories: Remembering words not presented in lists. <u>Journal of Experimental Psychology: Learning, Memory, and Cognition, 21,</u> 803-814.

Underwood, B.J. (1965). False recognition produced by implicit verbal responses. <u>Journal of Experimental Psychology, 70,</u> 122-129.

Note: List references in alphabetical order using first author's surname. Double-space references, no extra space between references.

*Center, no underline.*

↓

False Recall    16

Author Note

Jeanne S. Zechmeister, Department of Psychology; Eugene B. Zechmeister, Department of Psychology.

Portions of this research were presented at the Annual Meeting of the Psychonomic Society, November 1996. The authors thank the students in the first author's Research Methods in Psychology course at Loyola University of Chicago who participated in and discussed this study, and John J. Shaughnessy for his suggestions for this manuscript.

Send correspondence concerning this manuscript to Jeanne S. Zechmeister, Department of Psychology, Loyola University of Chicago, 6525 N. Sheridan Road, Chicago, IL 60626; e-mail: jzechme@luc.edu.

*Authors' department affiliations in first paragraph.*

*Acknowledge people who assisted with the research and manuscript preparation.*

*Last paragraph in Author Note specifies author's address for correspondence. Use this form exactly with your name and address.*

Footnotes

[1] The effect size, $r$, was derived from ANOVA output that presented $eta^2$ as a measure of effect size. Eta$^2$ represents the proportion of variance in the dependent variable that is accounted for by the independent variable. Eta$^2$ is analogous to $r^2$ in analyses involving one $df$ for the effect. The square root of $eta^2$ represents $r$, the magnitude of linear relationship between two variables. Cohen (1988) offers the following guidelines for interpreting the size of an effect using $r$: small effect, $r = .10$; medium effect, $r = .25$; large effect, $r = .40$.

[2] Simple main effect analyses were calculated by treating the comparison as a one-way ANOVA, as recommended by Keppel (1991) for mixed designs.

[3] We also examined whether immediate- vs. delayed-recall conditions influenced recognition in the ANOVA. Because this variable did not produce any statistically significant effects in the recognition analyses, it will not be discussed further.

*Note: Use footnotes sparingly in manuscript.*

*Type flush with left margin.*

*Line separates title from body of table.*

*Center column headings over appropriate columns.*

*Line separates headings from table data.*

*Line at end of table data.*

*Table "notes" are typed flush with left margin.*

*Table title, underlined, with first letters of major words in caps.*

False Recall    18

Table 1

Mean Proportions for Recognizing Items as "Old" at Time 1 and Time 2 (48-hr Delay)

|  | Studied and Recalled | Studied and Not Recalled | Distractor |
|---|---|---|---|
| Correct List Items | | | |
| Time 1 | .84 | .79 | .19 |
|  | (.12) | (.17) | (.12) |
| Time 2 | .76 | .56 | .18 |
|  | (.22) | (.16) | (.16) |
| False Critical Items | | | |
| Time 1 | .97 | .88 | .28 |
|  | (.12) | (.20) | (.13) |
| Time 2 | .91 | .64 | .17 |
|  | (.20) | (.24) | (.10) |

Note. Standard deviations are in parentheses. "Recalled" and "Not Recalled" refer to whether participants were asked to recall list items at Time 1, not whether these items were produced by participants during recall.

*Note: Use double-space in table. Place only one table on a page.*

*Center, no underline.*

False Recall    19

↓
Figure Caption

*Flush with left margin. Do not abbreviate "Figure."* →

<u>Figure 1.</u> Mean proportions of correct and false recall in the immediate- and delayed-recall conditions.

*Note: More than one figure caption may appear on a "Figure Captions" page.*

*The figure itself appears on a separate page at end of manuscript. If there is more than one figure, each appears on a separate page.*

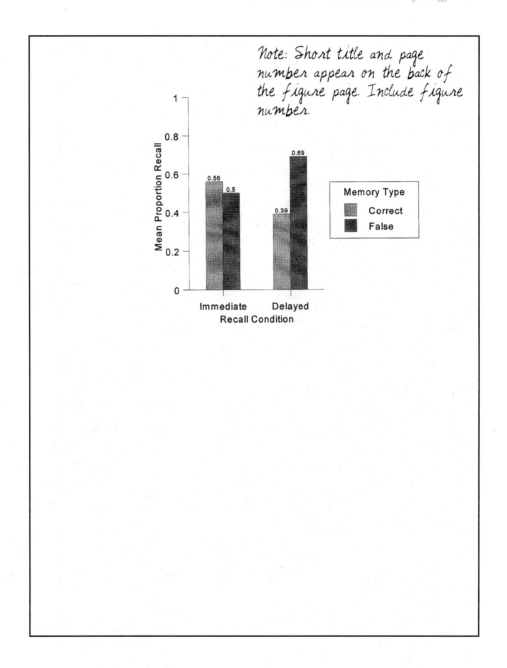

# Glossary

**ABAB design (reversal design)** A single-case experimental design in which an initial baseline stage (A) is followed by a treatment stage (B), a return to baseline (A), and then another treatment stage (B); the researcher observes whether behavior changes on introduction of the treatment, reverses when the treatment is withdrawn, and improves again when the treatment is reintroduced.

**ABBA counterbalancing** A technique for balancing stage-of-practice effects in the complete repeated measures design that involves presenting the conditions in one sequence (e.g., AB) followed by the opposite of the same sequence (e.g., BA).

**accidental sample** A type of nonprobability sample that results when availability and willingness to respond are the overriding factors used in selecting respondents; generally low in representativeness.

**actuarial prediction** Prediction of people's typical or average behavior based on reliable correlations between variables (e.g., predicting students' college GPA based on SAT scores).

**analytical comparisons** A statistical technique that can be applied (usually after obtaining a significant omnibus $F$-test) to locate the specific source of systematic variation in an experiment.

**applied research** See **basic versus applied research.**

**archival data** Source of evidence based on records or documents relating the activities of individuals, institutions, governments, and other groups; used as an alternative to or in conjunction with other research methods.

**baseline stage** First stage of a single-case experiment in which a record is made of the individual's behavior prior to any intervention.

**basic versus applied research** Whereas basic research mainly seeks knowledge about nature simply for the sake of understanding it better, applied research seeks knowledge that will modify or improve the present situation; however, basic and applied research are considered to have a reciprocal relationship, for example, when basic research is used to identify abstract

principles that can be applied in real-world settings, and when applied research is used to reveal possible limitations or extensions of these principles.

**behavior modification (behavior therapy)** The application of learning-conditioning principles in order to change behavior; the term behavior therapy is used when this application is with clinical populations.

**behavior therapy** See **behavior modification.**

**biased sample** A sample in which the distribution of characteristics is systematically different from that of the parent population.

**block randomization** The most common technique for carrying out random assignment in the random groups design; each block includes a random order of the conditions and there are as many blocks as there are subjects in each condition of the experiment.

**case study** An intensive description and analysis of a single individual.

**causal inference** Identification of the cause or causes of a phenomenon, by establishing covariation of cause and effect, a time-order relationship with cause preceding effect, and the elimination of plausible alternative causes.

**ceiling (and floor) effect** Measurement problem whereby the researcher cannot measure the effects of an independent variable or a possible interaction because performance has reached a maximum (minimum) in any condition of the experiment.

**checklist** Instrument used to record the presence or absence of something in the situation under observation.

**coding** The initial step in data reduction, especially with narrative records, in which units of behavior or particular events are identified and classified according to specific criteria.

**complex design** Experiment in which two or more independent variables are studied simultaneously.

**confederate** Someone in the service of a researcher who is instructed to behave in a certain way in order to help produce an experimental treatment.

**confidence intervals**   Indicate the range of values in which we can expect a population value to fall with a specified degree of confidence (e.g., .95).

**confounding**   Occurs when the independent variable of interest systematically covaries with a second, unintended independent variable.

**contamination**   Occurs when there is communication of information about the experiment between groups of participants.

**content analysis**   Any of a variety of techniques for making inferences by objectively identifying specific characteristics of messages, usually written communications but may be any form of message; used extensively in the analysis of archival data.

**control**   Key component of the scientific method whereby the effect of various factors possibly responsible for a phenomenon are isolated; three basic types of control are manipulation, holding conditions constant, and balancing.

**correlation**   Exists when two different measures of the same people, events, or things vary together; the presence of a correlation makes it possible to predict values on one variable by knowing the values on the second variable.

**correlation coefficient**   Statistic indicating how well two measures vary together; absolute size ranges from 0.0 (no correlation) to 1.00 (perfect correlation); direction of covariation is indicated by the sign of the coefficient, a plus ($+$) indicating that both measures covary in the same direction and a minus ($-$) indicating that the variables vary in opposite directions.

**correlational research**   Research whose goal is to identify predictive relationships among naturally occurring variables.

**counterbalancing**   A control technique for distributing (balancing) practice effects across the conditions of a repeated measures design. How counter-balancing is accomplished depends on whether a complete or an incomplete repeated measures design is used.

**cross-sectional design**   Survey research design in which one or more samples of the population are selected and information is collected from the samples at one time.

**data reduction**   Process in the analysis of behavioral data whereby results are meaningfully organized and statements summarizing important findings are prepared.

**debriefing**   Process following a research session through which participants are informed about the rationale for the research in which they par-

ticipated, about the need for any deception, and about their specific contribution to the research. Important goals of debriefing are to clear up any misconceptions and to leave participants with a positive feeling toward psychological research.

**deception**   Intentionally withholding information about significant aspects of a research project from a participant or presenting misinformation about the research to participants.

**demand characteristics**   Cues and other information used by participants to guide their behavior in a psychological study, often leading participants to do what they believe the observer (experimenter) expects them to do.

**dependent variable**   Measure of behavior used by the researcher to assess the effect (if any) of the independent variables.

**differential transfer**   Potential problem in repeated measures designs when performance in one condition differs depending on which of two other conditions precedes it.

**double-blind**   Both the participant and the observer are kept unaware (blind) of what treatment is being administered.

**ecological psychology**   Has as its goal the comprehensive description of individuals in everyday contexts.

**effect size**   Index of the strength of the relationship between the independent variable and dependent variable that is independent of sample size.

**element**   Each member of the population of interest.

**empirical approach**   Approach to acquiring knowledge that emphasizes direct observation and experimentation as a way of answering questions.

**ethnography**   Branch of anthropology that focuses on the systematic description (e.g., using naturalistic observation and participant observation) of the context and meanings of social interactions in a particular culture. May share similar goals with ecological psychology.

**ethogram**   A complete catalog of all the behavior patterns of an organism, including information as to frequency, duration, and context of occurrence.

**ethology**   Study of the behavior of organisms in relation to their natural environment; generally considered a branch of biology.

**event sampling**   Procedure whereby the observer records each event that meets a predetermined definition; more efficient method than time sampling when event of interest occurs infrequently.

**experimenter effects** Experimenters' expectations that may lead them to treat subjects differently in different groups or to record data in a biased manner.

**external validity** The extent to which the results of a research study can be generalized to different populations, settings, and conditions.

**extraneous variables** Potential independent variables that are not of direct interest to a researcher, but, in order to avoid confounding, must be controlled (e.g., nature of experimenters, size of groups tested).

**field experiment** Procedure in which one or more independent variables is manipulated by an observer in a natural setting to determine the effect on behavior.

**field notes** Verbal records of a trained observer that provide a running description of participants, events, settings, and behaviors.

**floor effect** See **ceiling effect.**

**F-test** Statistical test based on the analysis of variance, specifically the ratio of systematic variation and error variation. Under the null hypothesis both sources of variation represent error variation only and the expected value of $F$ is 1.00.

**Hawthorne effect** Changes in a person's behavior brought about by the interest shown in that person by significant others.

**hypothesis** A tentative explanation for a phenomenon.

**idiographic approach** Intensive study of an individual, with an emphasis on both individual uniqueness and lawfulness.

**independent groups design** Each separate group of subjects in the experiment represents a different condition as defined by the level of the independent variable.

**independent variable** Factor for which the researcher either selects or manipulates at least two levels in order to determine its effect on behavior.

**individual differences variable** A characteristic or trait that varies consistently across individuals, such as level of depression, age, intelligence, gender. Because this variable is formed from pre-existing groups (i.e., it occurs "naturally") an individual differences variable is sometimes called a *natural groups variable*. Another term sometimes used synonymously with individual differences variable is *subject variable*.

**inferential statistics** Means to test whether the differences in a dependent variable that are associated with various conditions of an experiment are reliable, that is, larger than would be expected on the basis of error variation alone.

**informed consent** Explicitly expressed willingness to participate in a research project based on clear understanding of the nature of the research, of the consequences of not participating, and of all factors that might be expected to influence willingness to participate.

**interaction** What occurs when the effect of one independent variable differs depending on the level of a second independent variable.

**internal validity** Degree to which differences in performance can be attributed unambiguously to an effect of an independent variable, as opposed to an effect of some other (uncontrolled) variable; an internally valid study is free of confounds.

**interobserver reliability** Degree to which two independent observers are in agreement.

**interrupted time-series design** See **simple interrupted time-series design** and **time series with nonequivalent control group design.**

**interviewer bias** Occurs when the interviewer tries to adjust the wording of a question to fit the respondent or records only selected portions of the respondent's answers.

**longitudinal design** Research design in which the same sample of respondents is interviewed (tested) more than once.

**main effect** Overall effect of an independent variable in a complex design.

**margin of error** In survey research, an estimate of the difference between a result obtained from a sample (e.g., the sample mean) and the corresponding true population value (e.g., population mean).

**matched groups design** Type of independent groups design in which the researcher forms comparable groups by matching subjects on a pretest task and then randomly assigning the members of these matched sets of subjects to the conditions of the experiment.

**measurement scale** One of four levels of physical and psychological measurement: nominal (categorizing), ordinal (ranking), interval (specifying distance between stimuli), and ratio (having an absolute zero point).

**mechanical subject loss** Occurs when a subject fails to complete the experiment because of equipment failure or because of experimenter error.

**meta-analysis** Analysis of results of several (often, very many) independent experiments investigating the same research area; the measure used in a meta-analysis is typically effect size.

**minimal risk**   A research participant is said to experience minimal risk when probability and magnitude of harm or discomfort anticipated in the research are not greater than that ordinarily encountered in daily life or during the performance of routine tests.

**multimethod approach**   Approach to hypothesis testing that seeks evidence by collecting data using several different measures of behavior; a recognition of the fact that any single measure of behavior can result from some artifact of the measuring process.

**multiple-baseline design (across subjects, across behaviors, across situations)**   A single-case experimental design in which the effect of a treatment is demonstrated by showing that behaviors in more than one baseline change as a consequence of the introduction of a treatment; multiple baselines are established for different individuals, for different behaviors in the same individual, or for the same individual in different situations.

$N = 1$ **designs**   See **single-case experiment.**

**narrative record**   Record intended to provide a more or less faithful reproduction of behavior as it originally occurred.

**natural groups design**   Type of independent groups design in which the conditions represent the selected levels of a naturally occurring independent variable, for example, the individual differences variable age.

**naturalistic observation**   Observation of behavior in a more or less natural setting without any attempt by the observer to intervene.

**nomothetic approach**   Approach to research that seeks to establish broad generalizations or laws that apply to large groups (populations) of individuals; the average or typical performance of a group is emphasized.

**nonequivalent control group design**   Quasi-experimental procedure in which a comparison is made between control and treatment groups that have been established on some basis other than through random assignment of participants to groups.

**nonprobability sampling**   A sampling procedure in which there is no way to estimate the probability of each element's being included in the sample; two common types are accidental sampling and purposive sampling.

**null hypothesis**   Assumption used as the first step in statistical inference whereby the independent variable is said to have had no effect.

**observer bias**   Systematic errors in observation often resulting from the observer's expectancies regarding the outcome of a study (i.e., expectancy effects).

**operational definition**   Procedure whereby a concept is defined solely in terms of the operations used to produce and measure it.

**participant observation**   Observation of behavior by someone who also has an active and significant role in the situation or context in which behavior is recorded.

**physical traces**   Source of evidence that is based on the remnants, fragments, and products of past behavior; used as an alternative to or in conjunction with other research methods.

**placebo control**   Procedure by which a substance that resembles a drug or other active substance but that is actually an inert, or inactive, substance is given to participants.

**plagiarism**   Presentation of another's ideas or work without clearly identifying the source.

**population**   Set of all the cases of interest.

**power**   Probability in a statistical test that a false null hypothesis will be rejected; power is related to the level of significance selected, the size of the treatment effect, and the sample size.

**practice effects**   Changes that participants undergo with repeated testing. Practice effects are the summation of both positive (e.g., familiarity with a task) and negative (e.g., boredom) factors associated with repeated measurement.

**privacy**   Right of individuals to decide how information about them is to be communicated to others.

**probability sampling**   Sampling procedure in which the probability that each element of the population will be included in the sample can be specified.

**program evaluation**   Research that seeks to determine whether a change proposed by an institution, government agency, or other unit of society is needed and likely to have an effect as planned or, when implemented, to actually have an effect.

**purposive sampling**   A type of nonprobability sampling in which the investigator selects the elements to be included in the sample on the basis of their special characteristics (e.g., recovering alcoholics).

**quasi-experiments**   Procedures that resemble those characteristics of true experiments, for example, that some type of intervention or treatment is used and a comparison is provided, but are lacking in the degree of control that is found in true experiments.

**random assignment**   Most common technique for forming groups as part of an independent groups design; the goal is to establish equivalent groups by balancing individual differences.

**random groups design**   Most common type of independent groups design in which subjects are randomly selected or randomly assigned to each group such that groups are considered comparable at the start of the experiment.

**random sampling**   See **simple random sampling.**

**reactivity**   Influence that an observer has on the behavior under observation; behavior influenced by an observer may not be representative of behavior when an observer is not present.

**regression (to the mean)**   Because some component of a test score is due to error (as opposed to true score), extreme scores on one test are likely to be closer to the mean on a second test, thus posing a threat to the validity of an experiment in which extreme groups are selected; the amount of this statistical regression is greater for less reliable tests.

**relevant independent variable**   Independent variable that has been shown to influence behavior, either directly, by producing a main effect, or indirectly, by resulting in an interaction in combination with a second independent variable.

**reliability**   A measurement is reliable when it is consistent.

**repeated measures designs**   Research designs in which each subject participates in all conditions of the experiment (i.e., measurement is repeated on the same subject).

**replication**   Repeating the exact procedures used in an experiment to determine whether the same results are obtained.

**representativeness**   A sample is representative to the extent that it has the same distribution of characteristics as the population from which it was selected; our ability to generalize from sample to population is critically dependent on representativeness.

**response bias**   Threat to the representativeness of a sample that occurs when some participants selected to respond to a survey systematically fail to complete the survey (e.g., due to failure to complete a lengthy questionnaire or to reply with a request to participate in a phone survey).

**risk/benefit ratio**   Subjective evaluation of the risk to a research participant relative to the benefit both to the individual and to society of the results of the proposed research.

**sample**   Something less than all the cases of interest; in survey research, a subset of the population actually drawn from the sampling frame.

**sampling frame**   Specific listing of all the members of the population of interest; an operational definition of the population.

**scientific method**   Approach to knowledge that emphasizes empirical rather than intuitive processes, testable hypotheses, systematic and controlled observation of operationally defined phenomena, data collection using accurate and precise instrumentation, valid and reliable measures, and objective reporting of results; scientists tend to be critical and, most importantly, skeptical.

**selection bias**   Threat to the representativeness of a sample that occurs when the procedures used to select a sample result in the over- or underrepresentation of a significant segment of the population.

**selective deposit**   Bias that results from the way physical traces are laid down and the way archival sources are produced, edited, or altered, as they are established; when present, the bias severely limits generality of research findings.

**selective subject loss**   Occurs when subjects are lost differentially across the conditions of the experiment as the result of some characteristic of each subject that is related to the outcome of the study.

**selective survival**   Bias that results from the way physical traces and archives survive over time; when present, the bias severely limits the external validity of research findings.

**sensitivity**   Refers to the likelihood in an experiment that the effect of an independent variable will be detected when that variable does, indeed, have an effect; sensitivity is increased to the extent that error variation is reduced (e.g., by holding variables constant rather than balancing them).

**simple interrupted time-series design**   Quasi-experimental procedure in which changes in a dependent variable are observed for some period of time both before and after a treatment is introduced.

**simple main effect**   Effect of one independent variable at one level of a second independent variable in a complex design.

**simple random sampling (random selection)**   Type of probability sampling in which each possible sample of a specified size in the population has an equal chance of being selected.

**single-case experiment**   A procedure that focuses on behavior change in one individual ($N = 1$) by systematically contrasting conditions within that individual while continuously monitoring behavior.

**situation sampling**  Random or systematic selection of situations in which observations are to be made with the goal of representativeness across circumstances, locations, and conditions.

**social desirability**  Pressures on survey respondents to answer as they think they should respond in accordance with what is most socially acceptable, and not in accordance with what they actually believe.

**spurious relationship**  What exists when evidence falsely indicates that two or more variables are associated.

**statistically significant**  When the probability of an obtained difference in an experiment is smaller than would be expected if error variation alone were assumed to be responsible for the difference, the difference is statistically significant.

**stratified random sampling**  Type of probability sampling in which the population is divided into subpopulations called strata and random samples are drawn from each of these strata.

**structured observation**  Variety of observational methods using intervention in which the degree of control is often less than in field experiments; frequently used by clinical and developmental psychologists when making behavioral assessments.

**successive independent samples design**  Survey research design in which a series of cross-sectional surveys is done and the same questions are asked of each succeeding sample of respondents.

**theory**  Logically organized set of propositions that serves to define events, describe relationships among events, and explain the occurrence of these events; scientific theories guide research and organize empirical knowledge.

**threats to internal validity**  Possible causes of a phenomenon that must be controlled so a clear cause-effect inference can be made.

**time sampling**  Selection of observation intervals either systematically or randomly with the goal of obtaining a representative sample of behavior.

**time series with nonequivalent control group design**  (See also **simple interrupted time-series design**.) Quasi-experimental procedure that improves on the validity of a simple time-series design by including a nonequivalent control group; both treatment and comparison groups are observed for a period of time both before and after the treatment.

**unobtrusive (nonreactive) measures**  Measures of behavior that eliminate the problem of reactivity, because observations are made in such a way that the presence of the observer is not detected by those being observed.

**validity**  The "truthfulness" of a measure; a valid measure is one that measures what it claims to measure.

# References

Abelson, R. P. (1985). A variance paradox: When a little is a lot. *Psychological Bulletin, 97*, 129–133.

Abelson, R. P. (1995). *Statistics as principled argument*. Hillsdale, NJ: Erlbaum.

Abelson, R. P. (1997). On the surprising longevity of flogged horses: Why there is a case for the significance test. *Psychological Science, 8*, 12–15.

Adair, J. G., Dushenko, T. W., & Lindsay, R. C. L. (1985). Ethical regulations and their impact on research practice. *American Psychologist, 40*, 59–72.

Addison, W. E. (1986). Agonistic behavior in preschool children: A comparison of same-sex versus opposite-sex interactions. *Bulletin of the Psychonomic Society, 24*, 44–46.

Adjang, O. M. J. (1986). Exploring the social environment: A developmental study of teasing in chimpanzees. *Ethology, 73*, 136–160.

Adler, A. (1973). *Practice and theory of individual psychology*, (P. Radin., Trans.) Totowa, NJ: Littlefield, Adams.

Adler, T. (1991, December). Outright fraud rare, but not poor science. *APA Monitor*, 11.

Albright, J. S., & Henderson, M. C. (1995). How real is depressive realism? A question of scales and standards. *Cognitive Therapy and Research, 19*, 589–609.

Allison, M. G., & Ayllon, T. (1980). Behavioral coaching in the development of skills in football, gymnastics, and tennis. *Journal of Applied Behavior Analysis, 13*, 297–314.

Allport, G. W. (1946). Letters from Jenny. *Journal of Abnormal and Social Psychology, 41*, (3, 4).

Allport, G. W. (1961). *Pattern in growth and personality*. New York: Holt, Rinehart and Winston.

Allport, G. W. (1965). *Letters from Jenny*. New York: Harcourt, Brace & World.

Altmann, J. (1974). Observational study of behavior: Sampling methods. *Behavior, 48*, 1–41.

Ambady, N., & Rosenthal, R. (1993). Half a minute: Predicting teacher evaluations from thin slices of nonverbal behavior and physical attractiveness. *Journal of Personality and Social Psychology, 64*, 431–441.

American Psychiatric Association. (1994). *Diagnostic and statistical manual of mental disorders* (4th ed.). Washington, DC: Author.

American Psychological Association. (1991). Five-year report of the policy and planning board, 1990; Five years of turbulence, change, and growth within APA. *American Psychologist, 46*, 678–688.

American Psychological Association. (1992). Ethical principles of psychologists and code of conduct. *American Psychologist, 47*, 1597–1611.

American Psychological Association. (1994). *Publication manual* (4th ed). Washington, DC: Author.

American Psychological Association. (1998). Summary report of journal operations, 1997. *American Psychologist, 53*, 983–984.

Anderson, C. A. (1989). Temperature and aggression: Ubiquitous effects of heat on occurrence of human violence. *Psychological Bulletin, 106*, 74–96.

Anderson, C. A., & Bushman, B. J. (1997). External validity of "trivial" experiments: The case of laboratory aggression. *Review of General Psychology, 1*, 19–41.

Anderson, C. A., Bushman, B. J., & Groom, R. W. (1997). Hot years and serious and deadly assault: Empirical tests of the heat hypothesis. *Journal of Personality and Social Psychology, 73*, 1213–1223.

Anderson, C. R. (1976). Coping behaviors as intervening mechanisms in the inverted-U stress-performance relationship. *Journal of Applied Psychology, 61*, 30–34.

Anderson, J. R. (1990). *The adaptive character of thought*. Hillsdale, NJ: Erlbaum.

Anderson, J. R. (1993). *Rules of the mind*. Hillsdale, NJ: Erlbaum.

Anderson, J. R., & Milson, J. R. (1989). Human memory: An adaptive perspective. *Psychological Review, 96*, 703–719.

Anderson, K. J., & Revelle, W. (1982). Impulsivity, caffeine, and proofreading: A test of the Easterbrook hypothesis. *Journal of Experimental Psychology: Human Perception and Performance, 8*, 614–624.

Anglin, J. M. (1993). Vocabulary development: A morphological analysis. *Monographs of the Society for Research in Child Development, 58* (10, Serial No. 238).

Asch, S. E. (1951). Effects of group pressure upon the modification and distortion of judgements.

In H. Guetzkow (Ed.), *Groups, leadership, and men* (pp. 177–190). Pittsburgh: Carnegie.

Asch, S. E. (1955). Opinions and social pressure. *Scientific American, 193*, 31–35.

Astin, A. W., Parrott, S. A., Korn, W. S., & Sax, L. J. (1997). *The American freshman: Thirty year trends*. Los Angeles: Higher Education Research Institute, UCLA.

Atkinson, R. C. (1968). Computerized instruction and the learning process. *American Psychologist, 23*, 225–239.

Atkinson, R. C., & Shiffrin, R. M. (1968). Human memory: A proposed system and its control processes. In K. W. Spence & J. T. Spence (Eds.), *The psychology of learning and motivation*, Vol. 2 (pp. 89–195). New York: Academic Press.

Azar, B. (1994a, December). Animal research threatened by activism. *APA Monitor*, 18.

Azar, B. (1994b, August). Computers create global research lab. *APA Monitor*, 1, 16.

Azar, B. (1994c, August). Research made easier by computer networks. *APA Monitor*, 16.

Azar, B. (1995, May). Board approves ways to spend science funds. *APA Monitor*, 25.

Azar, B. (1997, March). APA task force urges a harder look at data. *APA Monitor*, 26.

Bailey, J. M., Kim, P. Y., Hills, A., & Linsenmeier, J. A. W. (1997). Butch, femme, or straight acting? Partner preferences of gay men and lesbians. *Journal of Personality and Social Psychology, 73*, 960–973.

Banaji, M. R., & Crowder, R. G. (1989). The bankruptcy of everyday memory. *American Psychologist, 44*, 1185–1193.

Barash, D. P. (1977). Human ethology: Exchanging cheetahs for Chevrolets? *Environment and Behavior, 9*, 487–490.

Barker, R. G., Wright, H. F., Schoggen, M. F., & Barker, L. S. (1978). Day in the life of Mary Ennis. In R. G. Barker et al. (Eds.), *Habitats, environments, and human behavior* (pp. 51–98). San Francisco: Jossey-Bass.

Baron, J. N., & Reiss, P. C. (1985). Same time, next year: Aggregate analyses of the mass media and violent behavior. *American Sociological Review, 50*, 347–363.

Baron, R. M., & Kenny, D. A. (1986). The moderator-mediator variable distinction in social psychological research: Conceptual, strategic, and statistical considerations. *Journal of Personality and Social Psychology, 51*, 1173–1182.

Bartholomew, G. A. (1982). Scientific innovation and creativity: A zoologist's point of view. *American Zoologist, 22*, 227–335.

Bartlett, F. C. (1932). *Remembering: A study in experimental and social psychology*. Cambridge: Cambridge University Press.

Baumeister, R. F. (1995). Disputing the effects of championship pressures and home audiences. *Journal of Personality and Social Psychology, 68*, 644–648.

Baumeister, R. F., & Steinhilber, A. (1984). Paradoxical effects of supportive audiences on performance under pressure: The home field disadvantage in sports championships. *Journal of Personality and Social Psychology, 47*, 85–93.

Baumrind, D. (1985). Research using intentional deception: Ethical issues revisited. *American Psychologist, 40*, 165–174.

Berk, R. A., Boruch, R. F., Chambers, D. L., Rossi, P. H., & Witte, A. D. (1987). Social policy experimentation: A position paper. In D. S. Cordray & M. W. Lipsey (Eds.), *Evaluation Studies Review Annual*, Vol. 11 (pp. 630–672). Newbury Park, CA: Sage.

Bickman, L. (1976). Observational methods. In C. Selltiz, L. S. Wrightsman, & S. W. Cook (Eds.), *Research methods in social relations* (pp. 251–290). New York: Holt, Rinehart and Winston.

Blanchard, F. A., Crandall, C. S., Brigham, J. C., & Vaughn, L. A. (1994). Condemning and condoning racism: A social context approach to interracial settings. *Journal of Applied Psychology, 79*, 993–997.

Blanck, P. D., Bellack, A. S., Rosnow, R. L., Rotheram-Borus, M. J., & Schooler, N. R. (1992). Scientific rewards and conflicts of ethical choices in human subjects research. *American Psychologist, 47*, 959–965.

Bolgar, H. (1965). The case study method. In B. B. Wolman (Ed.), *Handbook of clinical psychology* (pp. 28–39). New York: McGraw-Hill.

Bond, C. F., Jr., & Titus, L. J. (1983). Social facilitation: A meta-analysis of 241 studies. *Psychological Bulletin, 94*, 265–292.

Booth, W. (1988). Chimps and research: Endangered? *Science, 241*, 777–778.

Boring, E. G. (1950). *A history of experimental psychology*. New York: Appleton-Century-Crofts.

Boring, E. G. (1954). The nature and history of experimental control. *American Journal of Psychology, 67*, 573–589.

Bourke, K. (1998, September). Now available on-line: Interactive experiments. *APS Observer*, 14–15.

Brainerd, C. J. (1978). *Piaget's theory of intelligence*. Englewood Cliffs, NJ: Prentice-Hall.

Brandt, R. M. (1972). *Studying behavior in natural settings*. New York: Holt, Rinehart and Winston: University Press of America, 1981.

Bridgewater, C. A., Bornstein, P. H., & Walkenbach, J. (1981). Ethical issues and the assignment of publication credit. *American Psychologist, 36,* 524–525.

Brigham, T. A., Meier, S. M., & Goodner, V. (1995). Increasing designated driving with a program of prompts and incentives. *Journal of Applied Behavior Analysis, 28,* 83–84.

Broach, D. (1992, June). Non-cognitive predictions of performance in radar-based air traffic control training. Paper presented at the Fourth Annual Convention of the American Psychological Society, San Diego, CA.

Bröder, A. (1998). Deception can be acceptable. *American Psychologist, 53,* 805–806.

Brown, R., & Kulik, J. (1977). Flashbulb memories. *Cognition, 5,* 73–99.

Browne, M. A., & Mahoney, M. J. (1984). Sport psychology. *Annual Review of Psychology, 35,* 605–625.

Burns, M. S., Haywood, H. C., & Delclos, V. R. (1987). Young children's problem-solving strategies: An observational study. *Journal of Applied Developmental Psychology, 8,* 113–121.

Campbell, A. (1981). *The sense of well-being in America.* New York: McGraw-Hill.

Campbell, A., Converse, P. E., & Rodgers, W. L. (1975). *The quality of American life; July–August, 1971.* Ann Arbor: ISR Social Science Archive.

Campbell, D. T. (1969). Reforms as experiments. *American Psychologist, 24,* 409–429.

Campbell, D. T., & Stanley, J. C. (1966). *Experimental and quasi-experimental designs for research.* Chicago: Rand McNally.

Campbell, R. (Ed.). (1992). *Mental lives: Case studies in cognition.* Oxford: Blackwell.

Candland, D. K. (1993). *Feral children and clever animals.* New York: Oxford University Press.

Carroll, J. M., & Russell, J. A. (1997). Facial expressions in Hollywood's portrayal of emotion. *Journal of Personality and Social Psychology, 72,* 164–176.

Caspi, A., Begg, D., Dickson, N., Harrington, H., Langley, J., Moffitt, T. E., & Silva, P. A. (1997). Personality differences predict health-risk behaviors in young adulthood: Evidence from a longitudinal study. *Journal of Personality and Social Psychology, 73,* 1052–1063.

Ceci, S. J. (1993). Cognitive and social factors in children's testimony. Master Lecture presented at the American Psychological Association Convention.

Chambers, J. H., & Ascione, F. R. (1987). The effects of prosocial and aggressive videogames on children's donating and helping. *Journal of Genetic Psychology, 148,* 499–505.

Cherlin, A. J., Furstenberg, F. F., Jr., Chase-Lansdale, P. L., Kiernan, K. E., Robins, P. K., Morrison, D. R., & Teitler, J. O. (1991). Longitudinal studies of effects of divorce on children in Great Britain and the United States. *Science, 252,* 1386–1389.

Chow, S. L. (1988). Significance test or effect size? *Psychological Bulletin, 103,* 105–110.

Christensen, L. (1988). Deception in psychological research: When is its use justified? *Personality and Social Psychology Bulletin, 14,* 664–675.

Cicchetti, D. (1998). Child abuse and neglect—usefulness of the animal data: Comment on Maestipieri and Carroll (1998). *Psychological Bulletin, 123,* 224–230.

Clark, H. H., & Schober, M. F. (1992). Asking questions and influencing answers. In J. M. Tanur (Ed.), *Questions about questions: Inquiries into the cognitive bases of surveys.* New York: Russell Sage Foundation.

Cohen, D. (1979). *J. B. Watson: The founder of behaviorism.* London: Routledge & Kegan Paul.

Cohen, J. (1988). *Statistical power analysis for the behavioral sciences* (2nd ed.). Hillsdale, NJ: Erlbaum.

Cohen, J. (1990). Things I have learned (so far). *American Psychologist, 45,* 1304–1312.

Cohen, J. (1992). A power primer. *Psychological Bulletin, 112,* 155–159.

Cohen, J. (1995). The earth is round ($p < .05$). *American Psychologist, 49,* 997–1003.

Cohen, N. J., McCloskey, M., & Wible, C. G. (1990). Flashbulb memories and underlying cognitive mechanisms: Reply to Pillemer. *Journal of Experimental Psychology: General, 119,* 97–100.

Connors, G. J., Collins, R. L., Dermen, K. H., & Koutsky, J. R. (1998). Substance use restraint: An extension of the construct to a clinical population. *Cognitive Therapy and Research, 22,* 75–87.

Converse, P. E., & Traugott, M. W. (1986, November 28). Assessing the accuracy of polls and surveys. *Science, 234,* 1094–1097.

Cook, T. D., & Campbell, D. T. (1979). *Quasi-experimentation: Design and analysis issues for field settings.* Chicago: Rand McNally.

Cordaro, L., & Ison, J. R. (1963). Psychology of the scientist: X. Observer bias in classical conditioning of the planarian. *Psychological Reports, 13,* 787–789.

Coren, S., & Porac, C. (1977). Fifty centuries of right-handedness: The historical record. *Science, 198,* 631–632.

Courneya, K. S., & Carron, A. V. (1992). The home advantage in sport competitions: A literature review. *Journal of Sport & Exercise Psychology, 14,* 13–27.

Cronbach, L. J. (1992). Four *Psychological Bulletin* articles in perspective. *Psychological Bulletin, 12,* 389–392.

Crossen, C. (1994). *Tainted truth: The manipulation of fact in America.* New York: Simon & Schuster.

Crusco, A. H., & Wetzel, C. G. (1984). The Midas touch: The effects of interpersonal touch on restaurant tipping. *Personality and Social Psychology Bulletin, 10,* 512–517.

Csikszentmihalyi, M., & Larson, R. W. (1987). Validity and reliability of the experience-sampling method. *Journal of Nervous and Mental Disorders, 175,* 526–533.

Curtiss, S. R. (1977). *Genie: A psycholinguistic study of a modern-day "wild child."* New York: Academic Press.

Dawes, R. M. (1991, June). *Problems with a psychology of college sophomores.* Paper presented at the Third Annual Convention of the American Psychological Society, Washington, DC.

Dawes, R. M., Faust, D., & Meehl, P. E. (1993). Statistical prediction versus clinical prediction: Improving what works. In G. Keren & C. Lewis (Eds.), *A handbook for data analysis in the behavioral sciences: Methodological issues* (pp. 351–367). Hillsdale, NJ: Erlbaum.

de Blois, S. T., Novak, M. A., & Bond, M. (1998). Object permanence in orangutans (*Pongo pygmaeus*) and squirrel monkeys (*Saimiri sciureus*). *Journal of Comparative Psychology, 112,* 137–152.

Delespaul, P. A. E. G. (1995). *Assessing schizophrenia in daily life: The experience sampling method.* Rijkjaniversiteit van Limburg (Maastricht, The Netherlands).

DeLoache, J. S., Pierroutsakos, S. L., Uttal, D. H., Rosengren, K. S., & Gottlieb, A. (1998). Grasping the nature of pictures. *Psychological Science, 9,* 205–210.

Dickie, J. R. (1987). Interrelationships within the mother-father-infant triad. In P. W. Berman & F. A. Pedersen (Eds.), *Men's transitions to parenthood: Longitudinal studies of early family experience* (pp. 113–143). Hillsdale, NJ: Erlbaum.

Diener, E., & Crandall, R. (1978). *Ethics in social and behavioral research.* Chicago: The University of Chicago Press.

Dittmar, M. L., Berch, D. B., & Warm, J. S. (1982). Sustained visual attention in deaf and hearing adults. *Bulletin of the Psychonomic Society, 19,* 339–342.

Divorce of the year. *Newsweek,* March 12, 1973, pp. 48–49.

Dolan, C. A., Sherwood, A., & Light, K. C. (1992). Cognitive coping strategies and blood pressure responses to real-life stress in healthy young men. *Health Psychology, 11,* 233–240.

Eagly, A. H., & Steffen, V. J. (1984). Gender stereotypes stem from the distribution of women and men into social roles. *Journal of Personality and Social Psychology, 46,* 735–754.

Eibl-Eibesfeldt, I. (1975). *Ethology: The biology of behavior.* New York: Holt, Rinehart and Winston.

Emerson, J. D. (1991). Introduction to transformation. In D. C. Hoaglin, F. Mosteller, & J. W. Tukey (Eds.), *Fundamentals of exploratory analysis of variance* (pp. 365–400). New York: Wiley.

Endersby, J. W., & Towle, M. J. (1996). Tailgate partisanship: Political and social expression through bumper stickers. *The Social Science Journal, 33,* 307–319.

Entwisle, D. R., & Astone, N. M. (1994). Some practical guidelines for measuring youth's race/ethnicity and socioeconomic status. *Child Development, 65,* 1521–1540.

Epley, N., & Huff, C. (1998). Suspicion, affective response, and educational benefit as a result of deception in psychology research. *Personality and Social Psychology Bulletin, 24,* 759–768.

Epstein, S. (1979). The stability of behavior: On predicting most of the people much of the time. *Journal of Personality and Social Psychology, 37,* 1097–1126.

Erber, R. (1991). Affective and semantic priming: Effects of mood on category accessibility and inference. *Journal of Experimental Social Psychology, 27,* 480–498.

Ericsson, K. A., & Charness, N. (1994). Expert performance: Its structure and acquisition. *American Psychologist, 49,* 725–747.

Ericsson, K. A., Chase, W. G., & Faloon, S. (1980). Acquisition of a memory skill. *Science, 208,* 1181–1182.

Estes, W. K. (1997). On the communication of information by displays of standard errors and confidence intervals. *Psychonomic Bulletin & Review, 4,* 330–341.

Evans, R., & Donnerstein, E. (1974). Some implications for psychological research of early versus late term participation by college students. *Journal of Research in Personality, 8,* 102–109.

Feeney, D. M. (1987). Human rights and animal welfare. *American Psychologist, 42,* 593–599.

Festinger, L., Riecken, H., & Schachter, S. (1956). *When prophecy fails.* Minneapolis: University of Minnesota Press.

Fine, M. A., & Kurdek, L. A. (1993). Reflections on determining authorship credit and authorship order on faculty-student collaborations. *American Psychologist, 48,* 1141–1147.

Fiore, S. (1994, May/June). The student notebook. *APS Observer*, p. 28.

Fischer, K., Schoeneman, T. J., & Rubanowitz, D. E. (1987). Attributions in the advice columns: II. The dimensionality of actors' and observers' explanations for interpersonal problems. *Personality and Social Psychology Bulletin, 13*, 458–466.

Fisher, C. B., & Fryberg, D. (1994). Participant partners: College students weigh the costs and benefits of deceptive research. *American Psychologist, 49*, 417–427.

Fossey, D. (1981). Imperiled giants of the forest. *National Geographic, 159*, 501–523.

Fossey, D. (1983). *Gorillas in the mist*. Boston: Houghton-Mifflin.

Fowler, R. D. (1992). Report of the chief executive officer: A year of building for the future. *American Psychologist, 47*, 876–883.

Frame, C. L., & Strauss, C. C. (1987). Parental informed consent and sample bias in grade-school children. *Journal of Social and Clinical Psychology, 5*, 227–236.

Frank, M. G., & Gilovich, T. (1988). The dark side of self- and social perception: Black uniforms and aggression in professional sports. *Journal of Personality and Social Psychology, 54*, 74–85.

Frick, R. W. (1995). Accepting the null hypothesis. *Memory & Cognition, 23*, 132–138.

Friedman, H. S., Tucker, J. S., Schwartz, J. E., Tomlinson-Keasy, C., Martin, L. R., Wingard, D. L., & Criqui, M. H. (1995). Psychosocial and behavioral predictors of longevity: The aging and death of the "Termites." *American Psychologist, 50*, 69–78.

Friedman, M. P., & Wilson, R. W. (1975). Application of unobtrusive measures to the study of textbook usage by college students. *Journal of Applied Psychology, 60*, 659–662.

Fromm, E. (1998). Lost and found half a century later: Letters by Freud and Einstein. *American Psychologist, 53*, 1195–1198.

Gabrieli, J. D. E., Fleischman, D. A., Keane, M. M., Reminger, S. L., & Morrell, F. (1995). Double dissociation between memory systems underlying explicit and implicit memory in the human brain. *Psychological Science, 6*, 76–82.

Gannon, L., Luchetta, T., Rhodes, K., Pardie, L., & Segrist, D. (1992). Sex bias in psychological research. *American Psychologist, 47*, 389–396.

Geller, E. S., Russ, N. W., & Altomari, M. G. (1986). Naturalistic observations of beer drinking among college students. *Journal of Applied Behavior Analysis, 19*, 391–396.

Gena, A, Krantz, P. J., McClannahan, L. E., & Poulson, C. L. (1996). Training and generalization of affective behavior displayed by youth with autism. *Journal of Applied Behavioral Analysis, 29*, 291–304.

Gillham, J. E., Reivich, K. J., Jaycox, L. H., & Seligman, M. E. P. (1995). Prevention of depressive symptoms in school children: Two-year follow-up. *Psychological Science, 6*, 343–351.

Goldstein, R. S., Minkin, B. L., Minkin, N., & Baer, D. M. (1978). Finders, keepers?: An analysis and validation of a free-found-ad policy. *Journal of Applied Behavior Analysis, 11*, 465–473.

Goodall, J. (1987). A plea for the chimpanzees. *American Scientist, 75*, 574–577.

Goodman, S. H., Lahey, B. B., Fielding, B., Dulcan, M., Narrow, W., & Regier, D. (1997). Representativeness of clinical samples of youths with mental disorders: A preliminary population-based study. *Journal of Abnormal Psychology, 106*, 3–14.

Graham, S. (1992). "Most of the subjects were White and middle class": Trends in published research on African Americans in selected APA journals, 1970–1989. *American Psychologist, 47*, 629–639.

Grammer, K., Schiefenhovel, W., Schleidt, M., Lorenz, B., & Eibl-Eibesfeldt, I. (1988). Patterns on the face: The eyebrow flash in crosscultural comparison. *Ethology, 77*, 279–299.

Gray, J. N., & Melton, G. B. (1985). The law and ethics of psychosocial research on AIDS. *Nebraska Law Review, 64*, 637–688.

Griffin, J. H. (1960). *Black like me*. New York: New American Library.

Grisso, T., Baldwin, E., Blanck, P. D., Rotheram-Borus, M. J., Schooler, N. R., & Thompson, T. (1991). Standards in research: APA's mechanisms for monitoring the challenges. *American Psychologist, 46*, 758–766.

Guerin, B. (1986). Mere presence effects in humans: A review. *Journal of Experimental Social Psychology, 22*, 38–77.

Haber, L. R., & Haber, R. N. (1982). Does silent reading involve articulation? Evidence from tongue twisters. *American Journal of Psychology, 95*, 409–419.

Haden, C. A. (1998). Reminiscing with different children: Relating maternal stylistic consistency and sibling similarity in talk about the past. *Developmental Psychology, 34*, 99–114.

Haden, C. A., Haine, R. A., & Fivush, R. (1997). Developing narrative structure in parent-child reminiscing across the preschool years. *Developmental Psychology, 33*, 295–307.

Hagen, R. L. (1997). In praise of the null hypothesis statistical test. *American Psychologist, 52,* 15–24.

Halpern, A. R., & Bower, G. H. (1982). Musical expertise and melodic structure in memory for musical notation. *American Journal of Psychology, 95,* 31–50.

Harlow, H. F., & Harlow, M. K. (1966). Learning to love. *American Scientist, 54,* 244–272.

Harnack, A., & Kleppinger, E. (1997). *Online! A reference guide to using Internet sources.* New York: St. Martin's Press.

Hart, B., & Risley, T. R. (1995). *Meaningful differences in the everyday experience of young American children.* Baltimore, MD: Paul H. Brookes.

Hartup, W. W. (1974). Aggression in childhood: Development perspectives. *American Psychologist, 29,* 336–341.

Hass, R. G., Katz, I., Rizzo, N., Bailey, J., & Eisenstadt, D. (1991). Cross-racial appraisal as related to attitude ambivalence and cognitive complexity. *Personality and Social Psychology Bulletin, 17,* 83–92.

Hays, R. (1980). Honesty requiring a self-initiated response. *Psychological Reports, 46,* 87–90.

Heath, L., & Davidson, L. (1988). Dealing with the threat of rape: Reactance or learned helplessness? *Journal of Applied Social Psychology, 18,* 1334–1351.

Heatherton, T. F., Mahamedi, F., Striepe, M., Field, A. E., & Keel, P. (1997). A 10–year longitudinal study of body weight, dieting, and eating disorder symptoms. *Journal of Abnormal Psychology, 106,* 117–125.

Heatherton, T. F., Nichols, P., Mahamedi, F., & Keel, P. K. (1995). Body weight, dieting, and eating disorder symptoms among college students 1982 to 1992. *American Journal of Psychiatry, 152,* 1623–1629.

Hedges, L. V. (1981). Distributional theory for Glass's estimator of effect size and related estimators. *Journal of Educational Statistics, 6,* 107–128.

Hersen, M., & Barlow, D. H. (1976). *Single-case experimental designs: Strategies for studying behavior change.* New York: Pergamon Press.

Hilts, P. J. (1995). *Memory's ghost: The nature of memory and the strange tale of Mr. M.* New York: Simon & Schuster.

Hippler, H. J., & Schwarz, N. (1987). Response effects in surveys. In H. J. Hippler, N. Schwarz, & S. Sudman (Eds.), *Social information processing and survey methodology* (pp. 102–122). New York: Springer-Verlag.

Hirschberg, N., & Itkin, S. (1978). Graduate student success in psychology. *American Psychologist, 33,* 1083–1093.

Hite, S. (1987). *Women and love: A cultural revolution in progress.* New York: Knopf.

Hoaglin, D. C., Mosteller, F., & Tukey, J. W. (Eds.). (1983). *Understanding robust and exploratory data analysis.* New York: Wiley.

Hoaglin, D. C., Mosteller, F., & Tukey, J. W. (Eds.). (1991). *Fundamentals of exploratory analysis of variance.* New York: Wiley.

Hofer, M. A., & Myers, M. M. (1996). Animal models in psychosomatic research. *Psychosomatic Medicine, 58,* 521–523.

Holden, C. (1987). Animal regulations: So far, so good. *Science, 238,* 880–882.

Holmbeck, G. N. (1997). Toward terminological, conceptual, and statistical clarity in the study of mediators and moderators: Examples from the child-clinical and pediatric psychology literatures. *Journal of Consulting and Clinical Psychology, 65,* 599–610.

Holsti, O. R. (1969). *Content analysis for the social sciences.* Reading, MA: Addison-Wesley.

Hops, J., Biglan, A., Sherman, L., Arthur, J., Friedman, L., & Osteen, V. (1987). Home observations of family interactions of depressed women. *Journal of Consulting and Clinical Psychology, 55,* 341–346.

Horn, W. F., & Heerboth, J. (1982). Single-case experimental designs and program evaluation. *Evaluational Review, 6,* 403–424.

Horton, S. V. (1987). Reduction of disruptive mealtime behavior by facial screening. *Behavior Modification, 11,* 53–64.

Howell, D. C. (1997). *Statistical methods for psychology* (4th ed.). Belmont, CA: Wadsworth.

Hughes, H. M., & Haynes, S. N. (1978). Structured laboratory observation in the behavioral assessment of parent-child interactions: A methodological critique. *Behavior Therapy, 9,* 428–447.

Hunt, M. (1997). *How science takes stock: The story of meta-analysis.* New York: Russell Sage Foundation.

Hunter, J. E. (1997). Needed: A ban on the significance test. *Psychological Science, 8,* 3–7.

Jackson, J. M., Buglione, S. A., & Glenwick, D. S. (1988). Major league baseball performance as a function of being traded: A drive theory analysis. *Personality and Social Psychology Bulletin, 14,* 46–56.

Jenni, D. A., & Jenni, M. A. (1976). Carrying behavior in humans: Analysis of sex differences. *Science, 194,* 859–860.

Jenni, M. A. (1976). Sex differences in carrying behavior. *Perceptual and Motor Skills, 43*, 323–330.

Johnson, D. (1990). Animal rights and human lives: Time for scientists to right the balance. *Psychological Science, 1*, 213–214.

Joswick, K. E. (1994). Getting the most from Psyc-LIT: Recommendations for searching. *Teaching of Psychology, 21*, 49–53.

Judd, C. M., Smith, E. R., & Kidder, L. H. (1991). *Research methods in social relations* (6th ed.). Fort Worth, TX: Holt, Rinehart and Winston.

Kagan, J., Reznick, J. S., & Snidman, N. (1988). Biological bases of childhood shyness. *Science, 240*, 167–171.

Kahneman, D., Fredrickson, B. L., Schreiber, C. A., & Redelmeier, D. A. (1993). When more pain is preferred to less: Adding a better end. *Psychological Science, 4*, 401–405.

Kahneman, D., & Tversky, A. (1973). On the psychology of prediction. *Psychological Review, 80*, 237–251.

Kardas, E. P., & Milford, T. M. (1996). *Using the Internet for social science research and practice*. Belmont, CA: Wadsworth.

Kazdin, A. E. (1978). Methodological and interpretive problems of single-case experimental designs. *Journal of Consulting and Clinical Psychology, 46*, 629–642.

Kazdin, A. E. (1980). *Behavior modification in applied settings* (rev. ed.). Homewood, IL: Dorsey Press.

Kazdin, A. E. (1982). Single-case experimental designs. In P. C. Kendall & J. N. Butcher (Eds.), *Handbook of research methods in clinical psychology* (pp. 416–490). New York: Wiley.

Kazdin, A. E. (1998). *Research designs in clinical psychology*. Boston: Allyn and Bacon.

Kazdin, A. E., & Erickson, L. M. (1975). Developing responsiveness to instructions in severely and profoundly retarded residents. *Journal of Behavior Therapy and Experimental Psychiatry, 6*, 17–21.

Keith, T. Z., Reimers, T. M., Fehrmann, P. G., Pottebaum, S. M., & Aubrey, L. W. (1986). Parental involvement, homework, and TV time: Direct and indirect effects on high school achievement. *Journal of Educational Psychology, 78*, 373–380.

Keith-Spiegel, P., & Koocher, G. P. (1985). *Ethics in psychology: Professional standards and cases*. New York: Random House.

Keller, F. S. (1937). *The definition of psychology*. New York: Appleton-Century-Crofts.

Kelley-Milburn, D., & Milburn, M. A. (1995). Cyberpsych: Resources for psychologists on the Internet. *Psychological Science, 6*, 203–211.

Kelman, H. C. (1967). Human use of human subjects: The problem of deception in social psychological experiments. *Psychological Bulletin, 67*, 1–11.

Kelman, H. C. (1972). The rights of the subject in social research: An analysis in terms of relative power and legitimacy. *American Psychologist, 27*, 989–1016.

Kenny, D. A. (1979). *Correlation and causality*. New York: Wiley.

Keppel, G. (1991). *Design and analysis: A researcher's handbook* (3rd ed.). Englewood Cliffs, NJ: Prentice-Hall.

Kiesler, S., Walsh, J., & Sproull, L. (1992). Computer networks in field research. In F. B. Bryant, J. Edwards, F. S. Tindale, E. J. Posavac, L. Heath, E. Henderson, & Y. Suarez-Balcazar (Eds.), *Methodological issues in applied social psychology: Vol. 2. Social psychological applications to social issues* (pp. 239–267). New York: Plenum.

Kimble, G. A. (1989). Psychology from the standpoint of a generalist. *American Psychologist, 44*, 491–499.

Kimmel, A. J. (1996). *Ethical issues in behavioral research: A survey*. Cambridge, MA: Blackwell.

Kimmel, A. J. (1998). In defense of deception. *American Psychologist, 53*, 803–805.

Kirk, R. E. (1996). Practical significance: A concept whose time has come. *Educational and Psychological Measurement, 56*, 746–759.

Kirkham, G. L. (1975). Doc cop. *Human Behavior, 4*, 16–23.

Kirsch, I. (1978). Teaching clients to be their own therapists: A case-study illustration. *Psychotherapy: Theory, Research and Practice, 15*, 302–305.

Kirsch, I., & Sapirstein, G. (1998). Listening to prozac but hearing placebo: A meta-analysis of antidepressant medication. *Prevention and Treatment* [On-line serial], *1*. Available: journals.apa.org/ prevention/volume1/ pre0010002a.html.

Klemmack, S. H., & Klemmack, D. L. (1976). The social definition of rape. In M. J. Walker & S. L. Brodsky (Eds.), *Sexual assault*. Lexington, MA: Lexington Books.

Krantz, J. H., Ballard, J., & Scher, J. (1997). Comparing the results of laboratory and World-Wide-Web samples on the determinants of female attractiveness. *Behavior Research Methods, Instruments, & Computers, 29*, 264–269.

Kratochwill, T. R., & Brody, G. H. (1978). Single subject designs: A perspective on the controversy over employing statistical inference and implications for research and training in behavior modification. *Behavior Modification, 2*, 291–307.

Kratochwill, T. R., & Levin, J. R. (Eds.). (1992). *Single-case research design and analysis.* Hillsdale, NJ: Erlbaum.

Kratochwill, T. R., & Martens, B. K. (1994). Applied behavior analysis and school psychology. *Journal of Applied Behavior Analysis, 27,* 3–5.

Kubany, E. S. (1997). Application of cognitive therapy for trauma-related guilt (CT-TRG) with a Vietnam veteran troubled by multiple sources of guilt. *Cognitive and Behavioral Practice, 4,* 213–244.

LaFrance, M., & Mayo, C. (1976). Racial differences in gaze behavior during conversations: Two systematic observational studies. *Journal of Personality and Social Psychology, 33,* 547–552.

Lakatos, I. (1978). *The methodology of scientific research.* London: Cambridge University Press.

Landers, S. (1987a, September). CARE urges protection for animals and labs. *APA Monitor,* 28–29.

Landers, S. (1987b, December). Lab checks: Rigid or reciprocal? *APA Monitor,* 6–7.

Landers, S. (1988, September). Adolescent study presents dilemma. *APA Monitor,* 6.

Langer, E. J. (1989). *Mindfulness.* Reading, MA: Addison-Wesley.

Langer, E. J. (1997). *The power of mindful learning.* Reading, MA: Addison-Wesley.

Langer, E. J., & Piper, A. I. (1987). The prevention of mindlessness. *Journal of Personality and Social Psychology, 53,* 280–287.

Langer, E. J., & Rodin, J. (1976). The effects of choice and enhanced personal responsibility for the aged: A field experiment in an institutional setting. *Journal of Personality and Social Psychology, 34,* 191–198.

Larose, S., & Roy, R. (1995). Test of reactions and adaptation in college (TRAC): A new measure of learning propensity for college students. *Journal of Educational Psychology, 87,* 293–306.

Larson, R. (1989). Beeping children and adolescents: A method for studying time use and daily experience. *Journal of Youth and Adolescence, 18,* 511–530.

Larson, R. W., Richards, M. H., Moneta, G., Holmbeck, G., & Duckett, E. (1996). Changes in adolescents' daily interactions with their families from ages 10 to 18: Disengagement and transformation. *Developmental Psychology, 32,* 744–754.

Latané, B., & Darley, J. M. (1970). *The unresponsive bystander: Why doesn't he help?* New York: Appleton-Century-Crofts.

Latané, B., Williams, K., & Harkin, S. (1979). Many hands make light the work: The causes and consequences of social loafing. *Journal of Personality and Social Psychology, 37,* 822–832.

Lau, R. R., & Russell, D. (1980). Attributions in the sports pages. *Journal of Personality and Social Psychology, 39,* 29–38.

Leavens, D. A., & Hopkins, W. D. (1998). Intentional communication by chimpanzees: A cross-sectional study of the use of referential gestures. *Developmental Psychology, 34,* 813–822.

Lenneberg, E. H. (1967). *Biological foundations of language.* New York: Wiley.

Levine, R. V. (1990). The pace of life. *American Scientist, 78,* 450–459.

Levine, R. V., West, L. J., & Reis, H. T. (1980). Perceptions of time and punctuality in the United States and Brazil. *Journal of Personality and Social Psychology, 38,* 541–550.

Linton, M. (1978). Real world memory after six years: An *in vivo* study of very long term memory. In M. M. Gruneberg, P. E. Morris, & R. N. Sykes (Eds.), *Practical aspects of memory* (pp. 69–76). New York: Academic Press.

Locke, T. P., Johnson, G. M., Kirigin-Ramp, K., Atwater, J. D., & Gerrard, M. (1986). An evaluation of a juvenile education program in a state penitentiary. *Evaluation Review, 10,* 281–298.

Loftus, E. F. (1979). *Eyewitness testimony.* Cambridge, MA: Harvard University Press.

Loftus, E. F. (1997a). Creating childhood memories. *Applied Cognitive Psychology, 11* (Special Issue), 575–586.

Loftus, E. F. (1997b). Memory for a past that never was. *Current Directions in Psychological Science, 6,* 60–65.

Loftus, E. F., & Burns, T. E. (1982). Mental shock can produce retrograde amnesia. *Memory & Cognition, 10,* 318–323.

Loftus, G. R. (1991). On the tyranny of hypothesis testing in the social sciences. *Contemporary Psychology, 36,* 102–105.

Loftus, G. R. (1993). A picture is worth a thousand $p$ values: On the irrelevance of hypothesis testing in the microcomputer age. *Behavior Research Methods, Instruments, & Computers, 25,* 250–256.

Loftus, G. R. (1996). Psychology will be a much better science when we change the way we analyze data. *Current Directions in Psychological Science, 5,* 161–171.

Loftus, G. R., & Masson, M. E. J. (1994). Using confidence intervals in within-subject designs. *Psychonomic Bulletin & Review, 1,* 476–490.

Lorge, I., & Chall, J. (1963). Estimating the size of vocabularies of children and adults: An analysis of methodological issues. *Journal of Experimental Education, 32,* 147–157.

Lovaas, O. I. (1993). The development of a treatment-research project for developmentally disabled and autistic children. *Journal of Applied Behavior Analysis, 26*, 617–630.

Lovaas, O. I., Newsom, C., & Hickman, C. (1987). Self-stimulatory behavior and perceptual reinforcement. *Journal of Applied Behavior Analysis, 20*, 45–68.

Lovaas, O. I., Schaeffer, B., & Simmons, J. Q. (1965). Building social behaviors in autistic children by use of electric shock. *Journal of Research in Personality, 1*, 99–109.

Lubin, B., Zuckerman, M., Breytspraak, L. M., Bull, N. C., Gumbhir, A. K., & Rinck, C. M. (1988). Affects, demographic variables, and health. *Journal of Clinical Psychology, 44*, 131–141.

Lucas, R. E., Diener, E., & Suh, E. (1996). Discriminant validity of well-being measures. *Journal of Personality and Social Psychology, 71*, 616–628.

Ludwig, T. E., Jeeves, M. A., Norman, W. D., & DeWitt, R. (1993). The bilateral field advantage on a letter-matching task. *Cortex, 29*, 691–713.

Lyons, C. A., & Ghezzi, P. M. (1995). Wagering on a large scale: Relationships between public gambling and game manipulations in two state lotteries. *Journal of Applied Behavior Analysis, 28*, 127–137.

Madigan, C. M. (1995, March 19). Hearing it right: Small turnout spoke. *Chicago Tribune*, pp. 1–2.

Maestripieri, D., & Carroll, K. A. (1998). Child abuse and neglect: Usefulness of the animal data. *Psychological Bulletin, 123*, 211–223.

Marx, M. H. (1963). The general nature of theory construction. In M. H. Marx (Ed.), *Theories in contemporary psychology* (pp. 4–46). New York: Macmillan.

Maser, J. D., & Seligman, M. E. P. (Eds.). (1977). *Psychopathology: Experimental models*. San Francisco: Freeman.

May, C. P., Hasher, L., Stoltzfus, E. R. (1993). Optimal time of day and magnitude of age differences in memory. *Psychological Science, 4*, 326–330.

McCain, L. J., & McCleary, R. (1979). The statistical analysis of the simple interrupted time-series quasi-experiment. In T. D. Cook & D. T. Campbell (Eds.), *Quasi-Experimentation: Design & analysis issues for field settings* (pp. 233–293). Chicago: Rand McNally.

McCloskey, M., Wible, C. G., & Cohen, N. J. (1988). Is there a special flashbulb-memory mechanism? *Journal of Experimental Psychology: General, 117*, 171–181.

McGrew, W. C. (1972). *An ethological study of children's behavior*. New York: Academic Press.

McGuire, W. J. (1997). Creative hypothesis generating in psychology: Some useful heuristics. *Annual Review of Psychology, 48*, 1–30.

McKinney, J. D., Mason, J., Perkerson, K., & Clifford, M. (1975). Relationship between classroom behavior and academic achievement. *Journal of Educational Psychology, 67*, 198–203.

McSweeney, A. J. (1978). Effects of response cost on the behavior of a million persons: Charging for directory assistance in Cincinnati. *Journal of Applied Behavior Analysis, 11*, 47–51.

Medvec, V. H., Madey, S. F., & Gilovich, T. (1995). When less is more: Counterfactual thinking and satisfaction among Olympic medalists. *Journal of Personality and Social Psychology, 69*, 603–610.

Meehl, P. E. (1954). *Clinical versus statistical prediction: A theoretical analysis and review of the literature*. Minneapolis: University of Minnesota Press.

Meehl, P. E. (1967). Theory-testing in psychology and physics: A methodological paradox. *Philosophy of Science, 34*, 103–115.

Meehl, P. E. (1978). Theoretical risks and tabular asterisks: Sir Karl, Sir Ronald, and the slow progress of soft psychology. *Journal of Consulting and Clinical Psychology, 46*, 806–834.

Meehl, P. E. (1990a). Appraising and amending theories: The strategy of Lakatosian defense and two principles that warrant it. *Psychological Inquiry, 1*, 108–141.

Meehl, P. E. (1990b). Why summaries of research on psychological theories are often uninterpretable. *Psychological Reports, 66*, 195–244 (Monograph Supplement 1-V66).

Meehl, P. E. (1993). Philosophy of science: Help or hindrance? *Psychological Reports, 72*, 707–733.

Melton, G. B., & Gray, J. N. (1988). Ethical dilemmas in AIDS research: Individual privacy and public health. *American Psychologist, 43*, 60–64.

Melton, G. B., Levine, R. J., Koocher, G. P., Rosenthal, R., & Thompson, W. C. (1988). Community consultation in socially sensitive research. *American Psychologist, 43*, 573–581.

Merritt, C. B., & Fowler, R. G. (1948). The pecuniary honesty of the public at large. *Journal of Abnormal and Social Psychology, 43*, 90–93.

Miles, M. B., & Huberman, A. M. (1994). *Qualitative data analysis* (2nd ed.). Thousands Oaks, CA: Sage.

Milgram, S. (1974). *Obedience to authority*. New York: Harper & Row.

Milgram, S. (1977). Subject reaction: The neglected factor in the ethics of experimentation. Hastings Center Report, October.

Milgram, S., Liberty, H. J., Toledo, R., & Wackenhut, J. (1986). Response to intrusion into waiting lines. *Journal of Personality and Social Psychology, 51*, 683–689.

Miller, G. A., & Wakefield, P. C. (1993). On Anglin's analysis of vocabulary growth. *Monographs of the Society for Research in Child Development, 58,* (10, Serial No. 238).

Miller, J. D. (1986, May). Some new measures of scientific illiteracy. Paper presented at the meeting of the American Association for the Advancement of Science, Philadelphia.

Miller, N. E. (1985). The value of behavioral research on animals. *American Psychologist, 40,* 423–440.

Miller, T. Q., Heath, L., Molcan, J. R., & Dugoni, B. L. (1991). Imitative violence in the real world: A re-analysis of homicide rates following championship prize fights. *Aggressive Behavior, 17,* 121–134.

Mook, D. G. (1983). In defense of external invalidity. *American Psychologist, 38,* 379–387.

Moore, B. R., & Stuttard, S. (1979). Dr. Guthrie and *Felis domesticus* or: Tripping over the cat. *Science, 205,* 1031–1033.

Morier, D., & Keeports, D. (1994). Normal science and the paranormal: The effect of a scientific method course on students' beliefs. *Research in Higher Education, 35,* 443–453.

Mosteller, F., & Hoaglin, D. C. (1991). Preliminary examination of data. In D. C. Hoaglin, F. Mosteller, & J. W. Tukey (Eds.), *Fundamentals of exploratory analysis of variance* (pp. 40–49). New York: Wiley.

Mulaik, S. A., Raju, N. S., & Harshman, R. A. (1997). There is a time and place for significance testing. In L. L. Harlow, S. A. Mulaik, & J. H. Steiger (Eds.), *What if there were no significance tests?* (pp. 65–115). Mahwah, NJ: Erlbaum.

Murray, B. (1998, December). The authorship dilemma: Who gets credit for what? *APA Monitor, 1,* 31.

Myers, D. G. (1998). *Psychology* (5th ed.). New York: Worth.

Myers, D. G. (1999). *Social psychology* (6th ed.). New York: McGraw-Hill.

Myers, D. G., & Diener, E. (1995). Who is happy? *Psychological Science, 6,* 10–19.

National Research Council (1996) *Guide for the care and use of laboratory animals.* A report of the Institute of Laboratory Animal Resources committee. Washington, DC: National Academy Press.

Neisser, I., & Harsch, N. (1992). Phantom flashbulbs: False recollections of hearing the news about *Challenger.* In E. Winograd & I. Neisser (Eds.), *Affect and accuracy in recall: Studies of "flashbulb memories"* (pp. 9–31). New York: Cambridge University Press.

Newcomb, T. M., Koenig, K. E., Flacks, R., & Warwick, D. P. (1967). *Persistence and change: Bennington College and its students after twenty-five years.* New York: Wiley.

Newhagen, J. E., & Ancell, M. (1995). The expression of emotion and social status in the language of bumper stickers. *Journal of Language and Social Psychology, 14,* 312–323.

New town blues: HUD abandons a disaster. *Time,* October 16, 1978, p. 84.

Novak, M. A. (1991, July). "Psychologists care deeply" about animals. *APA Monitor,* 4.

Orne, M. T. (1962). On the social psychology of the psychological experiment: With particular reference to demand characteristics and their implications. *American Psychologist, 17,* 776–783.

Ortmann, A., & Hertwig, R. (1997). Is deception necessary? *American Psychologist, 52,* 746–747.

Ortmann, A., & Hertwig, R. (1998). The question remains: Is deception acceptable? *American Psychologist, 53,* 806–807.

Osgood, C. E., & Walker, E. G. (1959). Motivation and language behavior: A content analysis of suicide notes. *Journal of Abnormal and Social Psychology, 59,* 58–67.

Parry, H. J., & Crossley, H. M. (1950). Validity of responses to survey questions. *Public Opinion Quarterly, 14,* 61–80.

Parsons, H. M. (1974). What happened at Hawthorne? *Science, 183,* 922–932.

Parsonson, B. S., & Baer, D. M. (1992). The visual analysis of data, and current research into the stimuli controlling it. In T. R. Kratochwill & J. R. Levin (Eds.), *Single-case research design and analysis* (pp. 15–40). Hillside, NJ: Erlbaum.

Pennebaker, J. W., Mayne, T. J., & Francis, M. E. (1997). Linguistic predictors of adaptive bereavement. *Journal of Personality and Social Psychology, 72,* 863–871.

Peterson, J. (1995). How are psychologists perceived by the public? *APA Monitor,* 31.

Pezdek, K., Finger, K., & Hodge, D. (1997). Planting false childhood memories: The role of event plausibility. *Psychological Science, 8,* 437–441.

Phillips, D. P. (1977). Motor vehicle fatalities increase just after publicized suicide stories. *Science, 196,* 1464–1465.

Phillips, D. P. (1978). Airplane accident fatalities increase just after newspaper stories about murder and suicide. *Science, 201,* 748–750.

Phillips, D. P. (1983). The impact of mass media violence on U.S. homicides. *American Sociological Review, 48,* 560–568.

Phillips, D. P., & Bollen, K. A. (1985). Same time, last year: Selective data dredging for negative findings. *American Sociological Review, 50,* 364–371.

Piaget, J. (1965). *The child's conception of number.* New York: Norton.

Pillemer, D. B. (1990). Clarifying the flashbulb memory concept: Comment on McCloskey, Wible, & Cohen (1988). *Journal of Experimental Psychology: General, 119,* 92–96.

Pingitore, R., Dugoni, B. L., Tindale, R. S., & Spring, B. (1994). Bias against overweight job applicants in a simulated employment interview. *Journal of Applied Psychology, 79,* 909–917.

Pishkin, V., & Shurley, J. T. (1983). Electrophysiological parameters in anxiety and failure: Evaluation of doxepin and hydroxyzine. *Bulletin of the Psychonomic Society, 21,* 21–23.

Pitman, R. K., Kolb, B., Orr, S. P., deJong, J., Yadati, S., & Singh, M. M. (1987). On the utility of ethological data in psychiatric research: The example of facial behavior in schizophrenia. *Ethology and Sociobiology, 8,* 111S–116S.

Plous, S. (1998). Signs of change within the animal rights movement: Results from a follow-up survey of activists. *Journal of Comparative Psychology, 112,* 48–54.

Popper, K. R. (1959). *The logic of scientific discovery.* New York: Basic Books.

Popper, K. R. (1976). *Unended quest.* Glasgow: Fontana/Collins.

Posavac, E. J., & Carey, R. G. (1997). *Program evaluation.* (5th ed.). Englewood Cliffs, NJ: Prentice-Hall.

Poulton, E. C. (1973). Unwanted range effects from using within-subject experimental designs. *Psychological Bulletin, 80,* 113–121.

Poulton, E. C. (1975). Range effects in experiments on people. *American Journal of Psychology, 88,* 3–32.

Poulton, E. C. (1982). Influential companions. Effects of one strategy on another in the within-subjects designs of cognitive psychology. *Psychological Bulletin, 91,* 673–690.

Poulton, E. C., & Freeman, P. R. (1966). Unwanted asymmetrical transfer effects with balanced experimental designs. *Psychological Bulletin, 66,* 1–8.

Powell, D. H., & Whitla, D. K. (1994). Normal cognitive aging: Toward empirical perspectives. *Current Directions in Psychological Science, 3,* 27–31.

Powell-Cope, G. M. (1995). The experience of gay couples affected by HIV infection. *Qualitative Health Research, 5,* 36–62.

Prentice, D. A., & Miller, D. T. (1992). When small effects are impressive. *Psychological Bulletin, 112,* 160–164.

Rachels, J. (1986). *The elements of moral philosophy.* New York: McGraw-Hill.

Richardson, D. R., Pegalis, L., & Britton, B. (1992). A technique for enhancing the value of research participation. *Contemporary Social Psychology, 16,* 11–13.

Riddoch, M. J., & Humphreys, G. W. (1992). The smiling giraffe: An illustration of a visual memory disorder. In R. Campbell (Ed.), *Mental lives: Case studies in cognition* (pp. 161–177). Oxford: Blackwell.

Riley, D. A. (1962). Memory for form. In L. Postman (Ed.), *Psychology in the making* (pp. 402–465). New York: Knopf.

Rimm, D. C., & Masters, J. C. (1979). *Behavior therapy: Techniques and empirical findings* (2nd ed.). New York: Academic Press.

Rindskopf, D. M. (1997). Testing "small," not null, hypotheses: Classical and Bayesian approaches. In L. L. Harlow, S. A. Mulaik, & J. H. Steiger (Eds.), *What if there were no significance tests?* (pp. 319–32). Mahwah, NJ: Erlbaum.

Rodman, J. L., & Burger, J. M. (1985). The influence of depression on the attribution of responsibility for an accident. *Cognitive Therapy and Research, 9,* 651–657.

Roethlisberger, F. J. (1977). *The elusive phenomena: An autobiographical account of my work in the field of organized behavior at the Harvard Business School.* Cambridge, MA: Division of Research, Graduate School of Business Administration (distributed by Harvard University Press).

Rollin, B. E. (1985). The moral status of research animals in psychology. *American Psychologist, 40,* 920–926.

Rosenfeld, A. (1981). Animal rights vs. human health. *Science, 81,* 18, 22.

Rosenhan, D. L. (1973). On being sane in insane places. *Science, 179,* 250–258.

Rosenthal, R. (1963). On the social psychology of the psychological experiment: The experimenter's hypothesis as unintended determinant of experimental results. *American Scientist, 51,* 268–283.

Rosenthal, R. (1966). *Experimenter effects in behav-ioral research*. New York: Appleton-Century-Crofts.

Rosenthal, R. (1976). *Experimenter effects in behavioral research*. (Enlarged ed.). New York: Irvington.

Rosenthal, R. (1990). How are we doing in soft psychology? *American Psychologist, 45,* 775–777.

Rosenthal, R. (1991). *Meta-analytic procedures for social research* (rev. ed.). Newbury Park, CA: Sage.

Rosenthal, R. (1994a). Interpersonal expectancy effects: A 30-year perspective. *Current Directions in Psychological Science, 3,* 176–179.

Rosenthal, R. (1994b). Science and ethics in conducting, analyzing, and reporting psychological research. *Psychological Science, 5,* 127–134.

Rosenthal, R., & Rosnow, R. L. (1991). *Essentials of behavioral research: Methods and data analysis* (2nd ed.). New York: McGraw-Hill.

Rosnow, R. L., & Rosenthal, R. (1995). "Some things you learn aren't so": Cohen's paradox, Asch's paradigm, and the interpretation of interaction. *Psychological Science, 6,* 3–9.

Ross, A. S., & White, S. (1987). Shoplifting, impaired driving, and refusing the Breathalyzer: On seeing one's name in a public place. *Evaluation Review, 11,* 254–260.

Rotter, J. B. (1966). Generalized expectancies for internal versus external control of reinforcement. *Psychological Monographs, 80* (1, Whole No. 609), 1–28.

Rozin, P., Markwith, M., & Stoess, C. (1997). Moralization and becoming a vegetarian: The transformation of preferences into values and the recruitment of disgust. *Psychological Science, 8,* 67–73.

Ruksznis, E. (1998, July/August). 10th annual convention: A decade of success, a future of promise. *APS Observer, 1,* 8–10, 18–19.

Rymer, R. (1993). *Genie: A scientific tragedy.* New York: Harper Collins.

Sackheim, H. A., Gur, R. C., & Saucy, M. C. (1978). Emotions are expressed more intensely on the left side of the face. *Science, 202,* 434–436.

Sacks, O. (1985). *The man who mistook his wife for a hat and other clinical tales.* New York: Harper & Row.

Sacks, O. (1995). *An anthropologist on Mars.* New York: Knopf.

Salomon, G. (1987). Basic and applied research in psychology: Reciprocity between two worlds. *International Journal of Psychology, 22,* 441–446.

Satterfield, J. M., & Seligman, M. E. P. (1994). Military aggression and risk predicted by explanatory style. *Psychological Science, 5,* 77–82.

Schacter, D. L. (1996). *Searching for memory.* New York: Basic Books.

Schaller, G. B. (1963). *The mountain gorilla.* Chicago: University of Chicago Press.

Schlenker, B. R., Phillips, S. T., Boniecki, K. A., & Schlenker, D. R. (1995a). Championship pressures: Choking or triumphing in one's own territory? *Journal of Personality and Social Psychology, 68,* 632–643.

Schlenker, B. R., Phillips, S. T., Boniecki, K. A., & Schlenker, D. R. (1995b). Where is the home choke? *Journal of Personality and Social Psychology, 68,* 649–652.

Schmidt, F. L. (1996). Statistical significance testing and cumulative knowledge in psychology: Implications for training of researchers. *Psychological Methods, 1,* 115–129.

Schmidt, F. L., & Hunter, J. E. (1997). Eight common but false objections to the discontinuation of significance testing in the analysis of research data. In L. L. Harlow, S. A. Mulaik, & J. H. Steiger. (Eds.), *What if there were no significance tests?* (pp. 37–64). Mahwah, NJ: Erlbaum.

Schmidt, W. C. (1997). World-Wide-Web survey research: Benefits, potential problems, and solutions. *Behavior Research Methods, Instruments, & Computers, 29,* 274–279.

Schnelle, J. F., Kirchner, R. E., Macrae, J. W., McNees, M. P., Eck, R. H., Snodgrass, S., Casey, J. D., & Uselton, P. H., Jr. (1978). Police evaluation research: An experimental and cost-benefit analysis of a helicopter patrol in a high-crime area. *Journal of Applied Behavior Analysis, 11,* 11–21.

Schoeneman, T. J., & Rubanowitz, D. E. (1985). Attributions in the advice columns: Actors and observers, causes and reasons. *Personality and Social Psychology Bulletin, 11,* 315–325.

Schulman, P., Castellon, C., & Seligman, M. E. P. (1989). Assessing explanatory style: The content analysis of verbatim explanations and the Attributional Style Questionnaire. *Behavioral Research and Therapy, 27,* 505–512.

Schulz, R., & Bazerman, M. (1980). Ceremonial occasions and mortality: A second look. *American Psychologist, 35,* 253–261.

Schuman, H., & Bobo, L. (1988). Survey-based experiments on white racial attitudes toward residential integration. *American Journal of Sociology, 94,* 273–299.

Schuman, H., Presser, S., & Ludwig, J. (1981). Context effects of survey responses to questions about abortion. *Public Opinion Quarterly, 45,* 216–223.

Schuman, H., & Scott, J. (1987). Problems in the use of survey questions to measure public opinion. *Science, 236,* 957–959.

Scoville, W. B., & Milner, B. (1957). Loss of recent memory after bilateral hippocampal lesions. *Journal of Neurology, Neurosurgery, and Psychiatry, 20*, 11–19.

Shapiro, K. J. (1998). *Animal models of human psychology: Critique of science, ethics, and policy.* Seattle, WA: Hogrefe & Huber.

Sharpe, D., Adair, J. G., & Roese, N. J. (1992). Twenty years of deception research: A decline in subjects' trust? *Personality and Social Psychology Bulletin, 18*, 585–590.

Shattuck, R. (1994). *The forbidden experiment: The story of the Wild Boy of Averyon.* New York: Kodansha.

Sieber, J. E., Iannuzzo, R., & Rodriguez, B. (1995). Deception methods in psychology: Have they changed in 23 years? *Ethics & Behavior, 5*, 67–85.

Simon, H. A. (1992). What is an "explanation" of behavior? *Psychological Science, 3*, 150–161.

Singer, B., & Benassi, V. A. (1981). Occult beliefs. *American Scientist, 69*, 49–55.

Singer, P. (1990). The significance of animal suffering. *Behavioral and Brain Sciences, 13*, 9–12.

Skinner, B. F. (1937). Two types of conditioned reflex: A reply to Konorski and Miller. *Journal of General Psychology, 16*, 272–279.

Skinner, B. F. (1966). Operant behavior. In W. K. Honig (Ed.), *Operant behavior: Areas of research and application* (pp. 12–32). New York: Appleton-Century-Crofts.

Smith, J. A., Harré, R., & Van Langenhove, L. (1995). Idiography and the case study. In J. A. Smith, R. Harré, & L. Van Langenhove (Eds.), *Rethinking psychology* (pp. 59–69). Thousand Oaks, CA: Sage.

Smith, M. A., & Leigh, B. (1997). Virtual subjects: Using the Internet as an alternative source of subjects and research environment. *Behavior Research Methods, Instruments, & Computers, 29*, 496–505.

Smith, P. K., & Lewis, K. (1985). Rough-and-tumble play, fighting, and chasing in nursery school children. *Ethology and Sociobiology, 6*, 175–181.

Smith, R. J. (1977). Electroshock experiment at Albany violates ethics guidelines. *Science, 198*, 383–386.

Smith, T. W. (1981). Qualifications to generalized absolutes: "Approval of hitting" questions on the GSS. *Public Opinion Quarterly, 45*, 224–230.

Sommer, R. (1968). Hawthorne dogma. *Psychological Bulletin, 70*, 592–595.

Spitz, R. A. (1965). *The first year of life.* New York: International Universities Press.

Stern, S. E., & Faber, J. E. (1997). The lost e-mail technique: Milgram's lost-letter technique in the age of the Internet. *Behavior Research Methods, Instruments, & Computers, 29*, 260–263.

Sternberg, R. J. (1986). A triangular theory of love. *Psychological Review, 93*, 119–135.

Sternberg, R. J. (1992, September). How to win acceptances by psychology journals: 21 tips for better writing. *APS Observer*, 12–13, 18.

Sternberg, R. J. (1997, September). What do students still most need to learn about research in psychology? *ABS Observer*, 14, 19.

Sternberg, R. J., & Williams, W. M. (1997). Does the Graduate Record Examination predict meaningful success in the graduate training of psychologists? A case study. *American Psychologist, 52*, 630–641.

Strauss, A., & Corbin, J. (1990). *Basics of qualitative research.* Newbury Park, CA: Sage.

Sun, M. (1981). Laetrile brush fire is out, scientists hope. *Science, 212*, 758–759.

Surwit, R. S., & Williams, P. G. (1996). Animal models provide insight into psychosomatic factors in diabetes. *Psychosomatic Medicine, 58*, 582–589.

Tassinary, L. G., & Hansen, K. A. (1998). A critical test of the waist-to-hip-ratio hypothesis of female physical attractiveness. *Psychological Science, 9*, 150–155.

Taylor, K. M., & Shepperd, J. A. (1996). Probing suspicion among participants in deception research. *American Psychologist, 51*, 886–887.

Taylor, S. J., & Bogdan, R. (1998). *Introduction to qualitative research methods: A guidebook and resource* (3rd ed.). New York: Wiley.

Terman, L. M. & Oden, M. A. (1947). *Genetic studies of genius: The gifted child grows up* (Vol. 4). Stanford, CA: Stanford University Press.

Thomas, L. (1992). *The fragile species.* New York: Charles Scribner's Sons.

Thompson, T. L. (1982). Gaze toward and avoidance of the handicapped: A field experiment. *Journal of Nonverbal Behavior, 6*, 188–196.

Tucker, J. S., Friedman, H. S., Schwartz, J. E., Criqui, M. H., Tomlinson-Keasey, C., Winograd, D. L., & Martin, L. R. (1997). Parental divorce: Effects on individual behavior and longevity. *Journal of Personality and Social Psychology, 73*, 381–391.

Tukey, J. W. (1977). *Exploratory data analysis.* Reading, MA: Addison-Wesley.

Tversky, A., & Kahneman, D. (1971). Belief in the law of small numbers. *Psychological Bulletin, 76*, 105–110.

Tversky, A., & Kahneman, D. (1974). Judgement under uncertainty: Heuristics and biases. *Science, 185*, 1124–1131.

Ulrich, R. E. (1991). Animal rights, animal wrongs and the question of balance. *Psychological Science, 2*, 197–201.

Ulrich, R. E. (1992). Animal research: A reflective analysis. *Psychological Science, 3*, 384–386.

Underwood, B. J. (1957). *Psychological research*. New York: Appleton-Century-Crofts.

Underwood, B. J. (1975). Individual differences as a crucible in theory construction. *American Psychologist, 30*, 128–134.

Underwood, B. J., & Shaughnessy, J. J. (1975). *Experimentation in psychology*. New York: Wiley: Robert E. Krieger, 1983.

Valentiner, D. P., Holahan, C. J., & Moos, R. H. (1994). Social support, appraisal of event controllability, and coping: An integrative model. *Journal of Personality and Social Psychology, 66*, 1094–1102.

VanBiervliet, A., Spangler, P. F., & Marshall, A. M. (1981). An ecobehavioral examination of a simple strategy for increasing mealtime language in residential facilities. *Journal of Applied Behavior Analysis, 14*, 295–305.

VanderStoep, S. W., & Shaughnessy, J. J. (1997). Taking a course in research methods improves reasoning about real-life events. *Teaching of Psychology, 24*, 122–124.

Van Meter, P., Yokoi, L., & Pressley, M. (1994). College students' theory of note-taking derived from their perceptions of note-taking. *Journal of Educational Psychology, 86*, 323–338.

Wallraff, H. G., & Sinsch, U. (1988). The role of "outward-journey information" in homing experiments with pigeons: New data on ontogeny of navigation and general survey. *Ethology, 77*, 10–27.

Ward, W. D., & Jenkins, H. M. (1965). The display of information and the judgement of contingency. *Canadian Journal of Psychology, 19*, 231–241.

Warwick, D. P., & Lininger, C. A. (1975). *The sample survey: Theory and practice*. New York: McGraw-Hill.

Watson, J. B. (1913). Psychology as the behaviorist views it. *Psychological Review, 20*, 158–177.

Watson, J. B. [1914] (1967). *Behavior: An introduction to comparative psychology*. New York: Holt, Rinehart and Winston.

Webb, E. J., Campbell, D. T., Schwartz, R. D., Sechrest, L., & Grove, J. B. (1981). *Non-reactive measures in the social sciences* (2nd ed.). Boston: Houghton-Mifflin.

Weigel, R. H., Loomis, J. W., & Soja, M. J. (1980). Race relations on prime time television. *Journal of Personality and Social Psychology, 39*, 884–893.

Weiner, H. (1996). Use of animal models in peptic ulcer disease. *Psychosomatic Medicine, 58*, 524–545.

Willems, E. P. (1969). Planning a rationale for naturalistic research. In E. P. Willems & H. L. Raush (Eds.), *Naturalistic viewpoints in psychological research* (pp. 44–71). New York: Holt, Rinehart and Winston.

Willems, E. P., & Raush, H. L. (Eds.). (1969). *Naturalistic viewpoints in psychological research*. New York: Holt, Rinehart and Winston.

Willingham, W. W. (1974). Predicting success in graduate education. *Science, 183*, 273–278.

Wilson, G. T. (1978). On the much discussed nature of the term "behavior therapy." *Behavior Therapy, 9*, 89–98.

Winer, B. J., Brown, D. R., & Michels, K. M. (1991). *Statistical principles in experimental design* (3rd ed.). New York: McGraw-Hill.

Winograd, E., & Neisser, U. (Eds.). (1992). *Affect and accuracy in recall: Studies of "flashbulb memories."* New York: Cambridge University Press.

Yeaton, W. H., & Sechrest, L. (1981). Critical dimensions in the choice and maintenance of successful treatments: Strength, integrity, and effectiveness. *Journal of Consulting and Clinical Psychology, 49*, 156–167.

Yeaton, W. H., & Sechrest, L. (1986). Use and misuse of no-difference findings in eliminating threats to validity. *Evaluation Review, 10*, 836–852.

Zechmeister, E. B., Chronis, A. M., Cull, W. L., D'Anna, C. A., & Healy, N. A. (1995). Growth of a functionally important lexicon. *Journal of Reading Behavior, 27*, 201–212.

Zechmeister, E. B., & Johnson, J. E. (1992). *Critical thinking: A functional approach*. Pacific Grove, CA: Brooks/Cole.

Zechmeister, E. B., & Nyberg, S. E. (1982). *Human memory: An introduction to research and theory*. Pacific Grove, CA: Brooks/Cole.

Zechmeister, J. S., & Zechmeister, E. B. (2000). Introductory textbooks and psychology's core concepts. *Teaching of Psychology*, in press.

# Credits

**Chapter 1** Page 3: Photo of Wilhelm Wundt © Corbis; photo of William James © Culver Pictures. Figure 1.1: Photos courtesy of Thomas A. Sebeok, Distinguished Professor Emeritus, Indiana University, Bloomington. Figure 1.2: Photo by Paula Shaughnessy. Figure 1.3: Original drawing by Fran Hughes. Figure 1.4: From Figure 3: page 453, of R. V. Levine (1990), "The pace of life," *American Scientist, 78,* 450–459. Copyright 1990 by Sigma Xi, The Scientific Research Society, Inc. Used with permission of the publisher and author. Figure 1.5: Photo © Corbis. Figure 1.6: Photo by Eugene B. Zechmeister.

**Chapter 2** Figure 2.1: Photos by Eugene B. Zechmeister and John J. Shaughnessy. Special thanks go to Erica, Linda, and Hilary Bryant, Earron Henderson and members of his social psychology class, Candy Baguilat, Lynda Cafasso, and Peter Bergquist for being willing subjects for these photos; we thank Bill Shofner for helping us obtain animal pictures. And let us not forget to identify John's dog, Emma. We also wish to acknowledge the cooperation of the Parmly Institute of Loyola University of Chicago as well as Rich Bowen for providing experimental settings for some of these photos. Ethical principles 6.06–6.26 of the American Psychological Association (1992), "Ethical principles of psychologists and code of conduct," *American Psychologist, 47,* 1597–1611. Copyright 1992 by the American Psychological Association. Reprinted by permission of the publisher. Neither the original nor this reproduction can be republished, photocopied, reprinted, or distributed in any form, without the prior written permission of the APA. Figure 2.2: Photo by Eugene B. Zechmeister. We wish to thank Jen Brockway and Bess Anderson for posing as undergraduate students. Figure 2.3: Photo of Eugene B. and Jeanne S. Zechmeister by a friendly passer-by. Figure 2.4: Original drawing by Fran Hughes. Figure 2.5: Photo © Martin Rogers/Stock Boston.

**Chapter 3** Figure 3.1: Photo by Eugene B. Zechmeister. Figure 3.2: Photo © Corbis/Farrell Grehan. Figure 3.3: Reprinted with permission from D. A. Jenni and M. A. Jenni (1976), "Carrying behavior in humans: Analysis of sex differences," *Science, 194,* 859–960. Figure 1, page 859. Copyright 1976 American Association for the Advancement of Science. Table 3.1: from J. R. Dickie, and S. C. Gerber (1980), "Training in social competence: The effect on mothers, fathers, and infants," *Child Development, 51,* 1248–1251. Materials from Jane Dickie, Psychology Department, Hope College, Holland, MI 49423. Table 3.3: From Table 2, page 550, of M. LaFrance and C. Mayo (1976), "Racial differences in gaze behavior during conversations: Two systematic observational studies," *Journal of Personality and Social Psychology, 33,* 547–552. Copyright 1976 by the American Psychological Association. Reprinted by permission of the publisher and author. Figure 3.4: Original drawing by Fran Hughes.

**Chapter 4** Table 4.1: Adapted from Table 3, page 621, of R. E. Lucas, E. Diener, & E. Suh (1996), "Discriminant validity of well-being measures," *Journal of Personality and Social Psychology, 71,* 616–628. Copyright 1996 by the American Psychological Association. Reprinted by permission of the publisher and author. Table 4.2: From Appendix Table 8, of A. Campbell (1981), *The sense of well-being in America,* New York: McGraw-Hill. Copyright 1981 by McGraw-Hill, Inc. Reprinted by permission of publisher. Figure 4.2: Adapted from Figure 1, page 1095, of D. P. Valentiner, C. J. Holohan, & R. H. Moos (1994), "Social support, appraisals of event controllability, and coping: An integrative model," *Journal of Personality and Social Psychology, 66,* 1094–1102. Copyright 1994 by the American Psychological Association. Reprinted by permission of the publisher and author. Figure 4.5: Original drawing by Fran Hughes. Figure 4.6: From Figure 7, page 13, of A. W. Astin, S. A. Parrott, W. S. Korn, & L. J. Sax (1997), *The American freshman: Thirty year trends,* Los Angeles: Higher Education Research Institute. Used with permision of the author and publisher.

**Chapter 5** Figure 5.1: Photo of Jeanne S. Zechmeister by Eugene B. Zechmeister. Table 5.1: Based on material from E. J. Webb, D. T. Campbell, R. D. Schwartz, L. Sechrest, and J. B. Grove, *Nonreactive measures in social sciences,* 2nd ed. (1981), Boston: Houghton Mifflin. Copyright 1981 by Harper &

Row, Publishers, Inc. (Copyright by Sage Publications, Inc. Adapted by permission of publisher and author.) Figure 5.2: Photo by Hope College Public Relations Department. Used with permission. Figure 5.3: Reprinted from Figure 1, page 1465, of D. P. Phillips (1977), "Motor vehicle fatalities increase just after publicized suicide stories." *Science, 196,* 1464–1465. Copyright 1977 American Association for the Advancement of Science. Reprinted by permission of publisher and author. Table 5.2: Adapted from material on pages 203–206 in R. M. Brandt (1972), *Studying behavior in natural settings,* New York: Holt, Rinehart & Winston. (Republished 1981 by University Press of America, Washington, D.C.). Used by permission of author. Figure 5.4: Adapted from Figure 2, page 83, and Figure 3, page 85, of C. A. Anderson (1989), "Temperature and aggression: Ubiquitous effects of heat on occurrence of human violence." *Psychological Bulletin, 106,* 74–96. Copyright 1989 by the American Psychological Association. Used with permission of publisher and author.

**Chapter 6** Table 6.3: Adapted from Table 1, page 177, in R. Rosenthal (1994), "Interpersonal expectancy effects: A 30-year perspective," *Current Directions in Psychological Science, 3,* 176–179. Copyright 1994 by the American Psychological Society. Used with permission of author and publisher. Figure 6.1: From Figure 1, page 319, of E. F. Loftus & T. E. Burns (1982), "Mental shock can produce retrograde amnesia," *Memory & Cognition, 10,* 318–323. Copyright 1982 by the Psychonomic Society, Inc. Used with permission of publisher and author. Figure 6.2: Photo by Jeanne S. Zechmeister. We wish to thank members of Jeanne S. Zechmeister's Spring 1996 research methods in psychology class for permission. Figure 6.3: Original drawing by Fran Hughes. Figure 6.4: Photo © Herb Snitzer/Stock Boston. Figure 6.5: Photo by Eugene B. Zechmeister. Figure 6.6: Photo courtesy of Judy DeLoache and from Figure 2 of J. S. DeLoache, S. L. Pierroutsakos, D. H. Uttal, K. S. Rosengren, & A. Gottlieb (1998), "Grasping the nature of pictures," *Psychological Science, 9,* 205–210. Figures 6.7 and 6.8: Based on data provided by Judy DeLoache and her colleagues and adapted from Figure 3 of a study by J. S. DeLoache, S. L. Pierroutsakos, D. H. Uttal, K. S. Rosengren, & A. Gottlieb (1998), "Grasping the nature of pictures," *Psychological Science, 9,* 205–210. Used with permission of publisher.

**Chapter 7** Figure 7.1: Original drawing by Fran Hughes. Figure 7.2: From Figure 1, page 434, of H. A. Sackheim, R. C. Gur, and M. C. Saucy (1978), *Science, 202,* 434–436. Copyright 1978 by American Association for the Advancement of Science. Used with permission of author and publisher.

**Chapter 8** Table 8.1: Based on Table 1, page 86, of R. G. Hass, I. Katz, N. Rizzo, J. Bailey, and D. Eisenstadt (1991), "Cross-racial appraisal as related to attitude ambivalence and cognitive complexity." *Personality and Social Psychology Bulletin, 17,* 83–92. Copyright 1991 by Sage Publications, Inc. Adapted by permission of the publisher and author. Figure 8.5: Based on data provided by John J. Shaughnessy. Figure 8.6: Based on data in Table 2, page 913, of R. Pingitore, B. L. Dugoni, R. S. Tindale, & B. Spring (1994), "Bias against overweight job applicants in a simulated employment interview," *Journal of Applied Psychology, 79,* 909.917. Copyright 1994 by the American Psychological Association. Used with permission of publisher and author. Figure 8.7: Original drawing by Fran Hughes. Table 8.5: From J. L. Rodman and J. M. Burger (1985), "The influence of depression on the attribution of responsibility for an accident." *Cognitive Therapy and Research, 9,* 651–657. Copyright 1985 by Plenum Publishing Corporation. Used with permission of publisher and author. Table 8.6 and Figure 8.8: From Figure 1, page 341, of M. L. Dittmar, D. B. Berch, and J. S. Warm (1982), "Sustained visual attention in deaf and hearing adults," *Bulletin of the Psychonomic Society, 19,* 339–342. Copyright 1982 by the Psychonomic Society. Adapted by permission of publisher and author.

**Chapter 9** Case study illustration: From I. Kirsch (1978), "Teaching clients to be their own therapists: A case study illustration," *Psychotherapy: Theory, Research and Practice, 15,* 302–305. Reprinted by permission of Donald K. Freedheim, Editor. Figure 9.1: Photo courtesy of Bibliotheque Nationale. Used with permission. Figure 9.2: Adapted from Figure 9.1, page 209, of A. E. Kazdin (1998), *Research design in clinical psychology* (3rd ed.), Boston: Allyn & Bacon. Used with permission of author and publisher. Figure 9.3: From Figure 1, page 60, of S. V. Horton (1987), "Reduction of disruptive mealtime behavior by facial screenings," *Behavior Modification, 11,* 53–64. Copyright 1987 by Sage Publications, Inc. Adapted by permission of publisher and author. Figure 9.4: From Figure 1, page 301, of M. G. Allison and T. Allyon (1980), "Behavioral coaching in the development of skills in football, gymnastics, and tennis," *Journal of Applied Behavioral Analysis, 13,* 297–304. Copyright 1980 by the Experimental

Analysis of Behavior, Inc. Reprinted by permission of publisher and author. Figure 9.6: Original drawing by Fran Hughes.

**Chapter 10** Figure 10.1: Photo © Archive Photos. Figure 10. 2: Original drawing by Fran Hughes. Figure 10.4: From Figures 5 and 6, page 416, of D. T. Campbell (1969), "Reforms as experiments." *American Psychologist, 24,* 409–429. Copyright 1969 by the American Psychological Association. Reprinted by permission of publisher and author. Figure 10.5: From Figure 1, page 257, of A. S. Ross and S. White (1987), "Shoplifting, impaired driving, and refusing the breathalyzer," *Evaluation Review, 11,* 254–260. Copyright 1987 by Sage Publications. Reprinted by permission by publisher and author. Figure 10.6: From A. J. McSweeney (1978), "Effects of response cost on the behavior of a million persons: Charging for directory assistance in Cincinnati," *Journal of Applied Behavior Analysis, 11,* 47–51. Copyright 1978 by the Society for the Experimental Analysis of Behavior, Inc. Reprinted by permission of publisher and author. Figure 10.7: From J. F. Schnelle, R. E. Kirchner, J. W. Macrae, M. P. McNees, R. H. Eck, S. Snodgrass, J. D. Casey, and P. H. Uselton, Jr. (1978), "Police evaluation research: An experimental and cost benefit analysis of a helicopter patrol in a high-crime area," *Journal of Applied Behavior Analysis, 11,* 11–21. Copyright 1978 by the Society for the Experimental Analysis of Behavior, Inc. Reprinted by permission of publisher and author. Figure 10.8: Based on Figure 2, page 444, of G. Salomon (1987), "Basic and applied research in psychology: Reciprocity between two worlds," *International Journal of Psychol-*

*ogy, 22,* 441–446. Reprinted by permission of Elsevier Science Publishers, Academic Publishing Division, and author.

**Appendix A** Permission to use statistical Tables A.2, A.3, and A.4 in Appendix A is acknowledged with tables in Appendix A. Table A.5: Based on Table 2.3.5, pages 36–37, in J. Cohen (1988), *Statistical power analysis for the behavioral sciences* (2nd ed.), Mahwah NJ: Erlbaum. Used with permission of the publisher. Table A.6: Based on Tables 8.3.12, 8.3.13, 8.3.14, & 8.3.15, pages 311–318, in J. Cohen (1988), *Statistical power analysis for the behavioral sciences* (2nd ed.), Mahwah NJ: Erlbaum. Used with permission of the publisher.

**Appendix B** Table B.1: Questionnaire used in a survey conducted by researchers at the Institute for Social Research (ISR), University of Michigan. Reprinted by permission of Willard Rodgers, ISR, Ann Arbor, MI 48106, and Sage Publications, Inc. Table B.2: Questionnaire given to authors, who were passengers on Amtrak's Chicago–St. Louis train, by representatives of the Illinois Department of Transportation.

**Appendix C** Extensive quotations from *Publication Manual of the American Psychological Association,* 4th ed. (1994). Washington, DC. Copyright 1994 by the American Psychological Association. Reprinted by permission of the publisher. Neither the original nor this reproduction can be republished, photocopied, reprinted, or distributed in any form, without the prior written permission of the APA.

# Name Index

# Subject Index